EATCS

Monographs on Theoretical Computer Science

Volume 24

Tamás Gergely László Úry

# First-Order Programming Theories

With 10 Figures

Springer-Verlag
Berlin Heidelberg New York
London Paris Tokyo
Hong Kong Barcelona
Budapest

*Authors*

Prof. Dr. Tamás Gergely
Applied Logic Laboratory
P. O. Box 675, 1539 Budapest, Hungary

Dr. László Úry
Applied Logic Laboratory
P. O. Box 675, 1539 Budapest, Hungary

*Editors*

Prof. Dr. Wilfried Brauer
Institut für Informatik, Technische Universität München
Arcisstrasse 21, D-8000 München 2, FRG

Prof. Dr. Grzegorz Rozenberg
Institute of Applied Mathematics and Computer Science
University of Leiden, Niels-Bohr-Weg 1, P. O. Box 9512
NL-2300 RA Leiden, The Netherlands

Prof. Dr. Arto Salomaa
Department of Mathematics, University of Turku
SF-20500 Turku 50, Finland

ISBN 3-540-54277-9 Springer-Verlag Berlin Heidelberg New York
ISBN 0-387-54277-9 Springer-Verlag New York Berlin Heidelberg

Library of Congress Cataloging-in-Publication Data
Gergely, T. (Tamás)
First-order programming theories / by Tamás Gergely and László Úry. p. cm. – (EATS monographs on theoretical computer science: v. 24) Includes bibliographical references and index.
ISBN 3-540-54277-9 (acid-free paper). – ISBN 0-387-54277-9 (U.S.: acid-free paper)
1. Electronic digital computers – Programming. I. Úry, László, 1953– . II. Title III. Series.
QA76.6.G4744 1991 005.1–dc20 91-27370


Printed in the United States of America



Data coversion by authors
45/3140 – 543210 – Printed on acid-free paper

# Preface

This work presents a purely classical first-order logical approach to the field of study in theoretical computer science sometimes referred to as the theory of programs, or programming theory.

This field essentially attempts to provide a precise mathematical basis for the common activities involved in reasoning about computer programs and programming languages, and it also attempts to find practical applications in the areas of program specification, verification and programming language design.

Many different approaches with different mathematical frameworks have been proposed as a basis for programming theory. They differ in the mathematical machinery they use to define and investigate programs and program properties and they also differ in the concepts they deal with to understand the programming paradigm.

Different approaches use different tools and viewpoints to characterize the data environment of programs. Most of the approaches are related to mathematical logic and they provide their own logic. These logics, however, are very eclectic since they use special entities to reflect a special world of programs, and also, they are usually incomparable with each other.

This Babel's mess irritated us and we decided to peel off the eclectic components and try to answer all the questions by using classical first-order logic. In our opinion, this is the logic even programmers and pragmatically oriented people are familiar with, and if this logic becomes appropriate to serve as a basis for programming theory, then this theory will satisfy the requirement that it speak about the world under consideration as simply as possible.

This work reflects our journey from the eclectic programming logics to the simple classical first-order logic, which furthermore turned out to be more powerful than the non-classical ones.

Putting this long journey into a book we had B. Mahr's full support and encouragement, for which we would like to thank him. We also acknowledge Springer-Verlag for their kind, willing and supportive cooperation and the unknown referees for their invaluable comments on our book. We are especially grateful to J. A. Ross, Copy Editor, for his scrupulous inspection of the manuscript and whose work hopefully led to a smooth reading of this book.

We are indebted to H. Andréka, I. Németi and I. Sain for our fruitful discussions of the subject in the past sixteen years. Special thanks go to our colleagues M. Erdélyi-Szabó, A. Juhos, Á. Kurucz and M. Szőts at the Applied Logic Laboratory, Budapest for their helpful comments and criticisms on reading the penultimate version of our manuscript. Finally, we thank our wives Lydia and Ágnes for their support and passionate involvement in bringing our book to this final shape.

Budapest, August 1991 Tamás Gergely, László Úry

# Contents

## Part II
## Extended Dynamic Logics



## Part III
## Temporal Characterization of Programs



## Part IV
## Programming Logic with Explicit Time

# Introduction

**Programming Theory.** The field of study dealing with programs and programming languages in theoretical computer science is usually referred to as *programming theory*, or *the theory of programs*. This field essentially deals with the formal investigation of the world of programs, including characterization of programs, description of program properties and checking whether a given program satisfies certain properties. In order to support this investigation, programming theory attempts essentially to provide an appropriate mathematical foundation. This theory also attempts to provide appropriate, theoretically well based methods and tools to support practical applications, e.g. in the field of program specification and verification and also in program design and in programming language development.

Conditionally we can divide programming theory into two main subfields. Programming languages and programs play the main role in the first subfield, while in the second one the languages which describe program properties have the leading role. We assign to the first area the research that aims to develop formal tools for the characterization of programming languages and programs from different aspects. First of all we should provide appropriate formal tools to define programs as formal objects. These tools consider programs from the syntactic aspect. This aspect deals with the "*how*" specification of programs, i.e. it analyses how a program is to be given, how it is constructed, how optimal or complex it is, etc. The programs, however, represent algorithms and are formal objects of a special kind. Namely, beyond the syntactic aspect they have a meaning connected with their execution. Execution of real programs takes place in real computers and results in changes in the contents of the storage units (registers) of the computers, which, in turn, form the data environment of the program under execution. Programming theory, however, deals with abstract programming languages and, accordingly, the execution of programs takes place in an appropriate "abstract" data environment which represents the computers.

Therefore, the semantics of a programming language is connected with the characterization of changes caused by the program's execution in the data environment. The semantics of programming languages deals with questions we may call "*what*"-questions, regarding what a program does or what properties it has.

Having defined the program semantics we can investigate the computational power of a programming language. Moreover, it is an important task to compare different programming languages with respect to their computational power. To carry out this task, the formal characterization of programming languages must be continued to the point where purely formal objects can be introduced to replace programming languages.

The main problems the second subfield deals with are connected with the selection of program properties that are interesting from theoretical and pragmatical points of view. Having selected the interesting properties, a formal language must be developed which facilitates the description of these properties and their investigation. We also require a formal calculus for the descriptive language which allows us to prove whether the program to be considered possesses any interesting properties.

**Mathematical Framework.** Programming theory should possess appropriate formal methods and tools to deal successfully with the problems arising in both subfields. Moreover, it would be desirable to have a mathematical foundation which could provide a unique framework and view for both subfields. Different approaches with different mathematical frameworks have been proposed as a basis for programming theory. They differ in the mathematical machinery they use to define and investigate programs and program properties and in the concepts they use to understand the programming paradigm.

What mathematical framework will be adequate to characterize programs and programming languages and to reason about them from both syntactic and semantic perspectives? *Mathematical logic is the only discipline which has a well developed culture to deal with the syntax and semantics of some formally defined languages.* However, in mathematical logic the meaning of a formal sentence is characterized by its interpretation in the appropriate models and by analysing its validity with respect to these models. Logic systems by nature are *static*, while the meaning of algorithms and so of programs connected with execution require *dynamic* consideration. Therefore, if we intend to use logic for developing a programming theory we have to find a solution for this contradictory situation which provides appropriate logical tools to represent the dynamic aspect of programs, namely their execution. While we are looking for the required solution the following questions about the handling of program meaning should be answered:

- What does a logic formulation characterize if it speaks about program execution?
- What computation processes appear in the selected logic during the formal characterization?
- Does program execution coincide with these computational processes?

These questions should be answered while dealing with the first subfield of programming theory when we intend to represent and characterize programs in the scope of mathematical logic and to develop a corresponding theory of computation. Of course, considering the second subfield of programming theory, above all program properties should be selected which are interesting from a theoretical or pragmatic point of view, and an appropriate language should be developed to describe and, possibly, to prove them. If we wish to develop this language in the framework of mathematical logic then appropriate answers to the above questions are also very important. We should also emphasize that the tools developed in the two subfields are almost disjoint from one another. Basically, there is no interrelation even in the case when these tools are logical.

**Programming Logic.** *Our aim in this book is to show how mathematical logic can be used to develop a programming theory such that both its subfields will be organically interrelated.* This interrelation can be obtained for example if the selected program properties are defined according to the logical tools used to represent program semantics and if the descriptive languages correspond to the purely logical characterization of programming languages. Let us see the logical tools developed for the second subfield. We call *the logic of programs,* or *programming logic*, the collection of formal tools of a programming theory, based on mathematical logic and used to reason about programs from the points of view of syntax and semantics.

Almost all programming logics are extensions of first-order classical logic, such as e.g. Floyd-Hoare language (Floyd [1967], Hoare [1969]), algorithmic logic (Engeler [1967], Salwicki [1970], Banachowski, Kreczmar, Mirkowska, Rasiova, Salviczki [1978]), dynamic logic (Pratt [1976], Harel [1979]), programming logic (Constable, O'Donnell [1978]) and temporal logic (Pnueli [1977]). Note that all these programming logics became non-classical in their tools and views after having expanded classical logic in order to handle the dynamic aspect of programs. Is it necessary to use non-classical logics in programming theory or is classical first-order logic, in itself, sufficient to answer all important questions? In contrast with the non-classical logic, the main advantages of classical first-order logic are that it is widely known, most programmers are familiar with it, and it possesses suitable model and proof theoretic tools for a programming theory.

This is why we aim to develop a programming theory by restricting ourselves entirely to the classical first-order logic framework. We will start with the investigation of the meaning of program execution in the scope of mathematical logic and with the development of the corresponding theory of computation. Then we continue the development of programming theory with the investigation of different non-classical programming logics. While discussing their disadvantages, we introduce a programming logic based on the pure classical first-order logic that eliminates all the disadvantages and is more powerful than the first-order non-classical logics. Before going into details about the programming logic proposed here, let us consider how the main technical problems connected with programs are solved in different programming logics.

One of the problems concerns how programs are represented in the syntax of the programming logic. In the Floyd-Hoare language and in dynamic logic, programs are treated as modalities. In the algorithmic logic introduced by Engeler [1967] and in the programming logic of Constable, O'Donnell [1978], programs appear as atomic formulas, while in the algorithmic logic considered by Salwicki [1970] programs appear rather as terms. Another viewpoint is expressed in the temporal logical approach where programs do not appear in the formulas at all, but remain implicit.

Another problem is connected with handling program semantics. Most of the programming logics emphasize the description of results of program execution rather than the program itself that carries them out. These programming logics use an *input-output* relational (which we call *denotational*) semantics.

Other programming logics consider the entire computational process by using trace semantics. Trace semantics presupposes the modeling of computer functioning which takes place in time. Thus programming logic aiming at the characterization of different program features should be capable of describing and characterizing the data environment of programs and describing features and characteristics related to time. There are different possibilities for realizing these concepts, namely:

(i) only data are built into the model construction; time appears in the metalanguage only;
(ii) time appears in addition to data in the descriptive language but model constructions deal with data only;
(iii) both data and time are handled by the descriptive language and both are built into the model constructions.

Note that all the programming logics mentioned above realize possibility (i) except for temporal logic. Those versions of programming logic that handle time only *implicitly*, i.e. only on the metalanguage level, describe the time connected with the execution of programs by the set of natural numbers, or, more precisely, by the standard model of arithmetic. Yet, at the same time, they describe the data in first-order theories, which means that non-standard data are also allowed and handled. (Note that "standard" and "non-standard" are used in the sense of the logic of arithmetic, see e.g. Mendelson [1964].) This results in a certain *asymmetry* in the theory of programming, and the power of proof will be insufficient, e.g. the programming logic will not be complete. This asymmetry has been emphasized and discussed in more detail in Gergely, Úry [1978, 1981]. If we provide a first-order theory at the same time as an *explicit* tool for handling time then, besides standard time moments, non-standard moments also come into the picture. This way the programming theory becomes *symmetric*.

In connection with non-standard time we note that in certain models the program, observed internally, can terminate after running for an "infinitely long" time. The termination in this case occurs at a time moment which is a non-standard number. However, the same run is infinite and non-terminating if observed externally. In connection with termination, McCarthy [1978] emphasized the necessity to investigate the relation between non-standard and standard models in the theory of programming as well. (See also Hájek [1981, 1986a, 1986b].)

The intermittent assertion method introduced by Burstall [1974] provides a consideration of program properties connected with time in a certain sense.

This method realizes possibility (ii). We mention that the well-founded-sets method used for proving program termination can also be considered as an explicit handling of time. It also realizes possibility (ii).

As we know, within the framework of logic, the first explicit time consideration was made by Kröger. He used ordinals to represent time (Kröger [1976,1977]) and realized possibility (ii). Temporal logic is the best-known method among those realizing possibility (iii) (see e.g. Kröger [1987] or Goldblatt [1987]).

**Hungarian School.** It is a natural wish to have a programming logic in the scope of classical (many sorted) first-order logic which also realizes possibility (iii), i.e. which handles both data and time explicitly and models computers so that the "abstract machine" contains elements representing data and time. This logic, which in this book is called time logic, was introduced in the late 1970s and was actively investigated under the name of non-standard dynamic logic by the "Hungarian school" of programming logic. This school was started by Andréka, Gergely, Németi [1977], Andréka, Németi [1978], Gergely [1978] and Gergely, Úry [1978]. The main objective of this school was the development of formal tools in the scope of classical first-order logic, to define program semantics and to describe program properties and investigate them by the use of appropriate proof systems. Initially, time logic was introduced in two versions differing in the definition of semantics. The first version used the so-called continuous trace semantics initiated by Andréka, Gergely, Németi [1977] and Andréka, Németi [1978], while the second one used the definable trace semantics proposed by Gergely, Úry [1978]. The activity of this school resulted a large number of papers with many interesting results among which we emphasize: Andréka [1983], Andréka, Németi, Sain [1979a, 1979b, 1981, 1982], Csirmaz [1981,1985], Gergely [1987], Gergely, Úry [1980a, 1980b, 1981, 1982], Németi [1982], Sain [1983,1985a,b,c, 1987, 1991]. In the second half of the 1980s the ideology together with the approach of this school became internationally known, and researchers of other countries also followed this approach; see e.g. Abadi [1989], Gonzáles, Artelejo [1985], Hájek [1986a, 1986b], Pásztor [1986], Leivant[1985], Makowsky, Sain [1989] and Richter, Szabó [1986]. The approach of the Hungarian school provided many new facilities for programming theory. For example, it allows one to characterize different program verification methods and to compare different programming logics with respect to their program verification power. This study was made in Sain [1985c,1991]. Another advantage of this approach is that it allows one to handle directly any new computational devices, added to a given programming language in order to augment its computational power, with the same programming logic, i.e. with the time logic without any modification. Remember that this is not the case e.g. in dynamic logic (cf. Meyer [1980], Harel [1984]).

**Our Objective.** In this book we wish to develop the first-order programming theory by dealing not only with the programming logic, i.e. with the second subfield of programming theory, but also with the first subfield. That is, we wish to augment the theory which has appeared as the result of the Hungarian school, with an appropriate computation theory preserving the main characteristic of the approach of this school, namely the *consistent usage of classical first-order logic*. That is, *we wish to extend the research started by the Hungarian school to both subfields of programming theory and to develop a first-order programming theory which deals with these subfields in an interrelated way*, such that, for example, it allows us to develop programming logics according to the requirements that have arisen in the first subfield and using some of the logical constructions developed there. Thus, for example, the development of different descriptive languages depends on the ways we define program semantics and also on the computation theory.

The present book is devoted to the development of the required programming theory. It is divided into a preparatory part and four numbered parts. The preparatory part provides the basic mathematical notions, notations and facts from (naive) set theory and mathematical logic. Special attention is devoted to the notion of inductive definability, which plays an important role in the formation of both subfields of our programming theory. We suggest reading Sections 1.2 and 1.4 even for readers who know mathematical logic at a professional level, because without these sections the book won't be understandable.

**Computation Theory.** The first numbered part, Part I, is devoted to the first subfield of programming theory and develops a computational theory in the framework of classical first-order logic. While developing a programming theory, we may, in principle, consider some concrete programming languages; however, for the theoretical investigation it is far more convenient to consider a programming language of abstract syntax. When choosing the syntax, such constructions are taken into account as are essential for many concrete programming languages (thus in the letters the abstract constructions appear in special form). We select the guarded command language introduced by Dijkstra [1976] as the basic programming language of our theory. This non-deterministic language is denoted by $P_\sigma$, where $\sigma$ is an arbitrary but fixed signature (similarity type), the symbols of which are used in the syntax of the programming language. We also use a version of $P_\sigma$ which augments the latter by random assignment, resulting in an infinite non-determinism. This language is denoted by $rP_\sigma$. The conglomerate of programming languages differing in the signature are denoted as $P$ and $rP$, respectively, and are called programming families.

In order to characterize a program execution, first we model a computer within the models of classical first-order logic. From the point of view of execution the characteristic feature of a computer is what sort of data it can understand and how it can manipulate them, i.e. what kinds of transformations can be made or what kinds of property about data can be discovered. Valuations establishing connection between variables and the elements of the universes of the models are used to represent storage units of the computer. This is how states in the data environment, i.e. in the model, will be defined.

There are two possibilities to represent the execution process. First, the changes in data environment are represented only by the first and the last "states". This is the *input-output* or *denotational semantics* of programs. Second, the entire computational process is represented by the sequences of states in the data environment. This is the *trace semantics* of the programs.

In order to approach the practical programming situation and to have more powerful programming languages we augment the basic nondeterministic programming language with different computational devices like stacks, counters, lists and sets in a *purely logical* way by the use of a specially developed type of *extension*, which allows us to appropriately extend the signature.

Since our approach is based on pure first-order logic the notion of computability is to be extended from the set of natural numbers, i.e. from the standard model of arithmetic, to the models of a given signature. Therefore, computation in non-standard models becomes a well defined useful notion.

By the use of a semantic representation of programs and by the new notion of computability, programming languages which differ in the number of stacks that may be used in the programs can be compared with respect to their computational power. This investigation is sometimes called *comparative schematology*. In comparative schematology as well as in programming theory, several abstract constructions have been suggested and investigated with respect to computability and to computational power in comparison with given programming languages. With respect to the computational power, these constructions simultaneously provided a formal characterization of the programming languages with the same computational power as these constructions themselves. The effective definitional schema introduced by Friedmann [1971] is one of most important of these constructions, which was used and further developed, e.g. by Shepherdson [1973] and Tiuryn [1981]. We also aim to develop abstract constructions by using appropriate logical tools to give a direct logical characterization of the following programming languages of our theory: $rP_\sigma$, $P_\sigma^1$, $rP_\sigma^1$, $P_\sigma^2$ and $rP_\sigma^2$. Here $rP_\sigma^i$ ($P_\sigma^i$) ($i = 1, 2$) denotes the programming language obtained by augmenting $rP_\sigma$ ($P_\sigma$) with the possibility to use $i$ stacks. The constructions we define are the set of recursively enumerable relations, the set of inductively defined relations and the set of effectively inductively definable relations, denoted as $Rec$, $I$ and $EI$, respectively. Note that the constructions developed by Moldestad, Stoltenberg-Hansen, Tucker [1978] and used for logical characterization of some abstract computational machinery are close to ours regarding their attitude of using inductive definability. Our logical characterization yields the following results:

$$\begin{array}{rcl} rP & \approx & Rec \\ P^1 & \approx & EI \\ rP^1 & \approx & I \\ P^2 & \approx & EI^c \end{array}$$

where the superscript $c$ indicates that the usage of the set of natural numbers together with the basic functions is allowed.

We emphasize two consequences of our logical characterization which allow the development of dynamic logic and its axiomatization in the classical first-order framework. Namely, it follows that *transitive and reflexive closure* plays the main role when we intend to characterize the denotational semantics of programs without stacks. However, this is not enough if the programs are with stacks. In this case *the solutions* of appropriate *fixed-point equations* are needed to define the required semantics. By axiomatizing the transitive and reflexive closure and the solutions of certain types of fixed-point equations we define two different programming logics in the scope of classical first-order logic.

In Part I we also generalize Church's thesis to our logical framework.

**Extended dynamic logics.** Part II is devoted to the consideration of the main program properties, and a version of dynamic logic is introduced on the base of our programming language $rP_\sigma$. We consider only the so-called regular dynamic logic since only it corresponds to our intuition on effective computability. Special attention is given to the investigation of the main properties of dynamic logic. Completeness is the focus of this investigation. It is shown that this descriptive language is incomplete, by proving the incompleteness of the Floyd-Hoare sublanguage of dynamic logic.

Different ways are then considered to make the Floyd-Hoare language complete. Two main possibilities are followed. The first one restricts the set of formulas allowed from the language in order to get completeness. The second possibility is to change the notion of completeness. Beyond the known property of relative completeness we introduce a new notion called stop completeness.

The main results of this part are connected with the development of two different programming logics in the scope of classical first-order logic which are defined in accordance with the logical characterization of programming languages, i.e. of programming families developed in Part I. This development is connected with making internal the formal notions that are used to describe program semantics. This internalization can be ensured by providing appropriate tools for defining these notions in the logic in question. First we show how dynamic logic can be developed in classical first-order logic by internalizing only the denotational semantics. This internalization is allowed by an appropriate axiomatization of reflexive and transitive closure. For the latter we use a special extended language based on the notion of *transitive extension.* By the use of this extended language we introduce two axiom systems $Ind_\sigma$ and $Ind^*_\sigma$ which differ in the formulas with respect to which the transfinite induction works. On the base of the transitive extension we introduce the extended dynamic logic which is to define two different and more concrete dynamic logics by using the axiom systems $Ind_\sigma$ and $Ind^*_\sigma$. These are the dynamic logic with *continuous denotational semantics* and that with *strongly continuous denotational semantics.* The first one we also call non-standard dynamic logic because it has all the necessary semantic properties that the dynamic logic developed by the Hungarian school has. The only difference is that the latter is developed in time logic, i.e. with explicit time consideration, while in our case the non-standard dynamic logic is just a first-order version of the regular dynamic logic without, for example, explicit time handling. Note that the continuous and definable denotational semantics are close in character to the continuous and definitional trace semantics respectively introduced in the framework of time logic. By the introduced extended language we define the *extended dynamic logic* whose important particular case is *non-standard dynamic logic*. Therefore, a counterpart of the main object of investigation of the Hungarian school, i.e. non-standard dynamic logic, is obtained by an appropriately constructed extension. We establish the compactness and the completeness of the extended dynamic logic and also that of the non-standard dynamic logic.

The role of the two axiom systems $Ind_\sigma$ and $Ind^*_\sigma$ is crucial in first-order characterization of the methods and of their derivation system to prove program properties. First we characterize the Floyd-Hoare method (denoted as $Cal_{FH}$) by the use of $Ind_\sigma$ and we establish its completeness with respect to $Ind_\sigma$, i.e. with respect to the continuous denotational semantics. Moreover, by using axiom schema $Ind^*_\sigma$ we are the first to succeed in giving a purely first-order axiomatic characterization of the calculus (denoted as $Cal_{DL}$) for the regular dynamic logic given by Harel [1979]. Sain [1984] also gives a characterization of this calculus, but within the framework of time logic supposing Peano axioms for the data structure.

However, dynamic logic is appropriate only to describe properties of programs which do not use stacks. This is connected with the pecularity of the Floyd-Hoare method that it considers only the properties of the data environment of the program under execution in a given moment of time independently of the properties before and after this moment. That is, this method describes program properties in a "context-free" way, supposing that a "state transformer" can describe execution, which, however, is not true when the use of stacks is allowed in the programs. In order to describe programs with one stack a new language was developed: the so-called *inductive logic*. This language is also obtained by an appropriate extension called inductive extension. This extension is defined such that it contains at least one solution of some well-defined set of fixed-point equations, since as we know from Part I it is necessary for characterizing the denotational semantics of the programs with stack. By the use of the extended language we axiomatize the main properties required from the semantics by introducing two axiom systems $\nabla Ind_\sigma$ and $\nabla Ind^*_\sigma$ with the same role as in the case of transitive extension. By using the axiom systems $\nabla Ind_\sigma$ and $\nabla Ind^*_\sigma$ we define in this framework the so-called *definable* and *strongly definable denotational semantics* which together with the inductive logic form the *dynamic logic with definable denotational semantics* and *that with strongly definable denotational semantics*, respectively.

We show that these dynamic logics are compact and complete. A derivation system called $I/O$-calculus and denoted as $Cal_{I/O}$ is developed which was suggested by L. Úry. This calculus is in character between the Floyd-Hoare calculus and that of the usual calculus of classical first-order logic. This calculus eliminates the main disadvantages of the Floyd-Hoare style methods connected with their above mentioned ideology, and so it becomes appropriate to prove properties of programs which use one stack. This calculus considers program execution along with establishing the program structure and some interrelations between the computational states representable at the structural level.

Inductive logic also allows the axiomatic characterization of derivation systems by using axioms systems $\nabla Ind_\sigma$ and $\nabla Ind^*_\sigma$. The first one can be used to characterize the Floyd-Hoare calculus, while the second one is appropriate to characterize the $I/O$-calculus.

**Temporal Logic.** First-order temporal logic is considered in Part III. The version introduced here has Kripke models which consist of data, time and functions. The functions are used to represent operational program semantics; however, they appear only at the metalevel, in the model definition, while the syntax does not contain them. Concerning time we define an axiom system $Nord$, which, however, does not ensure the existence of preceding time moments to the time moments differing from 0. The Kripke models will be built up by using the models of $Nord$ as time structures.

We consider only first-order descriptive languages, so their investigation, as one might expect, is more difficult than that of the propositional case. Moreover, some unexpected results have been found. Namely, while comparing the expressive power of (regular) dynamic logic and standard temporal logic it turns out that in the case of first-order logic they are incomparable, while in the propositional case (regular) dynamic logic is more powerful (cf. Harel [1984]). We show that there exists a temporal logical formula that cannot be interpreted in dynamic logic and we also show the existence of a dynamic logical formula not interpretable in temporal logic. However, if we restrict ourselves to countable models then a surprising result takes shape. While first-order dynamic logic can be interpreted in temporal logic, the latter remains non-interpretable in the former logic even now. These results show that first-order temporal logic is of interest for programming theory, despite Meyer's conclusion that temporal logic is theoretically of no interest (see p.28 of Meyer [1980]).

In this part we continue the axiomatic characterization of different program verification methods. Namely, we axiomatize three different induction principles by the axiom schemas $MInd_\sigma$, $MInd^B_\sigma$, $MInd^P_\sigma$. We show that these axiom systems characterize three different program verification methods: the Floyd-Hoare method, and two temporal logical methods suggested by Burstall [1974] under the name of the method of intermittent assertions and the method suggested by Pnueli [1977]. Note that these two methods are based on an arbitrary but fixed calculus of temporal logic. Let $Cal_B$ and $Cal_P$ denote these temporal logical methods, respectively. Moreover, we compare these methods with respect to their expressive power. We succeed in showing that the comparison of these program verification methods can already be established in the framework of first-order temporal logic. Note that the characterization and comparative investigation of these methods was first performed by Sain [1986] in the time-logic framework, which as we shall see is more powerful than temporal logic. We also emphasize that temporal logic methods are not adequate to describe program properties of programs which use stacks. This is so because the temporal logical methods remain context free with respect to the states of the program execution.

**Time Logic.** Part IV is devoted to the descriptive language called *time logic* which is introduced as an appropriate extension that explicitly considers data, time and possible data change at both the meta and the object levels. The set of possible data and the set of possible time moments are used to model the computer. The possible data changes (which are represented by appropriate functions) are used to characterize program execution or computer functioning. It is shown that time logic eliminates the disadvantages of both dynamic and temporal logics. Moreover, the dynamic and temporal logics can be embedded into this time logic. To all constructions of the previous logics, appropriate time-logical axioms will correspond which can be obtained by the embedding functions.Therefore, for example, the models used in different programming logics can be axiomatized in the models of time logic.

Using the time logic embedding of different descriptive languages we can establish their interrelation with respect to their expressive power. It will be shown that time logic is the most powerful, while the Floyd-Hoare language is the least powerful. Between them, though incomparable, the dynamic and temporal logics are situated. That is, we have the following net:

Time logic $TL_\sigma$

$\nearrow \quad \nwarrow$

Temporal logic $ML_\sigma$ $\qquad$ $DL_\sigma$ Extended dynamic logic

$\nwarrow \quad \nearrow$

Floyd-Hoare logic $HL_\sigma$

Below we will see how this net can be formulated more precisely.

We continue the axiomatic characterization of different program verification methods. First of all we characterize the calculi $Cal_{FH}$, $Cal_B$ and $Cal_P$ by embedding the axiom systems $MInd_\sigma$, $MInd_\sigma^B$ and $MInd_\sigma^P$ into the time logic. The axiom systems so obtained are denoted as $TInd_\sigma$, $TInd_\sigma^B$ and $TInd_\sigma^P$, respectively, and coincide with those established by Sain [1986].

Note that historically the first result in axiomatic characterization of these methods was obtained by Csirmaz [1981] who showed that $Cal_{FH}$ can be characterized by an appropriate induction axiom schema and that it is complete with respect to continuous trace semantics. A new and very elegant proof for this fact was given by Sain [1985a,1985b] and is much simpler than Csirmaz' proof.

While the induction axiom schemas concern data dependency on time, appropriate axioms should also be considered which characterize the set of functions that corresponds to possible data changes. These axioms are different versions of the *comprehension schemas* well known from axiomatic set theory. These axioms together with the inductive schemas are used to define different versions of regular time theory. We emphasize three of them, $Reg_\sigma^*$, $Reg_\sigma^\nabla$ and $Reg_\sigma$ which are used to axiomatically characterize $Cal_{DL}$, $Cal_{I/O}$ and $Cal_1$.

The latter is an arbitrary but fixed classical first-order calculus whose applicability is shown in Gergely, Úry [1981] and independently in Andréka, Németi, Sain [1982]. Note that the axiom systems $Reg_\sigma^*$ and $Reg_\sigma^\nabla$ are obtained by the corresponding translations of $Ind_\sigma^*$ and $\nabla Ind_\sigma^*$ into time logic. It is important to emphasize that the program verification method characterized by $Reg_\sigma^\nabla$ allows us to prove program properties for the programming languages $P_\sigma^1$ and $P_\sigma^2$. Comparison of these axiom systems shows how the corresponding verification methods are interrelated with respect to expressive (proof) power. The comparison results in the following net:

$$
\begin{array}{ccccc}
 & & Reg_\sigma & & \\
 & \nearrow & & \nwarrow & \\
TInd_\sigma^P & & & & Reg_\sigma^\nabla \\
\uparrow & & & & \uparrow \\
TInd_\sigma^B & & & & Reg_\sigma^* \\
 & \nwarrow & & \nearrow & \\
 & & TInd_\sigma & &
\end{array}
$$

Note that the first comparative investigation of the calculi $Cal_{FH}$, $Cal_B$, $Cal_P$ and $Cal_1$ was done by Sain [1986] (its English version is Sain [1991]) by the use of time-logical characterization. We also remark that the programming theory based on time logic is appropriate to express many important programming notions, such as total correctness and initial algebras, for example.

In order to have a comprehensive picture of the main tools developed in our first-order programming theory we sum up the main programming logics in the following table, where we indicate what type of semantics they use and show which axiomatizations they allow and which verification methods are characterized by them.

| Logic | Program Semantics | Axiom systems | | | | | |
|---|---|---|---|---|---|---|---|
| | | $P_\sigma$ | | | | $P_\sigma^1, P_\sigma^{1,c}$ | |
| Dynamic | Denotation | $Ind_\sigma$ | | | $Ind_\sigma^*$ | | |
| Inductive | Denotation | $\nabla Ind_\sigma$ | | | | $\nabla Ind_\sigma^*$ | |
| Temporal | Trace | $MInd_\sigma$ | $MInd_\sigma^B$ | $MInd_\sigma^P$ | | | |
| Time | Trace | $TInd_\sigma$ | $TInd_\sigma^B$ | $TInd_\sigma^P$ | $Reg_\sigma^*$ | $Reg_\sigma^\nabla$ | $Reg_\sigma$ |
| Method | | $Cal_{FH}$ | $Cal_B$ | $Cal_P$ | $Cal_{DL}$ | $Cal_{I/O}$ | $Cal_1$ |

This table at the same time sums up the main new results obtained in Parts II, III and IV while developing the second subfield of our programming theory in a strict interrelation with the programming languages, program semantics and computation theory obtained in Part I when developing the first subfield. This interrelation gives our programming theory a unique face of its own, which we hope our readers will recognize.

# Mathematical Background

Chapter 1

# Logic and Model Theory

The programming theory to be developed in this work is based on first-order classical logic. In order to follow this development we expect the reader to be familiar with the elements of classical mathematical logic and with the basic notions of (naive) set theory that we accept as our starting point.

We use all the set theoretic and logical ideas in the traditional sense as they are defined e.g. in Mendelson [1964] or in Chang, Keisler [1973]. The ideas which are not defined in this chapter but will be met in the work should be understood as defined in Chang, Keisler [1973].

In Section 1.1 we highlight all the notions and notations including those of set theory important for our purposes. Section 1.2 provides the main definitions for the abstract language concept together with that of the derivation system. We emphasize that according to our view a language is a pair comprising syntax and semantics which slightly differs from that of most of the textbooks in mathematical logic, whose notion of language corresponds to our notion of syntax. Note that this language concept has been introduced in Andréka, Gergely, Németi [1975a]. The basic notions of the many-sorted classical first-order language are given in Section 1.3. A special kind of relation is introduced in Section 1.4 to handle many-sorted relations. The notion of ultraproduct, which is an important tool to construct models, is given in Section 1.5. Arithmetic plays an important role in computation, and so it does too in the theory of programming. The main arithmetical ideas important for our investigation are listed in Section 1.6.

The reader familiar with mathematical logic at a professional level can skim over this chapter except for Sections 1.2 and 1.4. In order to understand the notations used throughout the book it is essential that (s)he become acquainted with these two sections.

## 1.1 Basic Mathematical Notions

We start by reviewing the basic mathematical notions - used throughout the book - together with the basic set-theoretic notions.

For informal logic, i.e. for the metalanguage, we use "$\rightarrow$" for "implies", "$\leftrightarrow$" or "iff" for "if and only if", "$\neg$" for "not", "$\wedge$" for "and", "$\vee$" for "or",

"$\exists$" for "there exists", "$\forall$" for "for all" and "$\rightleftharpoons$" for "equal by definition". We will also use quantification over a given set $A$ in the form $\forall x \in A$ or $\exists x \in A$.

The notation $\{x \mid \phi(x)\}$ denotes the family of all $x$ which satisfy $\phi$. $x \in A$ means that $x$ is an element of $A$. $A \subseteq B$ (or $B \supseteq A$) means that $A$ is a subset of $B$. If $A \subseteq B$ and $B \subseteq A$ then the sets $A$ and $B$ are equal, which is denoted by $A = B$. $A \subset B$ (or $B \supset A$) means that $A$ is a proper subset of $B$, i.e. $A \subseteq B$ and $A \neq B$. $Sb(A)$ denotes the set of all subsets of $A$. $Sb_{<\alpha}(A)$ denotes the set of all subsets of $A$ having cardinality less than $\alpha$. $\emptyset$ denotes the empty set. Note that for any set $A$ we have $\emptyset \in Sb(A)$. The set-theoretic operations union $\cup$, intersection $\cap$ and difference $\setminus$ have their usual meaning. If $A \cap B = \emptyset$, $A$ and $B$ are said to be disjoint. As usual, $\cup^*$ denotes the disjoint union.

With any sets $x, y$ we associate an ordered pair $(x, y) = \{\{x\}, \{x, y\}\}$. The ordered $n$-tuple $(x_1, ..., x_n)$ of the sets $x_1, ..., x_n$ is defined by induction on $n$ for any $n > 2$ as the ordered pair $((x_1, ..., x_{n-1}), x_n)$.

The set $\{(x_1, ..., x_n) \mid x_1 \in X_1, ..., x_n \in X_n\}$ is called the direct product of the sets $X_1, ..., X_n$ and it is denoted by

$$\prod_{i=1}^{n} X_i \text{ or } X_1 \times ... \times X_n \text{ or } \prod\{X_i \mid i = 1, ..., n\}$$

If $X_1 = ... = X_n = X$ then we simply write

$$X^n = \prod_{i=1}^{n} X.$$

As usual, take $X^0 \rightleftharpoons \{\emptyset\}$ and $X^1 \rightleftharpoons X$. For any $n > 0$ a set $R$ is said to be an $n$-ary relation iff $R \subseteq \prod\{X_i \mid i = 1, ..., n\}$ for some sets $X_1, ..., X_n$. We use the projection functions $\pi_i : \prod_1^n X_j \to X_i$. For any $x = (x_1, ..., x_n)$: $\pi_i(x) \rightleftharpoons x_i$.
Let $R$ be an $n$-ary relation on $X_1, ..., X_n$, i.e.

$$R \subseteq \prod_{i=1}^{n} X_i \text{ and } x_i \in X_i \text{ for } i = 1, ..., n.$$

We say that $x_1, ..., x_n$ are in relation $R$, (denoted as $R(x_1, ..., x_n)$) iff $(x_1, ..., x_n) \in R$. For binary relation $R$ we also use the notation $x_1 R x_2$ instead of $(x_1, x_2) \in R$.
Let $R \subseteq A \times B$, $Q \subseteq B \times C$ be two binary relations. As usual we use the following notations:

- $dom\ R \rightleftharpoons \{a \mid \exists b \in B\ (a, b) \in R\}$ (the domain of a relation)
- $R^{-1} \rightleftharpoons \{(b, a) \mid (a, b) \in R\}$ (the inverse relation)
- $rng\ R \rightleftharpoons dom\ R^{-1}$ (the range of a relation)
- $R \circ Q \rightleftharpoons \{(a, c) \mid \exists b\ (a, b) \in R \text{ and } (b, c) \in Q\}$ (the composition of two relations)
- $R\restriction_{X \times Y} \rightleftharpoons \{(a, b) \mid a \in X, b \in Y, (a, b) \in R\}$ (the restriction of the relation)

- $R\restriction_{X.} \rightleftharpoons R\restriction_{X \times B}$ (the restriction of the domain of the relation)
- $R\restriction_{.Y} \rightleftharpoons R\restriction_{A \times Y}$ (the restriction of the range of the relation)

An $(n+1)$-ary relation $F \subseteq \prod_{i=1}^{n+1} X_i$ is said to be a functional relation iff for any $(x_1, ..., x_n) \in \prod_{i=1}^{n} X_i$ and for any $x_{n+1}, x'_{n+1} \in X_{n+1}$ if $(x_1, ..., x_n, x_{n+1}) \in F$ and $(x_1, ..., x_n, x'_{n+1}) \in F$ then $x_{n+1} = x'_{n+1}$. Take

$$\begin{aligned} dom\ F &\rightleftharpoons \{(x_1, ..., x_n) \mid \exists x_{n+1} \in X_{n+1}\ (x_1, ... x_n, x_{n+1}) \in F\} \\ rng\ F &\rightleftharpoons \{x \mid \exists (x_1, ..., x_n) \in \textstyle\prod_{i=1}^{n} X_i\ (x_1, ..., x_n, x) \in F\} \end{aligned}$$

For any $n$-ary functional relation $F \subseteq \prod_{i=1}^{n+1} X_i$ we use the notations

(i) $F : X_1 \times .... \times X_n \rightarrow_p X_{n+1}$
(ii) $F(x_1, ..., x_n) = x_{n+1}$ iff $(x_1, ..., x_n, x_{n+1}) \in F$.

A functional relation $F : X_1 \times ... \times X_n \rightarrow_p X_{n+1}$ is onto or surjective iff $rng\ F = X_{n+1}$. $F$ is one-one or injective iff for any $x \in rng\ F$ there exists a unique $(x_1, ..., x_n) \in domF$ such that $F(x_1, ..., x_n) = x$. $F$ is said to be a bijection iff it is both onto and one-one.

A functional relation $F : \prod_{i=1}^{n} X_i \rightarrow_p X_{n+1}$ is sometimes said to be a partial function. A partial function $F : \prod_{i=1}^{n} X_i \rightarrow_p X_{n+1}$ is called a function iff $domF = \prod_{i=1}^{n} X_i$. The notation $F : \prod_{i=1}^{n} X_i \rightarrow X_{n+1}$ means that $F$ is a function.

Sometimes we use the $\lambda$-notation to define functions. Let $x \in A$ and $t$ be an expression depending on $x$. Let us define a function $f : A \rightarrow B$ such that for all $x \in A$, $f(x) \rightleftharpoons t$. This function is denoted by $\lambda x.t$ or $\lambda x \in A.t$.

${}^{A}B$ or $[A \rightarrow B]$ denotes the set of all functions from $A$ to $B$. In the case of partial functions we use the notation $[A \rightarrow_p B]$. Note that ${}^{A}B$ is also called the $A$-th power of $B$. If $F : A \rightarrow B$ is a function and $C \subseteq A$ then $F\restriction_C$ denotes the restriction of $F$ to the set $C \times B$. If $F : A \rightarrow_p B$ and $G : B \rightarrow_p C$ are two given functions then $F \circ G$ denotes their composition (in that order). This means that for an $a \in A$: $(F \circ G)(a) = G(F(a))$.

Let $I$ be a (perhaps infinite) set of indices and let us consider a fixed $I$-indexed family of sets $\{X_i \mid i \in I\}$. A function $f$ is called a *choice function* on this family if $dom\, f = I$ and for each $i \in I$, $f(i) \in X_i$. The direct product of the family of sets $\{X_i \mid i \in I\}$, denoted by

$$\prod_{i \in I} X_i \text{ or } \prod\{X_i \mid i \in I\},$$

is defined as the set of all choice functions belonging to this family of sets, i.e.

$$\prod_{i \in I} X_i \rightleftharpoons \{f \mid f \in [I \rightarrow \cup\{X_i \mid i \in I\}], \forall i \in I : f(i) \in X_i\}.$$

It is easy to see that if $I$ is finite then this definition is naturally isomorphic to the above defined notion of direct product.

We identify any ordinal with the set of all ordinals less than itself, i.e. $\alpha = \{\beta \mid \beta < \alpha\}$. Natural numbers are the finite ordinals. $\omega_0$ or $\mathbb{N}$ is the set of all natural numbers, i.e. the first infinite ordinal. We denote the class of all ordinals by $On$. As usual $\omega_1$ is the first non-countable ordinal. If $\alpha$ is an ordinal, $\alpha^+$ is the least cardinal greater than $\alpha$. $|A|$ denotes the cardinality of the set $A$.

$A^*$ denotes the set of all finite sequences of elements of $A$, i.e. the set of all $A$-valued functions defined on natural numbers. It means that $A^* = \bigcup\{^nA : n \in \mathbb{N}\}$. $\lambda$ denotes the empty sequence. Similarly $A^\infty$ denotes the set of all infinite sequences of elements of $A$. Thus, $A^\infty \rightleftharpoons {}^{\mathbb{N}}A$. $\langle x \rangle$ denotes the 1-length sequence with the only member $x$. $s_1 \circ s_2$ is the concatenation of two sequences. If $s_1$ is an infinite sequence then, by definition, $s_1 \circ s_2 = s_1$.

The set of finite and infinite sequences is denoted by $A^{\leq\omega}$, i.e. $A^{\leq\omega} \rightleftharpoons A^* \cup A^\infty$. Let $s \in A^{\leq\omega}$ be a sequence. $length(s)$ denotes the length of $s$. Obviously $length(\lambda) = 0$. We sometimes use $|s|$ to denote the length of a sequence.

Let $n \in \mathbb{N}$ and $s$ be a sequence of length $n$, consisting of elements of $A$. We often write $(s(0), s(1), ..., s(n-1))$ instead of $s$, i.e. we consider $s$ as an (ordered) n-tuple. If $i \leq n$ then we write $s\restriction_i$ for the sequence $(s(0), s(1), ..., s(i-1))$. We also use $in\, s$ and $out\, s$ instead of $s(0)$ and $s(length(s)-1)$, respectively. It may happen that $A$ is a function space, say $[V \to B]$. If $W \subseteq V$ and $s \in A^* \cup A^\infty$ then $s\restriction_W$ is a shorthand for the sequence $(s(0)\restriction_W, ..., s(i)\restriction_W, ...)$.

## 1.2 Derivation Systems

Given a formal language like a $\sigma$-type first-order one with formally defined syntax and semantics, we are able to describe and characterize different objects of interest. However, in order to support getting new formulas from some given ones or establishing the truth value of a formula of interest, appropriate formal tools are required.

First we introduce the main notions at an abstract level.

**(1.1) Definition.** *A language is a triple $\mathcal{L} = (F, M, \models)$, where $F$ and $M$ are a non-empty set and a class, respectively and $\models \subseteq M \times F$. $F$ is called the set of formulas, $M$ is called the class of models and $\models$ is called the validity relation.*

As usual, we use an infix notation, i.e. if $\phi \in F$ and $m \in M$ then instead of $(m, \phi) \in \models$ we write $m \models \phi$ and say that $\phi$ is true in $m$ or $m$ is a model of $\phi$. Let $A \subseteq F$, and let $m \in M$. We say that the set $A$ of formulas is true in the model $m$ iff for all $\phi \in A$: $m \models \phi$. Let $A \subseteq F$ be a fixed set of formulas. The models of $A$ (in the language $\mathcal{L}$) is the class $Mod(A)$ of models within which $A$ is true, i.e.

$$Mod(A) \rightleftharpoons \{m \mid m \models A\}.$$

Let $\mathcal{K} \subseteq M$ be a fixed class of models. The theory of $\mathcal{K}$ is the set $Th(\mathcal{K})$ of formulas which are true in all the models belonging to $\mathcal{K}$, i.e.

$$Th(\mathcal{K}) \rightleftharpoons \{\phi \mid \text{for all } m \in \mathcal{K} : m \models \phi\}.$$

The validity relation can be extended to a consequence relation in the following way. Let $A \subseteq F$ and $\chi \in F$ be fixed. We say that $\chi$ is a *consequence* of $A$ iff $\chi \in Th(Mod(A))$. In this case we simply write $A \models \chi$. The elements of the set $Th(Mod(\emptyset))$ are called the universally valid formulas (or tautologies) of the language $\mathcal{L}$, and this set is also denoted by $Th(\mathcal{L})$.

**(1.2) Definition.** *Let $F$ be a fixed set. A mapping $\vdash: Sb(F) \to Sb(F)$ is said to be a derivation system for $F$ iff it satisfies the following conditions:*

*(i) $A \subseteq \vdash(A)$ for any $A \subseteq F$.*
*(ii) If $A \subseteq \vdash(B)$ then $\vdash(A) \subseteq \vdash(B)$ for any $A, B \subseteq F$.*
*(iii) $\vdash(A) = \bigcup\{\vdash(B) \mid B \subseteq A$ and $B$ is finite $\}$ for any $A \subseteq F$.*

*If $\chi \in F$ and $\chi \in \vdash(A)$ then we say that $\chi$ is derivable from $A$, written as $A \vdash \chi$.*

Let $\mathcal{L}$ be a language. The validity relation $\models$ can be extended to a map $\models: Sb(F) \to Sb(F)$ by taking

$$\models(A) \rightleftharpoons \{\chi \in F \mid A \models \chi\}.$$

It is clear that $\models$ satisfies the properties (i)-(ii) of the above definition if we replace $\vdash$ by $\models$.

**(1.3) Definition.** *Let $\mathcal{L} = (F, M, \models)$ be a language and let $\vdash$ be a derivation system for $F$.*

*(a) The derivation system $\vdash$ is complete (with respect to $\mathcal{L}$) iff for all $A \subseteq F$, $\vdash(A) \supseteq \models(A)$.*
*(b) The derivation system $\vdash$ is sound (with respect to $\mathcal{L}$) iff for all $A \subseteq F$, $\vdash(A) \subseteq \models(A)$.*

Let us suppose that $\lceil\cdot\rceil : F \to \mathbb{N}$ is a one-one function, which is also called a *numeration*. If so then we have the right to speak about recursive and recursively enumerable sets of formulas. For example a set $A \subseteq F$ is recursive iff $\lceil A \rceil$ $(= \{\lceil\phi\rceil \mid \phi \in A\})$ is recursive as a subset of $\mathbb{N}$.

**(1.4) Definition.** *Let $\mathcal{L} = (F, M, \models)$ be a fixed language with numeration $\lceil\cdot\rceil$.*

*(a) Language $\mathcal{L}$ is called complete iff $Th(\mathcal{L})$ is recursively enumerable.*
*(b) Language $\mathcal{L}$ is called complete with respect to consequence iff for all $A \subseteq F$, $\models(A)$ is recursively enumerable in $A$.*

(c) *Let $A \subseteq F$ be a fixed set of formulas. The set $A$ is called axiomatizable iff there is a recursively enumerable set of axioms, say $Ax$, such that $Th(Ax) = Th(A)$.*

(d) *Language $\mathcal{L}$ is called compact iff for all $A \subseteq F$ and $\phi \in F$, if $A \models \phi$ then there is a finite $A' \subseteq A$ such that $A' \models \phi$.*

We are often interested not in the whole Th($\mathcal{L}$) but only in one of its subsets $E$.

**(1.5) Definition.** *Let $E \subseteq F$ be an arbitrary set of formulas. A derivation system $\vdash$ is complete with respect to $E$ iff*

*(i)* $\vdash$ *is sound with respect to* $\mathcal{L}$,

*(ii)* $E \subseteq \vdash(\emptyset)$.

**(1.6) Definition.** *A calculus is a partial map $K : Sb(F) \rightarrow_p Sb(F)$. A calculus is called finitary iff $A \in dom(K)$ implies that $A$ is finite.*

As usual, if $\phi \in K(\{\phi_1, ..., \phi_k\})$ where $\phi_1, ..., \phi_k, \phi \in F$, we write this fact as an inference rule:

$$\frac{\phi_1, ..., \phi_k}{\phi}.$$

We will see that any finitary calculus $K$ defines a derivation system. Let $A \subseteq F$ be fixed. Define $C_K(A)$ by taking

$$C_K(A) \rightleftharpoons \{\chi \mid \chi \in F, \exists B \subseteq A : \chi \in K(B)\}.$$

Any element of $C_K(A)$ is called a one-step consequence of $A$. The derivable formulas can be obtained by applying one-step consequence finitely many times. Take

$$\begin{aligned} K^0(A) &\rightleftharpoons A; \\ K^{n+1}(A) &\rightleftharpoons C_K(K^n(A)); \\ \vdash_K(A) &\rightleftharpoons \textstyle\bigcup_{n \in \mathbb{N}} K^n(A). \end{aligned}$$

**(1.7) Lemma.** *For any finitary calculus $K$, $\vdash_K$ is a derivation system.*

A calculus is called *recursive* iff the relation

$$R \rightleftharpoons \{((\phi_1, ..., \phi_n), \chi) \mid n \in \mathbb{N},\ \phi_1, ..., \phi_n, \chi \in F,\ \chi \in \vdash_K (\{\phi_1, ..., \phi_n\})\}$$

is recursive.

## 1.3 Basic Notions of Many-Sorted First-Order Language

First let us define the notion of a many-sorted similarity type, from which the language is going to be built up.

**(1.8) Definition.** *A triple $\sigma = (S, ar_r, ar_f)$ is said to be a many-sorted similarity type iff*

*(i) $S$ is a nonempty set called the set of sorts;*
*(ii) $ar_r$ and $ar_f$ are functions so that $rng\, ar_r \subseteq S^*$ and $rng\, ar_f \subseteq (S^* \setminus \{\lambda\})$ and $dom\ ar_r$, $dom\ ar_f$ and $S$ are pairwise disjoint sets.*

The functions $ar_r$ and $ar_f$ are called arity functions. The elements of $dom\, ar_r$ and $dom\, ar_f$ are said to be the relation symbols and function symbols, respectively. A function symbol $c$ with $ar_f(c) = \langle s \rangle$ is called an ($s$-sorted) constant symbol.

If $\sigma$ is a many-sorted similarity type then we use the following notations:

$$\begin{aligned} sort\ \sigma &\rightleftharpoons S \\ rel\ \sigma &\rightleftharpoons dom\, ar_r \\ func\ \sigma &\rightleftharpoons dom\, ar_f. \end{aligned}$$

For $i = 1, 2$, let $\sigma_i = (S^i, ar_r^i, ar_f^i)$ be two similarity types. We say that $\sigma_2$ is an expansion of $\sigma_1$ (or $\sigma_1$ is a reduction of $\sigma_2$) (written as $\sigma_1 \subseteq \sigma_2$) iff

- $S^1 \subseteq S^2$;
- $ar_r^1 = ar_r^2 \restriction dom\ ar_r^1$;
- $ar_f^1 = ar_f^2 \restriction dom\ ar_f^1$.

A similarity type $\sigma$ is said to be finite iff $|sort\ \sigma \cup rel\ \sigma \cup func\ \sigma| < \omega_0$. Throughout the work we deal mainly with finite similarity types. Instead of the functions $ar_r$ and $ar_f$ we use a unique function $ar$ defined on $dom\, ar_r \cup dom\, ar_f$ as follows:

$$ar(r) = \begin{cases} ar_r(r) & \text{if } r \in dom\, ar_r; \\ ar_f(r) & \text{if } r \in dom\, ar_f. \end{cases}$$

Thus the function $ar$ renders the corresponding sequence of sorts to each relation and function symbol of a similarity type $\sigma$, i.e.

(i) if $\rho \in rel\, \sigma$ then $ar(\rho) = (s_1, ..., s_n)$;
(ii) if $f \in func\, \sigma$ then $ar(f) = (s_1, ..., s_n; s_{n+1})$;

for some $n \in \mathbb{N}$ and $s_i \in sort\, \sigma\, (i = 1, ..., n+1)$.

Later we shall write $\rho : s_1, ..., s_n$ if $\rho \in rel\ \sigma$ and $ar(\rho) = (s_1, ..., s_n)$ and $f : s_1, ..., s_n \to s_{n+1}$ if $f \in func\ \sigma$ and $ar(f) = (s_1, ...s_n; s_{n+1})$, respectively.

If $\sigma$ is a similarity type for which $|sort\, \sigma| = 1$ then we use the following simplification of the function $ar$:

$$ar'(r) \rightleftharpoons \begin{cases} length(ar(r)) & \text{if } r \in rel\,\sigma; \\ length(ar(r)) - 1 & \text{if } r \in func\,\sigma. \end{cases}$$

Further on we write $ar$ instead of $ar'$ without danger of ambiguity.
Let $R$ be a new relation symbol (i.e. $R \notin (func\,\sigma \cup rel\,\sigma)$). $\sigma \cup \{R\}$ will denote the new similarity type obtained from $\sigma$ by adding the new symbol $R$. This means that if the arity of $R$ is $(s_1, ..., s_n)$ then

$$\sigma \cup \{R\} \rightleftharpoons (S \cup \{s_1, ..., s_n\}, ar \cup (R, (s_1, ..., s_n))).$$

We use the notation $\sigma \cup \{R_1, ..., R_k\}$ or $\sigma^R$ to express the fact that the new relation symbols $R_1$,...,$R_k$ are added to the similarity type $\sigma$.

Now we consider many-sorted models.

**(1.9) Definition.** *Let $\sigma$ be a many-sorted similarity type. A $\sigma$-type model is a function $\mathcal{A}$ with the following properties:*

*(i) for any $s \in sort\,\sigma$, $\mathcal{A}(s) = A_s$ is a nonempty set; $A \rightleftharpoons \bigcup\{A_s \mid s \in sort\,\sigma\}$ is said to be the universe of the model (sometimes we write $\mathcal{A}(\sigma) = A$);*
*(ii) for any $\rho \in rel\ \sigma$ such that $ar(\rho) = (s_1, ..., s_n)$*

$$\mathcal{A}(\rho) \subseteq \prod_{i=1}^{n} A_{s_i};$$

*(iii) for any $f \in func\ \sigma$ such that $ar(f) = (s_1, ..., s_n; s)$*

$$\mathcal{A}(f) : \prod_{i=1}^{n} A_{s_i} \to A_s.$$

*The class of all $\sigma$-type models is denoted by $Mod_\sigma$.*
*(iv) Let $\mathcal{A}$ be a $\sigma$-type model and let us suppose that a similarity type $\delta \subseteq \sigma$ is a reduction of $\sigma$. The $\delta$ type reduction of the $\sigma$-type model $\mathcal{A}$ (written as $\mathcal{A}\restriction_\delta$) is the unique $\delta$-type model $\mathcal{B}$ defined in the following way:*
- *for all $s \in sort\ \delta$: $\mathcal{B}(s) = \mathcal{A}(s)$;*
- *for all $f \in func\ \delta$: $\mathcal{B}(f) = \mathcal{A}(f)$;*
- *for all $r \in rel\ \delta$: $\mathcal{B}(r) = \mathcal{A}(r)$.*

*In this case we also say that $\mathcal{A}$ is an extension of $\mathcal{B}$.*

Sometimes we write $r_\mathcal{A}$ instead of $\mathcal{A}(r)$ for any $\mathcal{A} \in Mod_\sigma$ and for any symbol $r \in dom\,ar$. We use script capital letters for the models while for their universe the corresponding italic capital letters are used.

**(1.10) Definition.** *Let $\mathcal{A}$,$\mathcal{B}$ be two $\sigma$-type models. $\mathcal{B}$ is a submodel of $\mathcal{A}$ or $\mathcal{A}$ is an extension of $\mathcal{B}$ iff*

*(i) for any $s \in sort\ \sigma$, $B_s \subseteq A_s$*
*(ii) for any $\rho \in rel\ \sigma$ such that $ar(\rho) = (s_1, ..., s_n)$*

$$\rho_{\mathcal{B}} = \rho_{\mathcal{A}} \upharpoonright \prod_{i=1}^{n} B_{s_i};$$

*(iii) for any $f \in func\ \sigma$ such that $ar(f) = (s_1, ..., s_n; s)$*

$$f_{\mathcal{B}} = f_{\mathcal{A}} \upharpoonright (\prod_{i=1}^{n} B_{s_i}) \times B_s.$$

We remark that if $\mathcal{A}_i$ is a $\sigma_i$-type model ($i = 1, 2$) and $\sigma_1$ and $\sigma_2$ have no common sorts, function and relation symbols then we can define *the disjoint union* $\mathcal{A}_1 + \mathcal{A}_2$ as a minimal model which is an extension of both of them. Because we work with many-sorted languages, disjoint union can be constructed in an obvious manner taking $sort\ \sigma \rightleftharpoons sort(\sigma_1 \cup^* \sigma_2)$ and defining relations and operations naturally.

Let $R$ be a new relation symbol with respect to a given similarity type $\sigma$ and let $\mathcal{A}$ be a $\sigma$-type model. $(\mathcal{A}, Q)$ is a shorthand for a $\sigma \cup \{R\}$-type model $\mathcal{A}'$ the $\sigma$-type reduct of which is $\mathcal{A}$ and $\mathcal{A}'(R) = Q$.

Before we define the syntax of many-sorted first-order languages we need the following notions.

**(1.11) Definition.** *Let $S$ be a set of sorts and for each $s \in S$ let $V_s$ be a countably infinite (i.e. a denumerable) set which is disjoint from all other sets so far introduced. Let $V = \bigcup\{V_s \mid s \in sort\ \sigma\}$. $V_s$ is the set of $s$-sorted variables and $V$ is the set of $S$-sorted variables.*

Let $sort : V \to S$ be the function which renders to each variable its sort. Let $X$ and $Y$ be two arbitrary subsets of $V$. $Y$ is said to be a copy of $X$ iff

(i) $X \cap Y = \emptyset$;
(ii) there is bijection $\iota : X \to Y$;
(iii) for any $x \in X$, $sort(x) = sort(\iota(x))$

**(1.12) Definition.** *Let $\sigma$ be a many-sorted similarity type, and let $V$ be a set of $S$-sorted variables, where $S \rightleftharpoons sort\ \sigma$. For any $s \in sort\,\sigma$, the set of $s$-sorted $\sigma$-type terms $Term_s(\sigma, V)$ is the smallest set for which:*

*(i) $V_s \subseteq Term_s(\sigma, V)$;*
*(ii) if $f \in func\ \sigma$ such that $ar(f) = (s_1, ..., s_n; s)$ and $\tau_1, ..., \tau_n$ are terms of the sorts $s_1, ..., s_n$ , respectively (i.e. $\tau_i \in Term_{s_i}(\sigma, V)$ for each $i = 1, ..., n$) then $f(\tau_1, ..., \tau_n) \in Term_s(\sigma, V)$.*

The set of $\sigma$-type terms is the set $Term(\sigma, V) = \cup\{Term_s(\sigma, V) \mid s \in sort\ \sigma\}$. The terms of $Term_s(\sigma, V)$ which do not contain variables are called *closed* or *ground* terms. We define the function $sort : Term(\sigma, V) \to sort\,\sigma$ which renders to each term $\tau$ its sort, i.e. $sort(\tau) = s$ iff $\tau \in Term_s(\sigma, V)$.

**(1.13) Definition.** *The set of $\sigma$-type atomic formulas is the set $Atom(\sigma, V)$:*

$Atom(\sigma, V) = \{\rho(\tau_1, ..., \tau_n) \mid \rho \in rel\ \sigma,\ \tau_1,...,\tau_n \in Term(\sigma, V)$ and $ar(\rho) = (sort\,\tau_1, ..., sort\,\tau_n)\} \cup \{\tau_1 = \tau_2 \mid sort(\tau_1) = sort(\tau_2)\}$.

**(1.14) Definition.** *The set of first-order $\sigma$-type formulas is the smallest set $Form(\sigma, V)$ such that*

*(i)* $Atom(\sigma, V) \subseteq Form(\sigma, V)$;
*(ii) if $\phi, \psi \in Form(\sigma, V)$ and $v \in V$ then $(\neg\phi)$, $(\phi \wedge \psi)$ and $(\exists v \phi)$ also belong to $Form(\sigma, V)$.*

Let $Open(\sigma, V)$ be the set of those first-order $\sigma$-type formulas which do not contain quantifiers (called open formulas), i.e. $Open(\sigma, V)$ is defined like $Form(\sigma, V)$ with the only difference that condition (ii) has been changed to

*(ii') if $\phi, \psi \in Open(\sigma, V)$ then $(\neg\phi)$ and $(\phi \wedge \psi)$ belong to $Open(\sigma, V)$.*

We introduce the other logical connectives as abbreviations. Let $\phi, \psi \in Form(\sigma, V)$ and $v \in V$. Then we write

$\phi \vee \psi$ instead of $\neg(\neg\phi \wedge \neg\psi)$
$\phi \rightarrow \psi$ instead of $\neg\phi \vee \psi$
$\phi \leftrightarrow \psi$ instead of $(\phi \rightarrow \psi) \wedge (\psi \rightarrow \phi)$
$\forall v \phi$ instead of $\neg\exists v \neg\phi$.

Note that the logical connectives used in $Form(\sigma, V)$ and in the informal logic, i.e. in the metalanguage introduced in Section 1.1, are the same. However, from the context it is understandable whether the formal language $Form(\sigma, V)$ or the metalanguage is used.
Let us take two distinguished formulas of $Form(\sigma, V)$:

$$true \rightleftharpoons (x = x);$$
$$false \rightleftharpoons \neg(x = x).$$

Variables which are not in the scope of a corresponding quantifier are called *free*. The variables which are not free are said to be *bound*. Let $var(\phi)$ denote the set of all free variables occuring in $\phi$. If $var(\phi) \subseteq X$ then the notation $\phi(X)$ will often be used to indicate that free variables of $\phi$ belong to set $X$. Intuitively $X$ in $\phi(X)$ can also be understood as a vector of variables. If $var(\phi) = \{x\}$ then we shall write $\phi(x)$ instead of $\phi(\{x\})$. A formula $\phi$ without free variables is called a *sentence*.

A formula $\phi$ is in *prenex (normal) form* iff $\phi$ consists of a (possibly) empty string of quantifiers (called *quantifier prefix*) followed by an open formula (called *matrix*). We also say that $\phi$ is a prenex formula.

In order to define the semantics of a $\sigma$-type first-order language we must establish a connection between the syntax (i.e. the set of $\sigma$-type formulas) and the class of $\sigma$-type models. For this purpose, we need the following definitions. For any variable $v \in V$, any term $\tau \in Term(\sigma, V)$ and any formula $\phi \in$

$Form(\sigma, V)$, let $\phi[\tau/v]$ be the formula obtained from $\phi$ by replacing every free occurrence of $v$ in $\phi$ by $\tau$ such that there is no collision between the variable symbols of $\tau$ and those of $\phi$ occurring in the quantifiers. Thus some bound variables can be renamed. In the case of notation $\phi(v)$, instead of $\phi[\tau/v]$ we just write $\phi(\tau)$. Let $\phi[\tau_i/v_i]_{i=1}^n$ (or $\phi[\tau_i/v_i]_{i\in I}$) be the formula obtained from $\phi$ by replacing in parallel all free occurrences of the variables $v_i$ in $\phi$ by the corresponding $\tau_i$ ($i = 1, ..., n$ or $i \in I$).

Let $R_i$ be a relation symbol with arity $X_i \rightleftharpoons \{x_1, ..., x_{n_i}\}$ ($i = 1, ..., n$). For each $i$ ($i = 1, ..., n$) let $\psi_i \in Form_\sigma$ be a given formula. For an arbitrary $\phi \in Form_\sigma$ let $\phi[\psi_i/R_i]_{i=1}^n$ be the formula obtained from $\phi$ by replacing each occurrence of $R_i(\tau_1, ..., \tau_{n_i})$ by $\psi_i[\tau_j/x_j]_{j=1}^{n_i}$.

Let $\sigma$ be a fixed many-sorted similarity type. A numeration $\lceil\cdot\rceil : Form_\sigma \to \mathbb{N}$ is called *effective* iff recursive functions correspond to all logical operations defined on sorts, symbols, variables, terms and formulas (e.g. $\wedge$, $\exists$, substitution, forming terms, etc.). This means that for example the function

$$\lambda(n, m).\lceil \lceil n\rceil^{-1} \wedge \lceil m\rceil^{-1}\rceil : \mathbb{N} \times \mathbb{N} \to_p \mathbb{N}$$

is recursive. (For the details see Mendelson [1964].) One of the most famous effective codings is the so-called Gödel coding. For each similarity type $\sigma$ we fix a given effective numeration $\lceil\cdot\rceil$. Such statements as "the logic $\mathcal{L}$ is complete..." always mean that the formulas under consideration are first-order and the numeration used in Definition (1.4) is this fixed effective one.

**(1.15) Definition.** *Let $\sigma$ be a many-sorted similarity type and let $V$ be a set of sort$\sigma$-sorted variables. Let $\mathcal{A} \in Mod_\sigma$ be an arbitrary model. A partial valuation of the variables into a model $\mathcal{A}$ is a partial function $k : V \to_p A$ such that if $v \in dom\, k$ then $k(v) \in \mathcal{A}(sort(v))$. Let $pVal_\mathcal{A}$ be the set of all partial valuations, i.e.*

$$pVal_\mathcal{A} \rightleftharpoons \{k : V \to_p A \mid if\; x \in dom\, k\; then\; k(x) \in A(sort(x))\}.$$

A partial valuation $k \in pVal_\mathcal{A}$ can be considered as a partial function

$$k \in \prod\{[V_s \to_p A_s] \mid s \in sort\,\sigma\}.$$

Let $W \subseteq V$ be an arbitrary set of variables. A partial valuation $k \in Val_\mathcal{A}$ for which $dom\, k = W$ holds is called a *valuation on* $W$. Let

$$Val_\mathcal{A}[W] \rightleftharpoons \{k \in pVal_\mathcal{A} \mid dom\, k = W\}.$$

If $dom\, k = V$ is the set of all variables then we say that $k$ is a *valuation*. Let $Val_\mathcal{A}$ be the set of all valuations.

Let $k_1$ and $k_2$ be two arbitrary partial valuations from $pVal_\mathcal{A}$. Let $k_1 + k_2$ be the function defined as follows:

$$dom\,(k_1 + k_2) \rightleftharpoons dom\,k_1 \cup dom\,k_2;$$

$$(k_1 + k_2)(x) \rightleftharpoons \begin{cases} k_2(x) & \text{if } x \in dom\,k_2; \\ k_1(x) & \text{if } x \in dom\,k_1 \backslash dom\,k_2. \end{cases}$$

Let $x \in V_s$ and $a \in A_s$ for an arbitrary $s \in sort\,\sigma$ and let $k \in pVal_{\mathcal{A}}$. Then $k[a/x] = k + \{(x, a)\}$ is a new partial valuation which is the same as $k$ except at $x$ where it provides value $a$.

Let $X \subseteq V$ and $Y$ be a copy of $X$ with the bijection $\iota$. Then for any $k \in pVal_{\mathcal{A}}$ we can define a new partial valuation $k[Y/X] = \iota \circ k$. Let $\phi$ be a $\sigma$-type formula, and let $k$ be a partial valuation such that $Y \subseteq dom\ k$ and let $X \rightleftharpoons var(\phi)$. In this case $\mathcal{A} \models \phi[Y/X][k]$ iff $\mathcal{A} \models \phi[k[Y/X]]$.

Let $X$ be a set of variables and let $Y$ be a copy of $X$ with the bijection $\iota$. Let $k \in pVal_{\mathcal{A}}$ be a partial valuation such that $X \cup Y \subseteq dom\ k$. $k[X : Y]$ is the following partial valuation:

$$k[X : Y](v) \rightleftharpoons \begin{cases} k(v) & \text{if } v \in (dom\,k) \setminus (X \cup Y); \\ k(\iota(v)) & \text{if } v \in X; \\ k(\iota^{-1}(v)) & \text{if } v \in Y. \end{cases}$$

Thus $k[X : Y]$ valuates the variables of $X$ according to their copy in $Y$ and the variables of $Y$ according to the corresponding variables from $X$.

**(1.16) Definition.** *Let $\tau \in Term(\sigma, V)$, $\mathcal{A} \in Mod_\sigma$. Let $k \in pVal_{\mathcal{A}}$ such that $var(\tau) \subseteq dom\ k$. The meaning of a term $\tau$ in the model $\mathcal{A}$ with respect to a valuation $k$ (denoted as $\tau_{\mathcal{A}}[k]$) is defined as follows*

*(i) if $\tau$ is a variable $v$ then $\tau_{\mathcal{A}}[k] = k(v)$,*

*(ii) if $\tau$ is of the form $f(\tau_1, ..., \tau_n)$ where $f \in func\ \sigma$ such that $f : s_1, ..., s_n \to s$ then $f(\tau_1, ..., \tau_n)_{\mathcal{A}}[k] = f_{\mathcal{A}}(\tau_{1\mathcal{A}}[k], ..., \tau_{n\mathcal{A}}[k])$.*

**(1.17) Definition.** *Let $\mathcal{A} \in Mod_\sigma$ be fixed. For any $\phi \in Form(\sigma, V), k \in pVal_{\mathcal{A}}$ if $var(\phi) \subseteq dom\,k$ then we define the validity relation $\mathcal{A} \models \phi[k]$, by induction on the complexity of $\phi$, as follows:*

*(i) if $\phi \rightleftharpoons (\tau_1 = \tau_2)$ (where $\tau_1, \tau_2 \in Term_s(\sigma, V)$) we have $\mathcal{A} \models (\tau_1 = \tau_2)[k]$ iff $\tau_{1\mathcal{A}}[k] = \tau_{2\mathcal{A}}[k]$,*

*(ii) if $\phi \rightleftharpoons \rho(\tau_1, ..., \tau_n)$ then $\mathcal{A} \models \rho(\tau_1, ..., \tau_n)[k]$ iff $(\tau_{1\mathcal{A}}[k], ..., \tau_{n\mathcal{A}}[k]) \in \rho_{\mathcal{A}}$.*

*(iii) for any $\psi, \chi \in Form(\sigma, V)$ and $v \in V$*

*(a) if $\phi \rightleftharpoons \neg\psi$ then $\mathcal{A} \models (\neg\psi)[k]$ iff $\mathcal{A} \models \psi[k]$ does not hold,*

*(b) if $\phi \rightleftharpoons (\psi \wedge \chi)$ then $\mathcal{A} \models (\psi \wedge \chi)[k]$ iff $\mathcal{A} \models \psi[k]$ and $\mathcal{A} \models \chi[k]$,*

*(c) if $\phi \rightleftharpoons \exists v\psi$ then $\mathcal{A} \models \exists v\psi[k]$ iff there exists a partial valuation k' such that for any $z \in V$ if $z \neq v$ then $k(z) = k'(z)$ and $\mathcal{A} \models \psi[k']$.*

*A formula $\phi \in Form(\sigma, V)$ is valid in a model $\mathcal{A}$ (denoted by $\mathcal{A} \models \phi$) iff for each partial valuation $k \in pVal_{\mathcal{A}}$ for which $var(\phi) \subseteq dom\,k$, $\mathcal{A} \models \phi[k]$ holds. In this case we say that $\mathcal{A}$ is a model of $\phi$.*

**(1.18) Definition.** *A first-order $\sigma$-type many-sorted language is a triplet of the form* $(Form(\sigma, V), Mod_\sigma, \models)$.

Let $\mathcal{K}$ be an arbitrary class of $\sigma$-type models, i.e. $\mathcal{K} \subseteq Mod_\sigma$, and let $\phi \in Form(\sigma, V)$ be arbitrary. $\mathcal{K}$ satisfies $\phi$ iff each model of $\mathcal{K}$ satisfies it, i.e. $\mathcal{K} \models \phi$ iff for any $\mathcal{A} \in \mathcal{K}$, $\mathcal{A} \models \phi$ holds.

Let $Th : Sb(Mod_\sigma) \to Sb(Form(\sigma, V))$ be a mapping such that for any $\mathcal{K} \subseteq Mod_\sigma$, $Th(\mathcal{K}) \rightleftharpoons \{\phi : \phi \in Form(\sigma, V) \text{ and } \mathcal{K} \models \phi\}$. $Th(\mathcal{K})$ is said to be the theory of $\mathcal{K}$. Let $\Sigma \subseteq Form(\sigma, V)$. A model $\mathcal{A} \in Mod_\sigma$ satisfies $\Sigma$ iff it satisfies each formula of $\Sigma$, i.e. $\mathcal{A} \models \Sigma$ iff for each $\phi \in \Sigma$, $\mathcal{A} \models \phi$ holds.

Let $Mod : Sb(Form(\sigma, V)) \to Sb(Mod_\sigma)$ be a mapping such that for any $\Sigma \subseteq Form(\sigma, V)$:

$$Mod(\Sigma) = \{\mathcal{A} \mid \mathcal{A} \in Mod_\sigma \text{ and } \mathcal{A} \models \Sigma\}.$$

$Mod(\Sigma)$ is said to be the class of models of $\Sigma$.

**(1.19) Lemma.** *For any $\Sigma_1, \Sigma_2 \subseteq Form(\sigma, V)$ and $\mathcal{K}_1, \mathcal{K}_2 \subseteq Mod_\sigma$:*
*(i) $Th(\mathcal{K}_1) \supseteq Th(\mathcal{K}_2)$ for $\mathcal{K}_1 \subseteq \mathcal{K}_2$;*
*(ii) $Mod(\Sigma_1) \supseteq Mod(\Sigma_2)$ for $\Sigma_1 \subseteq \Sigma_2$.*

A formula $\phi \in Form(\sigma, V)$ is said to be a *tautology* iff $Mod(\{\phi\}) = Mod_\sigma$, i.e. iff it is valid in any $\sigma$-type model. Let $\Sigma \subseteq Form(\sigma, V)$ and $\phi \in Form(\sigma, V)$ be arbitrary. $\phi$ is said to be *a semantic consequence* of $\Sigma$ iff each model of $\Sigma$ satisfies $\phi$ as well, i.e. $Mod(\Sigma) \subseteq Mod(\{\phi\})$.

Let $Ax \subseteq Form(\sigma, V)$ be a given set of axioms and let $\Sigma, \Gamma \subseteq Form(\sigma, V)$ be two arbitrary sets of formulas. We say that $\Sigma$ and $\Gamma$ are equivalent (written as $\Sigma \equiv \Gamma$) iff for each model $\mathcal{A} \in Mod(Ax)$ and for each valuation $k \in Val_{\mathcal{A}}[V]$: $Ax \models \Sigma[k]$ iff $Ax \models \Gamma[k]$. If $\Sigma$ and $\Gamma$ consist of a simple formula, say $\phi$ and $\psi$, then we simply write $\phi \equiv \psi$. We emphasize that in the notation $\Sigma \equiv \Gamma$ we do not indicate $Ax$ because from the context it will be evident what set of axioms is considered.

If the set $V$ is known from the context we simply write $Form_\sigma$, $Term_\sigma$, $Atom_\sigma$, $Open_\sigma$ instead of the sets $Form(\sigma, V)$, $Term(\sigma, V)$, $Atom(\sigma, V)$ and $Open(\sigma, V)$, respectively.

Let $T \subseteq Form_\sigma$ be a set of sentences, i.e. a theory. $T$ has the *quantifier elimination property* if for each formula $\phi \in T$ there is a quantifier free (i.e. open) formula $\psi$ such that $T \models \phi$ iff $T \models \psi$.

Let the similarity type $\sigma'$ be an extension of the similarity type $\sigma$. By *a conservative extension of a theory* $T$ in $Form_\sigma$ we mean a theory $T' \supseteq T$ in $Form_{\sigma'}$ iff every model $\mathcal{A}$ of $T$ has an extension $\mathcal{A}'$ to a model of $T'$.

## 1.4 Relations in Many-Sorted Structures

Let us fix a $\sigma$-type model $\mathcal{A}$. Let $W \subseteq V$ be a finite set of variables with $|W| = n$. Fix an ordering $\{w_1, ..., w_n\}$ of $W$. A natural bijection $\iota$ can be defined between $Val_{\mathcal{A}}[W]$ and $\prod_{i=1}^{n} \mathcal{A}(sort(w_i))$ by taking $\iota(k) \rightleftharpoons (k(w_1), ..., k(w_n))$. Therefore a relation on $\prod_{i=1}^{n} \mathcal{A}(sort(w_i))$ can be identified with a relation on $Val_{\mathcal{A}}[W]$.

A $W$-type relation on $\mathcal{A}$ is a subset $\rho$ of $Val_{\mathcal{A}}[W]$. Clearly $\rho$ can be considered as a relation $\tilde{\rho}$ on $\prod_{i=1}^{n} \mathcal{A}(sort(w_i))$ by taking

$$\tilde{\rho} \rightleftharpoons \left\{(a_1, ..., a_n) \mid \cup_{i=1}^{n}\{(w_i, a_i)\} \in \rho\right\}.$$

If $W_1, ..., W_n$ are disjoint sets of variables and if we wish to refer the sets $W_i$ separately then we write $(W_1, ..., W_n)$ instead of $W_1 \cup ... \cup W_n$. If $W_j$ contains only one variable symbol, say $x$, we simply write $x$ instead of $\{x\}$. Thus $(W, x, y)$ is just the set $W \cup \{x\} \cup \{y\}$. Sometimes we add a new relation symbol $\rho$ to describe the properties of a $W$-type relation. In this case we say that $\rho$ has the arity $W$ (or $\rho$ is $W$-type) to express that there is an ordering $\{w_1, ..., w_n\}$ of $W$ such that the arity of $\rho$ is just $(sort(w_1), ..., sort(w_n))$.

Let $X, Y, Z$ be pairwise disjoint sets of variables. Some well known notions of binary relations can be generalized for $(X, Y)$-type relations as well. Let $\rho_1$ be an $(X, Y)$-type, $\rho_2$ be a $(Y, Z)$-type relation on $\mathcal{A}$. Having this form of types we can define

- $dom\ \rho_1 \rightleftharpoons \{a \in Val_{\mathcal{A}}[X] \mid \exists b \in Val_{\mathcal{A}}[Y] : \ a + b \in \rho_1\}$.
- $rng\ \rho_1 \rightleftharpoons \{b \in Val_{\mathcal{A}}[Y] \mid \exists a \in Val_{\mathcal{A}}[X] : \ a + b \in \rho_1\}$.
- $\rho_1 \circ \rho_2 \rightleftharpoons \{a + c \in Val_{\mathcal{A}}[X, Z] \mid a \in Val_{\mathcal{A}}[X], c \in Val_{\mathcal{A}}[Z], \exists b \in Val_{\mathcal{A}}[Y] :$ $a + b \in \rho_1 \wedge b + c \in \rho_2\}$.

Let us suppose that $Y$ is a copy of $X$. Then we can define the following operations on $(X, Y)$-type relations.

- $\rho_1^{-1} \rightleftharpoons \{b[Y/X] + a[X/Y] \mid (a, b) \in \rho_1\}$.
- $\Delta_{(X,Y)} \rightleftharpoons \{(a + a[X/Y]) | a \in Val_{\mathcal{A}}[X]\}$.
- $\rho_1 \circ \rho_2 \rightleftharpoons \rho_1 \circ \Delta_{(Y,X)} \circ \rho_2$. Be careful: the $\circ$ operation is defined for two different cases (see also above)!
- An $(X, Y)$-type relation $\rho$ is called *reflexive* iff $\Delta_{(X,Y)} \subseteq \rho$.
- An $(X, Y)$-type relation $\rho$ is called *transitive* iff $\rho \circ \rho \subseteq \rho$.
- The reflexive and transitive closure of an $(X, Y)$-type relation $\rho$ is the least reflexive and transitive relation $\rho'$ for which $\rho \subseteq \rho'$ hold. The transitive and reflexive closure of $\rho$ is denoted by $TRC(\rho)$.
- Let $\rho_i$ be an $X_i$-type relation (for $i = 1, 2$). If $X_1 \cap X_2 = \emptyset$ then the product $\rho_1 \times \rho_2$ of these two relations can be considered as an $X_1 \cup X_2$-type relation in the following way:

$$(k_1, k_2) \mapsto k_1 + k_2 \quad (\text{for any } k_i \in Val_{\mathcal{A}}[X_i]).$$

Let $\phi \in Form_\sigma$ with $var(\phi) \rightleftharpoons X \cup^* Y$. Let $k \in Val_{\mathcal{A}}[Y]$ be a given valuation. We sometimes use the following $X$-sorted relation

$$\phi_{\mathcal{A}}[k] \rightleftharpoons \{k_1 \in Val_{\mathcal{A}}[X] \mid \mathcal{A} \models \phi[k_1 + k]\}.$$

## 1.5 Ultraproducts

Ultraproduct construction is one of the basic methods of constructing models. It allows the construction of a new model from a given set of models. Let $I$ be a nonempty set. A *filter* $D$ over $I$ is a nonempty set $D \subseteq Sb(I)$ with the following properties:

(i) $\emptyset \notin D$;
(ii) $D$ is closed under finite intersection, i.e. $A, B \in D$ implies that $A \cap B \in D$;
(iii) for all $A \in D$, if $A \subseteq B$ then $B \in D$;

A set $D \subseteq Sb(I)$ is said to be an *ultrafilter* iff

(i) $D$ is a filter
(ii) for each $A \subseteq I$, either $A$ or $I \backslash A$ belongs to $D$.

An ultrafilter $D$ is called *principal* iff there is an element $i \in I$ such that for all $A \subseteq D$, $A \in D$ iff $i \in A$.

We emphasize that on any infinite set $I$ there is at least one non-principal ultrafilter. We also remark that the proof of this theorem requires the use of the axiom of choice. (See in Chang, Keisler [1973]).

Fix a similarity type $\sigma$ and let $\{\mathcal{A}_i \mid i \in I\}$ be an $I$-indexed family of $\sigma$-type models. Our aim is to construct a new model from this family. The Cartesian product construction does not work in general, i.e. the Cartesian product of a set of models of a theory will not be a model of this theory. However, the ultraproduct method helps us.

**(1.20) Definition.** *Let $\mathcal{K} \rightleftharpoons \{\mathcal{A}_i \mid i \in I\}$ be an $I$-indexed family of $\sigma$-type models and let $D$ be a filter on $I$. The reduced product of the family $\mathcal{K}$ is a $\sigma$-type model $\mathcal{B}$ (denoted by $\prod_{i \in I} \mathcal{A}_i/D$) such that:*

*(i) The universe of $\mathcal{B}$ is the set of all equivalence classes of $=_D$, where $=_D$ is defined as follows: let $f, g \in \prod_{i \in I} A_i$, $f =_D g$ iff*

$$\{i \in I \mid f(i) = g(i)\} \in D$$

*I.e. $\mathcal{B} \rightleftharpoons \{f_D \mid f \in \prod_{i \in I} A_i\}$ where $f_D = \{g \in \prod_{i \in I} A_i \mid f =_D g\}$. Sometimes we use the notation $[f]_D$ instead of $f_D$.*

*(ii) Let $r \in rel\ \sigma$ and $ar(r) = (s_1, ... s_n)$. Then $r_{\mathcal{B}}(f_D^1, ..., f_D^n)$ iff*

$$\{i \in I \mid r_{\mathcal{A}_i}(f^1(i), ..., f^n(i))\} \in D.$$

(iii) *Let* $f \in func\ \sigma$ *and* $ar(f) = (s_1, ..., s_n; s_{n+1})$*.Then*$f_{\mathcal{B}}(f_D^1, ..., f_D^n) = f_D^{n+1}$ *iff* $\{i \in I \mid f_{\mathcal{A}_i}(f^1(i), ..., f^n(i)) = f_{\mathcal{A}_i}^{n+1}(i)\} \in D$.

*If* $D$ *is an ultrafilter then* $\prod_{i \in I} \mathcal{A}_i/D$ *is said to be an ultraproduct of* $\{\mathcal{A}_i \mid i \in I\}$ *modulo* $D$*. If for all* $i \in I$, $\mathcal{A}_i = \mathcal{A}$ *then we write* $\mathcal{A}^I/D$ *instead of* $\prod_{i \in I} \mathcal{A}/D$ *and call it the* $I$*-th ultrapower of* $\mathcal{A}$ *modulo* $D$.

The main advantage of the ultraproduct construction is that the elementary properties of the family $\{\mathcal{A}_i \mid i \in I\}$ are preserved under ultraproduct. Let $\mathcal{B} \rightleftharpoons \prod_{i \in I} \mathcal{A}_i/D$ be the ultraproduct of a given family $\{\mathcal{A}_i \mid i \in I\}$. If $k \in Val_{\mathcal{B}}$ and $i \in I$ then, by using the projection functions, we can define a valuation $k_i$ in $\mathcal{A}_i$.

**(1.21) Theorem.** *(Los.) Let* $\{\mathcal{A}_i \mid i \in I\}$ *be a family of* $\sigma$*-type models and let* $D$ *be an ultrafilter over* $I$*. For any* $\sigma$*-type formula* $\phi \in Form_\sigma$*, and valuation* $k \in Val_{\mathcal{B}}$*, we have*

$$\prod_{i \in I} \mathcal{A}_i/D \models \phi[k] \text{ iff } \{i \in I \mid \mathcal{A}_i \models \phi[k_i]\} \in D.$$

For details about ultraproducts, see e.g. Chang, Keisler [1973] or Eklof [1977].

## 1.6 Arithmetic

Natural numbers, numerical relations and functions over them, together called arithmetic and the axiomatic theory of arithmetic, play a fundamental role in computer science. They are particularly important in the foundation of programming theory. Here we introduce the main ideas needed for our investigations. First of all we define a formal language that allows us to speak about natural numbers. Let $\eta$ be the following one-sorted similarity type:

$$\begin{aligned} 0 &:\to s \\ S, P &: s \to s \\ +, \cdot &: s, s \to s \\ \leq &: s, s \end{aligned}$$

Here $S$ and $P$ are the symbols for the successor and predecessor functions, respectively. For the function symbols $+$ and $\cdot$ we use the infix notation and write $a + b$ and $a \cdot b$ instead of $+(a, b)$ and $\cdot(a, b)$, respectively.

The $\eta$-type first-order language is appropriate to formulate statements on natural numbers. However, for the investigation we require an axiomatic theory for which we select Peano's axioms. Let

$$A_1 \rightleftharpoons \forall x \neg(S(x) = 0)$$

$$
\begin{aligned}
A_2 &\rightleftharpoons \forall x \forall y \big(S(x) = S(y) \rightarrow x = y\big) \\
A_3 &\rightleftharpoons \forall x (x + 0 = x) \\
A_4 &\rightleftharpoons \forall x \forall y \big(x + S(y) = S(x + y)\big) \\
A_5 &\rightleftharpoons \forall x (x \cdot 0 = 0) \\
A_6 &\rightleftharpoons \forall x \forall y \big(x \cdot S(y) = x \cdot y + x\big) \\
A_{7\phi} &\rightleftharpoons \Big(\phi[0/x] \wedge \forall x \big(\phi \rightarrow \phi[S(x)/x]\big)\Big) \rightarrow \forall x \phi \\
A_8 &\rightleftharpoons x \leq z \leftrightarrow \exists z (x + z = y) \\
A_9 &\rightleftharpoons \forall x (x \neq 0 \rightarrow S(P(x)) = x) \wedge P(0) = 0
\end{aligned}
$$

The axiom $A_{7\phi}$ is an axiom schema for induction. The set $PA$ of Peano's axioms is defined as follows:

$$PA \rightleftharpoons \{A_i \mid i = 1, ..., 6, 8, 9\} \cup \{A_{7\phi} \mid \phi \in Form_\eta\}$$

This axiomatic theory is often called Peano arithmetic. It is an important fact that $PA$ is not finitely axiomatizable. The intended model of $PA$ is the model with the universe $\mathbb{N}$ consisting of all the natural numbers over which the functions $0, S, +$ and $\cdot$ are defined as expected. This model is denoted as $\mathcal{N}$ and it is called the standard one. All models not isomorphic to $\mathcal{N}$ are called non-standard ones. For every infinite cardinal there are at least continuously many non-isomorphic models of $PA$ of that cardinality. The smallest submodel of every model of $PA$ is isomorphic to $\mathcal{N}$.

Let $PA_s$ denote Peano's axioms formulated in a sort $s$. Then Peano arithmetic corresponds to the sort $s$ in the case of a many-sorted similarity type which contains $\eta$ and whose set of sorts contains $s$.

For some purposes we will need another axiomatization of arithmetic. Let the one-sorted similarity type $\hat{\eta}$ consist of the function symbols $0$, $S$, $P$ of arities 0,1,1, respectively. It is clear that $\hat{\eta}$ is a reduction of $\eta$.

Let us consider the following axioms and axiom schema:

(i) $\forall x \neg \big(S(x) = 0\big)$;

(ii) $\forall x \forall y \big(S(x) = S(y) \rightarrow x = y\big)$;

(iii) $\forall x \big(x \neq 0 \rightarrow S(P(x)) = x\big) \wedge P(0) = 0$;

(iv) $\Big(\phi[0/x] \wedge \forall x \big(\phi \rightarrow \phi[S(x)/x]\big)\Big) \rightarrow \forall x \phi$, for any $\phi \in Form_\sigma$.

Let $Next'$ be the theory consisting of the axioms (i)–(iii), while let $Next$ be the theory $Next'$ augmented with the induction axiom schema (iv). It is clear that $PA \models Next$, which means that $\mathcal{N}{\restriction}_{\hat{\eta}}$ is also a model of $Next$.

Let $\mathcal{N}$ be the standard model of $PA$ with the universe $\mathbb{N}$. An important set of partial functions over $\mathbb{N}$ is that of the so-called recursive functions which are constructed from a given set of the so-called initial functions by applying finitely many times only some given rules (operations). Now we define the initial functions and the operations.

The initial functions:

(i) zero function $Z$ which is defined as $Z(a) = 0$ for all $a$;

(ii) successor function $S$; $S(a) = a + S(0)$ for all $a$;
(iii) projection functions $\pi_i^n$; for all $n \in \mathbb{N}$, $a_1, ..., a_n$ and for all $i = 1, ..., n$, $\pi_i^n(a_1, ..., a_n) = a_i$.

The operations:

(i) substitution: if $h$ is an $m$-ary and $g_1, ..., g_m$ are $n$-ary recursive functions then so is the $n$-ary function $f$ defined as

$$f(x_1, ..., x_n) \rightleftharpoons h(g_1(x_1, ..., x_n), ..., g_m(x_1, ..., x_n));$$

(ii) recursion: if $g$ is an $n$-ary and $h$ is an $(n+2)$-ary recursive function then the $(n+1)$-ary function defined as follows is also recursive:

$$f(x_1, ..., x_n, 0) \rightleftharpoons g(x_1, ..., x_n),$$
$$f(x_1, ..., x_n, S(y)) \rightleftharpoons h(x_1, ..., x_n, y, f(x_1, ..., x_n, y));$$

(iii) minimalization ($\mu$-operator): if $g(x_1, ..., x_n, y)$ is an $(n+1)$-ary recursive function then the function $\mu y(g = 0)$ defined by the following properties is recursive: $\mu y(g(x_1, ..., x_n, y) = 0)$ is the least $z$ such that for all $y \leq z$: $(x_1, ..., x_n, y) \in dom\ g$ and $g(x_1, ..., x_n, z) = 0$. If such $z$ does not exist then the function is undefined (at that argument).

Recursive functions can be coded similarly to the coding of terms or formulas. The code, however, in this case should allow an effective traceback. This means that the code should reflect how the recursive function is built up, i.e. from what initial functions and by the use of which operators it is constructed. Since the same recursive function can be obtained in various ways, the same recursive function can have more than one code, which distinguishes it from the case of terms and formulas.

In certain circumstances it is not sufficient to say that a function is recursive, but we have to know exactly how it is constructed, i.e. we have to know one of its codes. This is so, because it is undecidable whether two codes do determine the same recursive function. Therefore a recursive function is effectively given iff one of its codes is also given.

A set $B \subseteq \mathbb{N}$ is called *recursively enumerable* iff either $B$ is empty or there is a recursive function $f : \mathbb{N} \to \mathbb{N}$, such that $B = \{f(n) \mid n \in \mathbb{N}\}$. A set $B$ is said to be *recursive* iff both $B$ and its complement $\mathbb{N} \setminus B$ are recursively enumerable. A set $A \subseteq \mathbb{N}$ is *arithmetical* iff there is a formula $\phi(x) \in Form_\eta$ such that $A = \{a \in \mathbb{N} \mid \mathcal{N} \models \phi[a]\}$.

Let $H \subseteq \mathbb{N}$. We can speak about the set of *recursive functions with oracle* $H$ adding the characteristic function

$$\chi_H(n) \rightleftharpoons \begin{cases} 0 & \text{if } n \notin H; \\ 1 & \text{if } n \in H. \end{cases}$$

to the initial functions. A set $B \subseteq \mathbb{N}$ is called *recursively enumerable in* $H$ iff either $B$ is empty or there is a recursive function $f : \mathbb{N} \to \mathbb{N}$ with oracle $H$

such that $B = \{f(n) \mid n \in \mathbb{N}\}$. A set $B$ is said to be *recursive in $H$* iff both $B$ and its complement $\mathbb{N} \setminus B$ are recursively enumerable in $H$.

Let $\lceil \cdot \rceil : Form_\eta \to \mathbb{N}$ be a fixed effective numeration (e.g. the Gödel coding) of the $\eta$-type formulas. A subset $\Phi$ of $\eta$-type formulas is called recursive, recursively enumerable or arithmetical iff the set $\lceil \Phi \rceil$ of natural numbers is recursive, recursively enumerable or arithmetical, respectively.

**(1.22) Theorem.** *Neither the set of formulas $Th(\mathcal{N})$ nor $Form_\eta \setminus Th(\mathcal{N})$ are recursively enumerable.*

**(1.23) Theorem.** *The set $Th(\mathcal{N})$ is not arithmetical.*

This theorem corresponds to Tarski's theorem which says that the truth of the formulas of $Form_\eta$ is not definable in $\mathcal{N}$. The arithmetical sets can be classified with respect to the complexity of the formula that defines them. The complexity is measured according to quantifiers in the prenex form of the defining formula. The hierarchy is defined as follows:

In (i) and (ii) below, the formula $\phi \in Form_\eta$ can contain only bounded quantifiers, i.e. quantifiers of the form

- $\forall x(x \leq n \to \psi)$;
- $\exists x(x \leq n \wedge \psi)$.

(i) A $\Sigma_1^0$-formula is of the form $\exists Y \phi(X,Y)$.
(ii) A $\Pi_1^0$-formula is of the form $\forall Y \phi(X,Y)$.
(iii) If $\phi(X,Y)$ is a $\Sigma_n^0$-formula, then $\forall Y \phi(X,Y)$ is a $\Pi_{n+1}^0$-formula.
(iv) If $\phi(X,Y)$ is a $\Pi_n^0$-formula, then $\exists Y \phi(X,Y)$ is a $\Sigma_{n+1}^0$-formula.
(v) A $\Delta_n^0$-formula is logically equivalent both to a $\Sigma_n^0$- and a $\Pi_n^0$-formula.

A set $A \subseteq \mathbb{N}$ is called a $\Pi_n^0$-set ($\Sigma_n^0$-set, $\Delta_n^0$-set) iff there is a $\Pi_n^0$-formula ($\Sigma_n^0$-formula, $\Delta_n^0$-formula) $\phi(x)$ such that $A = \{a \in \mathbb{N} \mid \mathcal{N} \models \phi[a]\}$.

$\Delta_1^0$-sets are the recursive sets, the $\Sigma_1^0$-sets are the recursively enumerable sets and the $\Pi_1^0$-sets are the sets with recursively enumerable complements. With respect to this so-called arithmetical hierarchy the sets $Th(\mathcal{N})$ and $Form_\eta \setminus Th(\mathcal{N})$ of formulas do not belong to the $\Pi_n^0$- and $\Sigma_n^0$-sets (for any $n \in \mathbb{N}$).

**(1.24) Theorem.** *Let $cal : Sb(F) \to_p Sb(F)$ be a calculus. Let us suppose that $cal$ is a recursive function. Then the set of all formulas provable by $cal$ is recursively enumerable.*

*Proof.* Let $Q$ be the set of provable formulas. Since all proofs are finite they can be effectively enumerated. Since *cal* is recursive, the relation "$y$ is the code (Gödel number) of the proof of the formula $\phi_x$ which is coded by $x$" is decidable (recursive). Let $R(x,y)$ denote this relation. Hence $\phi_x$ is provable iff there exists an $y$ such that $R(x,y)$ is true. However, it is known that a set $A$ is recursively enumerable iff there exists a recursive predicate $R'(x,y)$ such that $x \in A$ iff $\exists y R'(x,y)$ holds. Therefore Q is recursively enumerable. □

This theorem means that all formulas provable by a recursive calculus form a $\Sigma_1^0$-set. Therefore, the gap between provable and the true in $\mathcal{N}$ formulas of $Form_\eta$ is extremely wide. This is also said in the following

**(1.25) Theorem.** *(Gödel's incompleteness theorem.) There exists a formula of $Form_\eta$ which is true in $\mathcal{N}$ but unprovable in PA.*

There is another formulation of Gödel's theorem which gives a negative answer to Hilbert's tenth problem. The latter asks if it is possible to give a recursive function that can tell of a given Diophantine equation with natural number coefficients whether it has a solution in natural numbers.

Diophantine equations are simply polynomials over $\mathcal{N}$ of the form

$$P(x_1, ..., x_n) = 0.$$

**(1.26) Theorem.** *(Matiyasevits, Tsudnovskii) Hilbert's tenth problem is unsolvable, i.e. there is no recursive function that could decide whether an equation*

$$P(x_1, ..., x_n) = 0$$

*has a solution in* $\mathbb{N}$.

A set $A$ of ordered $n$-tuples of natural number is called Diophantine if there is a polynomial $P(x_1, ..., x_n, y_1, ..., y_m)$ where $m \geq 0$ such that $A =$

$$\{(a_1, ..., a_n) \mid \exists y_1 ... \exists y_m(\mathcal{N} \models P(x_1, ..., x_n, y_1, ..., y_m) = 0[a_1/x_1, ..., a_n/x_n])\}.$$

**(1.27) Theorem.** *A set $A$ is Diophantine iff it is recursively enumerable.*

For details see e.g. Theorem 8.1 in Davis [1973].

Therefore, we can reformulate Gödel's theorem as follows:

**(1.28) Theorem.** *The set of all unsolvable (in $\mathbb{N}$) Diophantine equations is not recursively enumerable.*

Note that when we use this theorem we will have an arbitrary but fixed finite set of variables whose elements can only be used in the Diophantine equations. However, even for this case Theorem (1.28) remains true. If this were not the case then for each finite set of variables all the Diophantine equations would be solvable. This contradicts Theorem (1.28).

Now let us see another type of definability of sets over $\mathbb{N}$. Let us consider a $\eta$-type second-order language which allows quantification over relations and functions. A set is said to be ***analytical*** if it is definable by a second-order formula of the form

$$Q_1 R_1 ... Q_m R_m \phi(x_1, ..., x_n, R_1, ..., R_m),$$

where $R_1, ..., R_m$ are relation variables, $Q_i$ $(i = 1, ..., n)$ is either $\exists$ or $\forall$, and $\phi(x, R) \in Form_\eta$. A set $R \subseteq \mathbb{N}$ is said to be a $\Pi^1_1$-set iff $R$ is definable in $\mathcal{N}$ by a formula of the form

$$\forall R_1 ... \forall R_n \phi(R_1, ..., R_n, x),$$

for some $\phi \in Form_\eta$.

A set $R$ is $\Sigma^1_1$ if $\mathbb{N} \setminus R$ is $\Pi^1_1$ and $R$ is $\Delta^1_1$ if $R$ is both $\Sigma^1_1$ and $\Pi^1_1$. Note that the analytical hierarchy can be built up with respect to the complexity of the prefix consisting of the quantifiers over relations. We remark that each inductively definable set (see Chapter 2) on $\mathbb{N}$ is $\Sigma^1_1$. A set $A$ is said to be $\Pi^1_1$-complete (or maximal in $\Pi^1_1$) iff it is a $\Pi^1_1$-set and for any other $\Pi^1_1$-set $B$ there exists a recursive function $f$ such that $\forall x(x \in A \leftrightarrow f(x) \in B)$.

Chapter 2

# Inductive Definability

Developing a logic-based theory of programming, the chief concern is the logical definition of the main notions connected with programming. In order to deal successfully with this concern an appropriate definability theory has to be used. In our program-theoretic investigation, inductive definability will play a significant role in the establishment of certain relationship between models, computability and programs. In the present chapter we list the main concepts of this theory in accordance with Aczel [1977], Barwise [1975] and Moschovakis [1974].

Let $\mathcal{A} \in Mod_\sigma$ be arbitrary for an arbitrary but fixed similarity type $\sigma$. Almost all semantic notions of the programming theory can be represented by an appropriately selected set of valuations over the model $\mathcal{A}$. That is, for a given set $X$ of variables we intend to define an $X$-type relation $Q \subseteq Val_\mathcal{A}[X]$.

**(2.1) Definition.** *Let $\mathcal{A} \in Mod_\sigma$. A $Y$-type relation $Q \subseteq Val_\mathcal{A}[Y]$ is said to be first-order definable on $\mathcal{A}$ or simply definable on $\mathcal{A}$ iff there is a set of variables $X$, a formula $\phi \in Form_\sigma$ with $X \rightleftharpoons var(\phi)$ and a valuation $k \in Val_\mathcal{A}[X \setminus Y]$ such that $Y \subseteq X$, and for all $a \in Val_\mathcal{A}[Y]$ we have $a \in Q$ iff $\mathcal{A} \models \phi[k+a]$. The valuation $k$ is called the parameter of the definition. This relation $Q$ is denoted by $\phi_\mathcal{A}\restriction_k$.*

The definition of set $Q$ of valuations can also be given by introducing a new relation symbol $R$ which will correspond the set $Q$. Let us suppose that $R$ is *sort* $\sigma$-sorted. A formula $\phi(Y, P) \in Form_\sigma$ is said to be the *defining formula* of $Q$ with parameter $k \in Val_\mathcal{A}[P]$ iff

$$Q = \{a \in Val_\mathcal{A}[Y] \mid (\mathcal{A}, Q) \models (R(Y) \leftrightarrow \phi(Y, P))[a + k]\}.$$

Thus $Q$ consists of exactly those valuations $a \in Val_\mathcal{A}[Y]$ making the formula $R(Y) \leftrightarrow \phi(Y, P)$ valid with respect to the valuation $a + k$ in the model $(\mathcal{A}, Q)$. In other words the formula $\phi$ *explicitly defines* the relation $R$ which is denoted as $R(Y) = \phi(Y, P)$. If the formula $\phi$ may contain the new relation symbol $R$ as well (i.e. $\phi(Y, P) \in Form_{\sigma \cup \{R\}}$) then the definition $R(Y) = \phi(Y, P)$ is called *implicit*. Now let us see more precisely what an implicit definition is.

Let $R_1,...,R_n$ be new relation symbols with sorts belonging to *sort* $\sigma$. Let $\sigma^R$ denote the new similarity type. An *equation* in $\sigma$ is a triplet $(R, \phi, X)$ where $ar(R) = X$ and $\phi \in Form_{\sigma^R}$. The set of equations

$$E \rightleftharpoons \{(R_i, \phi_i, X_i) \mid i = 1..n\},$$

is called an *equation system* iff the following hold:

- $R_i$ and $R_j$ are different relation symbols if $i \neq j$.
- Let $P_i \rightleftharpoons var(\phi_i) \setminus X_i$ $(i = 1, ..., n)$. Then $\bigcup_{i=1}^{n} X_i \bigcap \bigcup_{i=1}^{n} P_i = \emptyset$.

  The elements of $\bigcup_{i=1}^{n} P_i$ are called *parameters*.

**(2.2) Definition.** *Let $E = \{(R_i, \phi_i, X_i) \mid i = 1, ..., n\}$ be an equation system in $\sigma$. Fix a model $\mathcal{A} \in Mod_\sigma$ and a parameter valuation $k \in Val_{\mathcal{A}}[\bigcup_{i=1}^{n} P_i]$. An $n$-tuple $(Q_1, ..., Q_n)$ of sets of valuations $Q_i \subseteq Val_{\mathcal{A}}[X_i]$ $(i = 1, ..., n)$ is a solution (or a fixed point) of $E$ with parameter $k$ iff for all $i = 1, ..., n$:*

$$(*) \qquad (\mathcal{A}, Q_1, ..., Q_n) \models \forall X_i (R_i(X_i) \leftrightarrow \phi_i(X_i, P_i))[k].$$

*Let $\beta^j = (Q_1^j, ..., Q_n^j)$ $(j = 1, 2)$ be two solutions of $E$ with parameter $k$. We say that $\beta^1$ is less than or equal to $\beta^2$ (denoted as $\beta^1 \subseteq \beta^2$) iff for all $i = 1, ..., n$, $Q_i^1 \subseteq Q_i^2$. We also use the notations $\beta^1 \supseteq \beta^2$, $\beta^1 \subset \beta^2$ and $\beta^1 \supset \beta^2$ with their obvious meaning.*

*A solution $\beta$ of the equation system $E$ is said to be the least solution (or the least fixed point) of $E$ with parameter $k$ iff each solution $\beta'$ of $E$ with parameter $k$ is greater than or equal to the solution $\beta$, i.e. $\beta \subseteq \beta'$.*

An equation system is often written in the form:

$$\begin{cases} R_1(X_1) & = & \phi_1(X_1, P_1) \\ \vdots & \vdots & \vdots \\ R_n(X_n) & = & \phi_n(X_n, P_n) \end{cases}$$

In general, not each equation system $E$ has a solution. In order to have one the formulas $\phi_i$ have to satisfy certain conditions. To define these conditions we investigate the fixed-point theory of the so-called monotone operators from a logical point of view.

Let $B$ be a non-empty set. A function of the form $\Gamma : Sb(B) \rightarrow Sb(B)$ is said to be a *monotone operator on* $B$ iff it preserves inclusion, i.e. $C \subseteq C' \subseteq B$ implies $\Gamma(C) \subseteq \Gamma(C')$.

**(2.3) Definition.** *For any monotone operator $\Gamma$ on $B$ and for any ordinal $v \in On$ let $I(\Gamma, v)$ be the set defined by transfinite recursion:*

$$I(\Gamma, v) \rightleftharpoons \Gamma(\bigcup\{I(\Gamma, \mu) \mid \mu < v\})$$

*As basis, $I(\Gamma, 0) = \Gamma(\emptyset)$. Let $I(\Gamma) \rightleftharpoons \bigcup\{I(\Gamma, v) \mid v \in On\}$ $(\subseteq Sb(B))$ which is said to be the relation defined inductively by $\Gamma$.*

**(2.4) Lemma.** *Let $B$ be a fixed non-empty set, and let $\Gamma : Sb(B) \rightarrow Sb(B)$ be a monotone operator. Then*

*(i) if $\upsilon, \mu \in On$ are such that $\upsilon \leq \mu$ then $I(\Gamma, \upsilon) \subseteq I(\Gamma, \mu)$; hence $I(\Gamma, \upsilon+1) = \Gamma(I(\Gamma, \upsilon))$.*
*(ii) Let $\lambda = max(|B|, \omega_0)$. For some ordinal $\kappa$ of cardinality less than or equal to $\lambda$ we have $I(\Gamma) = I(\Gamma, \kappa)$. The least infinite $\kappa$ of such ordinals is said to be the closure ordinal of $\Gamma$ denoted by $cl(\Gamma)$;*
*(iii) $I(\Gamma) = I(\Gamma, cl(\Gamma))$ is the least fixed point of $\Gamma$.*

*Proof.*

(i) This follows from the monotonicity of $\Gamma$ since for $\upsilon \leq \mu$

$$I(\Gamma, \upsilon) = \Gamma(\cup\{I(\Gamma, \xi) \mid \xi < \upsilon\}) \subseteq \Gamma(\cup\{I(\Gamma, \xi) \mid \xi < \mu\}) = I(\Gamma, \mu).$$

(ii) To contradict the claim, let us suppose that we have $\Gamma(I(\Gamma, \upsilon)) \neq I(\Gamma, \upsilon)$ for each $\upsilon < \lambda^+$. By using (i), $I(\Gamma, \upsilon + 1) \supset I(\Gamma, \upsilon)$. Then we can choose different elements $k_\upsilon \in B$ for any $\upsilon < \lambda^+$. Thus we obtain the set $K = \{k_\upsilon : \upsilon < \lambda^+\}$ such that $K \subseteq B$ and $|K| = \lambda^+$ which is a contradiction, since $|B| \leq \lambda$. So we have proved that there is a $\kappa < \lambda^+$ such that $I(\Gamma, \kappa) = I(\Gamma, \kappa+1)$. By transfinite induction on $\upsilon \in On$ one can check that if $\upsilon \geq \kappa$ then $I(\Gamma, \upsilon) = I(\Gamma, \kappa)$. Therefore $I(\Gamma, \kappa) = I(\Gamma)$.
(iii) It follows from (i) and (ii) that if $\kappa = cl(\Gamma)$ then

$$\Gamma(I(\Gamma)) = \Gamma(I(\Gamma, \kappa)) = I(\Gamma, \kappa + 1) = I(\Gamma, \kappa) = I(\Gamma).$$

On the other hand if $\Gamma(D) = D$ for some $D$, then by transfinite induction on $\zeta$ it can be shown that $I(\Gamma, \zeta) \subseteq D$. because using the induction hypothesis and the monotonicity of $\Gamma$

$$I(\Gamma, \zeta) = \Gamma(\cup\{I(\Gamma, \lambda) \mid \lambda < \zeta\}) \subseteq \Gamma(D) = D.$$

Therefore $I(\Gamma) = \cup\{I(\Gamma, \lambda) \mid \lambda \in On\} \subseteq D$. □

Now let us see how a relation can be defined inductively by the use of appropriate first-order formulas. Let $\sigma$ be an arbitrary many-sorted similarity type which does not contain the relation symbols $R_i$ $(i = 1, ..., n)$ with arities from *sort* $\sigma$.

**(2.5) Definition.** *The set $\Sigma^+(\sigma; R_1, ..., R_n)$ of positive existential formulas in which each $R_i$ $(i = 1, ..., n)$ occurs only positively is the smallest set $F$ of $\sigma \cup \{R_1, ..., R_n\}$-type formulas with the following properties:*

*(i) for any $\pi \in Atom_\sigma$, $\pi$ and $\neg\pi$ belong to $F$;*
*(ii) if $\tau = (\tau_1, ..., \tau_n)$ is an $n$-tuple of $\sigma$-type terms of the appropriate sorts then the formula $R_i(\tau)$ belongs to $F$ $(i = 1, ..., n)$;*
*(iii) if $\phi, \psi \in F$ and $x$ is any variable, then $\phi \wedge \psi$, $\phi \vee \psi$ and $\exists x\phi$ belong to $F$.*

For programming theory the following result of first-order logic is very important.

**(2.6) Theorem.** *Let $\phi \in \Sigma^+(\sigma; R)$ be arbitrary. Let $X = \{x_1, ..., x_m\} \rightleftharpoons var(\phi)$. There are open formulas of $Form_\sigma$ (not containing $R$)*

$$\Theta_1(X, Y, U_1, ..., U_k)\,(k \geq 1) \text{ and } \Theta_2(X, Y)$$

*with free variables as indicated such that*

$$(*) \qquad \phi(X) \leftrightarrow \exists U_1 ... \exists U_k \exists Y \left( (\Theta_1 \wedge \bigwedge_{i=1}^{k} R(U_i)) \vee \Theta_2 \right)$$

*is a tautology. (Here $sort(U_i) = ar(R)$).*

*Proof.* This proceeds in three parts. In the first, we suppose that the formula $\exists U(R(U))$ is true; in the second, we handle the case when $\exists U(R(U))$ is false; and in the last part we show how these two cases can be handled in the same manner.

(A) Let us suppose that $\exists U(R(U))$ holds. We prove by induction on the structure of $\phi$ that there is an open formula $\Theta_1(X, Y, U_1, ..., U_k)$ of $Form_\sigma$ such that

$$\phi \equiv \exists U_1 ... \exists U_k \exists Y \left(\Theta_1 \wedge \bigwedge_{i=1}^{k} R(U_i)\right).$$

(Remember that $\equiv$ is context sensitive. Here $\equiv$ means the equivalence with respect to the set of formulas $\{\exists U R(U)\}$.)

Case 1. $R$ does not occur in $\phi$. Then $\phi \equiv \phi \wedge \exists U(R(U))$ holds. Hence the prenex normal form (with $\exists U$ first) of $\phi \wedge \exists U(R(U))$ will be the desired formula.

Case 2. $\phi \rightleftharpoons R(\tau)$. Then $\phi \equiv \exists U(U = \tau \wedge R(U))$ is also valid.

Case 3. $\phi \rightleftharpoons \exists z \psi(z)$. By the induction hypothesis there is an open formula $\Theta(X, z, Y, U_1, ..., U_k)$ such that

$$\psi(X, z) \equiv \exists U_1 ... \exists U_k \exists Y \left(\Theta(X, z, Y, U_1, ..., U_k) \wedge \bigwedge_{i=1}^{k} R(U_i)\right).$$

Hence

$$\phi(X) \equiv \exists U_1 ... \exists U_k \exists Y \exists z \left(\Theta \wedge \bigwedge_{i=1}^{k} R(U_i)\right)$$

follows immediately.

Case 4. $\phi(X; R) \rightleftharpoons \phi'(X; R) \vee \phi''(X; R)$ or $\phi(X; R) \rightleftharpoons \phi'(X; R) \wedge \phi''(X; R)$. By induction hypothesis there are open formulas $\Theta', \Theta''$ such that

$$\phi'(X; R) \equiv \exists U'_1 ... \exists U'_{k_1} \exists Y' \left(\Theta'(X, Y', U'_1, ..., U'_{k_1}) \wedge \bigwedge_{i=1}^{k_1} R(U'_i)\right),$$

$$\phi''(X; R) \equiv \exists U''_1 ... \exists U''_{k_2} \exists Y'' \left(\Theta''(X, Y'', U''_1, ..., U''_{k_2}) \wedge \bigwedge_{j=1}^{k_2} R(U''_j)\right).$$

We can assume that all the variables of $Y'$, $Y''$, $U_i'$ and $U_j''$ ($i = 1, ..., k_1; j = 1, ..., k_2$) are distinct but $k_1$ and $k_2$ are equal to $k$ (since $\exists U(R(U))$ is supposed to be true). Supposing that the elements of $U_1,...,U_n$ and $Y$ are pairwise disjoint vectors of new variables,

$$\phi'(X; R) \vee \phi''(X; R) \equiv$$

$$\exists U_1 ... \exists U_k \exists Y \left( (\Theta'(X, Y, U_1, ..., U_k) \vee \Theta''(X, Y, U_1, ..., U_k)) \wedge \bigwedge_{i=1}^{k} R(U_i) \right)$$

and $\quad \phi'(X; R) \wedge \phi''(X; R) \equiv$

$$\exists U_1' ... \exists U_k' \exists U_1'' ... \exists U_k'' \exists Y' \exists Y'' \Big( \Theta'(X, Y', U_1', ..., U_k') \wedge$$

$$\Theta''(X, Y'', U_1'', ..., U_k'') \wedge \bigwedge_{i=1}^{k} R(U_i') \wedge \bigwedge_{i=1}^{k} R(U_i'') \Big).$$

are both true.

(B) Now let us consider the case when the formula $\neg\exists U(R(U))$ is true. Let $\phi^*$ be the formula obtained from $\phi$ by substituting the false formula $x \neq x$ (where $x$ is a new variable) instead of any occurrence of $R$ and by closing the new formula with $\exists x$. Assuming the validity of $\neg\exists U(R(U))$, we have that $\phi \equiv \phi^*$. Let $\Theta_2(X, Y)$ be the matrix of the prenex normal form of $\phi^*$.

(C) Let us consider the pair $(\Theta_1, \Theta_2)$ where the open formulas $\Theta_1$ and $\Theta_2$ were defined in parts (A) and (B), respectively. It is clear that this pair satisfies the statement of the theorem, so the formula

$$\phi(X) \leftrightarrow \exists U_1 ... \exists U_k \exists Y \left( (\Theta_1 \wedge \bigwedge_{i=1}^{k} R(U_i)) \vee \Theta_2 \right)$$

is a tautology. □

**(2.7) Definition.** *Let $\mathcal{A} \in Mod_\sigma$ be an arbitrary model and let us fix a finite set $X$ of variables. Let $R$ be a new relation symbol with arity $X$. Let us give a formula $\phi$ belonging to $\Sigma^+(\sigma; R)$ such that $var(\phi) \subseteq X$. By using $\phi$ we can define an operator ${}_{\mathcal{A}}\Gamma_\phi$ on $Val_{\mathcal{A}}[X]$ in the following way. For an arbitrary $Q \subseteq Val_{\mathcal{A}}[X]$ take ${}_{\mathcal{A}}\Gamma_\phi(Q) \rightleftharpoons \{k \in Val_{\mathcal{A}}[X] \mid (\mathcal{A}, Q) \models \phi[k]\}$.*

**(2.8) Theorem.** *For any $\mathcal{A} \in Mod_\sigma$ and $\phi(R) \in \Sigma^+(\sigma; R)$ the operator ${}_{\mathcal{A}}\Gamma_\phi$ is*

*(a) monotone, i.e. if $Q_1 \subseteq Q_2 \subseteq Val_{\mathcal{A}}[X]$ then ${}_{\mathcal{A}}\Gamma_\phi(Q_1) \subseteq {}_{\mathcal{A}}\Gamma_\phi(Q_2)$ (where $X = var(\phi(R))$) and*

*(b) finitary, i.e. there is an $n \in \mathbb{N}$ such that if $k \in {}_{\mathcal{A}}\Gamma_\phi(Q)$ then there is a $Q' \subseteq Q$ such that $|Q'| \leq n$ and $k \in {}_{\mathcal{A}}\Gamma_\phi(Q')$ also holds.*

*Proof.* This directly follows from Theorem (2.6). □

Now we introduce an important measurement for the positive existential formulas and for the operators defined by them. Let $\phi \in \Sigma^+(\sigma; R)$ be arbitrary. According to Theorem (2.6) there are formulas $\Theta_1$ and $\Theta_2$ such that the formula

$$\phi(X) \leftrightarrow \exists U_1 ... \exists U_k \exists Y \left( (\Theta_1 \wedge \bigwedge_{i=1}^{k} R(U_i)) \vee \Theta_2 \right)$$

is a tautology. The least number $k$ for which there are formulas $\Theta_1$ and $\Theta_2$ such that the above formula is a tautology is called the *rank* of the formula $\phi$ and it is denoted by $rank(\phi)$.

Let ${}_{\mathcal{A}}\Gamma_\phi$ be an operator defined by $\phi$ according to Definition (2.7). Define the *rank of* ${}_{\mathcal{A}}\Gamma_\phi$ (denoted by $rank_{\mathcal{A}}(\phi)$) to be the least $n$ such that if $k \in {}_{\mathcal{A}}\Gamma_\phi(Q)$ then there is a $Q' \subseteq Q$ such that $|Q'| \leq n$ and $k \in {}_{\mathcal{A}}\Gamma_\phi(Q')$ holds. We remark that $rank_{\mathcal{A}}(\phi) \leq rank(\phi)$.

The key to the relevance of inductive definability to computability is the following

**(2.9) Theorem.** *Let $B$ be a non-empty set and let $\Gamma$ be a monotone and finitary operator on $B$. The closure ordinal of $\Gamma$ is $\omega_0$.*

*Proof.* It is enough to prove that $I(\Gamma, \omega_0 + 1) = I(\Gamma, \omega_0)$. First we check that

$$(*) \qquad \cup\{I(\Gamma, n) \mid n \in \omega_0\} = I(\Gamma, \omega_0).$$

Using monotonicity, the right hand side contains the left hand side. To prove the other direction let $k \in I(\Gamma, \omega_0) = \Gamma(\cup\{I(\Gamma, n) \mid n \in \omega_0\})$. Since $\Gamma$ is finitary there is a finite $K \subset \cup\{I(\Gamma, n) \mid n \in \omega_0\}$ such that $k \in \Gamma(K)$ also holds. Since $\Gamma$ is monotone and $K$ is finite there is an $i \in \omega_0$ such that $K \subseteq I(\Gamma, i)$. This means that

$$k \in \Gamma(K) \subseteq \Gamma(I(\Gamma, i)) = I(\Gamma, i+1) \subseteq \cup\{I(\Gamma, n) \mid n \in \omega_0\},$$

which already proves (*). Applying $\Gamma$ to each side of equation (*) and using Lemma (2.4) (i) we get $I(\Gamma, \omega_0) = I(\Gamma, \omega_0 + 1)$. Using transfinite induction and the definition of the closure ordinal we get that $cl(\Gamma) = \omega_0$. □

**(2.10) Corollary.** *Let $R(X) = \phi(X)$ be a parameterless equation such that $\phi \in \Sigma^+(\sigma; R)$. Let $\mathcal{A} \in Mod_\sigma$ be given. The many-sorted relation ${}_{\mathcal{A}}I_\phi \rightleftharpoons I({}_{\mathcal{A}}\Gamma_\phi)$ is the least fixed point of the equation $R(X) = \phi(X)$.*

**(2.11) Definition.** *Let $\mathcal{A} \in Mod_\sigma$. A $Y$-type relation $Q \subseteq Val_{\mathcal{A}}[Y]$ is said to be inductively definable on $\mathcal{A}$ or simply inductive on $\mathcal{A}$ iff there is a set of variables $X$, a new relation symbol $R$ with arity $X$, a formula $\phi \in \Sigma^+(\sigma; R)$ and a valuation $k \in Val_{\mathcal{A}}[X \setminus Y]$ such that $Y \subseteq X$, and for all $a \in Val_{\mathcal{A}}[Y]$ we have $a \in Q$ iff $k + a \in {}_{\mathcal{A}}I_\phi$. This relation is also denoted by ${}_{\mathcal{A}}I_\phi\restriction k$. The valuation $k$ is called the parameter of the definition. Let $I_{\mathcal{A}}$ denote the set of all inductive relations on $\mathcal{A}$.*

**(2.12) Theorem.** *Let $R(X) = \phi(X,P)$ be an equation such that $\phi \in \Sigma^+(\sigma; R)$. Let a model $\mathcal{A} \in Mod_\sigma$ and a (parameter) valuation $k \in Val_\mathcal{A}[P]$ be given. There is a least fixed point $Q$ of this equation with parameter $k$ in $\mathcal{A}$. Moreover, $Q$ is inductively definable in $\mathcal{A}$.*

*Proof.* By Theorem (2.6) $\phi$ is of the form

$$\phi(X) \leftrightarrow \exists U_1 ... \exists U_k \exists Y \left( (\Theta_1 \wedge \bigwedge_{i=1}^{k} R(U_i)) \vee \Theta_2 \right)$$

Let $R^P$ be a new relation symbol with arity $X \cup P$. Take the following formula:

$$\phi^P(X,P) \leftrightarrow \exists U_1 ... \exists U_k \exists Y \left( (\Theta_1 \wedge \bigwedge_{i=1}^{k} R^P(U_i, P)) \vee \Theta_2 \right).$$

It is clear that $\phi^P \in \Sigma^+(\sigma; R^P)$. It is not hard to prove that ${}_\mathcal{A}I_{\phi^P}\restriction_k$ is the least fixed point of $R(X) = \phi(X,P)$ in $\mathcal{A}$ with parameter $k$. □

**(2.13) Theorem.** *Let $\sigma'$ be an extension of $\sigma$ obtained by adding new sorts and new constant symbols only of the new sorts. Let $\mathcal{A}' \in Mod_{\sigma'}$ be a fixed model and let $\mathcal{A} \rightleftharpoons \mathcal{A}'\restriction_\sigma$. Let $Q \subseteq Val_\mathcal{A}[X]$ be a given many-sorted set on a finite set $X$ of variables. $Q$ is inductive on $\mathcal{A}$ iff $Q$ is inductive on $\mathcal{A}'$.*

**(2.14) Theorem.** *Let $E \rightleftharpoons \{(R_i, \phi_i, X_i) \mid i = 1, ..., n\}$ be an equation system in $\sigma$ with parameters $P_i$ $(i = 1, ..., n)$. Let $\mathcal{A} \in Mod_\sigma$ and $k \in Val_\mathcal{A}[\cup_{i=1}^n P_i]$ be given. Let*

$$rank(E) \rightleftharpoons \max \{rank(\phi) \mid i = 1, ..., n\}.$$

*There is a least fixed point $\beta = (Q_1, ..., Q_n)$ of the equation system $E$ in $\mathcal{A}$ with parameter $k$. Moreover, every set $Q_i$ $(i = 1, ..., n)$ is inductively definable on $\mathcal{A}$ by a $rank(E)$-ranked formula, and this formula does not depend on $\mathcal{A}$.*

*Proof.* Let us extend $\sigma$ to a similarity type $\sigma'$ by adding a new sort *Label* and $n$ new constant symbols $L_i$ : *Label* $(i = 1, ..., n)$. Let us extend $\mathcal{A}$ to a model $\mathcal{A}'$ of $\sigma$ such that the interpretations of the symbols $L_i$ are different from each other. We show that $E$ has a least solution in $\mathcal{A}'$, which is inductively definable in $\mathcal{A}'$. It is clear that this is the least solution in $\mathcal{A}$ as well. According to the previous theorem this fact implies the statement of the theorem.

Let $u$ be a *Label*-sorted variable. We can suppose that the sets $X_i$ are disjoint from each other. Let $Y \rightleftharpoons (\cup_{i=1}^n X_i)\{u\} \cup (\cup_{i=1}^n P_i)$. Let $R'$ be a $Y$-sorted new relation symbol. Take

$$\phi \rightleftharpoons \bigvee_{i=1}^{n} \left( (u = L_i) \wedge \phi_i \left[ R(Y)[L_j/u]/R_j \right]_{j=1}^{n} \right).$$

Let $Q$ be the least fixed point of the equation $R(Y) = \phi(Y,P)$ in $\mathcal{A}'$ with parameter $k$. By Theorem (2.12) this $Q$ exists and is inductively definable in $\mathcal{A}'$. Let $k' \in Val_\mathcal{A}[Y]$ be an arbitrary but fixed valuation. Let

$k_i \rightleftharpoons k'\restriction(Y \setminus X_i) \setminus \{u\} + \{(u, L_i\} + k$. Take $Q_i \rightleftharpoons \{\ell \in Val_{\mathcal{A}}[X_i] \mid k_i + \ell \in Q\}$ $(i = 1, ..., n)$. One can check that $\beta \rightleftharpoons (Q_1, ..., Q_n)$ is the least solution of the equation system $E$ in $\mathcal{A}'$ with parameter $k$. From the definition of $Q_i$, it is obvious that each $Q_i$ $(i = 1, ..., n)$ is inductively definable in $\mathcal{A}'$, and the definition does not depend on $\mathcal{A}$. Since $rank(\phi) = rank(E)$ this formula is a $rank(E)$-ranked one. □

**(2.15) Theorem.** (Transitivity) *Let $\sigma$ be a fixed similarity type and let $E'$, $E$ be two equation systems in $\sigma$ such that for each equation $(R, \phi, X)$ belonging to $E$, $\phi \in \Sigma^+(\sigma; R_1, ..., R_n)$ and $E' \subseteq E$. Let $\beta = (Q_1, ..., Q_n)$ be the least fixed point of $E$ in $\mathcal{A}$ with parameter $k$. Take $\beta' \rightleftharpoons \{Q_i \mid$ there is an equation in $E'$ for $R_i\}$. Then $\beta'$ is the least solution of $E'$ in $\mathcal{A}$ with parameter $k$.*

**(2.16) Definition.** *Let $\sigma$ be a fixed many-sorted similarity type. The pair $(\Theta_1(X, Y, U_1, ..., U_k), \Theta_2(X, Y))$ of two $\sigma$-type open formulas is said to be an inductive definitional schema. Let $\mathcal{A}$ be a $\sigma$-type model. The relation ${}_{\mathcal{A}}I_{\phi}$ defined in $\mathcal{A}$ by the formula*

$$\phi(X) \rightleftharpoons \exists U_1 ... \exists U_k \exists Y \left( (\Theta_1(X, Y, U_1, ..., U_k) \wedge \bigwedge_{i=1}^{k} R(U_i)) \vee \Theta_2(X, Y) \right)$$

*is said to be the relation defined by $(\Theta_1(X, Y, U_1, ..., U_k), \Theta_2(X, Y))$ in $\mathcal{A}$. This relation is also denoted by ${}_{\mathcal{A}}I_{(\Theta_1, \Theta_2)}$.*

For the sake of simplicity we will not indicate the variables of the constituent formulas of the inductive definitional schema, though they cannot be guessed from the mentioned formulas themselves. However, all the time we suppose that these variables are given.

**(2.17) Lemma.** *Let $\mathcal{A} \in Mod_\sigma$ and fix a many-sorted relation $Q \subseteq Val_{\mathcal{A}}[Y]$. $Q$ is inductive on $\mathcal{A}$ iff there is a set $X$ of variables, an inductive definitional schema $(\Theta_1, \Theta_2)$ and a parameter $k \in Val_{\mathcal{A}}[X \setminus Y]$ such that $Y \subseteq X$ and for any $a \in Val_{\mathcal{A}}[Y]$:*

$$a \in Q \quad iff \quad k + a \in {}_{\mathcal{A}}I_{(\Theta_1, \Theta_2)}.$$

*Proof.* The statement is an immediate consequence of the corresponding definitions and Theorem (2.6). □

**(2.18) Example.** Let $\phi \in Form_\sigma$ be a formula with $var(\phi) = (X, X', P)$, where $X'$ is a copy of $X$ and $X, X'$ and $P$ are pairwise disjoint. Consider the following definition:

$$\tilde{\phi}(X, X', P) \rightleftharpoons (X = X') \vee \exists X'' \left( \phi(X, X'', P) \wedge \tilde{\phi}(X'', X', P) \right).$$

Fix a model $\mathcal{A} \in Mod_\sigma$ and a valuation $k \in Val_{\mathcal{A}}[P]$. Obviously,

$$TRC(\phi_{\mathcal{A}}\restriction k) \;=\; {}_{\mathcal{A}}I_{\tilde{\phi}}\restriction k.$$

We remark that the sets which are definable by the transitive and reflexive closure of a first-order definable relation are the same as the sets which are inductively definable by 1-ranked formulas.

**(2.19) Example.** Let $\sigma$ be a many-sorted similarity type and let $\mathcal{A}$ be a $\sigma$-type model. Fix a finite set $X$ of variables and a valuation $k \in Val_{\mathcal{A}}[X]$. The Herbrand universe ${}_{\mathcal{A}}H_\sigma(k)$ generated from $k$ in $\mathcal{A}$ is the least family $\{{}_{\mathcal{A}}H_s(k) \mid s \in sort\ \sigma\}$ such that

- for any $x \in X$, if $s = sort\ \sigma$ then $k(x) \in {}_{\mathcal{A}}H_s(k)$;
- for any $s \in sort_\sigma$, ${}_{\mathcal{A}}H_s(k) \subseteq A_s$;
- the family is closed for the function symbols of $\sigma$ interpreted in $\mathcal{A}$.

We note that if for all $s \in sort\ \sigma$ there is at least one constant symbol $c$ with sort $s$ then ${}_{\mathcal{A}}H_\sigma(\emptyset)$ is the smallest submodel of $\mathcal{A}$.

Now we show how the Herbrand universe can be defined inductively. For any $s \in sort\ \sigma$ let $y_s$ be a new variable symbol and $R_s$ a new $\{y_s\} \cup X$-sorted relation symbol. Take $Y \rightleftharpoons \{y_s \mid s \in sort\ \sigma\}$. For any function symbol $f : s_1, ..., s_n \to s$ let $U_f$ be a new vector of variables such that $U_f \rightleftharpoons \{u_1, ..., u_n\}$ and for all $i = 1, ..., n$ we have $sort(u_i) = s_i$. Consider the following fixed point equation system ($s \in sort\ \sigma$):

$$R_s(y_s, X) \;=\; \bigvee_{\substack{c \in func\ \sigma \\ sort(c)=s}} y_s = c \;\vee\; \bigvee_{\substack{x \in X \\ sort(x)=s}} y_s = x \;\vee$$

$$\bigvee_{ar(f)=(s_1,...,s_n;s)} \exists U_f\Big(y_s = f(U_f) \wedge \bigwedge_{u \in U_f} R_{sort(u)}(u, X)\Big),$$

It is an easy exercise to prove that the least fixed point of this equation system is just the Herbrand universe generated from a fixed parameter $k \in Val_{\mathcal{A}}[X]$. This means that the sets ${}_{\mathcal{A}}H_s(k)$ are inductive on $\mathcal{A}$ ($s \in sort\ \sigma$).

# Part I
# Computability

Chapter 3

# Introduction to Part I

Our main objective in this part is the development of a theory based on classical first-order logic which can serve as the foundation for a logic-based programming theory. Namely, this theory should deal with programs and with their logically meaningful semantics, and should also provide purely logical tools to extend programming languages with new computation devices or data structures. This theory should also be appropriate to investigate the programming languages for example from the viewpoint of their computational power, and to provide them with a sharp logical characterization.

The focus of interest of a programming theory is programs. A program consists of elementary actions called instructions and is just a precise plan of actions over its data environment. The notion of a program is closely related to that of an algorithm, which is one of the fundamental concepts of theoretical computer science. We consider an algorithm to be a precise prescription specifying a computational process that starts with some initial data and aims at the achievement of some desired result. Therefore, a program is simply the representation of an algorithm. What type of instructions are allowed and how they can be structured to represent an algorithm is an important question when we are looking for the basis of a programming theory. This basis is the programming language that is to provide the necessary tools to represent algorithms.

One can require to build up a theory of programming on such a programming language which is general enough to represent "all possible" algorithms, so it should be of maximal computational power. At the same time this language is required to have all the characteristic constructions a real programming language has, except those that represent mere decoration. The latter are more important not for theory but in practical work. So in order to develop a programming theory we intend to choose an abstract programming language that satisfies the above mentioned requirements.

We choose a nondeterministic programming language to be the basis for our programming theory. Before defining it, we fix a signature, i.e. a similarity type which provides us with the symbols from which a first-order language is built up. The expressions (the terms and formulas) of this language form the basis of the programming language and therefore they are used in the programs.

We select the guarded command language introduced by Dijkstra [1976] as our basic programming language, with the only difference that we omit the abort construct and the abort state. $P_\sigma$ will denote this language, where $\sigma$

is the fixed similarity type (alphabet). We augment this language by random assignment and so we obtain the language denoted as $rP_\sigma$. (See Section 4.1.) These programming languages are structured.

However, we define another version of the programming language $P_\sigma$ by using so-called transition graphs. In fact this is just a flowchart variant of $rP_\sigma$ denoted by $rG_\sigma$. (See Section 4.2.)

In programming theory the main object is the program and not the programming language. In the theory we aim to formally characterize the programs. For this we require two formalisms. The first one will deal with syntactic aspects and the second will deal with the semantics of the programs. The latter has a significant role, since programs as algorithms are a special kind of object with a specific meaning. Namely, an algorithm is static in its syntactic form, whereas it receives a meaning during its execution which is already dynamic. Therefore the intended meaning of an algorithm and thus of a program is connected with its execution. In our informal description of an algorithm, the computational process corresponded to the meaning, so now we have to define computational processes in a formal way. The programs expressed in the abstract programming language specify computational processes when they are executed in an idealized "computer". Therefore, the semantics of the algorithms, or more precisely of the programs, is based on the model of the computer itself. So this computer is to be characterized in such a way that it allows the definition of the computational processes.

The formal characterization of meaning is quite familiar in mathematical logic, since it has a well developed theory (and culture) - model theory - to deal with semantic questions. However, the formalization of idealized computers and of their computational processes meets some difficulties in mathematical logic. Namely, the essentially dynamic processes are to be represented by logical tools and methods which are static by nature. The main question is whether we can formalize this dynamism using purely logical tools.

The basic instruction of the programming language is the assignment. The variables name the memory registers of the computer where the programs will run. The logical consideration of the variables in the left hand side of the assignments is a crucial point.

In our programming language we use the same set of variables which is used in the definition of the first-order language. However, the variables on the left hand side of the assignment are considered as register name variables. These reflect the "virtual" memory registers of the abstract computer where the results of the symbolically given computations of the programs are to be stored. The registers are virtual because at this stage they are given only by the variables. So each program has its own virtual memory of a size equal to the number of variables used in the program. Hence the memory capacity of the computer is finite for each program. However, the possibility to extend the memory capacity dynamically, e.g. by the use of stacks, is an important condition for a programming language that is to be universal.

Since the programs of the basic programming language are built up from symbols of a fixed similarity type, say $\sigma$, to define their meaning we have to interpret them in the $\sigma$-type models (relation structures) of the corresponding $\sigma$-type first-order language. Therefore, the computer should be represented by these models. Intuitively, the computation processes too are to be defined over these models.

The changes in the values of the variables will be used to model the computational processes, i.e. the program executions. The variables will be concretized by the use of valuations which assign concrete elements in the universe of the model to the variables. We use two approaches to define computation processes. The first one, given in Section 4.1, defines the relation between the inputs and outputs of the program execution without characterizing how the output is obtained, while the second one takes account of the whole process of execution by defining a trace (see Section 4.2). As we shall see, the trace semantics is external to our first-order language. The denotations, on the other hand, which are the input-output relations, are internal, and are defined by the use of tools provided entirely by the first-order language. In Section 4.4 special attention will be payed to the canonical form of the programs.

The basic programming language, as we shall see in Section 7.2, is not universal. We could augment it directly by adding the necessary programming constructs. We prefer, however, to use a method which is closer to our logic approach. We extend the similarity type and the models so that the programming language constructed on this basis is augmented by the required new constructs, such as counters, lists, stacks, etc. (see Section 5.1).

Section 6.1 is devoted to the investigation of the programming language $rP_\sigma$ augmented with different numbers of stacks. Special attention is paid in Section 6.2 to the deterministic programming languages and to the question of whether a nondeterministic program can be simulated by a deterministic one. To investigate this question the notion of diagonalization will be introduced. A diagonalization of a nondeterministic program is a deterministic program which, in certain sense, enumerates all the possible outputs of the original program. It will be shown that the programming language should be augmented with at least two stacks to give it the diagonalizability property.

Computability is one of the basic notions of programming theory. It is related to the strict mathematical formalization of the intuitive idea of "mechanical calculation". The classical theory of recursive functions or of computing deals with computability. Different kinds of machinery such as recursive functions, register machines, normal algorithms and so on have been proposed for investigating computability (on which see for example Rogers [1967]). Programming languages provide new machinery for the theory of computability, as can be seen for example in Davis [1979] or in Cutland [1980].

Almost all approaches in the theory of computing deal with numerical computation, that is, with computation in the standard model of arithmetic. In contrast to these approaches, we aim to define and study computation on arbitrary models.

According to our logical approach as developed so far, the programs of a programming language of a fixed similarity type, say $\sigma$, get their shape in the $\sigma$-type models. This is where the computational processes also take place when the program execution is under consideration. Therefore, we formalize and investigate the notion of computability over these models.

The main notions are introduced in Section 7.1, where we also investigate what closure properties hold for the computable relations. A generalization of recursive relations is also introduced and studied.

In Chapter 6 a family of $\sigma$-type programming languages are introduced which differ in the number of stacks they allow one to use. A comparative analysis of these languages with respect to their computational power appears in Section 7.2, where a generalization of Church's thesis for the case of computations on the $\sigma$-type models is also introduced. Namely, in our computation theory the reformulated Church's thesis says that the effectively computable relations of a fixed relation structure are precisely the same as the relations computable by the stack extension.

The algorithms as prescriptions can be presented not only by the use of the abstract programming language but also in a purely logical way. We show this in Chapter 8 by using the notion of effective inductive definitional schemas based on the notion of inductive definability. A similar logical approach to defining the algorithmic prescriptions is considered by Moldestad, Stoltenberg-Hansen, Tucker [1978]. At the same time, the logical definition of algorithmic prescriptions gives us a purely logical characterization of the programming languages with one and two stacks.

Chapter 4

# Main Properties of Program Schemas

In this chapter we introduce a basic programming language by defining its syntax and semantics. The syntax is defined as a set of program schemas constructed with a given set of program constructs by using the terms and the open formulas of a fixed alphabet (similarity type). This ensures that the function and relation symbols from which the terms and formulas are built up are included in the program schemas. We take the traditional view of a programming language as syntactic: in this case the syntax is the set of program schemas of the given similarity type.

The semantics of the program schemas is defined by the characterization of the changes caused by the execution. The execution presupposes the interpretation of the symbols of the similarity type used in the programs. Therefore, the relational structures, i.e. the models, of the appropriate first-order logic of the same similarity type as that of the programming language represent the computer, or more precisely the data environment, where the program execution takes place.

Therefore, the program schemas are to be interpreted in the first-order models. The interpretation of a program schema in a given model is obtained by interpreting the function and relation symbols of the schema by the corresponding functions and relations of the model. Thus we obtain programs from a program schema. From now on we shall use the notion of program, which the reader is to understand from the context either as a program schema or as a concrete program.

We represent changes in the data environment of the programs by the use of a set of computational states. A computational state at any time comprises the values of all program variables at that time, i.e. a computational state characterizes the environment of the program to be considered at any time moment. We define the semantics in two ways. The first characterizes the sequence of all states reached during the program execution. This is called operational semantics. The second characterizes the semantics by providing only the initial and final states, i.e. the states from which the program starts and those which are obtained by its termination. This is the relational or, more precisely, input-output semantics which we also call denotational semantics.

In Section 4.1 the basic programming language is introduced as a structured language. Here we also introduce the input-output semantics of this language. The unstructured version of this programming language is given in

Section 4.2 in the form of graphs. This form makes it easier to understand operational or trace semantics.

An interesting question is whether the semantics will be internal (or definable within the corresponding first-order logic) or external (given as a special mathematical entity from the outside by the use of non-first-order logical tools). This question is analysed in Section 4.3, where it is shown that while the semantic characterization - by the computation paths called traces - is external, the input-output characterization, by the so-called denotations, is internal. Here the questions connected with program termination are also analysed. Section 4.4 is devoted to the investigation of the canonical form of programs of the basic programming language.

## 4.1 Basic Definitions of Program Schemas

We now define the programming language which will serve as the fundamental one throughout the rest of the book. This language is syntactically the same as Dijkstra's guarded command language, but its semantics is a slight modification of the original definition. (See Dijkstra [1976].)

Let $\sigma$ be an arbitrary many-sorted similarity type. We define the $\sigma$-type program schemas built up from the function and relation symbols of $\sigma$. From now on let $V$ denote a denumerable set of variables: $V = \cup\{V_s \mid s \in sort\ \sigma\}$.

**(4.1) Definition.** *The set of $\sigma$-type program schemas $P_\sigma$ is the least set satisfying the following properties:*

*(i) a)* **skip** $\in P_\sigma$ *(do nothing);*
*b)* **loop** $\in P_\sigma$ *(infinite cycle);*
*(ii) if $v \in V$, $\tau \in Term_\sigma$ and $v$ and $\tau$ are of the same sort then $(v := \tau)$ (assignment) belongs to $P_\sigma$;*
*(iii) if $\alpha_1, \alpha_2 \in Open_\sigma$ and $p_1, p_2 \in P_\sigma$ then*
*a) $(p_1; p_2)$ (composition);*
*b)* **if** $\alpha_1 \to p_1 \square \alpha_2 \to p_2$ **fi** *(conditional alternation);*
*c)* **do** $\alpha_1 \to p_1 \square \alpha_2 \to p_2$ **od** *(conditional repetition or repetitive command) belong to $P_\sigma$.*

Note that formulas in (iii)(b) and (c) are also called *guards* or *tests*. According to our understanding of the conditional alternation, if both of the guards fail then the program skips rather than aborts as in Dijkstra's original definition.

We illustrate the intuitive meaning of the guards by conditional repetition in (iii)(c). While executing the program **do** $\alpha_1 \to p_1 \square \alpha_2 \to p_2$ **od** one of the subprograms $p_1$ or $p_2$ will be executed repeatedly until both guards become false. If both guards are true then a non-deterministic choice is taken and then the corresponding subprogram will be executed. Otherwise that subprogram is chosen the guard of which is true. Using Pascal notation, the conditional repetition is equivalent to the following program:

**while** $\alpha_1 \vee \alpha_2$ **do**
  **if** $\alpha_1 \wedge \neg\alpha_2$ **then** $p_1$ **else**
  **if** $\neg\alpha_1 \wedge \alpha_2$ **then** $p_2$ **else**
    **choice** $(p_1, p_2)$;

The conditional constructs provide only a finite non-determinism to the programming language $P_\sigma$. However, we extend $P_\sigma$ by adding random assignments of the form $y :=?$. These assignments augment $P_\sigma$ by an infinite non-determinism, since the intended meaning of $y :=?$ is that $y$ gets a new non-deterministically chosen value.

**(4.2) Definition.** *The set of $\sigma$-type program schemas with random assignment is the least set $rP_\sigma$ that satisfies (i)-(iii) above and*

*(iv) if $v \in V$ then $(v := ?)$ (random assignment) belongs to $rP_\sigma$.*

The set $P_\sigma$ ($rP_\sigma$) is also called the basic programming language (with random assignment, respectively) and its elements are called programs or program schemas. It is obvious that $P_\sigma \subseteq rP_\sigma$.

A $\sigma$-type program $p \in rP_\sigma$ is said to be a program *without cycle* iff it does not contain conditional repetition (iii)(c) of Definition (4.1). We emphasize that a program without cycle may contain some infinite cycles **loop**.

The *complexity* of $\sigma$-type programs with random assignment is defined as follows:

(i) The complexity of all subprograms is less than that of the program.
(ii) Let $p$ be of the form **do** $\alpha_1 \to p_1 \Box \alpha_2 \to p_2$ **od** and take $q \rightleftharpoons$ **if** $\alpha_1 \to p_1 \Box \alpha_2 \to p_2$ **fi**. The complexity of $q$ is less than that of $p$.

Further on we use this complexity when we prove statements by induction on the sets $rP_\sigma$ and $P_\sigma$.

We note that a program schema $p$ of $rP_\sigma$ becomes a program by getting concrete meaning so that we fix a $\sigma$-type model and interpret the symbols of the similarity type $\sigma$ used in the schema $p$. However, further on we also use the notion of program even in the uninterpreted case. From the context it is unambiguous whether we mean a program or a program schema.

Consider the following alphabet

$$H_\sigma \rightleftharpoons V \cup \{\textbf{skip}, \textbf{loop}, :=, ?, ;, \textbf{if}, \textbf{fi}, \textbf{do}, \textbf{od}, (, ), \to, \Box, \wedge, \neg\} \cup rel\,\sigma \cup func\,\sigma$$

Obviously, $rP_\sigma \subseteq H_\sigma^*$.

**(4.3) Lemma.** *(On unique readability.) Let $p \in rP_\sigma \subseteq H_\sigma^*$ be arbitrary. One and only one of the following cases is true:*

- $p =$ **skip**;
- $p =$ **loop**;
- *there is a unique* $v \in V$ *and a unique* $\tau \in Term_\sigma$ *such that* $p = (v := \tau)$;
- *there is a unique* $v \in V$ *such that* $p = (v :=?)$;
- *there are unique* $\alpha_1, \alpha_2 \in Open_\sigma$ *and* $p_1, p_2 \in rP_\sigma$ *such that either*
  $p = (p_1; p_2)$ *or*
  $p =$ **if** $\alpha_1 \to p_1 \square \alpha_2 \to p_2$ **fi** *or*
  $p =$ **do** $\alpha_1 \to p_1 \square \alpha_2 \to p_2$ **od**.

*Proof.* By induction on the length of the programs. □

Now we introduce some frequently used program constructs as abbreviations.

**(4.4) Definition.** *Let* $n \in \mathbb{N}$ $(n \geq 2)$ *be given and for any* $1 \leq i \leq n$ *let* $p, p_i \in P_\sigma$ *and* $\alpha, \alpha_i \in Open_\sigma$ *and* $v \in V$ *be arbitrary.*

*(i)* **while** $\alpha$ **do** $p$ **od** $\rightleftharpoons$ **do** $\alpha \to p \square false \to$ **skip od**;
*(ii)* **repeat** $p$ **until** $\alpha \rightleftharpoons$ $p$; **while** $\neg\alpha$ **do** $p$ **od**;
*(iii)* $(1..i..n) : p_i \rightleftharpoons p_1; p_2; ...; p_n$
*(iv)* **if** $\alpha_1 \to p_1 \square \alpha_2 \to p_2 \square ... \square \alpha_n \to p_n$ **fi** $\rightleftharpoons$
**if** $\alpha_1 \to p_1 \square \alpha_2 \vee ... \vee \alpha_n \to$ **if** $\alpha_2 \to p_2 \square \alpha_3 \vee ... \vee \alpha_n \to$ **if** ... **fi fi fi** . *We also use the notation* **if** $\alpha \to p$ **fi** *instead of* **if** $\alpha \to p \square false \to$ **skip fi**
*(v)* **if** $\square$ $(1..i..n) : \alpha_i \to p_i$ **fi** $\rightleftharpoons$ **if** $\alpha_1 \to p_1 \square ... \square \alpha_n \to p_n$ **fi**
*(vi)* **do** $\alpha_1 \to p_1 \square \alpha_2 \to p_2 \square ... \square \alpha_n \to p_n$ **od** $\rightleftharpoons$
**while** $\alpha_1 \vee ... \vee \alpha_n$ **do if** $\alpha_1 \to p_1 \square, ..., \square \alpha_n \to p_n$ **fi od**;
*(vii)* **do** $\square (1..i..n) : \alpha_i \to p_i$ **od** $\rightleftharpoons$ **do** $\alpha_1 \to p_1 \square ... \square \alpha_n \to p_n$ **od**.

*Note that due to the nondeterminism often the order of the constituent programs* $p_i$ *or components* $\alpha_i \to p_i$ $(i = 1, ..., n)$ *in (iii), (v) and (vii) is irrelevant. In this case we will give a finite set of indices, say* $I$*, and* $(i \in I)$ *will be written instead of* $(1..i..n)$*. This means that in the program constructs defined in (iii),(v) and (vii) the programs may be understood with an arbitrary ordering of the given set* $I$ *of indices. In the case (iii) this may lead to ambiguity unless all the programs have specific properties.*

*(viii) Let* $X \subseteq V$ *be a finite set of variables, let* $Y$ *be a copy of* $X$*, and let* $\iota : X \to Y$ *be the corresponding bijection.* $X := Y$ *is a shorthand for* $(x \in X) : x := \iota(x)$ *and* $X = Y$ *is a shorthand for* $\bigwedge_{x \in X} x = \iota(x)$.
*(ix)* **choice** $(p_1, ..., p_n) \rightleftharpoons$ **if** $true \to p_1 \square ... \square true \to p_n$ **fi** .

To define the meaning of the programming language $rP_\sigma$, first the symbols of the similarity type $\sigma$ should be interpreted and then the exact meaning of the programs are to be defined on the basis of the above interpretation. The symbols of type $\sigma$ may be relational, functional or constant ones and it is straightforward to interpret them in appropriate relation structures, i.e. in $\sigma$-type first-order models. Therefore, it would be proper to define the semantics of $rP_\sigma$ within these models. This can be done if we consider the models as the data environment of the programs where program execution takes place. The program variables are to be interpreted in this data environment. To define program semantics, the computation process is to be represented in the data environment. The states of computation produce the values of all program variables at any time. So let us first consider how the notion of computation states can be defined in a fixed $\sigma$-type model.

For any program $p \in P_\sigma$ (or $p \in rP_\sigma$) let $var(p)$ denote the set of all variables occurring in the text of $p$. It can also be considered as a function $var : rP_\sigma \to Sb(V)$. We recall the definition of $X$-type relations:

**(4.5) Definition.** *Let $\mathcal{A}$ be an arbitrary but fixed $\sigma$-type model. For any set $X \subseteq V$ let us define the set of valuations of the variables of $X$ by taking*

$$Val_{\mathcal{A}}[\![X]\!] \rightleftharpoons \{f : X \to A \mid sort(f(x)) = sort(x)\}$$

*where $A = \cup\{A_i \mid i \in sort\sigma\}$.*

*If $X = V$ we write $Val_{\mathcal{A}}$ instead of $Val_{\mathcal{A}}[\![V]\!]$ and we write $Val_{\mathcal{A}}[\![p]\!]$ instead of $Val_{\mathcal{A}}[\![var(p)]\!]$. Similarly, when there is a function $var : F \to Sb(V)$ for some set $F$, and $var$ is obvious from the context we write $Val_{\mathcal{A}}[\![f]\!]$ instead of $Val_{\mathcal{A}}[\![var(f)]\!]$ ($f \in F$).*

For a given program $p$ the set of valuations $Val_{\mathcal{A}}[\![p]\!]$ is just the set of computation states of $p$ in $\mathcal{A}$. However, very often we use $Val_{\mathcal{A}}$ instead of $Val_{\mathcal{A}}[\![p]\!]$ since we do not want to have to change the set of variables in inductions on the complexity of programs.

Now we define the input-output semantics of a program $p \in rP_\sigma$.

**(4.6) Definition.** *For an arbitrary but fixed model $\mathcal{A} \in Mod_\sigma$ and for a program $p \in rP_\sigma$ let the denotation $Den_{\mathcal{A}}[\![p]\!]$ be defined by the following properties:*

*(i)* $Den_{\mathcal{A}}[\![\textbf{skip}]\!] \rightleftharpoons \{(a, a) \mid a \in Val_{\mathcal{A}}\}$.
*(ii)* $Den_{\mathcal{A}}[\![\textbf{loop}]\!] \rightleftharpoons \emptyset$.
*(iii)* $Den_{\mathcal{A}}[\![(v := \tau)]\!] \rightleftharpoons \{(a, a + (v, \tau_{\mathcal{A}}[a])) \mid a \in Val_{\mathcal{A}}\}$.
*(iv)* $Den_{\mathcal{A}}[\![(p_1; p_2)]\!] \rightleftharpoons Den_{\mathcal{A}}[\![p_1]\!] \circ Den_{\mathcal{A}}[\![p_2]\!]$.

*(v)* $Den_{\mathcal{A}}[\![\textbf{if } \alpha_1 \to p_1 \Box \alpha_2 \to p_2 \textbf{fi}]\!] \rightleftharpoons$
$\{(a_1, a_2) \mid \mathcal{A} \models \alpha_i[a_1]$ *and* $(a_1, a_2) \in Den_{\mathcal{A}}[\![p_i]\!]$, *for some* $i \in \{1, 2\}\} \cup$
$\{(a, a) \mid \mathcal{A} \models (\neg\alpha_1 \wedge \neg\alpha_2)[a]$ *and* $a \in Val_{\mathcal{A}}\}$.

*(vi)* $Den_{\mathcal{A}}[\![\textbf{do } \alpha_1 \to p_1 \Box \alpha_2 \to p_2 \textbf{ od}]\!] \rightleftharpoons$
$\{(a, b) \mid \exists k \geq 0\ \exists a_0 ... \exists a_k\ (a_0, ..., a_k \in Val_{\mathcal{A}}$ *and* $a_0 = a$ *and* $a_k = b)$ *and*
$\forall i \in \{1, ..., k\}\ \exists j \in \{1, 2\}\ (\mathcal{A} \models \alpha_j[a_{i-1}]$ *and* $(a_{i-1}, a_i) \in Den_{\mathcal{A}}[\![p_j]\!]$ *and*
$\mathcal{A} \models (\neg\alpha_1 \wedge \neg\alpha_2)[a_k])\}$.

*(vii)* $Den_{\mathcal{A}}[\![v :=?]\!] \rightleftharpoons \{(a_1, a_2) \mid a_1{\restriction}V \setminus \{v\} = a_2{\restriction}V \setminus \{v\}; a_1, a_2 \in Val_{\mathcal{A}}\}$.

*Let $X \subseteq V$ be a fixed set of variables such that $var(p) \subseteq X$. Let $X'$ be a new copy of $X$ with bijection $\iota$. Then we define the input-output of $p$ with respect to $X$ as the many-sorted relation*

$$Den_{\mathcal{A}}[\![p, X]\!] \rightleftharpoons \{(k, l) \mid \exists (a, b) \in Den_{\mathcal{A}}[\![p]\!]\ a{\restriction}_X = k \text{ and } b{\restriction}_X = l[X'/X]\}$$

*Obviously $Den_{\mathcal{A}}[\![p, X]\!] \subseteq Val_{\mathcal{A}}[X, X']$ $(= Val_{\mathcal{A}}[X] \times Val_{\mathcal{A}}[X'])$.*

It is clear that $Den_{\mathcal{A}}[\![p]\!] \subseteq Val^2_{\mathcal{A}}$ for any program $p$ of $rP_\sigma$, i.e. the denotation of $p$ in $\mathcal{A}$ is a binary relation on the corresponding set of states. On the basis of the above definition the denotation can be considered as a function $Den$ defined on $Mod_\sigma \times rP_\sigma$. If we fix a model $\mathcal{A} \in Mod_\sigma$ then we obtain the function $Den_{\mathcal{A}}$ defined on $rP_\sigma$. For a fixed program $p$ we have the function $Den[\![p]\!]$ defined on $Mod_\sigma$.

## 4.2 Flowchart Schemas

Sometimes the characterization of the programs of the programming language $rP_\sigma$ is more convenient if instead of the linear and structured "text form" of $rP_\sigma$, we use a "graph form" which represents the corresponding flowchart schema. For example, the definition of operational semantics by the use of traces is more transparent if the program is given in the graph form.

To define a graph we require two sets, one for the set of nodes and another for the set of edges. Let *Label* be a fixed set whose elements are called *labels*. This set will be the *set of nodes*. For defining the set of edges we need the following

**(4.7) Definition.** *A transition is either an assignment or a random assignment or an open formula. Let $Trans_\sigma$ denote the set of all $\sigma$-type transitions:*

$$\begin{aligned} Trans_\sigma \rightleftharpoons\ & \{x := \tau \mid x \in V, \tau \in Term_\sigma\} \cup && \textit{(assignments)} \\ & \{x :=? \mid x \in V\} \cup && \textit{(random assignments)} \\ & \{\phi \mid \phi \in Open_\sigma\} && \textit{(open formulas).} \end{aligned}$$

Let $t \in Trans_\sigma$ and let $\alpha$ be the following function:

$$\alpha(t) \rightleftharpoons \begin{cases} t & t \in Open_\sigma; \\ true & \text{otherwise.} \end{cases}$$

**(4.8) Definition.** *A triplet $(g, start_g, stop_g)$ is called a (finite) transition graph iff*

*(i) $g : Label \times Label \to_p Trans_\sigma$ is a partial function,*
*(ii) $dom\ g$ is finite,*

*(iii)* $start_g, stop_g \in Label$ *and they are different,*
*(iv)* $stop_g$ *has no outcoming edges, i.e. the set* $\{c \mid (stop_g, c) \in dom\ g\}$ *is empty.*

*Let* $rG_\sigma$ *denote the set of all transition graphs. Let* $G_\sigma$ *be the set of all transition graphs without random assignments, i.e.*

$$G_\sigma \rightleftharpoons \{g \in rG_\sigma \mid \{x :=? \mid x \in V\} \cap rng\ g = \emptyset\}.$$

A transition graph is a mathematically well based object that we use as a flowchart schema. Namely, the elementary actions (i.e. the transitions) are assignments and tests. The execution of a transition graph is just the execution of these actions in a non-deterministic order depending on their relative position in the graph.

Further on, we identify the transition graph with its first component, that is, with the partial function $g$. The usual notions for transition graphs are defined as follows.

**(4.9) Definition.**

*(a)* $dom\, g$ *is the set of edges of the graph* $g$.
*(b)* $node(g) \rightleftharpoons \pi_1(dom\, g) \cup \pi_2(dom\, g)$ *is the set of nodes of the graph* $g$. *Of course,* $node(g) \subseteq Label$ *is finite.*
*(c) The functions*
$rank_{in}(c) \rightleftharpoons |\{c' \mid (c', c) \in dom\, g\}|$
$rank_{out}(c) \rightleftharpoons |\{c' \mid (c, c') \in dom\, g\}|$
*are the rank functions for* $node(g)$. *They assign to any node the number of incoming and outcoming edges, respectively.*
*(d)* $var(g) \rightleftharpoons \bigcup\{var(g(c,c')) \mid (c,c') \in dom\, g\}$ *is the set of all variables of the graph* $g$.

Now we turn to define the operational and denotational semantics of a transition graph. The definition of the meaning of a single transition is simple and for this purpose we can use $\sigma$-type formulas. Let $t \in Trans_\sigma$ be given. Let $X$ be the set of all variables occurring in the transition $t$. Let $Y$ be a new copy of $X$ with bijection $\iota$. Take the following formula:

$$D_t(X,Y) \rightleftharpoons \begin{cases} (\iota(x) = \tau) \wedge \bigwedge_{z \in X \setminus \{x\}} \iota(z) = z & \text{if } t = (x := \tau),\ \tau \in Term_\sigma; \\ \bigwedge_{z \in X \setminus \{x\}} \iota(z) = z & \text{if } t = (x :=?),\ x \in V; \\ \phi \wedge \bigwedge_{z \in X} \iota(z) = z & \text{if } t = \phi,\ \phi \in Open_\sigma. \end{cases}$$

In order to define the meaning of the entire transition graph we also have to logically describe how the nodes change while executing the transitions.

However, from the logical point of view it is important to emphasize that the set *Label* is external with respect to the data structures. In order to make the expressions containing elements of *Label* internal we propose different methods. The easiest of them supposes that $Term_\sigma$ contains two ground terms $\top$ and

$\bot$ and allows the consideration only of those models that satisfy the formula $\top \neq \bot$. However, in the forthcoming chapters, we use much more complicated constructions that eliminate the set *Label*.

To describe internally the elements of *Label* we use a special "binary coding mechanism". Let $\top$ and $\bot$ be two ground terms of the same sort. Let $g \in rG_\sigma$ and $n \rightleftharpoons |node(g)|$. For each node $c \in node(g)$ let us choose corresponding (different) sequences $L_c \in \{\top, \bot\}^n$. Let $X_L$ and $Y_L$ be two $n$-long sequences of new variables of the same sort as $\top$ (or $\bot$). Consider the following formula:

$$onestep_g(X, X_L, Y, Y_L) \rightleftharpoons \bigvee_{(c,c') \in dom\ g} (X_L = L_c) \wedge (Y_L = L_{c'}) \wedge D_{g(c,c')}(X, Y).$$

The formula $onestep_g$ expresses the one-step transition of the transition graph $g$ correctly only in those models $\mathcal{A} \in Mod_\sigma$ where $\mathcal{A} \models \top \neq \bot$. It may happen that we cannot find ground terms $\top$, $\bot$ satisfying $\mathcal{A} \models \top \neq \bot$ or that there is no ground term in $Term_\sigma$ at all. To avoid this problem we extend both the similarity type $\sigma$ and its models.

Let $\eta^G$ be an $s^G$-sorted similarity type which contains only two constant symbols: $\top, \bot : s^G$. Let $\mathcal{G}$ be a fixed model for $\eta^G$ such that $|G| = 2$ and $\mathcal{G} \models \top \neq \bot$. For any similarity type $\sigma$ let $\sigma^G$ be the disjoint union of $\sigma$ and $\eta^G$. Similarly for any model $\mathcal{A} \in Mod_\sigma$ let $\mathcal{A}^G \rightleftharpoons \mathcal{A} + \mathcal{G}$, which belongs to $Mod_{\sigma^G}$. Our aim is to show how the semantics of a $\sigma$-type transition graph can be described by using $\sigma^G$-type first-order formulas.

In order to achieve our aim we do not need to have two distinct ground terms of the same sort in $Term_\sigma$. Therefore, we suppose that during this chapter we use the two constant symbol belonging to the similarity type $\eta^G$.

We intend to interpret the transition graphs in the $\sigma$-type models. Let $\mathcal{A} \in Mod_\sigma$ be arbitrary. The set of all possible (computational) paths in $\mathcal{A}$ is defined as follows

$$Path_{\mathcal{A}} \rightleftharpoons (Val_{\mathcal{A}} \times Label)^{\leq\omega}.$$

Let $a = (k, c)$ be an element of $Val_{\mathcal{A}} \times Label$, let $\ell$ be a fixed new variable corresponding to labels ($\ell \notin V$) and let $v \in V$. Then we shall write $a(\ell)$ instead of $\pi_2(a)$, and $a(v)$ instead of $\pi_1(a)(v)$. This means that we consider $a$ as a function defined on $V \cup^* \{\ell\}$.

Fix a transition graph $g \in rG_\sigma$ and let $(X, X_L, Y, Y_L)$ be the free variables of the formula $onestep_g$. Let $X_L \rightleftharpoons (x_L^1, \ldots, x_L^n)$, where $n = |node(g)|$. Let a computational path $s \in Path_{\mathcal{A}}$ and a natural number $i < length(s)$ be given. In this case $s(i) = (k, c)$, where $k \in Val_{\mathcal{A}}$ and $c \in Label$. By definition $L_c = (d_1, \ldots, d_n)$ where $d_i \in \{\top, \bot\}$ $(i = 1, \ldots, n)$. We can define a valuation on $X \cup X_L$ by taking:

$$\tilde{k} \rightleftharpoons k\restriction_X + \{(x_L^i, (d_i)_{\mathcal{A}}) \mid i = 1, \ldots, n\}.$$

Since $\tilde{k}$ depends on $s$ and $i$ (supposing that the binary coding mechanism is fixed once and for all) we denote this $\tilde{k}$ as $\tilde{s}(i)$.

**(4.10) Definition.** *Let $g$ be a transition graph. The set of all traces of $g$ in $\mathcal{A}$ is defined as follows:*

$$Trace_{\mathcal{A}}[\![g]\!] \rightleftharpoons \{s \in Path_{\mathcal{A}} \mid |s| \geq 1, s(0)(\ell) \in node(g) \text{ and } \forall i < length(s) - 1 : \ \mathcal{A}^G \models onestep_g(\tilde{s}(i), \tilde{s}(i+1)[Y/X, Y_L/X_L])\}$$

*We also need the "finitary" version of $Trace_{\mathcal{A}}[\![g]\!]$. Let $X \subseteq V$ be a finite set of variables such that $var(g) \subseteq X$. Then let $Trace_{\mathcal{A}}[\![g, X]\!] \rightleftharpoons Trace_{\mathcal{A}}[\![g]\!]\restriction_{X \cup \{\ell\}}$.*

The notation $Trace_{\mathcal{A}}[\![g]\!]$ does not indicate the following properties:

- what extension of $\mathcal{A}$ is used;
- what terms for $\top$ and $\bot$ in $onestep_g$ are used;
- how the coding vectors $L_c$ ($c \in node(g)$) are defined.

However, the set $Trace_{\mathcal{A}}[\![g]\!]$ does not depend on the particular selection of these items. We only have to suppose that $\mathcal{A}' \models \top \neq \bot$ (where $\mathcal{A}'$ is the particularly chosen extension of $\mathcal{A}$). Therefore the notation $Trace_{\mathcal{A}}[\![g]\!]$ is correct.

Using traces it is an easy task to define the denotation of transition graphs by means of the following

**(4.11) Definition.** *Let $\mathcal{A}$ be a fixed $\sigma$-type model. For any transition graph $g$ of $rG_\sigma$ the input-output relation or denotation of $g$ in $\mathcal{A}$ is defined by taking*

$$Den_{\mathcal{A}}[\![g]\!] \rightleftharpoons \Big\{(in\ s\restriction_V, out\ s\restriction_V) \ \Big|\ s \in Trace_{\mathcal{A}}[\![g]\!] \quad (in\ s)(\ell) = start_g, (out\ s)(\ell) = stop_g\Big\}.$$

*Obviously $Den_{\mathcal{A}}[\![g]\!] \subseteq Val_{\mathcal{A}} \times Val_{\mathcal{A}}$.*

*Let $X \subseteq V$ a fixed set of variables such that $var(g) \subseteq X$ and let $X'$ be a new copy of $X$ with bijection $\iota$. Then we define the input-output relation or denotation of $g$ with respect to $X$ in $\mathcal{A}$ as the many-sorted relation*

$$Den_{\mathcal{A}}[\![g, X]\!] \rightleftharpoons \{(k, k') \mid \exists (a, b) \in Den_{\mathcal{A}}[\![g]\!] \ a\restriction_X = k \text{ and } b\restriction_X = k'[X'/X]\}$$

*Obviously $Den_{\mathcal{A}}[\![g, X]\!] \subseteq Val_{\mathcal{A}}[X, X']$ $(= Val_{\mathcal{A}}[X] \times Val_{\mathcal{A}}[X'])$.*

By the use of transition graphs we define the graph representation of the programs of $rP_\sigma$.

**(4.12) Definition.** *Let $p \in rP_\sigma$ be arbitrary. The graph representation of $p$ denoted by $gr(p)$ is defined in Figs. 4.1–4.4 by induction on the complexity of $p$.*

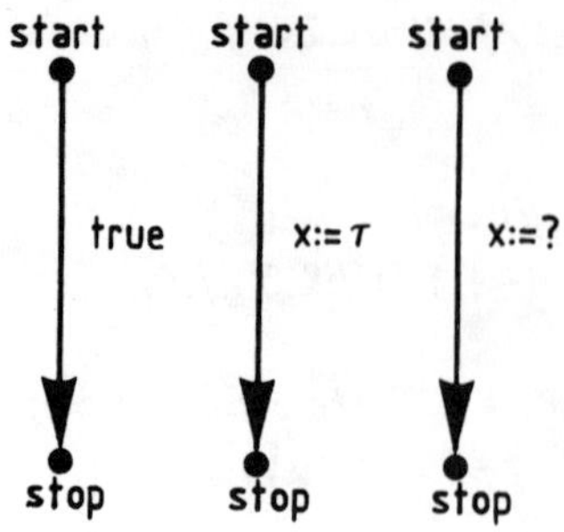


Fig. 4.1. Graph representation of programs **skip**, $x := \tau$ and $x :=?$, respectively

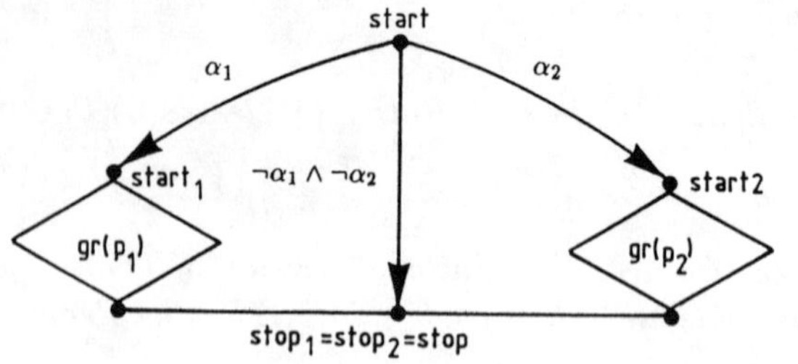


Fig. 4.3. Graph representation of program **if** $\alpha_1 \rightarrow p_1 \square \alpha_2 \rightarrow p_2$ **fi**

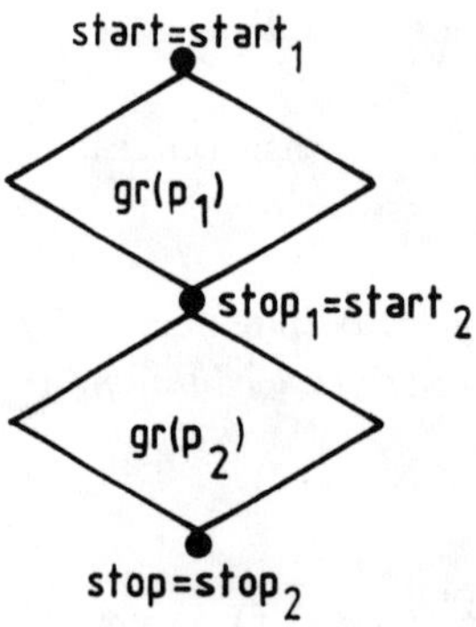


Fig. 4.2. Graph representation of program $p_1; p_2$

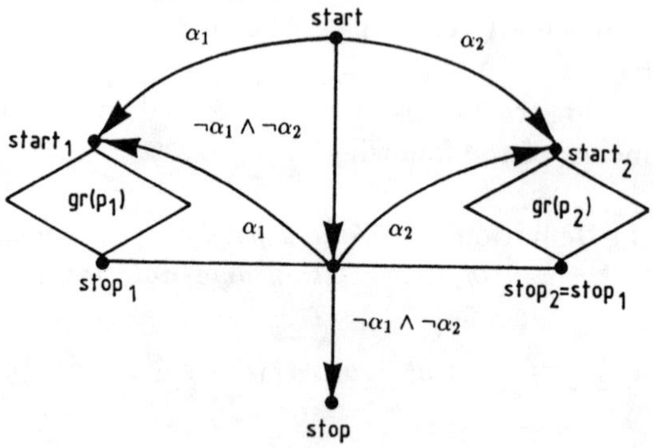


Fig. 4.4. Graph representation of program **do** $\alpha_1 \rightarrow p_1 \square \alpha_2 \rightarrow p_2$ **od**

We emphasize that the representation of the **if**...**fi** construct is a substructure of the representation of the **do**...**od** construct.

Having a program $p \in rP_\sigma$ we can define its denotation either according to Definition (4.6) or by the use of Definition (4.11) for the graph representation of $p$. What is the interrelation between these two denotations? The answer can be established by using the corresponding definitions.

**(4.13) Theorem.** *For any program $p \in rP_\sigma$, any finite set $X$ of variables ($var(p) \subseteq X$) and any model $\mathcal{A} \in Mod_\sigma$,*

$$Den_{\mathcal{A}}[\![p]\!] = Den_{\mathcal{A}}[\![gr(p)]\!];$$
$$Den_{\mathcal{A}}[\![p, X]\!] = Den_{\mathcal{A}}[\![gr(p), X]\!].$$

By using the graph representation of programs we have the possibility to define the operational semantics of $rP_\sigma$.

**(4.14) Definition.** *Let $\mathcal{A} \in Mod_\sigma$ be fixed. For any $p \in rP\sigma$ let*

$$Trace_{\mathcal{A}}[\![p]\!] \rightleftharpoons \{s \in Trace_{\mathcal{A}}[\![gr(p)]\!] \mid (in\, s)(\ell) = start_{gr(p)}\}.$$

Let $p \in rP_\sigma$ be fixed. Each element $s$ of $Trace_{\mathcal{A}}[\![p]\!]$ is called a *trace* of $p$ in $\mathcal{A}$ starting from the input $(in\, s)\restriction_V$. We say that a trace *ends* iff it is finite. In this case $(out\, s)\restriction_V$ is called the *output* of the trace $s$. We say that a trace $s$ of $p$ *terminates* iff it is finite and $(out\, s)(\ell) = stop_{gr(p)}$.

Given the trace in a node $c$ of a transition graph $g$ let us see what would intuitively make it possible to move to one of the nodes linked with $c$. It is evident that if the formula $\bigvee\{\phi \mid \exists c' g(c, c') = \phi\}$ is a tautology then at least one node $c'$ can always be reached from the node $c$. However, this condition is not supposed. Therefore, it may happen that from the node $c$ it is impossible to go any further because none of the open formulas $\phi$ on the outcoming edges of $c$ will be true or there is no node linked with $c$, i.e. the transition graph aborts in $c$. The formula $abort_g(X, X_L) \rightleftharpoons$

$$\bigvee_{c \in node(g) \setminus \{stop_g\}} \Big( (X_L = L_c) \wedge \bigwedge \{\neg\alpha(g(c, c')) \mid (c, c') \in dom\ g\} \Big)$$

describes this situation. To reflect this situation in the semantics as well, a special auxiliary node *abort* would be useful, though here we will not introduce it. Note that if we consider the graph representation $gr(p)$ of any program $p$ the formula $\neg abort_g$ is a tautology.

## 4.3 Main Properties of Programs

The semantics of the programming language $rP_\sigma$ has been defined in $\sigma$-type models by the introduction of special mathematical objects. It is an important question whether program semantics is definable in the $\sigma$-type first-order logic. The answer to this question depends on the definability of the mathematical objects employed to define the semantics. In the case of trace semantics the definition is based on sequences of computation states. Sequences, as we know, are not syntactic elements of a first-order classical language and they cannot be spoken about in such a language. Therefore, the operational semantics is external. We can expect that the case of input-output semantics is different since it is defined as a (many-sorted) relation.

The following theorem, which provides the fundamental property of input-output semantics defined by denotations, shows to what extent the input-output semantics is internal.

**(4.15) Theorem.** *Let us fix an arbitrary many-sorted similarity type $\sigma$.*

*(a) For any program $p \in rP_\sigma$ and model $\mathcal{A} \in Mod_\sigma$, if $X \supseteq var(p)$ is finite then $Den_\mathcal{A}[\![p, X]\!]$ is inductively definable in $\mathcal{A}$ by a formula independent of $\mathcal{A}$.*

*(b) For any transition graph $g \in rG_\sigma$ and model $\mathcal{A} \in Mod_\sigma$, if $X \supseteq var(g)$ is finite then $Den_\mathcal{A}[\![g, X]\!]$ is inductively definable in $\mathcal{A}$ by a formula independent of $\mathcal{A}$.*

*Proof.*

(a) Let us fix a program $p \in rP_\sigma$. Let $Den_\mathcal{A}[\![p, X]\!]$ have the arity $(X, Y)$ and let $\iota$ be the identity bijection between $X$ and $Y$. For any program $q$ whose complexity is less than or equal to that of $p$ let us add a new relation symbol $R_q$ of arity $(X, Y)$. For any $q$ we define a parameterless equation system $E_q$ independently of $\mathcal{A}$ such that if $\beta$ is the least fixed point of $E_q$ in $\mathcal{A}$ then $\beta_{R_q} = Den_\mathcal{A}[\![q, X]\!]$. By Theorem (2.14) this already proves the theorem. These sets of equations are constructed by induction on the complexity of $q$.

(i) If $q \rightleftharpoons$ **skip** then take $E_q \rightleftharpoons \{R_q(X,Y) = (X = Y)\}$. If $q \rightleftharpoons$ **loop** then take $E_q \rightleftharpoons \{R_q(X,Y) = (X \neq X)\}$.

(ii) If $q \rightleftharpoons (v := \tau)$ then take $E_q \rightleftharpoons \{R_q(X,Y) = \big(\iota(v) = \tau \wedge \bigwedge_{w \in X \setminus \{v\}} \iota(w) = w\big)\}$.

(iii) Let $q \rightleftharpoons (p_1; p_2)$. Add the equation $R_q(X,Y) = \exists Z(R_{p_1}(X,Z) \wedge R_{p_2}(Z,Y))$ to the set $E_{p_1} \cup E_{p_2}$. The resulting $E_q$ is appropriate.

(iv) Let $q \rightleftharpoons$ **if** $\alpha_1 \rightarrow p_1 \,\square\, \alpha_2 \rightarrow p_2$ **fi** then by the induction hypothesis let $E_{p_1}$ and $E_{p_2}$ be the respective equation systems defining $Den_\mathcal{A}[\![p_1, X]\!]$ and $Den_\mathcal{A}[\![p_2, X]\!]$. Add the following equation

$$R_q(X,Y) \rightleftharpoons (\neg\alpha_1 \wedge \neg\alpha_2 \wedge X = Y) \vee \bigvee_{i=1}^{2} \big(\alpha_i(X) \wedge R_{p_i}(X,Y)\big)$$

to the set $E_{p_1} \cup E_{p_2}$. Let $E_q$ be the equation system so obtained. $E_q$ is appropriate.

(v) Let $q \rightleftharpoons$ **do** $\alpha_1 \rightarrow p_1 \,\square\, \alpha_2 \rightarrow p_2$ **od** and let $q' \rightleftharpoons$ **if** $\alpha_1 \rightarrow p_1 \,\square\, \alpha_2 \rightarrow p_2$ **fi**. By the induction hypothesis let $E_{q'}$ be the equation system which inductively defines the relation $Den_\mathcal{A}[\![q', X]\!]$. Let $S_q$ be a new relation symbol with arity $(X, Y)$. Let us extend $E_{q'}$ to $E_q$ by adding the following two equations:

$$\begin{aligned} S_q(X,Y) &= R_{q'}(X,Y) \vee \exists Z(S_q(X,Z) \wedge R_{q'}(Z,Y)) \\ R_q(X,Y) &= S_q(X,Y) \wedge (\neg\alpha_1 \wedge \neg\alpha_2)[Y/X]. \end{aligned}$$

$E_q$ is appropriate.

(vi) If $q \rightleftharpoons (v :=?)$ then take the equation system:

$$E_q \rightleftharpoons \Big\{R_q(X,Y) = \bigwedge\{w = \iota(w) \mid w \in X \setminus \{v\}\}\Big\}.$$

(b) Let us extend the similarity type $\sigma$ to $\sigma^G$ by adding $\eta^G$ to the similarity type $\sigma$. Fix a transition graph $g \in rG_\sigma$ and let $X = var(g)$ and $Y$ be a new copy of $X$. We recall the formula $onestep_g \in Form_{\sigma^G}$. Let $(X, X_L, Y, Y_L)$ be the free variables of $onestep_g$ and let $L_c$ be the sequence corresponding to the node $c$. Let $(Z, Z_L)$ be a new copy of $(X, X_L)$. Take the formula

$$\phi(X,X_L,Y,Y_L) \rightleftharpoons (Y = X \wedge Y_L = X_L \wedge \bigvee_{c \in node(g)} X_L = L_c) \vee \\ \exists Z \exists Z_L \big(R(X,X_L,Z,Z_L) \wedge onestep_g(Z,Z_L,Y,Y_L)\big).$$

Now let $\mathcal{A}$ be an arbitrary $\sigma$-type model and let $\mathcal{A}^G = \mathcal{A} + \mathcal{G}$. Let $k \rightleftharpoons \{(X_L, L_{start_g}), (Y_L, L_{stop_g})\} \in Val_{\mathcal{A}^G}[X_L \cup Y_L]$. Let $Q \rightleftharpoons_{\mathcal{A}^G} I_\phi\restriction_k$. From Definition (4.11) using Definition (4.10) we immediately have that $Q = Den_{\mathcal{A}}[\![g, X]\!]$. By Corollary (2.10) and Theorem (2.12) the many-sorted relation $Q$ is inductively definable in $\mathcal{A}$. □

We remark that in the above theorem statement (a) follows from statement (b) since $Den_{\mathcal{A}}[\![p, X]\!] = Den_{\mathcal{A}}[\![gr(p), X]\!]$ according to Theorem (4.13).

Let us consider the following $\eta$-type program which outputs the sum of $x$ and $y$ in the variable $z$:

$$q \rightleftharpoons z := x; \textbf{do}\ y \neq 0 \rightarrow z := z+1; y := y-1 \ \Box false \rightarrow \textbf{skip od}\ .$$

The programs whose complexities are less than that of $q$ are the programs

$$\begin{aligned} q_1 &\rightleftharpoons \textbf{do}\ y \neq 0 \rightarrow z := z+1; y := y-1 \ \Box false \rightarrow \textbf{skip od}\ ; \\ q_2 &\rightleftharpoons \textbf{if}\ y \neq 0 \rightarrow z := z+1; y := y-1 \ \Box false \rightarrow \textbf{skip fi}\ ; \\ q_3 &\rightleftharpoons z := z+1; y := y-1; \end{aligned}$$

and the simple assignments. By using the method of the previous theorem the following equation system defines the denotational semantics of $q$ in an arbitrary $\eta$-type model:

$$\begin{aligned} R_{z:=x}(U,U') &= (z' = x) \wedge (x' = x) \wedge (y' = y) \\ R_{z:=z+1}(U,U') &= (z' = z+1) \wedge (x' = x) \wedge (y' = y) \\ R_{y:=y-1}(U,U') &= (y' = y-1) \wedge (x' = x) \wedge (z' = z) \end{aligned}$$

$$
\begin{aligned}
R_{\mathbf{skip}}(U,U') &= U' = U \\
R_{q_3}(U,U') &= \exists U''(R_{z:=z+1}(U,U'') \wedge R_{y:=y-1}(U'',U)) \\
R_{q_2}(U,U') &= (y \neq 0 \wedge R_{q_3}(U,U')) \vee (false \wedge R_{\mathbf{skip}}(U,U')) \\
&\quad \vee (y = 0 \wedge true \wedge U = U') \\
S_{q_1}(U,U') &= R_{q_2}(U'',U') \vee \exists U''(S_{q_1}(U,U'') \wedge R_{q_2}(U'',U')) \\
R_{q_1}(U,U') &= S_{q_1}(U,U') \wedge (U' = 0) \\
R_q(U,U') &= \exists U''(R_{z:=x}(U,U'') \wedge R_{q_1}(U'',U'))
\end{aligned}
$$

Now we show that under certain conditions the input-output semantics is not only implicitly but also explicitly definable. To establish this fact we first define and analyse the termination property of programs by using the notion of traces.

**(4.16) Definition.** *Let $\mathcal{K} \subseteq Mod_\sigma$ be an arbitrary class of $\sigma$-type models and $\phi \in Form_\sigma$. A program $p \in rP_\sigma$ has the $\phi$-start termination property in $\mathcal{K}$ iff for any $\mathcal{A} \in \mathcal{K}$ and $k \in Val_{\mathcal{A}}$, $\mathcal{A} \models \phi[k]$ implies that there is no infinite trace of $p$ starting from input $k$.*

**(4.17) Theorem.** *Let $p \in rP_\sigma$, $\mathcal{A}_i \in Mod_\sigma$ and $s_i \in Trace_{\mathcal{A}_i}[\![p]\!]$ ($i \in \mathbb{N}$) be such that $length(s_i) \geq i$. Moreover, let $D$ be a nonprincipal ultrafilter on $\mathbb{N}$ and $\mathcal{A} \rightleftharpoons \prod_{i\in\mathbb{N}} \mathcal{A}_i/D$ be the ultraproduct of $\mathcal{A}_i$'s ($i \in \mathbb{N}$). By using the traces $s_i$ we define a path $s \in Path_{\mathcal{A}}$. For $j \in \mathbb{N}$ and for $v \in V$ take*

$$s(j)(v) \rightleftharpoons [\lambda i \in \mathbb{N}. s_i'(j)(v)]_D;$$

*where $s_i'(j) = s_i(j)$ if $j < length(s_i)$ and is arbitrary otherwise. Now we turn to define $s(j)(l)$. Since the domain of $g$ is finite, there is a node $c_j \in Label$ and an index set $J_{c_j} \in D$ such that for every $i \in J_{c_j}$ we have $s_i(j)(l) = c_j$. Let $s(j)(l)$ be equal to this $c_j$. Let us denote this $s$ by $\prod_{i\in\mathbb{N}} s_i/D$. If so then $s \in Trace_{\mathcal{A}}[\![p]\!]$.*

*Proof.* Let $s$ be as in the theorem. Now for a fixed $j \in \mathbb{N}$ the following three sets belong to the ultrafilter $D$:

$$
\begin{aligned}
I_1 &\rightleftharpoons \{i \in \mathbb{N} \mid i > j+1\} \\
I_2 &\rightleftharpoons \{i \in \mathbb{N} \mid s_i(j)(l) = c_j\} \\
I_3 &\rightleftharpoons \{i \in \mathbb{N} \mid s_i(j+1)(l) = c_{j+1}\}
\end{aligned}
$$

Then $I \rightleftharpoons I_1 \cap I_2 \cap I_3 \in D$. Moreover, if $i \in I$ then $\mathcal{A}_i \models \alpha(g(c_j, c_{j+1}))[s_i(j)\restriction_V]$. Therefore, $\mathcal{A} \models \alpha(g(c_j, c_{j+1}))[s(j)\restriction_V]$, i.e.

$$\mathcal{A} \models onestep_g\left[\tilde{s}(j), \tilde{s}(j+1)[Y/X, Y_L/X_L]\right]$$

holds (the further conditions are trivial). □

**(4.18) Corollary.** *Let $Ax \subseteq Form_\sigma$ be a consistent set of formulas, $p \in rP_\sigma$ and $\phi \in Form_\sigma$ be arbitrary such that $p$ has the $\phi$-start termination property in*

*$Mod(Ax)$. Then there exists an $i \in \mathbb{N}$ such that for any model $\mathcal{A} \in Mod(Ax)$ and for any $s \in Trace_{\mathcal{A}}[\![p]\!]$, $\mathcal{A} \models \phi[in\, s\restriction_V]$ implies that $length(s) \leq i$.*

*Proof.* To gain a contradiction, let us suppose that for any $i \in \mathbb{N}$ there is a model $\mathcal{A}_i \in Mod(Ax)$ and a trace $s_i \in Trace_{\mathcal{A}_i}[\![p]\!]$ such that $\mathcal{A}_i \models \phi[in\, s_i\restriction_V]$ and $length(s_i) \geq i$. Take $\mathcal{A} = \prod\{\mathcal{A}_i \mid i \in \mathbb{N}\}/D$ (where $D$ is a nonprincipal ultrafilter on $\mathbb{N}$). Let $s$ be the trace constructed in Theorem (4.17). However, $s$ is an infinite trace of $p$ in $\mathcal{A}$ and $\mathcal{A} \models \phi[in\, s\restriction_V]$. Since $\mathcal{A} \in Mod(Ax)$ the program $p$ does not have the $\phi$-start termination property in $Mod(Ax)$. □

This corollary can be reformulated as follows. Let $Ax \subseteq Form_\sigma$ and $p \in rP_\sigma$ be given and let $\phi \in Form_\sigma$ be arbitrary. Let us suppose that $p$ has an arbitrarily long finite trace starting with an input satisfying $\phi$ in some models of $Ax$. Then $p$ also has an infinite trace of the same property.

Now we show that if the length of all the computational paths of a program is bounded then the corresponding denotation is first-order definable. To establish this property we introduce a restriction of the input-output relation by requiring that the input satisfies a given condition $\phi \in Form_\sigma$. Let $X \supset var(\phi)$ and be $Y$ a copy of $X$. Then

$$\begin{aligned} Den_{\mathcal{A}}[\![p]\!]\restriction_\phi &\rightleftharpoons \{(s_1, s_2) \mid \mathcal{A} \models \phi[s_1] \wedge (s_1, s_2) \in Den_{\mathcal{A}}[\![p]\!]\} \\ Den_{\mathcal{A}}[\![p, X]\!]\restriction_\phi &\rightleftharpoons \{(s_1\restriction_X, s_2[X/Y]\restriction_Y) \mid (s_1, s_2) \in Den_{\mathcal{A}}[\![p]\!]\restriction_\phi\} \end{aligned}$$

for any $p \in rP_\sigma$ and $\mathcal{A} \in Mod_\sigma$.

**(4.19) Theorem.** *Let $Ax \subseteq Form_\sigma$ be a consistent set of formulas, and let $p \in rP_\sigma$. Let $X \rightleftharpoons var(p) \cup var(\phi)$. Suppose that $p$ has the $\phi$-start termination property in $Mod(Ax)$ for some $\phi \in Form_\sigma$. Then there is a formula in $Form_\sigma$ which defines $Den_{\mathcal{A}}[\![p, X]\!]\restriction_\phi$ in any $\mathcal{A} \in Mod(Ax)$ and this formula does not depend on the model $\mathcal{A}$.*

*Particularly, if $p \in rP_\sigma$ does not contain any cycle then $Den_{\mathcal{A}}[\![p, X]\!]\restriction_\phi$ is first-order definable by a formula depending only on the program $p$.*

*Proof.* First we remark that by Corollary (4.18) there is an $i \in \mathbb{N}$ such that for any model $\mathcal{A} \in Mod(Ax)$, and for any trace $s \in Trace_{\mathcal{A}}[\![p]\!]$, if $\mathcal{A} \models \phi[(in\, s)\restriction_V]$ then $length(s) \leq i$. By using this fact we prove the theorem by induction on the complexity of $p$. Take two disjoint copies $Y$ and $Z$ of $X$ with bijections $\iota$ and $\iota'$, respectively. Now we define $Den_{\mathcal{A}}[\![p, X]\!]\restriction_\phi$ of arity $(X, Y)$.

(i) Let $p \rightleftharpoons$ **skip** . The formula $\phi(X) \wedge X = Y$ is appropriate.
(ii) Let $p \rightleftharpoons$ **loop** . The formula $\phi(X) \wedge X \neq X$ is appropriate.
(iii) Let $p \rightleftharpoons (v := \tau)$. $Den_{\mathcal{A}}[\![p, X]\!]\restriction_\phi$ is defined by the formula

$$\phi(X) \wedge \bigwedge\{\iota(w) = w \mid w \in X\backslash\{v\}\} \wedge (\iota(v) = \tau).$$

(iv) Let $p \rightleftharpoons (p_1; p_2)$. By the induction hypothesis there are formulas $\beta_1(X,Y)$ and $\beta_2(X,Y)$ which define $Den_{\mathcal{A}}[\![p_1, X]\!]\restriction_\phi$ and $Den_{\mathcal{A}}[\![p_2, X]\!]\restriction_{rng\, \beta_1}$, respectively. (Note that since $(p_1; p_2)$ has the $\phi$-start termination property on $Mod(Ax)$, $p_2$ necessarily has the $rng\ \beta_1$-start termination property on $Mod(Ax)$, where $rng\ \beta_1 \rightleftharpoons \exists Z \beta_1(Z,X)$. Then the formula $\exists Z(\beta_1(X,Z) \wedge \beta_2(Z,Y))$ defines $Den_{\mathcal{A}}[\![p, X]\!]\restriction_\phi$.

(v) Let $p \rightleftharpoons$ **if** $\alpha_1 \to p_1 \square \alpha_2 \to p_2$ **fi** . Let $\phi_i(X,Y)$ be the formula which by the induction hypothesis defines $Den[\![p_i, X]\!]\restriction_{\alpha_i \wedge \phi}$ for $i = 1,2$. The formula

$$\bigvee_{i=1}^{2} \phi_i(X,Y) \vee (\neg\alpha_1 \wedge \neg\alpha_2 \wedge X = Y)$$

defines $Den[\![p, X]\!]\restriction_\phi$.

(vi) Let $p \rightleftharpoons$ **do** $\alpha_1 \to p_1 \square \alpha_2 \to p_2$ **od** . Let $k \in \mathbb{N}$ be a natural number such that for any trace $s \in Trace_{\mathcal{A}}[\![p]\!]$, if $\mathcal{A} \models \phi[in(s)]$ then $length(s) \leq k$. To prove this case we also use induction on $k$. (The existence of $k$ follows from Corollary (4.18) and note that any program $p$ of the above form has at least one trace $s$ with $length(s) \geq 3$.) If the corresponding $k = 3$ then the denotation of $p$ equals that of **skip** and, by (i), $Den_{\mathcal{A}}[\![p, X]\!]\restriction_\phi$ is definable. In general, it is easy to see that the denotation of the program $p$ and that of the program

$$\textbf{if}\ \neg\alpha_1 \wedge \neg\alpha_2 \to \textbf{skip}\ \square\, \alpha_1 \to p_1; p \,\square\, \alpha_2 \to p_2; p\ \textbf{fi}$$

are the same. Now let us suppose that the assumptions of the theorem hold for any program with complexity less than or equal to $p$ and with maximum length of traces $k-1$ ($k > 3$). For any $i = 1,2$, let $\beta_i(X,Y)$ be the formula which defines $Den[\![p_i, X]\!]\restriction_{\phi \wedge \alpha_i}$ according to the induction hypothesis which we have for the subprograms of $p$. Let $\hat{\beta}_i \rightleftharpoons rng\, \beta_i$. In the first period of execution of $p$ if either $p_1$ or $p_2$ is executed then at most $k-1$ steps are left for the execution of $p$. For $i = 1,2$, let $\gamma_i$ be the formula which, by the induction hypothesis, defines $Den_{\mathcal{A}}[\![p, X]\!]\restriction_{\hat{\beta}_i}$. Let us consider the formula

$$(\neg\alpha_1 \wedge \neg\alpha_2 \wedge X = Y) \vee \bigvee_{i=1}^{2} \exists Z\Big(\beta_i(X,Z) \wedge \gamma_i(Z,Y)\Big).$$

Obviously, this formula defines $Den_{\mathcal{A}}[\![p, X]\!]\restriction_\phi$ in any model $\mathcal{A} \in Mod(Ax)$.

(vii) Let $p \rightleftharpoons (v :=?)$. It is obvious that the formula $\phi(X) \wedge \bigwedge\{\iota(w) = w \mid w \in X \setminus \{v\}\}$ defines $Den_{\mathcal{A}}[\![p, X]\!]\restriction_\phi$. □

A similar theorem holds for transition graphs too.

**(4.20) Definition.** *A $\sigma$-type model $\mathcal{A}$ is said to be recursively presented iff it satisfies the following properties:*

*(i)* *For each sort* $s \in sort(\sigma)$ *there is an injective (or 1-1) function* $\lceil s \rceil : A_s \rightarrow \mathbb{N}$ *such that* $rng \lceil s \rceil$ *is a recursively enumerable set of* $\mathbb{N}$.

*(ii)* *For each function symbol* $f : s_1, ..., s_n \rightarrow s$ *of* $\sigma$ *the partial function below is recursive:*

$$\langle \lceil s_1 \rceil^{-1}, ..., \lceil s_n \rceil^{-1} \rangle \circ f_{\mathcal{A}} \circ \lceil s \rceil : \mathbb{N}^n \rightarrow \mathbb{N}.$$

*(iii)* *For each relation symbol* $\rho : s_1, ..., s_n$ *of* $\sigma$ *the relation below is recursive:*

$$\langle \lceil s_1 \rceil, ..., \lceil s_n \rceil \rangle (\rho_{\mathcal{A}}) \subseteq \mathbb{N}^n$$

*(iv)* *A code is given for each recursive function and relation used in (i)-(iii).*

A model $\mathcal{A} \in Mod_\sigma$ is said to be finite iff its universe is finite, i.e. $| A | < \omega_0$. It is obvious that for any recursively presented model $\mathcal{A} \in Mod_\sigma$ there is another model $\mathcal{A}' \in Mod_\sigma$ such that the universes of $\mathcal{A}'$ are recursively enumerable subsets of $\mathbb{N}$ and $\mathcal{A}$ and $\mathcal{A}'$ are (recursively) isomorphic to each other. Although the class $C$ of all recursively presented models of $Mod_\sigma$ is not a set, by factorizing $C$ using model equivalence we obtain a set. Let $FRPM_\sigma$ be the *set* of all finite and recursively presented $\sigma$-type models with recursively enumerable universes.

**(4.21) Definition.** *Let* $P \subseteq rP_\sigma$ *be an arbitrary set of programs. The halting problem of* $P$ *with respect to the finite and recursively presented models is said to be decidable iff the set*

$$\{(p, a, \mathcal{A}) \mid \mathcal{A} \in FRPM_\sigma, p \in P, a \in Val_{\mathcal{A}}[var(p)] \text{ and } p \text{ has a terminating trace in } \mathcal{A} \text{ starting with } a\}$$

*is recursive.*

Note that by using an appropriate coding function the above set can be considered as a subset of $\mathbb{N}$, since $\mathcal{A}$ is finite and recursively presented.

**(4.22) Theorem.** *For any finite model* $\mathcal{A}$ *and any transition graph* $g \in rG_\sigma$ *there is an* $n \in \mathbb{N}$ *recursively depending only on* $|A|$ *and* $|node(g)|$ *such that if* $k \in dom\, Den_{\mathcal{A}}[\![g]\!]$ *then the transition graph* $g$ *has a terminating trace of length* $\leq n$ *starting from* $k$.

*Proof.* Let $u \rightleftharpoons max(|A|, |node(g)|)$ and let $m \rightleftharpoons |var(g)| + 1$. Take $n \rightleftharpoons u^m$. Obviously $|Val_{\mathcal{A}}[g] \times node(g)| \leq n$. Let $k \in dom\ Den_{\mathcal{A}}[\![g]\!]$ be arbitrary and let $s$ be a terminating trace of $g$ with $(in\, s{\restriction}_V) = k$. We show that if $|s| > n$ then $s$ can be shortened to a terminating trace $s'$ with $(in\, s'{\restriction}_V) = k$. If $|s| > n$ then there are $i, j \in \mathbb{N}$ such that $i < j$ and $s(i) = s(j)$. Hence the subtrace of $s$ between $i$ and $j$ can be dropped out and we get a shorter trace. □

**(4.23) Corollary.** *The halting problem of the programming language* $rP_\sigma$ *with respect to finite and recursively presented models is decidable.*

*Proof.* If a finite and recursively presented model is given then it is sufficient to try all possible traces up to the length $n$ to check whether a program $p \in rP_\sigma$ terminates in it. Because of the use of finite nondeterminism the set of all possible computation paths of length less than or equal to $n$ is finite and the halting problem is decidable. □

Note that the condition of recursive presentation is necessary. To show this let $\phi$ be either an undecidable statement or a statement of unknown truth value. For example, let $\phi$ be Fermat's famous conjecture. Let $\sigma$ be a one-sorted similarity type and let $c$ be a constant symbol and $\rho$ a unary relation symbol. Let us consider the finite model $\mathcal{A}$ with the universe $A = \{1\}$ such that $c_\mathcal{A} = 1$ and

$$\rho_\mathcal{A} = \begin{cases} \{1\} & \text{if } \phi \text{ is true;} \\ \emptyset & \text{otherwise.} \end{cases}$$

Let us take the program **if** $\rho(c) \rightarrow$ **loop** $\square \neg\rho(c) \rightarrow$ **skip fi**. It is undecidable whether this program terminates. To avoid this problem, condition (iv) is added to Definition (4.20).

## 4.4 Canonical Form of Programs

The denotation provides the meaning of a program by characterizing the input and output of the finite computational traces. By using the restricted version of the input-output characterization introduced above we can also define whether two programs are equivalent.

**(4.24) Definition.** *Let $\mathcal{K} \subseteq Mod_\sigma$ be a class of models and $\phi \in Form_\sigma$ be an arbitrary but fixed formula. Let $X \subseteq V$ be an arbitrary set of variables such that $var(\phi) \subseteq X$. Two programs $p, q \in rP_\sigma$ are said to be equivalent in $\mathcal{K}$ with respect to $\phi$ and $X$ (written as $p \equiv q \pmod{\mathcal{K}, \phi, \mathrm{X}}$) iff for all models $\mathcal{A} \in \mathcal{K}$ we have $Den_\mathcal{A}[\![p, X]\!]\restriction_\phi = Den_\mathcal{A}[\![q, X]\!]\restriction_\phi$.*

We use the notation $p \equiv q$ instead of $p \equiv q \pmod{Mod_\sigma, true, V}$. If any of $\mathcal{K} = Mod_\sigma$, $\phi = true$ or $X = V$ takes place then we omit the corresponding component from the definition. For example $p \equiv q \pmod{X}$ means that

$$p \equiv q \pmod{Mod_\sigma, true, X}.$$

By using this notion of program equivalence we investigate the programming language $rP_\sigma$ in order to find out whether there exists a canonical form for the programs of $rP_\sigma$. In order to establish canonical forms and also to develop programs playing an important role in the theoretical investigations of the forthcoming sections some special programs and formulas are required which we introduce below.

**(4.25) Lemma.** *For any finite similarity type $\sigma$ and finite set of variables $X$ there exists a $\sigma$-type open formula $one_\sigma(X)$ such that for an arbitrary $\sigma$-type model $\mathcal{A}$ and $k \in Val_\mathcal{A}[X]$: $\mathcal{A} \models one_\sigma(X)[k]$ iff for all $s \in sort(\sigma)$, $|_\mathcal{A}H_s(k)| \leq 1$, i.e. $one_\sigma(X)$ expresses that the Herbrand universe generated from $k$ has at most one element for each sort of $\sigma$.*

*Proof.* Let $S = sort(\sigma)$. Fix $X \subseteq V$. Let $\tau_s$ be a fixed $s$-sorted term such that $var(\tau_s) \subseteq X$. Let $S_X \subseteq S$ be the set of all $s \in S$ for which such a term exists. The intended meaning of $\tau_s$ is that its value is the only element of that sort in the Herbrand universe. The formula $one_\sigma(X)$ has to describe that:

- If a variable $x \in X$ has a sort $s$ then its value is equal to the value of $\tau_s$.
- Any function $f : s_1, ..., s_n \to s$ applied to the values of $(\tau_{s_1}, ..., \tau_{s_n})$ results the value of $\tau_s$.

A formula which describes the above is the following:

$$one_\sigma(X) \rightleftharpoons \bigwedge\{\tau_s = w \mid sort(w) = s, s \in S_X, w \in X\} \wedge$$
$$\bigwedge\{f(\tau_{s_1}, ..., \tau_{s_n}) = \tau_s \mid f : s_1, ..., s_n \to s, f \in func\,\sigma,\ s_i, s \in S_X\}.$$

□

**(4.26) Theorem.** *For any finite similarity type $\sigma$ and for any finite set of variables $X \subseteq V$ there exists a program $Init_\sigma(X) \in P_\sigma$ which provides two new distinct vectors $W_1$, $W_2$ as output for any $\sigma$-type model $\mathcal{A}$ and any input $k \in Val_\mathcal{A}$ satisfying $\mathcal{A} \models \neg one_\sigma(X)[k]$.*

*Proof.* Let $W_1$ be a set of variables containing exactly one variable $w_s$ for each sort $s$ of $sort\ \sigma$. Let $W_2$ be a new copy of $W_1$ with $\iota : W_1 \to W_2$. Let $H \rightleftharpoons \{(x, y) \mid x, y \in W_1 \cup W_2 \cup X, sort(x) = sort(y)\}$.

Take the following program:

$$\begin{aligned} Init_\sigma(X) \rightleftharpoons \textbf{if}\ & \square\,((v, w) \in H) : \neg(v = w) \to w_{sort(v)} := v; \iota(w_{sort(v)}) := w \\ & \square\,(f : s_1, ..., s_n \to s) \in func\ \sigma : \neg f(w_{s_1}, ..., w_{s_n}) = w_s \\ & \quad \to \iota(w_s) := f(w_{s_1}, ..., w_{s_n}) \\ \textbf{fi}. & \end{aligned}$$

As in the proof of (4.25), $\mathcal{A} \models \neg one_\sigma(X \cup W_1 \cup W_2)[k]$ can hold in two cases:

(i) for some $v$ and $w$ ($(v, w) \in H$): $k(v) \neq k(w)$;
(ii) there is a function symbol $f : s_1, ..., s_n \to s$ such that $f(k(w_{s_1}), ..., k(w_{s_n})) \neq k(w_s)$.

The first part of the **if...fi** construct corresponds to case (i) while the second part corresponds to case (ii). Since $\neg one_\sigma(X) \to \neg one_\sigma(X \cup W_1 \cup W_2)$ the program $Init_\sigma(X)$ suffices. □

We remark that $var(Init_\sigma(X)) = X \cup W_1 \cup W_2$. Furthermore we also note that it may happen that $Init_\sigma(X)$ provides two distinct vectors for $W_1$ and $W_2$

but the formula $one_\sigma(X)$ holds. This is so because $W_1$ contains a variable for each sort of $\sigma$. In general $Init_\sigma(X)$ provides two distinct vectors for $W_1$ and $W_2$ iff the formula $one_\sigma(X \cup W_1 \cup W_2)$ does not hold.

**(4.27) Lemma.** *For any program $p \in rP_\sigma$ let $X = var(p)$, and take the following program:*

$$p_1 \rightleftharpoons \textbf{if } one_\sigma(X^W) \to \textbf{skip } \Box \neg one_\sigma(X^W) \to Init_\sigma(X);$$
$$\textbf{while } W_1 \neq W_2 \textbf{ do choice } (p, W_1 := W_2)\textbf{od fi},$$

*where $X^W \rightleftharpoons X \cup W_1 \cup W_2$. Let $\hat{p} \rightleftharpoons W_1 :=?; W_2 :=?;\ p_1$. For any model $\mathcal{A} \in Mod_\sigma$, $Den_\mathcal{A}[\![\hat{p}, X]\!]$ is the reflexive and transitive closure of $Den_\mathcal{A}[\![p, X]\!]$. Moreover, if $p \in P_\sigma$ then $p_1$ also has this property, and $p_1 \in P_\sigma$.*

*Proof.* Let $X'$ be a new copy of $X$. $Den_\mathcal{A}[\![\hat{p}, X]\!]$ is an $(X, X')$-type relation on $\mathcal{A}$. In the case of $\hat{p}$, if it is possible, the assignments $W_1 :=?; W_2 :=?$ can generate two distinct values for $W_1$ and $W_2$. Otherwise the model $\mathcal{A}$ has only one element in each sort. In this case the first member of **if** ...**fi** part of the program $\hat{p}$ gives the possibility of the termination and gives the reflexive and transitive closure of $Den_\mathcal{A}[\![\hat{p}, X]\!]$.

In the case of $p \in P_\sigma$ obviously

$$TRC(Den_\mathcal{A}[\![p, X]\!])\restriction_{one_\sigma(X^W)} =$$
$$\{(k, k[X/X']) \mid k \in Val_\mathcal{A}[X], \mathcal{A} \models one_\sigma(X^W)[k]\}.$$

This corresponds to the first part of the **if**...**fi** construct in $p_1$. Otherwise (i.e. when $\neg one_\sigma(X^W)$ holds) $Init_\sigma(X)$ generates two distinct vectors for $W_1$ and $W_2$. In both cases ($p \in rP_\sigma$ or $p \in P_\sigma$) if $W_1 \neq W_2$ then the **do**...**od** construct in $p_1$ iterates the program $p$ until the second permanently true guard of **choice** is chosen. If we choose the first guard $k$ times and only then the second one we get the relation

$$Den_\mathcal{A}[\![\overbrace{p; ...; p}^{k \text{ times}}, var(p)]\!].$$

Since $k$ may be arbitrary we have $Den_\mathcal{A}[\![\hat{p}, X]\!] = TRC(Den_\mathcal{A}[\![p, X]\!])$. □

In order to construct a program $p \in rP_\sigma$ from a given transition graph $g \in rG_\sigma$ we need $|node(g)|$-many different entities to represent the set $Label \cap node(g)$ in data. Therefore, we define $n$ different vectors $L_i$ $(i = 1, ..., n)$, which get different values during the execution if this is at all possible. The role of vectors $L_i$ is similar to that of sequences $L_c$ (as in the proof of Theorem (4.15)(b)). However, instead of ground terms $\top$ and $\bot$ we use the values of two sets of variables coding the elements of *Label*. Moreover, these values are computed during the execution of the corresponding program. This means that instead of "compilation time" coding we have to use "run time" coding.

**(4.28) Lemma.** *Let $g \in rG_\sigma$ and let $n = |node(g)| \geq 2$. Let $X \rightleftharpoons var(p)$. There is a program $InitLabels(g)$ such that in any model $\mathcal{A} \in Mod_\sigma$ if $\mathcal{A} \models \neg one_\sigma(X)$ then it assigns pairwisely different values to a sequence of different sets of variables $L_{c_1}, ..., L_{c_n}$, where $node(g) = \{c_1, ..., c_n\}$. Moreover, $L_{c_2}, ..., L_{c_n}$ are copies of $L_{c_1}$.*

*Proof.* Let $X \rightleftharpoons var(g)$ and $W_1$, $W_2$ be new sets of variables defined as in Theorem (4.26). For any sort $s \in sort\ \sigma$ and for any $i, j \in node(g)$ let $x^s_{ij}$ be a new variable of $sort\ \sigma$. Take

$$L_i \rightleftharpoons \{x^s_{ij} \mid j \in node(g), s \in sort\ \sigma\} \quad (i \in node(g)).$$

(Note that all the sets $L_i$ can be considered as copies of each other). Finally let us define $InitLabels(g)$ as the following program:

$$Init_\sigma(X); \textbf{if } \Box(s \in sort\ \sigma) : w_s \neq \iota(w_s) \rightarrow (i, j \in node(g)) : G^s_{ij} \textbf{ fi},$$

where

$$G^s_{ij} \rightleftharpoons \begin{cases} x^s_{ij} := w_s & \text{if } i = j; \\ x^s_{ij} := \iota(w_s) & \text{if } i \neq j. \end{cases}$$

□

Now we show that in a well-defined sense any transition graph is equivalent to a program.

For any transition $t \in Trans_\sigma$ take

$$step(t) \rightleftharpoons \begin{cases} t & \text{if } t \notin Open_\sigma; \\ \textbf{skip} & \text{otherwise.} \end{cases}$$

For a fixed transition graph $g \in rG_\sigma$ with $node(g) = \{c_1, ..., c_n\}$ let $X \rightleftharpoons var(g)$ and take the following (*one step*) program (belonging to $rP_\sigma$):

$$\begin{array}{l}
os(g) \rightleftharpoons \textbf{if } L = L_{stop} \rightarrow \textbf{skip } \Box \\
\quad \textbf{if } \Box(i \in \pi_1(dom\ g)) : true \rightarrow \\
\quad\quad \textbf{if } L = L_i \wedge \neg \bigvee\{\alpha(g(i,j)) \mid (i,j) \in dom\ g\} \rightarrow \textbf{loop } \Box \\
\quad\quad\quad L = L_i \wedge \bigvee\{\alpha(g(i,j)) \mid (i,j) \in dom\ g\} \rightarrow \\
\quad\quad\quad\quad \textbf{if } \Box\,((i,j) \in dom\ g) : \alpha(g(i,j)) \rightarrow step(g(i,j)); L := L_j \textbf{fi} \\
\quad\quad \textbf{fi} \\
\quad \textbf{fi} \\
\textbf{fi}.
\end{array}$$

Note that $var(os(g)) = X \cup L \cup \bigcup\{L_c \mid c \in node(g)\}$. Here $L_c$ corresponds to the node $c$ of $g$, and $L$ to an arbitrary node of $g$. Later, when applying $os(g)$, every $L_c$ can be considered as a copy of $L$, and they will have different values. It can easily be seen that $os(g)$ skips if its input at $L$ is equal to $L_{stop}$. It goes into an infinite loop if all the outcoming edges from the input node are false and otherwise it chooses non-deterministically one of the true edges outcoming from the input node. Note that during the run of $os(g)$ only the value of $X$ and $L$ can change.

We remark that if we deal with programs of $rP_\sigma$ then the program $Init_\sigma(X)$ alone cannot be appropriately used since it can happen that during the program execution a random assignment $y :=?$ makes $one_\sigma(X)$ false. (See the difference between program $\hat{p}$ and $p_1$ in Lemma (4.27)!) This problem can be avoided with the help of a more complicated construction that checks the appearance of random assignments.

Let $TF_\sigma$ be the set of all truth value functions $h : rel\,\sigma \to \{true, false\}$. Let

$$one_\sigma(X;h) \rightleftharpoons one_\sigma(X) \wedge \bigwedge\{\rho(\tau_{s_1}, ..., \tau_{s_n}) \leftrightarrow h(\rho) \mid (\rho : s_1, ..., s_n) \in rel\ \sigma\},$$

where $\tau_{s_i}$ is the same as in the proof of (4.25). The formula $one_\sigma(X,h)$ expresses that the Herbrand universe generated from $X$ has at most one element of each sort and that $h$ is really a truth value function over the Herbrand universe. We say that a valuation $k \in Val_{\mathcal{A}}$ satisfies $h \in TF_\sigma$ iff $\mathcal{A} \models one_\sigma(X;h)[k]$. A trace $s$ of $g$ starts with a state satisfying $h$ iff $s(0)\restriction_V$ satisfies $h$.

Fix a transition graph $g$, a truth value function $h \in TF_\sigma$, a node $d \in node(g)$ and a variable $y \in var(g)$. Let us define two programs $run(g,h,d,y)$ and $run(g,h)$ as follows. Let the program $run(g,h,d,y)$ be **skip** if there exists a trace $\beta$ which starts with an input value $k$ for which $\mathcal{A} \models one_\sigma(X,h)[k]$, and the trace $\beta$ ends in the node $d$ and contains only one random assignment, which is just before $d$ and is $y :=?$. Otherwise let $run(g,h,d,y)$ be **loop**. Similarly let $run(g,h)$ be **skip** if there exists a terminating trace of $g$ starting from a state satisfying $h$ such that if this trace computes a random assignment $x :=?$ then it does not change the actual value of the variable $x$. Otherwise take $run(g,h) \rightleftharpoons$ **loop**. The program $run(g,h)$ could also be defined such that in the transition graph $g$ all occurrences of random assignments will be changed to **skip**. Let $g'$ be this new graph. Then $run(g,h)$ is **skip** iff there exists a terminating trace of $g'$ starting from a state satisfying $h$.

Note that $run(g,h)$ and $run(g,h,d,y)$ can be constructed from the graph $g$ in a recursive way. This is so because the construction is independent of the models, since supposing that $\mathcal{A} \models one_\sigma(X;h)[k]$ means that the truth value of any open formula is uniquely determined by $h$ itself. Furthermore, it is enough to investigate only finitely many traces, since, because of $\mathcal{A} \models one_\sigma(X)[k]$, it is enough to consider potential traces without repetitive crossing of the same nodes and with random assignments at most just before their last member.

Now we are ready to write down a program working similarly to the transition graph $g$. Let $Y \rightleftharpoons (X, W_1, W_2, L_{c_1}, ..., L_{c_n}, L)$, where the variables on the right-hand side are those of $InitLabels(g)$, as defined in Lemma (4.28), except $L$, which is a new copy of $L_{c_1}$. Furthermore, we suppose that the subprograms $InitLabels(g)$ and $os(g)$ use these variables as indicated in their definitions. Let $X^W \rightleftharpoons (X, W_1, W_2)$. Let $p'(g)$ be the program shown in Fig. 4.5.

$$
\begin{array}{l}
\textbf{if } one_\sigma(X) \to \textbf{choice } \Big( \textbf{if } \square(h \in TF_\sigma, y \in var(g), d \in node(g)) : \\
\qquad one_\sigma(X;h) \to \big(run(g,h,d,y); \\
\qquad\qquad y := ?; W_1 := ?; W_2 := ? \\
\qquad\qquad \textbf{if } one_\sigma(X^W) \to \textbf{loop fi}; \\
\qquad\qquad InitLabels(g); \\
\qquad\qquad L := L_d \\
\qquad\qquad \big) \\
\qquad \textbf{fi}, \\
\qquad \textbf{if } \square(h \in TF_\sigma) : one_\sigma(X;h) \to run(g,h)\,\textbf{fi} \\
\qquad \Big) \\
\square \\
\quad \neg one_\sigma(X) \to InitLabels(g); \\
\qquad L := L_{start} \\
\textbf{fi}.
\end{array}
$$

**Fig. 4.5** The program $p'(g)$

It is clear that $var(os(g)) \subseteq Y$. Now take the program

$$r(g) \rightleftharpoons \textbf{repeat } Y' := Y; os(g) \textbf{ until } Y' = Y.$$

At the end take $pr(g) \rightleftharpoons p'(g); r(g)$.

The following theorem expresses that the program $pr(g)$ defined above is really similar to the transition graph $g$.

**(4.29) Theorem.** *For any $g \in rG_\sigma$ if $X \rightleftharpoons var(g)$ then*

$$Den_{\mathcal{A}}[\![g, X]\!] = Den_{\mathcal{A}}[\![pr(g), X]\!].$$

In theoretical investigations it is useful to have a possibility to represent each object under consideration in a given form, which is usually called the canonical form. Let us see whether and how we have such a possibility for our theory of programming.

**(4.30) Theorem.** *(On canonical form.) For an arbitrary program $p \in rP_\sigma$ there are programs $p', p'' \in rP_\sigma$ without cycles such that*

$$p \equiv p';\ \textbf{repeat } Y' := Y; p'' \textbf{ until } Y' = Y \quad (\mathrm{mod}\ var(p))$$

*where $Y \supseteq var(p') \cup var(p'') \cup var(p)$ and $Y'$ is a new copy of $Y$. Moreover, if $p \in P_\sigma$ then $p'$ and $p''$ belong to $P_\sigma$.*

*Proof.* Let $can : rP_\sigma \to rP_\sigma$ be the map rendering to each $p \in rP_\sigma$ the program $can(p) \rightleftharpoons pr(gr(p))$. By definition, $can(p)$ has the desired form with $p' \rightleftharpoons p'(gr(p))$, $p'' \rightleftharpoons os(gr(p))$ and by Theorem (4.29),

$$p \equiv can(p) \quad (\text{mod } var(p))$$

since $var(gr(p)) = var(p)$.

If $p \in P_\sigma$ then the first part of the **choice** construction in $p'(gr(p))$ is equivalent to **loop** so it can be dropped out. Thus we may assume that $p'(gr(p))$ and hence $p'$ and $p''$ belong to $P_\sigma$ as well. □

From the above proof it can be seen that the program $p'$ has to establish two different values whose finite sequences serve as markers (values for $L_i$'s) in the remaining part of the canonical form. Therefore, if we consider such models only where two distinct elements are a priori required, then the canonical form becomes simple. Namely, we have the following

**(4.31) Corollary.** *For any program $p \in rP_\sigma$ there is a program $q$ without cycles and there are two new variables $c$ and $d$ of the same sort such that*

$$p \equiv \textbf{repeat } Y' := Y; q \textbf{ until } Y' = Y \quad (\text{mod } c \neq d, var(p)),$$

*where $Y = var(q) \supseteq var(p) \cup \{c, d\}$ and $Y'$ is a new copy of $Y$.*

*Proof.* Let $g = gr(p)$ and $p'(g)$, $os(g)$ be the same as previously, with the only difference that $X$ of $p'(g)$ is now equal to $var(g) \cup \{c, d\}$. Take

$$q \rightleftharpoons \textbf{if } c \neq d \rightarrow p'(g); c := d \,\square\, c = d \rightarrow os(g) \textbf{ fi}.$$

The required equivalence follows from the proof of Theorem (4.30). □

**(4.32) Corollary.** *Let us fix an arbitrary many-sorted similarity type $\sigma$. For any program $p \in rP_\sigma$, if $X \supseteq var(p)$ is a finite set of variables and $\mathcal{A} \in Mod_\sigma$ then $Den_{\mathcal{A}}[\![p, X]\!]$ is inductively definable in $\mathcal{A}$ by a 1-ranked formula independent of $\mathcal{A}$.*

*Proof.* Let

$$p \equiv p_1; \textbf{ repeat } Y' := Y; p_2 \textbf{ until } Y' = Y \quad (\text{mod } var(p))$$

be the canonical form of a given program $p \in rP_\sigma$. Let $Z$ be a new copy of $Y$. By Theorem (4.15) there are open formulas $\phi_i(Y, Y')$ which define $Den_{\mathcal{A}}[\![p_i, Y]\!]$ in any $\sigma$-type model $\mathcal{A}$. Let $R$ and $S$ be two new $(Y, Y')$-arity relation symbols. Take the following equation system $E$:

$$\begin{aligned} S(Y,Y') &= \phi_2(Y,Y') \vee \exists Z\,(S(Y,Z) \wedge \phi_2(Z,Y')); \\ R(Y,Y') &= \exists Z\,(\phi_1(Y,Z) \wedge S(Z,Y') \wedge \phi_2(Y',Y')) \end{aligned}.$$

It is clear that $rank(E) = 1$. By Theorem (2.14) let $\beta$ be the least solution of this equation in a given model $\mathcal{A} \in Mod_\sigma$. By Theorem (4.19) $\beta_R$ is equal to $Den_{\mathcal{A}}[\![p, X]\!]$. By Theorem (2.14), $\beta_R$ is inductively definable by a 1-ranked formula as well. □

Chapter 5

# Extension of Program Schemas

The basic programming language introduced so far should be considered as the minimal language in our investigation. It is sufficient for a programming logic to establish only some negative results by showing that something fails even in the case of this minimal language. However, for a programming logic we need a programming language which is universal in the computational sense, that is, in which any algorithm can be represented by an appropriate program. As we shall see in Chapter 7, the language $rP_\sigma$ is not such. Therefore, we need either another programming language or a special device to extend the language $rP_\sigma$ appropriately. We choose the latter approach and introduce a logical tool which ensures the required extension in a purely logical way.

A programming language may be extended in data structures and/or in computation devices. Extension in data structures means the possibility of (run-time) modification of the data environment of a program. This extension can be of two kinds: static and dynamic. Static extension introduces a new data structure that is unchanged throughout the life of the program. Dynamic extension allows the introduction of new data structures when they are needed, even during a program execution. Here we deal only with static extension, which may be used to augment the basic programming language with new fixed abstract data types.

Logically, extension can be realized by defining new relation and function symbols and also new sorts of variables that correspond to the new data structures.

The extension in computation devices provides new control structures in our case, i.e. new devices to manipulate data. In order to introduce a new control structure we have to provide all necessary functions and relations required to realize the new control. Therefore an extension in computation devices can also be defined as a static extension in data structures. A computation device supports the computation processes and it appears neither in the input nor in the output. The required extension can be defined as a data extension such that new sorts of data can be used during the computation only if they are not used in the input and output. For example, an array is such a new control structure, and the language has to be extended with appropriate functions to use it. However, when it is used for input as well, an array can also be a new data structure. In order for the extension to be a data or control structure, the language has to be extended with a new sort of variables which refers to the new data structure, for example to the array, but in the control case these new entities do not appear in the input and the output.

In the present work we only deal with the static extensions of the language $rP_\sigma$ with new control structures. The method of extension we introduce in Section 5.1 is purely logical, which differentiates our approach from the others. We show that the widely used control structures, e.g. stacks, lists and counters, can be defined as extensions.

Section 5.2 is devoted to the detailed investigation of set extensions of a programming language by allowing the usage of sets. In Section 5.3 we discuss the halting problem for the extensions.

Note that extension will be used not only for augmenting programming languages by different computational devices but also to construct new languages to describe program properties, as in Section 11.2.

## 5.1 Main Properties of Extensions

In this chapter we provide a purely logical method to extend the programming language $rP_\sigma$ by new control structures. First we extend the similarity type $\sigma$ by the new function and relation symbols necessary to realize the desired control structure. Then the class of models $Mod_\sigma$ is extended in order to provide the appropriate semantics of the extended programming language.

**(5.1) Definition.** *An extension of the similarity type $\sigma$ is a pair $(\delta, ext)$ where*

*(i)* $\delta \supseteq \sigma$;
*(ii)* $ext : Mod_\sigma \to Sb(Mod_\delta)$ *is an arbitrary function;*
*(iii) for arbitrary $\mathcal{A} \in Mod_\sigma$ and $\mathcal{B} \in ext(\mathcal{A})$ the $\sigma$-type reduct of $\mathcal{B}$ is $\mathcal{A}$, i.e. $\mathcal{B}\restriction_\sigma = \mathcal{A}$;*

*An extension is called strict iff for each $\mathcal{A} \in Mod_\sigma$, $ext(\mathcal{A}) \neq \emptyset$.*

We remark that in Part I we use only strict extensions. A very simple extension is the so-called empty extension. Just take $emp_\sigma \rightleftharpoons (\sigma, id_\sigma)$, where $id_\sigma : Mod_\sigma \to Sb(Mod_\sigma)$ is defined by $id_\sigma(\mathcal{A}) \rightleftharpoons \{\mathcal{A}\}$. It is clear that $emp_\sigma$ is an extension.

**(5.2) Definition.** *Let $\sigma$ and $\sigma'$ be two disjoint similarity types. Let $\mathcal{A} \in Mod_{\sigma'}$ be a fixed model. The extension of similarity type $\sigma$ with model $\mathcal{A}$ is defined by taking*

*(i)* $\delta \rightleftharpoons \sigma \cup^* \sigma'$;
*(ii) for each model $\mathcal{B} \in Mod_\sigma$ :* $ext(\mathcal{B}) \rightleftharpoons \{\mathcal{B} + \mathcal{A}\}$.

*Let $\sigma(\mathcal{A})$ denote this extension.*

**(5.3) Lemma.** *Let $(\sigma^1, ext^1)$ be an extension of the similarity type $\sigma$ and let $(\sigma^2, ext^2)$ be an extension of the similarity type $\sigma^1$. Then $(\sigma^2, ext^1 \circ ext^2)$ is also an extension of $\sigma$, where*

$$ext^1 \circ ext^2 \rightleftharpoons \lambda\mathcal{A} \in Mod_\sigma. \bigcup \{ext^2(\mathcal{B}) \mid \mathcal{B} \in ext^1(\mathcal{A})\}.$$

*Moreover, if both $ext^1$ and $ext^2$ are strict then $ext^1 \circ ext^2$ is strict as well.*

*Proof.* Obviously $\sigma \subseteq \sigma^1 \subseteq \sigma^2$. For each $\mathcal{A}' \in ext^1 \circ ext^2(\mathcal{A}))$: $\mathcal{A}'\restriction_\sigma = \mathcal{A}$. Therefore, $(\sigma_2, ext^1 \circ ext^2)$ is an extension of $\sigma$. To prove the strict case fix a model $\mathcal{A} \in Mod_\sigma$. By definition there is an $\mathcal{A}^1 \in ext^1(\mathcal{A})$ and there is an $\mathcal{A}^2 \in ext^2(\mathcal{A}^1)$. Since $\mathcal{A}^2 \in ext^1 \circ ext^2(\mathcal{A})$ thus $ext^1 \circ ext^2(\mathcal{A}) \neq \emptyset$. □

Therefore, an extension of $\sigma$ provides a new way of defining the semantics for the new syntactic elements too. If $(\delta, ext)$ is an extension of $\sigma$ then $rP_\delta$ is the programming language extended, together with the semantics defined accordingly, to the function $ext$ in the following way. Let us suppose that for any sort $s$ from $(sort\ \delta)\backslash(sort\ \sigma)$ we can fix a constant symbol $c_s$ of sort $s$. Let $W \rightleftharpoons \{x \mid x \in V$ and $sort(x) \in (sort\ \delta)\backslash(sort\ \sigma)\}$. Let $f_c \in Val_\mathcal{B}[W]$ be such that for any variable $x$ with $sort(x) = s$, $f_c(x) \rightleftharpoons (c_s)_\mathcal{A}$.

**(5.4) Definition.** *Let $(\delta, ext)$ be an extension of $\sigma$, and let $p \in rP_\delta$ be an arbitrary program and let $\mathcal{A} \in Mod_\sigma$ be fixed. Then the denotation of $p$ in the model $\mathcal{A}$, $ext\text{-}Den_\mathcal{A}[\![p]\!] \subseteq (Val_\mathcal{A}[V_{sort\sigma}])^2$ is defined as follows: for any $f, g \in Val_\mathcal{A}[V_{sort\sigma}]$ we have $(f, g) \in ext\text{-}Den_\mathcal{A}[\![p]\!]$ iff for $f' = f + f_c$ and for each $\mathcal{B} \in ext(\mathcal{A})$ there exists a valuation $g' \in Val_\mathcal{B}$ such that $(f', g') \in Den_\mathcal{B}[\![p]\!]$ and $g \subseteq g'$.*

Informally, this definition means that $(f, g) \in ext\text{-}Den_\mathcal{A}[\![p]\!]$ iff considering any extension $\mathcal{B}$ of $ext(\mathcal{A})$, if we start our program $p$ with the original input values on $\sigma$-sorted variables and with input values according to $c_s$ on the $s$-sorted variables, then there is a run of $p$ in $\mathcal{B}$ such that it stops with output values defined by $g$ on $\sigma$-sorted variables ($s \in sort\ \delta \setminus sort\ \sigma$).

Note that $ext\text{-}Den_\mathcal{A}[\![p]\!]$ does not contain input-output values of the variables in the new sorts from $(sort\ \delta)\backslash(sort\ \sigma)$, hence the extension has been obtained by introducing a control structure rather than a data structure.

Now we define the notion of extended computability.

**(5.5) Definition.** *Let $(\delta, ext)$ be an extension of $\sigma$ and let $\mathcal{A} \in Mod_\sigma$ be fixed.*

*(a) An $X$-type relation $R \subseteq Val_\mathcal{A}[X]$ where $sort(X) \subseteq sort\,\sigma$ is said to be ext-computable in $\mathcal{A}$ iff there is a program $p \in rP_\delta$ and a valuation $k \in Val_\mathcal{A}[V \setminus X]$ such that for any valuation $a \in Val_\mathcal{A}[X]$:*

$$a \in R \quad \textit{iff} \quad k + a \in dom\ ext\text{-}Den_\mathcal{A}[\![p]\!].$$

*For such $p$ and $k$ we say that $R$ is computable by the program $p$ with parameter $k$, or that program $p$ with parameter $k$ computes $R$.*

(b) *Let $P \subseteq rP_\delta$. The relation $R$ is called $P$-computable in $\mathcal{A}$ iff there is a program $p \in P$ with a parameter $k$ which computes $R$ in $\mathcal{A}$.*

Observe, that if $|ext(\mathcal{A})| = 1$ for each $\mathcal{A} \in Mod_\sigma$, then for any $k \in Val_\mathcal{A}$, $k \in dom\ ext\text{-}Den_\mathcal{A}[\![p]\!]$ iff $p$ can terminate with input $k + f_c$ in the unique extension $\mathcal{B} \in ext(\mathcal{A})$.

Note that taking the empty extension into account we obtain the notion of computability in the usual sense for the minimal language $rP_\sigma$. We remark that Definitions (5.4) and (5.5) - at least formally - depend on the choice of the constant symbols $c_s$. Let $\mathcal{A} \in Mod_\sigma$ and let $\mathcal{B} \in ext(\mathcal{A})$. Let $f_{c'}$ and $f_{c''} \in Val_W[\mathcal{B}]$ be such that for any variable $x \in W$ with $sort(x) = s$, $f_{c'}(x) = (c'_s)_\mathcal{B}$ and $f_{c''}(x) = (c''_s)_\mathcal{B}$, where $c'_s$ and $c''_s$ are (possibly the same) constant symbols of each sort $s \in (sort\ \delta) \setminus (sort\ \sigma)$. Let $ext\text{-}Den'$ and $ext\text{-}Den''$ denote the denotations defined by using $f_{c'}$ and $f_{c''}$ according to Definition (5.4), respectively. According to these definitions we obtain two notions of computable many-sorted relations: the $ext'$-computable and the $ext''$-computable ones. We remark that generally $ext\text{-}Den'_\mathcal{A}[\![p]\!] \neq ext\text{-}Den''_\mathcal{A}[\![p]\!]$.

**(5.6) Lemma.** *In any $\sigma$-type model $\mathcal{A}$ the set of ext-computable relations does not depend on the choice of constant symbols $c_s$.*

*Proof.* Using the notation before the lemma, it is enough to prove that the $ext'$-computable and the $ext''$-computable relations are the same. Let $R \subseteq Val_\mathcal{A}[X]$ be an $ext'$-computable $X$-type relation by a program $p$ and a parameter $k$, i.e. for any $a \in Val_\mathcal{A}[X] : k + a \in dom\,(ext\text{-}Den'_\mathcal{A}[\![p]\!])$ iff $a \in R$. Take the following program:

$$\hat{p} \quad \rightleftharpoons \quad (x \in var(p) \cap W) : x := c'_{sort(x)};\ p.$$

Obviously, for any $a \in Val_\mathcal{A}[X], k+a \in dom\ ext\text{-}Den''_\mathcal{A}[\![\hat{p}]\!]$ iff $a \in R$. Thus each $ext'$-computable relation is also an $ext''$-computable one. The other direction can be proved similarly. □

In order to compare any two extensions of $rP_\sigma$ we need the following notion.

**(5.7) Definition.** *Let $\sigma$ be a fixed similarity type and let $(\delta_i, ext_i)$ for $i = 1, 2$ be two given extensions of $\sigma$.*

(i) *These extensions have the same computational power (denoted as $ext_1 \approx ext_2$) iff the $ext_1$-computable and $ext_2$-computable relations are the same in any model of $Mod_\sigma$.*

(ii) *The extension $(\delta_1, ext_1)$ has more computational power than the extension $(\delta_2, ext_2)$ (denoted as $ext_1 \gtrsim ext_2$ or $ext_2 \lesssim ext_1$) iff each $ext_2$-computable relation is also $ext_1$-computable in any model of $Mod_\sigma$.*

(iii) *The extension $(\delta_1, ext_1)$ has definitely more computational power than the extension $(\delta_2, ext_2)$ (denoted as $ext_1 > ext_2$ or $ext_2 < ext_1$) iff $ext_1 \gtrsim ext_2$ but $ext_1 \not\approx ext_2$.*

To illustrate the above let us see how the extension is done when some important control structures are introduced.

**(5.8) Example.** (Counter.)

(i) Let $\sigma$ be an arbitrary similarity type such that $\omega \notin sort\ \sigma$. Let us add to $\sigma$ three new symbols: $0 :\to \omega$, $+1 : \omega \to \omega$, $-1 : \omega \to \omega$. Let $\sigma^c$ be the new type obtained in this way.

(ii) For any model $\mathcal{A} \in Mod_\sigma$ let $\mathcal{A}^c$ be the extension of $\mathcal{A}$ such that

$$\begin{aligned} \omega_{\mathcal{A}^c} &\rightleftharpoons \mathbb{N} \\ 0_{\mathcal{A}^c} &\rightleftharpoons 0 \\ +1_{\mathcal{A}^c}(x) &\rightleftharpoons x+1 \\ -1_{\mathcal{A}^c}(x) &\rightleftharpoons x-1 \end{aligned}$$

Let $counter(\mathcal{A}) \rightleftharpoons \{\mathcal{A}^c\}$ and take $counter_\sigma \rightleftharpoons (\sigma^c, counter)$.

We remark that if $\nu$ is the empty similarity type, then $counter_\sigma$ is the extension $\sigma(\mathcal{N}\restriction_{\nu^c})$. (For this notation see Definition (5.2).) We also note that the operation $+1$ is enough to compute all the recursive functions on $\mathbb{N}$, thus in any counter extension we can use the power of recursion theory.

**(5.9) Example.** (Stack.)

(i) Let $\sigma$ be arbitrary. For any $d \in sort\ \sigma$ let $d^s$ be a new sort (representing a stack for $d$-sorted elements) and let us add the following new symbols to $\sigma$:

$$\begin{aligned} tail^d &: d^s \to d^s \\ head^d &: (d^s, d) \to d \\ push^d &: (d^s, d) \to d^s \\ empty^d &: \to d^s \end{aligned}$$

Let $\sigma^s$ denote the similarity type so obtained.

(ii) For any model $\mathcal{A} \in Mod_\sigma$ let $\mathcal{A}^s$ be the extension of $\mathcal{A}$ such that $(\mathcal{A}^s)_{d^s} \rightleftharpoons (\mathcal{A}_d)^*$ (i.e. $\mathcal{A}^s_{d^s}$ is the set of all finite sequences of the elements of sort $\mathcal{A}_d$).

$$tail^d_{\mathcal{A}^s}(h) = \begin{cases} h' & \text{if } h = h' \circ \langle a \rangle \text{ for some } a \in \mathcal{A}_d; \\ empty^d_{\mathcal{A}^s} & \text{otherwise.} \end{cases}$$

$$head^d_{\mathcal{A}^s}(h, a_1) = \begin{cases} a & \text{if } h = h' \circ \langle a \rangle \text{ for some } a \in \mathcal{A}_d; \\ a_1 & \text{otherwise.} \end{cases}$$

$$push^d_{\mathcal{A}^s}(h, a) = h \circ \langle a \rangle$$

$$empty^d_{\mathcal{A}^s} = \lambda \text{ (the empty sequence from } (\mathcal{A}_d)^*\text{).}$$

Let $stack(\mathcal{A}) = \{\mathcal{A}^s\}$. Now take $stack_\sigma = (\sigma^s, stack)$.

Note that by the use of the stack extension the memory capacity becomes unbounded. This unbounded memory capacity can only be handled by the functions introduced above. By stack extension we can simulate counter extension as well. Namely, a stack simulates a counter if we forget about the content of the data which we push in or take off the stack. The pushing represents $+1$, taking off represents $-1$, while the empty stack represents 0. Therefore, simulating a counter we only consider how many data are in the stack. We emphasize that when speaking about stack extension, the constant symbols $c_d$ used in Definition (5.4) for $f_c$ are uniquely determined: $c_{d^s} = empty^d$.

**(5.10) Example.** (Elementary list)

(i) Let $\sigma$ be an arbitrary similarity type. First let us take the extension $\sigma^c$ of Example (5.8) and for any $d \in sort\ \sigma$ let us add $d^l$ (representing the lists of $d$-sorted elements) as a new sort. Then let us add the following new symbols to $\sigma^c$:

$$\begin{aligned} nil^d &: \to d^l \\ \circ^d &: d^l, d^l \to d^l \\ \langle . \rangle^d &: d \to d^l \\ first^d &: d^l, d \to d \\ last^d &: d^l, d \to d \\ butfirst^d &: d^l \to d^l \\ butlast^d &: d^l \to d^l \\ member^d &: d^l, \omega, d \to d \end{aligned}$$

Let $\sigma^l$ denote the similarity type so obtained.

(ii) For any model $\mathcal{A} \in Mod_\sigma$ let $\mathcal{A}^l$ be the extension of $\mathcal{A}^c$ such that

$$\begin{aligned} (\mathcal{A}^l)_{d^l} &\rightleftharpoons (\mathcal{A}_d)^* \\ nil^d_{\mathcal{A}^l} &\rightleftharpoons \lambda \text{ (the empty sequence of } (\mathcal{A}_d)^*) \\ \circ^d_{\mathcal{A}^l}(h_1, h_2) &\rightleftharpoons h_1 \circ h_2 \\ \langle . \rangle^d_{\mathcal{A}^l}(a) &\rightleftharpoons \langle a \rangle \\ first^d_{\mathcal{A}^l}(h, a_1) &\rightleftharpoons \begin{cases} a & \text{if } h = \langle a \rangle \circ h' \text{ for some } h', a; \\ a_1 & \text{otherwise.} \end{cases} \\ last^d_{\mathcal{A}^l}(h, b_1) &\rightleftharpoons \begin{cases} b & \text{if } h = h' \circ \langle b \rangle \text{ for some } h', b; \\ b_1 & \text{otherwise.} \end{cases} \\ butfirst^d_{\mathcal{A}^l}(h) &\rightleftharpoons \begin{cases} h' & \text{if } h = \langle a \rangle \circ h' \text{ for some } a, h'; \\ nil^d & \text{otherwise.} \end{cases} \\ butlast^d_{\mathcal{A}^l}(h) &\rightleftharpoons \begin{cases} h' & \text{if } h = h' \circ \langle b \rangle \text{ for some } h', b; \\ nil^d & \text{otherwise.} \end{cases} \\ member^d_{\mathcal{A}^l}(h, n, a) &\rightleftharpoons \begin{cases} h(n) & \text{if } |h| > n; \\ a & \text{otherwise.} \end{cases} \end{aligned}$$

Now take $list(\mathcal{A}) \rightleftharpoons \{\mathcal{A}^l\}$ and define $list_\sigma \rightleftharpoons (\sigma^l, list)$.

Note that list is a computational device widely used in programming practice. However, it does not increase the computational power of the programming language with respect to the stack extension as we can see from the following

**(5.11) Theorem.** *$list_\sigma$ and $stack_\sigma$ have the same computational power, i.e. $list_\sigma \approx stack_\sigma$*

*Proof.* Let $X$ be any finite set of *sort* $\sigma$-sorted variables, and let $\mathcal{A} \in Mod_\sigma$ be arbitrary. It is enough to prove that

(i) for any $p \in rP_{\sigma^s}$, $k \in Val_\mathcal{A}$, there is a program $p \in rP_{\sigma^l}$ and a valuation $k' \in Val_\mathcal{A}$ such that for any $a \in Val_\mathcal{A}[X]$:

$$(*) \qquad (k + a) \in dom\ stack\text{-}Den_\mathcal{A}[\![p]\!] \text{ iff } (k' + a) \in dom\ list\text{-}Den_\mathcal{A}[\![p']\!];$$

(ii) for any $p' \in rP_{\sigma^l}$, $k' \in Val_\mathcal{A}$, there is a program $p \in rP_{\sigma^s}$ and a valuation $k \in Val_\mathcal{A}$ such that for any $a \in Val_\mathcal{A}[X]$ (*) holds.

Consider first (i). For any $d \in sort\ \sigma$ let $\iota_d$ be a bijection between the $d^s$-sorted and $d^l$-sorted variables. Now make the following substitutions in the text of each $p \in rP_{\sigma^s}$ for any $d \in sort\ \sigma$:

| | | |
|---|---|---|
| $\iota_d(x)$ | for $x$ | (if $x$ is a $d^s$-sorted variable); |
| $nil^d$ | for $empty^d$; | |
| $butlast^d$ | for $tail^d$; | |
| $last^d$ | for $head^d$; | |
| $\hat{h} \circ^d \langle\hat{a}\rangle^d$ | for $push^d(h, a)$, | |

where $\hat{h}$ and $\hat{a}$ are obtained from $h$ and $a$, respectively, after the corresponding substitutions. Let the resulting program be denoted by $\hat{p}$. Now it is easy to show by induction, that $p' \rightleftharpoons \hat{p}$, $k' \rightleftharpoons k$ will satisfy (i), if we fix the constant symbols in the only possible way, i.e. $c_{d^s} \rightleftharpoons empty^d$, and $c_{d^l} \rightleftharpoons nil^d$.

The other direction (ii) is more complicated so we only sketch it. First the counterpart of lists is to be formed for which stacks can be appropriately used. All we have to do is to forget about the contents of the stacks. Each stack represents the number of its elements. The empty stack represents 0.

Using the reverse of the above substitutions we can arrange that $empty^d$, $tail^d$ and $head^d$ work appropriately. Consider the following $\sigma^l$-type term:

$$pu^d(l, a) \rightleftharpoons l \circ^d \langle a\rangle^d.$$

It is clear that $pu^d$ is computable by $push^d$. We need the following claim.

**Claim.** For any term $\tau \in Term_{\sigma_l}$ with variables $T$, we can construct a *deterministic* program (see (6.13)) $p_\tau \in det\text{-}P_{\sigma^l}$ with variables $X \cup \{y\}$ such that $X \supseteq T$, $\{y\} \cap T = \emptyset$ and

(i) $p_\tau$ does not contain the function symbols $first^d$, $butfirst^d$, $member^d$ and it uses $\circ^d$ and $\langle\cdot\rangle^d$ in the scope of the term $pu^d$ as described above;

(ii) for any $\mathcal{A} \in Mod_\sigma$, $\hat{k} \in Val_{\mathcal{A}'}$, $k \in Val_{\mathcal{A}'}[T]$, starting from the valuation $\hat{k} + k$, program $p_\tau$ stops, and the (unique) output value of $y$ is equal to $\tau_{\mathcal{A}'}[k]$.

The proof of the claim is left to the reader. Using the claim we can now construct an appropriate $p \in rP_{\sigma^\bullet}$ for $p' \in rP_{\sigma'}$ with $k \rightleftharpoons k'$. □

## 5.2 Set Extension

Now we show how the programming language $rP_\sigma$ can be augmented with sets as the control structure, i.e. how the set extension of $rP_\sigma$ can be defined. We want to define the set of all hereditarily finite sets generated from a given set of atoms (also called urelements). We give an elaborated construction since we have to neglect the "element" relation on the urelements. Let $H$ be an arbitrary non-empty set and for any $i \in \mathbb{N}$ define the set $Fin^i(H)$ by induction on $i$:

$$Fin^0(H) \rightleftharpoons H \times \{0\} \cup \{\emptyset\}$$
$$Fin^1(H) \rightleftharpoons \{(a,1) \mid a \in Sb_{<\omega_0}(Fin^0(H)), a \neq \emptyset\}$$
$$Fin^{i+1}(H) \rightleftharpoons \{(a,i+1) \mid a \in Sb_{<\omega_0}(\cup_{j=1}^{i} Fin^j(H)), \exists b \in a\ \pi_2(b) = i\} (i \geq 1)$$

This definition can be read as follows. Elements of $H$ are *atoms*. The empty set $\emptyset$ is a set. The atoms and the empty set together are called 0-ranked sets. The 0-ranked sets have no elements. The 1-ranked sets are the non-empty finite subsets of the set of 0-ranked sets. For $i \geq 1$, an $(i+1)$-ranked set is a finite set whose elements have rank $\leq i$ and which contains at least one element with rank $i$. Note that in general $H \cap Fin^0(H) \neq \emptyset$. There is a natural bijection $\iota_H : H \to (Fin^0(H) \setminus \{\emptyset\})$ by taking $\iota_H(a) \rightleftharpoons (a,0)$ for any $a \in H$.

**(5.12) Definition.** *The set of hereditarily finite sets generated from a nonempty set $H$ is $HFin(H) \rightleftharpoons \cup\{Fin^i(H) \mid i \in \mathbb{N}\}$. Let us define an element relation $\varepsilon$ on $HFin(H)$ by taking*

$$x \varepsilon y \textit{ iff } y \notin Fin^0(H) \textit{ and } x \in \pi_1(y).$$

*Moreover, let $atom_H \rightleftharpoons Fin^0(H) \setminus \{\emptyset\}$.*

**(5.13) Theorem.** *Let $H$ be a non-empty set. $(HFin(H), \varepsilon, \emptyset)$ is a model of the Zermelo-Fraenkel axiom system with urelements $atom_H$ and without an infinity axiom.*

For details about the Zermelo-Fraenkel axiom system with urelements and about this theorem see e.g. Jech [1971].

In order to use sets in the process of computation we need a computable function which can pick up the elements of a set and throw them into the process.

**(5.14) Definition.** *A function $f : HFin(H) \to HFin(H)$ is called a choice function iff, for all $x \in HFin(H)$, if $x \in atom_H$ or $x = \emptyset$ then $f(x) = \emptyset$, otherwise $f(x)\varepsilon x$.*

If $f$ is a choice function and a set $x$ has at least one element then $f(x)\varepsilon x$ always holds. Otherwise $f(x) = \emptyset$.

Now we are ready to define the set extension of the similarity type $\sigma$. For the sake of convenience we define the set-extension $set_\sigma$ of $\sigma$ only for one-sorted similarity types. Let $sort\ \sigma = \{d\}$ and fix a new sort, say $d^\in$. Let us add the following symbols to $\sigma$:

$$\begin{aligned}
\emptyset\ &: \to d^\in \\
\circ, \setminus\ &: d^\in, d^\in \to d^\in \\
atom &: d^\in \\
\in\ &: d^\in, d^\in \\
c\ &: d^\in \to d^\in \\
\iota\ &: d \to d^\in
\end{aligned}$$

Let $\sigma^\in$ denote this new similarity type. Now let us consider what the extension of the $\sigma$-type models looks like. Let $\mathcal{A}$ be an arbitrary model from $Mod_\sigma$. The set of models $set(\mathcal{A})$ consists of all the $\sigma^\in$-type models $\mathcal{B}$ for which the following hold:

(i) $\mathcal{B}\restriction_\sigma = \mathcal{A}$;
$\mathcal{B}_{d^\in} = HFin(A)$;

(ii)
a) $\emptyset_\mathcal{B} = \emptyset\ (\in Fin^0(A))$;
b) $atom_\mathcal{B} = atom_A$;
c) $\in_\mathcal{B} = \{(a, b) \mid a, b \in HFin(A), a\varepsilon b\}$;
d) $\iota_\mathcal{B}(a) = \iota_A(a)$;
e) $\setminus_\mathcal{B}(a, b) = a \setminus b$;
f) $\circ_\mathcal{B}(a, b) = a \cup \{b\}$;
g) $c_\mathcal{B}$ is an arbitrary choice function on $HFin(A)$.

We emphasize that the operations $\setminus, \cup, \{\cdot\}$ have their meaning with respect to the model $(HFin(H), \varepsilon, \emptyset)$ of the set theory. For example, $a \setminus b \rightleftharpoons \{x \mid x\varepsilon a$, but $\neg(x\varepsilon b)\}$.

We also note that the operations defined in e) and g) together provide the inverse of the operation defined in f). Since we consider only finite sets, almost all set-theoretical operations can be computed with these three operations. These operations are analogous to the operations $+1$ and $-1$.

**(5.15) Definition.** *The set extension of $\sigma$ is $set_\sigma = (\sigma^\in, set)$.*

The set-extension $rP_{\sigma^\in}$ of $rP_\sigma$ is said to be the set language and we describe its elements as set programs. We show how some well known relations and operations defined on sets can be computed by the use of $\sigma^{\in}$-type programs. We use the following notations: $\{u\} \rightleftharpoons \emptyset \circ u$; $true \rightleftharpoons \{\emptyset\}$; $false \rightleftharpoons \emptyset$.

**(5.16) Lemma.** *There is a set program which decides whether $y \in x$. Moreover, this program does not use the relation symbols $\in$ and atom.*

*Proof.* It is easy to verify that the following program is appropriate:

```
if c(x) = ∅ ∧ x \ {∅} = x → r := false □
   c(x) ≠ ∅ ∨ x \ {∅} ≠ x → u := c(x); z := x;
                     while z ≠ ∅ ∧ u ≠ y do z := z\{u};
                         if z = ∅ → skip □ z ≠ ∅ → u := c(z) fi od;
                     if u = y → r := true □ z = ∅ → r := false fi
fi.
```

□

**(5.17) Lemma.** *There is a set program which decides the relation atom. Moreover, the program does not use the symbol atom.*

*Proof.* It is easy to verify that the following program is suitable:

```
if c(x) ∈ x → r := false □ x = ∅ → r := false
                    □ c(x) ∉ x ∧ x ≠ ∅ → r := true fi.
```

□

**(5.18) Lemma.** *There is a set program which decides whether an element $x$ is a natural number or not (in the set theoretical sense).*

*Proof.* Let us take the following program:

```
y := x; r := true;
while y ≠ ∅ do u := y;
    while u ≠ ∅ do v := c(u); u := u\{v}; if y = v ∘ v → u := ∅ fi od;
    if y = v ∘ v → y := v □ y ≠ v ∘ v → y := ∅; r := false fi
od
```

This program is appropriate. □

**(5.19) Lemma.** *There is a program $p$ such that for any input set $x$ the program $p$ outputs the natural number $|x|$ (as a set).*

*Proof.* Let us take the following program

```
u := ∅;
if atom(x) → skip □
   ¬atom(x) → while x ≠ ∅ do u := u ∘ u; x := x\{c(x)} od
fi.
```

This program is appropriate. □

**(5.20) Lemma.** *There is a program $p$ such that for any pair of input sets $x$, $y$*

*the program p outputs the set $x \cup y$.*

*Proof.* Consider the following program:

**if** $atom(x) \rightarrow x := \emptyset$ **fi**; $z := x$;
**if** $atom(y) \rightarrow y := \emptyset$ **fi**;
**while** $y \neq \emptyset$ **do** $z := z \circ c(y)$; $y := y \setminus \{c(y)\}$ **od**.

This program is good. □

**(5.21) Lemma.** *There is a set program which computes $x \cap y$.*

*Proof.* This is trivial using the well known equality: $x \cap y = x \backslash (x \backslash y)$. □

Note that in our set language the choice function plays an important pragmatic role. Its use corresponds to the language SETL (see e.g. Shoenberg, Schwartz, Sharir [1981]). Without using the choice functions in programs the computation of well known set operations becomes more complicated, as can be seen in Pascal (see e.g. Alagić, Arbib [1978]).

**(5.22)** *Remark.* It is an open problem whether the extensions $set_\sigma$ and $list_\sigma$ have the same computational power, i.e. $set_\sigma \approx list_\sigma$.

It is an easy exercise to prove that any $list_\sigma$-computable relation is also $set_\sigma$-computable. To prove the other direction we can try to follow the proof of Theorem (5.11), but we have to overcome some technical problems. The first one appears when we try to code sets into lists. Our $list_\sigma$ extension contains elementary lists only, but the sets are hereditarily finite ones. Fortunately, the entire recursion theory is a part of the $list_\sigma$ extension so we can find an appropriate coding for sets. The second problem arises when we try to simulate the choice function $c$. We can try to simulate all the possible choice functions on a given set. Since all the sets are finite we can construct all these functions and can compute them in all cases. Thirdly, $c$ is a function, i.e. it gives the same value whenever evaluated for the same argument. This means that we have to save all the choice functions whenever used, which can be done by coding finite functions into lists. However, we cannot do anything with the fact that arbitrarily (finitely) many sets can appear while a program runs.

We note that in practice there is a "natural" ordering on the class of atoms, and this ordering induces a unique choice function on sets. Considering the extension $set'_\sigma$, which contains only those models within which this "natural" choice function is given, it is easy to prove that $list_\sigma \not\succeq set'_\sigma$. However, in general it may happen that $list_\sigma \not\succeq set_\sigma$.

## 5.3 Halting Problem for Extensions

Now we turn to investigate the halting problem in the case of the extended programming languages.

**(5.23) Definition.** *Let $(\delta, ext)$ be a fixed extension of a similarity type $\sigma$ and $rP_\delta$ be the extended programming language. Let $P \subseteq rP_\delta$ be a fixed programming language. The halting problem for the programming language $P$ with respect to finite and recursively presented models is decidable iff the set*

$$\{(p, a, \mathcal{A}) \mid \mathcal{A} \in FRPM_\sigma, p \in P \text{ and } a \in dom\ ext\text{-}Den_{\mathcal{A}}[\![p]\!]\}$$

*is recursive, i.e. it is decidable whether a program $p \in P$ starting with input $a$ terminates in all models $\mathcal{B} \in ext(\mathcal{A})$, where $\mathcal{A}$ (and not necesserily $\mathcal{B}$) is finite and recursively presented.*

One of the properties of extended programming languages is that the analogue of Corollary (4.23) does not hold for them in general.

**(5.24) Theorem.** *Let $\sigma$ be an arbitrary similarity type. The halting problem for the programming language $P_{\sigma^c}$ with respect to finite and recursively presented models is not decidable.*

*Proof.* By definition, for any model $\mathcal{A} \in Mod_\sigma$ its counter extension $counter(\mathcal{A})$ contains an isomorphic copy of the standard model $\mathcal{N}$ of arithmetic. It is known that the halting problem on $\mathcal{N}$ is undecidable. For example, we can consider a program $DE(\tau_1, \tau_2)$ of $P_{\sigma^s}$ which terminates only if a given Diophantine equation $\tau_1 = \tau_2$ is solvable (cf. Lemma (12.1)). But the solvability of this equation is undecidable (cf. Theorem (1.26)). □

Note that the Canonical Form Theorem (4.30) remains true even for the stack extension $rP_{\sigma^s}$ but with the difference that the correspondence between the programs of $rP_{\sigma^s}$ and the appropriate $p'$ and $p^*$ is not recursive. This non-recursiveness follows from Theorem (5.24) because in general it is undecidable whether the program $run(gr(p), h)$ is equal to **loop** or to **skip** . However, the correspondence becomes recursive in the case of Corollary (4.31) since the existence of two distinct values for $c$ and $d$ implies that $\neg one_\sigma(X)$ holds.

**(5.25) Theorem.** *Let $P^1_\sigma \subset P_{\sigma^s}$ contain those programs which use only one stack in each sort. The halting problem for the programming language $P^1_\sigma$ with respect to finite and recursively presented models is decidable.*

It is well known that the halting problem for the nondeterministic pushdown automata is decidable (see Aho, Ullman [1972]). It can be proved that the termination of a given program of $P^1_\sigma$ on a given recursively presented model can be recursively transferred into the halting problem for an appropriately defined push-down automaton. Therefore, by using this transformation the fact mentioned above implies Theorem (5.25).

It is interesting that if we are allowed to use only one stack in the programs then the statement of Theorem (5.24) changes into its opposite.

Chapter 6

# Program Schemas with Stacks

We have seen so far how the programming language $rP_\sigma$ can be augmented with new computational devices by the use of extension. From the viewpoint of computational power, as in Chapter 5, it is sufficient to augment the language $rP_\sigma$ with stacks. Therefore, for the theory it is sufficient to use the stack extension of $rP_\sigma$. However, the way the extension has been made does not limit the number of new devices usable in the programs. For example, according to Definition (5.1) infinitely many counters or stacks are allowed in the appropriate extension of $rP_\sigma$.

It is an interesting question how many stacks the programming language $rP_\sigma$ should be extended by in order to obtain a language of maximal computational power. In Section 6.1 we introduce several enlargements of $rP_\sigma$ which differ in the number of stacks we are allowed to use in the programs and we start to investigate how the enlargements obtained are related to each other from the viewpoint of computational power.

Section 6.2 is devoted to the deterministic programming languages with a finite number of stacks. It will be investigated whether nondeterministic programs can be simulated by deterministic ones. For this we introduce the notion of diagonalization. The diagonalization of program $p \in P$ ($\subseteq rP_{\sigma^s}$) is a deterministic program which enumerates all the possible outputs of the original program $p$ in some sense. It will be shown that $P_\sigma$ is not diagonalizable in general and it will not be so even if the usage of one stack will be allowed. The usage of at least two stacks should be allowed in the programming language $P$ in order to have a diagonalization for any program of $P$.

## 6.1 On the Number of Stacks

Up to now the extension has been introduced for infinitely many stacks, but now we restrict the number of stacks available in a program. In the first part of this section we deal with extensions of $rP_\sigma$ differing in the number of augmented stacks and with the possibility of testing whether the stacks are empty. Let $stack = (\sigma^s, stack)$ be as in Definition (5.9).

To distinguish between an arbitrary similarity type $\sigma$ and its stack-extension $\sigma^s$, let $V_\sigma$ and $V_s$ be the set of *sort* $\sigma$-sorted variables and the set of the *stack*-sorted variables, respectively, i.e. $V_s = \bigcup\{V_{d^s} \mid d \in sort\ \sigma\}$ or equivalently $V_s = \bigcup\{V_a \mid a \in sort\ \sigma^s)\}\backslash V_\sigma$.

According to the definition, the function *stack* associates a unique model $\mathcal{A}^s$ with any model $\mathcal{A} \in Mod_\sigma$. One would expect that if a fixed class of models is axiomatizable, say with a set $Ax$ of axioms, then its stack extension will also be so, i.e. $\{\mathcal{A}^s \mid \mathcal{A} \in Mod(Ax)\}$ will also be axiomatizable. However, this is not true, as it is shown in the following

**(6.1) Lemma.** *Let $\mathcal{A} \in Mod_\sigma$ and let $D$ be a non-principal ultrafilter on $\mathbb{N}$. Then there is no model $\mathcal{B} \in Mod_\sigma$ such that $\mathcal{B}^s$ isomorphic to $(\mathcal{A}^s)^{\mathbb{N}}/D$.*

*Proof.* Let us fix a sort $m \in sort\ \sigma$. For any $i \in \mathbb{N}$ let $b_i \in A_m$ be a fixed $m$-sorted element of the model $\mathcal{A}$. Define a sequence $d^i$ such that $d^0 \rightleftharpoons \langle b_0 \rangle$; $d^i \rightleftharpoons d^{i-1} \circ \langle b_i \rangle$ $(i \in \mathbb{N})$. It is obvious that $d \rightleftharpoons [\lambda i.(d^i)]_D$ is an element of the ultraproduct $(\mathcal{A}^s)^{\mathbb{N}}/D$. Let $e^0 \rightleftharpoons d$, $e^{j+1} \rightleftharpoons tail^m_{(\mathcal{A}^s)^{\mathbb{N}}/D}(e^j)$. Now let us consider the following set (for an arbitrary $j \in \mathbb{N}$):

$$\{i \mid e^j(i) = empty^m_{\mathcal{A}}\}.$$

This set is equivalent to the set $\{i \mid i \in \mathbb{N}, i < j\}$ which does not belong to the ultrafilter $D$. Therefore, for all $j \in \mathbb{N}$ $e^j \neq empty^m(\mathcal{A}^s)^{\mathbb{N}}/D$. However, in $\mathcal{B}^s$ such a $d$ does not exist. □

**(6.2) Corollary.** *Let $\mathcal{K} \subseteq Mod_\sigma$ be an axiomatizable class. Then the class*

$$stack(\mathcal{K}) \rightleftharpoons \bigcup\{stack(\mathcal{A}) | \mathcal{A} \in \mathcal{K}\}$$

*is not axiomatizable.*

*Proof.* For a contradiction, let us suppose that $stack(\mathcal{K})$ is an axiomatizable class of $\sigma^s$-type models. If so then this class is closed under ultraproducts. However, this is not the case according to Lemma (6.1). □

Now we define programming languages with different number of stacks. For the definition we could restrict the number of stack-sorted variables to the desired number of stacks. However, we select another possibility by introducing special programs from which the required program with the desired number of stacks can be built up.

**(6.3) Definition.** *For any sort $a \in sort\ \sigma$ let us fix an enumeration of $a^s$-sorted variables: $V_{a^s} \rightleftharpoons \{x^a_1, ..., x^a_n, ...\}$. For a given $H \subseteq rP_{\sigma^s}$ and for a given natural number $k \in \mathbb{N}$ let us define the following closure properties:*

*(i)* **skip** *and $v := \tau$ belong to $H$ for all $v \in V_\sigma$ and $\tau \in Term_\sigma$ such that $sort(v) = sort(\tau)$;*

*(ii) $v :=?$ belongs to $H$ for all $v \in V_\sigma$;*

*(iii)$^k$the programs*

$$\begin{array}{lcl} Empty_i^a & \rightleftharpoons & x_i^a := empty^a, \\ Push_i^a(\tau) & \rightleftharpoons & x_i^a := push^a(x_i^a, \tau), \\ Pop_i^a(v) & \rightleftharpoons & v := head^a(x_i^a, v);\ x_i^a := tail^a(x_i^a) \end{array}$$

*belong to H if* $a \in sort\,\sigma$, $0 < i \leq k$ *and* $sort(\tau) = sort(v) = a$;

*(iv) if* $p_1, p_2 \in H$ *and* $\phi_1, \phi_2 \in Open_\sigma$ *then* **if** $\phi_1 \to p_1 \Box \phi_2 \to p_2$ **fi** *and* **do** $\phi_1 \to p_1 \Box \phi_2 \to p_2$ **od** *belong to H;*

*(v)$^k$ if* $p_1, p_2 \in H$ *and* $\phi_1, \phi_2 \in Open_\sigma \cup \{x_i^a = empty^a \mid i \leq k, a \in sort\,\sigma\} \cup \{x_i^a \neq empty^a \mid i \leq k, a \in sort\,\sigma\}$ *then* **if** $\phi_1 \to p_1 \Box \phi_2 \to p_2$ **fi** *and* **do** $\phi_1 \to p_1 \Box \phi_2 \to p_2$ **od** *belong to H;*

*(vi) if* $p_1, p_2 \in H$ *then* $(p_1; p_2) \in H$.

*Let the programming languages* $P_\sigma^k$, $P_\sigma^{k,e}$, $rP_\sigma^k$, $rP_\sigma^{k,e}$ *be defined respectively as the minimal sets satisfying the closure properties as shown below*

$$\begin{array}{lcl} P_\sigma^k & \rightleftharpoons & (i) + (iii)^k + (iv) + (vi) \\ P_\sigma^{k,e} & \rightleftharpoons & (i) + (iii)^k + (v)^k + (vi) \\ rP_\sigma^k & \rightleftharpoons & (i) + (ii) + (iii)^k + (iv) + (vi) \\ rP_\sigma^{k,e} & \rightleftharpoons & (i) + (ii) + (iii)^k + (v)^k + (vi) \end{array}$$

*The superscripts k and e indicate that k stacks and the test of empty stacks are allowed, respectively.*

Observe that in the above definition, property (v)$^k$ ($k > 0$) is stronger than property (iv).

Instead of $x_i^a = empty^a$ we simply write $IsEmpty_i^a$. In the one-sorted case we omit the superscripts denoting the sorts. Note that sometimes we use the notations $Push_i(X)$ and $Pop_i(X)$ for a finite set $X$ of variables. This means that there is a given ordering $x_1,...,x_n$ on $X$ and

$$Push_i(X) \rightleftharpoons (1..k..n) : Push_i(x_k);$$
$$Pop_i(X) \rightleftharpoons (n..k..1) : Pop_i(x_k).$$

From the above definition we immediately have the following

**(6.4) Lemma.**

$$\begin{array}{ccccc} P_\sigma^k & \subset & P_\sigma^{k,e} & \subset & P_{\sigma^s} \\ \cap & & \cap & & \cap \\ rP_\sigma^k & \subset & rP_\sigma^{k,e} & \subset & rP_{\sigma^s} \end{array}$$

Since stacks are introduced as a new control structure, i.e. as a computational device and not as a data type, the meaning of a program can be defined straightforwardly in terms of denotations and traces.

**(6.5) Definition.** *For any program $p \in rP^k_\sigma$, model $\mathcal{A} \in Mod_\sigma$ and finite $X \supseteq var(p)$ let the meaning of $p$ in $\mathcal{A}$ be defined as follows:*

$$\begin{aligned} Den_{\mathcal{A}}[\![p]\!] &\rightleftharpoons stack\text{-}Den_{\mathcal{A}}[\![p]\!], \\ Den_{\mathcal{A}}[\![p, X]\!] &\rightleftharpoons stack\text{-}Den_{\mathcal{A}}[\![p, X]\!], \\ Trace_{\mathcal{A}}[\![p, X]\!] &\rightleftharpoons Trace_{\mathcal{A}^s}[\![p, X]\!]. \end{aligned}$$

**(6.6) Definition.** *Let $\sigma$ be a one-sorted similarity type which contains the similarity type of arithmetic. A model $\mathcal{A} \in Mod_\sigma$ is said to be arithmetical if it contains a submodel isomorphic to $\mathcal{N}$ and there is a function which codes the finite sequences of elements of $A$.*

More precisely, a model $\mathcal{A} \in Mod_\sigma$ is said to be arithmetical if $sort\,\sigma \rightleftharpoons \{s\}$ and $\sigma$ contains the following symbols: $+, * : s, s \to s$; $0, 1 :\to s$; $\beta : s, s, s \to s$; $(\cdot,\cdot)^\frown\cdot : s, s, s \to s$; $nat : s$ such that

(i) $(nat_{\mathcal{A}}, +_{\mathcal{A}}\restriction nat_{\mathcal{A}}, *_{\mathcal{A}}\restriction nat_{\mathcal{A}}, 0_{\mathcal{A}}, 1_{\mathcal{A}})$ is isomorphic to the standard model $\mathcal{N}$ of arithmetic;

(ii) $\mathcal{A} \models \forall n \forall a \forall x\; nat(n) \to$
$\exists! b \forall i < n\; (\beta(a, i, n) = \beta(b, i, n+1) \wedge \beta(b, n, n+1) = x \wedge (a, n)^\frown x = b)$
($i < n$ is a shorthand for $nat(i) \wedge \exists j(nat(j) \wedge i + j = n \wedge i \neq n)$.

Intuitively $\beta$ is a coding function for finite sequences: $\beta(a, i, n)$ is the $i$-th member of an $n$-long sequence coded by $a$. (ii) means that each sequence $a$ of length $n$ can be extended to an $(n+1)$-long sequence $b$ by adding a new element $x$ (as its $(n+1)$-th member). This sequence is coded by $(a, n)^\frown x$.

**(6.7) Theorem.** *Let $\mathcal{A} \in Mod_\sigma$ be an arithmetical model.*

*(A) Let $X \rightleftharpoons var(p)$. For an arbitrary $p \in rP_\sigma$, $Den_{\mathcal{A}}[\![p, X]\!]$ is first-order definable in $\mathcal{A}$.*

*(B) The $P_{\sigma^s}$ and $P_\sigma$-computable relations in $\mathcal{A}$ are the same. (Similarly the $rP_{\sigma^s}$ and $rP_\sigma$-computable relations in $\mathcal{A}$ are also the same.)*

*Proof.*

(A) We prove a stronger result. Let $g \in rG_\sigma$ and let

$$fin\text{-}Trace_{\mathcal{A}}[\![g, X]\!] \rightleftharpoons Trace_{\mathcal{A}}[\![g, X]\!] \cap (Val_{\mathcal{A}}[X] \times Label)^*$$

be the set of all finite traces of $g$ in $\mathcal{A}$. For an arbitrary transition graph $g \in rG_\sigma$, $fin\text{-}Trace_{\mathcal{A}}[\![g, X]\!]$ is first-order definable in $\mathcal{A}$ in the following sense. Let $X \rightleftharpoons var(g)$. Let us suppose that $Label \subseteq nat_{\mathcal{A}}$. There is a relation $Q \subseteq Val_{\mathcal{A}}[X, l] \times nat_{\mathcal{A}}$ such that

(i) $Q$ is first-order definable in $\mathcal{A}$;
(ii) $fin\text{-}Trace_{\mathcal{A}}[\![g, X]\!] = \{S \in (Val_{\mathcal{A}}[X \cup \{l\}])^* | \exists(k,t) \in Q,\ |s| = t, \forall i < t, \forall v \in X \cup \{l\} :\ S(i)(v) = \beta(k(v), i, t)\}$.

Using $Q$, Definition (4.11) and Theorem (4.13) we can conclude that $Den_{\mathcal{A}}[\![p, X]\!] = Den_{\mathcal{A}}[\![gr(p), X]\!]$ is first-order definable. To construct such a $Q$ we can simply rewrite Definition (4.10):

$$Q \rightleftharpoons \{(k,t) \mid \beta(k(l), 0, t) \in node(g), \forall i < t-1 \\ onestep_g(\{\beta(k(v), i, t) \mid v \in X \cup \{l\}\}, \{\beta(k(v), i+1, t) \mid v \in X \cup \{l\}\})\}$$

By using (ii) of the definition of arithmetic models one can check that the above $Q$ is appropriate.

(B) By using the coding function $\beta$ the contents of stacks can be represented by appropriate codes which belong to $A$. Indeed, for any stack variable $S_i$ let $c_i$ and $l_i$ be two new variables. The variable $l_i$ means the length of $S_i$ and for any $k < l_i$, $\beta(c_i, k, l_i)$ is the $k$-th element of $S_i$. Let $O_c$ be a code for the empty sequence.
(i) Let $p \rightleftharpoons Empty_i$. Then $p$ can be substituted by the program $c_i := O_c$; $l_i := 0$.
(ii) Let $p \rightleftharpoons Push_i(\tau)$. Then $p$ can be substituted by the following program:

$$l_i := l_i + 1; c_i := (c_i, l_i)\frown\tau.$$

(iii) Let $\phi \rightleftharpoons IsEmpty_i$. Then $\phi$ can be substituted by $l_i = 0$.
(iv) Finally let $p \rightleftharpoons Pop_i(x)$. Then $p$ can be substituted by the following program:

**if** $l_i > 1 \rightarrow l := 0; c := O_c$
    **while** $l < (l_i - 1)$ **do** $c := (c, l)\frown\beta(c_i, l, l_i)$; $l := l + 1$ **od** ;
    $x := \beta(c_i, l, l_i); c_i := c; l_i := l;$
$\square$
$l_i = 1 \rightarrow l_i := 0; x := \beta(c_i, 0, 1); c_i := O_c$
**fi** .

□

**(6.8) Theorem.** *Let $\sigma$ be a one-sorted similarity type. For all $k \in \mathbb{N}$ and $\mathcal{A} \in Mod_\sigma$ the $P_\sigma^{k,e}$-computable relations are the same as the $P_\sigma^k$-computable ones in $\mathcal{A}$.*

*Proof.* It is obvious that any $P_\sigma^k$-computable relation is also $P_\sigma^{k,e}$-computable. The opposite direction, i.e. the statement of the theorem, is not trivial. Moreover, we note that due to Theorem (5.24) the correspondence between $P_\sigma^{k,e}$-computable and $P_\sigma^k$-computable relations is not recursive. This means that there is no recursive function which forms a correspondence between $P_\sigma^{k,e}$ and

$P^k_\sigma$ such that to each program $p \in P^{k,e}_\sigma$ it assigns a program $p' \in P^k_\sigma$ which terminates for the same inputs as $p$ does.

Our proof is based on a concrete transformation which provides for each program $p \in P^{k,e}_\sigma$ the required program from $P^k_\sigma$. This transformation is based on rewriting the contents of the stacks for which we introduce two different markers $W_1$ and $W_2$. Marker $W_1$ is pushed on to the bottom of the stack and, after pushing a value, the other marker $W_2$ must be pushed down on to the stack, thus taking out an element from the obtained stack. If this element is $W_2$ then a "real" element follows, if it is $W_1$ then the stack is empty.

Now we define precisely the transformation in question by giving the following transformation rules. Let $p \in P^{k,e}_\sigma$ be arbitrary. Let $\widehat{p}$ be the program obtained from $p$ by the use of the following transformation rules:

(i) $Push_i(\tau)$ is replaced by $Push_i(\tau); Push_i(W_2)$,
(ii) $Pop_i(x)$ is replaced by

$$Pop_i(U_i);\ \textbf{if}\ U_i = W_1 \rightarrow Push_i(W_1) \,\Box\, U_i \neq W_1 \rightarrow Pop_i(x)\ \textbf{fi}\ ,$$

(iii) **if** $\alpha_1 \rightarrow p_1 \,\Box\, \alpha_2 \rightarrow p_2$ **fi** is replaced by

$$((1..i..k) : Pop_i(U_i);\ Push_i(U_i));$$
$$\textbf{if}\ \alpha_1[(U_i = W_1)/IsEmpty_i]^k_1 \rightarrow \widehat{p}_1 \,\Box\, \alpha_2[(U_i = W_1)/IsEmpty_i]^k_1 \rightarrow \widehat{p}_2\ \textbf{fi}\ ,$$

(iv) **do** $\alpha_1 \rightarrow p_1 \,\Box\, \alpha_2 \rightarrow p_2$ **od** is replaced by

$$((1..i..k) : Pop_i(U_i); Push_i(U_i));$$
$$\textbf{do}\ \alpha_1[(U_i = W_1)/IsEmpty_i]^k_1 \rightarrow \widehat{p}_1; ((1..i..k) : Pop_i(U_i); Push(U_i))\Box$$
$$\alpha_2[(U_i = W_1)/IsEmpty_i]^k_1 \rightarrow \widehat{p}_2; (i : 1..k) : [Pop_i(U_i); Push(U_i)]\textbf{od}\ ,$$

where each set of variable $U_i$ is a new copy of the set $W_1$ of variables occurring in $Init_\sigma(X)$ where $X \rightleftharpoons var(p) \cap V_\sigma$.

In order to have program equivalence with respect to the entire set of variables, the values of the auxiliary variables are to be saved. Therefore, we take an appropriate program *Move* to save these values and another program *Remove* to return the same values. We use the part of the first stack below $W_1$ to save the values of auxiliary variables. Without this, the equivalence between $p$ and $T(p)$ (defined later) would hold only with respect to mod $var(p)$. So take

$$Move \rightleftharpoons (1..i..k) : Push_1(U_i)); Push_1(W_1); Push_1(W_2);$$
$$Remove \rightleftharpoons Pop_1(U_1);\ \textbf{while}\ U_1 = W_2\ \textbf{do}\ Pop_1(U_1); Pop_1(U_1)\ \textbf{od}\ ;$$
$$Pop_1(W_2);\ Pop_1(W_1);\ (k..i..1) : Pop_1(U_i).$$

Finally let

$$T(p) \rightleftharpoons \textbf{if}\ one_\sigma(X) \rightarrow \textbf{if}\ \Box(h \in TF_\sigma) : one_\sigma(X,h) \rightarrow run(gr(p),h)\ \textbf{fi}\ \Box$$
$$\neg one_\sigma(X) \rightarrow Move; Init_\sigma(X);$$
$$((1..i..k) : Push_i(W_1));\ \widehat{p};\ Remove$$
$$\textbf{fi}\ .$$

We remark that the usage of $run(gr(p), h)$ makes the correspondence between $p$ and $T(p)$ non-recursive. The appropriateness of the program $T(p)$ is shown by the following

**Claim.** For any $p \in P_\sigma^{k,e}$, $Den_{\mathcal{A}}[\![p]\!] = Den_{\mathcal{A}}[\![T(p)]\!]$.

*Proof.* Let us see what we get by the above transformation. If the formula $one_\sigma(X, h)$ holds then $T(p)$ skips iff $p$ does so. If $one_\sigma(X)$ does not hold then first we save the values of all the auxiliary variables in the first stack. Then $Init_\sigma(X)$ generates two different values for the markers $W_1$ and $W_2$. After this $W_1$ is pushed down into all the stacks. In the end $\hat{p}$ simulates the computation of $p$. For example, if $p$ sometimes reaches a state in which the stacks have the contents shown in Fig. 6.1, then within the appropriate point of its path $\widehat{p}$ has its stacks with the contents shown in Fig. 6.2.

At the very end, *Remove* restores the saved values of new variables. This proves the claim and thus the theorem itself. □

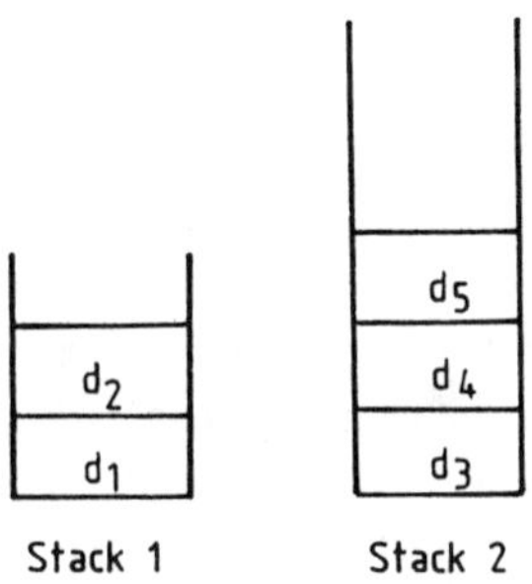


**Fig. 6.1.** The contents of the original stacks

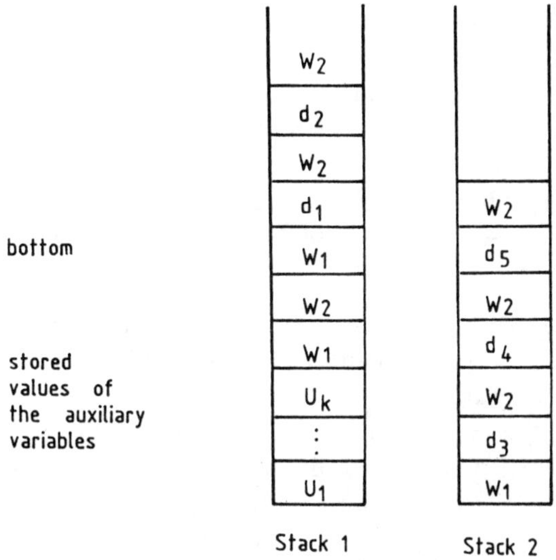


**Fig. 6.2.** The contents of the stacks of the transformed program. The first stack contains all the auxiliary variables and then a bottom marker $W_1$. All the other stacks contain only the bottom marker $W_1$

This theorem is not true for many-sorted similarity types because the program $Init_\sigma(X)$ provides one pair of distinct values only for a fixed sort. To repeat the above proof for a many-sorted similarity type $\sigma$ we need two distinct values $w_1^a$ and $w_2^a$ for each sort $a \in sort\,\sigma$. Whereas, if there are infinitely many stacks the theorem remains true.

Let both $P_\sigma^{ne} \subset P_{\sigma^\bullet}$ and $rP_\sigma^{ne} \subset rP_{\sigma^\bullet}$ denote the maximal programming language in which only formulas of $Open_\sigma$ can be used as guards and the emptiness of the stacks cannot be directly checked. That is, $P_\sigma^{ne} = \{P_\sigma^k | k \in \mathbb{N}\}$ and $rP_\sigma^{ne} = \{rP_\sigma^k | k \in \mathbb{N}\}$.

**(6.9) Theorem.** *Let $\sigma$ be an arbitrary many-sorted similarity type. In any model $\mathcal{A} \in Mod_\sigma$ the $P_\sigma^{ne}$- and the $P_{\sigma^\bullet}$-computable relations are the same. This implies that $P_{\sigma^\bullet} \approx \bigcup\{P_\sigma^k \mid k \in \mathbb{N}\}$. Similarly, in any model $\mathcal{A} \in Mod_\sigma$ the $rP_\sigma^{ne}$- and the $rP_{\sigma^\bullet}$-computable relations are the same. This implies that $rP_{\sigma^\bullet} \approx \bigcup\{rP_\sigma^k \mid k \in \mathbb{N}\}$.*

*Proof.* If we have a sufficient number of stacks at our disposal then we can use stacks of other sorts instead of those stacks of whose sort only one unique element exists in the Herbrand universe. This replacement can be done, since only the number of the elements of these sorts in the stacks are of interest. □

**(6.10) Theorem.** *Let $\sigma$ be a one-sorted similarity type. In any model $\mathcal{A} \in Mod_\sigma$ for all $k \geq 2$ the $P_\sigma^{k+1,e}$-computable relations are also $P_\sigma^k$ computable ones.*

*Proof.* For the sake of convenience we prove only the case $k = 2$. According to Theorem (6.8) it is sufficient to show that $P_\sigma^{3,e} \approx P_\sigma^{2,e}$. This can be proved by using the above method. One can write a program which stores all values into a chosen stack together with a marker. This marker is just the index of the real stack. By using another stack all the statements $Empty_i$, $Pop_i$, $Push_i$ and the test $IsEmpty_i$ can be simulated. □

**(6.11) Theorem.** *Let $\sigma$ be an arbitrary (many-sorted) similarity type. For all models $\mathcal{A} \in Mod_\sigma$ and for all $k \geq 2$, any $P_\sigma^{k,e}$-computable relation is also $P_\sigma^2$-computable in $\mathcal{A}$.*

*Proof.* By the use of Theorems (6.8) and (6.9) we obtain $P_\sigma^{k,e} \lesssim P_\sigma^{ne} \approx P_{\sigma^\bullet}$. It follows from Theorems (6.9) and (6.10) that for any one sorted similarity type $\sigma$, $P_{\sigma^\bullet} \approx P_\sigma^2$.

Now we sketch how this result can be extended to the many-sorted case. First we have to modify the formula $one_\sigma(X)$ and the program $Init_\sigma(X)$. Let $a \in sort\ \sigma$ and let $one_\sigma^a(X)$ be an open $\sigma$-type formula such that $\mathcal{A} \models one_\sigma^a(X)[k]$ iff $|_\mathcal{A}H_a(k)| \leq 1$. Let $Init'_\sigma(X)$ be a program belonging to $P_\sigma$ such that $Init'_\sigma(X)$ provides two distinct values for variable $w_1^a$ and $w_2^a$ for each sort $a \in sort\ \sigma$ for which $\neg one_\sigma^a(X)$ holds. It is obvious that the formulas $one_\sigma^a(X)$ ($a \in sort\ \sigma$) and the program $Init'_\sigma(X)$ can be constructed using the same ideas as in the proofs of Lemma (4.25) and Theorem (4.26).

When the formula $\neg one_\sigma^a(X)$ holds for all $a \in sort\ \sigma$, then by definition $Init'_\sigma(X)$ provides a pair of different values in each sort, i.e. in all data types. In this case the method used in the proof of Theorem (6.8) is appropriate here too.

Let us suppose that at least for one sort, say $a \in sort\ \sigma$, the formula $\neg one_\sigma^a(X)$ holds. Then $Init'_\sigma(X)$ provides two distinct elements of $A_a$, and with respect to the sort $a$ two stacks are equivalent to infinitely many stacks. Therefore, at our disposal there are infinitely many new stacks to code those stacks in the sort of which there are no two distinct values. In this case we can code a stack with the number of its elements.

In the case when for all $a \in sort\ \sigma$ the formula $one^a_\sigma(X)$ holds (i.e. $one_\sigma(X)$ holds) then we can use the programs $run(gr(p), h)$ as in the proof of Theorem (6.8).

We leave the elaboration of the details to the reader. □

**(6.12)** *Remark.* From the above, the question arises of whether the programming family $P^{1,e}$ has definitely more computational power than the family $P^1$. Note that for any similarity type $\sigma$ if there are at least two distinct elements then $P^{1,e}_\sigma \approx P^1_\sigma$. However, if there is at least one sort for which there are not two distinct elements then the stack will work as a counter with respect to this sort. Therefore, $P^{1,e}_\sigma$ will be equal to $P^{1,1c}_\sigma$, where $P^{1,1c}_\sigma$ denotes the set of all programs which can use one stack with the possibility to check its emptiness and only one counter-type variable. So the above question can be reformulated as follows: is $P^{1,1c} > P^1$ true for an appropriately chosen $\sigma$? But this question has been answered positively by Harnik [1975]. Note that according to Theorem (6.8), however, the answer is no for the one-sorted similarity types.

## 6.2 Deterministic Programming Languages

The corresponding deterministic sublanguage can be obtained from any programming language introduced in the previous chapter by allowing only deterministic choice instead of nondeterministic choice in the **if** ...**fi** and **do**...**od** constructs.

**(6.13) Definition.** *Let det-$P^n_\sigma$ be the minimal subset of $P^n_\sigma$ for which the following hold:*

*(i)* **skip** , $v := \tau$, $Pop^d_i(x)$, $Push^d_i(x)$ *and* $Empty^d_i$ *belongs to det-$P^n_\sigma$ (for $0 < i \leq n$);*

*(ii) det-$P^n_\sigma$ is closed under composition;*

*(iii) if $p_1, p_2 \in$ det-$P^n_\sigma$, $\phi_1, \phi_2 \in Open_\sigma$ and $\exists x(\phi_1 \wedge \phi_2)$ is logically false (i.e. in every model the formulas $\phi_1$ and $\phi_2$ cannot be true at the same time) then*

**if** $\phi_1 \rightarrow p_1 \square\ \phi_2 \rightarrow p_2$ **fi** *and*

**do** $\phi_1 \rightarrow p_1 \square\ \phi_2 \rightarrow p_2$ **od** *also belong to det-$P^n_\sigma$.*

*The elements of det-$P^n_\sigma$ are called deterministic programs.*

We remark that these programs are syntactically deterministic. A program can be called semantically deterministic if, for each model $\mathcal{A} \in Mod_\sigma$, $Den_{\mathcal{A}}[\![p]\!]$ is a partial function.

**(6.14) Definition.** *For any $P \subseteq P^n_\sigma$ let det-$P \rightleftharpoons$ (det-$P^n_\sigma$) $\cap\ P$.*

One would like to simulate programs of $P$ by the use of deterministic programs of *det-P*. However, this cannot be simply done because any deterministic program has at most one output value for each input value. Therefore we could augment the language *det-*$P_\sigma$ by a new instruction **output** $\tau$. By the use of this new instruction arbitrary output values can be obtained during even a single computational path. We choose another way to multiply the output values which does not require an auxiliary instruction.

**(6.15) Definition.** *Let $P \subseteq rP^n_\sigma$. The programming language $P$ is called diagonalizable iff for all programs $p \in P$ there are two programs $I(p), R(p) \in$ det-P such that for all $\mathcal{A} \in Mod_\sigma$:*

$$Den[\![p]\!] = \bigcup_{i \in \mathbb{N}} Den[\![I(p); (1..j..i) : R(p)]\!] \quad (\text{mod } var(p)),$$

*where $I(p)$ and $R(p)$ are called the initialization and the repetitive parts of p respectively. The pair $(I(p), R(p))$ is called the diagonalization of p in det-P.*

To make the definition below more understandable, we suggest identifying $I(p)$ with that part of the program p which extends to the point where the first output value appears. Similarly let $R(p)$ be identified with the part of the program $p$ between two successive output values. The following statement is immediate from the definition.

**(6.16) Lemma.** *If $(I(p), R(p))$ is a diagonalization of p in det-P then*

$$dom\, Den[\![p, var(p)]\!] = dom\, Den[\![I(p), var(p)]\!].$$

**(6.17) Theorem.** *For any $n \geq 2$ the programming language $P^n_\sigma$ is diagonalizable.*

*Proof.* As we have seen in Theorem (6.11) $P^2_\sigma \approx P^n_\sigma$ for any $n \geq 2$. From Theorem (6.9) it is obvious that $P_{\sigma^\bullet} = \cup\{P^n_\sigma \mid n \in \mathbb{N}\}$. Thus $P^n_\sigma \approx P_{\sigma^\bullet}$ for every $n \geq 2$. Therefore, we prove the theorem for the programming language $P_{\sigma^\bullet}$, which allows the usage of countably many stacks. By using several stacks as counters we make the entire arithmetic and all the recursive functions computable.

Let $p \in P^2_\sigma$ be fixed. We have to use Theorems (8.15) and (8.21) to construct $I(p)$ and $R(p)$. Let $X \rightleftharpoons var(p)$ and $F \subseteq (X \to Term_\sigma) \times Open_\sigma$ be as in Theorem (8.15). If $F = \emptyset$ then the program $p$ never terminates. In this case we can simply take $I(p) \rightleftharpoons$ **loop** and $R(p)$ as arbitrary. If $F \neq \emptyset$ then there is a recursive enumeration $f : \mathbb{N} \to F$. Let $n$ be a new variable. By using the fact that all recursive functions are computable by $P^2_\sigma$-programs, we can apply Theorem (8.21). This means that there are $P^2_\sigma$-programs which can evaluate terms and open formulas. Let $R(p)$ be such a program, which evaluates the open formula $\pi_2(f(n))$ and which, if the open formula is not true, increases $n$ by 1 until the formula first becomes true. In that case $R(p)$ continues its running with the evaluation of the terms $\pi_1(f(n-1))(x)$ for all $x \in X$. Then $R(p)$ terminates. $I(p)$ initializes all the auxiliary variables necessary to simulate arithmetic and then it takes $n := 0$ and runs like $R(p)$. □

**(6.18) Corollary.** *In any model $\mathcal{A} \in Mod_\sigma$ the $P^2_\sigma$-computable relations are also det-$P^2_\sigma$-computable.*

*Proof.* Follows from (6.16) and (6.17). □

Let $\sigma$ be a one-sorted similarity type containing the following symbols:

(a) $g, h : d \to d$;
(b) $\rho : d$.

Let us take the following two $P_\sigma$ programs:

$Gen_y \rightleftharpoons$ **if** $one_\sigma(x) \to$ **skip** $\Box$
$\neg one_\sigma(x) \to Init_\sigma(\{x\});\ t_1 := W_1;\ t_2 := W_2;\ y := x;$
**while** $t_1 \neq t_2$ **do** $y := g(y) \Box y := h(y) \Box t_1 := t_2$ **od**
**fi** .

$Leaftest \rightleftharpoons Gen_y;$ **if** $\rho(y) \to$ **skip** $\Box \neg\rho(y) \to$ **loop** **fi** .

Informally the program *Leaftest* is a search performed on the binary tree shown in Fig. 6.3.

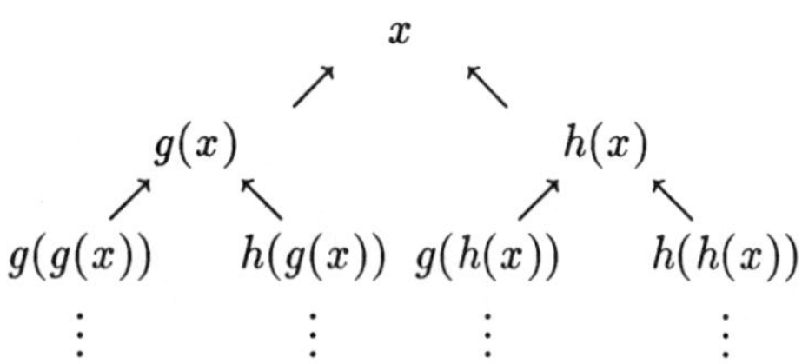


**Fig. 6.3** Leaftest

*Leaftest* searches on this tree in order to find a node whose value makes the predicate $\rho$ true. If such a node $y$ is found *Leaftest* returns $y$ as its output value, otherwise the program runs forever. Note that *Leaftest* is an important tool in comparative schematology introduced by Paterson, Hewitt [1970].

Let $Lf \rightleftharpoons dom\, Den_{\mathcal{A}}[\![Leaftest, \{x\}]\!]$. It is an easy exercise to check the following equivalence:

$$Lf = \Big\{a \big| \exists f_1 ... \exists f_n\ f_i \text{ is either } g \text{ or } h \text{ and } \mathcal{A} \models \rho\Big(f_n(f_{n-1}(...f_1(x)...))\Big)[a]\Big\}.$$

**(6.19) Lemma.** *The set $Lf$ is not computable in det-$P_\sigma$.*

*Proof.* This theorem was first stated and proved in Paterson, Hewitt [1970] (as Theorem 1) for a programming language which does not allow the use of the equation symbol. However, the original proof works in our case as well, because it is based on the fact that in a *det-*$P_\sigma$-program only a fixed number of values can be stored. □

**(6.20) Corollary.** *The programming language* $P_\sigma$ *is not diagonalizable.*

*Proof.* For a contradiction, let us suppose that *Leaftest* has a diagonalization in *det-*$P_\sigma$, i.e.

$$Den_{\mathcal{A}}[\![Leaftest]\!] = \bigcup_{i \in \mathbb{N}} Den_{\mathcal{A}}[\![I(Leaftest);\ (1..j..i) : R(Leaftest)]\!].$$

Take $PLt \rightleftharpoons I(Leaftest)$. Clearly, $PLt \in det\text{-}P_\sigma$ and

$$x \in dom\,(Den_{\mathcal{A}}[\![PLt, \{x\}]\!]) = dom\,(Den_{\mathcal{A}}[\![Leaftest, \{x\}]\!])$$

iff $x \in Lf$. Hence $PLt$ computes $Lf$ in *det-*$P_\sigma$, which contradicts Lemma (6.19). □

We note that the programming language $P_\sigma^1$ is not diagonalizable either. However, for the proof we need some methods which will be developed in Chapter 7, so we formulate this statement only in Chapter 7 as Corollary (7.23).

Chapter 7

# Computability

The theory of computability deals with the formal characterization of the "effectively computable" functions and relations. Different pieces of machinery, such as recursive functions, register machines, and normal algorithms, have been proposed for this aim. Programming languages provide a new technique for the formalization of computability, and at the same time they make it possible to deal with the characterization of the computable functions and relations adequately within the programming theory.

In this chapter we use the programming languages introduced so far to describe the main properties of computability. Almost all approaches consider numerical computations, i.e. the computation over the standard model of arithmetic. In contrast to these approaches, in Section 7.1 we define computability over arbitrary models and provide its general characterization. Among other things, we show what type of closure properties hold for computable relations. A generalization of recursive relation is also introduced and studied. Section 7.2 is devoted to the comparative analysis of the different families of programming languages. Moreover a generalization of Church's thesis is given for the case of computation over arbitrary first-order structures.

## 7.1 Computability over First-Order Structures

Computability is one of the basic notions of programming theory, which we define by the use of the $\sigma$-type programming languages for the relations of an arbitrary (many-sorted) $\sigma$-type model. We recall Definitions (5.5)(b) and (6.5):

**(7.1) Definition.** *Let us fix an arbitrary model $\mathcal{A} \in Mod_\sigma$ and let $P \subseteq rP_{\sigma^s}$ be arbitrary. A $W$-type relation $\rho \subseteq Val_{\mathcal{A}}[W]$ is said to be $P$-computable in $\mathcal{A}$ iff there is a program $p \in P$ and a valuation $k \in Val_{\mathcal{A}}[V \setminus W]$ such that for all valuations $a \in Val_{\mathcal{A}}[W]$*

$$a \in \rho \text{ iff } k + a \in dom\, Den_{\mathcal{A}}[\![p]\!].$$

*The set of all many-sorted relations which are $P$-computable in $\mathcal{A}$ is denoted by $P(\mathcal{A})$.*

Roughly speaking, a relation $\rho$ is $P$-computable in a model $\mathcal{A}$ iff there is a program $p \in P$ such that the set of inputs, for which the program $p$ starting with empty stacks has at least one terminating path, is just the set $\rho$ (this is true, since $|ext(\mathcal{A})| = 1$).

Let us suppose that a relation $\rho$ is $P$-computable and $p$ and $k$ are the corresponding program and parameter and $var(p) = W$. Let $W'$ be a copy of $W$. One can prove that $W$ can be substituted by $W'$ such that the new program computes the relation $\rho[W'/W]$ with parameter $k[W' : W]$.

**(7.2) Lemma.** *Let $P \subseteq rP_{\sigma^\bullet}$ be closed under the properties (i),(iv) and (vi) of Definition (6.3). Let $W \rightleftharpoons var(p) \cap V_\sigma$. Then for any program $p \in P$ the relation $Den_{\mathcal{A}}[\![p, W]\!]$ is $P$-computable.*

*Proof.* Let $p \in P$ be fixed. Let $W'$ be a new copy of $W$. Let us consider the following program $p' \rightleftharpoons p; \mathbf{if}\ \ W \neq W' \ \rightarrow \mathbf{loop\ fi}$ and fix a valuation $k \in Val_{\mathcal{A}}$. It is clear that for arbitrary valuations a $\in Val_{\mathcal{A}}[W]$ and $b \in Val_{\mathcal{A}}[W']$

$$k + (a + b) \in dom(Den_{\mathcal{A}}[\![p']\!]) \quad \text{iff} \quad a + b \in Den_{\mathcal{A}}[\![p, W]\!].$$

□

**(7.3) Corollary.** *Let the programming language $P$ be equal to any of $P_\sigma$, $rP_\sigma$, $P^{k,e}_\sigma$, $P^k_\sigma$, $rP^k_\sigma$ or $rP^{k,e}_\sigma$. Then for every program $p \in P$ the denotation of $p$ is $P$-computable in every model $\mathcal{A} \in Mod_\sigma$.*

Further on if $P = P^{k,e}_\sigma$ then instead of $P^{k,e}_\sigma$-computability we simply say $k$-computability, indicating the computability with $k$ stacks (including the $Empty_i$-test). Similarly we refer to $r$-$k$-computability instead of $rP^{k,e}_\sigma$-computability. In the case of $k = 0$ we speak about computability and $r$-computability instead of 0- and $r$-0-computability.

Let $EmptyAll \rightleftharpoons \mathbf{do}\ (d \in sort\ \sigma; 1..j..k) : \neg IsEmpty^d_j \rightarrow Pop^d_j(t_d)\ \mathbf{od}$ , where $t_d$ is a new variable symbol for each sort $d$.

**(7.4) Theorem.** *The set of $k$-computable and the set of $r$-$k$-computable relations are closed under intersection, union and product.*

*Proof.* Let $\mathcal{A} \in Mod_\sigma$ be an arbitrary but fixed model and let $W \subseteq V_\sigma$ be also fixed and finite and let $\rho_1, \rho_2 \subseteq Val_{\mathcal{A}}[W]$ be two $W$-type relations on $A$. Suppose that $\rho_1$ and $\rho_2$ are $k$-computable by programs $p_1, p_2 \in P^{k,e}_\sigma$, with parameters $k_1$ and $k_2$, respectively. Let $Z \rightleftharpoons var(p_1) \cap var(p_2) \cap V_\sigma$. We may suppose that $Z \subseteq W$ and for any $a \in Val_{\mathcal{A}}[W]$ and $i = 1, 2$:

$$a \in \rho_i \quad \text{iff} \quad k_i + a \in dom\ Den_{\mathcal{A}}[\![p_i]\!].$$

(i) To prove the closure under intersection let $Z'$ be a copy of $Z$ disjoint from $var(p_1) \cup var(p_2)$. Take the following program

$$p \rightleftharpoons Z' := Z;\ p_1;\ EmptyAll;\ Z := Z';\ p_2.$$

The execution of program $p$ starts with the execution of the program $p_1$ and then the program $p_2$ runs with a slight modification. To save the values of the common variables of $p_1$ and $p_2$ we use $Z'$. To ensure the starting of program $p_2$ with empty stacks we use the subprogram *EmptyAll*. Now let $k \rightleftharpoons k_1 + (k_2\restriction_{var(p_2)})$. One can prove that for any $a \in Val_{\mathcal{A}}[W]$: $a \in \rho_1 \cap \rho_2$ iff $k + a \in dom\ Den_{\mathcal{A}}[\![p]\!]$.

(ii) To prove the closure under union take the following program

$$p \rightleftharpoons \mathbf{if}\ true\ \rightarrow p_1\ \Box\ true \rightarrow p_2\ \mathbf{fi}\ .$$

Take $k \rightleftharpoons k_1 + (k_2\restriction_{var(p_2)})$. It is clear that for any

$$a \in Val_{\mathcal{A}}[W] : a \in \rho_1 \cup \rho_2 \quad \text{iff} \quad k + a \in dom\ Den_{\mathcal{A}}[\![p]\!].$$

(iii) Let $W_1, W_2 \subseteq V_\sigma$ be such that $W_1 \cap W_2 = \emptyset$ and suppose that $\rho_i \subseteq Val_{\mathcal{A}}[W_i]$, $i = 1, 2$. Let $p_1$ and $p_2$ be two programs such that $var(p_1) \cap var(p_2) \cap V_\sigma = \emptyset$ and for some valuations $k_1,\ k_2$, let $a \in \rho_i$ iff $k_i + a \in Den_{\mathcal{A}}[\![p_i]\!]$ $(i = 1, 2)$. Take $k \rightleftharpoons k_1 + k_2\restriction_{var(p_2)}$ and

$$p \rightleftharpoons p_1;\ EmptyAll;\ p_2,$$

where the program *EmptyAll* empties all the stacks which are either in $p_1$ or in $p_2$. Clearly $k + a \in dom\ Den_{\mathcal{A}}[\![p]\!]$ iff $a \in \rho_1 \times \rho_2$.

□

**(7.5) Theorem.**

*(A) Let $\mathcal{A} \in Mod_\sigma$ be an arbitrary but fixed model and let us suppose that for any finite $Y \subseteq V_\sigma$ there exists a program $any(Y) \in P_\sigma^k$ such that "for all valuations $a \in Val_{\mathcal{A}}$ and $c \in Val_{\mathcal{A}}[Y]$ there is a valuation $b \in Val_{\mathcal{A}}$ such that $(a, b) \in Den_{\mathcal{A}}[\![any(Y)]\!]$ and $b\restriction_Y = c$." Then the set of k-computable relations in $\mathcal{A}$ is closed under composition and under reflexive and transitive closure. Moreover, $rng\ Den_{\mathcal{A}}[\![p, var(p) \cap V_\sigma]\!]$ is k-computable for any k and $p \in P_\sigma^k$.*

*(B) The set of r-k-computable relations is closed under composition and under reflexive and transitive closure. Moreover, for any $p \in rP_\sigma^k$,*

$$rng\ Den_{\mathcal{A}}[\![p, var(p) \cap V_\sigma]\!]$$

*is r-k-computable.*

*Proof.*

(A)(i) To prove closure under composition let $\rho_1$ be an $(X, Y)$-type relation and $\rho_2$ be a $(Y, Z)$-type relation in $\mathcal{A}$. Let us suppose that for $i = 1, 2$ the program $p_i$ $(\in rP_\sigma^k)$ computes $\rho_i$ with parameter $k_i \in Val_{\mathcal{A}}[var(p_i)]$, i.e. if $a \in Val_{\mathcal{A}}[X]$, $b \in Val_{\mathcal{A}}[Y]$ and $c \in Val_{\mathcal{A}}[Z]$:

$$(a,b) \in \rho_1 \quad \text{iff} \quad k_1 + a + b \in dom\ Den_{\mathcal{A}}[\![p_1, X \cup Y]\!];$$
$$(b,c) \in \rho_2 \quad \text{iff} \quad k_2 + b + c \in dom\ Den_{\mathcal{A}}[\![p_2, Y \cup Z]\!].$$

We can suppose that $var(p_1) \cap var(p_2) \cap V_\sigma \subseteq Y$. Let $Y'$ be a copy of $Y$ disjoint from $X$ and $Z$. Take the following program

$$q \rightleftharpoons any(Y);\ Y' := Y;\ p_1;\ Y := Y';\ EmptyAll;\ p_2.$$

The program $q$ starts with a valuation for $(X, Z)$ and first generates (by using $any(Y)$) a valuation for $Y$ to be a candidate for an intput vector of $p_1$ and $p_2$. This is necessary, since $k$ below fixes the input values for $Y$. Take $k \rightleftharpoons k_1 + k_2\lceil_{var(p_2)}$. For any $a \in Val_{\mathcal{A}}[X]$ and $c \in Val_{\mathcal{A}}[Z]$ we have

$$a + c \in \rho_1 \circ \rho_2 \text{ iff } k + (a + c) \in dom\ Den_{\mathcal{A}}[\![q, Y \cup Z]\!].$$

(ii) To prove reflexive and transitive closure let $Y$ be a copy of $X$ and fix an $(X,Y)$-type relation $\rho$ in $\mathcal{A}$. Let us suppose that $p$ is a program which computes $\rho$ with parameter $k$; i.e. for all $a \in Val_{\mathcal{A}}[X]$, $b \in Val_{\mathcal{A}}[Y]$:

$$(a,b) \in \rho \quad \text{iff} \quad k + a + b \in dom\ Den_{\mathcal{A}}[\![p, X \cup Y]\!].$$

We can suppose that $var(any(Y)) \cap var(p) \cap V_\sigma \subseteq Y$ and variables of $Init_\sigma(X)$ differ from all other variables used. Let $U, Z$ be two different copies of $X$ which are also disjoint from $var(p)$. Take the following program $q$:

```
if X = Y → skip □
   X ≠ Y → Z := Y; while Z ≠ X do any(Y); U := Y;
                                   EmptyAll; p; X := U
                             od
fi .
```

The program $q$ first checks whether the formula $X = Y$ is true. If it is true then this is a good case because of reflexivity. In the opposite case the program $q$ first saves the value of $Y$ in $Z$. The subprogram **while** generates a new value for $Y$ and saves it in $U$. Then the program $p$ starts, and terminates only if the actual values of $X$ and $Y$ belong to $\rho$. Let us denote the successive values of $U$ by $U_0$, $U_1$, etc. Then by the above $(U_i, U_{i+1})$ belongs to $\rho$ for any $i$. The program terminates iff the last value of $U$ is equal to the initial value of $Y$ saved in $Z$. Therefore, the program $q$ starting with a value for $(X,Y)$ terminates iff for some $n$ it generates a sequence $U_0, U_1, \ldots$ such that for any $i \in \mathbb{N}$, $(U_i, U_{i+1}) \in \rho$ and $(X, U_0) \in \rho$ and at termination $U_n = Y$. Thus taking any parameter $k' \in Val_{\mathcal{A}}$ with $k'\lceil_{var(p) \cap V_\sigma} = k$ the program $q$ computes the relation $TRC(\rho)$.

(iii) To prove the $k$-computability of $rng\ Den_{\mathcal{A}}[\![p, X]\!]$ let $p \in rP^k_\sigma$ be arbitrary. Let $X \rightleftharpoons var(p)$ and let $X'$ be a copy of $X$. Furthermore let

$$\rho \rightleftharpoons rng\ Den_{\mathcal{A}}[\![p, X]\!] \subseteq Val_{\mathcal{A}}[X'].$$

We can suppose that the variables of the program $any(X)$ are disjoint from the set of variables $X'$. Let us take the following program

$$q \rightleftharpoons any(X);\ EmptyAll;\ p; \textbf{if } X' = X \rightarrow \textbf{skip} \ \Box X' \neq X \rightarrow \textbf{loop fi}\ .$$

This program starting with the input $X'$ terminates iff the program $p$ computes an output which is equal to $X'$. It is not difficult to verify that the program $q$ with an arbitrary parameter $k$ computes exactly $\rho$.

(B) The proof goes similarly to that in (A). We only have to use $Y :=?$ instead of $any(Y)$.

□

Now let us see whether $rng(Den_{\mathcal{A}}[\![p, var(p)]\!])$ is k-computable in every model $\mathcal{A}$ for any program $p \in P^k_\sigma$. To answer this question we need the following

**(7.6) Lemma.** *Let us consider the one-sorted similarity type $\sigma'$ with sort $\sigma' = \{s\}$ and function symbols $1 :\rightarrow s$; $+ : s, s \rightarrow s$. Fix a program $p \rightleftharpoons x := x + x$ and a natural number $n \in \mathbb{N}$. There exists a $\sigma'$-type model $\mathcal{A}$ such that $rng(Den_{\mathcal{A}}[\![p, \{x\}]\!])$ is not $n$-computable in $\mathcal{A}$.*

*Proof.* Let $\mathcal{B}$ be an arbitrary non-standard model of Peano arithmetic, and take $\mathcal{A} \rightleftharpoons \mathcal{B}\restriction_{\sigma'}$. To deduce a contradiction let us suppose that $q \in P^n_\sigma$ computes $rng(Den_{\mathcal{A}}[\![p, \{x\}]\!])$ i.e.

$$k + \{(x, a)\} \in domDen_{\mathcal{A}}[\![q]\!] \quad \text{iff} \quad \mathcal{A} \models \exists y(y + y = x)[a]$$

holds for an appropriate valuation $k$. Let $m \rightleftharpoons max\{k(x) \mid x \in var(q)\}$. If $m$ is a standard number then let $c$ be an arbitrary non-standard number, otherwise let $c \rightleftharpoons m \cdot m + 1$. The following claim shows that the program $q$ terminates for $c$ iff it terminates for the values greater than $c$. However, since there are infinitely many odd and even numbers greater than $c$ the program $q$ does not compute the required set, which leads to a contradiction.

**Claim.** For any $d \geq c$ the program $q$ has a terminating trace starting from $k + (x, d)$ iff $q$ has a terminating trace starting from $k + (x, c)$. This means that the termination does not depend on the value of $x$ over $c$.

*Proof of Claim.* Let $\{x_1, x_2, ..., x_r\}$ list all the variables of the program $q$. We may suppose that $x = x_1$. Since $\sigma'$ contains only the function symbol $+$ and the constant symbol 1 the value of the variables and also the entities in stacks of any member of any trace $s$ of the program $q$ starting from any valuation $\ell$ can be written in the following form:

$$(*) \qquad s(t)(x_j) \rightleftharpoons \alpha(t,j,0) + \alpha(t,j,1) \cdot \ell(x_1) + \ldots + \alpha(t,j,r) \cdot \ell(x_r),$$

where $\alpha(t,j,0), \ldots, \alpha(t,j,r)$ are standard natural numbers. Tests in program $q$ are built up from the atomic formulas of the form $\tau = \tau'$. If a test $\tau = \tau'$ is at the $t$-th step of a trace starting from the input $k + \{(x,d)\}$, where $d \geq c$, then since the values of the variables of $\tau$ and $\tau'$ are of the form (*) it is true that this equation is of the form

$$\beta_\tau(t,0) + \beta_\tau(t,1) \cdot d + \ldots + \beta_\tau(t,r) \cdot k(x_r) = \\ \beta_{\tau'}(t,0) + \beta_{\tau'}(t,1) \cdot d + \ldots + \beta_{\tau'}(t,r) \cdot k(x_r),$$

where $\beta_\tau(t,i)$ and $\beta_{\tau'}(t,i)$ $(0 \leq i \leq r)$ are standard natural numbers. Therefore

$$\beta_\tau(t,0) + \beta_\tau(t,2) \cdot k(x_2) \ldots + \beta_{\tau'}(t,r) \cdot k(x_r) \leq n \cdot m < c \leq d.$$

Thus the equality holds iff $\beta_\tau(t,1) = \beta_{\tau'}(t,1)$ and

$$\beta_\tau(t,0) + \beta_\tau(t,2) \cdot k(x_2) + \ldots + \beta_\tau(t,r) \cdot k(x_r) = \\ \beta_{\tau'}(t,0) + \beta_{\tau'}(t,2) \cdot k(x_2) + \ldots + \beta_{\tau'}(t,r) \cdot k(x_r).$$

Therefore, if $d \geq c$ then the truth values of tests do not depend on $d$. Therefore, if $d \geq c$ then the termination of $q$ does not depend on the value of $x$. □

**(7.7) Theorem.** *In general, rng* $Den_{\mathcal{A}}[\![p, var(p)]\!]$ *is not k-computable (where* $p \in P^k_\sigma$ *and* $\mathcal{A} \in Mod_\sigma$*).*

*Proof.* Let $\sigma'$ and $\mathcal{A} \in Mod_{\sigma'}$ be the same as in Lemma (7.6). Let $p \rightleftharpoons x := x + x$. It is obvious that $rng(Den_{\mathcal{A}}[\![p, \{x\}]\!]) = \{x \mid \exists y \in A\ (x = y + y)\}$. But this relation is not $k$-computable according to the above lemma. □

We intend to extend the notion of recursively enumerable sets from the standard model of arithmetic $\mathcal{N}$ to any model of any similarity type $\sigma$. Remember that recursive functions (and hence recursively enumerable sets) have been built up from a given set of initial functions by the use of some given operations. However, in the general case the minimalization is missing, therefore for this general definition of recursivity we have to use a new operation. The transitive reflexive closure will be this new operation and it will play the role of minimalization in the general case.

Let $\mathcal{A}$ be a $\sigma$-type model and let $R \subseteq Val_{\mathcal{A}}[X]$ be an $X$-type relation on $\mathcal{A}$. For a given set of variables $Y \subseteq X$ the $Y$-th *projection* of $R$ is the $Y$-type relation

$$\pi_Y(R) \rightleftharpoons \{a \in Val_{\mathcal{A}}[Y] \mid \exists k \in Val_{\mathcal{A}}[X \setminus Y]\ a + k \in R\}.$$

For a given valuation $k \in Val_{\mathcal{A}}[Y]$ the *parametrization* of $R$ with $k$ is the relation

$$R\!\restriction_k \rightleftharpoons \{a \in Val_{\mathcal{A}}[X \setminus Y] \mid k + a \in R\}.$$

**(7.8) Definition.** *Let $\mathcal{A} \in Mod_\sigma$ be fixed. The set of recursively enumerable relations in $\mathcal{A}$ is the minimal set $Rec_\mathcal{A}$ that satisfies the following properties:*

*(i) If $\phi$ is an atomic formula or a negation of an atomic formula of $Form_\sigma$ then*

$$K_\phi \rightleftharpoons \{k \in Val_\mathcal{A}[var(\phi)] \mid \mathcal{A} \models \phi[k]\}$$

*belongs to $Rec_\mathcal{A}$.*

*(ii) $Rec_\mathcal{A}$ is closed under*
- *union;*
- *intersection;*
- *projection;*
- *parametrization;*
- *product;*
- *renaming;*
- *transitive and reflexive closure.*

The next theorem shows that Definition (7.8) gives back the notion of recursively enumerable sets in recursion theory.

**(7.9) Theorem.** *Let $\eta$ be the similarity type of arithmetic and let $\mathcal{N}$ be the standard model of Peano arithmetic PA. The recursively enumerable relations in $\mathcal{N}$ are exactly the recursively enumerable subsets (in the sense of recursion theory) of $\mathbb{N}^k$ ($k \in \mathbb{N}$).*

We leave it to the reader to prove this theorem as well as the following

**(7.10) Lemma.** *Let $\phi \in Open_\sigma$. Then*

$$K_\phi \rightleftharpoons \{k \in Val_\mathcal{A}[var(\phi)] \mid \mathcal{A} \models \phi[k]\}$$

*belongs to $Rec_\mathcal{A}$.*

**(7.11) Lemma.** *$Rec_\mathcal{A}$ is closed under composition.*

*Proof.* For a fixed and finite $W \subseteq V$ it is clear that $Val_\mathcal{A}[W]$ is recursively enumerable. Let $X$, $Y$, $Z$ be finite subsets of V and let $R_1 \subseteq Val_\mathcal{A}[X,Y]$ and $R_2 \subseteq Val_\mathcal{A}[Y,Z]$. One can check that

$$R_1 \circ R_2 = \pi_{X \cup Z}\Big(\big(R_1 \times Val_\mathcal{A}[Z]\big) \cap \big(Val_\mathcal{A}[X] \times R_2\big)\Big).$$

□

**(7.12) Lemma.** *Building up a recursively enumerable relation by using the sets of Definition (7.8) (i) and operations of (ii) it is enough to use parametrization only once at the end of the sequence of operations.*

*Proof.* We prove this statement by induction on the structure of $R \in Rec_{\mathcal{A}}$. We choose only two cases, and leave the others to the reader.

(i) Let $R = (R_1 \upharpoonright_k) \cap R_2$. By definition there are sets of variables $X, Y$ and $Z$ such that
- $X, Y \subseteq Z,\ X \cup Y = Z,\ X \cap Y = \emptyset$;
- $R_1 \subseteq Val_{\mathcal{A}}[Z]$;
- $R_2 \subseteq Val_{\mathcal{A}}[X]$;
- $k \in Val_{\mathcal{A}}[Y]$.

Obviously $R = (R_1 \cap (R_2 \times Val_{\mathcal{A}}[Y])) \upharpoonright_k$.

(ii) Let $R = TRC(S \upharpoonright_k)$. By definition there are sets of variables $X, Y, Z$ and $W$ such that
- $Y$ is a copy of $X$, $W$ is a copy of $Z$;
- $X, Y, Z$ and $W$ are pairwise disjoint;
- $S \subseteq Val_{\mathcal{A}}[X, Y, Z]$.
- $k \in Val_{\mathcal{A}}[Y]$.

Take the following $((X, Z), (Y, W))$-type relation:

$$S_1 \rightleftharpoons (S \times Val_{\mathcal{A}}[W]) \cap (Val_{\mathcal{A}}[X, Y] \times K_{Z=W}).$$

It is an easy exercise to show that $TRC(S \upharpoonright_k) = TRC(S_1) \upharpoonright_{k + k'}$, where $\iota : Z \to W$ is the bijection and $\iota \circ k' = k$. We remark that $k' \in Val_{\mathcal{A}}[W]$. □

**(7.13) Theorem.** *For any $\mathcal{A} \in Mod_\sigma$ the recursively enumerable and the $rP_\sigma$-computable relations in $\mathcal{A}$ are the same.*

*Proof.* First we check the easier direction: any recursively enumerable relation is $rP_\sigma$-computable. It is evident that $K_\phi$ is $rP_\sigma$-computable by the program **if** $\phi \to$ **skip** $\Box \neg\phi \to$ **loop fi** . Taking into account Definition (7.1) and Theorems (7.4) and (7.5), we only have to prove that the $rP_\sigma$-computable relations are closed under projections. But this follows from Definition (7.1). Indeed, let $R \subseteq Val_{\mathcal{A}}[X]$ be a relation computable by a program $p \in rP_\sigma$ and a parameter $k \in Val_{\mathcal{A}}$. So for all $a \in Val_{\mathcal{A}}[X]$:

$$a \in R \quad \text{iff} \quad k + a \in dom(Den_{\mathcal{A}}[\![p]\!]).$$

Fix a set of variables $Y \subseteq X$ and take the following program: $p' \rightleftharpoons (x \in X \backslash Y) : x :=?; p$. We have for all $a \in Val_{\mathcal{A}}[Y]$:

$$a \in \pi_Y(R) \quad \text{iff} \quad k + a \in dom(Den_{\mathcal{A}}[\![p']\!]).$$

To prove the other direction we first establish the following

**Claim.** Fix a program $p \in rP_\sigma$ and let $X \rightleftharpoons var(p)$. Then $Den_{\mathcal{A}}[\![p, X]\!] \subseteq Val_{\mathcal{A}}[X, X']$ is recursively enumerable on $\mathcal{A}$.

*Proof of Claim.* By induction on the complexity of p. Let $\iota : X \to X'$ be the corresponding bijection.

(i) The case $p \rightleftharpoons$ **skip** is trivial.
(ii) Let $p \rightleftharpoons x := \tau$ and consider the following formula

$$\phi \rightleftharpoons \bigwedge\{y = \iota(y) \mid y \in var(\tau) \setminus \{x\}\} \ \wedge \ \iota(x) = \tau.$$

Obviously, $K_\phi = Den_{\mathcal{A}}[\![p, X]\!]$.
(iii) If $p \rightleftharpoons x :=?$ then consider the formula

$$\phi \rightleftharpoons \bigwedge\{y = \iota(y) \mid y \in var(\tau) \setminus \{x\}\} \wedge \iota(x) = \iota(x).$$

One can easily prove that $K_\phi = Den_{\mathcal{A}}[\![p, X]\!]$.

Let $Y \subseteq V$ be arbitrary but finite. $Val_{\mathcal{A}}[Y]$ is recursively enumerable since for $\phi \rightleftharpoons Y = Y$, $K_\phi = Val_{\mathcal{A}}[Y]$. Furthermore, if $Y' = \iota(Y)$ is a copy of $Y$ then the relation $\Delta_{(Y,Y')}$ is recursively enumerable, since for $\psi \rightleftharpoons \bigwedge\{y = \iota(y) | y \in Y\}$ we have $\Delta_{(Y,Y')} = K_\psi$.

(iv) Now let $p \rightleftharpoons (p_1; p_2)$. Let $X_i \rightleftharpoons var(p_i)$ $(i = 1, 2)$ and take $X \rightleftharpoons X_1 \cup X_2$, $Y_1 \rightleftharpoons X_1 \setminus X_2$, $Y_2 \rightleftharpoons X_2 \setminus X_1$, $\Delta_i \rightleftharpoons \Delta_{(Y_i, \iota(Y_i))}$ $(i = 1, 2)$. One can check that

$$Den_{\mathcal{A}}[\![p, X]\!] = Den_{\mathcal{A}}[\![p_1, X_1]\!] \times \Delta_2 \circ Den_{\mathcal{A}}[\![p_2, X_2]\!] \times \Delta_1.$$

Here $Den_{\mathcal{A}}[\![p_i, X_i]\!] \times \Delta_{2-i}$ is considered as a $((X_i \cup Y_{2-i}), (X_i^! \cup \iota(Y_{2-i})))$-type many-sorted relation, where $X_i^!$ is a new copy of $X_i$ $(i = 1, 2)$.

In (v) and (iv) we use the following construction. Let $X$ be a finite set of variables and $\iota$ be a bijection with $dom\ \iota \supseteq X$. Let $\Phi_\iota(X) \rightleftharpoons \bigwedge_{x \in X} x = \iota(x)$ and take $\Delta_\iota(X) \rightleftharpoons K_{\Phi_\iota}$. For an arbitrary $X$-type relation $R$ define its diagonal

$$Diag(R) \rightleftharpoons (R \times R) \cap \Delta_\iota(X).$$

It is clear that if $R$ is recursively enumerable then $Diag(R)$ is also recursively enumerable.

(v) Let $p \rightleftharpoons$ **if** $\alpha_1 \to p_1 \ \Box\ \alpha_2 \to p_2$ **fi** . Let $X \rightleftharpoons var(p)$, $X_i \rightleftharpoons var(p_i)$, $Z_i \rightleftharpoons var(p) \setminus var(\alpha_i)$, $Y_i = var(p) \setminus var(p_i)$ for $i = 1, 2$. Take $\psi \rightleftharpoons \neg(\alpha_1 \wedge \alpha_2)$ and let $Y \rightleftharpoons X \setminus var(\psi)$. Let $\iota$ be a bijection from $X$ to a new copy of $X$. Then we have

$$Den_{\mathcal{A}}[\![p, X]\!] = \bigcup_{i=1}^{2} (Diag(K_{\alpha_i}) \times \Delta_\iota(Z_i)) \circ (Den_{\mathcal{A}}[\![p_i, X_i]\!] \times \Delta_\iota(Y_i))$$
$$\cup (Diag(K_\psi) \times \Delta_\iota(Y)).$$

Here the composed relations are considered to be of $(X, \iota(X))$-type.
(vi) Let $p \rightleftharpoons$ **do** $\alpha_1 \to p_1 \ \Box\ \alpha_2 \to p_2$ **od** . Take $p' \rightleftharpoons$ **if** $\alpha_1 \to p_1 \ \Box\ \alpha_2 \to p_2$ **fi** . Let $X \rightleftharpoons var(p) = var(p')$, $Y = X \setminus (var(\alpha_1) \cup var(\alpha_2))$. Take $\phi \rightleftharpoons \alpha_1 \vee \alpha_2$, $\psi \rightleftharpoons \neg\alpha_1 \wedge \neg\alpha_2$. Let $\Delta \rightleftharpoons \Delta_{(Y, \iota(Y))}$. We have

$$Den_{\mathcal{A}}[\![p, X]\!] = TRC((Diag(K_\phi) \times \Delta) \circ Den_{\mathcal{A}}[\![p', X]\!]) \circ (Diag(K_\psi) \times \Delta).$$

This completes the proof of the claim.

Let $R \subseteq Val_{\mathcal{A}}[X]$ be an $X$-type relation computable by $p \in rP_\sigma$ with parameter $k$. By the claim, $Den_{\mathcal{A}}[\![p, var(p)]\!]$ is recursively enumerable. Take $k_1 \rightleftharpoons k\restriction_{var(p)\setminus X}$ and $R_1 \rightleftharpoons \pi_{var(p)}(Den_{\mathcal{A}}[\![p, var(p)]\!])\restriction_{k_1}$. One can check that $R = R_1$. □

## 7.2 Church's Thesis

Considering the different programming languages introduced in the previous sections, two questions arise. The *first question* is how the intuitively computable relations of a model are connected with the relations computable by our programming languages. The *second question* is which one of the programming languages has more computational power.

Note that comparative schematology is the field which deals with our second question. The comparative analysis of many other programming languages can be found in Chandra [1974]. Let us see what we mean by computable relations.

**(7.14) Definition.** *Let $\mathcal{A} \in Mod_\sigma$ be an arbitrary model. A relation $\rho \subseteq A^n$ is said to be effectively computable iff there is an effective program which, for a given n-tuple $(a_1, ..., a_n) \in A^n$, eventually halts and outputs a given value in case $(a_1, ..., a_n) \in \rho$, and never halts otherwise.*

The above is not a mathematical definition, since we have not formalized what an effective program is in general. Therefore, considering programs of different programming languages, different relations of an arbitrary data structure, i.e. of an arbitrary model, could be considered effectively computable. There are different possible answers to the first question and these vary in the programming languages whose programs will be considered and in the data structure, i.e. in the models whose relations and functions are investigated on computability. With respect to our languages, the answer, in the most general form, is as follows:

**(7.15) Thesis.** *For an arbitrary $\sigma$-type model $\mathcal{A}$ the effectively computable relations are just the $P_{\sigma^\bullet}$-computable relations.*

This statement is only a thesis because the notion of effective computability is not mathematical in nature, as we have already mentioned. Hence the statement can never be proved.

This thesis says that from the viewpoint of effective computation the programming language $P_{\sigma^\bullet}$ is appropriate in the sense that the relations computable by programs of $P_{\sigma^\bullet}$ are just the effectively computable ones. Note that the programming language $P_{\sigma^s}$ is universal in the following sense: taking any programming language $P$ obtained from $P_\sigma$ by augmenting it with lists or counters or sets, each $P$-computable relation is also $P_{\sigma^s}$ computable.

Note that the reason for which Thesis (7.15) considers only the programming language $P_{\sigma^s}$ and not $rP_{\sigma^s}$ is the following. Though, as we shall soon see, random assignment increases the computation power of a programming language, the usage of random assignment leads to non-effectiveness connected with the random selection of an element from a possibly infinite set.

Thesis (7.15) is a natural generalization of what is called Church's thesis. Some other answers to the first question will be given later. The second question is connected with Thesis (7.15), since it asks which of the programming languages is more powerful.

Let $\sigma$ be a fixed similarity type and let $\mathcal{A}$ be a $\sigma$-type model. Let $Rel_\mathcal{A}$ denote the set of all many-sorted relations on $\mathcal{A}$, i.e.

$$Rel_\mathcal{A} \rightleftharpoons \{R|R \text{ is an } X\text{-type relation in } \mathcal{A} \text{ for some finite } X \subseteq V\}.$$

Take $Rel_\sigma \rightleftharpoons \bigcup\{Rel_\mathcal{A}|\mathcal{A} \in Mod_\sigma\}$. A *computation family* is a function $C$ of the form

$$C : \cup_\sigma Mod_\sigma \to \cup_\sigma Sb(Rel_\sigma)$$

in such a way that for every similarity type $\sigma$, and for every $\sigma$-type model $\mathcal{A}$, $C(\mathcal{A}) \subseteq Rel_\mathcal{A}$. For a fixed similarity type $\sigma$, we use the notation $C_\sigma$ for the restriction of $C$ to the class of all $\sigma$-type models $C{\restriction}_{Mod_\sigma}$.

Let us suppose that for every similarity type $\sigma$ a fixed extension $(\delta_\sigma, ext_\sigma)$ is given. Let $Q$ be a function which assigns to each similarity type $\sigma$ a programming language $Q_\sigma \subseteq rP_{\delta_\sigma}$. In this case $Q$ generates a computation family also denoted by $Q$ in the following way: for each $\mathcal{A} \in Mod_\sigma$ take

$$Q(\mathcal{A}) \rightleftharpoons \{R \in Rel_\mathcal{A} \mid R \text{ is computable by a program } p \in Q_\sigma\}.$$

In this case we also speak about a *programming family* instead of a computation family. Here we list the most frequently used programming (computation) families:

| Notation | Extension | Programming language |
|---|---|---|
| $P(=P^0)$ | $emp_\sigma$ | $P_\sigma$ |
| $rP$ | $emp_\sigma$ | $rP_\sigma$ |
| $P^s$ | $stack_\sigma$ | $P_{\sigma^s}$ |
| $P^k$ | $stack_\sigma$ | $P^k_\sigma$ |
| $P^{k,e}$ | $stack_\sigma$ | $P^{k,e}_\sigma$ |
| $rP^s$ | $stack_\sigma$ | $rP_{\sigma^s}$ |
| $rP^k$ | $stack_\sigma$ | $rP^k_\sigma$ |
| $rP^{k,e}$ | $stack_\sigma$ | $rP^{k,e}_\sigma$ |
| $det\text{-}P^k$ | $stack_\sigma$ | $det\text{-}P^k_\sigma$ |
| $P^{k,\mathcal{B}}$ | $stack_\sigma(\mathcal{B})$ | $P^k_{\sigma(\mathcal{B})}$ |
| $P^{k,c}$ | $stack_\sigma(\mathcal{N})$ | $P^k_{\sigma^c}$ |
| $P^{ne}$ | $stack_\sigma$ | $P^{ne}_\sigma$ |

**(7.16) Definition.**

*(i)* *Let $C_1$ and $C_2$ be two computation families. We say that the computational power of $C_1$ is greater than that of $C_2$ (denoted by $C_1 \gtrsim C_2$ or $C_2 \lesssim C_1$) iff for all similarity types $\sigma$ and for all $\sigma$-type models $\mathcal{A}$ we have $C_1(\mathcal{A}) \supseteq C_2(\mathcal{A})$. If both $C_1 \gtrsim C_2$ and $C_1 \lesssim C_2$ are true then we write $C_1 \approx C_2$.*

*(ii)* *The computational power of $C_1$ is said to be strictly greater than that of $C_2$ (in notation $C_1 > C_2$ or $C_2 < C_1$) iff $C_1 \gtrsim C_2$ and there is at least one similarity type $\sigma$ and one model $\mathcal{A}$ such that $C_1(\mathcal{A}) \supset C_2(\mathcal{A})$.*

This definition generalizes Definition (5.7) for computation families generated not by extension.

If a computation family is given by a family of programming languages then instead of the computational power of that family we speak about the computational power of the given programming language. A comparison of the programming families introduced so far is made in the following

**(7.17) Theorem.** *The computational power of the defined programming families can be described by the following statements:*

*(i)* $P^0 < P^1 < P^n \approx P^{n,e} \approx P^{ne} \approx P^s < rP^n \approx rP^{n,e} \approx rP^{ne} \approx rP^s$ $(n \geq 2)$;

*(ii)* $P^1 < rP^1 < rP^2$;

*(iii)* $det\text{-}P^0 < det\text{-}P^1 < det\text{-}P^2 \approx det\text{-}P^n \approx det\text{-}P^s$ $(n \geq 2)$;

*(iv)* $det\text{-}P^0 < P^0, det\text{-}P^1 < P^1, det\text{-}P^2 \approx P^2 \approx P^{ne}$;

*(v)* *$det\text{-}P^1$ and $P^0$ are incomparable.*

*Proof.* Equalities in (i) directly follow from Theorems (6.9) and (6.11). Equalities in (iv) directly follow from Theorems (6.9), (6.11) and Corollary (6.18). From (iv) and (v) $det\text{-}P^2 \approx P^2 \approx P^s$ which implies $det\text{-}P^2 \approx det\text{-}P^n \approx det\text{-}P^s$ $(n \geq 2)$ in (iii).

The inequalities follow from the subsequent lemmas and theorems: $P^0 < P^1$ follows from Theorem (7.21), $P^1 < P^2$ from Corollary (7.20) and $P^s < rP^2$ from $P^2 \approx P^s$ (see (iv) and Lemma (7.18)). Lemmas (7.18) and (7.19) together prove (ii) and Theorems (7.21) and (7.22) together prove $det\text{-}P^0 < det\text{-}P^1$ in (iii), (iv) and (v). □

The results of the above theorem are summarized in Fig. 7.1.

**(7.18) Lemma.** *$rP^2 > P^2$ and $rP^1 > P^1$.*

*Proof.* Let $\sigma'$ and $\mathcal{A}$ be as in Lemma (7.6). Let $\rho = \{\alpha \in A \mid \exists\beta\ \alpha = \beta + \beta\}$. By Lemma (7.6) $\rho$ is not $P^2_\sigma$-computable. However, $\rho$ is computable by the following $rP_\sigma$-program:

$$y :=?;\ \textbf{if}\ y + y = x \rightarrow \textbf{skip}\ \Box\ y + y \neq x \rightarrow \textbf{loop fi}\ .$$

□

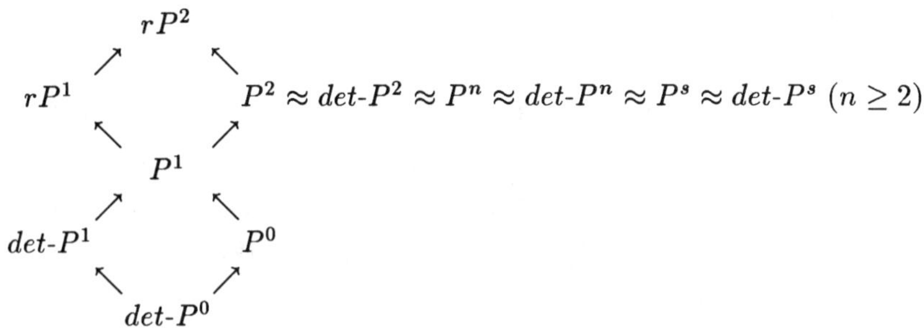


**Fig. 7.1.** Comparison of the programming families

**(7.19) Lemma.** *There is a similarity type $\sigma$ and a $\sigma$-type model $\mathcal{A}$ such that* $rP^2(\mathcal{A}) = P^2(\mathcal{A}) \neq P^1(\mathcal{A}) = rP^1(\mathcal{A})$.

*Proof.* See, e.g., Chandra [1974]. In fact, Chandra proved that $P^1 < det\text{-}P^{1,c}$. However, in his model $\mathcal{A}$, $rP^1(\mathcal{A}) = P^1(\mathcal{A})$ and $det\text{-}P^{1,c}(\mathcal{A}) = P^2(\mathcal{A}) = rP^2(\mathcal{A})$. □

**(7.20) Corollary.** $P^2 > P^1$ *and* $rP^2 > rP^1$.

**(7.21) Theorem.**
*(i)* $P^0 < P^1$ *and* $det\text{-}P^0 < det\text{-}P^1$.
*(ii)* $det\text{-}P^1 \lesssim P^0$ *does not hold.*

*Proof.* Let $\sigma$ be a $\{d\}$-sorted similarity type containing the following symbols: $L, R : d \to d$; $H : d, d \to d$; $\rho : d$. Consider the following inductively defined partial function:

$$f(x) \rightleftharpoons \begin{cases} x & \text{if } \rho(x); \\ H(f(L(x)), f(R(x))) & \text{if } \neg\rho(x). \end{cases}$$

The following $p_f \in det\text{-}P^{1,e}$-program computes $f$ in any $\sigma$-type model $\mathcal{A}$, i.e it terminates exactly for inputs $(x, y)$ with $y = f(x)$:

```
if one_σ(x,y)  → if ρ(x) → skip □ ¬ρ(x) → loop fi □
   ¬one_σ(x,y) → Init_σ(x,y);
                 if ρ(x)  → z := x □
                    ¬ρ(x) → x_1 := L(x); x_2 := R(x); end := W_2; Swap
                 fi;
                 if z = y → skip □ z ≠ y → loop fi
fi,
```

where *Swap* is the following program:

**while** $end \neq W_1$ **do**
  **if**

$$\rho(x_1) \wedge \neg\rho(x_2) \to Push_1(x_1, W_1, W_1); x_1 := L(x_2); x_2 := R(x_2) \,\square$$
$$\neg\rho(x_1) \wedge \rho(x_2) \to Push_1(x_2, W_2, W_2); x_1 := L(x_1); x_2 := R(x_1) \,\square$$
$$\neg\rho(x_1) \wedge \neg\rho(x_2) \to Push_1(x_2, W_1, W_2); x_1 := L(x_1); x_2 := R(x_1) \,\square$$
$$\rho(x_1) \wedge \rho(x_2) \to z := H(x_1, x_2); V := W_1; W := W_1;$$

  **while** $V = W \wedge \neg IsEmpty_1$ **do**
    $Pop_1(u, V, W)$;
    **if** $V = W_1 \wedge W = W_1 \to z := H(u, z) \,\square$
      $V = W_2 \wedge W = W_2 \to z := H(z, u) \,\square$
      $V \neq W \to Push_1(z, W_1, W_1); x_1 := L(u); x_2 := R(u)$
    **fi**
  **od** ;
  **if** $IsEmpty_1 \to end := W_1 \,\square\, \neg IsEmpty_1 \to$ **skip fi**

  **fi**
**od** .

It can be shown that *Swap* behaves in $\mathcal{A}$ in the following way. If exactly one of the items $L(x)$ and $R(x)$ belongs to $\rho_{\mathcal{A}}$ then the "good" item's $f$-value is the item itself. In this case *Swap* stacks the "good" item and the check continues for $L$- and $R$-values of the "wrong" one. The two markers, which are also pushed at the same time, mark whether an $L$-type or an $R$-type item was pushed before.

If both $L(x)$ and $R(x)$ do not belong to $\rho_{\mathcal{A}}$ then *Swap* always stacks $R(x)$, and the two markers show that the item below was pushed because of its "being wrong". In this case the check continues for $L(L(x))$ and $R(L(x))$. If the program finds an item $x$ with both $L(x)$ and $R(x)$ belonging to $\rho_{\mathcal{A}}$ then it computes $f(x) := H(L(x), R(x))$ and it pops a new item $u$. The markers show unambigously the reason why $u$ was stacked. Therefore, if $u$ is a "wrong" item then $f(x)$ is stacked instead of $u$ with markers showing that "the item below is good and is the $L$-value of something". If $u$ is "good" then $f(u)$ can be computed and a new item is taken out unless the stack is empty, which means that $z$ is the desired $f$-value of the original input.

By Theorem (6.8), there is a *det*-$P^1$ program too which computes $f$ in any $\sigma$-type model $\mathcal{A}$. However, Paterson, Hewitt [1970] states that there is no program $p \in P_\sigma$ such that it computes the same relation as $p$ does. Similarly to Lemma (6.19) the original proof works well for the programming language $P_\sigma$ too. Therefore, *det*-$P^1 \lesssim P^0$ does not hold. Thus *det*-$P^0 <$ *det*-$P^1$ and $P^0 < P^1$. $\square$

**(7.22) Theorem.**
*(i)* $det\text{-}P^0 < P^0$, $det\text{-}P^1 < P^1$, $det\text{-}P^1 < det\text{-}P^2$.
*(ii)* $P^0 \lesssim det\text{-}P^1$ *does not hold.*

*Proof.* The inequality $det\text{-}P^0 < P^0$ follows directly from the fact that $Leaftest$ belongs to $P^0_\sigma$ (see Corollary (6.18)) and from Lemma (6.19). To prove $det\text{-}P^1 < P^1$ we recall Theorem 5.4 from Harnik [1975] which states that $det\text{-}P^1 < det\text{-}P^2$. He gives a similarity type $\sigma$, a model $\mathcal{A} \in Mod_\sigma$ and a $det\text{-}P^2_\sigma$-computable relation $Q$ which is not $det\text{-}P^1_\sigma$-computable. We present the model $\mathcal{A}$ and the relation $Q$ and prove that $Q$ is $P^0_\sigma$-computable (and hence $P^1_\sigma$-computable). This proves that $det\text{-}P^1 < P^1$ and also proves that $P^0 \lesssim det\text{-}P^1$ does not hold.

Let $\sigma$ contain the following two symbols: $f : s \to s$; $\rho : s, s$. For an arbitrary $\mathcal{A} \in Mod_\sigma$ and a finite $X \subseteq V$ let $Q_\mathcal{A}$ be the following relation:

$$Q_\mathcal{A} \rightleftharpoons \Big\{k \in Val_\mathcal{A}[X] \mid \exists i, j \in \mathbb{N} \exists x, y \in X \ \mathcal{A} \models \rho\big(f^i(x), f^j(y)\big)[k]\Big\}.$$

Harnik proved that there is an $\mathcal{A}$ such that $Q_\mathcal{A}$ is not $det\text{-}P^1_\sigma$ computable. Now we give a $P_\sigma$-program which computes $Q_\mathcal{A}$:

$$p \rightleftharpoons \textbf{while } \neg\Phi \textbf{ do choice } \big((x \in X) : x := f(x)\big) \textbf{ od },$$

where $\Phi \rightleftharpoons \bigvee\{\rho(x, y) \mid x, y \text{ are different elements of } X\}$. □

**(7.23) Corollary.** $P^1_\sigma$ *is not diagonalizable.*

*Proof.* Indeed, if $P^1_\sigma$ were diagonalizable then according to Lemma (6.16) the $det\text{-}P^1_\sigma$- and the $P^1_\sigma$-computable relations would be the same, which would contradict the above theorem. □

Chapter 8

# On Inductive Definability of 1- and 2-Computable Relations

Up to now we have developed different logical tools in order to describe and investigate programming languages. However, from the logical viewpoint the programming languages remained external with respect to the logic, by the use of which the investigation took place. This raises an interesting question. Is it possible to give purely logical objects, which are internal to logic and which play the same role as programs? This question can be paraphrased as follows: Could programming languages be characterized in a purely logical way?

This characterization may be performed as follows. We develop special logical constructs such that the relations defined by them will be the same as those which are computable by the programming languages in question. That is, the logical characterization may be considered from the viewpoint of computational power. Such a construct is the set of all recursively enumerable relations, which are the same as the $P^0$-computable relations, and so the set characterizes the computational family $P^0$. In the present chapter we introduce the necessary constructs by the use of inductive definability in order to characterize the computational families which use stacks as well.

Section 8.1 deals with the construction of the logical equivalent of the computational family $P^1$ and $rP^1$. This construction will be the so-called effective inductively definable relations and the inductively definable relations, respectively. Section 8.2 is devoted to the logical characterization of programming languages with two (or equivalently more) stacks. For this aim we have to add the power of the standard model of arithmetic to augment the power of the corresponding inductive definability.

Note that in programming theory different abstract constructions have been introduced and investigated, first of all, from the viewpoint of computational power. The effective definitional schema developed by Friedmann [1971] is one of the first constructs in an abstract setting. This schema was later used and investigated by Shepherdson [1973] and by Tiuryn [1981]. From the point of view of the type of the abstract construct, the one developed by Moldestad, Stolenberg-Hansen, Tucker [1978] is close to ours, since it is also based on inductive definability. However, there is an important difference between all these abstract constructs and those we intend to develop. Namely, we require from these constructions a direct characterization of our programming languages, while the constructions mentioned above are used as tools for handling computation in an abstract manner.

## 8.1 Logical Characterization of 1-Computable Relations

It is an interesting question how the relations computable by a given programming language can be characterized in a purely logical way. Here we show that in the one-sorted case the 1-computable and the $r$-1-computable relations have this characterization by using a modification of inductive definability.

Let us fix a finite similarity type $\sigma$ for this chapter. We introduce a special type of formula by the use of the Herbrand universe defined in Chapter 2.

**(8.1) Definition.** *Let $\phi \in Form_\sigma, \mathcal{A} \in Mod_\sigma$ and $k \in Val_\mathcal{A}$ be arbitrary. $\exists u \in H_\sigma(X)$ (where $H_\sigma(X)$ is the Herbrand universe generated from the set $X$ of variables) is said to be a Herbrand quantifier. A formula of the form $\exists u \in H_\sigma(X)\phi$ is valid in $\mathcal{A}$ with respect to a valuation $k \in Val_\mathcal{A}$ iff there is an $a \in A$ such that*

*(i)* $\mathcal{A} \models \phi[k + \{(u, a)\}]$
*(ii) $a$ is an element of the Herbrand universe generated by the set $k(X)$.*

Instead of $\exists u_1 \in H_\sigma(X) ... \exists u_k \in H_\sigma(X)\phi$ we simply write $\exists U \in H_\sigma(X)\phi$ where $U = \{u_1, ... u_n\}$.

We remark that $\exists u \in H_\sigma(X)\phi$ is generally not first-order definable, since, as it is known, transitive and reflexive closures are first-order definable in a given $Ax$ iff in each model of $Ax$, $H_\sigma(X)$ is finite. However, the transitive and reflexive closures are not first-order definable in general (for details see Chapter 14).

**(8.2) Lemma.** *Let $\mathcal{A} \in Mod_\sigma$ be arbitrary but fixed and let $Y$ be a copy of $U$. The relation $HU(X, Y) \rightleftharpoons \exists U \in H_\sigma(X)\ Y = U$ is inductive in $\mathcal{A}$.*

*Proof.* For the sake of convenience we prove only the one-sorted case. Evidently, it is enough to prove the case of $U = \{u\}$ and $Y = \{y\}$. Let $X$ contain exactly $j$ variables $\{x_1, ..., x_j\}$. Let $S$ be a new $j + 1$-ary relation symbol. Take

$$\phi(X, y) \rightleftharpoons \bigvee_{i=1}^{j} y = x_i \vee$$

$$\bigvee \Big\{ \exists t_1 ... t_n \bigwedge_{i<n} (S(X, t_i) \wedge y = f(t_1 ... t_n)) \mid f : s_1, ..., s_n \to s \Big\}.$$

Observe that the formula $\phi(X, y)$ is positive existential. It is easy to verify that the relation ${}_\mathcal{A}I_\phi$ defined inductively by $\phi$ is the same as HU, i.e. in $\mathcal{A}$, ${}_\mathcal{A}I_\phi = HU_\mathcal{A}$. □

Recall the definition of inductive relation and inductive definitional schema from Definitions (2.11) and (2.16). Now we introduce an effective version of these notions.

**(8.3) Definition.** *Let $(\Theta_1(X,Y,U_1...U_h),\ \Theta_2(X,Y))$ be an inductive definitional schema. Let $\mathcal{A} \in Mod_\sigma$ be an arbitrary model. By Transitivity Theorem (2.9) the relation ${}_{\mathcal{A}}EI_{(\Theta_1,\Theta_2)}$ defined by the equation*

$$R(X) = \exists Y \exists Z_1 ... \exists Z_h \Big( \bigwedge_{i=1}^{h} HU(X,Z_i) \wedge HU(X,Y) \wedge$$
$$\Big( (\Theta_1(X,Y,Z_1,...,Z_h) \wedge \bigwedge_{i=1}^{h} R(Z_i)) \vee \Theta_2(X,Y) \Big) \Big)$$

*is inductively definable in $\mathcal{A}$. The relation ${}_{\mathcal{A}}EI_{(\Theta_1,\Theta_2)}$ is said to be effectively inductively defined by the inductive definitional schema $(\Theta_1,\Theta_2)$ in $\mathcal{A}$.*

**(8.4) Definition.** *Let $\mathcal{A} \in Mod_\sigma$. A many-sorted relation $\rho \subseteq Val_{\mathcal{A}}[X]$ is called effectively inductive in $\mathcal{A}$ iff there is an inductive definitional schema $(\Theta_1,\Theta_2)$ and a valuation $k \in Val_{\mathcal{A}}$ such that for each $a \in Val_{\mathcal{A}}[X]$ $a \in \rho$ iff $k + a \in {}_{\mathcal{A}}EI_{(\Theta_1,\Theta_2)}$.*

*Let us denote the set of all inductive relations and the set of all effectively inductive relations in $\mathcal{A}$ by $I(\mathcal{A})$ and $EI(\mathcal{A})$, respectively. In this way we define two computational families $I$ and $EI$.*

**(8.5) Lemma.** *If $\rho$ is effectively inductive in $\mathcal{A}$ then it is inductive in $\mathcal{A}$, i.e. $EI(\mathcal{A}) \subseteq I(\mathcal{A})$.*

*Proof.* The statement follows directly from the Transitivity Theorem (2.9) and from Lemma (8.2). □

**(8.6) Lemma.** *Let $X$ be a finite set of $\sigma$-sorted variables. There is a program $Herb(X) \in P^1_\sigma$ such that*

$$(a,b) \in Den_{\mathcal{A}}[\![Herb(X), X]\!] \subseteq Val_{\mathcal{A}}[X, X']$$

*iff $b \in Val_{\mathcal{A}}[X']$ is a vector of the Herbrand universe generated by the valuation $a$. Moreover, $Herb(X)$ does not modify the content of input stacks.*

*Proof.* For the sake of simplicity we just give the theorem for the one-sorted case. Let $m \rightleftharpoons max(max\{ar\ f | f \in func\ \sigma\}, n)$, and for all $j \leq m$ let $u_j$ be a new variable symbol. Let $T$ and $T'$ be two new copies of $W_1$. Now let $Herb(X)$ be the following program where we temporarily use the notations: **choice** $((1..i..n) : p_i)$ for **choice** $(p_1,...,p_n)$ and **choice** $((a \in A) : p_a)$ for **choice** $(p_{a_1},...,p_{a_k})$ where $A = \{a_1,...,a_k\}$.

$$
\begin{array}{l}
\textbf{if}\quad one_\sigma(X) \to \textbf{skip}\ \Box \\
\quad \neg one_\sigma(X) \to Init_\sigma(X); T := W_2; (1..j..m) : u_j := x_1; Push_1(W_1); Push_1(u_1); \\
\quad \textbf{while}\ T = W_2\ \textbf{do choice}\ \Big(\textbf{choice}\ ((f \in func\ \sigma) : u_1 := f(u_1, ..., u_{ar\ f})), \\
\qquad\qquad \textbf{choice}\ ((1..i..n) : Push_1(W_2);\ Push_1(u_i)), \\
\qquad\qquad \textbf{choice}\ ((1..i..n) : Pop_1(u_i);\ Pop_1(T')); \\
\qquad\qquad \textbf{if}\ T' = W_1 \to\ Push_1(T');\ Push_1(u_1)\ \textbf{fi}, \\
\qquad\qquad \textbf{choice}\ ((1..i..n, 1..j..m) : u_j := x_i), \\
\qquad\qquad T := W_1\Big) \\
\qquad \textbf{od}\ ; \\
\quad (1..i..n) : x_i := u_i;\ T' := W_2; \\
\quad \textbf{while}\ T' = W_2\ \textbf{do}\ Pop_1(u_1);\ Pop_1(T')\ \textbf{od} \\
\textbf{fi}\ .
\end{array}
$$

□

**(8.7) Lemma.** *Let $(\Theta_1, \Theta_2)$ be an inductive definitional schema. Fix a model $\mathcal{A} \in Mod_\sigma$. Then ${}_{\mathcal{A}}EI_{(\Theta_1,\Theta_2)}$ is 1-computable in $\mathcal{A}$.*

*Proof.* Let $\Theta_1(X, Z, U_1, ..., U_k)$, $\Theta_2(X, Z)$ be an inductive definitional schema. Let

$$S(X) = \exists U_1...U_k\ Z \in H_\sigma(X)\Big((\Theta_1(X, Z, U_1, ..., U_k) \wedge \bigwedge_{i=1}^{k} S(U_i)) \vee \Theta_2(X, Z)\Big)$$

be the fixed point equation defining $EI_{(\Theta_1,\Theta_2)}$. Let $\hat{X}$ and $V$ be new copies of $X$. Take the following program $p(\Theta_1,\Theta_2)$:

$$
\begin{array}{l}
Push_1(X); \\
\textbf{while}\ \neg IsEmpty_1 \to \\
\textbf{do} \\
\quad Pop_1(V);\ (1..i..k) : \hat{X} := V; Herb(\hat{X}); U_i := \hat{X}; \\
\quad \hat{X} := V; Herb(\hat{X}); Z := \hat{X}; \\
\quad \textbf{if}\ \Theta_2(V, Z) \to \textbf{skip}\ \Box \\
\qquad \neg\Theta_2(V, Z) \wedge \Theta_1(V, Z, U_1, ..., U_k) \to (1..i..k) : Push_1(U_i)\Box \\
\qquad \neg\Theta_2(V, Z) \wedge \neg\Theta_1(V, Z, U_1, ..., U_k) \to \textbf{loop} \\
\quad \textbf{fi} \\
\textbf{od}\ .
\end{array}
$$

It is clear that with an arbitrary parameter $k$ the program $p(\Theta_1, \Theta_2)$ computes $EI_{(\Theta_1,\Theta_2)}$ in $\mathcal{A}$. □

**(8.8) Lemma.** *Let $(\Theta_1, \Theta_2)$ be an inductive definitional schema. Fix a model $\mathcal{A} \in Mod_\sigma$. Then ${}_{\mathcal{A}}I_{(\Theta_1,\Theta_2)}$ is $rP^1_\sigma$-computable in $\mathcal{A}$.*

*Proof.* The proof of Lemma (8.7) works with the following substitutions:

$$
\begin{array}{lll}
(v \in U_i) : v :=? & \text{for} & \hat{X} := V; Herb(\hat{X}); U_i := \hat{X} \\
(v \in Z) : v :=? & \text{for} & \hat{X} := V; Herb(\hat{X}); Z := \hat{X}
\end{array}
$$

□

**(8.9) Theorem.** *Let $\sigma$ be a many-sorted similarity type. Then $EI_\sigma \lesssim P^1_\sigma$, $I_\sigma \lesssim rP^1_\sigma$.*

*Proof.* The statement follows from Lemmas (8.7)and (8.8). □

Now we turn to prove that any relation 1-computable in $\mathcal{A}$ is effectively inductive on $\mathcal{A}$. First we need some definitions and lemmas.

The graph representation defined in Chapter 4.2 is appropriate for extended programming languages too. Let us consider the programming language $rP^1_\sigma$ obtained by augmenting $rP_\sigma$ with one stack. Then for any $p \in rP^1_\sigma$ the graph representation of $p$ belongs to $rG_{\sigma^s}$. Therefore, the set $Trans_{\sigma^s}$ can be used for defining the graph representation of programs of $rP^1_\sigma$. For the sake of simplicity, however, we use in the graph representation $Pop_1(x)$ instead of the two composed assignment statements. That is, instead of two consecutive edges $x := head(s_1, x)$; $s_1 := tail(s_1)$ we use only one, namely $Pop_1(x)$. In the following we do not indicate the index of $Pop$ and $Push$ because there is only one stack.

**(8.10) Definition.** *Let $T \subset Trans_\sigma$ be given. For a trace $s \in Trace_{\mathcal{A}^s}[\![g]\!]$ take*

$$node(s,T) \rightleftharpoons \{a \mid \exists i < |s|-1 \; s(i)(l) = a, g(s(i)(l), s(i+1)(l)) \in T\}.$$

*Take*

$$\begin{aligned} T^+ &\rightleftharpoons \{Push(\tau) \mid \tau \in Term_\sigma\},\\ T^- &\rightleftharpoons \{Pop(x) \mid x \in V\} \text{ and}\\ T^0 &\rightleftharpoons \{x := \tau \mid x \in V, \tau \in Term_\sigma\} \cup \{\phi \mid \phi \in Open_\sigma\} \cup \{x :=? \mid x \in V\}. \end{aligned}$$

*(a) A trace $s$ is called normal iff $node(s,T^+) = node(s,T^-) = \emptyset$.*
*(b) A trace $s$ is called monotone iff $node(s,T^-) = \emptyset$.*
*(c) A trace $s$ is called positive iff for all $r \leq |s|$, $|node(s\restriction_r, T^+)| \geq |node(s\restriction_r, T^-)|$.*
*(d) A trace $s$ is called balanced iff it is positive and $|node(s,T^+)| = |node(s,T^-)|$.*

**(8.11) Lemma.** *Fix a one-sorted similarity type $\sigma$. Let $p \in P^{1,e}_\sigma (p \in rP^{1,e}_\sigma)$. There is a program $p' \in P^1_\sigma$ ($p' \in rP^1_\sigma$, respectively) such that $p \equiv p'$ (mod $var(p)$), and any trace of $p'$ is positive and $p'$ does not contain the command $Empty_1$.*

*Proof.* We recall that for a one-sorted similarity type $\sigma$, $P^{1,e}_\sigma = P^1_\sigma$ and $rP^{1,e}_\sigma = rP^1_\sigma$. Let $p \in P^{1,e}_\sigma$ ($p \in rP^{1,e}_\sigma$) be arbitrary. There is a program $p_1 \in P^{1,e}_\sigma$ ($p_1 \in rP^{1,e}_\sigma$) such that $p \equiv p_1$ and for any $\mathcal{A} \in Mod_\sigma$, every trace of $Trace_{\mathcal{A}^s}[\![gr(p_1)]\!]$ is positive and $p_1$ does not contain $Empty_1$. Namely, replace each occurrence of $Empty_1$ in $p$ by

**while** $\neg IsEmpty_1$ **do** $Pop_1(y)$ **od**,

where $y$ is a new variable, and replace each occurrence of $Pop_1(x)$ in $p$ by

$$\mathbf{if}\ IsEmpty_1 \rightarrow \mathbf{skip}\ \Box\ \neg IsEmpty_1 \rightarrow Pop_1(x)\ \mathbf{fi}.$$

Let us denote the resulted program by $p_1$. It is clear that $p_1$ has the required propeties.

Now consider the program $T(p_1)$ ($\in P^1_\sigma$ or $rP^1_\sigma$) defined in the proof of Theorem (6.8). By Theorem (6.8), $p_1 \equiv T(p_1)$ and it can be seen from the structure of $T(p_1)$ that $T(p_1)$ does not contain the command $Empty_1$, and any of its traces is positive. □

**(8.12) Theorem.** *Let $\sigma$ be a many-sorted similarity type and $\mathcal{A} \in Mod_\sigma$ be fixed. Let $p \in rP^1_\sigma$ be a program such that it does not contain the constant symbols $Empty^s$ (for $s \in sort\ \sigma$) and each trace of $Trace_\mathcal{A}[\![p]\!]$ is positive. Then $Den_\mathcal{A}[\![p, var(p)]\!]$ is inductive in $\mathcal{A}$. Moreover, if $p \in P^1_\sigma$ then $Den_\mathcal{A}[\![p, var(p)]\!]$ is effectively inductive in $\mathcal{A}$.*

*Proof.* Let $p$, $\mathcal{A}$ be as above and take $g \rightleftharpoons gr(p)$. We give parallel inductive definitions for the input-output relations along normal, monotone, balanced and positive traces of $g$. According to the Theorem (2.15), this means that $Den_\mathcal{A}[\![p, var(p)]\!]$ is inductive in $\mathcal{A}$. First we check the following informal recursive equations for traces given in Bachus-Naur form:

| | | | |
|---|---|---|---|
| (i) | *trace* | = | *positive* |
| (ii) | *normal* | = | $\lambda \mid normal \odot T^0$ |
| (iii) | *monotone* | = | $\lambda \mid monotone \odot T^0 \mid monotone \odot T^+$ |
| (iv) | *balanced* | = | $normal \mid normal \odot T^+ \odot balanced \odot T^- \odot normal$ |
| (v) | *positive* | = | $monotone \mid balanced \mid positive \odot positive$ |

where $s_1 \odot s_2$ is defined iff $out\ s_1 = in\ s_2$ and if $s_1 = s \circ \langle a \rangle$ then $s_1 \odot s_2 \rightleftharpoons s \circ s_2$. Moreover, we take $s_1 \odot \lambda \rightleftharpoons s_1$ and $\lambda \odot s_2 \rightleftharpoons s_2$.

The correctness of definition (i) follows from the assumption of the theorem. The correctness of (ii) and (iii) is trivial. To prove (iv) let $s \in Trace_{\mathcal{A}^\bullet}[\![g]\!]$ be a balanced trace. If $node(s, T^+) = node(s, T^-) = \emptyset$ then it is a normal trace. Otherwise $s$ contains at least one *Pop* statement. Consider the last occurrence of the *Pop* statement. The remaining part of the trace must be normal. Now take the first *Push* statement of this trace. Obviously, the trace before the first *Push* statement is normal. Since the trace itself is balanced, the trace between the first *Push* and the last *Pop* statements must also be balanced.

To prove (v) let $s \in Trace_{\mathcal{A}^\bullet}[\![g]\!]$ be a positive trace. If $|node(s, T^+)| = |node(s, T^-)|$ then $s$ is balanced. So we may suppose that $|node(s, T^+)| > |node(s, T^-)|$. If $|node(s, T^-)| = 0$ then $s$ is monotone. Therefore

$$|node(s, T^+)| > |node(s, T^-)| > 0.$$

We have to check that $s$ is the concatenation of two positive traces. Let us suppose that there is a non-empty initial segment $r$ of $s$ which is balanced. In this case let $s_1$ be the maximal of all such balanced subtraces of $s$. Let $s_2$ be such that $s = s_1 \odot s_2$. Otherwise let $s_1$ be the subtrace of the $s$ up to the first *Push* command. In the first case $s_2 \neq \lambda$ since $s$ is not balanced. In each initial segment of $s_2$ the number of *Push* commands is not less than the number of *Pop* commands. Otherwise $s_1$ would not be the maximal balanced subsequence of $s$. In the second case $s_2$ must be positive, otherwise $s$ would have a balanced initial segment.

Our last task is to turn these informal recursive equations into inductive ones. Let $X = var(g)$ and let $Y, Z$ be two copies of $X$. For any pair $a, b \in node(g)$ let $N_{ab}$, $M_{ab}$, $B_{ab}$ and $P_{ab}$ be new $(X, Y)$-type relation symbols. These new symbols will describe the input-output semantics between $a$ and $b$ of normal, monotone, balanced and positive traces, respectively. First we define the relations $T^0_{ab}$, $T^+_{ab}$ as first-order ones:

$$T^0_{ab}(X,Y) \quad \rightleftharpoons \quad \begin{cases} onestep_g((X,a),(Y,b)) & \text{if } g(a,b) \in T^+; \\ false & \text{otherwise.} \end{cases}$$

$$T^+_{ab}(X,Y) \quad \rightleftharpoons \quad \begin{cases} X = Y & \text{if } g(a,b) \in T^+; \\ false & \text{otherwise.} \end{cases}$$

**Normal traces**

$$N_{ab}(X,Y) = \bigvee\{\exists Z\ N_{ac}(X,Z) \wedge T^0_{cb}(Z,Y) \mid c \in node(g)\} \vee \bigvee_{a=b}(X = Y).$$

**Monotone traces**

$$M_{ab}(X,Y) = \bigvee\{\exists Z\ M_{ac}(X,Z) \wedge T^0_{cb}(Z,Y) \mid c \in node(g)\} \vee \bigvee\{\exists Z\ M_{ac}(X,Z) \wedge T^+_{cb}(Z,Y) \mid c \in node(g)\} \bigvee_{a=b}(X = Y).$$

**Balanced traces** Let $Z_1$, $Z_2$, $Z_3$ and $Z_4$ be four new copies of $X$ and let $\iota_i : X \to Z_i$ be the corresponding bijections $(i = 1, ..., 4)$.

$$\begin{aligned} &B_{ab}(X,Y) = \\ &\quad N_{ab}(X,Y) \vee \\ &\quad \bigvee\{\exists Z_1 ... \exists Z_4\ N_{ac_1}(X,Z_1) \wedge T^+_{c_1c_2}(Z_1,Z_2) \wedge B_{c_2c_3}(Z_2,Z_3) \wedge \\ &\quad N_{c_4b}(Z_4,Y) \wedge \iota_4(x) = \tau[\iota_1(x)/x]_{x\in X} \wedge \bigwedge\{\iota_4(v) = \iota_3(v) \mid v \neq x, v \in X\} \\ &\quad \mid c_1, c_2, c_3, c_4 \in dom\, g, g(c_1,c_2) = Push(\tau), g(c_3,c_4) = Pop(x)\}. \end{aligned}$$

**Positive traces**

$$P_{ab}(X,Y) = M_{ab}(X,Y) \vee$$
$$B_{ab}(X,Y) \vee$$
$$\bigvee\{\exists Z\ P_{ac}(X,Z) \wedge P_{cb}(Z,Y) \mid c \in node(g)\}.$$

We think that all these equations may be trivial, except for balanced traces. Unlike all the other equations this equation is not only for composition and union. Let us consider the following decomposition of a balanced trace $s$:

$$\begin{array}{ccccccccccccc} X & N_{ac_1} & Z_1 & T^{+}_{c_1c_2} & Z_2 & & B_{c_2c_3} & & Z_3 & T^{-}_{c_3c_4} & Z_4 & N_{c_4b} & Y \\ a & \longrightarrow & c_1 & \longrightarrow & c_2 & & \longrightarrow & & c_3 & \longrightarrow & c_4 & \longrightarrow & b \end{array}$$

The program at label $c_3$ executes a statement $Pop(x)$. The value of $x$ at label $c_4$ (being equal to the value of $\iota_4(x) \in Z_4$) cannot be computed from the values of $Z_3$ since $x$ is coming from the stack. Since $B_{c_2c_3}$ is balanced, the value of $\tau$ at label $c_1$ (or equivalently at $c_2$) gives the correct value of $x$ at $c_4$. The part of $s$ between $c_2$ and $c_3$ is balanced, therefore the value $\tau$ pushed at $c_1$ is the stack element taken out at $c_4$. So we can describe the value of $x$ at $c_4$ by taking $\iota_4(x) = \tau[\iota_1(x)/x]_{x \in X}$. $\bigwedge\{\iota_3(v) = \iota_4(v) \mid v \neq x, v \in X\}$ which guarantees that only $x$ can get a new value at $c_3$. We remark that in the case of $p \in P^1_\sigma$ all quantifiers can be replaced by appropriate Herbrand quantifiers. □

**(8.13) Theorem.** *Let $\sigma$ be a one-sorted similarity type. $EI_\sigma \approx P^1_\sigma \approx P^{1,e}_\sigma$ and $I_\sigma \approx rP^1_\sigma \approx rP^{1,e}_\sigma$.*

*Proof.* One direction of this theorem follows from Theorem (8.9). The other direction follows from Lemma (8.11) and Theorems (6.8) and (8.12).

Let now $\sigma$ be a many-sorted similarity type such that it contains two distinct constant symbols $c_s$ and $d_s$ for each sort $s \in sort\ \sigma$. If we consider only those models of $Mod_\sigma$ for which $\bigwedge_{s \in sort\ \sigma}(c_s \neq d_s)$ holds then Lemma (8.11) remains true for this case. Therefore, Theorem (8.13) holds for many-sorted similarity types as well, for those models.

**(8.14) Corollary.** *Let $\sigma$ be a fixed one-sorted similarity type. Let $\mathcal{A} \in Mod_\sigma$ be arbitrary. The inductive and 1-computable relations in $\mathcal{A}$ are the same iff there is a program $any(Y) \in P^1_\sigma$ simulating the random assignment $Y :=?$.*

*Proof.* This statement means that the $P^1_\sigma$-computable and the $rP^1_\sigma$-computable relations are the same in $\mathcal{A}$. Thus the statement follows from Lemmas (8.7) and (8.8) and Theorem (8.13). □

## 8.2 On the Role of Natural Numbers

In the present section we give the logical characterization of the computational family $P^2$ by using the effective inductively definable relations allowing the usage of arithmetic. This computation family is denoted by $EI^c$. While we define the equivalence of $P^2$ and $EI^c$ with respect to computational power we use the auxiliary fact that the computation families $P^2$ and $P^{1,c}$ have the same computational power.

Remember that the programming language $P^2_\sigma$ for an arbitrary similarity type $\sigma$ handles arithmetic, since by coding natural numbers as the length of stacks one can define all the operations and relations of arithmetic by appropriate programs. Let us investigate how $P^2_\sigma$-programs can be characterized by starting from arithmetic and $P_\sigma$. This investigation will consider which properties of arithmetic are significant and which should be added to $P_\sigma$ and to arithmetic for this characterization. Informally, we want to find a solution for the "equation" $P_\sigma + \mathcal{N} + ? = P^2_\sigma$. Moreover, we also would like to describe those $\sigma$-type models $\mathcal{B}$ which can replace $\mathcal{N}$ in this equation. Coding of the elements of the Herbrand universe generated from the inputs of program without random assignment will play an important role in this description. Note that this is the reason why the results below cannot be extended for programming languages with random assignment.

First let us formulate a recursion-theoretic theorem which will be appropriate to emphasize those properties of coding which are necessary for our aim.

**(8.15) Theorem.** *Let $p \in P^2_\sigma$ be arbitrary but fixed. Take $X \rightleftharpoons var(p)$, let $\iota : X \to X'$ be a copy of $X'$. There is a set $F \subseteq [X \to Term_\sigma] \times Open_\sigma$ with the following properties:*

*(A)(i) for each $(f, \alpha) \in F : var(\alpha) \subseteq X$;*

*(ii) for each $\mathcal{A} \in Mod_\sigma$; $k \in Val_\mathcal{A}[X]$, $k' \in Val_\mathcal{A}[X']$: $(k, k') \in Den_\mathcal{A}[\![p, X]\!]$ iff there is an $(f, \alpha) \in F$ such that $\mathcal{A} \models \alpha[k]$ and for each $x \in X$: $f(x)_\mathcal{A}[k] = k'(\iota(x))$;*

*(B) F is recursively enumerable (with respect to Gödel coding of $\sigma$-type terms and open formulas).*

*Proof.* Let $p \in P^2_\sigma$ be as in the theorem. First we construct a program $\tilde{p} \in P^2_\eta$ which runs similarly to $p$ but instead of "real data" it operates on codes of terms. This means that for each program variable $x_i$ there is another variable $f_i \in V_{sort\ \eta}$ which contains the code (Gödel number) of a term $\lceil f_i \rceil^{-1}$ whose value is the actual value of $x_i$. This also means that if, say, the program $p$ executes an assignment $x := \tau$ then $\tilde{p}$ computes the code of the term $\tau[\lceil f_i \rceil^{-1}/x_i]$. Similarly, if $p$ executes a command of the form $Push_i(\tau)$ then $\tilde{p}$ computes the code of $\tau[\lceil f_i \rceil^{-1}/x_i]$ and this natural number (i.e. the code itself) is pushed into the i-th stack. These steps can be carried out because we use effective coding and in this case the mentioned operations are recursive, therefore these operations can be computed by $P_\eta$-programs. We must be careful while simulating tests. Since $\tilde{p} \in P^2_\eta$ the program $\tilde{p}$ is not able to check that a test $\beta$ is true or not. To solve this problem the program $\tilde{p}$ built up a "big" open formula, more precisely, a code for this big open formula which is stored in a new variable $\alpha$. Let us see how the program $\tilde{p}$ simulates a program **if** $\beta_1 \to p_1 \Box \beta_2 \to p_2$ **fi**, which is a subprogram of $p$. $\tilde{p}$ thinks that all the three possibilities $\beta_1$, $\beta_2$ and $\neg\beta_1 \wedge \neg\beta_2$ may become true. Let $\gamma$ be one of these three formulas. First the code of the formula $\gamma[\lceil f_i \rceil^{-1}/x_i]$ is computed and then the code for the conjunction of this formula and the formula coded by $\alpha$ is computed. The code so obtained is the new value for $\alpha$. After this $\tilde{p}$ simulates $p_1$, $p_2$ or **skip**, depending on which of the formulas $\beta_1$, $\beta_2$ or $\neg\beta_1 \wedge \neg\beta_2$ was chosen.

Take

$$F \rightleftharpoons \{(\lambda x.\lceil k'(x)\rceil^{-1}, \lceil k(\alpha)\rceil^{-1}) | k' \in rng\ Den_{\mathcal{A}}[\![\tilde{p}, X]\!]\}.$$

By Theorems (7.5) (A) and (7.9) the set $F$ is recursively enumerable. It is not hard but it is very tiresome to prove that $F$ also satisfies the property (A) of the theorem. We leave this part of the proof to the reader. $\Box$

Now let us consider how the above properties of coding can be formulated in general. Let $\mu$ be an arbitrary but given similarity type. For an arbitrary $\mu$-type model $\mathcal{B}$ let ${}_{\mathcal{B}}[\,]$ be the function $Term(\mu, \emptyset) \to B$ which renders to each ground term $\tau$ the value $\tau_{\mathcal{B}}[\,]$ in the model $\mathcal{B}$.

**(8.16) Definition.** *Let $\mathcal{B} \in Mod_\mu$ be a fixed model. A coding schema in $\mathcal{B}$ for an arbitrary similarity type $\sigma$ consists of four functions*

$$\mathcal{Q}_t : Term_\sigma \to Term(\mu, \emptyset)$$
$$\mathcal{Q}_o : Open_\sigma \to Term(\mu, \emptyset)$$
$$\mathcal{Q}_v : V_{sort\ \sigma} \to V_{sort\ \mu}$$
$$\mathcal{Q}_p : P^2_\sigma \to P_\mu$$

*such that $\mathcal{Q}_t \circ {}_{\mathcal{B}}[\,]$, $\mathcal{Q}_o \circ {}_{\mathcal{B}}[\,]$ and $\mathcal{Q}_v$ are injective functions. Their (partial) inverse functions are denoted by $obj_t$, $obj_o$, $obj_v$, respectively.*

We intend to use a coding schema mainly for simulating $P^2_\sigma$-programs by $P_\mu$-programs. The function $\mathcal{Q}_p$ just does it. Since we do not want to suppose that $\mu \subseteq \sigma$, then the definition of "what simulation is" requires some tricks for which the other coding functions $\mathcal{Q}_t$, $\mathcal{Q}_o$ and $\mathcal{Q}_v$ have been introduced. Now we give the precise definition of "simulation".

**(8.17) Definition.** *A coding schema $\mathcal{Q}$ in $\mathcal{B}$ satisfies the program abstraction property iff there is a variable symbol $\alpha \in V_{sort\ \mu}$ such that for all $p \in P^2_\sigma$ and $\mathcal{A} \in Mod_\sigma$:*

$Den_{\mathcal{A}}[\![p, X]\!] =$

$$\{(k, k') \in Val_{\mathcal{A}}[X, X'] \mid \exists \ell, \ell'\ (\ell, \ell') \in Den_{\mathcal{B}}[\![\mathcal{Q}_p(p)]\!] \text{ such that}$$
$$\forall v \in X\ \ell(\mathcal{Q}_v(v)) = \mathcal{Q}_t(v) \text{ and}$$

$$\forall v \in X \ obj_t(\ell'(\iota_U(\mathcal{Q}_v(v))))_{\mathcal{A}}[k] = k'(\iota_X(v)) \ and$$
$$\mathcal{A} \models obj_o(l'(\iota_U(\alpha)))[k]\},$$

*where $X \rightleftharpoons var(p)$, $X'$ is a copy of $X$ with bijection $\iota_X$ and hence $Den_{\mathcal{A}}[\![p, X]\!] \subseteq Val_{\mathcal{A}}[X, X']$. Moreover, $U \rightleftharpoons var(\mathcal{Q}_p(p))$ and $U'$ is a new copy of $U$ with the bijection $\iota_U$.*

The above definition means that $\mathcal{Q}_p(p)$ for a given program $p \in P^2_\sigma$ computes the codes of all $(f, \alpha) \in F$ of Theorem (8.15) according to the coding schema $\mathcal{Q}$.

Now we define two programs, one of which computes the value of a coded term while the other decides whether a coded open formula is true.

**(8.18) Definition.**

*(i) A coding schema $\mathcal{Q}$ in $\mathcal{B}$ satisfies the data abstraction property with respect to $\sigma$ iff for each sorts $d \in sort\ \sigma$ and for each finite set $X \subset V_{sort\,\sigma}$ there is a program $pT_{(d,X)} \in P^1_{\sigma(\mathcal{B})}$ with $var(pT_{(d,X)}) \supseteq X \cup \{\beta\} \cup \{y_d\} \rightleftharpoons U$ (where $\beta \in V_\mu$, $y_d \notin X$ and $sort(y_d) = d$) such that for each $\mathcal{A} \in Mod_\sigma$*

$$Den_{\mathcal{A}+\mathcal{B}}[\![pT_{(d,X)}, U]\!] = \{(k, k') \in Val_{\mathcal{A}+\mathcal{B}}[U, U'] \mid obj_t(k(\beta))_{\mathcal{A}}[k] = k'(y_d)\}.$$

*(ii) A coding schema $Q$ in $\mathcal{B}$ satisfies the formula abstraction property with respect to $\sigma$ iff for all finite set $X \subset V_{sort\,\sigma}$ there is a program $pO_X \in P_{\sigma^1(\mathcal{B})}$ such that for all $\mathcal{A} \in Mod_\sigma$:*

$$dom\ Den_{\mathcal{A}+\mathcal{B}}[\![pO_X, X \cup \{\beta\}]\!] = \{k \in Val_{\mathcal{A}+\mathcal{B}}[X \cup \{\beta\}] \mid \mathcal{A} \models obj_o(k(\beta))[k]\}$$

*where $\beta \in V_\mu$.*

**(8.19) Lemma.** *Let $\mathcal{Q}$ be a coding schema in $\mathcal{B}$ which satisfies all program, data and formula abstraction properties. If so then $P^2_\sigma \lesssim P^{1,\mathcal{B}}_\sigma$.*

*Proof.* Let $p \in P^2_\sigma$ be an arbitrary program. Take $X \rightleftharpoons var(p)$. Let us suppose that $X \cap var(\mathcal{Q}_p(p)) = \emptyset$. Let $\tilde{p}$ be the following program:

$$\begin{aligned}\tilde{p} \rightleftharpoons\ & X' := X;\ (x \in X) : \mathcal{Q}_v(x) := \mathcal{Q}_t(x);\ \mathcal{Q}_p(p);\ \beta := \alpha;\ pO_X;\\ & (x \in X) : [X := X'; \beta := \mathcal{Q}_v(x); pT_{(sort(x),X)}; \iota_X(x) := y_{sort(x)}];\\ & X := X'.\end{aligned}$$

It is clear that $\tilde{p} \in P^{1,\mathcal{B}}_\sigma$ and $dom\ Den[\![p, X]\!] = dom\ Den[\![\tilde{p}, X]\!]$. This proves the fact that $P^2_\sigma \lesssim P^{1,\mathcal{B}}_\sigma$. □

**(8.20) Definition.** *A model $\mathcal{B} \in Mod_\mu$ is called a universal coding domain iff for all finite similarity types $\sigma$ there is a coding schema in $\mathcal{B}$ having all program, data and formula abstraction properties with respect to $\sigma$.*

**(8.21) Theorem.** *Any model of PA is a universal coding domain.*

*Proof.* A fully detailed proof would require several pages. However, the main stream of the proof is really very simple. Let $\mathcal{A} \in Mod(PA)$ be fixed. It is clear that $\mathbb{N} \subseteq A$. We only use this part of $A$. Fix a finite similarity type $\sigma$ and let $Q$ be an arbitrary effective coding of $Term_\sigma$, $Open_\sigma$, $V_\sigma$ and $P^2_\sigma$. We show that $Q$ has all the program, data and formula abstraction properties with respect to the similarity type $\sigma$. Indeed, the program abstraction property follows from Theorem (8.15). Now we have to define programs $pO_X$ and $pT_{(d,X)}$ for all $d$, $X$. However, it is enough to consider how a real compiler or a BASIC interpreter evaluates expressions using arithmetic and exactly one stack. Any of these programs is appropriate. □

**(8.22) Corollary.** *Any infinite Herbrand model is a universal coding domain.*

*Proof.* The main idea of the proof is in showing that arithmetic is computable in any infinite Herbrand model. We cannot say that it is definable because it is not true. However, we can construct programs which behave like functions $S$, $P$, $\cdot$, etc. Moreover, we can prove that these objects satisfy the well known properties of arithmetic, namely $PA$. In the end we can use Theorem (8.21). □

**(8.23) Corollary.** *For an arbitrary similarity type $\sigma$, $P^{1,c}_\sigma \approx P^2_\sigma$.*

*Proof.* It is clear that $P^{1,c}_\sigma \lesssim P^2_\sigma$. Indeed, $P^2_\sigma \approx P_{\sigma^s}$ and $P_{\sigma^c} \lesssim P_{\sigma^s}$ imply this statement. To prove that $P^2_\sigma \lesssim P^{1,c}_\sigma$ we first remark that $\mathcal{N} \models PA$. Using Theorem (8.21) we get that $\mathcal{N}$ is a universal coding domain. So we can apply Lemma (8.19) for $\mathcal{N}$ and get $P^2_\sigma \lesssim P^{1,\mathcal{N}}_\sigma = P^{1,c}_\sigma$. □

In order to provide a logical characterization of $P^2_\sigma$ let us consider a modification of the notion of (effectively) inductive relations. Let $\mathcal{A} \in Mod_\sigma$ be arbitrary and let $s$ be a new sort such that $s \notin sort\ \sigma$. Take the similarity type $\eta$ ($sort\ \eta = \{s\}$) and the standard model of arithmetic $\mathcal{N}$ such that its universe is considered to be $s$-sorted. Let $\mathcal{A}+\mathcal{N}$ be the extension of the model $\mathcal{A}$ by the standard model of arithmetic. Let $I^c_\sigma$ be the set of inductive relations on the models of $Mod_\sigma$ where the defining formula contains $\eta$-type formulas interpreted on $\mathcal{N}$ as subformulas. Also let $EI^c_\sigma$ be the set of effectively inductive relations on the models of $Mod_\sigma$ for which, in the (effectively) inductive schemas, the usage of $\eta$-type formulas interpreted on $\mathcal{N}$ is allowed. Note that this type of extension equips the programming languages with counters.

**(8.24) Definition.**

(a) *Let $\mathcal{A}$ be a $\sigma$-type model and let $X \subset V$. An $X$-type relation $R$ in $\mathcal{A}$ is called inductively definable in $\mathcal{A}$ by counters iff there is an inductive definitional schema $(\Theta_1, \Theta_2)$ and a valuation $k$ such that*

*(i)* $\Theta_1, \Theta_2 \in Form_{\sigma^c}$;
*(ii)* $k \in Val_{\mathcal{A}^c}[var(\Theta_1) \cup var(\Theta_2)]$;
*(iii)* *for any* $a \in Val_{\mathcal{A}}[X]$, $a \in R$ *iff* $(k + a) \in_{\mathcal{A}^c} I_{(\Theta_1, \Theta_2)}$.

*(b) An* $X$*-type relation* $R$ *on* $\mathcal{A}$ *is called effectively inductively definable on* $\mathcal{A}$ *by counters iff there is an inductive definitional schema* $(\Theta_1, \Theta_2)$ *which defines* $R$ *effectively inductively.*

*(c)* $I^c(\mathcal{A})$ *and* $EI^c(\mathcal{A})$ *denote the set of all relations inductively definable by counters and effectively inductively definable in* $\mathcal{A}$ *by counters, respectively.*

$EI$, $I$, $EI^c$, $I^c$ are functions defined on $\cup Mod_\sigma$. Taking this fact into account, they are computation families, and the computational power of these families can be considered according to Definition (7.16).

**(8.25) Theorem.** *For any one-sorted similarity type* $\sigma$:
*(i)* $P^2_\sigma \approx P^{1,c}_\sigma \approx EI^c_\sigma$;
*(ii)* $rP^{1,c}_\sigma \approx I^c_\sigma$

*Proof.*
(i) $P^{1,c}_\sigma \approx EI^c_\sigma$ follows from Theorem (8.13). $P^2_\sigma \approx P^{1,c}_\sigma$ has been proved in Corollary (8.23).
(ii) The statement (ii) simply follows from (i). □

**(8.26)** *Remark.* It is an open question whether $rP^2 > I^c$.

We summarize the results of Chapter 8 in Fig. 8.1.

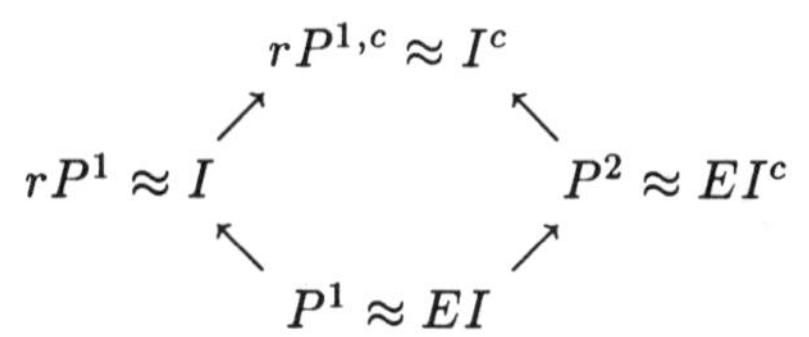


**Fig. 8.1.** Comparison of inductive definability and computability

Part II

# Extended Dynamic Logics

Chapter 9

# Introduction to Part II

The first significant steps in developing a unique logically based programming theory have been made in Part I. These steps resulted in a computation theory in the scope of first-order classical logic. To accomplish the development of our programming theory we have to make efforts to develop appropriate tools with the same scope to deal with the characterization of the programming languages and programs provided as formal objects by the computation theory. Moreover these tools should allow the required characterization in accordance with our computation theory. Part II is devoted to accomplishing the required development programming theory, that is, it is devoted to the development of the second subfield of programming theory in harmony with the first subfield outlined in Part I.

Characterization of the mentioned formal objects may concern some syntactic aspects and some semantic ones. The syntactic aspects consider the program texts and describe some properties referring to the type of commands and operators used in these texts. The semantic aspects consider the program meaning and deal with the properties of the program executions.

The required characterization may be made in at least the following two approaches. We define some properties which are selected for a certain reason and then we look for appropriate formal tools to describe these properties and deal with them. The same approach may group the properties, e.g. according to the formal tools that can be used to handle them. However, the other approach considers the object which we intend to characterize and provides appropriate tools to describe the object itself. Then by the use of the corresponding formalism any interesting property can be defined. This means that for semantically interesting properties of programs we develop formal tools to define the objects that represent program semantics and then by using these tools we handle any property of the program execution. We start in Chapter 10 with the consideration of some widely used program properties and their classification into safety, liveness and precedence groups according to Lamport [1983], Manna, Pnueli [1983] and Kröger [1987]. Aiming at the consideration of program properties the emphasis is transferred from the programming languages to the so-called descriptive languages that allows characterization of programming languages and programs from a semantic viewpoint. That is, while in computation theory the main objects are the programming languages, in the second subfield of programming theory the descriptive languages are the focus of interest. These languages should be appropriate to describe the necessary program properties and to investigate them. It is also required to have a formal calculus for the descriptive languages which allow proof of whether a program to be considered possesses any interesting properties.

Most of the formal descriptive languages emphasize the description of results of program executions rather than the program executions themselves. These languages use the input-output semantics of programs. The widely used dynamic logic and its Floyd-Hoare sublanguage are examples of these descriptive languages.

In Chapter 11 we define a version of dynamic logic for programming languages considered in Part I. This logic deals with two kinds of syntactic entities, formulas and programs. In this version we allow only open formulas in tests of the programs, since only this case corresponds to our intuition of effective computability. The logic considered here coincides with regular dynamic logic (cf. e.g. Meyer, Winklmann [1982]). We learn what program properties can be expressed by this version of dynamic logic and we focus on the investigation of its completeness.

It will be shown that not only is this dynamic logic incomplete but its important Floyd-Hoare sublanguage is too. We will consider different approaches to make this sublanguage complete. The first approach will restrict the set of formulas allowed to be used for describing program properties. However, as we will see, almost all pragmatically interesting restricted sets of dynamic logical formulas connected with partial correctness will be incomplete. The second approach modifies the classical notion of completeness. As is known, relative completeness (see Cook[1978]), and particularly arithmetical completeness, which presupposes an oracle that handles all tautologies of arithmetic, is appropriate for dynamic logic (see Harel [1979]). Dynamic logic is also $\omega$-complete, which means that if we add an inference rule to the calculus (called the $\omega$-rule) with infinitely many antecedents then the true dynamic logical statements can be proved. However, since we require an effective notion of proof this way of obtaining completeness is not satisfactory for us.

Therefore we will introduce a new notion of completeness, so-called Den-completeness, with a rather programming-theoretic motivation. This new notion fullfills the requirement of being the notion of effective proof but, as we will see, the Floyd-Hoare language will be incomplete even in this new sense with respect to the pragmatically important partial correctness theories.

Having seen these negative results we introduce a new approach which allows us to turn dynamic logic into a complete logic preserving the traditional notion of completeness. We also expect this approach to provide us with a dynamic logic which is harmonious with our computation theory. The logical tools necessary for developing the required dynamic logic will be introduced in Chapter 13. Note that among these tools a significant role will be played by a modification of the notion of extension introduced and used in Chapter 5 for augmenting the programming language $rP_\sigma$ with new computational devices.

The main characteristic of our approach is that we intend to provide tools with which we can give logical objects that allow the definition of program semantics inside the descriptive language. The so-called semantic function is the tool which embeds the programming language into the extended classical first-order language. By the use of the modified extension and of the semantic function, the extended dynamic logic will be introduced in a general setting together with an axiomatic calculus.

We will define different extensions and also different semantic functions by means of which different dynamic extended logics will be introduced. In Chapter 14 we develop the transitive extension which allows us to internalize reflexive and transitive closure of input-output relations. On the base of this extension we define a special extended language through which we introduce two axiom systems $Ind_\sigma$ and $Ind^*_\sigma$. We will study how transitive extension allows one to define the denotational semantics of programs. By the use of transitive extension and the axiom systems $Ind_\sigma$ and $Ind^*_\sigma$ we define the dynamic logic with continuous denotational semantics and that with strongly continuous denotational semantics. The first one will also be called non-standard dynamic logic because it has all the necessary semantic properties that the dynamic logic developed by the Hungarian school possesses. We will show that these new dynamic logics are already compact and complete. Then we introduce the Hoare calculus for these dynamic logics and we prove completeness. A first-order axiomatic characterization of the Hoare calculus will be established. The chapter ends with the comparision of different dynamic logics with respect to their logical power.

In Chapter 15 we will develop a version of dynamic logic allowing the description of properties of programs that may use stacks. It is known that the traditionally defined dynamic logic is not approapariate for this characterization because the Floyd-Hoare method used considers only the properties of the data environment of the program under execution at a given moment of time independently of the properties before and after this moment. That is, this method describes program properties in a "context-free" way, supposing that "state transformer" can describe the execution, which however is not true when the use of stacks is allowed in the programs. In order to describe programs with one stack a new language will be developed in Chapter 15, the so-called inductive logic. This language is also obtained by an appropriate extension called inductive extension. This extension is defined such that it contains at least one solution of some well-defined set of fixed-point equations, since as we know from Part I this is necessary for characterizing the denotational semantics of the programs with stack. By the use of the extended language we axiomatize the main properties required from the semantics by introducing two axiom systems $\nabla Ind_\sigma$ and $\nabla Ind^*_\sigma$ with the same role as in the case of transitive extension.

We will show how the inductive extension can be used to define the denotational semantics of programs with one stack. By the use of inductive logic and the axiom systems $\nabla Ind_\sigma$ and $\nabla Ind^*_\sigma$ we define the dynamic logic with definable denotational semantics and that with strongly definable denotational semantics, respectively. We show that these dynamic logics are compact and complete. A derivation system called $I/O$-calculus will be given which in character lies between the Floyd-Hoare calculus and that of the usual calculus of the classical first-order logic. This calculus eliminates the main ideological disadvantages of the Floyd-Hoare style methods mentioned above, and so it becomes appropriate to prove properties of programs which use one stack. This calculus considers the program execution along with establishing the program structure and some interrelations between the computational states representable at the structural level.

Inductive logic allows also the axiomatic characterization of derivation systems by using axiom systems $\nabla Ind_\sigma$ and $\nabla Ind^*_\sigma$. The first one can be used to characterize the Floyd-Hoare calculus, while the second one is appropriate to characterize the $I/O$-calculus.

The chapter ends with the comparative study of all the dynamic logics considered in Part II.

Chapter 10

# Description of Program Properties

Having formally defined the notions of programs and their executions over the abstract models of computers it is an important question how programs can be characterized. The first possibility is to consider how the programs are built up, i.e. what programming constructs participate in their definitions and how. The number of cycles or the number of constructs built into one another can be determined. However, this type of characterization is purely syntactic, of course, and considers programs only as texts. But the essence of programs is hidden in their execution, which takes place in the data environment and is represented by the definition of semantics of programming languages. Therefore, the semantic characterization of programs is necessary to reflect the pragmatic essence and to answer the question of what a program does. For this characterization, appropriate properties concerning program execution should be selected. According to the computation theory developed in Part I, these properties should concern the computation states from which the computational paths are formed and also to the traces themselves. For example a property like "the program terminates" refers to the finiteness of computation paths and also to the existence of a "terminal" state. However, this tight connection of properties with computation states suggests another view. Namely, the semantic characterization of programs should start with the appropriate definition of the program semantics, i.e. either of the denotations or of the traces. Since we aim to develop the programming theory in the scope of classical first-order logic, this definition should be stated using appropriate logical tools. Having given the logical definition of semantics, the same language will be appropriate to characterize the denotations or the traces. However, before starting to realize our view, which prefers the definition of the semantics to that of the description of program properties, we give a rough survey of the main properties.

Many different properties can be introduced; however, it is more useful to group them. Lamport [1977] distinguishes two groups of properties: the *safety* or *invariance* properties and the *liveness* or *eventuality* properties. Informally, a safety property states that some bad things never happen, or in other words, that a good property is true, forever. A liveness property states that some good things eventually happen either at one time or at a given number of time moments.

*Precedence* properties form another group. These properties refer to certain families of states and deal with their interrelation (see e.g. Manna, Pnueli

[1983]). The reader interested in more detailed investigation and classification of program properties is refered to Kröger [1987] or Manna, Pnueli [1988].

Let us consider the three groups of properties mentioned above, i.e. safety (or invariance) properties, liveness (or eventuality) properties and precedence properties.

First we consider some of the well known safety properties.

**(10.1) Definition.** *Let $\phi$, $\psi \in Form_\sigma$, $\mathcal{A} \in Mod_\sigma$ be fixed and let $p \in rP_\sigma$ be an arbitrary program.*

| Notion | Definition |
|---|---|
| Program p is partially correct in $\mathcal{A}$ w.r.t. $\phi$ and $\psi$ (which are called pre- and postconditions, respectively). | Each terminating computation path of $p$ in $\mathcal{A}$ starting from a state of property $\phi$, terminates in a state of property $\psi$. |
| Program $p$ has a global invariant $\psi$ in $\mathcal{A}$ w.r.t. the precondition $\phi$. | Each state of each computational path of $p$ in $\mathcal{A}$, which starts from a state of property $\phi$, is of property $\psi$. |
| Program $p$ has a generalized invariant $\psi$ in $\mathcal{A}$ w.r.t. the precondition $\phi$. | Each computational path of $p$ in $\mathcal{A}$, which starts from a state of property $\phi$, reaches states of property $\psi$ infinitely many times. |

Now we define some liveness properties.

**(10.2) Definition.** *Let $\phi$, $\psi \in Form_\sigma$, $\mathcal{A} \in Mod_\sigma$ be fixed and let $p \in rP_\sigma$ be an arbitrary program.*

| Notion | Definition |
|---|---|
| Program $p$ is quasi-totally correct in $\mathcal{A}$ with respect to the precondition $\phi$ and the postcondition $\psi$. | There exists a computational path of $p$ in $\mathcal{A}$ which starts from a state of property $\phi$ and terminates in a state of property $\psi$. |
| Program $p$ quasi-terminates in A with respect to the precondition $\phi$. | Program $p$ is quasi-totally correct in $\mathcal{A}$ with respect to the precondition $\phi$ and the postcondition *true*. |
| Program $p$ is pseudo-totally correct in $\mathcal{A}$ with respect to the precondition $\phi$ and the postcondition $\psi$. | Program $p$ is partially correct and quasi-totally correct in $\mathcal{A}$ with respect to the precondition $\phi$ and the postcondition $\psi$. |
| Program $p$ is totally correct in $\mathcal{A}$ with respect to the precondition $\phi$ and the postcondition $\psi$. | Each computational path of $p$ in $\mathcal{A}$, which starts from a state of property $\phi$, terminates and the terminal state is of property $\psi$. |

Now let us see some precedence properties.

**(10.3) Definition.** *Let $\phi$, $\psi_0, \psi_1 \in Form_\sigma$, $\mathcal{A} \in Mod_\sigma$ be fixed and let $p \in rP_\sigma$ be an arbitrary program.*

| Notion | Definition |
|---|---|
| Program $p$ has the weak accessibility property in $\mathcal{A}$ w.r.t. the precondition $\phi$ and the transients $\psi_0$, $\psi_1$ (denoted by $\phi \succ_w \psi_0, \psi_1$). | Each computational path of $p$ in $\mathcal{A}$, which starts from a state of property $\phi$, and reaches a state of property $\psi_0$, later also reaches a state of property $\psi_1$. |
| Program $p$ has the accessibility property in $\mathcal{A}$ w.r.t. the precondition $\phi$ and the transients $\psi_0$, $\psi_1$ (denoted by $\phi \succ \psi_0, \psi_1$). | Program $p$ has the $\phi \succ_w \psi_0, \psi_1$ property and each computational path of $p$ in $\mathcal{A}$ which starts from a state of property $\phi$, reaches a state of property $\psi_0$. |

An interesting variant of precedence properties deals with program equivalence.

**(10.4) Definition.** *Let $p_1$, $p_2 \in rP_\sigma$ be arbitrary programs and let $\mathcal{A} \in Mod_\sigma$ be fixed.*

| Notion | Definition |
|---|---|
| Program $p_1$ simulates program $p_2$ in $\mathcal{A}$. | Each computational path of $p_1$ in $\mathcal{A}$ is also a computational path of $p_2$ in $\mathcal{A}$. |
| Programs $p_1$ and $p_2$ are Trace-equivalent in $\mathcal{A}$. | Computational paths of $p_1$ and those of $p_2$ coincide in $\mathcal{A}$. |

Our main goal is to develop those languages which enable us to describe the properties of programs. For this purpose we need formal tools to characterize the computational paths of programs, i.e. the program semantics. In Part I, two different ways were introduced for this characterization: the denotational (or input-output relational) and the trace semantics. The first way characterizes the inputs and the outputs of computational paths providing the input-output semantics. The second reflects the changes of the values of program variables during the whole computation. This approach uses the notion of trace and it provides the trace semantics of programs.

The above informally defined properties of programs can be formally described by using the formal semantic definitions. To illustrate how program properties can be semantically characterized, i.e. formalized, let us see some safety properties first.

**(10.5) Definition.** *Let $\phi$, $\psi \in Form_\sigma$, $\mathcal{A} \in Mod_\sigma$ be fixed and let $p \in rP_\sigma$ be an arbitrary program.*

| Notion | Semantic characterization |
|---|---|
| Program $p$ is partially correct in $\mathcal{A}$ w.r.t. $\phi$ and $\psi$. | For each state $s_1 \in Val_{\mathcal{A}} \times \{start_{gr(p)}\}$ with $\mathcal{A} \models \phi[\pi_1(s_1)]$, if $s_2 \in Val_{\mathcal{A}} \times \{stop_{gr(p)}\}$ is a state with the property $(\pi_1(s_1),\pi_1(s_2)) \in Den_{\mathcal{A}}[\![p]\!]$ then $\mathcal{A} \models \psi[\pi_1(s_2)]$. |
| Program $p$ has a global invariant $\psi$ in $\mathcal{A}$ w.r.t. $\phi$. | For each computation path $a \in Trace_{\mathcal{A}}$ $[\![p]\!]$, if $\mathcal{A} \models \phi[in\ a]$ then for each state $s$ of $a$ in $\mathcal{A}$, $\mathcal{A} \models \psi[\pi_1(s)]$. |

Note that here the semantic characterization of the first notion uses the input-output relation while that of the second uses trace semantics. Now let us see an example of how these two semantics can be used for formalizing liveness properties.

**(10.6) Definition.** *Let $\phi$, $\psi \in Form_\sigma$, $\mathcal{A} \in Mod_\sigma$ be fixed and let $p \in rP_\sigma$ be an arbitrary program.*

| Notion | Semantic characterization |
|---|---|
| Program $p$ is quasi-totally correct in $\mathcal{A}$ w.r.t. $\phi$ and $\psi$ | For all state $s_1 \in Val_{\mathcal{A}} \times \{start_{gr(p)}\}$ if $\mathcal{A} \models \phi[s_1]$ then there exists state $s_2 \in Val_{\mathcal{A}} \times \{start_{gr(p)}\}$ such that $(s_1, s_2) \in Den_{\mathcal{A}}[\![p]\!]$ and $\mathcal{A} \models \psi[s_2]$ |
| Program $p$ has the accessibility property $\phi \succ \psi_0, \psi_1$ in $\mathcal{A}$. | For each path $a \in Trace_{\mathcal{A}}[\![p]\!]$ of $p$ in $\mathcal{A}$, if $\mathcal{A} \models \phi[\pi_1(in\ a)]$ there is an $i \leq \lvert a \rvert - 1$ such that $\mathcal{A} \models \psi_0[\pi_1(a(i))]$ and for all $i \leq \lvert a \rvert - 1$ if $\mathcal{A} \models \psi_0[\pi_1(a(i))]$ then there is a $j \geq i$ for which $\mathcal{A} \models \psi_1[\pi_1(a(j))]$. |

The above two definitions illustrate our view on the primary role of program semantics against the program properties. In these definitions, first we used the denotational semantics and then the trace semantics to formalize the program properties. Therefore, according to our view, the properties of programs can be also classified by the semantic construction which they refer to.

In our programming theory we can distinguish $Den$-based and $Trace$-based properties, depending on the semantic constructions used in their characterization. However, in order to define these properties, first of all appropriate formal languages should be developed to define and axiomatically characterize denotations and traces, and only then can we turn to the definition of the corresponding program properties. In the next chapter we start the realization of this plan with the investigation of the well known dynamic logic and its Floyd-Hoare sublanguage.

Chapter 11

# Den-based Descriptive Languages

Programs operate on their data environments. If we are interested in the change caused by the execution of a program in its environment then the input-output semantics, defined as a binary relation on data sequences, is suitable. A great variety of program properties is connected with the relational semantics, e.g. partial correctness, quasi-total correctness, pseudo-total correctness, etc.

Let us see a descriptive language to describe these properties and to decide whether a program has the properties in question. We introduce a slight modification of the well known and thoroughly investigated dynamic logic. About the latter see e.g. Harel [1984]. Here we establish some basic properties of this dynamic logic.

Let us fix a (possibly) many-sorted similarity type $\sigma$ and a countable set $V$ of variables. Remember that any member of $V$ is of a sort, i.e. there is a function $sort : V \to S$. $V_s = sort^{-1}(s)$ is the set of $s$-sorted variables.

**(11.1) Definition.** *Let $rP_\sigma$ be the $\sigma$-type programming language with random assignment and let $Atom_\sigma$ be the set of all $\sigma$-type atomic formulas. The syntax of the dynamic logic is the least set $rD_\sigma$ satisfying the following properties:*

*(i) $Atom_\sigma \subseteq rD_\sigma$;*
*(ii) for any dynamic logic formulas $\phi, \psi \in rD_\sigma$ and variable $v \in V$ the formulas $(\neg\phi)$, $(\phi \wedge \psi)$ and $(\exists v\phi)$ belong to $rD_\sigma$;*
*(iii) for any formula $\phi \in rD_\sigma$ and program $p \in rP_\sigma$, $([p]\phi)$ belongs to $rD_\sigma$.*

We introduce the dual logic operators as abbreviations:

$$\begin{array}{rcl} (\forall v\phi) & \rightleftharpoons & (\neg(\exists v(\neg\phi))); \\ (\phi \vee \psi) & \rightleftharpoons & (\neg((\neg\phi) \wedge (\neg\psi))); \\ (\langle p\rangle\phi) & \rightleftharpoons & (\neg([p](\neg\phi))). \end{array}$$

Moreover, let $\phi \to \psi \rightleftharpoons ((\neg\phi) \vee \psi)$. For the sake of convenience, the "superfluous" parentheses will be omitted in the subsequent notations.

The main idea of $rD_\sigma$ is to integrate programs into a descriptive language by allowing programs to be modal operators. For instance, if $p \in rP_\sigma$ is a program and $\phi$ is a formula then a new formula $[p]\phi$ can be formed. Informally, the meaning of "$[p]\phi$" is "whenever the execution of $p$ terminates, the formula $\phi$

holds at the termination" and the meaning of "$\langle p\rangle\phi$" is "there is a terminating computational path of $p$ which satisfies $\phi$ at the termination".

The semantics of dynamic-logic formulas can be derived from the relational semantics of programs and from the formula-semantics adapted from the relational semantics for modal logic introduced by Kripke, as e.g. in Fisher, Ladner [1979].

However, we define the semantics by the use of the class of $\sigma$-type models and the Kripke-style relational semantics will be imitated by the denotations defined in (4.6). Fix a program $p \in rP_\sigma$ and a model $\mathcal{A} \in Mod_\sigma$. Remember that the denotation of program $p$ is a relation $Den_{\mathcal{A}}[\![p]\!]$ such that $Den_{\mathcal{A}}[\![p]\!] \subseteq Val_{\mathcal{A}} \times Val_{\mathcal{A}}$. $Den_{\mathcal{A}}$ can also be considered as a function: $Den_{\mathcal{A}} : rP_\sigma \rightarrow Sb(Val_{\mathcal{A}} \times Val_{\mathcal{A}})$.

The validity relation, which establishes a connection between $rD_\sigma$ and $Mod_\sigma$, will be defined as an extension of the validity relation $\models$ of classical first-order logic. However, for the sake of simplicity we write $\models$ for the validity relation of dynamic logic, too.

**(11.2) Definition.** *Let us fix an arbitrary $\sigma$-type model $\mathcal{A}$ and let $k \in Val_{\mathcal{A}}$ be also arbitrary. The $k$-validity of a formula of $rD_\sigma$ in $\mathcal{A}$ (denoted by $\mathcal{A} \models \phi[k]$) is defined inductively in the following way:*

*(i) for any $\phi \in Atom_\sigma$, $\mathcal{A} \models \phi[k]$ iff it holds in the classical logic sense;*

*(ii) for any $\phi$, $\psi \in rD_\sigma$ and $v \in V$:*
- *$\mathcal{A} \models \phi \wedge \psi[k]$ iff $\mathcal{A} \models \phi[k]$ and $\mathcal{A} \models \psi[k]$;*
- *$\mathcal{A} \models \neg\phi[k]$ iff $\mathcal{A} \not\models \phi[k]$;*
- *$\mathcal{A} \models \exists v\phi[k]$ iff there is a valuation $l$ such that for any variable $w \neq v$ of $V$, $k(w) = l(w)$ and $\mathcal{A} \models \phi[l]$;*

*(iii) for any program $p \in rP_\sigma$ and $\phi \in rD_\sigma$, $\mathcal{A} \models [p]\phi[k]$ iff for any valuation $l$ such that $(k,l) \in Den_{\mathcal{A}}[\![p]\!]$ we have $\mathcal{A} \models \phi[l]$.*

*A formula $\phi \in rD_\sigma$ is said to be valid in $\mathcal{A}$ iff it is $k$-valid for any valuation $k$ of $Val_{\mathcal{A}}$.*

*The language $rDL_\sigma \rightleftharpoons (rD_\sigma, Mod_\sigma, \models)$ is the $\sigma$-type dynamic logic which is a descriptive language for the $\sigma$-type programming language $rP_\sigma$.*

We will also need two sublanguages of $rDL_\sigma$ differing only in their programming language, whose programs are used in (iii) of the above definition. These languages are $DL_\sigma$ and *det-*$DL_\sigma$ which are obtained by allowing only programs without random assignment and only deterministic programs, respectively. The corresponding sets of dynamic logic formulas are denoted as $D_\sigma$ and *det-*$D_\sigma$, respectively.

We emphasize that the dynamic logic defined here corresponds to the regular dynamic logic (cf. Harel [1984]). In our work we will not deal with other, logically more expressive, dynamic logics (e.g. the dynamic logic which allows the use of first-order formulas as tests) because we restrict ourselves only to the programs which in our view conform to Church's thesis.

From the above definition we immediately get the following

**(11.3) Lemma.** *$\mathcal{A} \models \langle p\rangle\phi[k]$ iff there is a valuation $k^*$ such that $(k, k^*) \in Den_{\mathcal{A}}[\![p]\!]$ and $\mathcal{A} \models \phi[k^*]$.*

Note that Definition (11.2) can be interpreted as a definition for a Kripke-style semantics. Indeed, for a fixed model $\mathcal{A} \in Mod_\sigma$, we consider the set of valuations, i.e. the set of states as the possible worlds of a Kripke model and $Den_{\mathcal{A}}[\![p]\!]$ for an arbitrary program $p \in rP_\sigma$ as the accessibility relation. Namely, $\mathcal{A} \models [p]\phi[k]$ means that the formula $[p]\phi$ is valid in the world $k$ iff $\phi$ is valid in all worlds $l$ which can be reached from the world $k$ by executing the program $p$.

The next lemma demonstrates that the logic operators $[\cdot]$ and $\langle\cdot\rangle$ in dynamic logic formulas really behave like "real" modal operators.

**(11.4) Lemma.** *Let us suppose that $X \rightleftharpoons var(\phi \to \psi)$. The following formulas of $rD_\sigma$ are tautologies:*

*(i)* $([p]\phi \land \langle p\rangle true) \to \langle p\rangle\phi$;
*(ii)* $\langle p\rangle(\phi \land \psi) \to (\langle p\rangle\phi \land \langle p\rangle\psi)$;
*(iii)* $[p](\phi \land \psi) \leftrightarrow ([p]\phi \land [p]\psi)$;
*(iv)* $\langle p\rangle(\phi \lor \psi) \leftrightarrow (\langle p\rangle\phi \lor \langle p\rangle\psi)$;
*(v)* $\forall X(\phi \to \psi) \to ([p]\phi \to [p]\psi)$;
*(vi)* $\forall X(\phi \to \psi) \to (\langle p\rangle\phi \to \langle p\rangle\psi)$;
*(vii)* $\neg[p]\phi \leftrightarrow \langle p\rangle\neg\phi$.

*Proof.* The statements immediately follow from the appropriate definitions. However, let us see, as an illustration, how (ii) can be proved. Let $\mathcal{A} \in Mod_\sigma$ be arbitrary and let us suppose that $\mathcal{A} \models \langle p\rangle(\phi \land \psi)[k]$. By Lemma (11.3) this means that there exists a valuation $k^*$ such that $(k, k^*) \in Den_{\mathcal{A}}[\![p]\!]$ and $\mathcal{A} \models (\phi \land \psi)[k^*]$. From this, by (ii) of Definition (11.2) we have $\mathcal{A} \models \phi[k^*]$ and $\mathcal{A} \models \psi[k^*]$. Therefore we obtain $\mathcal{A} \models \langle p\rangle\phi[k]$ and $\mathcal{A} \models \langle p\rangle\psi[k]$ from which, by using (ii) of Definition (11.2) again, $\mathcal{A} \models (\langle p\rangle\phi \land \langle p\rangle\psi)[k]$ follows.

Note that the implication in (ii) does not hold in the opposite direction since according to (ii) of Definition (11.2) $\mathcal{A} \models (\langle p\rangle\phi \land \langle p\rangle\psi)[k]$ is equivalent to $\mathcal{A} \models \langle p\rangle\phi[k]$ and $\mathcal{A} \models \langle p\rangle\psi[k]$. Therefore by definition there is a valuation, say $k_1$, for the first formula and there is another valuation, say $k_2$, for the second one such that the condition of Lemma (11.3) holds. Since valuations $k_1$ and $k_2$ may be different, $\mathcal{A} \models \langle p\rangle(\phi \land \psi)[k]$ does not follow from $\mathcal{A} \models \phi[k_1]$ and $\mathcal{A} \models \psi[k_2]$. □

However, in $rDL_\sigma$ there are many famous tautologies which correspond to the program constructs, as shown by the following

**(11.5) Lemma.** *Let $\mathcal{A}$ be a fixed $\sigma$-type model. Let $p \in rP_\sigma$ be a given program and let $\phi$, $\psi \in Form_\sigma$ be a given precondition and a given postcondition,* *respectively. Then*

*(i)* *If p does not contain any* **do...od** *commands then* $\phi \to [p]\psi$ *is equivalent to a* $\sigma$*-type first order formula.*
*(ii)* *Let us suppose that* $p \rightleftharpoons (p_1; p_2)$ *and there is a formula* $\psi' \in Form_\sigma$ *such that* $\mathcal{A} \models \phi \to [p_1]\psi'$ *and* $\mathcal{A} \models \psi' \to [p_2]\psi$. *Then* $\mathcal{A} \models \phi \to [p]\psi$.
*(iii)* *Let us suppose that* $p \rightleftharpoons$ **if** $\alpha_1 \to p_1 \Box \alpha_2 \to p_2$ **fi** . $\mathcal{A} \models \phi \to [p]\psi$ *iff for* $i = 1, 2$, $\mathcal{A} \models \phi \wedge \alpha_i \to [p_i]\psi$ *and* $\mathcal{A} \models \neg\alpha_1 \wedge \neg\alpha_2 \wedge \phi \to \psi$.
*(iv)* *Let us suppose that* $p \rightleftharpoons$ **do** $\alpha_1 \to p_1 \Box \alpha_2 \to p_2$ **od** *and there is a* $\kappa \in Form_\sigma$ *such that* $\mathcal{A} \models \phi \to \kappa$, $\mathcal{A} \models \kappa \wedge \neg\alpha_1 \wedge \neg\alpha_2 \to \psi$ *and* $\mathcal{A} \models \kappa \wedge (\alpha_1 \vee \alpha_2) \to [q]\kappa$, *where* $q \rightleftharpoons$ **if** $\alpha_1 \to p_1 \Box \alpha_2 \to p_2$ **fi** . *Then* $\mathcal{A} \models \phi \to [p]\psi$.

We remark that the statements in (ii) and (iv) cannot be reversed.

Let us consider the dynamic logic *det-DL*$_\sigma$.

**(11.6) Lemma.** *The following formulas are tautologies in det-D*$_\sigma$:
*(i)* $\langle p\rangle\phi \to [p]\phi$;
*(ii)* $\langle p\rangle\phi \leftrightarrow [p]\phi \wedge \langle p\rangle true$;
*(iii)* $\langle p\rangle(\phi \wedge \psi) \leftrightarrow (\langle p\rangle\phi \wedge \langle p\rangle\psi)$.
*(iv)* *Let X be a finite set of variables such that* $var(p) \subseteq X$. *Let Y and Z be two new copies of X. The following formula is also a tautology:*

$$(\langle p\rangle X = Y \wedge \langle p\rangle X = Z) \to Y = Z.$$

The main virtue of a descriptive language is to provide a general framework within which different concepts are connected with program properties that can be defined by the $\sigma$-type dynamic logic.

**(11.7) Lemma.** *Let* $\mathcal{A} \in Mod_\sigma, \phi, \psi \in Form_\sigma$ *and* $p \in rP_\sigma$ *be arbitrary.*

*(i)* *The following notions are definable in dynamic logic:*

| Notion | Dynamic-logic formula |
|---|---|
| p is partially correct in $\mathcal{A}$ w.r.t. the precondition $\phi$ and the postcondition $\psi$. | $\mathcal{A} \models \phi \to [p]\psi$ |
| p is quasi-totally correct in $\mathcal{A}$ w.r.t. the precondition $\phi$ and the postcondition $\psi$. | $\mathcal{A} \models \phi \to \langle p\rangle\psi$ |
| p quasi-terminates in $\mathcal{A}$ w.r.t. the precondition $\phi$. | $\mathcal{A} \models \phi \to \langle p\rangle true$ |
| p is pseudo-totally correct in $\mathcal{A}$ w.r.t. the precondition $\phi$ and the postcondition $\psi$. | $\mathcal{A} \models \phi \to \langle p\rangle true \wedge [p]\psi$ |

*(ii) The notion "p is totally correct in* $\mathcal{A}$ *with respect to the precondition* $\phi$ *and the postcondition* $\psi$*" is also definable in* $DL_\sigma$.

Note that the statement (ii) is not obvious. It is based on König's lemma. For any $p \in P_\sigma$ one can construct a formula $repeat_p \in rD_\sigma$ such that for all $\mathcal{A} \in Mod_\sigma$, $k \in Val_\mathcal{A}$ we have $\mathcal{A} \models repeat_p[k]$ iff $p$ has at least one infinite computational path starting from $k$ (cf. Theorem 3.39 in Harel [1984]). Now the formula $\phi \to ([p]\psi \wedge \neg repeat_p)$ is equivalent to the total correctness of $p$ with respect to the precondition $\phi$ and the postcondition $\psi$. Statement (ii) is not true for the dynamic logic with random assignment, since König's lemma does not hold for trees with infinite degrees.

Note that in the case of $rDL_\sigma$ we have no real duality between the dynamic logic formulas $\phi \to [p]\psi$ and $\phi \to \langle p\rangle\psi$ (the latter is equivalent to the formula $\neg(\phi \wedge [p]\neg\psi)$) since the corresponding notions (partial correctness and quasi-total correctness) are not dual ones, i.e. one cannot be obtained from the other by replacing the logic connectives with the corresponding dual ones. However, for the deterministic case, that is, for $det\text{-}DL_\sigma$, Lemmas (11.6) (ii) and (11.7) result in the following

**(11.8) Corollary.** *For $det\text{-}DL_\sigma$ the notions of quasi-total correctness, pseudo-total correctness and total correctness are the same.*

This means that in the deterministic case the notions of partial and total correctness are complementary even in their dynamic logic definition (cf. Manna [1969] and Harel [1980]).

In dynamic logic the semantics of a program $p$ can be defined and, consequently, several interrelated notions can also be defined.

**(11.9) Lemma.** *Let $p$ and $q$ be arbitrary programs of $rP_\sigma$ such that $var(p) = var(q) = X$ and let $Y$, $Z$ be two new copies of $X$. For these programs the following notions are definable in $rDL_\sigma$:*

| Notion | Dynamic-logic formula |
|---|---|
| Input-output relational semantics of program $p$. | $\langle p\rangle X = Y (\rightleftharpoons \delta_p(X,Y))$ |
| The execution of program $p$ is deterministic. | $\forall X \forall Y \forall Z(\delta_p(X,Y) = \delta_p(X,Z)) \to Y = Z$ |
| Program $p$ satisfies a given input-output relation $\chi(X,Y)$ which is a program free formula of $rDL_\sigma$. | $\forall X \forall Y(\delta_p(X,Y) \to \chi(X,Y))$ |
| Program $p$ simulates program $q$. | $\forall X \forall Y(\delta_q(X,Y) \to \delta_p(X,Y))$ |
| Programs $p$ and $q$ are equivalent. | $\forall X \forall Y(\delta_p(X,Y) \leftrightarrow \delta_q(X,Y))$ |

Note that the program $p$ in the second line of the table is not deterministic, only its execution is supposed to be so.

*Proof.* We prove only the first row of the table. Let $\iota : X \to Y$ be the corresponding bijection. The dynamic logic formula of this row is of the property that in any model $\mathcal{A} \in Mod_\sigma$ and for all $k, k^* \in Val_\mathcal{A}[X]$ we have

$$\mathcal{A} \models \langle p\rangle X = Y[k + k^*\restriction_Y] \text{ iff } (k, k^*[X : Y]) \in Den_{\mathcal{A}}[\![p, X]\!].$$

To check it let us fix $k$ and $k^*$ such that $\mathcal{A} \models \langle p\rangle(X = Y)[k + k^*\restriction_Y]$ holds. By definition there is a $k' \in Val_{\mathcal{A}}$ such that $\mathcal{A} \models X = Y[k']$ and $(k+k^*\restriction_Y, k') \in Den_{\mathcal{A}}[\![p]\!]$. Immediately $k'\restriction_X = \iota \circ (k'\restriction_Y)$. Since $Y \cap var(p) = \emptyset$ we have $(k + k^*\restriction_Y)\restriction_Y = k^*\restriction_Y = k'\restriction_Y$. Thus $k'\restriction_X = \iota \circ (k^*\restriction_Y)$. Hence $(k\restriction_X, k^*[X : Y]\restriction_X) \in Den_{\mathcal{A}}[\![p, X]\!]$.

The opposite direction can be proved similarly. □

Remember that, as we have seen in Chapter 6, the programming families $P^2_\sigma$ and $P^3_\sigma$ have the same computational power. However, if we do not allow the usage of equality in tests, then we cannot prove this equivalence. It is the most famous open question of the comparative schematology. Several proofs in Part I make direct use of the presence of equality in tests. The above theorem is also a good example for the power of equality, since a lot of programming notions become definable by simply using the symbol "=" with its usual meaning.

**(11.10) Theorem.** *The dynamic logic is not compact, i.e. there is a similarity type $\sigma$ such that the logic $DL_\sigma$ is not compact and thus neither is $rDL_\sigma$.*

*Proof.* The statement means that there is an infinite set of dynamic-logic formulas $\Phi \subseteq D_\sigma$ and a formula $\phi \in D_\sigma$ such that $\Phi \models \phi$, but for every finite subset $\Phi' \subseteq \Phi$, $\Phi' \not\models \phi$.

Let the similarity type $\sigma$ contain a constant symbol 0 and a unary function symbol +1 and two unary relation symbols $Q$ and $R$. Let us consider the following program:

$$p \rightleftharpoons \textbf{do } y = 0 \to x := x + 1 \;\Box\; y = 0 \to y := 0 + 1 \textbf{ od}$$

Obviously $p \in P_\sigma$. For this $p$ we can define the dynamic-logic formula $\phi$ describing partial correctness of $p$ with respect to the precondition $Q(x) \wedge y = 0$ and postcondition $R(x)$: $\phi \rightleftharpoons (Q(x) \wedge y = 0) \to [p]R(x)$. Now we define programs $p_n$ $(n \in \mathbb{N})$ by induction as follows:

$$\begin{array}{lcl} p_0 & \rightleftharpoons & \textbf{skip} \\ p_1 & \rightleftharpoons & \textbf{if } y = 0 \to x := x + 1 \;\Box\; y = 0 \to y := 0 + 1 \textbf{ fi} \\ \vdots & & \vdots \\ p_{n+1} & \rightleftharpoons & p_n; p_1 \end{array}$$

The dynamic-logic formula describing the partial correctness of the program $p_n$ is $\phi_n \rightleftharpoons (Q(x) \wedge y = 0) \to [p_n]R(x)$. Let $\Phi = \{\phi_n \mid n \in \mathbb{N}\}$. It is clear that $\Phi \models \phi$. Now we show that there is no finite subset $\Phi' \subseteq \Phi$ such that $\Phi' \models \phi$.

Let us suppose that $\Phi' \subseteq \Phi$ and $m$ is such that $m > max\{n|\phi_n \in \Phi'\}$. Clearly $\phi_m$ does not belong to $\Phi'$. Let us consider the standard model $\mathcal{N}$ of arithmetic where the symbols 0 and +1 are interpreted as usual. Let us interpret $Q$ and $R$ as follows:

$$Q_{\mathcal{N}}(x) \rightleftharpoons \begin{cases} \mathit{false} & \text{if } x \neq 0; \\ \mathit{true} & \text{if } x = 0. \end{cases}$$

$$R_{\mathcal{N}}(x) \rightleftharpoons \begin{cases} \mathit{false} & \text{if } x = m; \\ \mathit{true} & \text{otherwise.} \end{cases}$$

The figure below illustrates these interpretations.

$$\begin{array}{ccccccccccc} Q & & \neg Q & & \neg Q & & & \neg Q & & \neg Q & & \neg Q \\ 0 & \longrightarrow & 1 & \longrightarrow & 2 \rightarrow & \cdots\cdots\cdots & \rightarrow & m\text{-}1 & \longrightarrow & m & \longrightarrow & m{+}1 \\ R & & R & & R & & & R & & \neg R & & R \end{array}$$

Let $\mathcal{N}'$ denote this model. One can check that $\mathcal{N}' \models \Phi'$, however $\mathcal{N}' \not\models \phi$ (more precisely $\mathcal{N}' \not\models \phi[0/x, 0/y]$). Hence $\Phi' \not\models \phi$. □

We remark that the logic *det-*$DL_\sigma$ is not compact either, but to prove this statement we have to use a more elaborated example.

Having established that the dynamic logic is not compact let us see what about its completeness.

**(11.11) Theorem.** *The set of all tautologies of* $rDL_\sigma$ *is not recursively enumerable, i.e. the dynamic logic* $rDL_\sigma$ *is not complete.*

*Proof.* The statement follows from the incompleteness of a (recursive) sublanguage of $DL_\sigma$ which will be proved in the next theorem. □

The avoidance of incompleteness is a fundamental goal in programming logic research. The easiest way to eliminate incompleteness is to modify the notion of completeness. Such a notion as "arithmetical completeness" (see Cook [1975]) illustrates this approach. Another way is connected with the use of the $\omega$-rule. This approach changes recursive enumerability to $\Pi^1_1$-completeness, see e.g. Mirkowska [1980] or Goldblatt [1982] on this approach.

$\Pi^1_1$-completeness is an essential property of $rDL_\sigma$, as shown by Theorem (11.12) below.

Let us suppose that $\tilde{\sigma}$ contains a unary function symbol $f$, and two constant symbols 0 and 1. For any variable $x$, let $p_x$ be the following program:

$$j := 1;\ x := z;\ \textbf{while}\ j = 1 \textbf{do}\ \mathit{true} \rightarrow j := 0 \ \Box\ \mathit{true} \rightarrow x := f(x)\ \textbf{od}\,.$$

By the use of this program we can formulate the following

**(11.12) Theorem.** *The set of all tautologies of* $rDL_{\tilde{\sigma}}$ *is a* $\Pi^1_1$*-complete set. Moreover, the sublanguages of* $rDL_{\tilde{\sigma}}$ *consisting of formulas of the following forms are* $\Pi^1_1$*-complete:*

*(i)* $\langle p_y \rangle [p_x] \phi$;

*(ii)* $\exists y[p_x]\phi$;
*(iii)* $\exists y \exists w[p_x]\psi$;
*(iv)* $\langle p_y; p_w\rangle[p_x]\psi$.

*Here $\phi$ and $\psi$ range, respectively, over existential and arbitrary open formulas of $Form_{\bar{\sigma}}$, respectively.*

The proof of this theorem can be found e.g. in Harel, Meyer, Pratt [1977] or in Harel [1984].

Though the dynamic logic $DL_\sigma$ is incomplete, there is a notion of completeness which is appropriate even for this language. Namely, the notion of relative completeness, introduced by Cook [1978], can be used as was done by Harel [1978] (see also Harel [1979]). One of the essential notions of the calculus given by Harel [1979] is the direct handling of infinite descending computations by the so-called *convergence rule* based on the following property of dynamic logic. Let $\phi \in rD_\sigma$ and suppose that the variable n does not appear in the programs $p_1$ and $p_2$. Then, for a given model $\mathcal{A} \in Mod_\sigma$, we have

$$\frac{\begin{array}{c}\mathcal{A} \models \phi(n+1) \wedge (\alpha_1 \vee \alpha_2) \rightarrow \langle \textbf{if } \alpha_1 \rightarrow p_1 \,\Box\, \alpha_2 \rightarrow p_2 \textbf{fi } \rangle \phi(n), \\ \mathcal{A} \models \phi(0) \rightarrow \neg\alpha_1 \wedge \neg\alpha_2\end{array}}{\mathcal{A} \models \phi(n) \rightarrow \langle \textbf{do } \alpha_1 \rightarrow p_1 \,\Box\, \alpha_2 \rightarrow p_2 \textbf{ od } \rangle \phi(0)}$$

This property allows us to handle the appropriate terminations of programs. However, to enable us to use a rule based on this property, the universe of the model $\mathcal{A}$ must contain a set isomorphic to the set of natural numbers. These models play an essential role in the calculus introduced by Harel [1984] and in the new notion of completeness, called arithmetical completeness. This is so, because completeness is established relatively to any arithmetical model. (See Definition (6.6) for the definition of the arithmetical model and for the coding function $\beta$.)

The essential idea is to exploit the existence of first-order equivalents, in arithmetical models, to all formulas of $rDL_\sigma$.

**(11.13) Theorem.** *There exists a recursive function $h$ which assigns to each closed formula of $rDL_\sigma$ a $\sigma$-type first-order formula such that in each arithmetic model $\mathcal{A}$ and for any dynamic-logic formula $\phi$ the following holds:*

$$(*) \qquad \mathcal{A} \models \phi \quad \textit{iff} \quad \mathcal{A} \models h(\phi)$$

*Proof.* The construction of $h(\phi)$ can be made by induction on the complexity of $\phi$. The only non-trivial case is when $\phi$ is of the form $[p]\psi$. By Theorem (4.30) there are programs $p'$ and $\hat{p}$ free of **do...od** construct such that

$$p \equiv p'; \textbf{ while } \alpha \textbf{ do } p'' \textbf{ od} \quad (\text{mod } var(p)).$$

The programs $p'$ and $p''$ do not contain any **do...od** commands so there are open formulas $\xi'$ and $\xi''$ which define the denotation of the programs $p'$ and

$p''$, respectively. Moreover, let $X \rightleftharpoons var(p)$, let $X'$ be a new copy of $X$ and $Y \rightleftharpoons var(p;p';p'') \cup var(\alpha)$. It is clear that $X \subseteq Y$. Let $F$ be a new copy of $Y$. Let $\iota_X : X \to F$ and $\iota_{X'} : X' \to F$ be corresponding injections. Let $Q$ be a new copy of $F$. Let $\iota_Q : F \to Q$ be the corresponding bijection. Let $F(i)$ be a shorthand for the following ordered set of terms: $\{\beta(f,i,t) | f \in F\}$. Now we are ready to define the denotation of $p$ by taking the following formula:

$$\gamma_p(X,X') \rightleftharpoons \exists t \exists F\Big( \bigwedge_{x \in X} x = \beta(\iota_X(x),0,t) \wedge \bigwedge_{x' \in X'} x' = \beta(\iota_{X'}(x'),t-1,t) \wedge$$
$$\xi'(F(0),F(1)) \wedge \neg\alpha(F(t-1)) \wedge \forall i\big((1 \le i < t-1) \to \xi''(F(i),F(i+1))\big)\Big)$$

Now we can set

$$h(\phi) \rightleftharpoons \forall X'\big(\gamma_p(X,X') \to \psi[X'/X]\big).$$

□

From the completeness of the first-order language and from Theorem (11.13) we immediately have the required completeness of $rDL_\sigma$ with respect to arithmetical models.

**(11.14) Theorem.** *For every arithmetical model $\mathcal{A}$ the set of true formulas of $rDL_\sigma$ is recursively enumerable with respect to all first-order formulas being true in $\mathcal{A}$.*

Of course, the validity problem of $rDL_\sigma$ in arithmetical models remains $\Pi^1_1$-hard, i.e. the valid formulas of $rDL_\sigma$ form a $\Pi^1_1$-complete set. However, with respect to the set of all formulas which are true in a fixed arithmetical model the validity of the dynamic-logic formulas is only recursively enumerable. The $\Pi^1_1$-hardness is buried in the set of first-order formulas valid in $\mathcal{A}$.

Another possibility of giving a complete calculus for $rDL_\sigma$ is based on the algorithmic logic traditions developed by Salwicki [1970] on the ideas of Engeler [1967]. Here the following $\omega$-rule handles the **do...od** construct:

$$\frac{\{\phi \to [(1..i..n) : \textbf{if } \alpha_1 \to p_1 \Box \alpha_2 \to p_2 \textbf{fi}; \ \textbf{if } \alpha_1 \vee \alpha_2 \to \textbf{loop fi}]\,\psi \ \mid n \in \mathbb{N}\}}{\phi \to [\textbf{do } \alpha_1 \to p_1 \Box \alpha_2 \to p_2 \textbf{ od}]\psi}$$

**(11.15) Theorem.** *There is an axiomatic calculus with the above $\omega$-rule which is complete for $rDL_\sigma$.*

*Proof.* See e.g. in Harel [1979]. □

Now let us consider an important sublanguage of $rDL_\sigma$, which describes only the partial correctness of programs.

**(11.16) Definition.** *The $\sigma$-type Floyd-Hoare language $rHL_\sigma$ is a sublanguage of $rDL_\sigma$ such that its syntax $rH_\sigma$ consists of the formulas of the form $\phi \rightarrow [p]\psi$ where $\phi$ and $\psi$ are $\sigma$-type first-order formulas, i.e.*

$$rHL_\sigma \quad \rightleftharpoons \quad (rH_\sigma, Mod_\sigma, \models).$$

We will also use two sublanguages $HL_\sigma$ and $det\text{-}HL_\sigma$ with the syntax $H_\sigma$ and $det\text{-}H_\sigma$ which correspond to the dynamic logics $DL_\sigma$ and $det\text{-}DL_\sigma$, respectively.

Now we give a short historical review of the Floyd-Hoare language and of its way of describing and proving of the partial correctness of programs. Naur [1966] and Floyd [1967] can be regarded as the first contributors to the area of proving the correctness of programs. In their works the invariant assertion method is described. According to this method, a proof of the partial correctness of a program, given in a flowchart form, is carried out in the following way: We fix some points in the program such that there is at least one point in every cycle of the flowchart, and we attach assertions to these points, and verify implication between pairs of the assertions, assuming that the path connecting the corresponding points is indeed taken.

This establishes the truth of the postcondition, whenever the precondition is true and the program does terminate. This method, usually referred to as "Floyd's method", does not specify those points to which assertions are to be attached and thus, depending on how they are chosen, the proof can take the form of an induction over a natural part of the data manipulated by the program. Hoare [1969] developed this method further by fixing the points chosen in each cycle and by describing the method as an axiom system, writing $\phi\{p\}\psi$ for "$p$ is partially correct with respect to the precondition $\phi$ and the postcondition $\psi$", and by introducing rules of inference which allow to prove partial correctness of a program by splitting it up and thus reducing its complexity.

**(11.17) Definition.**

*(i) Following the traditional form of partial correctness formulas we write $\phi\{p\}\psi$ instead of $\phi \rightarrow [p]\psi$, i.e. the syntax of $rHL_\sigma$ is*

$$rH_\sigma \rightleftharpoons \{\phi\{p\}\psi \mid \phi, \psi \in Form_\sigma \text{ and } p \in rP_\sigma\}.$$

*(ii) Let $\mathcal{K} \subseteq Mod_\sigma$ be arbitrary. $rHL_\sigma^{\mathcal{K}}$ will denote the Floyd-Hoare language $(rH_\sigma, \mathcal{K}, \models)$. If $\mathcal{K} = Mod(Ax)$ for some $Ax$ then we write $rHL_\sigma^{Ax}$ instead of $rHL_\sigma^{\mathcal{K}}$.*

In a similar way we can define the languages $HL_\sigma^{Ax}$ and $det\text{-}HL_\sigma^{Ax}$ by using only programs belonging to $P_\sigma$ and $det\text{-}P_\sigma$, respectively.

**(11.18) Definition.** *Let $\mathcal{K} \subseteq Mod_\sigma$ be an arbitrary class of models. The partial correctness theory for $\mathcal{K}$ is the set*

$$rPC(\mathcal{K}) \rightleftharpoons \{\chi \in rH_\sigma \mid \mathcal{A} \models \chi \textit{ for all } \mathcal{A} \in \mathcal{K}\}.$$

*If* $\mathcal{K} = Mod(Ax)$ *then we write* $rPC(Ax)$ *instead of* $rPC(\mathcal{K})$.

In a similar way we can define the partial correctness theories $PC(\mathcal{K})$ and $det\text{-}PC(\mathcal{K})$ by using only programs belonging to $P_\sigma$ and $det\text{-}P_\sigma$, respectively.

**(11.19) Theorem.** *Let* $\sigma$ *be a fixed similarity type and let* $\mathcal{A}$ *and* $\mathcal{B}$ *be two given* $\sigma$*-type models with* $Th(\mathcal{A}) = Th(\mathcal{B})$. *Then* $PC(\{\mathcal{A}\}) = PC(\{\mathcal{B}\})$.

*Proof.* Let $\mathcal{A}$ and $\mathcal{B}$ be as in the theorem. Let us fix a program $p \in P_\sigma$ and let $X \rightleftharpoons var(p)$. Recall the set $F \subseteq [X \to Term_\sigma] \times Open_\sigma$ from Theorem (8.15). Let $\phi$, $\psi \in Form_\sigma$ be arbitrary formulas. By using $F$ we can construct the following formulas:

$$\Phi_{f,\alpha} \rightleftharpoons \forall X \phi(X) \wedge \alpha(X) \to \psi[f(x)/x]_{x \in X},$$

where $(f, \alpha) \in F$. It is clear that $\Phi_{f,\alpha} \in Form_\sigma$. Now using Theorem (8.15) we get the following:

$$\phi\{p\}\psi \in PC(\mathcal{A}) \quad \text{iff} \quad \{\Phi_{f,\alpha} \mid (f, \alpha) \in F\} \subseteq Th(\mathcal{A}).$$

Applying this fact to the model $\mathcal{B}$ we get the desired result. □

Note that this theorem does not hold for all dynamic-logic formulas. That is, there exist a similarity type $\sigma$, a formula $\chi \in rD_\sigma \setminus rH_\sigma$ and two $\sigma$-type models, say $\mathcal{A}$ and $\mathcal{B}$, such that $Th(\mathcal{A}) = Th(\mathcal{B})$, $\mathcal{A} \models \chi$, but $\mathcal{B} \not\models \chi$. Consider the similarity type of arithmetic and let $p \rightleftharpoons$ **while** $y \neq 0$ **do** $y := y - 1$ **od** and let $\chi \rightleftharpoons \langle p \rangle true$, which expresses that the program $p$ always terminates. It is clear that $\chi$ is valid in the standard model $\mathcal{N}$ of the axiom system $PA$ but is false in an arbitrary non-standard model of $Th(\mathcal{N})$.

Chapter 12

# The Problem of Completeness

Besides the description of program properties, programming logics are also expected to provide appropriate tools for proving the existence of these properties at concrete programs. Therefore, an appropriate calculus is required to permit the proof of formulas of the descriptive language. Moreover, we expect this calculus to be realizable in some intuitive sense, i.e. to correspond to our requirement of having an effective proof concept. Completeness of a descriptive language requires the recursive enumerability of the appropriate formulas. On the other hand, concerning the calculus, it is required to enumerate all the appropriate formulas.

In this chapter we investigate the completeness of dynamic logic. We show that, in general, it is incomplete and we investigate whether there exist complete sublanguages and also how the notion of completeness can be changed in order to obtain completeness with respect to the new notions. Section 12.1 is devoted to the investigation of the completeness of dynamic logic. However, instead of analysing the whole language, we confine ourselves to its important sublanguage, the Floyd-Hoare language, which, as we have seen, is appropriate to deal with the partial correctness property of programs. Moreover, we investigate the completeness of the calculus introduced by Hoare for this language. We prove the incompleteness of this calculus first by following the proof given by Wand [1978], then we give our own proof.

Section 12.2 deals with a restriction of partial correctness theories which is obtained by using pragmatic considerations of programming. However, we will see that with respect to restrictions within the termination suggested by the pragmatically interesting cases, the Floyd-Hoare language remains incomplete. Eventually we introduce in Section 12.3 a new notion of completeness which corresponds to a certain program-theoretic and also pragmatic motivation. It considers only provable formulas of the Floyd-Hoare language whose program components simulate the programs under investigation. The Floyd-Hoare language is expected to be complete with respect to these simulation programs.

## 12.1 Incompleteness Results

The partial correctness property plays a prominent part in the formal verification of concrete programs, and historically it was the first one of the formal proof for which appropriate logical tools were developed. As we have seen in Chapter 11 this property can be expressed in $rDL_\sigma$ by formulas of the form $\phi \to [p]\psi$. Thus, to handle the partial correctness property of programs we do not need the entire syntax $rD_\sigma$ but only a part of it, namely, the set of Floyd-Hoare formulas, i.e $rH_\sigma$.

We note that in the first period of dealing with the partial correctness property the question of completeness was neglected. The main activity was meant to extend the possibilities of Floyd-Hoare language to deal with more and more computational devices. To achieve this aim newer and newer rules have been introduced without considering the influence of these rules on completeness. Gergely, Szöts [1978] pioneered emphasizing the incompleteness of the Floyd-Hoare language considering the standard model of arithmetic. Besides this result here we also present some well known results for the case when the similarity type $\eta$ of arithmetic is considered. Moreover, let $\mathcal{K}$ contain only one semantic structure, namely the standard model $\mathcal{N}$ of arithmetic.

To establish the incompleteness of different partial correctness theories in the standard model of arithmetic, there is a useful method, based on the undecidability of the Diophantine equations. For this method, the existence of a program which solves a given Diophantine equation is essential.

Let $Ax \subseteq Form_\sigma$ be given. We say that $Ax$ *contains arithmetic* iff $\eta \subseteq \sigma$; $PA \subseteq Ax$ and there is a $\sigma$-type model $\mathcal{N}'$ such that $\mathcal{N}' \models Ax$ and $\mathcal{N}'\restriction_\eta = \mathcal{N}$.

**(12.1) Lemma.** *Let $Ax$ be an axiom system containing arithmetic. For any terms $\tau_1, \tau_2 \in Term_\eta$ there is a program $DE(\tau_1, \tau_2) \in det\text{-}P_\eta$ such that it terminates in any model $\mathcal{A}$ of $Ax$ iff the Diophantine equation $\tau_1 = \tau_2$ has at least one solution in $\mathcal{N}$.*

*Proof.* Let $X \rightleftharpoons var(\tau_1) \cup var(\tau_2)$. Let $u$ be a new variable. Take

$$\begin{aligned} q \quad \rightleftharpoons \quad & (x \in X) : x := ?; \\ & (x \in X) : (u := 0;\ \textbf{while}\ u \neq x\ \textbf{do}\ u := u + 1\ \textbf{od}\ ); \\ & \textbf{if}\ \tau_1 = \tau_2 \to \textbf{skip}\ \square\ \neg\tau_1 = \tau_2 \to \textbf{loop fi}\ . \end{aligned}$$

We remark that the subprogram in the second line checks whether the selected $x$ is a standard natural number belonging to $\mathbb{N}$.

Theorem (6.7) implies that $P(\mathcal{N}) = rP^2(\mathcal{N})$. Therefore, by Theorem (6.17) program $q$ can be diagonalized. Suppose that $(I(q), R(q))$ is the corresponding diagonalization of $q$, where both $I(q)$ and $R(q)$ are from $det\text{-}P_\sigma$.

Let $DE(\tau_1, \tau_2) \rightleftharpoons I(q)$. By Lemma (6.16) we learn that this program is appropriate. □

**(12.2) Theorem.**

*(i) $PC(\{\mathcal{N}\})$ is not recursively enumerable;*
*(ii) $PC(\{\mathcal{N}\})$ is recursive in the first-order theory $Th(\{\mathcal{N}\})$ of $\mathcal{N}$.*

*Proof.*
(i) To gain a contradiction we suppose that $PC(\{\mathcal{N}\})$ is recursively enumerable. For any $\tau_1$, $\tau_2 \in Term_\eta$ let us take the program $DE(\tau_1, \tau_2)$ defined in Lemma (12.1). It is clear that $true\{DE(\tau_1 = \tau_2)\}false \in PC(\{\mathcal{N}\})$ iff the equation $\tau_1 = \tau_2$ is not solvable in $\mathcal{N}$. According to our supposition the following set $H \rightleftharpoons$

$$\{true\{DE(\tau_1, \tau_2)\}false \mid \tau_1, \tau_2 \in Term_\eta, \mathcal{N} \models true\{DE(\tau_1, \tau_2)\}false\}$$

is recursively enumerable and therefore, the set

$$\hat{H} \rightleftharpoons \{\tau_1 = \tau_2 \mid \tau_1 = \tau_2 \text{ is not solvable in } \mathcal{N}\}$$

is also recursively enumerable. However this contradicts the fact that the set $\hat{H}$ of Diophantine equations having no solution in natural numbers is not recursively enumerable (see Theorem (1.26)).
(ii) The statement is an immediate consequence of Theorem (6.7).

□

**(12.3) Theorem.** *Let $Ax \subseteq Form_\sigma$ be an arbitrary set of axioms containing arithmetic. Then $PC(Ax)$ is not recursively enumerable.*

*Proof.* This is similar to the proof of (12.2) and so is left to the reader. □

**(12.4) Definition.** *Let $\sigma$ be an arbitrary similarity type. Let $\vdash$ be any fixed complete calculus for $Form_\sigma$. Let $\Phi \subseteq Form_\sigma$ be a fixed set of formulas. The $\Phi$-Hoare calculus (denoted by $\vdash_H^\Phi$) is the extension of $\vdash$ with the following inference rules (where $Ax \subseteq Form_\sigma$ is a consistent set of first-order formulas and $\chi$, $\phi$, $\psi$, $\phi'$, $\psi'$, $\alpha_i \in \Phi$):*

*(i) $Ax \vdash_H^\Phi \phi\{\mathbf{skip}\}\phi$ and $Ax \vdash_H^\Phi \phi\{\mathbf{loop}\}\mathbf{true}$;*
*(ii) if $\phi[\tau/v] \in \Phi$ then $Ax \vdash_H^\Phi \phi\{v := \tau\}\phi[\tau/v]$;*
*(iii) if $Ax \vdash_H^\Phi \phi\{p_1\}\chi$ and $Ax \vdash_H^\Phi \chi\{p_2\}\psi$ then $Ax \vdash_H^\Phi \phi\{p_1; p_2\}\psi$;*
*(iv) if $Ax \vdash_H^\Phi \phi \wedge \alpha_i\{p_i\}\psi$ for $i = 1, 2$ and $Ax \vdash (\phi \wedge \neg\alpha_1 \wedge \neg\alpha_2) \to \psi$ then $Ax \vdash_H^\Phi \phi\{\mathbf{if}\ \alpha_1 \to p_1 \Box \alpha_2 \to p_2 \mathbf{fi}\ \}\psi$;*
*(v) if $Ax \vdash_H^\Phi \phi \wedge (\alpha_1 \vee \alpha_2)\{\mathbf{if}\ \alpha_1 \to p_1 \Box \alpha_2 \to p_2\ \mathbf{fi}\ \}\phi$ then $Ax \vdash_H^\Phi \phi\{\mathbf{do}\ \alpha_1 \to p_1 \Box \alpha_2 \to p_2 \mathbf{od}\ \}\phi \wedge \neg\alpha_1 \wedge \neg\alpha_2$;*
*(vi) if $Ax \vdash \phi \to \phi'$, $Ax \vdash \psi' \to \psi$ and $Ax \vdash_H^\Phi \phi'\{p\}\psi'$ then $Ax \vdash_H^\Phi \phi\{p\}\psi$;*
*(vii) if $Ax \vdash \phi \to \forall v\psi(v)$ and $\phi \to \forall v\psi(v) \in \Phi$ then $Ax \vdash_H^\Phi \phi\{v :=?\}\psi$.*

*If $\Phi = Form_\sigma$ then we speak about the Hoare calculus and simply write $\vdash_H$ instead of $\vdash_H^{Form_\sigma}$.*

Note that in (v) the formula $\phi$ is called an inductive assertion (or an invariant) which remains true during the execution of the repetitive command.

From Definition (12.4) we immediately can obtain the following

**(12.5) Lemma.** *Let $Ax$ and $\Phi$ be as in Definition (12.4). Moreover, let us suppose that $\Phi$ is closed under Boolean combinations. Let $\phi\{p\}\psi \in rH_\sigma$ be fixed.*

*(i)* $Ax \vdash_H^\Phi \phi\{x := \tau\}\psi$ *iff* $Ax \vdash \phi \to \psi[\tau/x]$;

*(ii)* $Ax \vdash_H^\Phi \phi\{p_1; p_2\}\psi$ *iff there is a formula* $\phi' \in \Phi$ *such that* $Ax \vdash_H^\Phi \phi\{p_1\}\phi'$ *and* $Ax \vdash_H^\Phi \phi'\{p_2\}\psi$;

*(iii)* $Ax \vdash_H^\Phi \phi\{$**while** $\alpha$ **do** $p$ **od** $\}\psi$ *iff there is a formula* $\phi' \in \Phi$ *such that* $Ax \vdash_H^\Phi \phi' \wedge \alpha\{p\}\phi'$ *and* $Ax \vdash \phi \to \phi'$, $Ax \vdash (\phi' \wedge \neg\alpha) \to \psi)$.

**(12.6) Lemma.** *For an arbitrary $\Phi \subseteq Form_\sigma$ the calculus $\vdash_H^\Phi$ is sound, i.e. for any consistent set $Ax \subseteq \Phi$ and for any $\phi$, $\psi \in \Phi$ and $p \in rP_\sigma$, $Ax \vdash_H^\Phi \phi\{p\}\psi$ implies $Ax \models \phi\{p\}\psi$.*

*Proof.* By induction on the structure of $p$ according to (i)-(vii) of Definition (12.4) and using Lemma (12.5). □

Now let us explore the completeness of the Hoare calculus. First we restrict $rP_\sigma$ to the programs free of **do...od** commands.

**(12.7) Lemma.** *Let $Ax \subseteq Form_\sigma$ be arbitrary and let $p \in rP_\sigma$ be an arbitrary program without any* **do...od** *command. Then for any $\phi$, $\psi \in Form_\sigma$, $Ax \vdash_H \phi\{p\}\psi$ iff $Ax \models \phi\{p\}\psi$.*

*Proof.* One direction follows from Lemma (12.6). The other direction is proved by induction on the structure of $p$.

(i) Let $p \rightleftharpoons$ **skip**. $Ax \models \phi\{\mathbf{skip}\}\psi$ implies $Ax \models \phi \to \psi$. $Ax \vdash_H \phi\{\mathbf{skip}\}\psi$ by the completeness of $\vdash$ and by the rules (i) and (vi). The case of **loop** is proved similarly.

(ii) Let $p \rightleftharpoons (v := \tau)$. $Ax \models \phi\{v := \tau\}\psi$ implies $Ax \models \phi \to \psi[\tau/v]$. By the completeness of $\vdash$ and by Theorem (12.5) (i) we obtain $Ax \vdash_H \phi\{v := \tau\}\psi$.

(iii) Let $p \rightleftharpoons (p_1; p_2)$. Let $X \rightleftharpoons var(p) \cup var(\phi) \cup var(\psi)$ and let $Y$ be a copy of $X$. Let us suppose that $Ax \models \phi\{p\}\psi$. Then by Theorem (4.19) there exists a formula $\phi_1(X, Y) \in Form_\sigma$ such that $Ax \models \phi_1(X, Y)$ iff $(X, Y) \in Den_{\mathcal{A}}[\![p_1, X]\!]\restriction_\phi$ for any $\mathcal{A} \in Mod(Ax)$. This means that for the formula $\hat{\phi} \rightleftharpoons \exists Z\phi_1(Z, X)$, $Ax \models \phi\{p_1\}\hat{\phi}$ and $Ax \models \hat{\phi}\{p_2\}\psi$ hold. Hence by the induction hypothesis we have $Ax \vdash_H \phi\{p_1\}\hat{\phi}$ and $Ax \vdash_H \hat{\phi}\{p_2\}\psi$. Therefore, we obtain $Ax \vdash_H \phi\{p_1; p_2\}\psi$ by the rule (iii) of Definition (12.4).

(iv) Let $p \rightleftharpoons$ **if** $\alpha_1 \to p_1 \,\Box\, \alpha_2 \to p_2$ **fi** . Let us suppose that $Ax \models \phi\{p\}\psi$. Thus $Ax \models (\phi \wedge \alpha_i)\{p_i\}\psi$ for $i = 1, 2$ and $Ax \models (\phi \wedge \neg\alpha_1 \wedge \neg\alpha_2) \to \psi$. Hence we have $Ax \vdash_H \phi \wedge \alpha_i\{p_i\}\psi$ $(i = 1, 2)$ by the induction hypothesis and $Ax \vdash (\phi \wedge \neg\alpha_1 \wedge \neg\alpha_2) \to \psi$ by the completeness of $\vdash$. By the use of the rule (iv), we obtain $Ax \vdash_H \phi\{p\}\psi$.

(v) Let $p \rightleftharpoons (v :=?)$ and let us suppose that $Ax \models \phi\{v :=?\}\psi$. Thus $Ax \models \phi \to \forall v\psi$. By the completeness of the first-order calculus we have $Ax \vdash \phi \to \forall v\psi$. By (vii) of Definition (12.4) we obtain $Ax \vdash_H \phi\{v :=?\}\psi$.

□

Let us formulate Cook's relative completeness theorem (see in Cook [1978]):

**(12.8) Theorem.** *The calculus $\vdash_H$ is complete with respect to $\mathcal{N}$, i.e. for any $\phi$, $\psi \in Form_\eta$ and $p \in P_\eta$, $Th(\mathcal{N}) \vdash_H \phi\{p\}\psi$ iff $\mathcal{N} \models \phi\{p\}\psi$.*

The above theorem can be proved by the use of the fact that the semantic function *Den* is definable (see Theorem (11.13)) by $\eta$-type formulas in $\mathcal{N}$. Note that this theorem can be generalized for any model in which the semantics can be defined by first-order formulas. Arithmetic model, for example, are appropriate for this generalization.

Now we show that the Hoare calculus is not complete for $HL_\sigma$. First we follow the proof given by Wand [1978].

**(12.9) Theorem.** *(Incompleteness.) Respectively there is a similarity type $\sigma$, a model $\mathcal{A} \in Mod_\sigma$ and a formula $\chi = \phi\{p\}\psi$ such that $Th(\mathcal{A}) \not\vdash_H \chi$ but $\mathcal{A} \models \chi$.*

*Proof.* Let $\sigma$ contain one unary function symbol $f : d \to d$ and three unary relation symbols $q, \hat{q}, r : d$. Let $A \rightleftharpoons \mathbb{N} \cup^* \hat{\mathbb{N}}$ (I.e. $A$ is the union of two disjoint copies of $\mathbb{N}$)

(i)

$$f_{\mathcal{A}}(x) \quad \rightleftharpoons \quad \begin{cases} n-1 & \text{if } x = n \in \mathbb{N} \\ \hat{n}-1 & \text{if } x = \hat{n} \in \hat{\mathbb{N}} \end{cases};$$

(ii) $q_{\mathcal{A}}(x)$ iff $x = 0$;
(iii) $\hat{q}_{\mathcal{A}}(x)$ iff $x = \hat{0}$;
(iv) $r_{\mathcal{A}}(x)$ iff $x = n^2 - 1$ for some $n \in \mathbb{N}$.

Consider the program $p \rightleftharpoons$ **while** $\neg q(x) \wedge \neg\hat{q}(x)$ **do** $x := f(x)$ **od** . Obviously, $\mathcal{A} \models r(x)\{p\}q(x)$. Let $\chi \rightleftharpoons r(x)\{p\}q(x)$. Let the formula $u(x) \rightleftharpoons \neg q(x) \wedge \neg\hat{q}(x)$. We show that the formula $\chi$ is not provable from $Th(\mathcal{A})$. If $\chi$ were provable from $Th(\mathcal{A})$ then its proof should be of the following form:

$$\frac{r(x)\{\textbf{while } u(x) \textbf{ do } x := f(x) \textbf{od }\}q(x)}{r(x) \to \kappa(x),\ \dfrac{\kappa(x) \wedge u(x)\{x := f(x)\}\kappa(x)}{\kappa(x) \wedge u(x) \to \kappa[f(x)/x]}\ ,\ \kappa(x) \wedge \neg u(x) \to q(x)}$$

This is a proof for $\chi$ iff for the formula $\kappa$ the following hold in $\mathcal{A}$:

(a) $\kappa(x) \wedge \neg q(x) \wedge \neg\hat{q}(x) \to \kappa[f(x)/x]$;
(b) $r(x) \to \kappa(x)$;
(c) $\kappa(x) \wedge (q(x) \vee \hat{q}(x)) \to q(x)$.

From (b) we can deduce that $\mathcal{A} \models \kappa[n^2-1]$ for each $n \in \mathbb{N}$ and from (c) we have that $\mathcal{A} \models \neg\kappa[\hat{0}]$. Now (a) implies that $\mathcal{A} \models \kappa[n]$ and $\mathcal{A} \models \neg\kappa[\hat{n}]$ for all $n \in \mathbb{N}$. Thus $x \in \kappa_{\mathcal{A}}$ iff $x \in \mathbb{N}$.

Now the non-provability of $\chi$ follows from the lemma below, since if $\rho$ is not first-order definable then $\chi$ cannot be proved. □

**(12.10) Lemma.** *Let $\rho = \mathbb{N} \subseteq \mathbb{N} \cup^* \hat{\mathbb{N}}$. $\rho$ is not definable by a $\sigma$-type first-order formula.*

*Proof.* See in Wand [1978]. □

Now we give another construction to prove the incompleteness of the Hoare calculus. Recall the similarity type $\hat{\eta}$ and the axiom system $Next$ from Chapter 1. Let $\mathcal{A} \rightleftharpoons \mathcal{N}{\restriction}_{\hat{\eta}}$.

**(12.11) Theorem.** *There is no formula $\gamma \in Form_{\hat{\eta}}$ such that for all $a, b, c \in \mathbb{N}$, $\mathcal{A} \models \gamma[a, b, c]$ iff $a = b + c$.*

The theorem is a consequence of the fact that the theory $Next$ has the property of quantifier elimination.

Let us take the following program

$$p \rightleftharpoons y := x;\; z := 0;\; \mathbf{while}\; y \neq 0\; \mathbf{do}\; y := P(y);\; z := S(z)\; \mathbf{od}\,.$$

By the use of this program we give another proof for the incompleteness of the Hoare calculus.

**(12.12) Theorem.**
*(i) $\mathcal{A} \models true\{p\}x = z$ but*
*(ii) $Th(\mathcal{A}) \nvdash_H true\{p\}x = z$.*

*Proof.*
(i) This statement is trivial. Moreover, the truth of the formula $true\{p\}x = z$ can be proved by the use of Peano's axioms $PA$, i.e. $PA \vdash_H true\{p\}x = z$.
(ii) For a contradiction let us suppose that there is a proof of $true\{p\}x = z$. By Lemma (12.5) this proof has to be of the form:

$$\dfrac{\dfrac{true\{y := x; z := 0\}\phi_1}{true \to \phi_1[x/y, 0/z]}\;,\;\; \dfrac{\phi_1\{\mathbf{while}\; y \neq 0 \mathbf{do}\; y := P(y); z := S(z)\mathbf{od}\;\}x = z}{\phi_1 \to \phi_2\,,\; \phi_2 \wedge y = 0 \to x = z,\;\; \dfrac{\phi_2 \wedge y \neq 0\{y := P(y); z := S(z)\}\phi_2}{\phi_2 \wedge y \neq 0 \to \phi_2[P(y)/y, S(z)/z]}}}{true\{p\}x = z}$$

This is a proof iff the following formulas are theorems of $Th(\mathcal{A})$:

- $true \to \phi_1[x/y, 0/z], \phi_1 \to \phi_2$;
- $\phi_2 \wedge y = 0 \to x = z$;

- $\phi_2 \wedge y \neq 0 \rightarrow \phi_2[P(y)/y, S(z)/z]$.

Therefore in any model of $Th(\mathcal{A})$ the following formulas are true:

$$\phi_2(x, x, 0);$$
$$\phi_2(x, 0, x);$$
$$(\phi_2(x, y, z) \wedge y \neq 0) \rightarrow \phi_2[P(y)/y, S(z)/z].$$

Hence, taking $\phi_2(x, 0, x)$ as the basis of induction one can check by induction that in the model $\mathcal{A}$ for all $y$ and $z$ there exists a unique $x$ such that $\phi_2(x, y, z)$. Thus the formula $\phi_2$ defines the function $+$ in $\mathcal{A}$: $x = y + z$, which is impossible according to Theorem (12.11).

□

Both Wand's and our proof reflect that something is missing from the Hoare calculus, since in both cases an invariant assertion is needed from the corresponding first-order logic. Therefore, the necessary formulas are missing not only from $rHL_\sigma$ but from the entire $rDL_\sigma$ as well. Hence, not only $rHL_\sigma$ but also the entire $rDL_\sigma$ is incomplete. The weakness of the Hoare calculus is emphasized in the theorem below which shows that incompleteness can hold even in cases when the partial correctness theory is fairly simple.

**(12.13) Theorem.** *There exists a similarity type $\sigma$ and a $\sigma$-type model $\mathcal{A}$ such that*

*(i) $PC(\{\mathcal{A}\})$ is recursive in the first-order theory of $\mathcal{A}$, i.e. in $Th(\mathcal{A})$;*
*(ii) $\vdash_H$ is not complete with respect to $Th(\mathcal{A})$.*

*Proof.* See in Bergstra, Chmielinska, Tiuryn [1982]. □

## 12.2 On Restricted Partial Correctness Theories

It would be useful to find a satisfactory solution for establishing completeness in a certain sense for dynamic logic or for its appropriate sublanguage to reveal the cause of incompleteness. For this let us throw new light upon Theorems (12.2) and (12.3) by considering the following notion of completeness. Let $E \subseteq rH_\sigma$ be an arbitrary set of Floyd-Hoare formulas. The Floyd-Hoare language $rHL_\sigma^{Ax}$ for a given set $Ax$ of axioms is said to be complete with respect to $E$ if there exists a recursively enumerable set $H \subseteq rPC(Ax)$ such that $E \subseteq H$. Accordingly, Theorem (12.3) says that the Floyd-Hoare language $rHL_\sigma^{Ax}$ is not complete with respect to $rPC(Ax)$. As we have seen in Theorems (12.2) and (12.3) the sets $rPC(\{\mathcal{N}\})$ and $rPC(Ax)$ are not recursively enumerable. By analysing these statements we can see that these sets contain far too many programs, e.g. the nonterminating ones as well. So these sets are too large. Let us try to restrict the partial correctness theory to formulas interesting only from a programming point of view such that the new theory becomes recursively enumerable. The first possibility is to narrow the partial correctness theory by using pragmatical considerations of programming to give restriction within the termination. The rest of this section is devoted to the analysis of this restriction, while the next section discusses another possibility.

The approach of this section (i.e. asking if completeness with respect to some suitable $E$ holds) was initiated in Andréka, Gergely, Németi [1977]. All problemes raised there have been solved in Gergely, Úry [1981] with the exception of one solved in Andréka, Németi, Sain [1979b].

**(12.14) Definition.** *Let $\Theta \subseteq Form_\sigma$ and $\mathcal{K} \subseteq Mod_\sigma$ be arbitrary. The set of programs, terminating in all models of the class $\mathcal{K}$ after starting with any input that satisfies one of the preconditions of $\Theta$, is defined as follows:*

$$stop(\Theta, \mathcal{K}) \rightleftharpoons \{p \in P_\sigma \mid \forall \mathcal{A} \in \mathcal{K}, \forall \phi \in \Theta \quad p \text{ satisfies the } \phi\text{-start termination property in } \mathcal{A}\}.$$

An important property of terminating programs is the boundedness of their paths.

**(12.15) Lemma.** *Let $Ax \subseteq Mod_\sigma$ be a consistent set of axioms and $\mathcal{K} \rightleftharpoons Mod(Ax)$. Let $\phi \in \Theta$ and $p \in stop(\Theta, \mathcal{K})$ be arbitrary. Then there is an $i \in \mathbb{N}$ such that for any model $\mathcal{A} \in \mathcal{K}$ and for any path $s \in Trace_{\mathcal{A}}[\![p]\!]$ if $\mathcal{A} \models \phi[in\, s{\restriction}_V]$ holds then $length(s) \leq i$.*

*Proof.* The statement follows from Corollary (4.18). □

Now let us introduce a restriction of the partial correctness theory.

**(12.16) Definition.** *Let $\mathcal{K}$, $\mathcal{V} \subseteq Mod_\sigma$ be arbitrary, such that $\mathcal{V} \subseteq \mathcal{K}$. Take*

$$PC(\mathcal{K}, \mathcal{V}) \rightleftharpoons \{\phi\{p\}\psi \mid \mathcal{K} \models \phi\{p\}\psi, p \in stop(\{\phi\}, \mathcal{V}), \phi, \psi \in Form_\sigma, p \in P_\sigma\}$$

**(12.17) Theorem.** *Let $Ax$ be an axiom system containing arithmetic and let $\mathcal{K} = Mod(Ax)$. Then*

*(i) $PC(\mathcal{K}, \emptyset)$ is not recursively enumerable;*
*(ii) $PC(\mathcal{K}, \{\mathcal{N}\})$ is not recursively enumerable;*
*(iii) $PC(\mathcal{K}, \mathcal{K})$ is recursively enumerable.*

*Proof.* Statement (i) directly follows from Theorem (12.3) since $PC(\mathcal{K}, \emptyset) = PC(\mathcal{K})$. Now we prove the statement (ii). Let us fix a Diophantine equation $t_1 = t_2$ such that

$$\mathcal{K} \not\models \forall x \neg(t_1 = t_2) \text{ but } \mathcal{N} \models \forall x \neg(t_1 = t_2)$$

(by Theorem (1.28) such an equation exists). For any $\tau_1, \tau_2 \in Term(\sigma, V\backslash\{y,u\})$ let us consider the following program

$$R(\tau_1, \tau_2) \rightleftharpoons \textbf{if } \neg(t_1 = t_2) \rightarrow y := 0 \;\square\; t_1 = t_2 \rightarrow DE(\tau_1, \tau_2);\;\; y := 1 \textbf{ fi}$$

where the program $DE(\tau_1, \tau_2)$ has been defined in Lemma (12.1), and $u$ is the new variable in this program. To prove the statement we need the following

**Claim 1.**

(a) For any $\tau_1, \tau_2 \in Term(\sigma, V\backslash\{y,u\})$, $\mathcal{K} \models true\{R(\tau_1,\tau_2)\}y = 0$ iff the equation $\tau_1 = \tau_2$ is not solvable in the standard model $\mathcal{N}$.
(b) $R(\tau_1, \tau_2)$ terminates in $\mathcal{N}$ with respect to any precondition, i.e. $R(\tau_1, \tau_2) \in stop\{\{true\}, \{\mathcal{N}\})$.

*Proof of Claim 1.* Let $\tau_1, \tau_2 \in Term(\sigma, V\backslash\{y,u\})$ be arbitrary, and suppose that $n = |var(t_1) \cup var(t_2)|$. First we prove the "only if" part of the statement (a). Let us suppose that $Ax \models true\{R(\tau_1,\tau_2)\}y = 0$ and let $\mathcal{A} \in \mathcal{K}$ be such that for some $a_1, ..., a_n \in \mathcal{A}, \mathcal{A} \models t_1 = t_2[a_1/x_1, \ldots, a_n/x_n]$.

If an arbitrary but given Diophantine equation $\tau_1 = \tau_2$ has a solution in the natural numbers then the program $DE(\tau_1, \tau_2)$ has a terminating trace in $\mathcal{A}$ and so there is a trace of $R(\tau_1, \tau_2)$ in $\mathcal{A}$, starting with the input data $(a_1, ..., a_n)$, which terminates with output $y = 1$. This contradicts our supposition.

Now we consider the other direction of the statement (a). Let us suppose that the equation $\tau_1 = \tau_2$ is not solvable in $\mathcal{N}$. Then for every $\mathcal{A} \in \mathcal{K}$, $DE(\tau_1, \tau_2)$ does not have any terminating trace in $\mathcal{A}$. Thus, whenever $R(\tau_1, \tau_2)$ terminates in a model $\mathcal{A}$, it terminates with the output value $y = 0$.

Now we turn to prove the statement (b) of Claim 1. Since $\mathcal{N} \models \forall x \neg(t_1 = t_2)$, for any valuation $k$ every path of the program $R(\tau_1, \tau_2)$ starting from $k$ terminates (with output $y = 0$). So Claim 1 has been proved.

Now we complete the proof of the statement (ii). Let

$$\Theta \quad \rightleftharpoons \quad \{true\{R(\tau_1, \tau_2)\}y = 0 \mid \tau_1, \tau_2 \in Term(\sigma, V\backslash\{y,u\})\}.$$

It is clear that $\Theta$ is recursive. By Claim 1 it is evident that the set $U \rightleftharpoons \Theta \cap PC(\mathcal{K}, \{\mathcal{N}\})$ is recursively equivalent to the set of Diophantine equations unsolvable in natural numbers. Therefore, by using the recursivity of $\Theta$ we can conclude that the set $H$ is not recursively enumerable and nor is $PC(\mathcal{K}, \{\mathcal{N}\})$.

Statement (iii) can be proved by the use of Theorem (4.19) which states that if $\phi\{p\}\psi \in PC(\mathcal{K}, \mathcal{K})$ then $Den[\![p, var(p)]\!]\restriction_\phi$ is definable in $\mathcal{K}$. However, it is not clear whether the correspondence between the true partial correctness assertions and the definable formulas is recursive. So we need the following

**Claim 2.** For any similarity type $\sigma$ and for any $p \in P_\sigma$ there is a number $i(p) \in \mathbb{N}$ such that for each $\phi \in Form_\sigma$ there is a $\sigma$-type formula $stop_{i(p),p,\phi}$ with the following property: for an arbitrary set of formulas $Ax \subseteq Form_\sigma$, $Ax \models stop_{i(p),p,\phi}$ iff in any model $\mathcal{A} \in Mod(Ax)$ the length of any trace of $p$, starting from a state which satisfies $\phi$, is less than $i(p)$. Moreover, the connections between $p$ and $i(p)$ and between $i(p)$, $p$, $\phi$ and the formula $stop_{i(p),p,\phi}$ is recursive.

*Proof of Claim 2.* Let us recall variables $W_1$ and $W_2$ from the program $Init_\sigma(X)$ of Theorem (4.26). Moreover, recall formulas $onestep_g$ and $\alpha$ from Definition (4.10). Now let $g \rightleftharpoons gr(p)$ and take $i(p)$ as the length of a maximal length Hamilton path (i.e. a path with different nodes) in the graph $g$. For any $h \in TF_\sigma$ define the following $\sigma$-type formula:

$$is\_loop(p,h) \rightleftharpoons \begin{cases} true & \text{if } run(p,h) = \mathbf{loop}; \\ false & \text{otherwise.} \end{cases}$$

Let $i \rightleftharpoons i(p)$. Now we are ready to define the formula $stop_{i,p,\phi}$:

$$stop_{i,p,\phi} \rightleftharpoons \forall W_1 \forall W_2 \Bigg( W_1 \neq W_2 \to \forall X_1 \forall L_1 ... \forall X_i \forall L_i$$

$$\Big( \bigwedge_{j=1}^{i-1} onestep_g(X_j, L_j, X_{j+1}, L_{j+1}) \wedge L_1 = start_g \wedge \phi[X_1/X] \to$$

$$\bigwedge_{(L_i,L) \in dom\, g} \neg\alpha(g(L_i, L)) \Big) \Bigg) \wedge$$

$$\forall W_1 \forall W_2 (W_1 = W_2) \to \forall X \Big( \bigwedge_{h \in TF_\sigma} \phi \wedge one_\sigma(X, h) \to \neg is\_loop(p,h) \Big).$$

It is clear that this formula is appropriate and the mentioned connections are recursive ones. □

Note that the proof of (ii) of Theorem (12.17) also implies that there is no recursive set $H$ such that $PC(\mathcal{K}, \{\mathcal{N}\}) \subseteq H \subseteq rPC(\mathcal{K})$. Hence $HL_\sigma^{\mathcal{K}}$ is not complete with respect to $PC(\mathcal{K}, \{\mathcal{N}\})$ if $\mathcal{K} = Mod(Ax)$ for an $Ax$ containing arithmetic.

From the point of view of programming theory it would have been desirable if the Floyd-Hoare language $HL_\sigma^{Ax}$ had proved to be complete with respect to $PC(\mathcal{K}, \{\mathcal{N}\})$ because it is quite natural to demand the termination of the programs in the standard model. But this is not the case. The above theorem says that the partial correctness theory $PC(\mathcal{K}, \{\mathcal{N}\})$ is still far too large.

The completeness of $HL_\sigma^{Ax}$ with respect to $PC(\mathcal{K}, \mathcal{K})$ requires far too strong conditions of the program: to terminate in every model of a given class $\mathcal{K}$. This does not fit in with the programmer's intuition, which considers only the "standard world". Thus, it would be useful to find such a partial correctness theory with respect to which the language $HL_\sigma^{Ax}$ would prove to be complete with the demand of termination of programs in as few non-standard models as possible. The definition of such a theory seems to be fairly difficult, if it is possible at all.

## 12.3 Den-Completeness

In the previous sections the Floyd-Hoare language has been considered from a logical point of view and the classical notion of completeness has been modified by following a logical motivation. Here we introduce another notion of completeness with a rather programming-theoretic motivation. Namely, we wish to "simulate" Floyd-Hoare formulas with those formulas which are already surely provable. That is, given an arbitrary Floyd-Hoare formula $\phi\{p\}\psi \in H_\sigma$ then instead of its direct proof we wish to find such a program $p' \in P_\sigma$ that the formula $\phi\{p'\}\psi$ can already be proved. Of course, if we had no further assumptions on program $p'$, then a program which never terminates could be appointed to $p'$ and this would result in a useless notion. Therefore, we have to give further assumptions which make the sense precise in which the program $p'$ "simulates" $p$.

We will investigate what type of completeness notion we may obtain by providing the required additional assumption in two different ways:

(i) any output of $p$ is also an output of $p'$;
(ii) any, in a certain sense standard, output is also an output of $p'$.

Investigation of these kind of questions was raised in Andréka, Gergely, Németi [1977] but only for deterministic programs.

To gain positive results we have to use programs with two stacks as well. So we must modify all the notions defined in the previous chapters:

$$\begin{array}{lcl}
{}_2H_\sigma & \rightleftharpoons & \{\phi\{p\}\psi \mid \phi,\psi \in Form_\sigma \text{ and } p \in P^2_\sigma\} \\
{}_2HL^{\mathcal{K}}_\sigma & \rightleftharpoons & ({}_2H_\sigma, \mathcal{K}, \models) \\
{}_2PC(\mathcal{K}) & \rightleftharpoons & \{\chi \in {}_2H_\sigma \mid \mathcal{K} \models \chi\} \\
{}_2PC(\mathcal{K},\mathcal{V}) & \rightleftharpoons & \{\phi\{p\}\psi \mid \mathcal{K} \models \phi\{p\}\psi, p \in stop(\{\phi\},\mathcal{V}), \\
 & & \qquad \phi,\psi \in Form_\sigma, p \in P^2_\sigma\}
\end{array}$$

**(12.18) Definition.** *Let* $\mathcal{V} \subseteq Mod_\sigma$ *and* $\phi$, $\phi'$, $\psi$, $\psi' \in Form_\sigma$ *and* $p, p' \in P^2_\sigma$. *We say that* $(\phi', p', \psi')$ *is stronger than* $(\phi, p, \psi)$ *with respect to denotation in* $\mathcal{V}$ *(written as* $(\phi, p, \psi) \prec^{\mathcal{V}} (\phi', p', \psi')$ *iff the following conditions hold:*

- $\mathcal{V} \models \phi \to \phi'$;
- $\mathcal{V} \models \psi' \to \psi$;
- *for all* $\mathcal{A} \in \mathcal{V}$, $Den_{\mathcal{A}}[\![p]\!]\restriction_\phi \subseteq Den_{\mathcal{A}}[\![p']\!]\restriction_\phi$.

The last condition of the above definition means that if a program $p$ starts with an input satisfying a precondition $\phi$ then all the corresponding output values of $p$ are to be among the output values of $p'$ starting with the same input. In other words, program $p'$ is better than program $p$ with regard to the denotation in $\mathcal{V}$.

**(12.19) Definition.** *Let us fix two classes $\mathcal{V}, \mathcal{K} \subseteq Mod_\sigma$ of models such that $\mathcal{V} \subseteq \mathcal{K}$. Let $H \subseteq {}_2PC(\mathcal{K})$ be fixed. ${}_2HL_\sigma^\mathcal{K}$ is called $\mathcal{V}$-Den-complete with respect to $H$ iff there is a recursively enumerable set $E \subseteq {}_2PC(\mathcal{K})$ such that for all $\phi\{p\}\psi \in H$ there is a program $p'$ and there are formulas $\phi'$, $\psi' \in Form_\sigma$ such that*

*(i)* $\phi'\{p'\}\psi' \in E$;
*(ii)* $(\phi, p, \psi) \prec^\mathcal{V} (\phi', p', \psi')$.

*If $\mathcal{V} = \mathcal{K}$ we simply say Den-completeness instead of $\mathcal{V}$-Den-completeness.*

Now we introduce a subset of ${}_2PC(Ax)$ with respect to which ${}_2HL_\sigma^\mathcal{K}$ will be Den-complete. Let

$${}_2PCO(\mathcal{K}, \mathcal{V}) \rightleftharpoons \{\phi\{p\}\psi \in {}_2PC(\mathcal{K}, \mathcal{V}) \mid \psi \in Open_\sigma\}.$$

**(12.20) Theorem.** *Let $\mathcal{K}$ and $\mathcal{V}$ be as in Definition (12.19). The language ${}_2HL_\sigma^\mathcal{K}$ is $\mathcal{V}$-Den-complete with respect to the set ${}_2PCO(\mathcal{K}, \mathcal{V})$.*

*Proof.* First we define a recursively enumerable set $E$. Let us fix a finite set of variables $Z$ and an open $\sigma$-type formula $\psi$. Let $Y \rightleftharpoons var(\psi)$. Recall the program $Herb(Y \cup Z)$ of Lemma (8.6). Let us define a program $p_{Z,\psi}$ which takes a vector of the Herbrand universe $H_\sigma(Z \cup Y)$ generated by the program $Herb(Z \cup Y)$ and tests whether $\psi$ holds for the actual output value $Y$. If $\psi$ holds then $p_{Z,\psi}$ terminates, otherwise it loops. Take

$$p_{Z,\psi} \rightleftharpoons Herb(Z \cup Y);\ \textbf{if}\ \psi(Y) \rightarrow \textbf{skip} \ \Box\ \neg\psi(Y) \rightarrow \textbf{loop fi}\ .$$

Obviously, $\mathcal{K} \models true\{p_{Z,\psi}\}\psi$. Let us take

$$E \rightleftharpoons \{true\{p_{Z,\psi}\}\psi \mid \phi \in Form_\sigma, Z \subseteq V \text{ is finite}, \psi \in Open_\sigma\}.$$

It is obvious that the set $E$ is recursively enumerable. Let us suppose that $\phi\{p\}\psi \in {}_2PCO(\mathcal{K}, \mathcal{V})$. Let $Z \rightleftharpoons var(p)$. It is not hard to check that

$$(\phi, p, \psi) \prec^\mathcal{V} (true, p_{Z,\psi}, \psi).$$

□

**(12.21) Corollary.** *Let $Ax \subseteq Form_\sigma$ be an arbitrary consistent set of formulas. If $Ax$ has the quantifier elimination property then ${}_2HL_\sigma^{Ax}$ is Den-complete with respect to ${}_2PC(Ax)$.*

The notion of Den-completeness would be useful for programming theory and practice if the Floyd-Hoare language ${}_2HL_\sigma^\mathcal{K}$ were Den-complete with respect to the entire ${}_2PC(\mathcal{K})$. This would mean that to an arbitrary program $p \in P_\sigma^2$ satisfying given pre- and postconditions there would exist such a program $p' \in P_\sigma^2$ which would be better than $p$ with respect to the denotation in $\mathcal{K}$, and the properties of $p'$ could be proved. But this is not the case.

**(12.22) Theorem.** *The Floyd-Hoare language* ${}_2HL_\eta^{\{\mathcal{N}\}}$ *is Den-complete with respect neither to* ${}_2PC(\{\mathcal{N}\})$ *nor to* ${}_2PC(\{\mathcal{N}\}, \{\mathcal{N}\})$.

*Proof.* Let us fix a recursively innumerable but first-order definable unary relation $R$ in $\mathbb{N}$. Let $\psi(x)$ be the formula of $Form_\eta$ defining $R$ in $\mathcal{N}$.

For a contradiction, let us suppose that ${}_2HL_\eta^{\{\mathcal{N}\}}$ is Den-complete with respect to ${}_2PC(\{\mathcal{N}\}, \{\mathcal{N}\})$. By definition there is a recursively enumerable set $E$ with properties of Definition (12.19). Consider the set

$$\Pi \quad \rightleftharpoons \quad \{p \mid true\{p\}\psi \in E \text{ and } \psi' \to \psi\}.$$

Since $E$ is recursively enumerable, so is $\Pi$. Using Cantor diagonalization and Gödel coding one can check that there is a program $prog(\Pi) \in P_\eta^2$ with the following property:

$$Den_{\mathcal{N}}[\![prog(\Pi), \{x\}]\!] = \cup\{Den_{\mathcal{N}}[\![p, \{x\}]\!] \mid p \in \Pi\}.$$

Using the definition of $\Pi$ we get $rng\, Den_{\mathcal{N}}[\![prog(\Pi), \{x\}]\!] \subseteq R$. We prove that $rng\, Den_{\mathcal{N}}[\![prog(\Pi), \{x\}]\!]$ is just the set $R$. Indeed, let $k \in R$ and consider the following Floyd-Hoare formula: $\chi \rightleftharpoons true\{x := k\}\psi$. It is clear that $\chi \in {}_2PC(\{\mathcal{N}\}, \{\mathcal{N}\})$. Therefore, by the indirect assumption there is a $p' \in \Pi$ and a formula $\psi'$ such that $(true, x := k, \psi) \prec^{\{\mathcal{N}\}} (true, p', \psi')$. Hence $R \subseteq rng\, Den_{\mathcal{N}}[\![prog(\Pi), \{x\}]\!]$.

So we have proved that $R$ is the range of the denotation of the program $prog(\Pi)$ in $\mathcal{N}$. Using Theorem (7.5) (A) we get a program $\hat{p}$ such that $R$ is the domain of the denotation of $\hat{p}$. Applying Theorem (7.9) we get that $R$ is recursively enumerable which contradicts our original assumption. □

According to Theorem (12.20) and Corollary (12.21) Den-completeness can be used when the postconditions can be given as open formulas. But this seems to be insufficient even for programming theory, e.g. in the standard model of arithmetic. To illustrate this let us see the theory $Next$ introduced in Chapter 1 which, as we know, has the quantifier elimination property.

Let $\hat{\eta}$ be the similarity type of the axiom system $Next$. It is evident that $rP_{\hat{\eta}}(\mathcal{N}\restriction_{\hat{\eta}}) = rP_\eta(\mathcal{N})$ in standard models. However, many of the postconditions given in $PA$ cannot be formalized by the use of $Next$. Therefore, Corollary (12.21) is not of great significance for the programming theory and thus, in general, the notion of Den-completeness is not of much use for programming practice except for the cases when open formula specification exists, e.g. the case of a system of equations to be solved with a given exactness.

Let us try the other way round, i.e. when we expect program $p'$ to terminate for all, in a certain sense standard, input data for which the original program $p$ terminates. First let us define the notion of standard data.

**(12.23) Definition.**

*(i)* *A set $Ax \subseteq Form_\sigma$ of axioms is said to be of Herbrand-type iff $Ax$ is complete with respect to the quantifier-free closed (i.e. ground) formulas. This*

*means that for each ground atomic formula (including equality)* $\rho(\tau_1, ..., \tau_n)$ *of* $Atom_\sigma$ *either* $Ax \models \rho(\tau_1, ..., \tau_n)$ *or* $Ax \models \neg\rho(\tau_1, ..., \tau_n)$.

*(ii) A class* $\mathcal{K} \subseteq Mod_\sigma$ *of models is called Herbrand-type iff there is a Herbrand-type set* $Ax$ *of axioms such that* $Mod(Ax) = \mathcal{K}$.

Let $\mathcal{K}$ be a Herbrand-type class of $\sigma$-type models. If for every sort $s \in sort\ \sigma$ the similarity type $\sigma$ contains at least one constant symbol then for each model $\mathcal{A} \in \mathcal{K}$ one can define its standard part by taking

$$\mathcal{A}^{st} \rightleftharpoons (A^{st}, \{\rho_{\mathcal{A}} \restriction A^{st} \mid \rho \in rel\ \sigma \cup func\ \sigma\}),$$

where $A^{st} = \{\tau_{\mathcal{A}} \mid \tau \in Term_\sigma \text{ is ground }\}$. Clearly, for any $\mathcal{A}, \mathcal{B} \in \mathcal{K}$, $\mathcal{A}^{st}$ is isomorphic to $\mathcal{B}^{st}$.

**(12.24) Definition.** *A Herbrand-type model class* $\mathcal{K}$ *has a standard model iff for every (or equivalently for some) model* $\mathcal{A} \in \mathcal{K}$, $\mathcal{A}^{st} \models Th(\mathcal{K})$ *(or equivalently* $\mathcal{A}^{st} \in \mathcal{K}$*) holds.*

**(12.25) Definition.** *Let* $\mathcal{K}$ *be a Herbrand-type class of models. Let us fix a model* $\mathcal{A} \in \mathcal{K}$. *A valuation* $k \in Val_{\mathcal{A}}$ *is called standard iff for all* $v \in dom\ k$ *there is a ground term* $\tau$ *of* $Term_\sigma$ *such that* $k(v) = \tau_{\mathcal{A}}$ *(i.e.* $rng\ k \subseteq A^{st}$*).*

**(12.26) Definition.** *Let* $Ax \subseteq Form_\sigma$ *be of Herbrand-type with a standard model* $St(Ax)$. *A formula* $\phi \in Form_\sigma$ *is called absolute with respect to* $Ax$ *iff for every model* $\mathcal{A} \in Mod(Ax)$ *and for all standard valuations* $k \in Val_{\mathcal{A}}$, $\mathcal{A}^{st} \models \phi[k]$ *implies that* $\mathcal{A} \models \phi[k]$.

**(12.27) Theorem.** *Every existential* $\eta$*-type formula is absolute with respect to* $PA$.

*Proof.* It is obvious that $PA$ is of Herbrand-type with standard model $\mathcal{N}$. The absoluteness of a positive existential formula can be proved by formula-induction and we leave it to the reader. □

**(12.28) Definition.** *Let* $Ax \subseteq Form_\sigma$ *be of Herbrand-type with a standard model* $St(Ax)$. *Let* $H \subseteq {}_2PC(Ax)$. *The Floyd-Hoare language* ${}_2HL_\sigma^{Ax}$ *is said to be weak-complete with respect to* $H$ *iff it is* $\{St(Ax)\}$*-Den-complete with respect to* $H$.

From Theorem (12.22) and Theorem (12.27) we get the following

**(12.29) Corollary.** *The Floyd-Hoare language* ${}_2HL_\eta^{\{\mathcal{N}\}}$ *is not weak-complete with respect to* ${}_2PC(\{\mathcal{N}\})$.

**(12.30) Definition.** *Let* $Ax \subseteq Form_\sigma$ *be of Herbrand-type with a standard model* $St(Ax)$. *We say that* $Ax$ *satisfies the induction elimination property iff there*

*is a recursive function which renders to each inductive definitional schema* $(\Theta_1, \Theta_2)$ $(\Theta_1, \Theta_2 \in Form_{\sigma^c})$ *a formula* $\psi(\Theta_1, \Theta_2) \in Form_{\sigma^c}$*, absolute with respect to* $Ax$*, in such a way that*

$$_{St(Ax)^c}EI_{(\Theta_1,\Theta_2)} = \psi(\Theta_1, \Theta_2)_{St(Ax)^c}.$$

*We recall that* $_{St(Ax)^c}EI(\Theta_1, \Theta_2)$ *is the relation effectively inductively defined by* $(\Theta_1, \Theta_2)$ *in* $St(Ax)^c$ *(cf. Definition (8.3)).*

**(12.31) Theorem.** *The axiom system* $PA$ *satisfies the induction elimination property.*

**(12.32) Definition.** *Let us suppose that* $Ax$ *satisfies the induction elimination property. A formula* $\phi \in Form_\sigma$ *is said to be effectively represented in* $Ax$ *iff there is an inductive definitional schema* $(\Theta_1, \Theta_2)$ $(\Theta_1, \Theta_2 \in Open_{\sigma^c})$ *such that* $Ax \models \psi(\Theta_1, \Theta_2) \leftrightarrow \phi$*. We say that* $\phi$ *is effectively represented by* $(\Theta_1, \Theta_2)$*.*

Let $_2PCW(Ax) \rightleftharpoons \{\phi\{p\}\psi \in {}_2PC(Ax) \mid \psi$ is effectively represented in $Ax\}$.

**(12.33) Theorem.** *Let us suppose that* $Ax \subseteq Form_\sigma$ *satisfies the induction elimination property. The Floyd-Hoare language* $_2HL_\sigma^{Ax}$ *is weak-complete with respect to* $_2PCW(Ax)$*.*

*Proof.* Let $Ax$ be a Herbrand-type set of axioms which has a standard model $St(Ax)$. Let us suppose that $Ax$ satisfies the induction elimination property. Let $(\Theta_1, \Theta_2)$ be an inductive definitional schema. By Theorem (8.7) there is a program $IP(\Theta_1, \Theta_2) \in P_\sigma^2$ such that in $St(Ax)^c$:

$$(*) \qquad _{St(Ax)^c}EI_{(\Theta_1,\Theta_2)} \rightleftharpoons dom\, Den_{St(Ax)^c}[\![IP(\Theta_1, \Theta_2), Y]\!].$$

where $Y \rightleftharpoons var(IP(\Theta_1, \Theta_2))$. Let $Z$ be an arbitrary finite set of variables. Since $Ax$ is of Herbrand-type, for any $s \in sort\ \sigma$ there is at least one constant symbol, say $c_s$. Let $MakeConst \rightleftharpoons (x \in Z \cup Y) : x := c_{sort(x)}$. Let $Y'$ be a new copy of $Y$. In the end take the following program:

$$p_{Z,(\Theta_1,\Theta_2)} \rightleftharpoons MakeConst;\ Herb(Z \cup Y);\ EmptyAll;$$
$$Y' := Y; IP(\Theta_1, \Theta_2); Y := Y'.$$

We prove that $true\{p_{Z,(\Theta_1,\Theta_2)}\}\psi \in {}_2PC(Ax)$. Indeed, by using (*) and the fact that for any model $\mathcal{A} \in Mod(Ax)$ $St(Ax)$ is isomorphic to $\mathcal{A}^{st}$ we get that:

$$(**) \qquad Den_{\mathcal{A}^c}[\![p_{Z,(\Theta_1,\Theta_2)}, Y]\!] = \{(k, k') \mid \mathcal{A}^{st} \models \psi(\Theta_1, \Theta_2)[k']\}.$$

Since $\psi(\Theta_1, \Theta_2)$ is absolute with respect to $Ax$, so any output of $p_{Z,(\Theta_1,\Theta_2)}$ in any model $\mathcal{A}$ of $Ax$ also satisfies $\psi$ in the whole model $\mathcal{A}$. Now we are ready to define $E \rightleftharpoons \{\phi\{p_{Z,(\Theta_1,\Theta_2)}\}\psi \mid (\Theta_1, \Theta_2)$ is an inductive definitional schema, $Z \subseteq V$ is finite and $Ax \models \psi \leftrightarrow \psi(\Theta_1, \Theta_2)\}$.

Clearly $E$ is recursively enumerable since the correspondence between $(\Theta_1, \Theta_2)$ and $\psi(\Theta_1, \Theta_2)$ is recursive. By the above, $E \subseteq {}_2PC(Ax)$. Now let $\phi\{p\}\psi \in {}_2PCW(Ax)$ be arbitrary. By definition there is an inductive definitional schema $(\Theta_1, \Theta_2)$ such that $Ax \models \psi \leftrightarrow \psi(\Theta_1, \Theta_2)$. Take $Z \rightleftharpoons var(\phi) \cup var(p)$. Applying (**) we get $(\phi, p, \psi) \prec^{St(Ax)} (\phi, p_{Z,(\Theta_1,\Theta_2)}, \psi)$. Thus ${}_2HL_\sigma^{Ax}$ is weak-complete with respect to ${}_2PCW(Ax)$. □

**(12.34) Theorem.** *The Floyd-Hoare language* ${}_2HL_\eta^{PA}$ *is not complete with respect to* ${}_2PCW(PA)$.

*Proof.* Similar to the proof of Theorem (12.17), (i). □

Chapter 13

# Dynamic Logic Generated by Extension

As we have seen, the $\sigma$-type dynamic logic and even its Floyd-Hoare sublanguage are incomplete. The efforts made in the previous chapter to make dynamic logic complete did not bring us pragmatically satisfactory results. Therefore, we now look for another way to obtain a pragmatically satisfactory complete dynamic logic. First of all we require that this way should allow us to preserve the classical notion of completeness and should also provide us with the expected dynamic logic in the scope of classical first-order logic. The latter requirement follows from our original aim to develop programming theory in this scope. Moreover, we also require to develop the dynamic logic in compliance with the computation theory developed in Part I. In the present chapter we introduce the main logical tools which can be used to develop different programming logic as classical first-order languages. These tools are based on the notion of extension introduced in Chapter 5 and are used to augment the programming language $rP_\sigma$ with different computational devices.

We show how the so-called extended dynamic logic can be introduced and in what sense the logical power of different dynamic logics can be compared. Moreover, we give a method which allows us to give an axiomatic calculus for the extended dynamic logic in the spirit of the axiomatization given by Harel [1979] for the regular dynamic logic.

First of all, we define the language which we obtain on the base of an extension of some given similarity type.

**(13.1) Definition.** *Let $(\delta, ext)$ be a fixed extension of a given similarity type $\sigma$. The language $\mathcal{L}^{ext}$ generated by ext is the language given as the following triplet:*

$$(Form_\delta, Mod(ext), \models_{ext}),$$

*where*

*(i) $Mod(ext) \rightleftharpoons \cup\{ext(\mathcal{A}) \mid \mathcal{A} \in Mod_\sigma\}$;*

*(ii) for an arbitrary set $\Phi \subseteq Form_\delta$ and for any formula $\phi \in Form_\delta$ we have $\Phi \models_{ext} \phi$ iff for every model $\mathcal{A} \in Mod_\sigma$ and for every model $\mathcal{B} \in ext(\mathcal{A})$, $\mathcal{B} \models \Phi$ implies $\mathcal{B} \models \phi$.*

We note that $\models_{ext}$ and $\models$ are the same as validity relations (i.e. $\models_{ext} = \models\restriction_{Form_\delta \times Mod(ext)}$) but they differ as consequence relations since in general

$Mod(ext) \subset Mod_\sigma$. Given two fixed similarity types $\sigma$ and $\delta$, there are, if any, many possible extensions. However, sometimes it is important to have an extension distinguished in a certain sense. A maximal extension will play this role.

**(13.2) Definition.** *Let $Ax_\sigma \subseteq Form_\sigma$, $Ax_\delta \subseteq Form_\delta$ be fixed and let $(\delta, ext)$ be an extension of $\sigma$. $(\delta, ext)$ is called maximal with respect to $(Ax_\sigma, Ax_\delta)$ iff*

*(i) for each model $\mathcal{A} \in Mod(Ax_\sigma)$:*

$$ext(\mathcal{A}) = \{\mathcal{B} \mid \mathcal{A} \text{ is the } \sigma\text{-type reduct of } \mathcal{B} \text{ and } \mathcal{B} \models Ax_\sigma \cup Ax_\delta\}.$$

*and $ext(\mathcal{A}) \neq \emptyset$;*

*(ii) for each model $\mathcal{A} \in Mod_\sigma \setminus Mod(Ax_\sigma)$, $ext(\mathcal{A}) = \emptyset$.*

We note that if $(\delta, ext)$ is an extension of $\sigma$ which is maximal with respect to $(Ax_\sigma, Ax_\delta)$ then the set $Ax_\sigma \cup Ax_\delta$ of formulas is a conservative extension of $Ax_\sigma$. By definition, for any model $\mathcal{A} \in Mod(Ax_\sigma)$, $ext(\mathcal{A}) \neq \emptyset$. So there is a $\mathcal{B} \in ext(\mathcal{A})$ such that $\mathcal{B} \models Ax_\sigma \cup Ax_\delta$ and the $\sigma$-type reduct of $\mathcal{B}$ is $\mathcal{A}$. Therefore, we immediately get the following

**(13.3) Lemma.** *Let $\sigma$ and $\delta$ be be two fixed similarity types such that $\sigma \subseteq \delta$. Let $Ax_\sigma \subseteq Form_\sigma$ and $Ax_\delta \subseteq Form_\delta$ be also given. If $Ax_\sigma \cup Ax_\delta$ is a conservative extension of $Ax_\sigma$ then there is a (unique) extension $(\delta, ext)$ maximal with respect to $(Ax_\sigma, Ax_\delta)$.*

**(13.4) Theorem.** *Let $\sigma$ be a fixed simularity type and let $(\delta, ext)$ be an extension of $\sigma$ maximal with respect to $(Ax_\sigma, Ax_\delta)$ (where $Ax_\sigma \subseteq Form_\sigma$ and $Ax_\delta \subseteq Form_\delta$). The generated language $\mathcal{L}^{ext}$ is compact. Moreover, if $Ax_\sigma$ and $Ax_\delta$ are recursively enumerable then $\mathcal{L}^{ext}$ is complete with respect to consequence.*

*Proof.* By using the maximality of $ext$ for any $\Phi \subseteq Form_\delta$ and $\phi \in Form_\delta$ we have that $\Phi \models_{ext} \phi$ iff $\Phi \cup Ax_\sigma \cup Ax_\delta \models \phi$. Therefore, we can apply the compactness and completeness of the first-order logic and get the desired results. □

Let $\sigma$ be a fixed similarity type and let $(\delta, ext)$ be a given extension of $\sigma$. Let us suppose that a translation function $D : rP_\sigma \to Form_\delta$ is given which is supposed to describe the program semantics. This means that for each program $p \in rP_\sigma$ with the variables $X \rightleftharpoons var(p)$ there is a new copy $X'$ of $X$ such that $var(D(p)) \subseteq X \cup X'$. In this case $D$ is said to be a *semantic function*. We extend this function to a function $\tilde{D} : rD_\sigma \to Form_\delta$ in the following way:

(i) if $\phi \in Form_\sigma$ then $\tilde{D}(\phi) \rightleftharpoons \phi$;

(ii) if $\phi, \psi \in rD_\sigma$ and $v \in V_{sort\,\sigma}$ then

$$\tilde{D}(\phi \wedge \psi) \quad \rightleftharpoons \quad \tilde{D}(\phi) \wedge \tilde{D}(\psi);$$

$$\tilde{D}(\neg\phi) \rightleftharpoons \neg\tilde{D}(\phi);$$
$$\tilde{D}(\exists v\phi) \rightleftharpoons \exists v(\tilde{D}(\phi));$$

(iii) if $p \in rP_\sigma$, $\phi \in rD_\sigma$ then

$$\tilde{D}([p]\phi) \rightleftharpoons \forall X'(D(p)(X, X') \to \tilde{D}(\phi)[X'/X]),$$

where $X = var(p)$, $X'$ is an appropriate new copy of $X$.

(iv) We note that $\tilde{D}(\langle p\rangle\phi)$ is logically equivalent to the formula:

$$\tilde{D}(\langle p\rangle\phi) \rightleftharpoons \exists X'(D(p)(X, X') \wedge \tilde{D}(\phi)[X'/X]).$$

The function $\tilde{D}$ is also called a semantic function. By using this extended function we can define a new logic as follows.

**(13.5) Definition.** *Let $(\delta, ext)$ be an extension of a given similarity type $\sigma$. Let $D : rP_\sigma \to Form_\delta$ be a semantic function. The extended dynamic logic generated by extension $(\delta, ext)$ and semantic function $D$ is the language*

$$rDL_\sigma^{ext,D} \rightleftharpoons (rD_\sigma, Mod(ext), \models'_{ext}),$$

*where if $\mathcal{B} \in Mod(ext)$ and $\phi \in rD_\sigma$ then $\mathcal{B} \models'_{ext} \phi$ iff $\mathcal{B} \models_{ext} \tilde{D}(\phi)$.*

Note that we can think of this language $rDL_\sigma^{ext,D}$ as the embedding of the set $rD_\sigma$ of dynamic-logic formulas into the language $\mathcal{L}^{ext}$. It is clear that similarly we can define the extended dynamic logics $DL_\sigma^{ext,D}$ and $det\text{-}DL_\sigma^{ext,D}$.

By Theorem (13.4) we immediately get the following

**(13.6) Theorem.** *Let $\sigma$ be a fixed similarity type and let $(\delta, ext)$ be an extension of $\sigma$ maximal with respect to $(Ax_\sigma, Ax_\delta)$ (where $Ax_\sigma \subseteq Form_\sigma$ and $Ax_\delta \subseteq Form_\delta$). Let $D : rP_\sigma \to Form_\delta$ be a given semantic function. The extended dynamic logic $rDL_\sigma^{ext,D}$ generated by $(\delta, ext)$ and $D$ is compact. Moreover, if $Ax_\sigma$ and $Ax_\delta$ are recursively enumerable and $D$ is recursive, then the extended dynamic logic $rDL_\sigma^{ext,D}$ is complete with respect to consequence.*

Having fixed an extension $(\delta, ext)$ and a semantic function $D : rP_\sigma \to Form_\delta$ we want to give an extension $(\delta, st)$ which is called *the standard part* of $ext$ and within which the validity of $rD_\sigma$-formulas in "standard models" coincides with the usual definition. This means that

(a) for each model $\mathcal{A} \in Mod_\sigma$, $\emptyset \neq st(\mathcal{A}) \subseteq ext(\mathcal{A})$ is given and

(b) for each model $\mathcal{A} \in Mod_\sigma$, for each dynamic-logic formula $\phi \in rD_\sigma$ and for each $\mathcal{B} \in st(\mathcal{A})$ we have that $\mathcal{A} \models \phi$ iff $\mathcal{B} \models'_{ext} \phi$ (or equivalently $\mathcal{B} \models_{ext} \tilde{D}(\phi)$).

The property (b) guarantees that for non-standard models $\tilde{D}(\phi)$ can also be considered as a formula which describes the corresponding program properties. The following two lemmas (corresponding to Lemmas (11.4) and (11.6)) strengthen this feeling.

**(13.7) Lemma.** *Let $\phi,\psi \in rD_\sigma$ and let us suppose that $X \rightleftharpoons var(\phi \to \psi)$. The following formulas of $rD_\sigma$ are tautologies in an arbitrary extended dynamic logic $rDL_\sigma^{ext,D}$:*

*(i)* $([p]\phi \wedge \langle p\rangle true) \to \langle p\rangle\phi$;
*(ii)* $\langle p\rangle(\phi \wedge \psi) \to (\langle p\rangle\phi \wedge \langle p\rangle\psi)$;
*(iii)* $[p](\phi \wedge \psi) \leftrightarrow ([p]\phi \wedge [p]\psi)$;
*(iv)* $\langle p\rangle(\phi \vee \psi) \leftrightarrow (\langle p\rangle\phi \vee \langle p\rangle\psi)$;
*(v)* $\forall X(\phi \to \psi) \to ([p]\phi \to [p]\psi)$;
*(vi)* $\forall X(\phi \to \psi) \to (\langle p\rangle\phi \to \langle p\rangle\psi)$;
*(vii)* $\neg[p]\phi \leftrightarrow \langle p\rangle\neg\phi$.

**(13.8) Lemma.** *Let $p \in rP_\sigma$ and $\phi \in Form_\sigma$ be given. Let $X \rightleftharpoons var(p)$ and let $Y$ and $Z$ be two new copies of $X$. Let us suppose that $p$ is semantically deterministic, i.e. $ext \models \big([p](X = Y) \wedge [p](X = Z)\big) \to (Y = Z)$. Then the following formulas are tautologies in the extended dynamic logic $rDL_\sigma^{ext,D}$:*

*(i)* $\langle p\rangle\phi \to [p]\phi$;
*(ii)* $\langle p\rangle\phi \leftrightarrow [p]\phi \wedge \langle p\rangle true$;
*(iii)* $\langle p\rangle(\phi \wedge \psi) \leftrightarrow (\langle p\rangle\phi \wedge \langle p\rangle\psi)$.

However, in $rDL_\sigma^{ext,D}$ a lot of well-known program properties are generally not valid. Namely, the statements (ii) and (iv) of Lemma (11.5) are not valid in an arbitrary extended dynamic logic. So we have to choose an appropriate set $\Psi \subseteq Form_\delta$ of axioms to describe these properties. The set $\Psi$ is called also a semantic characterization since axioms of $\Psi$ generally formulate properties of program denotation and traces, i.e of properties of the semantic function $D$.

In the following chapters we will define several extensions and try to give appropriate semantic functions $D : rP_\sigma \to Form_\delta$. Except for one case, the definition of $D$ is not difficult at all. The results of Chapters 18 and 19 show that dynamic logic is not definable in temporal logic, which means that in the case of temporal logic the required semantic function $D$ defined on $rP_\sigma$ does not exist. However, if we restrict ourselves to the set of formulas $H_\sigma$ then by using some new constructions we can directly give the function $\tilde{D}$ instead of $D$.

Up till now we have been speaking about $rP_\sigma$-programs. But we have also to consider how formulas describing the properties of *stack*-programs can be handled in our theoretical framework. This means that we have also to consider semantic functions of the form $D : rP_\sigma^i \to Form_\delta$ ($i = 1, 2$). In this way we can build up the extended dynamic logics ${}_iDL_\sigma^{ext,D}$, ${}_irDL_\sigma^{ext,D}$ and *det*-${}_iDL_\sigma^{ext,D}$, respectively. Here $i = 1, 2$ shows the number of stacks. The sets of formulas of the above logics are $D_\sigma^i$, $rD_\sigma^i$ and *det*-$D_\sigma^i$, respectively.

By using different extensions we get different logics to express the same properties. It is a natural question how the logical power of these languages can be compared. First we introduce a relationship between two languages that considers which one of them has more true formulas from a given set.

**(13.9) Definition.** *Let* $\mathcal{L}_i \rightleftharpoons (F_i, M_i, \models_i)$ *be two languages* ($i = 1,2$). *Let us suppose that a set* $F$ *of formulas is given such that* $F \subseteq F_1 \cap F_2$. *The language* $\mathcal{L}_1$ *is logically more powerful than the language* $\mathcal{L}_2$ *with respect to* $F$ *(written as* $\mathcal{L}_1 >_F \mathcal{L}_2$ *or* $\mathcal{L}_2 <_F \mathcal{L}_1$*) iff*

*(i) for every* $Ax \subseteq F_1 \cap F_2$ *and for any formula* $\chi \in F$, $Ax \models_2 \chi$ *implies* $Ax \models_1 \chi$ *but*

*(ii) there is an* $Ax \subseteq F_1 \cap F_2$ *and a formula* $\chi \in F$ *such that* $Ax \models_1 \chi$ *and* $Ax \not\models_2 \chi$.

This general notion on the relationship of the languages we will use in the comparative study of different extended dynamic logics.

**(13.10) Definition.** *Let* $(\delta_i, ext_i)$ ($i = 1,2$) *be two given extensions of a given similarity type* $\sigma$. *Let us suppose that for* $i = 1,2$ *two semantic functions* $D_i : rP_\sigma \to Form_{\delta_i}$ *are given.* $rDL_\sigma^{ext_1,D_1}$ *is logically more powerful than* $rDL_\sigma^{ext_2,D_2}$ *with respect to* $rH_\sigma$ *(written as* $rDL_\sigma^{ext_1,D_1} >_{rH_\sigma} rDL_\sigma^{ext_2,D_2}$ *or* $rDL_\sigma^{ext_2,D_2} <_{rH_\sigma} rDL_\sigma^{ext_1,D_1}$*) iff*

*(i) for each* $Ax \subseteq Form_\sigma$ *and* $\chi \in rH_\sigma$ $Ax \models'_{ext_2} \chi$ *implies* $Ax \models'_{ext_1} \chi$ *but*

*(ii) there is an* $Ax \subseteq Form_\sigma$ *and a* $\chi \in rH_\sigma$ *such that* $Ax \models'_{ext_1} \chi$ *and* $Ax \not\models'_{ext_2} \chi$.

It is an interesting question how the extended dynamic logic $rDL_\sigma^{ext,D}$ can be proof-theoretically supported. We show that an appropriate axiomatic calculus can be given to this logic analogously to the axiomatization given by Harel [1979] for the regular dynamic logic. Taking into account the peculiarities of the extended dynamic logic we provide a method to build up an axiomatic calculus for it. One of the main tricks of this method is that we slightly modify the syntax $rD_\sigma$ by allowing the use of $\delta$-type formulas as pre- and postconditions for $\sigma$-type programs. To realize this modification let us define the set $rD_{\delta,\sigma}$ as the least set satisfying the following properties:

(i) $(Form_\sigma \subseteq)$ $Form_\delta \subseteq rD_{\delta,\sigma}$;

(ii) $rD_{\delta,\sigma}$ is closed under Boolean combinations and quantifications over variables belonging to $V_{sort\,\sigma}$;

(iii) if $p \in rP_\sigma$ and $\phi \in rD_{\delta,\sigma}$ then $[p]\phi \in rD_{\delta,\sigma}$ also holds.

It is clear that if a semantic function $D : rP_\sigma \to Form_\delta$ is given then $\tilde{D}$ is also definable for the set $rD_{\delta,\sigma}$ of formulas. In this way we can obtain a new extended logic $\mathcal{L}_{\delta,\sigma}^D \rightleftharpoons (rD_{\delta,\sigma}, Mod(ext), \models'_{ext})$. The following completeness theorem shows that if a calculus $\vdash_C$ proves that the program semantics is first-order definable then this calculus is complete with respect to the extended logic defined above.

**(13.11) Theorem.** *Let us suppose that* $(\delta, ext)$ *is an extension of* $\sigma$ *maximal with respect to* $(Ax_\sigma, Ax_\delta)$ *and let* $D : rP_\sigma \to Form_\delta$ *be a given semantic function.*

*Let us suppose that* $\vdash_C$ *is a sound calculus for the language* $\mathcal{L}^D_{\delta,\sigma}$. *Moreover, let us suppose that*

*(i) if* $\phi \in Form_\delta$ *and* $ext \models \phi$ *then* $\vdash_C \phi$;
*(ii) for any* $\phi \in rD_{\delta,\sigma}$ *there is a formula* $\phi^P \in Form_\delta$ *such that* $\vdash_C \phi \leftrightarrow \phi^P$.

*Then the calculus* $\vdash_C$ *is complete with respect to the extended dynamic logic* $rDL^{ext,D}_\sigma$.

*Proof.* Let $Ax \subseteq rD_\sigma$ and $\phi \in rD_\sigma$ be fixed and let us suppose that $Ax \models_{ext} \phi$. We aim to prove that $Ax \vdash_C \phi$. By assumption (ii) there is a formula $\phi^P \in Form_\delta$ such that $\vdash_C \phi \leftrightarrow \phi^P$. Thus $Ax \models_{ext} \phi^P$. For each element $\chi$ of $Ax$ there is a formula $\chi^P$ such that $\vdash_C \chi \leftrightarrow \chi^P$. By using the same argument as above we get that $\vdash_C Ax \equiv Ax^P$, where $Ax^P \rightleftharpoons \{\chi^P \mid \chi \in Ax\}$. Particularly, $ext \models Ax \equiv Ax^P$ also holds, which means that $Ax^P \models_{ext} \phi^P$. Since $ext$ is maximal, by Theorem (13.6) we get that there is a finite set of formulas $\Sigma \subseteq Ax^P$ such that $\Sigma \models_{ext} \phi^P$ or equivalently $ext \models \wedge\Sigma \to \phi^P$ holds. Since $\wedge\Sigma \to \phi^P$ is a $\delta$-type first-order formula by using (i) we get that $\vdash_C \wedge\Sigma \to \phi^P$ or equivalently $\Sigma \vdash_C \phi^P$. Therefore $Ax^P \vdash_C \phi^P$. Using the property of the formulas of the form $(\cdot)^P$ and first-order arguments we get $Ax \vdash_C \phi$. □

Now we give a more detailed calculus for $rDL^{ext,D}_\sigma$.

**(13.12) Definition.** *Let* $(\delta, ext)$ *be a given extension of* $\sigma$ *which is maximal with respect to* $(Ax_\sigma, Ax_\delta)$. *Let us suppose that a semantic function* $D : rP_\sigma \to Form_\delta$ *is given. The calculus* $\vdash_{dyn}$ *consists of the following axioms and rules.*

*(A) Axioms*

$T$ *all instances of the tautologies of the propositional logic and all the elements of* $Ax_\sigma \cup Ax_\delta$;

$R_{skip}$ $[\mathbf{skip}]\phi \leftrightarrow \phi$;

$R_{:=}$ $[x := \tau]\phi \leftrightarrow \phi[\tau/x]$;

$R_?$ $[x :=?]\phi \leftrightarrow \forall y\phi[y/x]$;

$R_;$ $[(p_1; p_2)]\phi \leftrightarrow [p_1]([p_2]\phi)$;

$R_{if}$ $[\mathbf{if}\ \alpha_1 \to p_1 \,\square\, \alpha_2 \to p_2 \mathbf{fi}]\phi \leftrightarrow (\neg\alpha_1 \wedge \neg\alpha_2 \to \phi) \wedge \bigwedge_1^2 (\alpha_i \to [p_i]\phi)$.

$R_{do}$ $[\mathbf{do}\ \alpha_1 \to p_1 \,\square\, \alpha_2 \to p_2 \mathbf{od}]\phi \leftrightarrow$
$$\forall Y\big(D(\mathbf{do}\ \alpha_1 \to p_1 \,\square\, \alpha_2 \to p_2\mathbf{od})(X,Y) \to \phi[Y/X]\big);$$

*(B) Inference rules*

$$(MP)\ \frac{\phi, \phi \to \psi}{\psi}; \quad (G[])\ \frac{\phi \to \psi}{[p]\phi \to [p]\psi}; \quad (G\exists)\ \frac{\phi \to \psi}{\exists x\phi \to \exists x\psi}.$$

We remark that this calculus is not sound in general. Indeed, the axioms $R_{skip}$-$R_{do}$, which express the usual requirements for the corresponding program constructs, might not be sound with respect to the semantics generated by a given semantic function $D$. However, the axioms $T$ and $R_{do}$ and the inference rules are sound with respect to an arbitrary semantic function $D$.

**(13.13) Theorem.** *If the calculus $\vdash_{dyn}$ is sound with respect to $\mathcal{L}^{ext,D}_{\delta,\sigma}$ then it satisfies conditions (i) and (ii) of Theorem (13.11) and therefore it is complete with respect to the extended dynamic logic $rDL^{ext,D}_{\sigma}$.*

*Proof.* First we remark that since $\vdash_{dyn}$ contains an entire "real" first-order calculus $(T, MP, G\exists)$ and $ext$ is maximal with respect to $(Ax_\sigma, Ax_\delta)$, condition (i) obviously holds. Now we prove condition (ii) by induction on the complexity of the formulas $\phi \in rD_{\delta,\sigma}$.

(a) Let $\phi \in Form_\sigma \cup Form_\delta$. By using (i) we get that $\vdash_{dyn} \phi \leftrightarrow \phi$, i.e. $\phi^P \rightleftharpoons \phi$ is appropriate.

(b) Let $\phi \rightleftharpoons \neg\psi$. By the induction hypothesis we have that $\vdash_{dyn} \psi \leftrightarrow \psi^P$ for an appropriate formula $\psi^P \in Form_\delta$. Using the axioms of T we get that $\vdash_{dyn} \neg\psi \leftrightarrow \neg\psi^P$. Hence $\phi^P \rightleftharpoons \neg\psi^P$ is appropriate.

(c) Let $\phi \rightleftharpoons \psi_1 \vee \psi_2$. By the induction hyptohesis there are two formulas $\psi_1^P, \psi_2^P \in Form_\delta$ such that $\vdash_{dyn} \psi_i \leftrightarrow \psi_i^P$ (for $i = 1, 2$). It is clear that $\phi^P \rightleftharpoons \psi_1^P \vee \psi_2^P$ is appropriate.

(d) The case $\phi \rightleftharpoons \exists\psi$ is similar to the cases (b) and (c). If $\vdash_{dyn} \psi \leftrightarrow \psi^P$ for a formula $\psi^P \in Form_\delta$ then by using the axioms of T and the rule $G\exists$ we get that $\vdash_{dyn} \exists v\psi \leftrightarrow \exists v\psi^P$. Hence $\phi^P \rightleftharpoons \exists v\psi^P$ is appropriate.

(e) Let $\phi \rightleftharpoons [p]\psi$. By the induction hypothesis there exists a formula $\psi^P \in Form_\delta$ such that $\vdash_{dyn} \psi \leftrightarrow \psi^P$. By using $G[]$ we get that $\vdash_{dyn} [p]\psi \leftrightarrow [p]\psi^P$.
By induction we define a formula $\phi'$ such that $\vdash_{dyn} [p]\psi^P \leftrightarrow \phi'$. By using axioms of (T) we get $\vdash_{dyn} [p]\psi \leftrightarrow \phi'$, which means that $\phi'$ is appropriate for $([p]\psi)^P$. Now let us suppose that for any first-order formula $\chi \in Form_\delta$ and for any subprogram $q$ of $p$ there is a formula $\beta \in Form_\delta$ such that $\vdash_{dyn} [q]\chi \leftrightarrow \beta$. By using this hypothesis we construct the formula $\phi^P$.
   (i) Let $p \rightleftharpoons$ **skip**. By axiom $R_{skip}$ we get $\vdash_{dyn} [\mathbf{skip}]\psi^P \leftrightarrow \psi^P$.
   (ii) Let $p \rightleftharpoons (x := \tau)$. By axiom $R_{:=}$ we get $\vdash_{dyn} [x := \tau]\psi^P \leftrightarrow \psi^P[\tau/x]$.
   (iii) Let $p \rightleftharpoons (x :=?)$. By axiom $R_?$ we get $\vdash_{dyn} [x :=?]\psi^P \leftrightarrow \forall y\psi^P[y/x]$.
   (iv) Let $p \rightleftharpoons (p_1; p_2)$. Using the induction hypothesis we get formulas $\beta_1, \beta_2 \in Form_\delta$ such that $\vdash_{dyn} [p_2]\psi^P \leftrightarrow \beta_1$ and $\vdash_{dyn} [p_1]\beta_1 \leftrightarrow \beta_2$. By the axioms of T and $R_;$ and by the rule $G[]$ we obtain $\vdash_{dyn} [(p_1; p_2)]\psi^P \leftrightarrow \beta_2$.
   (v) Let $p \rightleftharpoons$ **if** $\alpha_1 \to p_1 \Box \alpha_2 \to p_2$ **fi**. By the induction hypothesis there are formulas $\beta_1, \beta_2 \in Form_\delta$ such that for $i = 1, 2$, $\vdash_{dyn} [p_i]\psi^P \leftrightarrow \beta_i$. With the help of the axioms of T and $R_{if}$ we get

$$\vdash_{dyn} [\mathbf{if}\ \alpha_1 \to p_1 \Box \alpha_2 \to p_2 \mathbf{fi}]\psi^P \leftrightarrow (\neg\alpha_1 \wedge \neg\alpha_2 \to \psi^P) \wedge \bigwedge_{i=1}^{2} (\alpha_i \to \beta_i).$$

   (vi) If $p \rightleftharpoons$ **do** $\alpha_1 \to p_1 \Box \alpha_2 \to p_2$ **od** then we get the appropriate formula from $R_{do}$ without using the induction hypothesis on subprograms.

□

The above theorem shows that the really interesting question is how we axiomatize the modalities $[p]\phi$ and $\langle p\rangle\phi$. The axiomatization proposed above is appropriate, though the rule $R_{do}$ has no atomistic construction, i.e. it does not depend on the properties of the subprograms.

Chapter 14

# Continuous Denotational Semantics

The development of a programming logic in the scope of classical first-order logic is connected with making the formal notions, used to describe program properties, internal. This can be ensured by defining the definability of these notions in the logic in question. Here we show how dynamic logic can be developed in classical first-order logic by internalizing the denotation *Den* only. This internalization can be achieved by an appropriate axiomatization of reflexive and transitive closure. For the latter we introduce in Section 14.1 the so-called transitive extension and the corresponding extended language. This language will be appropriate to introduce two axiom systems $Ind_\sigma$ and $Ind^*_\sigma$. In this section it will also be shown how these axiom systems can be used to define the denotational semantics. In Section 14.2, by using the axiom systems $Ind_\sigma$ and $Ind^*_\sigma$ we introduce the dynamic logic with continuous denotational semantics $DL^{ns}_\sigma$ and that with strongly continuous denotational semantics $DL^{ns*}_\sigma$. The first one we also call non-standard dynamic logic. These logics realize our aim to define dynamic logic in the scope of classical first-order logic. Moreover, they preserve the classical notion of completeness, and we will show that they are compact and complete. Considering the Hoare calculus and its generalization we will show that these calculi are complete with respect to the continuous and the strongly continuous denotational semantics, respectively. These results at the same time provide a first-order characterization of the Hoare calculus and of its generalization. Then we compare the different dynamic logics with respect to their logical power. In Section 14.3 we will give an axiomatic calculus not only for the Floyd-Hoare sublanguage but for the entire extended dynamic logic by a variant of the calculus $\vdash_{dyn}$ introduced in the previous chapter. Having the denotation definable in the extended dynamic logics we study in Section 14.4 how the latter can handle program equivalence.

In this chapter we will deal with graph representation of programs in order to define appropriate semantic functions. Since we would have the first-order definition of these functions, it is vital importance to code the elements of the set *Label* into the first-order language. For this we follow the easiest way according to which we have to suppose that the similarity type $\sigma$ contains at least two distinct ground terms $\top$ and $\bot$ of the same sort and we consider only those models in which the formula $\top \neq \bot$ holds. According to the remark after Definition (4.10), in these models there is a first-order formula *onestep* which expresses what the relation *onestep* does in the graph representation.

The supposition of the existence of two different ground terms can be omitted as shown at the end of Chapter 15. However, the formalism which we would have to use would make the following constructions more complicated.

## 14.1 Transitive Extension

Intuitively it is evident that the main problem in defining the denotation *Den* is connected with the definition of program iteration. Since denotational semantics renders a relation to a program, the reflexive and transitive closure of this relation corresponds to iteration. We are interested in internalizing, thus we deal with the formulas defining the relations. Therefore the main question is whether the reflexive and transitive closure of an arbitrary formula is definable. The following lemma is a corollary of Theorem (7.13) and it shows that this is the proper question.

**(14.1) Lemma.** *If for every definable relation of a fixed $\sigma$-type first-order language, the reflexive and transitive closure is definable, then for any program $p \in rP\sigma$, its denotation is also definable.*

We note that in general the reflexive and transitive closure of the definable relations is not definable in an axiomatizable class of models.

Let $\sigma$ be a one-sorted similarity type, $\mathcal{A} \in Mod_\sigma$ be fixed. Let $R \subseteq A \times A$ be a binary relation in $\mathcal{A}$. For any $a, b \in A$ define their $R$-length:

$$d_R(a,b) \rightleftharpoons \begin{cases} 1 & \text{if } (a,b) \notin TRC(R); \\ \frac{n}{1+n} & \text{if } (a,b) \in TRC(R) \text{ and } n = min\{m \in \mathbb{N} \mid \exists a_0, ..., a_m : \\ & \qquad a_0 = a, a_m = b, \forall 0 \leq i < m \ (a_i, a_{i+1}) \in R\}. \end{cases}$$

(It is an easy exercise to prove that $d_R$ is a metric on $A$.) Define the $R$-diameter of $\mathcal{A}$ as

$$diag_R(\mathcal{A}) \rightleftharpoons sup\{d_R(a,b) \mid (a,b) \in TRC(R)\}.$$

It is clear that $diag_R(\mathcal{A}) \leq 1$.

**(14.2) Theorem.** *Let $\sigma$ be a one-sorted similarity type and let $Ax \subseteq Form_\sigma$ be a fixed axiom system. Let $\phi \in Form_\sigma$ such that $var(\phi) = \{x, x'\}$ and $x \neq x'$. The following two conditions are equivalent:*

*(i) there is a formula $\hat{\phi} \in Form_\sigma$ such that in any $\mathcal{A} \in Mod(Ax)$: $TRC(\phi_\mathcal{A}) = \hat{\phi}_\mathcal{A}$;*

*(ii) there is a real number $r < 1$ such that for all $\mathcal{A} \in Mod(Ax)$: $diag_{\phi_\mathcal{A}}(\mathcal{A}) \leq r$.*

*Proof.* (ii)$\Rightarrow$(i) is trivial. Indeed, let $r$ be as in (ii) and let us suppose that $n \in \mathbb{N}$ is such that $\frac{n}{1+n} \geq r$. In this case in any model $\mathcal{A}$ of $Ax$:

$$(*) \qquad TRC(\phi_{\mathcal{A}}) = \bigcup_{i \leq n} (\phi_{\mathcal{A}})^i.$$

It is obvious that the right-hand side of (*) is first-order definable by a formula $\hat{\phi}$ in $Ax$.

To prove (i)⇒(ii) let $\hat{\phi}$ be as in (i). To get a contradiction let us suppose that there is no appropriate $r$ in (ii). This means that for all $i \in \mathbb{N}$ there is a model $\mathcal{A}_i$ and there are two elements $a_i$, $b_i \in A_i$ such that $d_{\phi_{\mathcal{A}_i}}(a_i, b_i) > \frac{i}{1+i}$ and $(a_i, b_i) \in TRC(\phi_{\mathcal{A}_i})$. Let $D$ be a non-principal ultrafilter over $\mathbb{N}$ and let $\mathcal{B} \rightleftharpoons \prod_{i \in \mathbb{N}} \mathcal{A}_i / D$. Obviously, $\mathcal{B} \in Mod(Ax)$. We define two elements of $B$: $a \rightleftharpoons [\lambda i.a_i]_D$; $b \rightleftharpoons [\lambda i.b_i]_D$. Using Łos lemma (Theorem 1.21) we get that $(a, b) \in \hat{\phi}_{\mathcal{B}}$, since for every $i \in \mathbb{N}$: $(a_i, b_i) \in \hat{\phi}_{\mathcal{A}_i}$. According to (i) $(a, b) \in TRC(\phi_{\mathcal{B}})$. This means that for some $m \in \mathbb{N}$: $(a, b) \in (\phi_{\mathcal{B}})^m$. On the other hand, for every $i > m$ $(a_i, b_i) \notin (\phi_{\mathcal{A}_i})^m$ since $d_{\phi_{\mathcal{A}_i}}(a_i, b_i) > \frac{i}{1+i} > \frac{m}{1+m}$. Hence $(a, b) \notin (\phi_{\mathcal{B}})^m$, because $D$ is non-principal. This gives the contradiction. □

In general, the transitive and reflexive closure is definable only in second-order logic. This is why different versions of the latter e.g. $\omega$-logic, or weak second-order logic are used in developing programming logic. Salwicki [1970] is an example of using $\omega$-logic, while Laivant [1985] and Makowski, Sain [1987] are examples of the application of weak second-order logic.

Still requiring to remain in the scope of first-order logic, we investigate what conditions should be satisfied in order to obtain definability of the reflexive and transitive closure. To any open formula $\phi$ of a classical first-order language we render a formula $\phi^*$ with the intention that it denotes the reflexive and transitive closure of $\phi$. This intention can be expressed with the following infinitely long formula:

$$\begin{aligned}
\phi^*(X, X') \quad \equiv \quad & (X = X') \vee \phi(X, X') \vee \\
& \exists X_0 (\phi(X, X_0) \wedge \phi(X_0, X')) \vee \\
& \vdots \\
& \exists X_0 \exists X_1 ... \exists X_n (\phi(X, X_0) \wedge \phi(X_0, X_1) \wedge ... \wedge \phi(X_n, X')) \vee \\
& \vdots
\end{aligned}$$

Obviously this formula does not belong to any classical first-order language. According to Chapter 13, in order to stay within the scope of classical first-order logic we have to axiomatize the properties of the new symbols to ensure that $\phi^*$ is really the required closure of $\phi$. During the search for this axiomatization and the development of dynamic logic we use the notion of extension of a similarity type which is introduced in Definition (5.1) and used for defining new programming constructs to extend the programming language $rP_\sigma$ in a purely logical way (see Chapter 5).

**(14.3) Definition.** *For a similarity type $\sigma$ let us define the following set:*

$$\Delta_\sigma \rightleftharpoons \{(\phi, X, X', P) \mid \phi \in Open_\sigma, X \cup X' \cup P \supseteq var(\phi),$$
$$X' \text{ is a copy of } X \text{ and } X, X', P \text{ are pairwise disjoint sets}\}.$$

*The elements of $\Delta_\sigma$ are called $\sigma$-type $\Delta$-formulas. Sometimes we just write $\phi(X, X', P)$ instead of $(\phi, X, X', P)$.*

A $\Delta$-formula $(\phi, X, X', P)$ expresses the fact that in any model the formula $\phi$ can be considered as a $(X, X')$-type relation, hence the reflexive and transitive closure of this relation can be formulated. By using Definition (5.1) we give an extension of $\sigma$ which is appropriate to the description of the properties of the reflexive and transitive closure.

**(14.4) Definition.**
*(A) Let us fix a similarity type $\sigma$. A triple $(\delta, ext, *)$ is called a transitive extension of $\sigma$ iff*
  *(i) $(\delta, ext)$ is an extension of $\sigma$ (see Definition (5.1));*
  *(ii) $* : \Delta_\sigma \to Form_\delta$ is a function such that for each $(\phi, X, X', P) \in \Delta_\sigma$, $var(*(\phi, X, X', P)) \subseteq var(\phi)$. Instead of $*(\phi, X, X', P)$ we simply write $\phi^*(X, X', P)$.*
*(B) Let $Ax \subseteq Form_\delta$. We say that ext is a model of $Ax$ (written as $ext \models Ax$) iff for each $\mathcal{A} \in Mod_\sigma$ and for each $\mathcal{B} \in ext(\mathcal{A})$: $\mathcal{B} \models Ax$.*
*(C) Let $Ax_1$, $Ax_2 \subseteq Form_\delta$. $Ax_2$ is a semantic consequence of $Ax_1$ (written as $Ax_1 \models_{ext} Ax_2$) iff for each $\mathcal{A} \in Mod_\sigma$ and for each $\mathcal{B} \in ext(\mathcal{A})$: $\mathcal{B} \models Ax_1$ implies $\mathcal{B} \models Ax_2$.*

For the sake of convenience, if we say that a transitive extension *ext* is given then we mean that there is a given similarity type $\sigma$, an extension $(\delta, ext)$ of it and an appropriate function $*$.

We introduce two axiom systems $Ind_\sigma$ and $Ind^*_\sigma$ which provide us two different axiomatizations for the properties of the transitive and reflexive closure.

**(14.5) Definition.** *Let $(\delta, ext, *)$ be a transitive extension of $\sigma$. Let us consider the following axiom schemas and axiom systems:*

$Cl_{\phi(X,X',P)}$ *(reflexive and transitive closure of $\phi$) :*
$$\forall X \phi^*[X/X'] \land \forall X \forall Y \forall X' (\phi^*[Y/X'] \land \phi[Y/X] \to \phi^*);$$

$Tr_{\phi(X,X',P)}(\psi)$*(transfinite induction on $\psi$ with respect to $\phi^*$) :*
$$\forall X (\psi[X/X'] \land \forall Y \forall X' (\phi^*[Y/X'] \land \psi[Y/X'] \land \phi[Y/X] \to \psi) \to \forall X \forall X' (\phi^* \to \psi);$$

*We note that in the axiom $Tr_{\phi(X,X',P)}(\psi)$ the formula $\psi$ can contain an arbitrary set of parameters, e.g. $X$ itself!*

$$Ind_\sigma \rightleftharpoons \{Cl_{\phi(X,X',P)} \mid \phi(X,X',P) \in \Delta_\sigma\} \cup \{Tr_{\phi(X,X',P)}(\psi) \mid \phi(X,X',P) \in \Delta_\sigma, \psi \in Form_\sigma\}.$$

*Let $SForm_\sigma$ be the least subset of $Form_\delta$ satisfying the following properties:*

- $Form_\sigma \subseteq SForm_\sigma$;
- $\phi \in \Delta_\sigma$ *implies that* $\phi^* \in SForm_\sigma$;
- *if* $\phi \in SForm_\sigma$ *and* $Y$ *is an arbitrary copy of* $X \rightleftharpoons var(\phi)$ *then* $\phi[Y/X] \in SForm_\sigma$;
- $SForm_\sigma$ *is closed under Boolean combinations and quantifications over variables belonging to* $V_{sort\,\sigma}$.

$$Ind^*_\sigma \rightleftharpoons \{Cl_\phi \mid \phi \in \Delta_\sigma\} \cup \{Tr_\phi(\psi) \mid \phi \in \Delta_\sigma, \psi \in SForm_\sigma\}.$$

The axiom schema $Cl_\phi$ formulates that $\phi^*$ is really closed under $\phi$, informally $id \subseteq \phi^*$ and $\phi^* \circ \phi \subseteq \phi^*$. Unfortunately, we cannot formulate the minimality of the solution of this equation system because of the lack of set theory or of a higher-order logic. However, by using transfinite induction we can formulate some regularity along the considered iteration. Moreover, we have defined two versions of regularity differing in the domains from which the formulas describing the properties of the iterations can be selected. These versions of regularity yield different program semantics. We note that $Ind^*_\sigma$ implies that if $\phi$, $\psi \in \Delta_\sigma$ and $\phi \equiv \psi$ then $\phi^* \equiv \psi^*$ also holds. To show how $Ind_\sigma$ can be used we remark that the formula $(X = Y)^*$ is equivalent to $X = Y$ in any transitive extension $(\delta, ext, *)$ with $ext \models Ind_\sigma$. However, $Ind^*_\sigma$ is a really stronger axiom system as the following lemmas show.

**(14.6) Lemma.** *Let $(\delta, ext, *)$ be a given transitive extension such that $ext \models Ind^*_\sigma$. Let $\phi(X, X', P) \in \Delta_\sigma$ be fixed. Then*

$$ext \models \exists Z(\phi(X,Z,P) \wedge \phi^*(Z,Y,P)) \rightarrow \phi^*(X,Y,P).$$

*Proof.* Take $\psi(X,X',P,P') \rightleftharpoons \phi[P'/X,X/X'] \rightarrow \phi^*[P'/X]$. We want to prove the antecedent of $Tr_\phi(\psi)$ for every parameter $P$ and $P'$. $Cl_\phi$ proves $\phi(P',X,P) \rightarrow \phi^*(P',X,P)$, i.e. $\forall X\psi[X/X']$. The "interesting part" of the antecedent is of the following form:

$$\forall P \forall P' \forall Y \forall X' \Big( (\phi^*(X,Y,P) \wedge (\phi(P',X,P) \rightarrow \\ \rightarrow \phi^*(P',Y,P)) \wedge \phi(Y,X',P) \wedge \phi(P',X,P)) \rightarrow \phi^*(P',X,P) \Big)$$

which also holds by $Cl_\phi$. Thus, applying $Tr_\phi(\psi)$ and the first-order implication $\forall p(a(p) \rightarrow b(p)) \rightarrow (\forall x a(x) \rightarrow \forall x b(x))$, we obtain that

$$\forall P \forall P' \forall X \forall X' ((\phi^*(X,X',P) \wedge \phi(P',X,P)) \rightarrow \phi^*(P',X',P))$$

which, by using the first-order equivalence $\forall x(a(x) \rightarrow b) \leftrightarrow (\exists x a(x) \rightarrow b)$, is just the statement desired. □

**(14.7) Lemma.** *Let $(\delta, ext, *)$ be a given transitive extension such that $ext \models Ind^*_\sigma$. Let $\phi(X, X', P) \in \Delta_\sigma$ be fixed.*

$$ext \models \exists Z\,(\phi^*(X, Z, P) \wedge \phi^*(Z, Y, P)) \rightarrow \phi^*(X, Y, P),$$

*or, informally, $\phi^* \circ \phi^* \subseteq \phi^*$.*

*Proof.* Take $\psi(X, Y, P, P') \rightleftharpoons \phi^*(P', X, P) \rightarrow \phi^*(P', Y, P)$ and prove similarly to the previous lemma. □

**(14.8) Lemma.** *Let $(\delta, ext, *)$ be a given transitive extension such that $ext \models Ind^*_\sigma$. Let $\phi(X, X', P) \in \Delta_\sigma$ be fixed. Then*

*(i)* $ext \models \phi^*(X, X', P) \leftrightarrow (X = X') \vee \exists U(\phi^*(X, U, P) \wedge \phi(U, X', P))$;
*(ii)* $ext \models \phi^*(X, X', P) \leftrightarrow (X = X') \vee \exists U(\phi(X, U, P) \wedge \phi^*(U, X', P))$.

*Proof.* Both statements can be proved in the similar way, so we prove only (ii). Take $\psi \rightleftharpoons (X = X') \vee \exists U(\phi(X, U, P) \wedge \phi^*(U, X', P))$. To prove the antecedent of $Tr_{\phi(X,X',P)}(\psi)$ let us suppose that $\phi^*(X, Y, P) \wedge \psi(X, Y, P) \wedge \phi(Y, Z, P)$ holds in $ext$. If $X \neq Y$ then by using $\psi(X, Y, P)$ we get a $U$ such that $\phi(X, U, P) \wedge \phi^*(U, Y, P)$ is valid. By using $Cl_\phi$ we can conclude that $\phi^*(U, Y, P) \wedge \phi(Y, Z, P)$ implies $\phi^*(U, Z, P)$. Therefore $\psi(X, Z, P)$ also holds. If $X = Y$ then $\phi(X, Z, P) \wedge \phi^*(Z, Z, P)$ holds, so $\psi(X, Z, P)$ also holds with $U \rightleftharpoons Z$. Since $\psi(X, X, P)$ is a tautology we get from $Tr_{\phi(X,X',P)}(\psi)$ that $ext \models \forall P \forall X \forall Y\,(\phi^*(X, X', P) \rightarrow \psi(X, X', P))$. The other inclusion, i.e.

$$ext \models \forall P \forall X \forall Y\, \psi(X, X', P) \rightarrow (\phi^*(X, X', P))$$

follows from Lemma (14.6). □

We show how the "standard" notion of reflexive and transitive closure can be defined as a special transitive extension.

**(14.9) Definition.** *Fix a similarity type $\sigma$. The standard transitive extension $(\sigma^*, cst, *)$ of $\sigma$ is defined as follows*

*(i)* $\sigma^* \rightleftharpoons \sigma \cup \{\hat{\phi} : sort(X, X', P) \mid (\phi, X, X', P) \in \Delta_\sigma\}$, *where each $\hat{\phi}$ is a new relation symbol of the indicated sort;*
*(ii)* *For any $(\phi, X, X', P) \in \Delta_\sigma$ let $\phi^*(X, X', P) \rightleftharpoons \hat{\phi}(X, X', P)$;*
*(iii)* *$cst(\mathcal{A})$ contains exactly one model $\mathcal{B}$ within which for every $\Delta$-formula $\phi \in \Delta_\sigma$ the relation $\hat{\phi}_{\mathcal{B}}$ is the relation ${}_{\mathcal{A}}I_\Phi$ defined inductively in $\mathcal{A}$ by the formula*

$$\Phi \rightleftharpoons (X = X') \vee \exists X''\,(\phi(X, X'', P) \wedge \hat{\phi}(X'', X', P)).$$

*In other words, ${}_{\mathcal{A}}I_\Phi$ is the least fixed point of the following equation:*

$$R(X, X', P) \equiv (X = X') \vee \exists X''\,(\phi(X, X'', P) \wedge R(X'', X', P)).$$

**(14.10) Lemma.** $cst \models Ind^*_\sigma$.

*Proof.* This follows directly from the fact that for any $\phi \in \Delta_\sigma$, the closure ordinal of the operator ${}_{\mathcal{A}}\Gamma_\phi$ is $\omega_0$. Thus any axiom of $Ind^*_\sigma$ can be proved by induction on $\mathbb{N}$. □

**(14.11) Definition.** *Let $(\delta, ext, *)$ be a transitive extension of a similarity type $\sigma$. Let $rP^\flat_\sigma$ denote the set of all programs belonging to $rP_\sigma$ without any* **do...od** *commands. For any program $p \in rP_\sigma$ and for any finite set of variables $X$ ($\supseteq var(p)$) we define a $\delta$-type formula $D[\![p, X]\!]$ as follows.*

*(i) By Theorem (4.15), if $p \in rP^\flat_\sigma$ there is a formula $D[\![p,X]\!]$ which defines the many-sorted relation $Den_{\mathcal{A}}[\![p,X]\!]$ in an arbitrary model $\mathcal{A} \in Mod_\sigma$.*
*(ii) By Theorem (4.30), there is a function $\widetilde{can} : rP_\sigma \setminus rP^\flat_\sigma \to rP^\flat_\sigma \times Open_\sigma \times rP^\flat_\sigma$ such that for each program $p \in rP_\sigma \setminus rP^\flat_\sigma$ the following holds:*

$$p \equiv can(p) \rightleftharpoons \pi_1(\widetilde{can});\ \textbf{while}\ \pi_2(\widetilde{can})\ \textbf{do}\ \pi_3(\widetilde{can})\ \textbf{od}\quad (\text{mod } var(p)).$$

*We use the notations $p'$, $p^\alpha$ and $p''$, respectively, instead of $\pi_i(\widetilde{can})$ ($i = 1,2,3$). Moreover, we may suppose that if some $q$ is of the form $q_1;$* **while** *$\beta$* **do** *$q_2$* **od**, *then $p' = q_1$, $p^\alpha = \beta$ and $p'' = q_2$.*
*Let $Y \rightleftharpoons var(p; p'; p'') \cup var(p^\alpha)$. Let $Y'$ and $Y_1$ be two new copies of $Y$. Let $W \rightleftharpoons Y \setminus var(p)$ and let $W'$ be the copy of in $Y'$. It is clear that*

$$\Xi \rightleftharpoons \Big((p^\alpha \wedge D[\![p'', Y]\!]) \vee (\neg p^\alpha \wedge (Y = Y'))\Big)$$

*can be considered as a $\Delta$-formula: $\big(\Xi, Y, Y', \emptyset\big)$. Now let*

$$D[\![p, var(p)]\!] \rightleftharpoons \exists W \exists W' \exists Y_1 \big(D[\![p', Y]\!][Y_1/Y] \wedge \Xi^*[Y_1/Y] \wedge \neg p^\alpha[Y'/Y]\big).$$

*If $X \subseteq var(p)$ let $Z \rightleftharpoons X \setminus var(p)$ and let $Z'$ be its copy on $X'$, which is a new copy of $X$. Take*

$$D[\![p, X]\!] \rightleftharpoons D[\![p, var(p)]\!] \wedge (Z = Z').$$

By using the notations of this definition we immediately get the following

**(14.12) Lemma.** *The equivalence below holds in an arbitrary transitive extension and for an arbitrary program $p \in rP_\sigma \setminus rP^\flat_\sigma$:*

$$ext \models \Xi \equiv D[\![\textbf{if}\ p^\alpha \to p''\ \Box \neg p^\alpha \to \textbf{skip fi}, Y]\!],$$

*where $Y \rightleftharpoons var(can(p))$.*

From the Canonical Form Theorem (4.30) we immediately have the following

**(14.13) Theorem.** *Let cst be the standard transitive extension of a fixed similarity type $\sigma$. Then for every $p \in rP_\sigma$ and for any model $\mathcal{A} \in Mod_\sigma$ if $\mathcal{A} \models \top \neq \bot$ then*

$$Den_{\mathcal{A}}[\![p, var(p)]\!] = D[\![p, var(p)]\!]_{\mathcal{B}}$$

*holds, where $\{\mathcal{B}\} = cst(\mathcal{A})$.*

This theorem shows that, in some sense, *cst* does indeed describe the "normal" situation, i.e. when the programs are executed in the standard model of arithmetic.

The following statement has been proved in González, Artalejo [1985].

**(14.14) Theorem.** *Let ext be a fixed transitive extension. Let us suppose that $\mathcal{A} \in Mod_\sigma$ is a model such that for any $p \in rP_\sigma, Den_{\mathcal{A}}[\![p, var(p)]\!]$ is definable in $\mathcal{A}$. Let us suppose that for a model $\mathcal{B} \in ext(\mathcal{A})$, $\mathcal{B} \models Ind_\sigma$ holds. Moreover, let us suppose that any element $a \in A$ is definable in $\mathcal{A}$ by a $\sigma$-type first-order formula $\phi$. Then for every $p \in rP_\sigma$*

$$Den_{\mathcal{A}}[\![p, var(p)]\!] = D[\![p, var(p)]\!]_{\mathcal{B}}.$$

One of the main disadvantages of the axiom system $Ind_\sigma$ is that the operation $*$ defined in Definition (14.4) cannot be extended such that it becomes iterable. This means that we cannot define the formulas such as $\phi^{**}$ or $(\phi \wedge (\psi^*))^*$ appropriately. However, $Ind^*_\sigma$ is strong enough to define the $*$ operation on the formulas belonging to $SForm_\sigma$ as well. Moreover, some induction principles can also be proved for this extended $*$ operation.

In order to make the necessary extension we introduce three new logical connectives $\circ$, $\cup$ and *star* with the intended meaning of composition, union and iteration, respectively.

**(14.15) Definition.** *Let us define the set of extended $\Delta$-formulas $e\Delta_\sigma$ as the least set with the following properties:*

*(i)* $\Delta_\sigma \subseteq e\Delta_\sigma$;
*(ii)* *if* $\Delta_i \rightleftharpoons (\phi_i, X_i, X'_i, P_i) \in e\Delta_\sigma$ $(i = 1, 2)$ *such that* $X'_1 = X_2$ *then* $(\Delta_1 \circ \Delta_2, X_1, X'_2, P_1 \cup P_2) \in e\Delta_\sigma$;
*(iii)* *if* $\Delta_i \rightleftharpoons (\phi_i, X_i, X'_i, P_i) \in e\Delta_\sigma$ $(i = 1, 2)$ *such that* $X_1 = X_2$ *and* $X'_1 = X'_2$ *then* $(\Delta_1 \cup \Delta_2, X_1, X'_1, P_1 \cup P_2) \in e\Delta_\sigma$;
*(iv)* *if* $\Delta \rightleftharpoons (\phi, X, X', P) \in e\Delta_\sigma$ *then* $(star(\Delta), X, X', P) \in e\Delta_\sigma$;

**(14.16) Definition.** *Let $(\delta, ext, *)$ be a fixed transitive extension of $\sigma$. A function $Red : e\Delta_\sigma \to SForm_\sigma$ is called a reduction function in ext iff it satisfies the following properties ($\alpha \equiv \beta$ abbreviates $ext \models \top \neq \bot \to \alpha \leftrightarrow \beta$):*

*(i)* *if* $\Delta \rightleftharpoons (\phi, X, X', P) \in \Delta_\sigma$ *then* $Red(\Delta) \equiv \phi$ *and* $Red(star(\Delta)) \equiv \phi^*$;
*(ii)* *if* $\Delta_1, \Delta_2 \in e\Delta_\sigma$ *then*

$$Red(\Delta_1 \circ \Delta_2)(X_1, X_2', P_1 \cup P_2) \equiv \exists X_2\, Red(\Delta_1)(X_1, X_2, P_1) \wedge Red(\Delta_2)(X_2, X_2', P_2);$$

*(iii) if* $\Delta_1$, $\Delta_2 \in e\Delta_\sigma$ *then*

$$Red(\Delta_1 \cup \Delta_2)(X_1, X_1', P_1 \cup P_2) \equiv Red(\Delta_1)(X_1, X_1', P_1) \vee Red(\Delta_2)(X_1, X_1', P_2);$$

*(iv) if* $(\Delta, X, X', P) \in e\Delta_\sigma$ *then for* $star(\Delta)$ *the axiom* $Cl_{Red(\Delta)}$ *and the axiom schema* $\{Tr_{Red(\Delta)}(\psi) | \psi \in SForm_\sigma\}$ *holds, where*

$Cl_{Red(\Delta)}$ *(reflexive and transitive closure of* $Red(\Delta)$*)* :

$$\forall X\, Red(star(\Delta))[X/X'] \wedge \forall X \forall Y \forall X' \big(Red(star(\Delta))[Y/X'] \wedge Red(\Delta)[Y/X] \rightarrow Red(star(\Delta))\big)$$

$Tr_{Red(\Delta)}(\psi)$*(transfinite induction on* $\psi$ *with respect to* $Red(star(\Delta))$*)* :

$$\forall X \Big(\psi[X/X'] \wedge \forall Y \forall X' (Red(star(\Delta))[Y/X'] \wedge \psi[Y/X'] \wedge Red(\Delta)[Y/X] \rightarrow \psi)\Big) \rightarrow \forall X \forall X' (Red(star(\Delta)) \rightarrow \psi)$$

$Red(\Delta)$ *is called the reduction of the extended* $\Delta$*-type formula* $\Delta \in e\Delta_\sigma$.

**(14.17) Theorem.** *Let* $\sigma$ *be a similarity type and let* $(\delta, ext, *)$ *be one of its transitive extensions. If* $ext \models Ind_\sigma^*$ *then the reduction function in* $ext$ *(if it exists) is uniquely determined up to equivalence.*

*Proof.* This can be proved by using induction on the structure of the $\Delta$-formulas. The cases (i)-(iii) of Definition (14.15) are trivial using the properties (i)-(iii) of Definition (14.16). The case (iv) for *star* can be established by the use of induction since the range of a reduction function belong to $SForm_\sigma$. □

We will prove that if $Ind_\sigma^*$ holds in a transitive extension then the unique reduction function can be constructed. In order to define the function *Red* we construct the graph representation of the formulas of $e\Delta_\sigma$.

**(14.18) Definition.** *A* $\Delta$*-graph is a quadruple* $(g, X, X', P)$ *where* $X$, $X'$ *and* $P$ *are pairwise disjoint sets of variables,* $X'$ *is a copy of* $X$ *and* $g$ *is a function of the form* $Label \times Label \rightarrow_p Open_\sigma$ *such that*

*(i)* $dom\, g$ *is finite;*
*(ii) for any* $(a, b) \in dom\, g$, $var(g(a, b)) \subseteq X \cup X' \cup P$.

For $\Delta$-graphs we use the same notations as for the transition graphs (see Definition (4.9)). Let $(g, X, X', P)$ be an arbitrary $\Delta$-graph. Take the following formula:

$$\xi_g \rightleftharpoons \bigvee_{c,c' \in node(g)} (l = c \wedge l' = c' \wedge g(c,c')(X, X', P)).$$

Since $\xi$ is an open formula it can be considered as a $\Delta$-formula: $(\xi, X \cup \{l\}, X' \cup \{l'\}, P)$. Thus the $\delta$-type formula $\xi_g^*$ exists. If $g$ is clear from the context then we omit the subscript.

Let $\Lambda \subseteq node(g)$ be given. $\xi\restriction_\Lambda$ is a shorthand for the formula $\xi$ generated by the $\Delta$-graph $g\restriction_\Lambda$.

**(14.19) Definition.** *Let $(g, X, X', P)$ be a $\Delta$-graph. Let $a$, $b \in node(g)$ be fixed. Take*

$$\Lambda_{ab} \rightleftharpoons \{c \mid \text{ there is a directed path from } a \text{ to } b \text{ via } c\}.$$

*Take $G_{ab} \rightleftharpoons node(g) \setminus (\Lambda_{ab} \cup \{a, b\})$. The pair $(a, b)$ splits the graph $g$ iff the following hold:*

*(i) there is no edge between $G_{ab}$ and $\Lambda_{ab}$;*
*(ii) there is no edge from $G_{ab}$ to $b$;*
*(iii) there is no edge from $a$ to $G_{ab}$.*

Recall that $\equiv$ is context sensitive. In the next lemma the axiom system with respect to which $\equiv$ has a meaning is obviously the set $Ind_\sigma^* \cup \{top \neq \bot\}$.

**(14.20) Lemma.** *Let $(\delta, ext, *)$ be a transitive extension of $\sigma$ such that $ext \models Ind_\sigma^* \cup \{top \neq \bot\}$. Let $(g, X, X', P)$ be a $\Delta$-graph. In this case for all $a$, $c \in node(g)$ the following properties hold:*

*(i)* $$\xi^*((a,Z),(c,Z')) \equiv \bigvee_{(b,c) \in dom\ g} \exists Z''(\xi^*((a,Z),(b,Z'')) \wedge \xi((b,Z''),(c,Z'))).$$

*(ii)*

$$\xi^*((a,Z),(c,Z')) \equiv \bigvee_{(a,b) \in dom\ g} \exists Z''(\xi((a,Z),(b,Z'')) \wedge \xi^*((b,Z''),(c,Z'))).$$

*(iii) If $b \in node(g)$ such that each directed path between $a$ and $c$ contains $b$ then*

$$\xi^*((a,Z),(c,Z')) \equiv \exists Z''(\xi^*((a,Z),(b,Z'')) \wedge \xi^*((b,Z''),(c,Z'))).$$

*(iv) Let us suppose that $b$ is a node such that $(a, b)$ splits the graph and $c \notin \Lambda_{ab}$. Then*

$$\xi^*((a,Z),(c,Z')) \equiv \exists Z''((\xi\restriction_{\Lambda_{ab}})^*((a,Z),(b,Z'')) \wedge \xi^*((b,Z''),(c,Z'))).$$

*(v) Let us suppose that $b$ is a node such that $(b, c)$ splits the graph and $a \notin \Lambda_{bc}$. Then*

$$\xi^*((a,Z),(c,Z')) \equiv \exists Z''(\xi^*(((a,Z),(b,Z'')) \wedge (\xi\restriction_{\Lambda_{ab}})^*(b,Z''),(c,Z'))).$$

*Proof.* We only outline the proof. Statements (i) and (ii) follow from (i) and (ii) of Lemma (14.8), respectively. Statement (iii) follows from (iv) and (v), while the latters can be proved by using appropriate intermediate statements. For (iv) the following equivalence, obtained by omitting the assumption $c \notin \Lambda_{ab}$, should be proved by induction:

$$\xi^*((a,Z),(c,Z')) \equiv \xi^*((a,Z),(c,Z'))\vee \\ \exists Z''((\xi{\restriction}\Lambda_{ab})^*((a,Z),(b,Z'')) \wedge \xi^*((b,Z''),(c,Z'))).$$

An analogous equivalence should be proved for the establishment of statement (v). □

**(14.21) Definition.** *Let $\Delta \in e\Delta_\sigma$ be arbitrary. The graph representation $gr(\Delta)$ of $\Delta$ is a $\Delta$-graph with two special nodes of $gr(\Delta)$ called $start_\Delta$ and $stop_\Delta$ and it is defined by induction on the complexity of the formula $\Delta$ as shown in Figs. 14.1–14.4. Let $\xi$ be the formula defined for $\Delta$-graph $gr(\Delta)$ after Definition (14.18). Let us define $Red(\Delta)$ as $\xi^*[start_\Delta/l, stop_\Delta/l']$.*

**Fig. 14.1.** Graph representation of formula $\phi \in \Delta_\sigma$

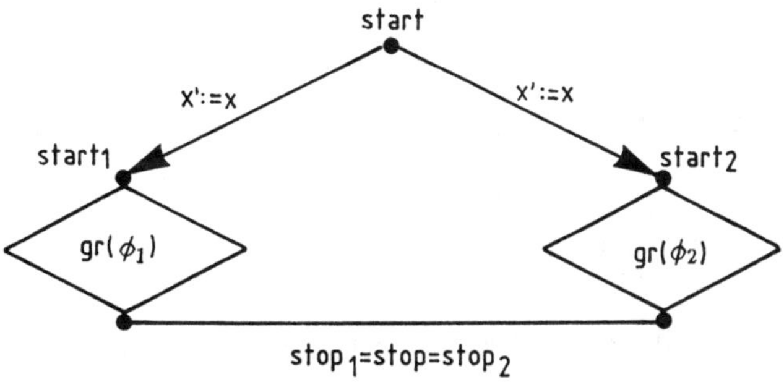


**Fig. 14.2.** Graph representation of operation ∪

**(14.22) Theorem.** *Let $(\delta, ext, *)$ be an inductive extension such that $ext \models Ind^*_\sigma$. The function $Red : e\Delta_\sigma \to SForm_\sigma$ defined in Definition (14.21) is a reduction function in ext.*

*Proof.* The proof goes by induction on the complexity of an $e\Delta_\sigma$-formula $\Delta$ by using statements (iii)-(v) of Lemma (14.20). Let us check the case of $\Delta \rightleftharpoons \Delta_1 \circ \Delta_2$. Recall the definition of the $\Delta$-graph $gr(\Delta)$ from Definition (14.21). It is clear that both $(start_{\Delta_1}, stop_{\Delta_1})$ and $(start_{\Delta_2}, stop_{\Delta_2})$ split the $\Delta$-graph $gr(\Delta)$, so we can use Lemma (14.20) and by the induction hypothesis we can prove that in *ext*

$$Red(\Delta)(X,X'') \equiv \exists X'(Red(\Delta_1)(X,X') \wedge Red(\Delta_2)(X',X'')).$$

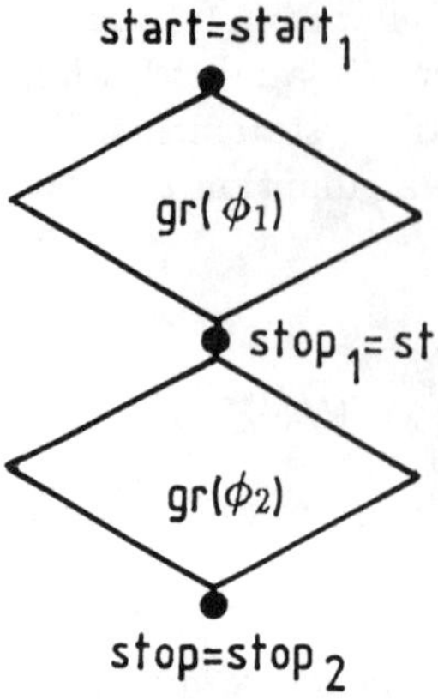


**Fig. 14.3.** Graph representation of operation $\circ$

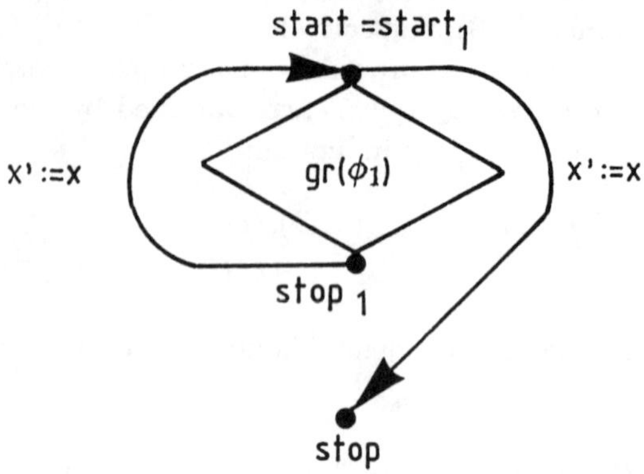


**Fig. 14.4.** Graph representation of operation *star*

Let $(\Delta, X, X', P) \in e\Delta_\sigma$ be an arbitrary extended $\Delta$-formula. We should prove that the axiom $Tr_{Red(\Delta)}(\psi)$ is true for any transitive extension satisfying $Ind^*_\sigma$. Let us suppose that the antecendent of this axiom holds, i.e. $\psi(X, X, P)$ and the formula

$$\forall Y \forall X' \Big(\xi^*_{star(\Delta)}(X, start_{star(\Delta)}, Y, stop_{star(\Delta)}) \wedge \psi(X, Y, P) \wedge \\ \xi^*_\Delta(Y, start_\Delta, X', stop_\Delta) \rightarrow \psi(X, X', P)\Big)$$

are true. Take

$$\psi'(X, \ell, X', \ell', P) \rightleftharpoons (\ell = start_\Delta) \wedge \Big((\ell' = stop_{star(\Delta)} \wedge \psi(X, X', P)) \vee \\ \exists Y\big(\psi(X, Y, P) \wedge \xi^*_\Delta(Y, start_\Delta, X', \ell')\big)\Big).$$

Fix $\ell \rightleftharpoons start_\Delta$. It is clear that $\psi'(X, \ell, X, \ell, P)$ is true since $\xi^*_\Delta(X, \ell, X, \ell)$ is true. We prove that the following formula is also true:

$$\forall Y \forall k \forall X \ell' \Big(\xi^*_{star(\Delta)}(X, \ell, Y, k) \wedge \\ \psi'(X, \ell, Y, k, P) \wedge \xi_{star(\Delta)}(Y, k, X', \ell') \rightarrow \psi'(X, \ell, X', \ell', P)\Big).$$

To prove it let us suppose that

$$\xi^*_{star(\Delta)}(X, \ell, Y, k) \wedge \psi'(X, \ell, Y, k) \wedge \xi_{star(\Delta)}(Y, k, X', \ell')$$

is true. We recall

$$\xi_{star(\Delta)}(Y, k, X', \ell') \equiv \xi_\Delta(Y, k, X', \ell') \vee (k = stop_\Delta \wedge \ell' = start_\Delta \wedge Y = X') \vee \\ (k = start_\Delta \wedge \ell' = stop_{star(\Delta)} \wedge Y = X').$$

If $\xi_\Delta(Y,k,X',\ell')$ is true then using $Cl_\Delta$ we get that $\psi'(X',\ell',P)$ is also true. If $\ell'$ is $start_\Delta$ or $stop_\Delta$ then using the original induction hypothesis we get that $\psi(X,X',\ell')$ is true and hence $\psi'(X',\ell',P)$ must be true.

Now using the succedent of $Tr_{\xi_{star(\Delta)}}(\psi')$ for $l' = stop_{star(\Delta)}$ we get the succedent of $Tr_{Red(\Delta)}(\psi)$. □

*From now on Red will denote the unique reduction function for extensions ext satisfying $ext \models Ind^*_\sigma$.*

The following theorem shows that $Ind^*_\sigma$ is also strong enough to prove certain properties of the *star* operation defined for extended $\Delta$-formulas. First let us introduce some notations. Let $(\phi, X, X', P) \in e\Delta_\sigma$ be a fixed extended $\Delta$-formula. Take

$$\begin{aligned} dom\ \phi &\rightleftharpoons \exists X' Red(\phi)(X,X',P); \\ rng\ \phi &\rightleftharpoons \exists X' Red(\phi)[X'/X, X/X'](X',X,P). \end{aligned}$$

**(14.23) Theorem.** *Let $(\delta, ext, *)$ be a fixed transitive extension such that $ext \models Ind^*_\sigma$. Then the following statements hold in ext:*

$$\begin{aligned} If_{\phi_1\phi_2}: \quad & \forall X\big(\neg(dom\,\phi_1 \wedge rng\,\phi_2) \wedge \neg(dom\,\phi_2 \wedge rng\,\phi_1)\big) \rightarrow \\ & \qquad (Red(star(\phi_1 \cup \phi_2)) \leftrightarrow Red(star(\phi_1) \cup star(\phi_2)) \\ Comp_{\phi_1\phi_2}: \quad & \forall X\, \neg(dom\,\phi_1 \wedge rng\,\phi_2) \rightarrow \big(Red(star(\phi_1 \cup \phi_2)) \leftrightarrow \\ & \qquad Red(star(\phi_1) \circ star(\phi_2))\big) \\ Iter_\phi: \quad & Red(star(star(\phi))) \leftrightarrow Red(star(\phi)) \end{aligned}$$

*where $\phi_1(X,X',P_1)$, $\phi_2(X,X',P_2)$, $\phi(X,X',P) \in e\Delta_\sigma$.*

*Proof.* We prove only the statement $Comp_{\phi_1\phi_2}$. It is clear that $Red(star(\phi_1) \circ star(\phi_2)) \rightarrow Red(star(\phi_1 \cup \phi_2))$. To check the other direction take the following formula

$$\psi(Y) \rightleftharpoons Red(star(\phi_1) \circ star(\phi_2))(X,Y,P).$$

We prove that the antecedent of $Tr_{Red(\phi_1 \cup \phi_2)}(\psi)$ (the transfinite induction axiom of Definition (14.16)) holds, i.e.

$$Red(star(\phi_1 \cup \phi_2))(X,Y,P) \wedge \psi(Y) \wedge Red(\phi_1 \cup \phi_2)(Y,Z,P) \rightarrow \psi(Z) \text{ is true.}$$

Let us suppose that the antecedent of the above formula holds. From $\psi(Y)$ follows that there is a set of variables $W$ such that the formula

$$Red(star(\phi_1))(X,W,P) \wedge Red(star(\phi_2))(W,Y,P)$$

holds. If $W = Y$ then $\psi(Z)$ obviously holds since $\neg dom\ \phi_1(Y)$ is true. Otherwise $rng\ \phi_2(Y)$ holds, which means that $\phi_2(Y, Z)$ holds. Thus $Red(star(\phi_2))(W, Z)$ also holds.

Now we can use the consequent of the rule $Tr_{Red(\phi_1 \cup \phi_2)}(\psi)$ which proves exactly what we wanted to check. □

**(14.24) Theorem.** *Let $(\delta, ext, *)$ be a transitive extension of $\sigma$ such that $ext \models Ind^*_\sigma$. Let $(\phi, X, X', P) \in e\Delta_\sigma$. The equation*

$$(*) \qquad Red((X = X') \cup (Q \circ \phi)) \equiv Q$$

*has a least $SForm_\sigma$-definable solution $Q$ in ext denoted by $(Y\phi)$.*

*Proof.* Take $(Y\phi) \rightleftharpoons Red(star(\phi))$. By Lemma (14.8) $(Y\phi)$ is a fixed-point of (*). Let us suppose that $\alpha(X, X', P') \in SForm_\sigma$ is an other solution of (*). By using $Tr_{(Y\phi)}(\alpha)$ we prove that $ext \models (Y\phi) \to \alpha$. In order to prove the antecedent of this axiom let us suppose that $ext \models (Y\phi)(X, Y, P) \wedge \alpha(X, Y, P') \wedge Red(\phi)(Y, Z, P)$. By using the fact that $\alpha$ is a solution of (*) we get that $ext \models \alpha(X, Z, P')$. So by using the succedent of $Tr_{Red(\phi)}(\alpha)$ we get $ext \models \forall P \forall P \forall X \forall Y((Y\phi)(X, Y, P) \to \alpha(X, Y, P'))$. □

Now we turn to show that the denotation of programs in $Ind^*_\sigma$ can be defined by formula induction as well. Therefore we obtain an atomic definition for the denotation of programs in contrast with Definition (14.11). For any program $p \in rP_\sigma$ and for any finite $X \subseteq V_{sort\ \sigma}$, if $var(p) \subseteq X$ then an extended $\Delta$-formula $(D'[\![p, X]\!], X, X', \emptyset)$ can be given by induction on the complexity of $p$ as follows:

$$D'[\![x := \tau, X]\!](X, X') \rightleftharpoons \iota(x) = \tau \wedge \bigwedge\{\iota(u) = u \mid u \in X \setminus \{x\}\}$$

$$D'[\![x :=?, X]\!](X, X') \rightleftharpoons \bigwedge\{\iota(u) = u \mid u \in X \setminus \{x\}\}$$

$$D'[\![(p_1; p_2), X]\!] \rightleftharpoons D'[\![p_1, X]\!] \circ D'[\![p_2, X]\!]$$

$$D'[\![\textbf{if } \alpha_1 \to p_1 \,\Box \alpha_2 \to p_2 \textbf{ fi}, X]\!](X, X') \rightleftharpoons (\neg\alpha_1 \wedge \neg\alpha_2 \wedge X' = X) \cup \bigcup_{i=1}^{2} (\alpha_i \wedge X' = X) \circ D'[\![p_i, X]\!](X, X')$$

$$D'[\![\textbf{do } \alpha_1 \to p_1 \,\Box \alpha_2 \to p_2 \textbf{ od}, X]\!](X, X') \rightleftharpoons star(((\alpha_1 \vee \alpha_2) \wedge X = X') \circ D'[\![\textbf{if } \alpha_1 \to p_1 \,\Box \alpha_2 \to p_2 \textbf{ fi}, X]\!]) \circ (\neg\alpha_1 \wedge \neg\alpha_2 \wedge X' = X),$$

where $p_1$, $p_2 \in rP_\sigma$, $X \subseteq V_{sort\ \sigma}$ is finite and $X'$ is a copy of $X$ with the bijection $\iota : X \to X'$.

Now we show that $Ind^*_\sigma$ proves that the two denotations $D$ and $D'$ are equivalent.

**(14.25) Theorem.** *Let us fix a transitive extension* $(\delta, ext, *)$ *of a given similarity type* $\sigma$ *such that* $ext \models Ind^*_\sigma$. *Then for all* $p \in rP_\sigma$ *and for all finite* $X \subseteq V_{sort\ \sigma}$ $(var(p) \subseteq X)$

$$ext \models Red(D'[\![p, X]\!]) \leftrightarrow D[\![p, X]\!].$$

*Proof.* Follows directly from Theorems (14.17), (14.22) and (14.23). □

**(14.26) Theorem.** *Let us fix a transitive extension* $(\delta, ext, *)$ *of* $\sigma$. *The following two induction axiom schemas are equivalent:*

$$Tr_{\phi(X,X',P)}(\psi):$$
$$\forall X\, (\psi[X/X'] \wedge \forall Y \forall X' (\phi^*[Y/X'] \wedge \psi[Y/X'] \wedge \phi[Y/X] \rightarrow \psi) \rightarrow \forall X \forall X' (\phi^* \rightarrow \psi);$$

$$\widetilde{Tr}_{\phi(X,X',P)}(\psi):$$
$$\forall X\, \Big(\psi[X/X'] \wedge \forall Y \forall X' (\phi^*[Y/X'] \wedge \psi[Y/X'] \wedge \phi[Y/X] \rightarrow \psi) \rightarrow \forall X' (\phi^* \rightarrow \psi)\Big);$$

*where* $\phi \in \Delta_\sigma$, $\psi \in SForm_\sigma$.

*Proof.* For an arbitrary $\phi \in \Delta_\sigma$, $\{\widetilde{Tr}_\phi(\psi) \mid \psi \in SForm_\sigma\} \models \{Tr_\phi(\psi) \mid \psi \in SForm_\sigma\}$ is trivial by using simple first-order equivalences. To prove the other direction let $\psi \in SForm_\sigma$ be fixed and let $var(\psi) \subseteq X \cup X' \cup P'$, where $X$, $X'$ and $P'$ are pairwise disjoint. Let

$$\tilde{\psi} \rightleftharpoons \forall Y \forall Z\, (\psi(X, X, P') \wedge \phi^*(X, Y, P) \wedge \psi(X, Y, P') \wedge \phi(Y, Z, P) \rightarrow \psi(X, Z, P')).$$

Clearly $var(\tilde{\psi}) \subseteq X \cup X' \cup P'$ and $\tilde{\psi} \in SForm_\sigma$. Using $Tr_\phi(\tilde{\psi})$ we can prove $\widetilde{Tr}_\phi(\psi)$. □

We remark that the corresponding theorem is not true for $Ind_\sigma$. The main reason why the above proof does not work in this case is that $\tilde{\psi} \notin Form_\sigma$.

## 14.2 Non-standard Dynamic Logic

Now we have all the necessary tools to define different extended dynamic logics. With the help of Definitions (13.1), (13.2) and (13.5) we can define the appropriate extended similarity types and the extended dynamic logics we are looking for. However, for the required definition we also need a semantic function $D$ for which we take the one in Definition (14.11).

**(14.27) Definition.** *Let* $\sigma$ *be a given similarity type. Let* $\sigma^*$ *and* $* : \Delta_\sigma \rightarrow Form_{\sigma^*}$ *be as in Definition (14.9) (i) and (ii).*

*(A) Let $(\sigma^*, ns, *)$ be the unique transitive extension maximal with respect to $(\{\top \neq \bot\}, Ind_\sigma)$. The extended dynamic logic*

$$rDL_\sigma^{ns} \rightleftharpoons rDL_\sigma^{ns,D} = (rDL_\sigma, Mod(ns), \models'_{ns})$$

*is called the non-standard dynamic logic or the dynamic logic with continuous denotational semantics.*

*(B) Let $(\sigma^*, ns*, *)$ be the unique transitive extension maximal with respect to $(\{\top \neq \bot\}, Ind_\sigma^*)$. The extended dynamic logic*

$$rDL_\sigma^{ns*} \rightleftharpoons rDL_\sigma^{ns*,D} = (rD_\sigma, Mod(ns*), \models'_{ns*})$$

*is called the dynamic logic with strongly continuous denotational semantics.*

Note that the adjective continuous has nothing common with the same notion used in any other mathematical disciplines, e.g. in topology. Its use has a historical basis: in Andréka, Németi [1978] the relations representing program meaning were called continuous if they satisfied some induction axiom schemas.

By using Theorem (13.6) we immediately get the following

**(14.28) Corollary.** *The non-standard dynamic logic $rDL_\sigma^{ns}$ and the dynamic logic with strongly continuous denotational semantics $rDL_\sigma^{ns*}$ are compact and complete with respect to the consequence.*

Having established the completeness of the above dynamic logics it is interesting to see how a Hoare-type calculus can be used for these logics. To answer this question first we introduce a Hoare calculus for transition graphs.

**(14.29) Definition.** *Let us fix a similarity type $\sigma$ and a set of formulas $Ax \subseteq Form_\sigma$ and a non-empty set of formulas $\Phi \subseteq Form_\sigma$. Let $\vdash$ be a complete first-order calculus. Let $g \in rG_\sigma$ be a transition graph and let $\phi$, $\psi$ be first-order formulas of $Form_\sigma$.*

*(A) A function $\kappa : node(g) \to \Phi$ is called a $\Phi$-invariant of $g$ with respect to $Ax$ iff*

$$Ax \cup \{\top \neq \bot\} \vdash \forall X \forall Y \big(\kappa(i)(X) \land onestep((X,i),(Y,j)) \to \kappa(j)[Y/X]\big).$$

*(B) We say that $\phi\{g\}\psi$ is $\Phi$-Hoare-provable from $Ax$ (written by $Ax \vdash_H^\Phi \phi\{g\}\psi$) iff there is a $\Phi$-invariant $\kappa : node(g) \to \Phi$ of $g$ with respect to $Ax$ such that:*

*(i) $Ax \cup \{\top \neq \bot\} \vdash \phi \to \kappa(start_g)$;*

*(ii) $Ax \cup \{\top \neq \bot\} \vdash \kappa(stop_g) \to \psi$.*

*If $\Phi = Form_\sigma$ then we just speak about Hoare-provable formulas and omit the superscript $\Phi$ in the notation.*

**(14.30) Theorem.** *Let $Ax \subseteq Form_\sigma$ be a set of axioms and let $\Phi \subseteq Form_\sigma$ be a fixed set of formulas closed under Boolean combinations. Let $g \in rG_\sigma$, $p \in rP_\sigma$ and $\phi$, $\psi \in \Phi$ be given such that each guard in $g$ and $p$ belongs to $\Phi$. Then*

*(i)* $Ax \vdash_H^\Phi \phi\{g\}\psi$ *implies* $Ax \cup \{\top \neq \bot\} \vdash_H^\Phi \phi\{pr(g)\}\psi$
*(ii)* $Ax \cup \{\top \neq \bot\} \vdash_H^\Phi \phi\{p\}\psi$ *implies* $Ax \vdash_H^\Phi \phi\{gr(p)\}\psi$
*(iii)* $Ax \cup \{\top \neq \bot\} \vdash_H^\Phi \phi\{p\}\psi$ *iff* $Ax \cup \{\top \neq \bot\} \vdash_H^\Phi \phi\{can(p)\}\psi$

*Proof.* We prove only statement (ii). Statement (i) can be proved similarly and statement (iii) follows from statements (i) and (ii). The proof of (ii) goes by induction on the complexity of $p$. We check only the program constructions:

(a) $Ax \vdash_H^\Phi \phi\{p_1; p_2\}\psi$ iff there are formulas $\phi', \mu, \psi'$ of $\Phi$ such that the formulas $\phi \to \phi'$, $\phi'\{p_1\}\mu$, $\mu\{p_2\}\psi'$, $\psi' \to \psi$ are true in $Ax \cup \{\top \neq \bot\}$. By the induction hypothesis, for $i = 1,2$ let $\kappa_i : node\, gr(p_i) \to \Phi$ be an invariant proving $\phi'\{p_1\}\mu$ and $\mu\{p_2\}\psi'$, respectively. Taking into account that $stop_{gr(p_1)}$ and $start_{gr(p_2)}$ label the same node of $gr(p)$, the following $\Phi$-invariant $\kappa : node(gr(p)) \to \Phi$ proves $\phi\{p\}\psi$:

$$\kappa(l) \rightleftharpoons \begin{cases} \kappa_1(l) & \text{if } l \in node(gr(p_1)) \setminus \{stop_{gr(p_1)}\}; \\ \kappa_2(l) & \text{if } l \in node(gr(p_2)) \setminus \{start_{gr(p_2)}\}; \\ \mu & \text{if } l = stop_{gr(p_1)} = start_{gr(p_2)}. \end{cases}$$

(b) $Ax \vdash_H^\Phi \phi\{\textbf{if } \alpha_1 \to p_1 \,\Box\, \alpha_2 \to p_2 \textbf{ fi }\}\psi$ iff there are formulas $\phi'$, $\psi$' of $\Phi$ such that the following formulas are provable in $Ax \cup \{\top \neq \bot\}$: $\phi \to \phi'$, $\phi' \wedge \alpha_i\{p_i\}\psi'$ $(i = 1,2)$, $\phi' \wedge \neg\alpha_1 \wedge \neg\alpha_2 \to \psi', \psi' \to \psi$. For $i = 1,2$ let $\kappa_i : node\ gr(p_i) \to \Phi$ be a $\Phi$-invariant proving $\phi' \wedge \alpha_i\{p_i\}\psi'$. Take $\kappa = \kappa_1 \cup \kappa_2 \cup \{(start, \phi')\}$ ($(start, \phi') \in \kappa$ means that $\kappa(start) = \phi'$) It is evident that $\kappa$ is an invariant of $gr(p)$ proving $\phi\{gr(p)\}\psi$ in $Ax$.

(c) $Ax \vdash_H^\Phi \phi\{\textbf{do } \alpha_1 \to p_1 \,\Box\, \alpha_2 \to p_2 \textbf{ od }\}\psi$ iff there are formulas $\phi'$, $\psi$' of $\Phi$ such that $\phi \to \phi'$, $\phi' \wedge (\alpha_1 \vee \alpha_2)\{\textbf{if } \alpha_1 \to p_1 \Box \alpha_2 \to p_2 \textbf{fi }\}\phi'$, $\phi' \wedge \neg\alpha_1 \wedge \neg\alpha_2 \to \psi'$ are provable in $Ax$. Take $q \rightleftharpoons \textbf{if } \alpha_1 \to p_1 \,\Box\, \alpha_2 \to p_2 \textbf{ fi}$ . Let $\kappa : node(gr(q)) \to \Phi$. Take

$$\kappa' = \kappa \cup \{(start, \phi')\} \cup \{(stop, \phi' \wedge \neg\alpha_1 \wedge \neg\alpha_2)\}.$$

It is easy to see that $\kappa'$ is an appropriate $\Phi$-invariant.

□

**(14.31) Definition.** *Let $(\delta, ext, *)$ be a given transitive extension of a given similarity type $\sigma$. Let $Ax \subseteq Form_\sigma$, $\phi$ and $\psi \in Form_\sigma$ be given.*

*(i)* *Let $p \in rP_\sigma$ be arbitrary. The formula $\phi\{p\}\psi$ is generalized Hoare-provable from $Ax$ (written as $Ax \vdash_{eH} \phi\{p\}\psi$) iff $Ax \cup Ind_\sigma^* \vdash_H^{SForm_\sigma} \phi\{p\}\psi$.*
*(ii)* *Let $g \in rG_\sigma$ be arbitrary. The formula $\phi\{g\}\psi$ is generalized Hoare-provable from $Ax$ (written as $Ax \vdash_{eH} \phi\{g\}\psi$) iff $Ax \cup Ind_\sigma^* \vdash_H^{SForm_\sigma} \phi\{g\}\psi$.*

The following theorem characterizes both the continuous and the strongly continuous denotational semantics.

**(14.32) Theorem.** *Let $Ax \subseteq Form_\sigma$ and let $\phi\{p\}\psi \in rH_\sigma$ be fixed.*

*(i) $Ax \vdash_H \phi\{p\}\psi$ iff $Ax \models'_{ns} \phi\{p\}\psi$;*
*(ii) $Ax \vdash_{eH} \phi\{p\}\psi$ iff $Ax \models'_{ns*} \phi\{p\}\psi$.*

*Proof.* The soundness of the Hoare and of the generalized Hoare calculus follows from Theorem (14.33). The other direction of the statements (i) and (ii) follows from Theorem (14.34) and Theorem (14.35), respectively. □

**(14.33) Theorem.** *The Hoare calculus and the generalized Hoare calculus are sound with respect to the continuous denotational and the strongly continuous denotational semantics, respectively.*

*Proof.* First we prove the case of strongly continuous denotational semantics. Let us suppose that for some formula $\phi\{p\}\psi \in H_\sigma$, $Ax \vdash_{eH} \phi\{p\}\psi$. By the statement (iii) of Theorem (14.30) we get $Ax \vdash_{eH} \phi\{can(p)\}\psi$. Using the notations of Definition (14.11), by Lemma (12.5) the proof of the last formula must be of the form:

$$(*)\qquad \cfrac{\phi\{p';\textbf{while } p^\alpha \textbf{ do } p'' \textbf{ od}\}\psi}{\phi\{p'\}\phi'\ ,\quad \cfrac{\phi'\{\textbf{while } p^\alpha \textbf{ do } p'' \textbf{ od}\}\psi}{\phi' \to \kappa\,,\ \kappa \wedge \neg p^\alpha \to \psi, \kappa \wedge p^\alpha\{p''\}\kappa,}}$$

where $\kappa \in SForm_\sigma$.

Since $p'$ does not contain any **do...od** commands, $Ax \vdash_{eH} \phi\{p'\}\phi'$ implies $Ax \cup \{\top \neq \bot\} \cup Ind^*_\sigma \models \phi\{p'\}\phi'$, hence $Ax \models'_{ns*} \phi\{p'\}\phi'$. Let $\tilde{p} \rightleftharpoons$ **while** $p^\alpha$ **do** $p''$ **od**. We will prove that $Ax \cup \{\top \neq \bot\} \models'_{ns*} \phi'\{\tilde{p}\}\psi$, which is equivalent to the following:

$$(**)\qquad Ax \cup \{\top \neq \bot\} \cup Ind^*_\sigma \models \phi' \wedge D[\![\tilde{p}]\!] \to \psi[Y'/Y],$$

where $Y \rightleftharpoons var(p^\alpha) \cup var(p'')$. By definition the canonical form of $\tilde{p}$ is itself, so

$$D[\![\tilde{p}]\!] \rightleftharpoons (p^\alpha \wedge D[\![p'', Y]\!])^* \wedge \neg p^\alpha[Y'/Y].$$

By the third line of the proof tree (*) we get that $Ax \cup \{\top \neq \bot\} \vdash \kappa \wedge p^\alpha \wedge D[\![p'', Y]\!] \to \kappa[Y'/Y]$. Since $\kappa \in SForm_\sigma$, the transfinite induction axiom $Tr_{p^\alpha \wedge D[\![p'',Y]\!]}(\kappa)$ belongs to $Ind^*_\sigma$, thus we get

$$Ax \cup \{\top \neq \bot\} \cup Ind^*_\sigma \models \kappa \wedge (p^\alpha \wedge D[\![p'', Y]\!])^* \to \kappa[Y'/Y].$$

Hence, taking into account the third line of (*) again, we can deduce that

$$(**)\qquad Ax \cup \{\top \neq \bot\} \cup Ind^*_\sigma \vdash \phi' \wedge D[\![\tilde{p}]\!] \to \psi[Y'/Y],$$

Then from the soundness of the first-order calculus we obtain (**).

The case of non-standard dynamic logic can be proved similarly. We have to note that in this case $\kappa$ also belongs to $Form_\sigma$. □

The following completeness theorem was first established by Csirmaz [1981] for his continuous trace semantics in the scope of a first-order logic, which differs from the non-standard dynamic logic considered in this chapter. An elegant and simple proof was later given by Sain [1985a], again for the continuous trace semantics and also in the scope of the logic defined by Csirmaz [1981]. Note that if $Ax$ contains arithmetic then the completeness theorem is almost trivial. See this case in Andréka, Németi [1978], where the continuous trace semantics was first considered.

**(14.34) Theorem.** *Fix a similarity type $\sigma$. Let $Ax \subseteq Form_\sigma$ be an arbitrary consistent set of formulas, let $p \in rP_\sigma$ be an arbitrary $\sigma$-type program, and let $\phi$ and $\psi$ ($\in Form_\sigma$) be pre- and postconditions, respectively. Then*

$$Ax \models'_{ns} \phi\{p\}\psi \quad \textit{implies} \quad Ax \vdash_H \phi\{p\}\psi.$$

*Proof.* Let $can(p)$ be the canonical form of $p$ and let us use the notations of Definition (14.11) and the equivalence of Lemma (14.12). Now let us suppose that $Ax \models'_{ns} \phi\{p\}\psi$ which, by definition, is equivalent to $Ax \models_{ns} \phi\{can(p)\}\psi$. By (iii) of Theorem (14.30), to show that $Ax \vdash_H \phi\{p\}\psi$ it is enough to construct a Hoare-proof of $\phi\{can(p)\}\psi$.

Let $\phi' \rightleftharpoons \exists Z'(\phi[Z/Z'] \wedge D[\![p', Z]\!](Z, Z')[Z : Z'])$. Then by (iv) of Lemma (14.12) and by the definition of $\phi'$

$$Ax \models'_{ns} \phi\{p'\}\phi'$$
$$Ax \models'_{ns} \phi'\{\tilde{p}\}\psi,$$

where $\tilde{p} \rightleftharpoons$ **while** $p^\alpha$ **do** $p''$ **od**. Since $p'$ does not contain any **do...od** commands, $Ax \models'_{ns} \phi\{p'\}\phi'$ iff $Ax \models \phi\{p'\}\phi'$ iff (by Lemma (12.7)) $Ax \cup \{\top \neq \bot\} \vdash_H \phi\{p'\}\phi'$. Now we will prove that $Ax \cup \{\top \neq \bot\} \vdash_H \phi'\{\tilde{p}\}\psi$.

Let $\Xi \rightleftharpoons p^\alpha \wedge D[\![p'', Y]\!]$. By definition of $ns$ and by the compactness theorem, $Ax \models'_{ns} \phi'\{\tilde{p}\}\psi$ implies that there is a finite $T \subseteq Ind_\sigma$ such that $Ax \cup \{\top \neq \bot\} \cup T \models \tilde{D}(\phi'\{\tilde{p}\}\psi)$. Let $T \rightleftharpoons \{Tr_{\phi_i}(\psi_i) \mid 1 \leq i \leq m\} \cup \{Cl_{\mu_j} \mid 1 \leq j \leq n\}$ and let $\Phi \rightleftharpoons \{\phi_1, ..., \phi_m\}$, $M \rightleftharpoons \{\mu_1, ..., \mu_n, \Xi\} \setminus \Phi$. For each $\Delta$-formula $\alpha(X_\alpha, Y_\alpha, P_\alpha) \in \Phi$ let $\Theta_\alpha \rightleftharpoons \{\psi_i \mid 1 \leq i \leq m \text{ and } \phi_i = \alpha\}$. Let $\Psi_\alpha \rightleftharpoons \{\wedge\Theta | \Theta \subseteq \Theta_\alpha\}$. For each $v \in \Psi_\alpha$ let $Q_v \rightleftharpoons var(v) \setminus (X_\alpha \cup Y_\alpha \cup P_\alpha)$. Since the variables of $Q_v$ occur bound in $Ind_\sigma$, it can be supposed that $v$, $v' \in \Psi_\alpha$ and $v \neq v'$ implies $Q_v \cap Q_{v'} = \emptyset$. Let $V_\alpha$ and $W_\alpha$ be two new copies of $X_\alpha$ and for every $v \in \Psi_\alpha$ let

$$cl_\alpha(v) \rightleftharpoons v[X_\alpha/Y_\alpha] \wedge \forall V_\alpha \forall W_\alpha (v[V_\alpha/Y_\alpha] \wedge \alpha[V_\alpha/X_\alpha, W_\alpha/Y_\alpha] \rightarrow v[W_\alpha/Y_\alpha])$$

(then $var(cl_\alpha(v)) \subseteq X_\alpha \cup P_\alpha \cup Q_v$).

Let $\Gamma_\alpha \rightleftharpoons \bigwedge\{\forall Q_v(cl_\alpha(v) \to v) \mid v \in \Psi_\alpha\}$, then $var(\Gamma_\alpha) \subseteq X_\alpha \cup Y_\alpha \cup P_\alpha$. It is easy to prove that the following formulas are tautologies:

(i) $\Gamma_\alpha[X_\alpha/Y_\alpha]$;
(ii) $\forall V_\alpha \forall W_\alpha(\Gamma_\alpha[V_\alpha/Y_\alpha] \wedge \alpha[V_\alpha/X_\alpha, W_\alpha/Y_\alpha] \to \Gamma_\alpha[W_\alpha/Y_\alpha])$.

Let us fix an arbitrary $\delta$-type model $\mathcal{B}$ and a valuation $k \in Val_{\mathcal{B}}[X_\alpha \cup P_\alpha]$ and let

$$\Psi_{\alpha\beta} \rightleftharpoons \{v_\beta[k + k_Q^v] \mid v \in \Psi_\alpha, k_Q^v \in Val_{\mathcal{B}}[Q_v]\}.$$

It is easy to verify that

(a) $\Psi_{\alpha\beta}[k]$ is closed under intersection;
(b) $\Gamma_{\alpha\mathcal{B}}[k] = \cap\{v_{\mathcal{B}}[k + k_Q^v] \mid v \in \Psi_\alpha, k_Q^v \in Val_{\mathcal{B}}[Q_v], \mathcal{B} \models cl_\alpha(v)[k + k_Q^v]\}$;
(c) $\Gamma_{\alpha\mathcal{B}}[k] \in \Psi_{\alpha\beta}[k]$.

Now we show that, if $\mathcal{B}$ and $k$ are fixed as above, then for every $v \in \Psi_\alpha$ and for every $k_Q^v \in Val_{\mathcal{B}}[Q_v]$

$$(*) \qquad \mathcal{B} \models T(v)[k + k_Q^v],$$

where

$$T(v)(X_\alpha, P_\alpha, Q_v) \rightleftharpoons (v[X_\alpha/Y_\alpha] \wedge \forall V_\alpha \forall W_\alpha(\Gamma_\alpha[V_\alpha/Y_\alpha] \wedge v[V_\alpha/Y_\alpha] \wedge \alpha[V_\alpha/X_\alpha, W_\alpha/Y_\alpha] \to v[W_\alpha/Y_\alpha])) \to \forall Y_\alpha(\Gamma_\alpha \to v).$$

If the consequent of $T(v)$ holds then (*) holds too. Assume that $\mathcal{B} \models \exists Y_\alpha(\Gamma_\alpha \wedge \neg v)[k + k_Q]^v$. Then $(\Gamma_\alpha \wedge v)_{\mathcal{B}}[k + k_Q^v] = \Gamma_{\alpha\mathcal{B}}[k] \cap v_{\mathcal{B}}[k + k_Q^v]$ (which belongs to $\Psi_{\alpha\beta}[k]$ by (a) and (b)) is smaller than $\Gamma_{\alpha\mathcal{B}}[k]$, thus by (c) $\mathcal{B} \not\models cl_\alpha(\Gamma_\alpha \wedge v)[k + k_Q^v]$. Therefore, either $\mathcal{B} \not\models (\Gamma_\alpha \wedge v[X_\alpha/Y_\alpha][k + k_Q^v]$ occurs and hence by (i) $\mathcal{B} \not\models v[X_\alpha/Y_\alpha][k + k_Q]$ or the following holds:

$$\mathcal{B} \models \exists V_\alpha \exists W_\alpha((\Gamma_\alpha \wedge v)[V_\alpha/Y_\alpha] \wedge \alpha[V_\alpha/X_\alpha, W_\alpha/Y_\alpha] \wedge \neg(\Gamma_\alpha \wedge v)[W_\alpha/Y_\alpha])[k + k_Q^v].$$

In both cases the antecedent of $T(v)$ does not hold in $\mathcal{B}$ with the valuation $k + k_Q^v$, which we wanted to prove.

Now for $\alpha \in M$ let $\Gamma_\alpha \rightleftharpoons true$. Let

$$\Sigma \rightleftharpoons \{\Gamma_\alpha(X_\alpha, Y_\alpha, P_\alpha) \leftrightarrow \hat{\alpha}(X_\alpha, Y_\alpha, P_\alpha) \mid \alpha \in M \cup \Phi\}.$$

We show that $Ax \cup \{\top \neq \bot\} \cup \Sigma \models Ax \cup \{\top \neq \bot\} \cup T$. Namely, the validity of the transfinite induction axioms follows from (*). The closure axioms obviously hold by (i) and (ii).

Since $Ax \cup T \cup \{\top \neq \bot\} \models \tilde{D}(\phi'\{\tilde{p}\}\psi)$ and each $\hat{\alpha}$ is a new symbol of $\delta$ with respect to $\sigma$, by the definition of $D[\![\tilde{p}, Y]\!]$ (cf. Definition (14.11)) we get

(iii) $Ax \cup \{\top \neq \bot\} \models \phi' \wedge \Gamma_\Xi \wedge \neg p^\alpha \to \psi[Y'/Y]$,

(obviously, if $\Xi \in \Phi$ then $Y = X_\Xi$, $Y' = Y_\Xi$, i.e. $var(\Gamma_\Xi) \subseteq Y \cup Y' \cup P_\Xi$).

Let $\mu \rightleftharpoons \exists Z'((\phi' \wedge \Gamma_{\Xi})[Z : Z'])$. (i) and (iii) imply $Ax \cup \{\top \neq \bot\} \models \phi' \to \mu$ and $Ax \models \mu \wedge \neg p^\alpha \to \psi$, respectively. By (ii) $Ax \cup \{\top \neq \bot\} \models \mu \wedge \Xi \to \mu[Y'/Y]$. Since $\Xi$ is just the denotation of the program $q \rightleftharpoons$ **if** $p^\alpha \;\to\; p''$ **fi** (cf. the equivalence of Lemma (14.12)), which contains no **do...od** command, we obtain that $Ax \cup \{\top \neq \bot\} \vdash_H \mu\{q\}\mu$. By definition this means that

$$Ax \cup \{\top \neq \bot\} \vdash_H \mu \wedge p^\alpha\{p''\}\mu.$$

In the end the following formulas give the desired Hoare-proof of $\phi'\{\tilde{p}\}\psi$:

$$Ax \cup \{\top \neq \bot\} \vdash \phi' \to \mu;$$
$$Ax \cup \{\top \neq \bot\} \vdash \mu \wedge \neg p^\alpha \to \psi;$$
$$Ax \cup \{\top \neq \bot\} \vdash_H \mu \wedge p^\alpha\{p''\}\mu.$$

□

**(14.35) Theorem.** *Fix a similarity type $\sigma$. Let $Ax \subseteq Form_\sigma$ be an arbitrary consistent set of formulas, let $p \in rP_\sigma$ be an arbitrary $\sigma$-type program, let $\phi$ and $\psi$ ($\in Form_\sigma$) be pre- and postconditions, respectively. Then*

$$Ax \models'_{ns*} \phi\{p\}\psi \quad \textit{implies} \quad Ax \vdash_{eH} \phi\{p\}\psi.$$

*Proof.* Let us suppose that for some $\phi\{p\}\psi \in rH_\sigma$, $Ax \models'_{ns*} \phi\{p\}\psi$ and let us suppose that $p$ does not contain any **do...od** commands. In this case $Ax \models'_{ns*} \phi\{p\}\psi$ is equivalent to $Ax \models \phi\{p\}\psi$ and by Theorem (12.7) we get $Ax \vdash_{eH} \phi\{p\}\psi$. Now let $p'$, $p''$, $p^\alpha$ and $Y$ be as in Definition (14.11). Let $Y'$ be a new copy of $Y$. Take $\phi'(Y) \rightleftharpoons \exists Y'(\phi(Y') \wedge D[\![p', Y]\!][Y' : Y])$. By Definition (14.11), Lemma (14.12) and the definition of the semantic function $\tilde{D}$ we get

(1) $$Ax \models'_{ns*} \phi\{p'\}\phi';$$
(2) $$Ax \models'_{ns*} \phi'\{\textbf{while } p^\alpha \textbf{ do } p'' \textbf{ od}\}\psi;$$

Since $p'$ does not contain any **do...od** commands by (1), we get

(3) $$Ax \vdash_{eH} \phi\{p'\}\phi'.$$

Let $\Xi \rightleftharpoons p^\alpha \wedge D[\![p'', Y]\!]$. Take $\kappa(Y) \rightleftharpoons \exists Y'(\phi'(Y') \wedge \Xi^*[Y' : Y])$. By definition and by the use of Definition (14.11) statement (2) is semantically equivalent to the following $\sigma^*$-type first-order formula: $\phi'(Y) \wedge \Xi^*(Y, Y') \wedge \neg p^\alpha \to \psi(Y')$. Hence, by using the definition of $\kappa$ we get the following:

(4) $$Ax \models'_{ns*} \phi'(Y) \to \kappa(Y)$$
(5) $$Ax \models'_{ns*} \kappa(Y) \wedge \neg p^\alpha \to \psi(Y)$$

By using the definition of $\kappa$ again and $Cl_{\Xi(Y,Y',\emptyset)}$ we can check that $Ax \models'_{ns*} \kappa(Y) \wedge \Xi(Y, Y') \to \kappa(Y')$. Since $\Xi$ is equivalent to the denotation of the program $q \rightleftharpoons$ **if** $p^\alpha \;\to\; p''$ **fi** we obtain $Ax \models'_{ns*} \kappa\{q\}\kappa$. However, $q$ does not contain any repetitive commands, thus we can use the well known program equivalences and get

$$(6) \qquad Ax \models'_{ns*} \kappa \wedge p^\alpha\{p''\}\kappa$$

According to the first lines of the proof we can substitute $\models'_{ns*}$ in the statements (4)-(6) by $\vdash_{eH}$. After this substitution (3)-(6) give a Hoare-proof for the formula $\phi\{can(p)\}\psi$. By using the statement (iii) of Theorem (14.30) we get $Ax \vdash_{eH} \phi\{p\}\psi$. □

**(14.36) Theorem.** *Let $\hat\eta$ be the similarity type of the axiom system $Next'$ (see Chapter 1) and let us suppose that $\hat\eta \subseteq \sigma$. Let $Next'$ contain the following axioms:*

$$\forall x(0 \neq x+1);$$
$$\forall x \forall y(x+1 = y+1 \rightarrow x = y);$$
$$\forall x(x \neq 0 \rightarrow (x-1)+1 = x);$$
$$0 - 1 = 0.$$

*Then $PA$ is definable in $Ind^*_\sigma \cup Next'$.*

*Proof.* Let us consider the maximal transitive extension $ns*$. First let us define the universe of the arithmetic. Let us consider the $\Delta$-formula $\alpha \rightleftharpoons (u' = u+1, \{u\}, \{u'\}, \emptyset)$. By definition take $\zeta(n) \rightleftharpoons Red(star(\alpha))(0,n)$. It is clear that $Next' \models_{ns*} \zeta(0) \wedge \forall n(\zeta(n) \rightarrow \zeta(n+1))$. Our aim is to prove that all the axioms of $PA$ hold. However, first we have to define addition and product as well.

Take the following $\Delta$-formula $\xi(x,y,z,x',y',z') \rightleftharpoons$

$$(x' = x+1 \wedge y' = y \wedge z' = z+1) \vee (x' = x \wedge y' = y+1 \wedge z' = z+1).$$

Let $sum(x',y',z') \rightleftharpoons \xi^*(0,0,0,x',y',z')$. By using Lemma (14.8) we get that the following formula is true:

$$\text{(i)} \quad sum(x',y',z') \leftrightarrow (x' = y' = z' = 0) \vee \exists x \exists y \exists z(x' = x+1 \wedge y' = y \wedge z' = z+1) \vee (x' = x \wedge y' = y+1 \wedge z' = z+1) \wedge sum(x,y,z)).$$

The next three statements immediately follow from (i) and $Next'$:

(ii) $sum(x,y,0) \leftrightarrow x = y = 0$;
(iii) $x \neq 0 \rightarrow (sum(x,y,z) \leftrightarrow sum(x-1,y+1,z))$;
(iv) $y \neq 0 \rightarrow sum(x,y,z) \leftrightarrow sum(x+1,y-1,z)$;

We remark that an induction axiom $Tr_\alpha(\phi)$ turns into the natural induction axiom along $\zeta$. We suppose that all the variables are bounded by $\zeta$. However, for the sake of simplicity we do not indicate this bound explicitly in the following formulas (v)-(viii). By using $Next'$, (ii)-(iv) and induction rules of the form $Tr_\alpha(\phi)$, we can prove the following statements:

(v) $sum(x, y, z) \leftrightarrow sum(y, x, z)$;
(vi) $sum(x, 0, z) \leftrightarrow x = z$;
(vii) $sum(0, y, z) \leftrightarrow y = z$;
(viii) $\exists! z sum(x, y, z)$.

By using (viii) the formula *sum* defines a function. Let denote this function, as usual, by $+$. $x+0 = x$ simply follows from (vi). In order to prove $x+(y+1) = (x+y)+1$ we have to prove by induction the following formula

(ix) $sum(x, y, z) \rightarrow sum(x, y+1, z+1)$.

The product of two numbers can be defined by the following formula:

$$\xi'(x, y, z, x', y', z') \rightleftharpoons (x' = x \wedge y' = y + 1 \wedge \\ sum(z, x, z')) \vee (x' = x + 1 \wedge y' = y \wedge sum(z, y, z')));$$

Now take $prod(x, y, z) \rightleftharpoons \xi^*(0, 0, 0, x, y, z)$. Using the same methods as in the case of *sum* we can prove that *prod* defines a function and satisfies the well-known properties. In the end the induction axioms of $PA_\eta$ obviously hold since any induction axiom of $PA_\eta$ also belongs to $Ind^*_\sigma$ (and it is of the form $Tr_\alpha(\cdot)$). □

**(14.37) Theorem.** *There is a similarity type $\sigma$, an axiom system $Ax$ and a formula $\chi \rightleftharpoons \phi\{p\}\psi \in H_\sigma$ such that*

$$Ax \not\models'_{ns} \chi \text{ but } Ax \models'_{ns*} \chi.$$

*Proof.* By Theorems (14.33) and (14.34) it is enough to construct a similarity type $\sigma$, a set of axioms $Ax \subseteq Form_\sigma$, a transitive extension $(\sigma^*, ns*, *)$ of $\sigma$ maximal with respect to $(\{\top \neq \bot\}, Ind^*_\sigma)$ and a formula $\phi\{p\}\psi$ such that

$$Ax \vdash_{eH} \phi\{p\}\psi \text{ but } Ax \cup \{\top \neq \bot\} \not\vdash_H \phi\{p\}\psi.$$

By Theorem (14.34) this proves the statement of this theorem.

Recall the similarity type $\hat{\eta}$ from Chapter 1. Let $\sigma \rightleftharpoons \hat{\eta}$ and let $\mathcal{A}$ be the model in Theorem (12.12). Let $(\sigma^*, ns*, *)$ be the unique extension of $\sigma$ maximal with respect to $(\{\top \neq \bot\}, Ind^*_\sigma)$. Take $Ax \rightleftharpoons Th(\mathcal{A})$. Recall the program $p$ from Theorem (12.11), i.e. let

$$p \rightleftharpoons z := 0; y := x; \textbf{ while } y \neq 0 \textbf{ do } y := y - 1; z := z + 1 \textbf{ od}.$$

By Theorem (12.12) we have $Ax \not\vdash_H true\{p\}x = z$. We are going to prove that $Ax \vdash_{eH} true\{p\}x = z$. Let $Next'$ be the axiom system of the previous theorem. It is clear that $Next' \subseteq Th(\mathcal{A})$. We can prove that $Next' \vdash_{eH} true\{p\}z = x$. Let us take $sum(y, z, x)$ as the invariant of the **while** loop. This formula is really an invariant (with respect to $Ind^*_\sigma \cup Next'$) since:

$Next' \vdash_{eH} true\{z := 0; y := x\}z = 0 \wedge y = x$

$Next' \cup Ind^*_\sigma \vdash (z = 0 \wedge y = x) \rightarrow sum(y, z, x)$ by (vi)

$Next' \vdash_{eH} sum(y, z, x) \wedge y \neq 0\{y := y - 1; z := z + 1\}sum(y, z, x)$ by (iii)

$Next' \cup Ind^*_\sigma \vdash sum(y, z, x) \wedge y = 0 \rightarrow z = x$ by (vii)

and the aboves give a generalized Hoare-proof of the formula $true\{p\}z = x$. □

Let us see how the different dynamic logics are related to each other.

**(14.38) Corollary.** *There is a similarity type* $\sigma$ *such that*

$$rDL_\sigma >_{rH_\sigma} rDL^{ns*}_\sigma >_{rH_\sigma} rDL^{ns}_\sigma.$$

*Proof.* Let $\sigma \rightleftharpoons \hat{\eta}$ be as in Theorem (14.36). The set of all tautologies of $rDL_\sigma$ form a $\Pi^1_1$-complete set, (see Theorem (11.12)) thus $rDL_\sigma >_{rH_\sigma} rDL^{ns*}_\sigma$ obviously holds. $rDL^{ns*}_\sigma >_{rH_\sigma} rDL^{ns}_\sigma$ is a simple consequence of Theorem (14.37). □

## 14.3 Axiomatic Calculus for the Extended Dynamic Logic

In the previous section the Hoare calculus and its generalization have been introduced and investigated for the Floyd-Hoare sublanguage of the non-standard dynamic logic and of the dynamic logic with strongly continuous denotational semantics. In this section we introduce an axiomatic calculus for the entire extended dynamic logic $rDL^{ns*}_\sigma$. For this we use the method of axiomatization given in Chapter 13 which resulted the calculus $\vdash_{dyn}$.

As we have mentioned in Chapter 12 dynamic logic is complete with respect to the arithmetic models. The latter can be axiomatized by the axiom system *Next*. Moreover, in order to build up an axiomatic calculus for the extended dynamic logic similar to that introduced by Harel [1979] we have to represent the latter in our first-order scope. This representation can be done by the axiom system $Ind^*_\sigma$. In other words this means that the axiomatic calculus of regular dynamic logic introduced by Harel [1979] is characterized by $Ind^*_\sigma$ in the scope of classical first-order logic. Therefore, if $\sigma$ is a similarity type containing $\hat{\eta}$ we will consider the transitive extension $ns'$ maximal with respect to $(Next', Ind^*_\sigma)$. Let $\vdash_{ns'}$ be the calculus obtained from $\vdash_{dyn}$ by dropping out $R_{do}$ and by adding the following two rules:

$$(I)\ \frac{\phi \wedge (\alpha_1 \vee \alpha_2) \rightarrow [\textbf{if}\ \alpha_1 \rightarrow p_1 \ \Box\ \alpha_2 \rightarrow p_2\ \textbf{fi}]\phi,\ \ \phi \wedge \neg\alpha_1 \wedge \neg\alpha_2 \rightarrow \psi}{\phi \rightarrow [\textbf{do}\ \alpha_1 \rightarrow p_1 \ \Box\ \alpha_2 \rightarrow p_2\ \textbf{od}]\psi}$$

$$(C)\ \frac{\zeta(x) \wedge \phi(x+1) \rightarrow \langle\textbf{if}\ \alpha_1 \rightarrow p_1 \ \Box\ \alpha_2 \rightarrow p_2\ \textbf{fi}\rangle\phi(x),\ \phi(0) \rightarrow \neg\alpha_1 \wedge \neg\alpha_2}{\zeta(x) \wedge \phi(x) \rightarrow \langle\textbf{do}\ \alpha_1 \rightarrow p_1 \ \Box\ \alpha_2 \rightarrow p_2\ \textbf{od}\rangle\phi(0)}$$

**(14.39) Theorem.** *The calculus* $\vdash_{ns'}$ *is sound and complete with respect to the extended dynamic logic* $rD_\sigma^{ns'}$. *That is, for any* $Ax \subseteq rD_\sigma$ *and* $\phi \in rD_\sigma$ *we have that*

$$Ax \models'_{ns'} \phi \quad \text{iff} \quad Ax \cup Next' \cup Ind^*_\sigma \vdash_{ns'} \phi.$$

*Proof.* By using Theorem (13.11) we have to prove that the assumptions (i) and (ii) of the mentioned theorem hold. We can repeat the proof of Theorem (13.13); however, we have to give a new proof for the case (e) since the axiom $R_{do}$ has been dropped out from the set of inference rules of the calculus $\vdash_{dyn}$. To prove the case (e) we define an ordering on programs. Let $p,\ p' \in rP_\sigma$ be two fixed programs. $p \prec p'$ iff $p$ is a subprogram of $p'$ or there is a program $q$ which is a subprogram of $p'$ or is equal to the program $p'$ such that $q$ is of the form **do** $\alpha_1 \to p_1 \,\Box\, \alpha_2 \to p_2$ **od** and $p =$ **if** $\alpha_1 \to p_1 \,\Box\, \alpha_2 \to p_2$ **fi** . It is an easy exercise to prove that $\prec$ is transitive and for any $p' \in rP_\sigma$ there are only finitely many $p$ such that $p \prec p'$. If $p \prec p'$ then we say that $p$ is simpler than $p'$.

Now we can formulate our induction hypothesis for the case (e). Let $p$ and $\psi$ be fixed. Let us suppose that for any $\chi \in Form_\delta$ and for any program $p'$ simpler than $p$ there is a formula $\beta \in Form_\delta$ such that $\vdash_{ns'} \langle p'\rangle\chi \leftrightarrow \beta$. Fix a first order formula $\psi^p \in Form_\delta$ such that $\vdash_{ns'} \langle p\rangle\psi \leftrightarrow \langle p\rangle\psi^p$. By induction we construct a formula $\phi^p$ such that $\vdash_{ns'} \langle p\rangle\psi \leftrightarrow \phi^p$.

The cases (i)-(v) are the same as in the proof of Theorem (13.13). We have only to give a new proof for the case $p \rightleftharpoons$ **do** $\alpha_1 \to p_1 \,\Box\, \alpha_2 \to p_2$ **od** . Let $X \rightleftharpoons var(p)$ and take $q \rightleftharpoons$ **if** $\alpha_1 \to p_1 \,\Box\, \alpha_2 \to p_2$ **fi** . We construct a formula $\Phi_\psi(X,n) \in Form_\delta$ which intuitively expresses the following statement: "*There is a trace of program* $p$ *with input* $X$ *which terminates at most after* $n$ *iterations of the program* $q$ *and its output satisfies* $\psi^p$". Our aim is to construct this formula $\Phi_\psi(X,n)$ and prove that $\vdash_{ns'} \langle p\rangle\psi^p \leftrightarrow \exists n\big(\zeta(n) \wedge \Phi_\psi(X,n)\big)$. That is, the formula $\phi^p \rightleftharpoons \exists n\big(\zeta(n) \wedge \Phi_\psi(X,n)\big)$ is appropriate.

First we show how this formula can be constructed. Let $R$ be a new relation symbol with arity $(X,n)$ and consider the fixed point equation:

$$R(X,n) = (\neg\alpha_1 \wedge \neg\alpha_2 \wedge (n=0) \wedge \psi^p)\vee$$
$$\exists Y \exists m(m+1=n \wedge R(Y,m) \wedge ((\alpha_1 \vee \alpha_2) \wedge \gamma(X,Y))),$$

where $Ax \cup Next' \cup \{\top \neq \bot\} \vdash_{ns'} \langle q\rangle(X=Y) \leftrightarrow \gamma(X,Y)$ (by the induction hypothesis).

Let $\Phi_\psi(X,n)$ be the least $SForm_\sigma$-definable fixed point of this equation. By using the fixed point properties we immediately get the following:

$$(1) \qquad ns' \models \forall n\Big(\zeta(n) \to \big(\Phi_\psi(X,n+1) \to \langle q\rangle\Phi_\psi(X,n)\big)\Big);$$

$$(2) \qquad ns' \models \Phi_\psi(X,0) \to \neg\alpha_1 \wedge \neg\alpha_2.$$

It is clear that $q$ is simpler than $p$, therefore we can use the induction hypothesis. So, there is a formula $\beta$ such that

(3). $$\vdash_{ns'} \langle q\rangle \Phi_\psi(X,n) \leftrightarrow \beta$$

By using (1), the soundness of $\vdash_{ns'}$ and the axioms of $T$ we get

$$ns' \models \forall n\big(\zeta(n) \wedge \Phi_\psi(X,n+1) \to \beta\big).$$

However, this formula is a first-order one, hence we can conclude that

(4) $$\vdash_{ns'} \forall n\big(\zeta(n) \wedge \Phi_\psi(X,n+1) \to \beta\big).$$

From (3) and (4) by using the appropriate tautologies of $T$ we obtain

(5) $$\vdash_{ns'} \forall n\big(\zeta(n) \to (\Phi_\psi(X,n+1) \to \langle q\rangle \Phi_\psi(X,n))\big).$$

Since the formula in (2) is a first-order one we immediately have that

(6) $$\vdash_{ns'} \Phi_\psi(X,0) \to \neg\alpha_1 \wedge \neg\alpha_2.$$

By the use of the inference rule (C) we can obtain from (5) and (6)

(7) $$\vdash_{ns'} \exists n\big(\zeta(n) \wedge \Phi_\psi(X,n) \to \langle p\rangle \Phi_\psi(X,0)\big).$$

On the other side, $ns' \models \Phi_\psi(X,0) \to \psi^p$ takes place according to the definition of $\Phi_\psi$. Since this is also a first-order formula we obtain $\vdash_{ns'} \Phi_\psi(X,0) \to \psi^p$. By the use of inference rule $G[]$ the axioms of $T$ get from this we

(8) $$\vdash_{ns'} \langle p\rangle \Phi_\psi(X,0) \to \langle p\rangle \psi^p.$$

From (7) and (8) by using the appropriate tautologies of $T$ we obtain the following

(9) $$\vdash_{ns'} \exists n\big(\zeta(n) \wedge \Phi_\psi(X,n)\big) \to \langle p\rangle \psi^p.$$

Now let us consider the other direction, i.e. $\vdash_{ns'} \langle p\rangle\psi^p \to \exists n\big(\zeta(n) \wedge \Phi_\psi(X,n)\big)$. By the use of the appropriate tautologies of $T$ this statement is equivalent to $\vdash_{ns'} \forall n\big(\zeta(n) \to \neg\Phi_\psi(X,n)\big) \to \neg\langle p\rangle\psi^p$ which is equivalent to

(10) $$\vdash_{ns'} \forall n\big(\zeta(n) \to \neg\Phi_\psi(X,n)\big) \to [p]\neg\psi^p.$$

In order to prove (10) let us consider the following facts which follow from the appropriate definitions:

(11) $$ns' \models \forall n\big(\zeta(n) \to \neg\Phi_\psi(X,n)\big) \wedge (\alpha_1 \vee \alpha_2) \to [q]\neg\forall n\big(\zeta(n) \to \neg\Phi_\psi(X,n)\big);$$

(12) $$ns' \models \forall n\big(\zeta(n) \to \neg\Phi_\psi(X,n)\big) \wedge \neg\alpha_1 \wedge \neg\alpha_2 \to \neg\psi^p.$$

Hence it is straightforward to obtain (by using appropriate axioms of $T$):

(13) $$\vdash_{ns'} \forall n\big(\zeta(n) \to \neg\Phi_\psi(X,n)\big) \wedge (\alpha_1 \vee \alpha_2) \to [q]\neg\forall n\big(\zeta(n) \to \neg\Phi_\psi(X,n)\big);$$

(14) $$\vdash_{ns'} \forall n\big(\zeta(n) \to \neg\Phi_\psi(X,n)\big) \wedge \neg\alpha_1 \wedge \neg\alpha_2 \to \neg\psi^p.$$

By using (13) and (14) and the rule $I$ we get (10). □

## 14.4 On Program Equivalence

Program equivalence can be defined with the help of the denotations of the programs. Since the denotations are definable in extensions, program equivalence can also be handled by their use.

For this section, let $(\delta, ext, *)$ be a transitive extension of a fixed similarity type $\sigma$.

**(14.40) Definition.** *Let $p$, $q \in rP_\sigma$ be two arbitrary programs and let $X \rightleftharpoons var(p) \cup var(q)$. Programs $p$ and $q$ are said to be equivalent in $ext$ (written $p \equiv_e q$) iff $D[\![p, X]\!]_{\mathcal{B}} = D[\![q, X]\!]_{\mathcal{B}}$ for any $\mathcal{B} \in Mod(ext)$.*

Another possibility of defining program equivalence is connected with the input-output characterization of programs. For this we need the following

**(14.41) Definition.** *Let $p \in rP_\sigma$ be an arbitrary program. The partial correctness theory of $p$ in $ext$ is defined as the set of preconditions and postconditions with respect to which $p$ is partially correct, i.e.*

$$PC(ext, p) \rightleftharpoons \{(\phi, \psi) : \phi, \psi \in Form_\sigma \text{ and } ext \models' \phi\{p\}\psi\}.$$

The connection between denotational equivalence (which uses only semantic notions) and the partial correctness theories (which use appropriate formulas, i.e. syntactic entities) is established by the following

**(14.42) Theorem.** *Two programs $p, q \in rP_\sigma$ are equivalent in $ext$ iff they have the same partial correctness theory in $ext$, i.e. $p \equiv_e q$ iff $PC(ext, p) = PC(ext, q)$.*

*Proof.* Let $X \rightleftharpoons var(p) \cup var(q)$. It is clear that if $D[\![p, X]\!]_{\mathcal{B}} = D[\![q, X]\!]_{\mathcal{B}}$ holds for any $\mathcal{B} \in Mod(ext)$ then $PC(ext, p) = PC(ext, q)$. In order to prove the other direction let us suppose that $Y = var(p)$ and let $Z$ be a copy of $Y$. Let $\phi \rightleftharpoons (Y = Z)$ and $\psi_p \rightleftharpoons D[\![p, X]\!](Z, Y)$. By the definition of $\psi_p$, $\mathcal{B} \models \phi\{p\}\psi_p$ for any model $\mathcal{B} \in Mod(ext)$, i.e $(\phi, \psi_p) \in PC(ext, p)$.

Therefore, by our supposition $PC(ext, p) = PC(ext, q)$ and hence $(\phi, \psi_p) \in PC(ext, q)$ also holds. However, because of the definition of $\psi_p$ for an arbitrary program $p' \in rP_\sigma$ with $var(p') \subseteq X$, $(\phi, \psi_p) \in PC(ext, p')$ iff for all $a \in Val_{\mathcal{B}}[X]$ and $b \in Val_{\mathcal{B}}[X']$, $(a, b) \in D[\![p', X]\!]_{\mathcal{B}}$ implies $(a, b) \in D[\![p, X]\!]_{\mathcal{B}}$. This means that $D[\![q, X]\!]_{\mathcal{B}} \subseteq D[\![p, X]\!]_{\mathcal{B}}$. Similarly we can prove that $D[\![p, X]\!]_{\mathcal{B}} \subseteq D[\![q, X]\!]_{\mathcal{B}}$. □

An important proof-theoretical advantage of $DL_\sigma^{ext}$ is provided by the following

**(14.43) Theorem.** *If $(\delta, ext, *)$ is a transitive extension maximal with respect to $(Ax, \Sigma)$ and the sets $Ax$ and $\Sigma$ are recursively enumerable then the set of pairs of programs equivalent in ext is recursively enumerable.*

*Proof.* By Definition (14.11) the denotation of any program $p \in rP_\sigma$ is definable in $Form_\delta$. To enumerate the pairs $(p, q)$ of programs denotationally equivalent in $ext$ is the same as to enumerate the consequences of $Ax \cup \Sigma$ of the form

$$\forall Y \forall Z\ D[\![p, var(p) \cup var(q)]\!](Y, Z) \leftrightarrow D[\![q, var(p) \cup var(q)]\!](Y, Z).$$

Since the correspondence between a program and the formula defining its denotation is recursive, the statement holds. □

**(14.44) Theorem.** *The set of pairs of programs that are equivalent in cst is not recursively enumerable.*

*Proof.* Recall the program $DE(\tau_1, \tau_2)$ from Lemma (12.1). Let us consider the following set

$$P \rightleftharpoons \{\textbf{if}\ \wedge Next' \rightarrow DE(\tau_1, \tau_2) \Box \neg \wedge Next' \rightarrow \textbf{loop fi}\ \mid \tau_1, \tau_2 \in Form_\eta\}.$$

It is not hard to prove that a program $p$ is equivalent to **loop** in any model of $cst$ iff the corresponding Diophantine equation $\tau_1 = \tau_2$ is not solvable in $\mathbb{N}$.

Now let us suppose that the program equivalence in $cst$ is recursively enumerable. In this case the set of those elements of $P$ which are equivalent to the program **loop** is also recursively enumerable, i.e. the set of unsolvable (in $\mathcal{N}$) equations is recursively enumerable. However, this contradicts Theorem (1.28). □

## 14.5 Constructing Transitive Extensions

Consider the following axiom and axiom schema:

$$\begin{aligned} Cl_\phi^+ &\rightleftharpoons \forall X \forall Y (\phi^*(X, Y, P) \rightarrow (X = Y) \vee \exists Z (\phi(X, Z, P) \wedge \phi^*(Z, Y, P))), \\ Ind_\sigma^+ &\rightleftharpoons Ind_\sigma \cup \{Cl_\phi^+ \mid \phi \in \Delta_\sigma\} \end{aligned}$$

We have proved in Lemma (14.8) that $Ind_\sigma^* \models Ind_\sigma^+$. Extending the notion introduced in Definition (14.41) let

$$PC(ext, Ax) \rightleftharpoons \{\phi\{p\}\psi \in rH_\sigma \mid Ax \models_{ext} \phi\{p\}\psi\},$$

where $Ax \subseteq Form_\delta$ and $(\delta, ext, *)$ is a given transitive extension. The main aim of this section is to prove that $PC(ns, Ind_\sigma) = PC(ns, Ind_\sigma^+)$. However, for this purpose we need some preliminary steps.

*In this section we always suppose that $Ax$ is such an axiom system that $\top \neq \bot \in Ax$.*

**(14.45) Lemma.** *Let $\mathcal{B} \in Mod(ns)$ be a fixed model. Let us define a new model $\tilde{\mathcal{B}}$ such that $\tilde{\mathcal{B}}\restriction_\sigma = \mathcal{B}\restriction_\sigma$ and for any relation symbol $\phi^*$ take $\phi^*_{\tilde{\mathcal{B}}} \rightleftharpoons \phi_{\mathcal{B}} \circ \phi^*_{\mathcal{B}} \cup id_{\mathcal{B}}$. Then $\tilde{\mathcal{B}} \in Mod(ns)$.*

*Proof.* It is clear that for any $\phi \in \Delta_\sigma$, $Cl_\phi$ holds in $\tilde{\mathcal{B}}$ since $\phi^*_{\mathcal{B}} \circ \phi_{\mathcal{B}} \subseteq \phi^*_{\tilde{\mathcal{B}}}$. To prove the induction axioms fix a $\phi \in \Delta_\sigma$, a $\psi \in Form_\sigma$ and a parameter valuation $k^P \in Val_{\mathcal{A}}[P]$. Let us consider the antecedent of $Tr_\phi(\psi)$:

$$(*)\;\; \psi(X,X,P) \wedge \forall Y \forall Z (\phi^*(X,Z,P) \wedge \phi(Z,Y,P) \wedge \psi(X,Z,P) \rightarrow \psi(X,Y,P)).$$

Let us suppose that $k_1 \in Val_{\mathcal{A}}[X]$ is such that (*) holds in $\tilde{\mathcal{B}}$. Let $Q^s \rightleftharpoons \{k_2 \in Val_{\tilde{\mathcal{B}}}[X] \mid \tilde{\mathcal{B}} \models \phi[k_1 + k_2[X/Y] + k^P]\}$. Let $P'$ be a new copy of $X$ and take $\hat{\psi} \rightleftharpoons \psi[P'/X]$. Fix a $k_2 \in Q^s$. By definition $\tilde{\mathcal{B}} \models \hat{\psi}[k_1 + k_2[X/Y] + k^P]$. Now one can check that the antecedent of $Tr_\phi(\hat{\psi})$ holds in $\mathcal{B}$ for valuation $k^P + k_2$. Now using the consequent of this axiom in $\mathcal{B}$ (for all $k_2 \in Q^s$) we can conclude the consequent of $Tr_\phi(\psi)$ in $\tilde{\mathcal{B}}$. □

Recall the notion of $\omega^+$-saturated models from Chang, Keisler [1973]. Let $\sigma$ be an arbitrary similarity type and let $P \subseteq V$ be an arbitrary set of variables such that $|P| < \omega^+$. For any $p \in P$ let $c_p$ be a new constant symbol with arity $sort(p)$. Let $\sigma^P$ denote the extension of $\sigma$ with all the constant symbols $c_p$ $(p \in P)$. If $\mathcal{A} \in Mod_\sigma$ is a given $\sigma$-type model and $k^P \in Val_{\mathcal{A}}[P]$ then $(\mathcal{A}, k^P)$ denotes the unique $\sigma^P$-type extension of $\mathcal{A}$ for which $c_p$ is interpreted as $k^P(p)$ $(p \in P)$.

A $\sigma$-type model is called $\omega^+$-saturated iff for each countable set of parameters $P$, for each finite set of variables $X$, for each set of formulas $\Phi \subseteq Form_{\sigma^P}$ and for each valuation $k^P \in Val_{\mathcal{A}}[P]$, if $C$ is a new copy of $X$, $X \cap P = \emptyset$, $var(\phi) \subseteq X \cup P$ $(\phi \in \Phi)$, and the set of formulas

$$Th((\mathcal{A}, k^P)) \cup \{\phi[C/X][c_p/p]_{p \in P} \mid \phi \in \Phi\}$$

is consistent then there is a valuation $k^X \in Val_{\mathcal{A}}[X]$ such that

$$(\mathcal{A}, k^X + k^P) \models \{\phi[C/X][c_p/p]_{p \in P} \mid \phi \in \Phi\}.$$

It is well known (see e.g. Chang, Keisler [1973] Lemma (5.1.4)) that any model $\mathcal{A}$ has an $\omega^+$-saturated elementary extension.

A model $\mathcal{B}$ is said to be an elementary extension of $\mathcal{A}$ iff $\mathcal{B}$ is an extension of $\mathcal{A}$ and for every formula $\phi$ and valuation $k$: $\mathcal{A} \models \phi[k]$ iff $\mathcal{B} \models \phi[k]$.

Now let us define the following sequences of models: $\mathcal{B}^0 \rightleftharpoons \mathcal{B}$ and for any $n \in \mathbb{N}$, $\mathcal{B}^{n+1} \rightleftharpoons \widetilde{\mathcal{B}^n}$. We remark that $\phi^*_{\mathcal{B}^n} = \phi^n_{\mathcal{B}} \circ \phi^*_{\mathcal{B}} \cup id_{\mathcal{B}}$. By using the above lemma one can prove by induction that $\mathcal{B}^n \in Mod_\sigma(ns)$ $(n \in \mathbb{N})$. Let us define the $\delta$-type model $\mathcal{B}^\infty$ by taking $\mathcal{B}^\infty(\phi^*) \rightleftharpoons \cap_{n \in \mathbb{N}} \mathcal{B}^n(\phi^*)$.

**(14.46) Lemma.** *Let us suppose that $\mathcal{B} \in Mod_\sigma(ns)$ is $\omega^+$-saturated. Then*

*(i) $\mathcal{B}^\infty \in Mod_\sigma(ns)$ and $\mathcal{B}^\infty \models Ind^+_\sigma$.*

*(ii) Let $\chi \in rH_\sigma$ be a given partial correctness formula. If for all $n \in \mathbb{N}$, $\mathcal{B}^n \not\models' \chi$ then $\mathcal{B}^\infty \not\models' \chi$.*

*Proof.* It is clear that $\mathcal{B}^\infty$ satisfies the closure axiom. To prove the induction schema let us suppose that there is a parameter valuation $k^P \in Val_\mathcal{B}[P]$ and valuation $k \in Val_\mathcal{B}[X]$ such that the antecedent (*) holds in $\mathcal{B}^\infty$ but its consequent fails in $\mathcal{B}$. This means that the antecedent of this axiom must fail in each model $\mathcal{B}^i$ ($i \in \mathbb{N}$). So there are valuations $k^i \in Val_\mathcal{B}[Y]$ such that

$$(**)\ \mathcal{B}^i \models \exists Z(\phi^*(X,Y,P)\wedge\phi(Y,Z,P)\wedge\psi(X,Y,P)\wedge\neg\psi(X,Z,P))[k+k^i+k^P].$$

Let $\theta \rightleftharpoons \phi(Y,Z,P)\wedge\psi(X,Y,P)\wedge\neg\psi(X,Z,P)$. By using (**) and the fact that for all $n \in \mathbb{N}$, $\phi^*_{n+1} \subseteq \phi^*_n$ we get that any finite subset of the set

$$\{(\phi^n \circ \phi^* \cup id)(X,Y,P) \wedge \theta \wedge \psi(X,X,P) \mid n \in \mathbb{N}\}$$

is satisfiable in $\mathcal{B}$. Since $\mathcal{B}$ is $\omega^+$-saturated the whole set is satisfiable in $\mathcal{B}$. However, if $\ell_X$ and $\ell_Y$ satisfy all the above formulas then the antecedent of (*) in $\mathcal{B}^\infty$ does not hold. We have a contradiction, i.e. we have proved that $\mathcal{B}^\infty$ belongs to $Mod_\sigma(ns)$. We remark that $\mathcal{B}^\infty \models Cl^+_\phi$ is obvious. □

**(14.47) Theorem.** *Let $Ax \subseteq Form_\sigma$. Then*

$$PC(ns, Ax \cup Ind_\sigma) = PC(ns, Ax \cup Ind^+_\sigma).$$

*Proof.* We remark that $PC(ns, Ax \cup Ind_\sigma) = PC(ns, Ax)$. So we can reformulate the statement of the theorem as follows: $Ind^+_\sigma$ is conservative over $Ind_\sigma$ with respect to the partial correctness assertions. It is obvious that $PC(ns, Ax \cup Ind_\sigma) \subseteq PC(ns, Ax \cup Ind^+_\sigma)$. To prove the other direction let us suppose that there is a $\chi \in rH_\sigma$ such that $\chi \in PC(ns, Ax \cup Ind^+_\sigma) \setminus PC(ns, Ax \cup Ind_\sigma)$. We can suppose that

$$\chi \rightleftharpoons \phi\{\textbf{while } p^\alpha \textbf{ do } p'' \textbf{ od}\}\psi.$$

Let $p \rightleftharpoons$ **while** $p^\alpha$ **do** $p''$ **od** and let $\Xi \rightleftharpoons D[\![p'', Y]\!] \in \Delta_\sigma$. Let $\Xi$ be as in Definition (14.11). It is not hard to check that $\tilde{\mathcal{B}} \models' \chi$ iff $\mathcal{B} \models' \tilde{\phi}\{p\}\psi$. Take $\tilde{\phi}(Y) \rightleftharpoons \exists Z(\phi(Z) \wedge \Xi(Z,Y))$. First we prove that there is a model $\mathcal{B} \in Mod_\sigma(ns)$ such that $\mathcal{B} \models Ax$ but $\tilde{\mathcal{B}} \not\models_{ns} \chi$. For a contradiction let us suppose that for all $\mathcal{B} \in Mod_\sigma(ns)$ if $\mathcal{B} \models Ax$ then $\tilde{\mathcal{B}} \models_{ns} \chi$. This means that $Ind_\sigma \cup Ax \models_{ns} \tilde{\phi}\{p\}\psi$. By Theorem (14.34), $\tilde{\phi}\{p\}\psi$ is Floyd-Hoare provable in Ax, and so let $\kappa$ be the corresponding invariant of $p''$ in $Ax$. Hence

(i) $Ind_\sigma \cup Ax \models \tilde{\phi} \to \kappa$;
(ii) $Ind_\sigma \cup Ax \models \kappa(X) \wedge p^\alpha \wedge \Xi(X,X') \to \kappa(X')$;
(iii) $Ind_\sigma \cup Ax \models \kappa(X) \wedge \neg p^\alpha \to \psi(X)$.

By using this $\kappa$ we can give a Floyd-Hoare proof for $\chi$ as well. Indeed, take $\tilde{\kappa} \rightleftharpoons \phi \vee \kappa$.

(a) $Ind_\sigma \cup Ax \models \phi \to \tilde{\kappa}$ is obvious from the definition of $\tilde{\kappa}$.

(b) Let us suppose that $\tilde{\kappa}(X) \wedge \Xi(X, X')$ is true. If $\kappa$ is also true then (ii) implies $\kappa(X')$ and therefore $\tilde{\kappa}(X')$. Now let us suppose that $\phi(X)$ is true. Then $\tilde{\phi}(X')$ is true and by (i) we again get $\kappa(X')$.

(c) Let us suppose that $\tilde{\kappa}(X) \wedge \Xi(X, X)$ is true. Then either $\kappa(X)$ is true or $\tilde{\phi}(X)$ is true and by (i) $\kappa(X)$ follows. Using (iii) we get that $\psi(X)$ is also true.

So we have proved that $Ax \vdash_H \chi$, which is a contradiction. Hence there is a model $\mathcal{B}$ with the desired properties.

In a similar way, by induction we can prove that if for all $\mathcal{B} \in Mod(Ax)$ $\mathcal{B}^{n+1} \models' \chi$ then for all $\mathcal{B} \in Mod(Ax)$ $\mathcal{B}^n \models' \chi$. Using the previously constructied $\mathcal{B}$ we get that for each $n \in \mathbb{N}$ we can construct a model $\mathcal{C}_n$ such that $\mathcal{C}_n \models Ax$ and $(\mathcal{C}_n)^n \not\models' \chi$.

Fix an $n \in \mathbb{N}$. It is obvious from the construction $\mathcal{B}^n$ that there is a formula $\chi^n \in SForm_\sigma$ (not depending on $\mathcal{B}$) such that $\mathcal{B}^n \models \neg\chi$ iff $\mathcal{B} \models \chi^n$. Using the properties of $\mathcal{C}_n$ we get that for all $i \geq n$, $C_i \models \chi^n$. Let $\mathcal{C} \rightleftharpoons \prod_{n\in\mathbb{N}} \mathcal{C}_n/D$ be an ultraproduct of the models $C_n$ by a nonprincipal ultrafilter. It is obvious that $\mathcal{C} \models Ax \cup Ind_\sigma \cup \neg\chi$. Moreover, for all $n \in \mathbb{N}$, $\mathcal{C} \models \neg\chi^n$. Let $\mathcal{B}$ be an $\omega^+$-saturated elementary extension of $\mathcal{C}$. By definition $\mathcal{B} \in Mod(ns)$, $\mathcal{B} \models Ax \cup \neg\chi$ and for all $n \in \mathbb{N}$, $\mathcal{B} \models \neg\chi^n$. This means that for all $n \in \mathbb{N}$, $\mathcal{B}^n \models \neg\chi$. Using Lemma (14.46) we get that $\mathcal{B}^\infty \models \neg\chi$ and $\mathcal{B} \models Ax \cup Ind_\sigma^+$. This last fact leads to a contradiction. □

**(14.48) Definition.** *Let us fix a $\Delta$-formula $(\phi, X, X', \emptyset)$ without parameters. Let $\mathcal{B} \in Mod_\sigma(ns)$ and a valuation $k \in Val_\mathcal{B}[X]$ be given. A many-sorted relation $Q \subseteq Val_\mathcal{B}[X]$ is called a weakly transitive extension of $\phi$ in $\mathcal{B}$ starting from $k$ iff:*

*(i) for each $\ell \in Q$ there is an $\ell'$ such that $\mathcal{B} \models \phi[\ell, \ell'[X/X']]$;*

*(ii) for each first-order definable (in $\mathcal{B}$) relation $R \subseteq Val_\mathcal{B}[X]$ if $k \in R$ and for each $\ell$, $\ell' \in Q$: $\ell \in R$ and $\mathcal{B} \models \phi[\ell, \ell'[X/X']]$ implies $\ell \in R$ then $Q \subseteq R$.*

*A weakly transitive extension $Q$ of $\phi$ in $\mathcal{B}$ starting from $k$ is called deterministic iff there is a* unique *sequence $k_i \in Q$ ($i \in \mathbb{N}$) such that $k_0 = k$ and for each $i \in \mathbb{N}$, $\mathcal{B} \models \phi[k_i, k_{i+1}[X/X']]$.*

**(14.49) Lemma.** *Let us suppose that for each $n \in \mathbb{N}$ $R_i$ is a (parametrically) first-order definable weakly transitive extension of $\phi$ in $\mathcal{B}$ starting from $k$ such that $R_{n+1} \subseteq R_n$. Let us suppose that $\mathcal{B}$ is $\omega^+$-saturated. Then $\bigcap_{n\in\mathbb{N}} R_n$ is also a weakly transitive extension of $\phi$ in $\mathcal{B}$ with respect to $k$.*

**(14.50) Theorem.** *Let us suppose that $Ax \not\vdash_H \phi\{p\}\psi$, where*

$$p \rightleftharpoons \textbf{while } p^\alpha \textbf{ do } p'' \textbf{ od}.$$

*Let $\Xi \rightleftharpoons D[\![p'', Y]\!]$. Then there is a model $\mathcal{B} \in Mod_\sigma(ns)$, there are two valuations $k$, $\ell \in Val_\mathcal{B}[Y]$ and there is a deterministic weakly transitive extension $R$ of $\Xi$ in $\mathcal{B}$ with respect to $k$ such that*

- $\mathcal{B} \models \phi[k]$ *but* $\mathcal{B} \models \neg\psi[\ell]$;
- $\ell \in R$.

*Proof.* We recall Theorem (14.47) which states that

$$PC(ns, Ax) = PC(ns, Ind_\sigma^+ \cup Ax).$$

Now let $\mathcal{B}$ be a model such that $\mathcal{B} \not\models' \phi\{p\}\psi$ and $\mathcal{B} \models Ind_\sigma^+$. Let $\Xi \rightleftharpoons D[\![p'', X]\!]$. We can suppose that $\mathcal{B}$ is $\omega^+$-saturated. Let $k_0, \ell \in Val_{\mathcal{A}}[X]$ be two valuations which prove that $\mathcal{B} \not\models' \phi\{p\}\psi$. Then:

- $\mathcal{B} \models \phi[k_0]$;
- $\mathcal{B} \models \neg\psi[\ell]$.
- $\mathcal{B} \models D[\![p, X]\!][k_1, \ell[X/X']]$, or equivalently
$$\mathcal{B} \models \left(\Xi^*(X, X') \wedge \neg p^\alpha[X'/X]\right)\left[k_1, \ell[X/X']\right].$$

Let $k_i$ ($i \in \mathbb{N}$, $i \geq 1$) be a sequence of valuations such that

(i) $\Xi^*\left[k_i, \ell[X'/X]\right]$;
(ii) $\Xi\left[k_i, k_{i+1}[X'/X]\right]$ ($i \in \mathbb{N}$).

We construct a sequence $Q_i$ ($i \in \mathbb{N}$) of weakly transitive extensions of $\Xi$ in $\mathcal{B}$ starting from $k_1$. Let us consider the following relation $Q_i$ in the model $\mathcal{B}$ by taking:

$$Q_i \rightleftharpoons \{k_j \mid j \leq i\} \cup \{k \mid \mathcal{B} \models \Xi^*[k_i, k[X'/X]]\}.$$

It is not hard to prove that there is a $\sigma$-type first-order formula, say $\theta_i$, which defines by appropriately chosen parameters the many-sorted relation $Q_i$ in $\mathcal{B}$. Let $R$ be an arbitrary first-order definable relation in $\mathcal{B}$, and let $\psi$ be the formula which defines the relation $R$ in $\mathcal{B}$. Using axiom $Tr_\Xi(\theta_i \wedge \psi)$ we can prove that property (ii) of Definition (14.48) holds. This means that $Q_i$ is a weakly transitive extension of $\Xi$ in $\mathcal{B}$ starting from $k_1$. (Moreover, if we replace $\Xi_{\mathcal{B}}^*$ for $Q_i$ then we again get a model of $Ind_\sigma^+$.) By axiom $Cl_\Xi^+$ we get that $\ell \in Q_i$ and $Q_{i+1} \subseteq Q_i$ ($i \in \mathbb{N}$). Let $R \rightleftharpoons \cap_{i \in \mathbb{N}} Q_i$. By Lemma (14.49) $R$ is also a weakly transitive extension of $\Xi$ in $\mathcal{B}$ starting from $k_1$. $\ell \in R$ because of $\ell \in Q_i$ ($i \in \mathbb{N}$). From the construction of $R$ and $Q_i$ ($i \in \mathbb{N}$) we can conclude that $R$ is deterministic. So $R$ is appropriate. □

Chapter 15

# Definable Denotational Semantics

In this chapter we show how an appropriate first-order language can be built up to describe the properties of $rP^1_\sigma$-programs. Here we also use the logical tools introduced in Chapter 13, and the method of the development of the required dynamic logics is similar to that used in the previous chapter. We have proved in Part I that $rP^1_\sigma \approx I$ for a one-sorted similarity type $\sigma$. Thus first we present a logic within which any fixed-point equation of the form $R(X) \equiv \phi(X, P)$ ($\phi \in \Sigma^+(\sigma, R)$) has a solution. Secondly, we show how the semantics of $rP^1_\sigma$ can be defined, and using this definition we give an appropriate semantic function $\hat{\cdot} : rD^1_\sigma \to Form_\delta$. Finally we give similar characterizations and completeness results to those in Chapter 14.

As in Chapter 14, here we will also use the graph representation of programs in the construction of the semantic functions. Therefore, to obtain first-order definability we follow the method of coding the elements of *Label*, supposing that the similarity type $\sigma$ contains two different ground terms $\top$ and $\bot$ of the same sort and supposing that the formula $\top \neq \bot$ is true in the models under consideration.

Let us suppose that for any $i \in \mathbb{N}$ and for any finite $X \subseteq V_{sort\ \sigma}$ a new relation symbol $R^i_X$ of sort $X$ is given. Let

$$\Omega \rightleftharpoons \{R^i_X \mid i \in \mathbb{N}, X \subseteq V_{sort\ \sigma} \text{ is finite}\}.$$

We recall the definition of positive existential formulas from Chapter 2. Let

$$\begin{aligned}
\Sigma^+_\sigma &\rightleftharpoons \cup\{\Sigma^+(\sigma; R) \mid R \in \Omega\},\\
I^+(\sigma; R^i_X) &\rightleftharpoons \{\phi \in \Sigma^+(\sigma; R^i_X) \mid var(\phi) \subseteq X\} \quad (R^i_X \in \Omega)\\
I^+_\sigma &\rightleftharpoons \cup\{I^+(\sigma; R) \mid R \in \Omega\}.
\end{aligned}$$

**(15.1) Definition.** *Let us fix a similarity type $\sigma$. A triplet $(\delta, ext, \nabla)$ is called an inductive extension of $\sigma$ iff*
*(i) $(\delta, ext)$ is an extension of $\sigma$ (see Definition (5.1)) and $\Omega \subseteq \delta$;*
*(ii) $\nabla : I^+_\sigma \to Form_\delta$ is a function such that for each $\phi \in I^+_\sigma$ $var(\nabla\phi) \subseteq var(\phi)$ (i.e. if $\phi \in I^+(\sigma; R^i_X)$ for an $R^i_X \in \Omega$ then $var(\nabla\phi) \subseteq X$).*

Note that here we do not distinguish three groups $X$, $X'$ and $P$ of variables as we did in Definition (14.3) because we can obtain all necessary cases by dividing $X$ appropriately.

We introduce two axiom systems $\nabla Ind_\sigma$ and $\nabla Ind^*_\sigma$ which provide two different axiomatizations of the properties of inductive definitions.

**(15.2) Definition.** *Let $(\delta, ext, \nabla)$ be an inductive extension of $\sigma$. For each $R^i_X \in \Omega$ and $\phi \in I^+(\sigma; R^i_X)$ let us consider the following axiom schemas:*

$Cl'_\phi$ *(closure property of $\phi$):*

$$\phi[\nabla\phi/R^i_X] \to \nabla\phi$$

$Tr'_\phi(\psi)$*(transfinite induction on $\psi$ with respect to $\nabla\phi$):*

$$\Big(\forall X \forall Y_1 ... \forall Y_k (\bigwedge_{j=1}^{k} (\nabla\phi \wedge \psi)[Y_j/X] \wedge \phi[\vee_{j=1}^{k} X = Y_j/R^i_X] \to \psi) \wedge$$

$$\forall X(\phi[false/R^i_X] \to \psi)\Big) \to \forall X(\nabla\phi \to \psi)$$

*where $k$ is the rank of $\phi$, and for each $j = 1, ..., k$, $Y_i$ is a new copy of $X$. We remark that $\psi$ can contain variables other than $X$. These variables can be considered as parameters. Because of the definition of validity there is a "hidden" universal quantification over parameters in the axiom schema $Tr'_\phi(\psi)$.*

$\nabla Ind_\sigma \rightleftharpoons \{Cl'_\phi \mid \phi \in I^+_\sigma\} \cup \{Tr'_\phi(\psi) \mid \phi \in I^+_\sigma, \psi \in Form_\sigma\}$.

*Let $\nabla Form_\sigma$ be the minimal subset of $Form_\delta$ satisfying the following properties:*

- $Form_\sigma \subseteq \nabla Form_\sigma$;
- $\phi \in I^+_\sigma$ *implies that* $\nabla\phi \in \nabla Form_\sigma$;
- $\phi \in \nabla Form_\sigma$, *$Y$ is an arbitrary copy of* $X \rightleftharpoons var(\phi)$ *implies* $\phi[Y/X] \in \nabla Form_\sigma$;
- $\nabla Form_\sigma$ *is closed under Boolean combinations and quantifications over variables belonging to* $V_{sort\,\sigma}$.

$\nabla Ind^*_\sigma \rightleftharpoons \{Cl'_\phi \mid \phi \in I^+_\sigma\} \cup \{Tr'_\phi(\psi) \mid \phi \in I^+_\sigma, \psi \in \nabla Form_\sigma\}$.

Let $E \subseteq \Omega \times \Sigma^+_\sigma$ be a finite set. Let us suppose that $E = \{(R_i, \phi_i) \mid i \leq n\}$. For $i = 1, ..., n$ let $X_i \rightleftharpoons ar(R_i)$, $P_i \rightleftharpoons var(\phi_i) \setminus X_i$. If $\phi_i \in \Sigma^+(\sigma; R_1, ..., R_n)$ for $i = 1, ..., n$, $(\cup_{i=1}^n X_i) \cap (\cup_{i=1}^n P_i) = \emptyset$ and $R_i \neq R_j$ $(i \neq j)$ then the set $E$ is called a *fixed-point equation system* (or simply *fixed-point equation* in the case of $n = 1$). Elements of $(\cup_{i=1}^n P_i)$ are called *parameters*.

A *solution* of this equation system in *ext* is a function $\alpha : \{R_i \mid i \leq n\} \to \nabla Form_\sigma$ such that for each $i$ $(1 \leq i \leq n)$:

$$(*) \qquad ext \models \alpha(R_i) \leftrightarrow \phi_i[\alpha(R_j)/R_j]_{j=1}^n.$$

We define an ordering on the solutions. Let $\alpha$, $\beta$ be two solutions in *ext* of the equation system $E$. The solution $\alpha$ is less than or equal to the solution $\beta$ (written as $\alpha \subseteq \beta$) iff for each $i$ $(1 \leq i \leq n)$:

$$ext \models \alpha(R_i) \to \beta(R_i).$$

An equation system $E \subseteq \Omega \times \Sigma_\sigma^+$ is written in the form:

$$\begin{cases} R_1(X_1) & \equiv & \phi_1(X_1, P_1) \\ \vdots & \vdots & \vdots \\ R_n(X_n) & \equiv & \phi_n(X_n, P_n) \end{cases}$$

We remark that for a small value of $n$, say 2, we write a solution in the form $(\alpha_1, \alpha_2)$, which means that we write $\alpha_i$ instead of $\alpha(R_i)$.

**(15.3) Lemma.**

(i) *Let $(\delta, ext, \nabla)$ be an inductive extension of $\sigma$ such that $ext \models \nabla Ind_\sigma$. Let $\phi \in I^+(\sigma; R)$, where $R \in \Omega$. For each $\kappa \in Form_\sigma$ if $ext \models \phi[\kappa/R] \to \kappa$ then $ext \models \nabla\phi \to \kappa$. Thus $\nabla\phi$ is less than or equal to any $Form_\sigma$-definable fixed-point in $ext$ of the equation $R \equiv \phi$.*

(ii) *Let $(\delta, ext, \nabla)$ be an inductive extension such that $ext \models \nabla Ind^*_\sigma$. Let $\phi \in I^+(\sigma; R)$, where $R \in \Omega$. $\nabla\phi$ is the least $\nabla Form_\sigma$-definable solution of the fixed-point equation $R(X) \equiv \phi$ $(X \rightleftharpoons ar(R))$ in $ext$.*

*Proof.*

(i) Let us suppose that the assumptions of statement (i) hold. In this case we use the induction axiom schema $Tr'_\phi(\kappa)$ $(\in \nabla Ind_\sigma)$. We check first that the antecedent of this axiom schema holds. Since $\phi$ is positive with respect to $R$ we get that $ext \models \forall X(\phi[false/R] \to \phi[\kappa/R])$. By $ext \models \forall X(\phi[\kappa/R] \to \kappa)$ we can conclude that $ext \models \forall X(\phi[false/R] \to \kappa)$. Now let us suppose that

$$\bigwedge_{i=1}^{k} (\nabla\phi \wedge \kappa)[Y_i/X] \wedge \phi[\vee_{i=1}^{k} X = Y_i/R]$$

holds in $ext$. By using the first member of this conjunction we get that $\vee_{i=1}^{k} X = Y_i \to \kappa$ is true in $ext$. So using monotonicity again we can conclude that $ext \models \phi[\vee_{i=1}^{k} X = Y_i/R] \to \phi[\kappa/R]$. Using the assumption about $\kappa$ and the second member of the conjunction above we get that $ext \models \kappa$. So we have proved that the antecedent of the induction axiom $Tr'_\phi(\kappa)$ holds. Using the consequent of the same axiom schema we get that $ext \models \nabla\phi \to \kappa$. We remark that we cannot prove that $\nabla\phi$ itself is a fixed-point of the equation $R(X) \equiv \phi$ in $ext$.

(ii) We prove that $\nabla\phi$ *is* a fixed-point of the equation $R(X) \equiv \phi$. By the positivity of $\phi$ with respect to $R$ and by using $Cl'_\phi$

$$ext \models \phi[\phi[\nabla\phi/R]/R] \to \phi[\nabla\phi/R].$$

Taking $\kappa \rightleftharpoons \phi[\nabla\phi/R]$ and applying (i) we get that $ext \models \nabla\phi \to \phi[\nabla\phi/R]$. ($Tr'_\phi(\kappa)$ could be applied, because $ext \models \nabla Ind^*_\sigma$.) Hence by the use of $Cl'_\phi$ again, $ext \models \nabla\phi \leftrightarrow \phi[\nabla\phi/R]$.

The fact that $\nabla\phi$ is the least $\nabla Form_\sigma$-definable fixed-point can be proved similarly as in (i).

□

The parametric version of the fixed-point theorem of Lemma (15.3) (ii) is proved in the following

**(15.4) Lemma.** *Fix an inductive extension $(\delta, ext, \nabla)$ of the similarity type $\sigma$ such that $ext \models \nabla Ind^*_\sigma$. Let $R \in \Omega$, $\phi \in \Sigma^+(\sigma; R)$ be given. The fixed-point equation*

$$(*) \qquad R(X) \quad \equiv \quad \phi(X, P)$$

*has a least $\nabla Form_\sigma$-definable solution in ext which is denoted by $(Y_R\phi)$.*

*Proof.* Let us suppose that $\phi$ is equivalent to the following formula (cf. Theorem (2.4)):

$$\exists Y \exists U_1 ... \exists U_k \Big( (\Theta_1(X, Y, U_1, ..., U_k, P) \wedge \bigwedge_{i=1}^{k} R(U_i)) \vee \Theta_2(X, Y, P) \Big).$$

Construct the following formula $\phi^P$:

$$\exists Y \exists U_1 \exists P_1 ... \exists U_k \exists P_k \Big( (\Theta_1(X, Y, U_1, ..., U_k, P) \wedge \bigwedge_{i=1}^{k} P_i = P \wedge \bigwedge_{i=1}^{k} Q(U_i, P_i)) \vee \Theta_2(X, Y, P) \Big)$$

It is obvious that $var(\phi^P) \subseteq ar(Q)$, i.e. $\phi^P \in I^+(\sigma, Q)$. Take $(Y_R\phi) \rightleftharpoons \nabla\phi^P$. It is an easy exercise to prove that this is indeed the least $\nabla Form_\sigma$-definable solution of the equation (*) in *ext*. □

**(15.5) Theorem.** *For $n \geq 1$ any equation system*

$$(1) \qquad \begin{cases} R_1(X_1) & \equiv & \phi_1(X_1, P_1) \\ \vdots & \vdots & \vdots \\ R_n(X_n) & \equiv & \phi_n(X_n, P_n) \end{cases}$$

*has a least $\nabla Form_\sigma$-definable solution in an inductive extension ext satisfying $\nabla Ind^*_\sigma \cup \{\top \neq \bot\}$.*

*Proof.* For the sake of convenience let $n = 2$. We can suppose that $X_1 \cap X_2 = \emptyset$. Let $n$ be a new variable such that $sort(n) \rightleftharpoons sort(\top)$ and let $Q \in \Omega$ be such that $ar(Q) \rightleftharpoons (n, X_1, X_2, P_1 \cup P_2)$. Let $\hat{X}_1$, $\hat{X}_2$ be new copies of $X_1$ and $X_2$, respectively. Consider the following equation

$$Q \equiv (n = \top \wedge \psi_1) \vee (n = \bot \wedge \psi_2) \tag{2}$$

where $\psi_1$ and $\psi_2$ are the following formulas:

$$\psi_1 \rightleftharpoons \phi_1[\exists \hat{X}_2\, Q(\top, X_1, \hat{X}_2, P_1 \cup P_2)/R_1, \exists \hat{X}_1\, Q(\bot, \hat{X}_1, X_2, P_1 \cup P_2)/R_2]$$
$$\psi_2 \rightleftharpoons \phi_2[\exists \hat{X}_2\, Q(\top, X_1, \hat{X}_2, P_1 \cup P_2)/R_1, \exists \hat{X}_1\, Q(\bot, \hat{X}_1, X_2, P_1 \cup P_2)/R_2]$$

Let $\Phi$ be the formula on the right hand side of the equation (2). By Lemma (15.4) let $\alpha \rightleftharpoons (Y_Q\Phi)$ be the least $\nabla Form_\sigma$-definable solution of (2) in *ext*. Take

$$\alpha_1 \rightleftharpoons \exists \hat{X}_2\, \alpha(\top, X_1, \hat{X}_2, P_1 \cup P_2)$$
$$\alpha_2 \rightleftharpoons \exists \hat{X}_1\, \alpha(\bot, \hat{X}_1, X_2, P_1 \cup P_2).$$

It is an easy exercise to prove that in *ext* the pair $(\alpha_1, \alpha_2)$ is a solution of (1). To prove that this is the least $\nabla Form_\sigma$-definable solution let $(\beta_1, \beta_2)$ be another solution of (1) in *ext*. Take

$$\beta \rightleftharpoons (n = \top \wedge \beta_1) \vee (n = \bot \wedge \beta_2).$$

By using first-order equivalences and the axiom $\{\top \neq \bot\}$ we get that $\beta$ is also a solution of (2). Therefore $\alpha \subseteq \beta$. Now using the same axioms and logical equivalences we get that $(\alpha_1, \alpha_2) \subseteq (\beta_1, \beta_2)$. Thus we have proved that $(\alpha_1, \alpha_2)$ is the least $\nabla Form_\sigma$-definable solution in $\nabla Ind^*_\sigma \cup \{\top \neq \bot\}$. □

We show how the "standard" notion of inductive definitions can be defined as a special inductive extension.

**(15.6) Definition.** *Fix a similarity type $\sigma$. The standard inductive extension $(\sigma^\nabla, ist, \nabla)$ of $\sigma$ is defined as follows*

*(i)* $\sigma^\nabla \rightleftharpoons \sigma \cup \{\hat{\phi} \mid \phi \in I^+_\sigma\}$, *where if $\phi \in I^+(\sigma; R^i_X)$ then $\hat{\phi}$ is a new relation symbol of the sort $X$;*

*(ii) for any $\phi \in I^+_\sigma$ let $\nabla\phi \rightleftharpoons \hat{\phi}(X)$;*

*(iii) for each $\mathcal{A} \in Mod_\sigma$, $ist(\mathcal{A})$ contains exactly one model $\mathcal{B}$ for which the following hold:*

- *the $\sigma$-type reduct of $\mathcal{B}$ is equal to $\mathcal{A}$;*
- *for every formula $\phi \in I^+_\sigma$ the relation $\hat{\phi}_\mathcal{B}$ is the relation ${}_\mathcal{A}I_\phi$ defined inductively in $\mathcal{A}$ by the formula $\phi$.*

**(15.7) Lemma.** $ist \models \nabla Ind^*_\sigma$.

*Proof.* This follows directly from the fact that for any $\phi \in I^+_\sigma$, the closure ordinal of the operator ${}_\mathcal{A}\Gamma_\phi$ is $\omega_0$. Thus any axiom of $\nabla Ind^*_\sigma$ can be proved by induction on $\mathbb{N}$. □

We show how an arbitrary inductive extension $(\delta, ext, \nabla)$ generates a transitive extension. Let $\phi(X, X', P)$ be a given $\Delta$-formula. Let $R \in \Omega$ be a relation symbol with arity $(X, X', P)$. Let

$$\tilde{\phi}(X, X', P) \rightleftharpoons \exists Y((\phi(Y, X', P) \wedge R(X, Y, P)) \vee (X = X').$$

It is clear that $rank\ \tilde{\phi} = 1$.

Define $\phi^* \rightleftharpoons \nabla\tilde{\phi}$. It is clear that $\phi^* \in Form_\delta$. Taking $ext^\nabla \rightleftharpoons ext$ we have defined a transitive extension $(\delta, ext^\nabla, *)$.

**(15.8) Theorem.** *Let $(\delta, ext, \nabla)$ be an inductive extension and let $(\delta, ext^\nabla, *)$ be the transitive extension generated by it.*

*(i) $ext \models \nabla Ind_\sigma$ implies $ext^\nabla \models Ind_\sigma$;*
*(ii) $ext \models \nabla Ind^*_\sigma$ implies $ext^\nabla \models Ind^*_\sigma$.*

*Proof.* It is clear that $*$ is a function of the appropriate form. For a fixed $\phi \in \Delta_\sigma$ the axiom schema $Cl_\phi$ can be proved by using the axiom schema $Cl'_{\tilde{\phi}}$. To prove the transfinite induction axioms let $\psi \in Form_\delta$. It is an easy but tiresome exercise to prove that the axiom schema $Tr'_{\tilde{\phi}}(\psi)$ implies the axiom schema $Tr_\phi(\psi)$. □

Let $g \in rG^1_\sigma$ be arbitrary and let $X \rightleftharpoons var(g)$. Let us suppose that there is a set $Type \rightleftharpoons \{N, M, P, B\}$ with four distinct elements disjoint from *Label*. Intuitively the elements of *Type* correspond to different types of traces considered in the proof of Theorem (8.12).

Let $m \rightleftharpoons |Type \cup node(g)|$. Using terms $\top$, $\bot$ and Lemma (4.28) there are $m$ distinct vectors of ground terms $C_1,...,C_m$ such that if $\top \neq \bot$ then for every $i$, $j$ $(1 \le i < j \le m)$ $C_i \neq C_j$ and $|C_i| = |C_j|$. Let $L$ be a set of variables containing $|C_1|$-many $sort(\top)$-sorted variables. Let $L_1$ and $L_2$ be two new copies of $L$. Let $\iota : Type \cup node(g) \to m$ be a fixed bijection. Instead of $C_{\iota(a)+1}$ we simply write $a$, and identify any element $a \in Type \cup node(g)$ with its code $C_{\iota(a)}$.

Let $X'$, $Y$, $Z_1,...,Z_4$ be six new copies of $X$. For $i = 1,...,4$ let $\iota_i : X \to Z_i$ be the corresponding bijection. Let $\Psi_1(g)$ be the disjunction of the following $\sigma$-type formulas:

$$\bigvee_{u \in \{N,M\}} (L = u) \wedge (a = c) \wedge (X = X'),$$

$$(L = N) \wedge \bigvee_{\substack{b \in node(g) \\ g(b,c) \in T^0}} \exists Y\Big(\Upsilon(N, a, b, X, Y) \wedge onestep_g((Y, b), (X', c))\Big),$$

$$(L = M) \wedge \bigvee_{\substack{b \in node(g) \\ g(b,c) \in T^0 \cup T^+}} \exists Y\Big(\Upsilon(M, a, b, X, Y) \wedge onestep_g((Y, b), (X', c))\Big),$$

$$(L = P) \wedge \Upsilon(M, a, c, X, X'),$$
$$(L = P) \wedge \Upsilon(B, a, c, X, X'),$$
$$(L = P) \wedge \bigvee_{b \in node(g)} \exists Y (\Upsilon(P, a, b, X, Y) \wedge \Upsilon(P, b, c, Y.X')),$$
$$(L = B) \wedge \Upsilon(N, a, c, X, X'),$$
$$(L = B) \wedge \bigvee_{\substack{c_1,c_2,c_3,c_4 \in node(g) \\ g(c_1,c_2)=Push_1(\tau) \in T^+ \\ g(c_3,c_4)=Pop_1(x) \in T^-}} \exists Z_1 ... \exists Z_4 \Big( \Upsilon(N, a, c_1, X, Z_1) \wedge (Z_1 = Z_2) \wedge$$
$$\Upsilon(B, c_2, c_3, Z_2, Z_3) \wedge \iota_4(x) = \tau[Z_1/X] \wedge \bigwedge \{\iota_4(v) = \iota_3(v) \mid v \in X \setminus \{x\}\} \wedge$$
$$\Upsilon(N, c_4, c, Z_4, X')\Big).$$

It is clear that $var(\Psi_1(g)) \subseteq X \cup X' \cup L$ and $\Psi_1(g) \in I^+(\sigma; \Upsilon)$. Now take

$$\Psi(g) \rightleftharpoons \bigvee_{a,c \in node(g)} (L_1 = a \wedge L_2 = c \wedge \Psi_1(g)).$$

It is obvious that $\Psi(g) \in \Sigma^+(\sigma; \Upsilon)$ and $var(\Psi(g)) \subseteq X \cup X' \cup L \cup L_1 \cup L_2$.

For any program $p \in rP^1_\sigma \setminus rP_\sigma$ let $pos(p)$ be such a program that $p \equiv pos(p)(\text{mod } var(p))$, any trace of $pos(p)$ is positive and $pos(p)$ does not contain the command $Empty_1$. By Lemma (8.11) such a program exists.

We note that $\Psi(g)$ defined above is a rewritten version of the recursive equations given in the proof of Theorem (8.12). This means that the following statement is a simple corollary of this theorem.

**(15.9) Corollary.** *Let $p \in rP^1_\sigma$ and $\mathcal{A} \in Mod_\sigma$ be fixed. Let $g \rightleftharpoons gr(pos(p))$. If $\mathcal{A} \models \top \neq \bot$ then*

$$Den_{\mathcal{A}}[\![p, var(p)]\!] = {}_{\mathcal{A}}I_{\Psi(g)} \restriction \{(P, start_g, stop_g)\} \times Val_{\mathcal{A}}[X, X'].$$

We recall Theorem (8.9). Let $\phi \in \Sigma^+(\sigma; R)$ be an arbitrary formula. Let $p(\phi) \in rP^1_\sigma$ be the program which computes in an arbitrary model $\mathcal{A} \in rP^1_\sigma$ the relation ${}_{\mathcal{A}}I_\phi$ inductively defined by $\phi$ in $\mathcal{A}$.

**(15.10) Theorem.** *Let $\sigma$ be a one-sorted similarity type. The denotation of $rP^1_\sigma$-programs is definable in any inductive extension $(\sigma^\nabla, ext, \nabla)$ containing the inductive extension ist. That is, for any program $p \in rP^1_\sigma$ and finite $X \supseteq var(p)$ there is a formula $D_1[\![p, X]\!]$ such that*

*(i) for each $p \in rP^1_\sigma$, $D_1[\![p, X]\!] \in \nabla Form_\sigma$;*
*(ii) for each $p \in rP_\sigma$, $D_1[\![p, X]\!] = D[\![p, X]\!]$;*
*(iii) for any model $\mathcal{A} \in Mod_\sigma$, $\mathcal{B} \in st(\mathcal{A}) \subseteq ext(\mathcal{A})$ and $p \in rP^1_\sigma$ if $\mathcal{A} \models \top \neq \bot$ then $Den_{\mathcal{A}}[\![p, X]\!] = D_1[\![p, X]\!]_{\mathcal{B}}$.*

*Moreover, if* $ext \models \nabla Ind^*_\sigma \cup \{\top \neq \bot\}$ *then*

*(iv) for every* $\phi \in I^+(\sigma; R)$, $ext \models dom\ D_1[\![p(\phi), X]\!] \leftrightarrow \nabla\phi$.

*Proof.* First let $p \in rP_\sigma$. Take

$$D_1[\![p, X]\!] \rightleftharpoons D[\![p, X]\!][\nabla\tilde{\phi}/\hat{\phi}].$$

Now let us fix a program $p \in rP^1_\sigma \setminus rP_\sigma$ and let $X \rightleftharpoons var(p)$. Let $X'$ be a new copy of $X$ and consider the following program $\tilde{p} \rightleftharpoons p;$ **if** $X = X' \rightarrow$ **skip** $\square X \neq X' \rightarrow$ **loop fi**. It is clear that in any model $\mathcal{A}$, $dom\ Den_{\mathcal{A}}[\![\tilde{p}, X, X']\!] = Den_{\mathcal{A}}[\![p, X]\!]$. Let $Z \rightleftharpoons var(\tilde{p})$ and let $Z'$ be its new copy. Now take

$$D_1[\![p, X]\!](X, Y) \rightleftharpoons \exists W \exists Z' \left(Y_\Upsilon \Psi\left(gr(pos(\tilde{p}))\right)\right)(P, start_g, stop_g, Z, Z').$$

It is clear that the conditions (i)-(iii) hold. The proof of condition (iv) is very technical and tiresome, so we only outline it. First we have to check that Lemma (8.6) is true in our first-order case. This means that in $Den_{\mathcal{A}}[\![Herb(X), X)]\!]$ we have to substitute $D_1$ for $Den$ and the Herbrand universe is the set defined as the least $\nabla Form_\sigma$-definable fixed-point of the equation system of Example (2.19).

Lemma (8.6) also states that $Herb(X)$ does not modify the content of the input stacks. This in our case can be formulated by using the following denotation function instead of $D_1$:

$$\exists W \exists Z' \left(Y_\Upsilon \Psi\left(gr(pos(\tilde{p}))\right)\right)(B, start_g, stop_g, Z, Z').$$

With this change the first-order version of Lemma (8.6) remains true.

Then, having proved this lemma and using the graph representation of $p(\phi)$ and the axioms of $\nabla Ind^*_\sigma$, we can prove (iv). We remark that this proof simulates an $I/O$-proof for an appropriate partial correctness assertion for the program $p(\phi)$ (see Definition (15.17)). □

Now we prove that if the stacks can be coded in data then the above definition gives the "usual" denotation of programs with stacks. Let us fix an inductive extension $(\delta, ext, \nabla)$ of a similarity type $\sigma$ and a set $Ax$ of axioms such that $Ax \subseteq Form_\delta$ and $\mathcal{A} \models Ax$ implies $ext\mathcal{A} \neq \emptyset$. For the sake of convenience let us suppose that $sort\ \sigma \rightleftharpoons \{d\}$, that there is a formula $\alpha \in \Sigma^+(\sigma; R)$ with $R \in \Omega$, that there are three distinct variables $x_1$, $x_2$ and $y$ such that the arity of $R$ is $(x_1, x_2, y)$ and that the least $\nabla Form_\sigma$-definable solution of the fixed-point equation $R(x_1, x_2, y) \equiv \alpha$ in $ext$ is an injective function of type $d, d \to d$. Then $Ax \cup \nabla Ind^*_\sigma$ implies the following formula in $ext$:

$$\forall x_1 \forall x_2 \exists y \nabla\alpha(x_1, x_2, y) \wedge$$
$$\forall y_1 \forall y_2 \forall x_1 \forall x_2 \left(\nabla\alpha(x_1, x_2, y_1) \wedge \nabla\alpha(x_1, x_2, y_2) \to (y_1 = y_2)\right).$$

If so then we say that $ext$ has a *pairing function.*

Let us suppose that the inductive extension $ext$ has a pairing function and $ext \models \nabla Ind^*_\sigma$. We define an inductive extension $(\delta \cup \sigma^s, ext^s, \nabla^s)$ in the following way. Let $\mathcal{A} \in Mod_\sigma$ and $\mathcal{B} \in ext(\mathcal{A})$ such that $\mathcal{B} \models Ax$. We define a $\delta \cup \sigma^s$-type extension $\mathcal{B}^s$ of $\mathcal{B}$ by taking the $d^s$-sorted universe of $\mathcal{B}^s$ as the $Seq$-component of the least $\nabla Form_\sigma$-definable fixed-point of the following equation system:

$$\begin{aligned} R(x_1, x_2, y) &\equiv \alpha(x_1, x_2, y) \\ Seq(x_1) &\equiv (x_1 = \bot) \vee \exists x_2 \exists d_2 \big(Seq(x_2) \wedge R(x_2, d, x_1)\big). \end{aligned}$$

By using the fact that $\nabla\alpha$ is a pairing function we can prove that the following formula is true in $Ax \cup \nabla Ind_\sigma^*$:

$$Seq(x) \to (x = \bot) \vee \exists! x_2 \exists! d_2 \big(Seq(x_2) \wedge R(x_2, d_2, x)\big).$$

Using this fact we can define the stack operations in an obvious manner. We remark that all these formulas belong to $\Sigma_\sigma^+$:

$$\begin{aligned} fhead(x, d, d') &\rightleftharpoons (x = \bot \wedge d = d') \vee \\ &\qquad \exists d_2 \exists x_2 \big(Seq(x_2) \wedge R(x_2, d_2, x) \wedge (d' = d_2)\big); \\ fpush(x, d, x') &\rightleftharpoons R(x, d, x'); \\ ftail(x, x') &\rightleftharpoons (x = \bot \wedge x' = \bot) \vee \\ &\qquad \exists d_2 \exists x_2 \big(Seq(x_2) \wedge R(x_2, d_2, x) \wedge (x' = x_2)\big); \\ fempty(x) &\rightleftharpoons x = \bot. \end{aligned}$$

For any $\mathcal{A} \in Mod_\sigma$ take $ext^s(\mathcal{A}) \rightleftharpoons \{\mathcal{B}^s \mid \mathcal{B} \models Ax\}$. It is clear that $(\delta \cup \sigma^s, ext^s)$ is an extension of $\sigma^s$.

Now we turn to define an appropriate function $\nabla^s$. Let $\phi \in I_{\sigma^s}^+(\sigma^s, R)$. Using the above definitions there is a formula $f\phi \in \Sigma^+(\sigma \cup \{R, Seq\})$ which is logically equivalent to the formula $\phi$ in any model $\mathcal{B}^s$ of $ext^s$. Let $S \in \Omega$ be a new relation symbol with $ar(S) = ar(\phi) = X$. Consider the fixed-point equation system

$$\begin{aligned} R(x_1, x_2, y) &\equiv \alpha(x_1, x_2, y); \\ Seq(x) &\equiv (x = \bot) \vee \exists x_2 \exists d_2 \big(Seq(x_2) \wedge R(x_2, d_2, x)\big); \\ S(X) &\equiv f\phi(X). \end{aligned}$$

By Theorem (15.5) this equation system has a least $\nabla Form_\sigma$-definable solution $\beta : \{R, Seq, S\} \to \nabla Form_\sigma$. Take $\nabla\phi \rightleftharpoons \beta(S)$. So we have defined the inductive extension $(\delta \cup \sigma^s, ext^s, \nabla^s)$. Since for any $\phi \in I_\sigma^+$, $\nabla^s\phi \in \nabla Form_\sigma$ it is an easy exercise to prove that $\mathcal{B}^s \models Ind_{\sigma^s}^*$.

We remark that $\mathcal{B}^s{\restriction}_{\sigma^s}$ is generally not isomorphic to the stack extension $\mathcal{A}^s$ of $\mathcal{A}$.

By Definition (14.11) there is a formula $D'[\![p, X]\!]$ which describes the semantics of an arbitrary program $p \in rP_{\sigma^s}$ in the extension $ext^s$, and by definition $D'[\![p, X]\!] \in \nabla Form_\sigma$. $\square$

**(15.11) Corollary.** *Let $(\delta, ext, \nabla)$ be an arbitrary extension of a fixed similarity type $\sigma$ and let $Ax \subseteq Form_\delta$ be such that $ext \models \nabla Ind^*_\sigma$ and $ext$ has a pairing function. Then for any program $p \in rP^1_\sigma$ with $X \rightleftharpoons var(p)$:*

$$ext \models \mathcal{B} \models D'[\![p, X]\!] \leftrightarrow D_1[\![p, X]\!].$$

This statement means that the axiom system $\nabla Ind^*_\sigma$ is strong enough to prove that the trace semantics of programs with simulation of stack operations (given by the formula $D'$) and the denotation semantics given by the direct use of inductive definition techniques (described by the formula $D_1$) are the same.

Most of the extensions considered in Chapter 5 can also be inductively defined. Therefore, the machinery used above to simulate stack operators can be also applied to define semantics for other extended programming languages, e.g. for *list*- and *set*-extensions. For more details see Section 26.3.

Having defined the program semantics we develop the corresponding extended dynamic logics (for main definitions see Chapter 13).

**(15.12) Definition.** *Let us fix a similarity type $\sigma$ and an inductive extension $(\delta, ext, \nabla)$ of it. The inductive logic (generated by $ext$) ${}_1DL^{ext}_\sigma$ is the language*

$$(rD^1_\sigma, Mod(ext), \models'_{ext}).$$

**(15.13) Definition.** *Let $\sigma$ be a given similarity type. Let $\sigma^\nabla$ and $\nabla : I^+_\sigma \to Form_{\sigma^\nabla}$ be as in Definition (15.6) (i) and (ii).*

*(A) Let $(\sigma^\nabla, df, \nabla)$ be the unique inductive extension maximal with respect to $(\{\top \neq \bot\}, \nabla Ind_\sigma)$. The inductive logic*

$${}_1DL^{df}_\sigma \rightleftharpoons (rD^1_\sigma, Mod(df), \models'_{df})$$

*is called the dynamic logic with definable denotational semantics.*

*(B) Let $(\sigma^\nabla, df*, \nabla)$ be the unique inductive extension maximal with respect to $(\{\top \neq \bot\}, \nabla Ind^*_\sigma)$. The inductive logic*

$${}_1DL^{df*}_\sigma \rightleftharpoons (rD^1_\sigma, Mod(df*), \models'_{df*})$$

*is called the dynamic logic with strongly definable denotational semantics.*

**(15.14) Corollary.** *The dynamic logics with definable denotational and strongly definable denotational semantics are compact and complete with respect to consequence.*

*Proof.* This statement is an obvious consequence of Theorem (13.6), since both $\nabla Ind_\sigma$ and $\nabla Ind^*_\sigma$ are recursive sets. □

**(15.15) Corollary.** *Let $(\delta, ext, \nabla)$ be a given inductive extension of the similarity type $\sigma$. Let $\chi \in rD_\sigma$ be a dynamic logical formula such that $ext \models \chi$. Then $ext^\nabla \models \chi$.*

*Proof.* The statement of the corollary follows from Theorems (15.8) and (15.10). □

**(15.16) Definition.** *Let $g \in rG^1_\sigma$ be fixed, let $\Psi(g) \in I^+(\sigma; \Upsilon)$ be the same as in Corollary (15.9) and let $Ax$, $\Phi \subseteq Form_\sigma$. A formula $\kappa \in \Phi$ with $var(\kappa) \subseteq var(\Upsilon)$ is called a $\Phi$-invariant of the transition graph $g$ with respect to $Ax$ iff*

$$Ax \cup \{\top \neq \bot\} \vdash \Psi(g)[\kappa/\Upsilon] \rightarrow \kappa.$$

**(15.17) Definition.** *Let $p \in rP^1_\sigma$, $Ax$, $\Phi \subseteq Form_\sigma$ and $\chi = \phi\{p\}\psi \in {}_1H_\sigma$ be fixed. Let $g \rightleftharpoons gr(pos(p))$.*

*(A) $\chi$ is $\Phi$-provable from $Ax$ by the $\sigma$-type I/O-calculus (written as $Ax \vdash^{\sigma,\Phi}_U \chi$) iff there is a $\Phi$-invariant $\kappa$ of $g$ with respect to $Ax$ with the following properties:*

$$Ax \cup \{\top \neq \bot\} \vdash \forall X \forall Y (\phi \wedge \kappa(P, start_g, stop_g, X, Y) \rightarrow \psi[Y/X]).$$

*(B) If $\Phi = Form_\sigma$ then instead of "$\Phi$-provable from $Ax \cup \nabla Ind_\sigma$ by the $\sigma$-type I/O-calculus" we say "provable from $Ax$ by the I/O-calculus", and write $\vdash_U$.*

*(C) Let $(\delta, ext, \nabla)$ be an inductive extension of $\sigma$. If $\Phi = \nabla Form_\sigma$ then instead of "$\Phi$-provable from $Ax \cup \nabla Ind^*_\sigma$ by the $\delta$-type I/O-calculus" we say "provable from $Ax$ by the generalized I/O-calculus", and write $\vdash_{eU}$. This means that for all $\chi \in {}_1H_\sigma$ $Ax \vdash_{eU} \chi$ iff $Ax \cup \nabla Ind^*_\sigma \vdash^{\delta, \nabla Form_\sigma}_U \chi$, by definition.*

**(15.18) Theorem.** *Let $Ax \subseteq Form_\sigma$ and let $\phi\{p\}\psi \in {}_1H_\sigma$ be given.*

*(i) $Ax \vdash_U \phi\{p\}\psi$ iff $Ax \models'_{df} \phi\{p\}\psi$;*
*(ii) $Ax \vdash_{eU} \phi\{p\}\psi$ iff $Ax \models'_{df*} \phi\{p\}\psi$.*

*Proof.* The soundness of the I/O- and of the generalized I/O-calculus follows from Theorem (15.19). The other direction of the statement (i) and (ii) follows from Theorem (15.20) and Theorem (15.21), respectively. □

**(15.19) Theorem.** *Let $(\delta, ext, \nabla)$ be a fixed inductive extension of $\sigma$. The I/O-calculus and the generalized I/O-calculus are sound with respect to the set ${}_1H_\sigma$ of formulas.*

*Proof.* Let us suppose that $Ax \vdash_U \phi\{p\}\psi$ and $Ax \vdash_{eU} \phi\{p\}\psi$, respectively. Let $\kappa$ be the appropriate invariant. In the first case by the definition of the I/O-calculus and by Lemma (15.3) (i), we get that $Ax \cup \nabla Ind_\sigma \cup \{\top \neq \bot\} \vdash$

$\nabla\Upsilon(gr(\tilde{p})) \rightarrow \kappa$. In the second case by using statement (iii) instead of statement (i) of Lemma (15.3) we get $Ax \cup \nabla Ind^*_\sigma \cup \{\top \neq \bot\} \vdash \nabla\Psi(g) \rightarrow \kappa$. By using Definitions (15.9), (15.17) (A), Theorem (15.10) and the soundness of the calculus $\vdash$, we can conclude that $\phi\{p\}\psi$ is valid in $Ax \cup \nabla Ind_\sigma \cup \{\top \neq \bot\}$ and in $Ax \cup \nabla Ind^*_\sigma \cup \{\top \neq \bot\}$. By using the maximality of *df* and *df*$*$ with respect to $(\{\top \neq \bot\}, \nabla Ind_\sigma)$ and $(\{\top \neq \bot\}, \nabla Ind^*_\sigma)$ we get that $Ax \models'_{df} \phi\{p\}\psi$ and $Ax \models_{df*} \phi\{p\}\psi$, respectively. □

**(15.20) Theorem.** *Fix a similarity type $\sigma$, an $Ax \subseteq Form_\sigma$, and a formula $\phi\{p\}\psi \in {}_1H_\sigma$. Then*

$$Ax \models'_{df} \phi\{p\}\psi \quad \textit{implies} \quad Ax \vdash_U \phi\{p\}\psi.$$

*Proof.* Let us suppose that $p \in rP_\sigma$. By using Corollary (15.15) and Theorem (14.34) we know that $Ax \vdash_H \phi\{p\}\psi$ holds. Using Theorem (14.30) we can conclude that $Ax \vdash_H \phi\{gr(p)\}\psi$. Let $\kappa : node(gr(p)) \rightarrow Form_\sigma$ be a generalized Hoare-proof of this partial correctness assertion. Take $\mu(P, a, c, X, X') \rightleftharpoons \kappa(c)$. Since $p \in rP_\sigma$, $\mu$ is thus an I/O-proof of the formula $\chi$.

Now let $p \in rP^1_\sigma \setminus rP_\sigma$. In this case we must repeat the proof of Theorem (14.34). We omit this proof because there is no further value in repeating it. Moreover, in some sense this proof is simpler than the original one, because we do not have to take care of the structure of the canonical form of $p$, and may use the graph representation of $p$ at once. □

**(15.21) Theorem.** *Fix a similarity type $\sigma$, an $Ax \subseteq Form_\sigma$, and a formula $\phi\{p\}\psi \in {}_1H_\sigma$. Then*

$$Ax \models'_{df*} \phi\{p\}\psi \quad \textit{implies} \quad Ax \vdash_{eU} \phi\{p\}\psi.$$

*Proof.* Let us suppose that $Ax \models_{df*} \phi\{p\}\psi$. Take $g \rightleftharpoons gr(pos(\tilde{p}))$, $\kappa \rightleftharpoons D_1$ (see the proof of Theorem (15.10)). By Definition (15.17) and by the maximality of *df*$*$ with respect to $(\{\top \neq \bot\}, \nabla Ind^*_\sigma)$ we can conclude that

$$Ax \cup \nabla Ind^*_\sigma \cup \{\top \neq \bot\} \models \forall X(\phi \wedge \kappa(P, start_g, stop_g, X, Y) \rightarrow \psi[Y/X])$$
$$Ax \cup \nabla Ind^*_\sigma \cup \{\top \neq \bot\} \models \Psi(g)[\kappa/\Upsilon] \rightarrow \kappa.$$

Since the calculus $\vdash$ is complete with respect to the first-order consequence $\models$ we get that $\kappa$ is a $\nabla Form_\sigma$ invariant of $gr(pos(\tilde{p}))$ and satisfies Definition (15.17), (A). Thus $Ax \vdash_{eU} \phi\{p\}\psi$. □

Let us investigate whether the proof power of dynamic logics will be greater if they are generated by different inductive extensions for programs free of stacks instead of the transitive ones.

**(15.22) Theorem.** *For an appropriate one-sorted similarity type $\sigma$*

$$_1rDL_\sigma^{ist} >_{rH_\sigma} {}_1rDL_\sigma^{df*} >_{rH_\sigma} {}_1rDL_\sigma^{df}.$$

*Proof.* Follows immediately from Theorems (14.37) and Theorem (15.18). □

**(15.23) Theorem.** *Let $\phi\{p\}\psi \in rH_\sigma$ be given and let $Ax \subseteq Form_\sigma$ be fixed. $Ax \vdash_H \phi\{p\}\psi$ iff $Ax \vdash_U \phi\{p\}\psi$.*

*Proof.* By using completeness results, namely Theorems (14.32) and (15.18), it is enough to prove that

$$Ax \models'_{ns} \phi\{p\}\psi \text{ iff } Ax \models'_{df} \phi\{p\}\psi.$$

Let us suppose that $Ax \models_{ns} \phi\{p\}\psi$ and there is a $\mathcal{B} \in Mod(df)$ such that $\mathcal{B} \not\models_{df} \phi\{p\}\psi$. By Definition (14.11) and Theorems (15.8) and (15.10) we get that $\mathcal{B}^* \in Mod(ns)$ and $\mathcal{B} \not\models \phi\{p\}\psi$ which is a contradiction. Now let us suppose that $Ax \models_{df} \phi\{p\}\psi$ but there is a $\mathcal{B} \in Mod(ns)$ such that $\mathcal{B} \not\models \phi\{p\}\psi$. Let us extend $\mathcal{B}$ to a model $\mathcal{B}^\nabla$ in the following way. Let $\phi \in \Delta_\sigma$ be fixed. Let $\rho$ be the relation symbol in $\sigma^\nabla$ that corresponds to the formula $\tilde{\phi} \in \Sigma^+(\sigma, R)$. Take $\rho_{\mathcal{B}^\nabla} \rightleftharpoons \phi^*_{\mathcal{B}}$. For every other $\rho$ let $\rho_{\mathcal{B}^\nabla} \rightleftharpoons {}_{\mathcal{B}'}I_\rho$, where $\mathcal{B}' \rightleftharpoons \mathcal{B}{\restriction}_\sigma$. It is clear that $\mathcal{B}^\nabla \models \nabla Ind_\sigma$. By using the definition of $\mathcal{B}^\nabla$ and Corollary (15.15), we get that $\mathcal{B}^\nabla \not\models \phi\{p\}\psi$ which is a contradiction. □

**(15.24) Corollary.** $DL_\sigma^{ns} \approx_{H_\sigma} {}_1DL_\sigma^{df}$.

We remark that this corollary is true for the set $D_\sigma$ of formulas as well, i.e. $DL_\sigma^{ns} \approx_{D_\sigma} {}_1DL_\sigma^{df}$. This statement can be proved by constructing a Hoare-like calculus for the set $D_\sigma$ and proving that both $DL_\sigma^{ns}$ and ${}_1DL_\sigma^{df}$ are complete with respect to this calculus.

**(15.25)** *Remark.* It is an open question whether $DL_\sigma^{ns*} <_{H_\sigma} {}_1DL_\sigma^{df*}$ or not. We conjecture that generally this is true.

The following diagram shows the interrelation of the logical power of the defined extended logics with respect to the set $H_\sigma$ of Floyd-Hoare formulas, thus it sums up our investigations in Chapters 13 and 15. An upward arrow ($\uparrow$) means that the logical power of the upper language is greater than that of the lower one.

$$\begin{array}{ccccc} DL^{cst} & \approx & DL & \approx & DL^{ist} \\ & & \uparrow & & \\ & & {}_1DL^{df*} & & \\ & & \uparrow ? & & \\ & & {}_1DL^{ns*} & & \\ & & \uparrow & & \\ DL^{ns} & = & DL^{df} & & \end{array}$$

**(15.26)** *Remark.* Let $\sigma$ be a many-sorted similarity type such that $\hat{\eta} \subseteq \sigma$. Theorem (15.10) remains true for $P^2_\sigma$ programs. Hence our whole theory of $rP^1_\sigma$-programs can be built up for $P^2_\sigma$-programs as well in inductive extensions maximal with respect to $(Next' \cup \{\top \neq \bot\}, \nabla Ind_\sigma)$ or with respect to $(Next' \cup \{\top \neq \bot\}, \nabla Ind^*_\sigma)$.

**(15.27)** *Remark.* In Chapters 14 and 15 we used the supposition of the existence of two distinct ground terms $\top$ and $\bot$ in the similarity type $\sigma$. However, this assumption can be eliminated. Let us specify how this elimination can be performed. The distinct ground terms were used

(i) in the definitions of the semantic functions *Red*, $D$, $D'$ and $D_1$;
(ii) in the definition of Hoare-calculus and of the I/O-calculus for the transition graphs;
(iii) in the proof of Theorem (15.5).

For the sake of simplicity let us suppose that the given similarity type $\sigma$ is one-sorted. In order to illustrate how to give a first-order definition of the semantic functions of (i) let us consider for example the semantic function $D$. Fix a program $p \in rP_\sigma$ and let $\tilde{\phi}$ be the formula obtained from the formula $D[\![p, var(p)]\!]$ replacing the ground terms $\top$ and $\bot$ by two distinct new variables $w_1$ and $w_2$, respectively. It is easy to see that

$$Ind^*_\sigma \models ((w_1 \neq w_2) \wedge (u_1 \neq u_2)) \rightarrow (\tilde{\phi} \leftrightarrow \tilde{\phi}[u_1/w_1, u_2/w_2]),$$

where $u_1$ and $u_2$ are new copies of $w_1$ and $w_2$. However, this is not true in the axiom system $Ind_\sigma$. Let $g \rightleftharpoons gr(p)$ and recall the program $run(g, h)$ from Section 4.4 defined after Lemma (4.28) which is either **skip** or **loop** . Therefore we can define the denotation of the program $p$ in the axiom system $Ind^*_\sigma$ in the following way:

$$\hat{D}[\![p, X]\!](X, Y) \rightleftharpoons \exists w_1 \exists w_2 (w_1 \neq w_2 \wedge \tilde{\phi}(X, Y)) \vee$$
$$\Big(\forall w_1 \forall w_2 (w_1 = w_2) \wedge \bigwedge_{h \in TF_\sigma} one_\sigma(\{w_1, w_2\}; h) \rightarrow (X = Y \wedge run(g, h) = \mathbf{skip}\ )\Big).$$

Note that $run(g, h) = \mathbf{skip}$ is equal to *true* or *false*, thus the above formula belongs to $SForm_\sigma$. Since the connection between the program $p$ and the formula $\hat{D}[\![p, X]\!]$ is recursive we can apply Theorem (13.6). Theorem (5.25) is required to give a similar construction for $rP^1_\sigma$-programs.

In order to eliminate the symbols $\top$ and $\bot$ from the definitions of Hoare-calculus and the I/O-calculus we can use the following method. First we prove the partial correctness formula $\phi\{p\}\psi$ from the axiom system $Ax \cup \{\exists w_1 \exists w_2 (w_1 \neq w_2)\}$ by the use of the original calculus. Then we have to consider the axiom system $Ax \cup \{\forall w_1 \forall w_2 (w_1 = w_2)\}$ and prove the following formula from it:

$$\bigwedge_{\substack{h \in TF_\sigma \\ run(g,h) = \mathbf{skip}}} (\phi \wedge one_\sigma(\{w_1, w_2\})) \rightarrow \psi[X/Y].$$

In order to eliminate the symbols $\top$ and $\bot$ from the proof of Theorem (15.5) we can use the full power of Definition (2.11) which allows us to use parameters of the universes of the models under consideration. Therefore, in this proof we can replace $\top$ and $\bot$ by new variables $w_1$ and $w_2$. In any model where $\neg\forall w_1 \forall w_2 (w_1 = w_2)$ is true, we can select distinct values for parameters $w_1$ and $w_2$. This fact guarantees that the pair $(\alpha_1, \alpha_2)$ is the least solution of the equation system (1) of Theorem (15.5).

Part III

# Temporal Characterization of Programs

Chapter 16

# Introduction to Part III

As we have seen, dynamic logic is based on input-output relational semantics. The expressive power of this descriptive language permits us to define many different program properties, including those connected with the "history" of execution. In order to characterize program semantics in this language, a computer is modelled by the data environment of the programs, and computer functioning, which is just data manipulation, represented by change of data. However, this functioning goes on in time, namely in time moments which depend on the construction of the computer and are generated by the computer's "inner clock". In the programming theories considered so far, time has been considered only at the metalevel, not allowing us to refer to time in the object language, i.e. in the descriptive language. In order to make a more refined model of a computer we represent it with both data environment and "inner clock". For the latter we have to provide tools for explicit time consideration.

The data manipulation providing the functioning is the change of data in time. Data change provided by the execution of a program occurs within a time interval characteristic for the computer. More precisely, the execution of a command occurs in a corresponding time cycle. Let us denote the set of disjoint time intervals by $T$. From a theoretical point of view the time intervals of $T$ can be considered as time moments, supposing that change takes place instantly. We also assume that changes cannot occur spontaneously, e.g. due to a breakdown, but only in a prescribed way. Similarly we assume that the machine itself can work infinitely long, never stopping due to breakdown or power loss. Thus a computer stops only if it is programmed to do so.

According to the above it is clear that at least two sets are required to characterize an abstract computer: the set of possible data and the set of possible time moments. Moreover, to characterize the functioning on the level of program execution the set of all possible data changes in time should be taken, i.e. a set of functions from $T$ to possible data. Therefore, a descriptive language which is able to provide an entire characterization of program execution should possess models consisting of three components: data structure, time structure and set of functions. By the use of these components we will obtain a Kripke-style semantics of our temporal logic. While developing an appropriate descriptive language we have at least two possibilities. The above constituents are defined in the models but are only partially represented in the syntax or, both syntax and semantics have appropriate constructions to reflect this situation.

The first possibility will be realized by a version of temporal logic developed here in Part III, while the second possibility will be realized by a classical first-order many-sorted language, called time logic, in Part IV.

Returning to the viewpoint of program semantics, we emphasize that after the input-output relational semantics handled by dynamic logic we intend to develop a descriptive language which is able to handle trace semantics as well.

Historically, the descriptive language based on temporal logic was the first that fulfilled the above requirement. Moreover, it realizes the first possibility from the two mentioned above. This descriptive language considers time as a modality by turning the program-based modalities of dynamic logic into modalities with a temporal interpretation. These modalities allow us to speak about the chronological order of computation states and about different types of occurrence of states.

The first method that deals with trace semantics was proposed by Burstall [1974]. It was called the method of "intermittent assertions" and was oriented to prove both partial and total correctness. This method differs from the Floyd-Hoare method at least in the following two respects. The characterization of programs through their execution is permitted and the calculus contains further induction type rules. The method was subsequently popularized by Manna, Waldinger [1978].

The possibility of using modalities with the temporal interpretation "always" and "sometimes" was already mentioned in connection with program verification in Burstall [1974].

This idea was followed by Pnueli [1977] to provide a formal interpretation of the intermittent assertion method by means of temporal logic. The temporal logic approach is applied to further investigation of the intermittent assertion method in Apt, Delporte [1983] and Sain [1985c]. The method is also used for parallel programs (see e.g. in Apt, Delporte [1983] and in Kröger [1987]).

For the sake of historical completeness we note that temporal-like operators were also elaborated in Kröger [1976 ,1977] to deal with program semantics. Following Pnueli [1977], a huge number of investigations have been devoted to the temporal logic approach. Kröger [1987] and Manna, Pnueli [1988] provide a comprehensive overview of the results obtained by this approach. In the mentioned works natural numbers provide the time moments for the temporal logic at the metalevel. In the 0-order (i.e. propositional) case this standard time view proved to be sufficient for the programming theory. However, this view is not appropriate in the first-order case, since it leads for example to incompleteness. Therefore, in order to handle this case appropriately the time structure for the temporal logic is required to be defined in a general manner. Andréka, Németi, Sain [1991] provides a survey of temporal logic with general time structure used for programming theory.

Many important questions still remain open in the case of the first-order temporal logic approach. The main question concerns the expressive power of the descriptive language, first of all in comparison with dynamic logic. The propositional temporal logic is expressible in dynamic logic (see e.g. Harel [1984]). This is the reason why Meyer [1980] concludes that the temporal logic approach is theoretically of no interest. However, what about the first-order case?

In the next chapter we introduce the main notions of first-order temporal logic, its syntax without using the *until* modality and a Kripke-style semantics. The time structure of this semantics will be defined by the use of an axiom system *Nord* which does not ensure the existence of a preceding time moment to any element differing from the first time moment 0. It is shown that temporal logic is incomplete with respect to the so-called standard Kripke models. However, without restricting the models to the standard ones this logic is complete, and a complete calculus is given.

In Chapter 18 we show how temporal logic can be used to describe program execution, which will allow the definition of program semantics in this logic as well. This implies that the temporal logic approach can be used to describe different program properties and to reason about programs as shown at the end of the chapter. The next three chapters are devoted to the comparative study of temporal and dynamic logics with respect to their descriptive power. In Chapter 19 we investigate whether dynamic logic is more general than the standard temporal logic, i.e. whether the latter can be embedded into dynamic logic, and we show that this is not the case. Chapter 20 is devoted to the investigation of the question of the embedding in the opposite direction, i.e. whether the standard temporal logic is more general than the dynamic logic: the answer proves to be negative.

In Chapter 21 a surprising result is obtained when the interrelation of the dynamic and and the standard temporal logics is investigated for models with a countable universe. We emphasize that this result is the opposite of that we had in the propositional case where temporal logic proves to be more powerful.

Up to Chapter 21 we compare the dynamic logic and the standard temporal logic, since they have a common model-theoretic background. Starting from Chapter 22 we consider temporal logic not only with standard Kripke models, but with arbitrary ones, and we provide a pure temporal logical characterization of three well known program verification methods. These methods are the Floyd-Hoare method, and two temporal logical methods, the first suggested by Burstall [1974] under the name of the method of intermittent assertions and the second suggested by Pnueli [1977].

The temporal logic characterization of these methods will be mathematically transparent and simple. Namely, we axiomatize three different induction principles by appropriate axiom schemas.

In Chapter 22 we also compare these methods with respect to their expressive power and show that the comparison of these program verification methods can also be established in the framework of first-order temporal logic. For this comparison we extend the axiom system *Nord* by a new axiom which ensures the existence of the previous time moment. Note that the characterization and comparative investigation of these methods was first performed by Sain [1986] in a time-logic framework which, as we shall see, is more powerful than temporal logic. In our temporal logic framework we provide the basic results of the comparison of the methods mentioned above with respect to their partial and total correctness theories.

Chapter 17

# Temporal Logic

Temporal logic is based on modal logic which uses the standard two modalities $\Box$ and $\Diamond$ interpreted as "necessity" and "possibility". Kripke [1963] elaborated a formal semantics for modal logic. Prior [1957] first suggested a temporal interpretation of the modalities, "always" for $\Box$ and "sometimes" for $\Diamond$. Following von Wright [1965] a new modality, the "next" time operator, denoted by $\circ$, was added to $\Box$ and $\Diamond$, and the temporal logic obtained was investigated in Prior [1967]. Prior's temporal logic contains operators for referring to both past and future. From Prior's work different temporal logics have been developed with different temporal operators. These logics realize different views of time such as the linear or branching time view; for example Pnueli [1977] adapted Prior's temporal logic with the linear time view to describe program properties following an idea of Burstall [1974]. This temporal logic uses the future fragment only and it contains the temporal operators "sometimes", "always" and "next". The time view is linear and semantically represented by natural numbers.

In the present work we also realize the linear time view by using discrete time represented by natural numbers. However, we add another temporal operator "first" to the above mentioned operators "always", "sometimes" and "next".

Let us fix two disjoint denumerable sets $V_l$ and $V_g$ of variables whose elements are said to be *local* and *global variables*, respectively. The set of global variables is the same as the set of variables used in the previous parts, i.e. $V_g \rightleftharpoons V$. The value of a local variable can be changed in time, while the value of each global variable remains unchanged in time. As we shall see, this temporal logic does not allow us to quantify over local variables, which implies that practically every formula can be considered universally closed with respect to the local variables.

In the case of many-sorted similarity types each variable has a sort too. Therefore, a function $sort : (V_l \cup V_g) \to S$ must be given to the set S of sorts. Moreover we suppose that a fixed sort-preserving bijection $\dot{} : V_g \to V_l$ is given. This implies that for any sort $s \in sort\ \sigma$ denumerably many local variables exist.

In our temporal logic we use new logical operators which allow us to formulate propositions the truth values of which depend on time and are related to some reference point (the present time). For example, we intend to describe statements like "a formula is always true from now on", "a formula will be sometimes true", "a formula will be true in the next moment", etc. The required new logical operators are introduced as modalities.

**(17.1) Definition.** *Let us fix an S-sorted similarity type $\sigma$. The set of $\sigma$-type temporal-logical formulas is defined as the minimal set $Mform_\sigma$ of formulas satisfying the following properties:*

*(i) $Atom(\sigma, V_g \cup V_l) \subseteq Mform_\sigma$;*
*(ii) for any formulas $\phi$, $\phi_1$, $\phi_2 \in Mform_\sigma$, $(\neg\phi)$, $(\phi_1 \vee \phi_2)$ belong to $Mform_\sigma$;*
*(iii) for any formulas $\phi \in Mform_\sigma$ and global variable $v \in V_g$, $(\forall v\phi)$ belongs to $Mform_\sigma$;*
*(iv) for any formula $\phi \in Mform_\sigma$, $(1\phi)$, $(\Box\phi)$ and $(\circ\phi)$ belong to $Mform_\sigma$.*

For the sake of convenience the "superfluous" parentheses will be omitted in the subsequent notations. The intuitive meaning of the modal operators is as follows:

$1\phi$ $\phi$ is true at the first time moment;
$\Box\phi$ $\phi$ is always true from now on;
$\circ\phi$ $\phi$ true at the next time-moment.

The last modality implicitly expresses the fact that time consists of perfectly isolated time moments, i.e. time is discrete. $\Diamond\phi$ is a shorthand for $\neg\Box\neg\phi$ meaning that $\phi$ will be true sometimes in the future. The semantics of temporal formulas can be defined by means of Kripke models.

Recall the similarity type $\eta$ of Section 1.6, which is a one-sorted similarity type with the only sort $s$. We use $x < y$ as a shorthand for $x \leq y \wedge y \not\leq x$. We often write $x + 1$ instead of $S(x)$. Let $Nord$ be an $\eta$-type axiom system describing the following properties:

- $\leq$ is an ordering (reflexive, transitive, symmetric);
- $\leq$ is linear, i.e. either $x \leq y$ or $y \leq x$;
- 0 is a "$\leq$-least" element, i.e. $0 \leq x$;
- $S$ is a successor with respect to $\leq$, i.e. $x \leq x + 1$ and $x < y \to x + 1 \leq y$.

We note that in the axiom system $Nord$ it is not provable that at any time moment (except for 0) there is a previous time moment. Since we will sometimes need this property we introduce a new axiom system $Npre$ by adding the axiom

- $\forall x \exists y (x \neq 0 \to y + 1 = x)$;

**(17.2) Definition.** *A $\sigma$-type Kripke model is a triplet $(\mathcal{A}, T, K)$, where $\mathcal{A} \in Mod_\sigma$ (called data structure) and $T \in Mod(Nord)$ (called time structure) and*

$$K \subseteq \bigcup_{s \in sort\ \sigma} [T \to A_s],$$

*such that for all $s \in sort\ \sigma$, $K \cap [T \to A_s] \neq \emptyset$.*

*If* $K = \bigcup_{s \in sort\,\sigma}[T \to A_s]$ *then* $(\mathcal{A}, \mathcal{T})$ *will be written instead of* $(\mathcal{A}, \mathcal{T}, K)$.

**(17.3) Definition.** *Let us fix a* $\sigma$*-type Kripke model* $(\mathcal{A}, \mathcal{T}, K)$. *A valuation in* $(\mathcal{A}, \mathcal{T}, K)$ *is a function* $k : (V_g \cup V_l) \to A \cup K$ *such that*

*(a)* *if* $v \in V_g$ *then* $k(v) \in A$ *and* $sort(k(v)) = sort(v)$,
*(b)* *if* $v \in V_l$ *and* $sort(v) = s$ *then* $k(v) \in K \cap [T \to A_s]$.

*The set of all valuations in* $(\mathcal{A}, \mathcal{T}, K)$ *is denoted by* $Val_{(\mathcal{A},\mathcal{T},K)}$.

**(17.4) Definition.** *Let* $(\mathcal{A}, \mathcal{T}, K)$ *be a Kripke model. Let us define the value of a term* $\tau$ *with respect to a valuation* $k$ *and a time moment* $t \in T$ *by taking*

$$\tau_{\mathcal{A}}[k,t] = \begin{cases} k(\tau)(t) & \text{if } \tau \in V_l; \\ k(\tau) & \text{if } \tau \in V_g; \\ f_{\mathcal{A}}(\tau_{1\mathcal{A}}[k,t], ..., \tau_{n\mathcal{A}}[k,t]) & \text{if } \tau = f(\tau_1, ..., \tau_n). \end{cases}$$

Now we are ready to define the validity of temporal-logic formulas.

**(17.5) Definition.**

*(i)* *Let* $(\mathcal{A}, \mathcal{T}, K)$ *be a Kripke model, let* $k$ *be a valuation in it and let* $t \in T$ *be a fixed time moment. We define the validity of temporal-logic formulas with respect to* $k \in Val_{(\mathcal{A},\mathcal{T},K)}$ *and* $t \in T$ *inductively as follows:*

- $(\mathcal{A}, \mathcal{T}, K) \models \rho(\tau_1, ..., \tau_n)[k,t]$ *iff* $(\tau_{1\mathcal{A}}[k,t], ..., \tau_{n\mathcal{A}}[k,t]) \in \rho_{\mathcal{A}}$;
- $(\mathcal{A}, \mathcal{T}, K) \models (\phi_1 \vee \phi_2)[k,t]$ *iff* $(\mathcal{A}, \mathcal{T}, K) \models \phi_1[k,t]$ *or* $(\mathcal{A}, \mathcal{T}, K) \models \phi_2[k,t]$;
- $(\mathcal{A}, \mathcal{T}, K) \models (\neg\phi)[k,t]$ *iff* $(\mathcal{A}, \mathcal{T}, K) \not\models \phi[k,t]$;
- $(\mathcal{A}, \mathcal{T}, K) \models (\forall v \phi)[k,t]$ *iff for each valuation* $\ell$ *if* $\ell(w) = k(w)$ *for any* $w \neq v$ *then* $(\mathcal{A}, \mathcal{T}, K) \models \phi[\ell,t]$;
- $(\mathcal{A}, \mathcal{T}, K) \models (1\phi)[k,t]$ *iff* $(\mathcal{A}, \mathcal{T}, K) \models \phi[k,0]$;
- $(\mathcal{A}, \mathcal{T}, K) \models (\Box\phi)[k,t]$ *iff* $(\mathcal{A}, \mathcal{T}, K) \models \phi[k,t^*]$ *for every* $t^* \geq t$
- $(\mathcal{A}, \mathcal{T}, K) \models (\circ\phi)[k,t]$ *iff* $(\mathcal{A}, \mathcal{T}, K) \models \phi[k,t+1]$.

*(ii)* *A temporal-logic formula* $\phi$ *is said to be valid in* $(\mathcal{A}, \mathcal{T}, K)$ *at moment* $t$ *iff it is valid with respect to each valuation* $k \in Val_{(\mathcal{A},\mathcal{T},K)}$ *at moment* $t$, *i.e.* $(\mathcal{A}, \mathcal{T}, K) \models \phi[t]$ *iff* $(\mathcal{A}, \mathcal{T}, K) \models \phi[k,t]$ *for every* $k \in Val_{(\mathcal{A},\mathcal{T},K)}$.

*(iii)* *A temporal-logic formula* $\phi$ *is said to be valid in* $(\mathcal{A}, \mathcal{T}, K)$ *with respect to the valuation* $k$ *iff it is valid at each time moment* $t \in T$ *with respect to the given valuation* $k$, *i.e.* $(\mathcal{A}, \mathcal{T}, K) \models \phi[k]$ *iff* $(\mathcal{A}, \mathcal{T}, K) \models \phi[k,t]$ *for every time moment* $t$.

*(iv)* *A temporal-logic formula* $\phi$ *is valid in* $(\mathcal{A}, \mathcal{T}, K)$ *iff it is valid at each time moment* $t \in T$ *and with respect to any valuation* $k \in Val_{(\mathcal{A},\mathcal{T},K)}$, *i.e.* $(\mathcal{A}, \mathcal{T}, K) \models \phi$ *iff for every* $t \in T$, $k \in Val_{(\mathcal{A},\mathcal{T},K)}$, $(\mathcal{A}, \mathcal{T}, K) \models \phi[k,t]$.

Let us denote the class of all $\sigma$-type Kripke models by $MMod_\sigma$. According to the above definitions the $\sigma$-type temporal logic $ML_\sigma$ is the triplet $(Mform_\sigma, MMod_\sigma, \models)$.

Let $Th(\mathcal{K}) \rightleftharpoons \{\phi \in Mform_\sigma \mid \mathcal{K} \models \phi\}$ denote the theory of the class $\mathcal{K} \subseteq MMod_\sigma$ of models and let $MMod(Ax) \rightleftharpoons \{(\mathcal{A}, \mathcal{T}, K) \mid (\mathcal{A}, \mathcal{T}, K) \models Ax\}$ denote the model class of the set $Ax \subseteq MMod_\sigma$ of axioms.

Remember that $\mathcal{N}$ denotes the standard model of arithmetic with the set $\mathbb{N}$ of natural numbers as universe on which the relation $\leq$ and functions $S$, $P$, $0$, $+$ and $\cdot$ are understood as usual.

**(17.6) Definition.** *A Kripke model $(\mathcal{A}, \mathcal{T}, K)$ is called standard iff $\mathcal{T} = \mathcal{N}$ and $K = \bigcup_{s \in sort\, \sigma}[T \to A_s]$.*

Now let us investigate the completeness of temporal logic with respect to standard Kripke models.

**(17.7) Theorem.** *The tautologies of $Mform_\sigma$ with respect to standard Kripke models constitute a $\Pi^1_1$-complete set.*

*Proof.* It is clear that the tautologies of $Mform_\sigma$ form at most a $\Pi^1_1$-complete set. To prove the theorem we construct a recursive subset of the tautologies and prove that this set is $\Pi^1_1$-complete. For the proof we need some methods to be defined later in Chapter 21. So we give this proof after Theorem 21.5. □

**(17.8) Corollary.** *The temporal logic $ML_\sigma$ is not complete with respect to standard Kripke models.* □

**(17.9) Definition.** *A temporal sentence is a temporal-logic formula including no free global variables. The following calculus is to derive temporal sentences from sets of temporal sentences. Let $\vdash_M$ be the calculus consisting of the following axioms and inference rules, where $x \in V_g$:*

*(1) Axioms and rules of predicate calculus:*
- *(1.1) propositional tautologies (of classical logic);*
- *(1.2) $\forall x\phi \to \phi[\tau/x]$ where $var(\tau) \cap V_l = \emptyset$;*
- *(1.3) $\phi, \phi \to \psi \vdash_M \psi$ (modus ponens);*
- *(1.4) Equality axioms.*

*(2) Axioms for formulas $\phi$ including no local variables:*
- *(2.1) $\Box\phi \leftrightarrow \phi$;*
- *(2.2) $1\phi \leftrightarrow \phi$;*
- *(2.3) $\circ\phi \leftrightarrow \phi$.*

*(3) Axiom and rule for local variables. Let $y$, $y' \in V_l$.*
- *(3.1) $\Box\exists x(x = y)$;*
- *(3.2) $\phi \vdash_M \phi[y'/y]$;*

*(4) Distributivity axioms. Let $M$ be $1$, $\circ$ or $\Diamond$.*
- *(4.1) $M(\phi_1 \vee \phi_2) \leftrightarrow M\phi_1 \vee M\phi_2$;*

*(4.2)* $M\neg\phi \leftrightarrow \neg M\phi$;
*(4.3)* $M\forall x\phi \leftrightarrow \forall x M\phi$;
*(5) Axioms of the time structure.*
*(5.1)* $\Diamond\phi_1 \wedge \Box\phi_2 \rightarrow \Diamond(\phi_1 \wedge \phi_2)$;
*(5.2)* $11\phi \leftrightarrow 1\phi$;
*(5.3)* $\Diamond 1\phi \rightarrow 1\phi$;
*(5.4)* $\Box\Box\phi \rightarrow \Box\phi$;
*(5.5)* $\Box\phi \leftrightarrow \phi \wedge \circ\Box\phi$;
*(5.6)* $1\Box\phi \rightarrow \Box\phi$;
*(5.7)* $\Box(\Diamond\phi_1 \vee \neg\phi_2) \vee \Box(\neg\phi_1 \vee \Diamond\phi_2)$;
*(5.8)* $\Diamond \circ \phi \rightarrow \circ\Diamond\phi$;
*(6) Generalization rules for modal quantifiers:*
*(6.1)* $\phi \vdash_M 1\phi$;
*(6.2)* $\phi \vdash_M \circ\phi$;
*(6.3)* $\phi \vdash_M \Box\phi$;

**(17.10) Theorem.** *(Completeness of calculus) The calculus $\vdash_M$ is complete and sound for $ML_\sigma$. This means that for any $Ax \subseteq Mform_\sigma$ and $\phi \in Mform_\sigma$, $Ax \models \phi$ iff $Ax \vdash_M \phi$.*

**(17.11) Corollary.** *The language $ML_\sigma$ is compact and complete with respect to the consequence relation.*

Note that the last statement also follows from the fact that according to Definition (26.1), temporal logic can be recursively embedded into time logic, which is compact and complete.

**(17.12)** *Remark.* We emphasize that the syntax of our temporal logic does not contain a construction like *until* (see e.g. Pnuelli [1977]). In the 0-order (i.e. propositional) case the modality *until* is necessary to express a large number of program properties, however, in the first-order case this is not true. In the following chapters we show how different programming notions and properties can be formulated in first-order temporal logic without *until*. Of course, it is not true that *until* is definable in our temporal logic. However, if *until* occurs only positively and universally in a temporal logic formula, then this formula has an equivalent within our temporal logic.

To demonstrate this fact let us suppose that a given similarity type $\sigma$ contains three different constant symbols 1, 2 and 3 of the same sort. Let $y$ be a new local variable with the same sort. Define the following formula:

$$Break(y) \rightleftharpoons 1(y=1 \vee y=2) \wedge 1\Box\big(y=1 \rightarrow \circ(y=1 \vee y=2)\big) \wedge \\ 1\Box\big((y=2 \vee y=3) \rightarrow \circ(y=3)\big).$$

It is not hard to check that if $Break(y)$ is valid in a Kripke model then the value of $y$ must be of the form $\{1\}^*2\{3\}^*$. Take

$$Enable(\psi, y) \rightleftharpoons 1\Box((y = 1 \to \neg\psi) \wedge (y = 2 \to \psi)).$$

The formula *Enable* expresses that if the value of $y$ is 1 or 2 at a time moment then the formula $\psi$ is false or true at that time moment, respectively. So the formula $Break(y) \wedge Enable(\psi, y)$ forces that the only time moment when y=2 is true is also the first time moment when $\psi$ is true. Hence

$$\phi\#\psi \rightleftharpoons (Break(y) \wedge Enable(\psi, y)) \to 1\Box(y = 1 \to \phi)$$

expresses in standard models that $\phi$ remains true until the first time moment when $\psi$ becomes true. However, the formula $\exists z\phi\#\psi$, for example, is not the correct translation of the corresponding temporal logic formula with *until*.

Chapter 18

# Temporal Logical Description of Program Properties

Now let us see how the $\sigma$-type temporal logic $ML_\sigma$ can be used to reason about programs and how program properties can be described. The temporal logic of programs will not mention programs explicitly, but it will operate on the computational paths realizing the execution of a program. This is one of the fundamental differences between the viewpoints of temporal logic and dynamic logic, since the latter does not directly operate on the computation but only on their input and output elements, yet it can directly refer to many programs.

In order to describe the program execution by means of temporal logic we require to refer to the elements of the set *Label* used in the graph representation of programs. This can be achieved by supposing that the similarity type $\sigma$ contains a sort $l$ and two $l$-sorted ground terms $\bot$ and $\top$. With the help of these constant symbols the elements of *Label* can be coded by appropiate $\sigma$-type first-order formulas. Let $g \in rG_\sigma$ be a fixed transition graph. For a transition graph $g$ we recall the formula $onestep_g(X, X_l, Y, Y_l)$ from Chapter 4. Remember that $X = var(g)$, $X_l$ is a set of variables large enough to code all the elements of $node(g)$ and $Y$, $Y_l$ are new copies of $X$ and $X_l$, respectively. All these variables are global. Now let us consider the local copies of $X$ and $X_l$ denoted by $\check{X}$ and $\check{X}_l$, respectively. These variables serve to describe the changes of the values of the program variables during the program execution.

Let us define the following version of the formula $onestep_g$:

$$localstep_g(X, X_l, Y, Y_l) \rightleftharpoons$$
$$onestep_g(X, X_l, Y, Y_l) \vee \big(abort_g(X, X_l) \wedge Y_l = X_l \wedge Y = X\big).$$

Note that this formula expresses that during the execution, the program under consideration either steps forward, which is described by the formula $onestep_g$, or it remains in place. We will explain later why we must modify the formula $onestep_g$ in this way. Here the formula $abort_g(X, X_l)$ expresses that the program reaches a node from which there are no valid outgoing edges. A possible version of $abort_g(X, X_l)$ is the following formula:

$$\bigwedge_{\substack{c,c' \in\, node(g) \\ (c,c') \in dom\ g}} \neg\exists Y \exists Y_L (X_l = L_c \wedge Y_l = L_{c'} \wedge D_{g(c,c')}(X, X_l, Y, Y_l)).$$

Note that if the graph $g$ is of the form $gr(p)$ for some,program $p \in rP_\sigma$ then $abort_g$ can be only in the node $stop_g$.

Let $U$, $V$ and $U_l$, $V_l$ be new (global) copies of $X$ and $X_l$, respectively. Consider the following temporal-logic formula $A_{step}$:

$$A_{step} \rightleftharpoons \forall U \forall U_l \Big( U = \check{X} \wedge U_l = \check{X}_l \rightarrow$$
$$\exists V \exists V_l \big( localstep_g(U, U_l, V, V_l) \wedge \circ(V = \check{X} \wedge V_l = \check{X}_l) \big) \Big).$$

It is clear that $var(A_{step}) = \check{X} \cup \check{X}_l$. We remark that $A_{step}$ depends on $g$.

In order to describe program execution we consider the standard Kripke model. We build up the necessary formulas with respect to this model, which afterwards can be used as a definition for all the other models. This strategy should be followed because the necessary notions are at our disposal only with respect to the standard model.

Let a time moment $t \in \mathbb{N}$ and a valuation $k \in Val_{(\mathcal{A},\mathcal{N})}$ be given. We can define a valuation of $V_g$ in the following way: $k(t) \rightleftharpoons \lambda y \in V_g.k(\check{y})(t)$. It is clear that $k(t) \in Val_{\mathcal{A}}$.

**(18.1) Lemma.** *Let $\mathcal{A}$ be an arbitrary $\sigma$-type model such that $\mathcal{A} \models \bot \neq \top$. Let $t \in \mathbb{N}$ and $k \in Val_{(\mathcal{A},\mathcal{N})}$ be given. $(\mathcal{A},\mathcal{N}) \models A_{step}[k,t]$ iff one of the following statements hold:*

*(i)* $\mathcal{A} \models abort_g[k(t)]$ *and* $k(t) = k(t+1)$ *or*
*(ii)* $\mathcal{A} \models onestep_g[k(t) + k(t+1)[X/Y, X_l/Y_l]]$.

*Proof.* Let us suppose that $k' \rightleftharpoons k + (U, k(\check{X})(t)) + (U_l, k(\check{X}_l)(t))$. By the definition of $A_{step}$, $(\mathcal{A},\mathcal{N}) \models A_{step}[k,t]$ is equivalent to

$$(\mathcal{A},\mathcal{N}) \models \exists V \exists V_l (localstep_g(U, U_l, V, V_l) \wedge \circ(V = \check{X} \wedge V_l = \check{X}_l))[k', t].$$

It is clear that $k'' \rightleftharpoons k' + (V, k(\check{X})(t+1)) + (V_l, k(\check{X}_l)(t+1))$ is the only valuation such that $(\mathcal{A},\mathcal{N}) \models \circ(V = \check{X} \wedge V_l = \check{X}_l)[k'', t]$ or equivalently $(\mathcal{A},\mathcal{N}) \models (V = \check{X} \wedge V_l = \check{X}_l)[k'', t+1]$. Thus we get that that $(\mathcal{A},\mathcal{N}) \models A_{step}[k,t]$ is equivalent to

$$\mathcal{A} \models localstep_g[k(t) + k(t+1)[X/Y, X_l/Y_l]].$$

This statement is obviously equivalent to the disjunction of the statements (i) and (ii). □

Now we turn to prove that in some sense $A_{step}$ describes the traces of the transition graph $g$. First we need some auxiliary definitions. Let $k \in Val_{(\mathcal{A},\mathcal{N})}$ be a valuation. With the help of $k$ we can define a path $tr(k) \in Path_{\mathcal{A}}$ by taking $tr(k) \rightleftharpoons \lambda t \in \mathbb{N}.k(t)$. It is clear that $tr(k)$ belongs to $[\mathbb{N} \to Val_{\mathcal{A}}]$. Now let us fix a valuation $k \in Val_{(\mathcal{A},\mathcal{N})}$ and a time moment $t \in \mathbb{N}$. Let $k^{(-t)}$ denote the following valuation: $k{\restriction}_{V_g} + \lambda y \in V_l.\lambda s \in \mathbb{N}.k(y)(s+t)$.

Let $H$ be a fixed set. For an arbitrary $s \in H^* \setminus \{\lambda\}$ let $Infty(s)$ denote a new sequence obtained from $s$ by repeating the last element of $s$ infinitely many times. Thus for any $n \in \mathbb{N}$:

$$Infty(s)(n) \rightleftharpoons \begin{cases} s(n) & \text{if } n < |s|; \\ out\, s & \text{if } n \geq |s|. \end{cases}$$

For an element $s$ of $H^\infty$ take $Infty(s) \rightleftharpoons s$. From the definitions and Lemma (18.1) we immediately get the following

**(18.2) Theorem.** *Let $\sigma$ be a fixed similarity type containing two distinct ground terms $\bot$ and $\top$ of the same sort and let $g \in rG_\sigma$ be a given transition graph. Let $(\mathcal{A}, \mathcal{N})$ be an arbitrary $\sigma$-type standard Kripke model such that $\mathcal{A} \models \bot \neq \top$. Let $t \in \mathbb{N}$ be a fixed natural number and let $k \in Val_{(\mathcal{A},\mathcal{N})}$ be a given valuation. $(\mathcal{A}, \mathcal{N}) \models \Box A_{step}[k, t]$ iff there is a finite or infinite trace $\beta$ of $g$ such that*

$$Infty(\beta) = tr\big(k^{(-t)}\big).$$

Using the above formulas we can formalize how a transition graph $g$ works starting from the label $start_g$ with input $X$.

**(18.3) Definition.** *Let $\sigma$ be a fixed similarity type containing two distinct ground terms $\bot$ and $\top$ of the same sort and let $g \in rG_\sigma$ be a given transition graph. The formula, expressing the way the transition graph works, is as follows.*

$$work(g) \rightleftharpoons 1\big(X = \check{X} \wedge \check{X}_l = start_g\big) \wedge 1\Box A_{step}(\check{X}, \check{X}_l)$$

This definitions can be applied to an arbitrary program $p \in rP_\sigma$ taking $gr(p)$ instead of $g$. For the sake of simplicity we write $p$ instead of $gr(p)$, i.e. $stop_p$ is a shorthand for $stop_{gr(p)}$ and $work(p)$ is a shorthand for $work(gr(p))$. We remark that $var(work(p)) \subseteq X \cup \check{X} \cup \check{X}_l$, where $\check{X}$ and $\check{X}_l$ are local copies of $X$ and $X_l$, respectively.

**(18.4) Theorem.** *The notions listed in Table 18.1 are formalized in temporal logic $ML_\sigma$. This formalization is correct with respect to those standard Kripke models within which $\bot \neq \top$ holds.*

*Proof.* We prove only the case of partial correctness. All the other cases can be proved similarly taking into account the fact that these properties speak about "all possible paths of a program".

Let $\mathcal{A} \in Mod_\sigma$ be a model such that $\mathcal{A} \models \bot \neq \top$ and let us fix a partial correctness assertion $\phi\{p\}\psi \in rH_\sigma$. We aim to prove that $\mathcal{A} \models \phi\{p\}\psi$ iff

$$(*) \qquad (\mathcal{A}, \mathcal{N}) \models \big(work(p) \wedge \phi\big) \rightarrow 1\Box\big(\check{X}_l = stop_p \rightarrow \psi[\check{X}/X]\big).$$

First let us suppose that $\mathcal{A} \models \phi\{p\}\psi$ holds. We prove (*). Let $\tilde{k} \in Val_{(\mathcal{A},\mathcal{N})}$ be a valuation such that $(\mathcal{A}, \mathcal{N}) \models \big(work(p) \wedge \phi\big)[\tilde{k}]$. Thus $\mathcal{A} \models \phi\big[\tilde{k}{\restriction}_X\big]$ and $\tilde{k}{\restriction}_X = k(0){\restriction}_X$. By Theorem (18.2) there is a trace $\beta$ of $p$ in $\mathcal{A}$ starting from

**Table 18.1.** Formalization of program properties

| Notion | Temporal-logical formula |
|---|---|
| $p$ is partially correct w.r.t. precondition $\phi$ and postcondition $\psi$ | $(work(p) \wedge \phi) \rightarrow 1\Box(\check{X}_l = stop_p \rightarrow \psi[\check{X}/X])$ |
| $p$ is totally correct w.r.t. precondition $\phi$ and postcondition $\psi$ | $(work(p) \wedge \phi) \rightarrow \Diamond\check{X}_l = stop_p \wedge 1\Box(\check{X}_l = stop_p \rightarrow \psi[\check{X}/X])$ |
| $\psi$ is a global invariant for $p$ w.r.t $\phi$ | $(work(p) \wedge \phi) \rightarrow 1\Box\psi[\check{X}/X]$ |
| $\psi$ is a generalized global invariant for $p$ w.r.t $\phi$ | $(work(p) \wedge \phi) \rightarrow 1\Box\Diamond\psi[\check{X}/X]$ |
| program $p$ has the $\phi \succ_w \psi_0, \psi_1$ property | $(work(p) \wedge \phi) \rightarrow 1\Box(\psi_0[\check{X}/X] \rightarrow \Diamond\psi_1[\check{X}/X])$ |
| program $p$ has the $\phi \succ \psi_0, \psi_1$ property | $(work(p) \wedge \phi) \rightarrow 1\Diamond\psi_0[\check{X}/X] \wedge 1\Box(\psi_0[\check{X}/X] \rightarrow \Diamond\psi_1[\check{X}/X])$ |

$start_p$ such that $Infty(\beta) = tr(k)$. If $\beta$ is an infinite trace then $\check{X} = stop_p$ never holds, i.e. (*) holds with the valuation $\tilde{k}$. Otherwise, if $\check{X} = stop_p$ holds sometimes, then $\beta$ is a terminating trace. Since $\mathcal{A} \models \phi\{p\}\psi$ and $\mathcal{A} \models \phi[in\beta]$ we get that $\mathcal{A} \models \psi[out\ \beta]$. However, if for some $s \in \mathbb{N}$ $(\mathcal{A}, \mathcal{N}) \models \check{X} = stop_p[\tilde{k}, s]$ then $out\ \beta = \tilde{k}(s)$. Thus

$$(\mathcal{A}, \mathcal{N}) \models 1\Box(\check{X}_l = stop_p \rightarrow \psi[\check{X}/X])[\tilde{k}].$$

The other direction can be proved using a similar argument. □

We have seen that $ML_\sigma$ is also a language suitable for describing program properties. Thus we have two descriptive languages. Both logics, the dynamic and the temporal ones, can be used to describe program properties. Which of these languages, however, is more convenient to use? How are their expressive powers related to each other? These questions will be answered in the following chapters.

Chapter 19

# Is Temporal Logic Expressible in Dynamic Logic?

As is well known, temporal logic can be defined in dynamic logic (cf. Harel [1984]) in the propositional case. This fact was used by Meyer [1980] when he stated that temporal logic is uninteresting from a scientific point of view.

However, by increasing the order of the language this idealistic picture changes. Namely, as the theorem below shows, in the first-order case temporal logic cannot be embedded into dynamic logic. Therefore, the growth of complexity of the language results in the growth of its scientific importance.

**(19.1) Theorem.** *There exists a temporal-logic formula $\phi \in Mform_\sigma$ for which there is no dynamic-logic formula $\delta \in rD_\sigma$ such that for all models $\mathcal{A} \in Mod_\sigma$ $(\mathcal{A}, \mathcal{N}) \models \phi$ iff $\mathcal{A} \models \delta$.*

*Proof.* Let $\phi \rightleftharpoons \exists x \Box (x \neq y)$, where $y \in V_l$. We show that this formula is appropriate. For this we need the following claims:

**Claim 1.** For any model $\mathcal{A} \in Mod_\sigma$, $(\mathcal{A}, \mathcal{N}) \models \exists x \Box (x \neq y)$ iff $|A| > \omega_0$.
*Proof of Claim 1.* Let us suppose that $(\mathcal{A}, \mathcal{N}) \models \exists x \Box (x \neq y)$. By definition this means that for any time moment $t \in \mathbb{N}$ and for any valuation $k$, $(\mathcal{A}, \mathcal{N}) \models \exists x \Box (x \neq y)[k, t]$. Then $(\mathcal{A}, \mathcal{N}) \models \exists x \Box (x \neq y)[k, 0]$ and therefore, by definition, there exists a valuation $l_k$ such that for every $t^* \in \mathbb{N}$ $l_k(x) \neq k(y)(t^*)$. This means that for every function $k(y) \in [\mathbb{N} \to A]$ there is an element $l_k(x)$ of $A$ which is out of $rng\ k(y)$, i.e. $|A| > \omega_0$.

For the other direction, if $|A| > \omega_0$ then for every valuation $k$ $k(y)$ is a function of $[\mathbb{N} \to A]$ with $A \setminus rng\ k(y) \neq \emptyset$. Let the valuation $l_k$ be defined as follows. $l_k(w) = k(w)$ if $w \neq x$ and let $l_k(x)$ be an arbitrary element of $A \setminus rng\ k(y)$. This $l_k$ verifies $(\mathcal{A}, \mathcal{N}) \models \exists x \Box (x \neq y)[k, t]$ for every $t \in \mathbb{N}$, which proves Claim 1.

**Claim 2.** Every dynamic-logic formula $\delta \in rD_\sigma$ which has a model $\mathcal{A} \in Mod_\sigma$ such that $|A| > \omega_0$ has a countable model $\mathcal{B} \in Mod_\sigma$ ($|B| = \omega_0$).

*Proof of Claim 2.* As is known, $rD_\sigma \lesssim L_{\omega_1, \omega}$, i.e. first-order dynamic logic is a part of the infinitary language with the formation rules of the classical first-order language where in addition infinite conjunctions $\bigwedge\{\phi_i \mid i \in \mathbb{N}\}$ are allowed (see e.g. Theorem (3.30) in Harel [1984]).

To be precise we note that the mentioned theorem considers a constructive $L_{\omega_1, \omega}$ language which itself is less than $L_{\omega_1, \omega}$. Since $\omega_1$ is a regular cardinal then we can use Corollary (3.1.4) of Dickmann [1985], according to which any formula of $L_{\omega_1,\omega}$ having a model also has a model of power $< \omega_1$. This completes the proof of Claim 2.

Now we are ready to prove the theorem. Let $(\mathcal{A},\mathcal{N}) \models \exists x \Box (x \neq y)$. To gain a contradiction let us suppose that there exists a dynamic-logic formula $dyn(\exists x \Box (x \neq y))$ such that

$$(*) \qquad \mathcal{A} \models dyn(\exists x \Box (x \neq y))$$

By Claim 1, $\mathcal{A}$ is an uncountable model, i.e. $|A| > \omega_0$. At the same time by Claim 2, $dyn(\exists x \Box x \neq y)$ has a countable model, say $\mathcal{B}$ ($|B| \leq \omega_0$). But by Claim 1, $(\mathcal{B},\mathcal{N}) \not\models \exists x \Box (x \neq y)$. □

We would expect that temporal logic could be interpreted in dynamic logic concerning only the countable models which were important to fit into the programmer's intuition. But this is not the case as the following theorem shows.

**(19.2) Theorem.** *There exists a temporal-logic formula $\phi \in Mform_\sigma$ for which there is no dynamic-logic formula $\delta \in rD_\sigma$ such that for every countable model $\mathcal{A}$, $\mathcal{A} \models \delta$ iff $(\mathcal{A},\mathcal{N}) \models \phi$.*

*Proof.* Let us take the following temporal-logic formula

$$\phi \rightleftharpoons \Diamond(\exists x \Box (x = y)) \to \exists x (1 \Box (x \neq y)),$$

(where $y$ is a local, $x$ is a global variable). It is easy to see that for an arbitrary model $\mathcal{A} \in Mod_\sigma$ if $(\mathcal{A},\mathcal{N}) \models \phi$ then $|A| \geq \omega_0$. To translate the formula $\phi$ into $rD_\sigma$ we need a formula $\delta_{fin}$ such that for any model $\mathcal{A} \in Mod_\sigma$, $\mathcal{A} \models \delta_{fin}$ iff $|A| < \omega_0$. If such a formula existed then $\neg\delta_{fin}$ would be an appropriate translation of $\phi$. However, according to Theorem 6 of Meyer, Parikh [1981] there is no such a formula in $rD_\sigma$. □

However, if we define the dynamic logic by using an extended programming language, say $rP_{\sigma^*}$ (or equivalently $rP^2_\sigma$) then the above formula $\phi$ could be interpreted in the corresponding dynamic logic. If we consider dynamic logic with random and array assignments then there exists the required formula $\delta_{fin}$ (see Lemma 7 in Meyer, Parikh [1981]).

Of course, this does not yet prove the possibility of interpreting temporal logic in the extended logic, say in $rD_{\sigma^*}$, with respect to the countable models.

The above theorem also emphasizes an important difference between temporal logic and dynamic logic. Namely, considering a single program, temporal logic speaks about its computation traces, but only about all possible ones at once. On the other hand dynamic logic cannot operate directly with the computation processes themselves, but only with their "extremal" points which appear in the input-output characterization, yet can refer directly to many programs. Therefore in dynamic logic, computation traces can be imitated by programs built up from appropriately selected computational devices. Namely, we need the possibility of using unbounded memory in the programs. This is why only a dynamic logic based on an appropriately extended programming language is able to interpret the temporal-logic formula $\phi$ of Theorem (19.2).

As we have seen from the above theorems, temporal logic cannot be translated into dynamic logic. What about the other direction?

Chapter 20

# Is Dynamic Logic Expressible in Temporal Logic?

In this chapter we complete the investigation of the interrelation of temporal and dynamic logics by showing that they are incomparable. For this we have to prove that temporal logic cannot define dynamic logic.

**(20.1) Theorem.** *There exists a dynamic-logic formula $\delta \in rD_\sigma$ for which there is no temporal-logic formula $\phi \in Mform_\sigma$ such that $\mathcal{B} \models \delta$ iff for all models $\mathcal{B} \in Mod_\sigma$ $(\mathcal{B}, \mathcal{N}) \models \phi$.*

*Proof.* It is enough to construct two models $\mathcal{A}$ and $\mathcal{A}'$ such that for any temporal-logic formula $\phi$

(*) $$(\mathcal{A}, \mathcal{N}) \models \phi \text{ iff } (\mathcal{A}', \mathcal{N}) \models \phi,$$

but for some dynamic-logic formula $\delta$

(**) $$\mathcal{A} \not\models \delta \text{ and } \mathcal{A}' \models \delta.$$

Now if for some $\phi_\delta \in Mform_\sigma$ $\mathcal{B} \models \delta$ iff $(\mathcal{B}, \mathcal{N}) \models \phi_\delta$ for any model $\mathcal{B} \in Mod_\sigma$, then especially $(\mathcal{A}, \mathcal{N}) \not\models \phi_\delta$ and $(\mathcal{A}', \mathcal{N}) \models \phi_\delta$ which contradicts (*).

Since the proof is rather complicated, we first sketch it.

(1) We construct the models $\mathcal{A}$ and $\mathcal{A}'$.
(2) We exhibit a program *pr* such that $\delta \rightleftharpoons \langle pr \rangle true \in rD_\sigma$ satisfies (**).
(3) After introducing some auxiliary definitions, we introduce the property of $n$-similarity ($n \in \mathbb{N}$) for pairs of valuations $(k, k')$ where $k \in Val_{(\mathcal{A},\mathcal{N})}$, $k' \in Val_{(\mathcal{A}',\mathcal{N})}$.
(4) We show that for any $n \in \mathbb{N}$
   (a) for all $k' \in Val_{(\mathcal{A}',\mathcal{N})}$ there is a valuation $k \in Val_{(\mathcal{A},\mathcal{N})}$ such that $k$ and $k'$ are $n$-similar;
   (b) for all $k \in Val_{(\mathcal{A},\mathcal{N})}$ there is a valuation $k' \in Val_{(\mathcal{A}',\mathcal{N})}$ such that $k$ and $k'$ are $n$-similar.
(5) We define a function $norm : MForm_\sigma \to \mathbb{N}$, representing the complexity of temporal-logic formulas.
(6) We show that if $k \in Val_{(\mathcal{A},\mathcal{N})}$ and $k' \in Val_{(\mathcal{A}',\mathcal{N})}$ are $n$-similar, and $norm(\phi) \leq n$ for a $\phi \in MForm_\sigma$, then for all $t \in \mathbb{N}$

$$(\mathcal{A}, \mathcal{N}) \models \phi[k, t] \text{ iff } (\mathcal{A}', \mathcal{N}) \models \phi[k', t].$$

Now we show that (4) and (6) together already prove (*). By Definition (16.5), $(\mathcal{B},\mathcal{N}) \models \phi$ means that for all $t \in \mathbb{N}$, $k \in Val_{(\mathcal{B},\mathcal{N})}$ $(\mathcal{B},\mathcal{N}) \models \phi[k,t]$. Now let $\phi \in MForm_\sigma$ be any formula for which $(\mathcal{A},\mathcal{N}) \models \phi$. We have to prove $(\mathcal{A}',\mathcal{N}) \models \phi$. Consider now any $t$ and $k'$. Let $m \rightleftharpoons norm(\phi)$. By (4)(a), we can choose a valuation $k \in Val_{(\mathcal{A},\mathcal{N})}$ such that $k$ and $k'$ are $m$-similar. Since $(\mathcal{A},\mathcal{N}) \models \phi$, we get that $(\mathcal{A},\mathcal{N}) \models \phi[k,t]$, from which, by (6), $(\mathcal{A}',\mathcal{N}) \models \phi[k',t]$. This already proves one direction of (*), since $t$ and $k'$ were arbitrary. The other direction of (*) can be proved similarly; we only have to use (4)(b) instead of (4)(a). Since (2) itself proves (**), it remains to realize steps (1)-(6) above, which takes up most of the rest of this chapter.

**Step 1.** Let $C$ be a set of cardinality $\omega_1$, i.e. $|C| = \omega_1$. Let $\gamma \in C$ be a fixed element. For every $p \in C$ let

$$S_p \rightleftharpoons \{(w,I,n,p,c) \mid I \subset C, n \in \mathbb{N}, c \in C, w \in Tree(I,n)\},$$

where $Tree(I,n) \rightleftharpoons I^* \cup \{w \circ \langle c \rangle \circ w' \mid w \in I^*, c \in C \backslash I, w' \in C^*, |w'| \leq n\}$ (recall that for a sequence $s$ its length is denoted by $|s|$). Let $S \rightleftharpoons \cup\{S_p \mid p \in C\}$, $A' \rightleftharpoons C \cup S$, $A \rightleftharpoons C^* \cup A'$ (here we note that the one-element sequence differs from its only element, and we may suppose that $C$, $C^*$ and $S$ are pairwise disjoint sets).

For any subset $D \subseteq A$ and relation $r \subseteq A \times A$ let us define $Par(D) \rightleftharpoons \{p \in C \mid \exists w \in C^* \exists J \subset C \exists n \in \mathbb{N} \exists c \in C$ such that $(w,I,n,p,c) \in D\}$, $Par(r) \rightleftharpoons Par(dom\, r) \cup Par(rng\, r)$. $Par(D)$ and $Par(r)$ are called the (set of) parameters of $D$ and $r$, respectively. Now let us define the functions $f : A \to A$, $g : A \times A \to A$ as follows

$$f(x) \rightleftharpoons \begin{cases} c & \text{if } x \in S \text{ and } x \text{ is of the form } (w,I,n,p,c); \\ \gamma & \text{if } x \in C^* \\ x & \text{if } x \in C. \end{cases}$$

$$g(x,y) \rightleftharpoons \begin{cases} (w \circ \langle x \rangle, I, n, p, c) & \text{if } x \in C,\ y \in S,\ y \text{ is of the form} \\ & \qquad (w,I,n,p,c) \text{ and } w \circ \langle x \rangle \in Tree(I,n); \\ y \circ \langle x \rangle & \text{if } x \in C \text{ and } y \in C^*; \\ \gamma & \text{otherwise} \end{cases}$$

Let us consider a one-sorted similarity type $\sigma$ with $sort\ \sigma = \{s\}$, $rel\ \sigma = \emptyset$, $func\ \sigma = \{\hat{\gamma}, \hat{f}, \hat{g}\}$ where $\hat{\gamma} :\to s$, $\hat{f} : s \to s$ and $\hat{g} : s,s \to s$. Now we define two models $\mathcal{A}$ and $\mathcal{A}'$ with universes $A$ and $A'$, respectively. For $\mathcal{A}$ let $\hat{\gamma}_\mathcal{A} \rightleftharpoons \gamma$, $\hat{f}_\mathcal{A} \rightleftharpoons f$, $\hat{g}_\mathcal{A} \rightleftharpoons g$, while for $\mathcal{A}'$ let $\hat{\gamma}_{\mathcal{A}'} \rightleftharpoons \gamma$, $\hat{f}_{\mathcal{A}'} \rightleftharpoons f{\restriction}A'$, $\hat{g}_{\mathcal{A}'} \rightleftharpoons g{\restriction}A' \times A'$. We note that this definition is correct, since $\{\gamma\}$, $rng(f{\restriction}A')$, $rng(g{\restriction}A' \times A') \subseteq A'$.

**Step 2.** Let $pr$ be the following program

$$pr \rightleftharpoons \textbf{while } y \neq \hat{\gamma} \textbf{ do } x :=?; y := g(f(x),y) \textbf{ od}\ .$$

Consider the dynamic-logic formula $\delta \rightleftharpoons \langle pr \rangle true$. Obviously, $\delta$ is valid in a model $\mathcal{B}$ iff starting with any valuation, the trace of $pr$ contains at least one terminating path. Our model construction implies that if the input value of $y$ is from $C$ or $S$ then $p$ contains at least one terminating path, i.e. $\mathcal{A}' \models \delta$. (If $y$ starts with an element of $C$ then the **do...od** cycle runs at most once. Otherwise $y$ starts with an element of $S$ having the form $(w, I, n, p, c)$, and if $x$ takes a value form $C \setminus I$, then the **do...od** cycle will stop in at most $n$ steps.) If the input value of $y$ is from $C^*$ then $pr$ never stops, i.e. $\mathcal{A} \not\models \delta$. Thus $\delta$ satisfies (**).

**Step 3.** Let us define $diag\ C \rightleftharpoons \{(c,c) \mid c \in C\}$. Let $r \subseteq A \times A$ be any relation. We shall define $ext_n(r)$, the $n^{th}$ extension of $r$ ($n \in \mathbb{N}$), by induction. Instead of $ext_n(r)$ we simply write $r_n$.

$$
\begin{aligned}
r_0 &\rightleftharpoons r \cup diag\, C \\
r_{m+1} &\rightleftharpoons r_m \cup \{(g(c,a), g(c,b)) \mid (a,b) \in r_m, c \in C\} \cup \\
&\qquad \{(a,b) \mid (g(c,a), g(c,b)) \in r_m, g(c,a) \neq \gamma \neq g(c,b), c \in C\}.
\end{aligned}
$$

It is easy to show, by induction, that

**(20.2) Lemma.** *If $r$, $r'$, $r'' \subseteq A \times A$; $m$, $n \in \mathbb{N}$ and $m < n$ then*

*(a)* $r \subseteq r_m \subseteq r_n$;
*(b)* *if* $r' \subseteq r$ *then* $r'_m \subseteq r_m$;
*(c)* *if* $r = r' \cup r''$ *then* $r_m = r'_m \cup r''_m$;
*(d)* $Par(r_m) = Par(r)$.

Let $r \subseteq A \times A'$ be any relation. $r$ is $n$-similarity (denoted as $r \in Sim_n$) for an $n \in \mathbb{N}$ iff

(i) $r_n$ is a functional and injective relation;
(ii) if $c \in C$; $x$, $g(c,x) \in dom\ r_n$ then $r_n(g(c,x)) = g(c, r_n(x))$;
(iii) if $a \in S$ and $a$ is of the form $(w, I, m, p, c)$ then $r(a) = (w, I, m, q, c)$, where $q \in C$;
(iv) if $a \in C^*$ then $r(a) = (a, I, m, p, \gamma) \in S$ where $I \subset C$, $n \leq m \in \mathbb{N}$, $p \in C$ and there is a $w \in C^*$ such that $|w| \geq n$ and $a \circ w \in Tree(I, m)$.

Note that conditions (i) and (ii) concern the $n^{th}$ extension of $r$, while (iii) and (iv) concern $r$ itself. We also note that if $r_n$ is functional and injective then $r$ has the same properties too (cf. Lemma (20.2a)).

**(20.3) Lemma.** *If $r \in Sim_n$ then*

*(a)* *if* $m \leq n$ *then* $r_m$ *is functional and injective;*
*(b)* *if* $m \leq n$ *then* $r \in Sim_m$;
*(c)* *if* $r' \subseteq r$ *then* $r' \in Sim_n$.

*Proof.* (a) and (b) follow from Lemma (20.2a), while (c) follows from Lemma (20.2b), using also the definition of $m$-similarity. □

**(20.4) Lemma.** *If* $r \in Sim_n$ *then*

(a) $C \subseteq dom\ r_n$ *and* $r_n(c) = c$ *for all* $c \in C$;
(b) *if* $x \in dom\ r_n$ *then* $r_n(f(x)) = f(r_n(x))$.

*Proof.* Statement (a) follows from the definition of $r_0$ and Lemma (20.3a). To prove (b), from (a) and the definition of $f$ we have

- if $x \in C$: $r_n(f(x)) = r_n(x) = x = f(x) = f(r_n(x))$;
- if $x \in C^*$: by property (iv) of $n$-similarity $r_n(x)$ is of the form $(x, I, m, p, \gamma)$, thus $r_n(f(x)) = r_n(\gamma) = \gamma = f((x, I, m, p, \gamma)) = f(r_n(x))$;
- if $x \in S$: $x$ is of the form $(w, I, m, p, c)$ and by property (iii) of $n$-similarity $r_n(x)$ is of the form $(w, I, m, q, c)$, thus $r_n(f(x)) = r_n(c) = c = f((w, I, m, q, c)) = f(r_n(x))$.

□

If $k \in Val_{(\mathcal{A},\mathcal{N})}$, $k' \in Val_{(\mathcal{A}',\mathcal{N})}$ then let us define

$$r(k, k') \rightleftharpoons \{(k(x), k'(x)) \mid x \in V_g\} \cup \{(k(y)(t), k'(y)(t)) \mid y \in V_l, t \in \mathbb{N}\},$$

where $V_g$ and $V_l$ denote the set of global and local variables, respectively. It is easy to see that $r(k, k') \subseteq A \times A'$. We say that $k$ and $k'$ are $n$-similar (denoted $Sim_n(k, k')$) iff $r(k, k') \in Sim_n$.

**Step 4.**

**(20.5) Lemma.** *If* $k' \in Val_{(\mathcal{A}',\mathcal{N})}$, *then for all* $n \in \mathbb{N}$ *there is a valuation* $k \in Val_{(\mathcal{A},\mathcal{N})}$ *such that* $Sim_n(k, k')$.

*Proof.* Let $k$ be the same as $k'$. Thus we have to prove that $r \rightleftharpoons r(k', k') \in Sim_n$. It is easy to show by induction that $r_n = \{(a, a) \mid a \in dom\ r_n\}$. Thus properties (i) and (ii) of $n$-similarity are trivial. Property (iii) is satisfied with $q = p$, while property (iv) is trivial, since $C^* \cap dom\ r = \emptyset$. □

**(20.6) Lemma.** *If* $k \in Val_{(\mathcal{A},\mathcal{N})}$, *then for all* $n \in \mathbb{N}$ *there is a valuation* $k' \in Val_{(\mathcal{A}',\mathcal{N})}$ *such that* $Sim_n(k, k')$.

*Proof.* Let $D(k) \rightleftharpoons \{k(x) \mid x \in V_g\} \cup \{k(y)(t) \mid y \in V_l, t \in \mathbb{N}\}$, which (after defining $k'$) will be equal to $dom\, r(k, k')$. First we define a partial function $h : C^* \to S$. Let $p \in C$ be a parameter such that $S_p \cap D(k) = \emptyset$. Since $|Par(D(k))| \leq |D(k)| \leq \omega_0 < \omega_1 = |C|$, therefore $C \setminus Par(D(k)) \neq \emptyset$, and so any $p \in C \setminus Par(D(k))$ will do. Furthermore, let

$$J \rightleftharpoons \{c \in C \mid c \text{ occurs in some sequence of } C^* \cap D(k)\}.$$

Since $|D(k)| \leq \omega_0$, we have that $|J| \leq \omega_0$ and so $J \subset C$. Therefore we can define $h$ as follows:

- $dom\ h \rightleftharpoons Tree(J,n) \subset C^*$;
- $h(a) \rightleftharpoons (a, J, n, p, \gamma) \in S$ for all $a \in dom\ h$.

Note that, because of the definition of $J$, $C^* \cap D(k) \subseteq Tree(J,n) = dom\ h$. Now we can define $k'$. For all $x \in V_g$, $y \in V_l$, $t \in \mathbb{N}$ let

$$k'(x) \rightleftharpoons \begin{cases} k(x) & \text{if } k(x) \in C \cup S; \\ h(k(x)) & \text{if } k(x) \in C^*. \end{cases}$$

$$k'(y)(t) \rightleftharpoons \begin{cases} k(y)(t) & \text{if } k(y)(t) \in C \cup S; \\ h(k(y)(t)) & \text{if } k(y)(t) \in C^*. \end{cases}$$

It is left to prove that with this $k'$, $r \rightleftharpoons r(k,k') \in Sim_n$. Let $r' \rightleftharpoons r\restriction_{S\cdot}, r'' \rightleftharpoons r\restriction_{C^*\cdot}$. It is easy to show by induction that the following properties hold for all $m \leq n$:

(a) $r_m = r'_m \cup r''_m$;
(b) $r'_m = \{(a,a) \mid a \in dom\ r'_m\} \supseteq diag\ C$;
(c) $r''_m = \{(a, h(a)) \mid a \in dom\ r''_m \setminus C\} \cup diag\ C$
(especially $dom\ r''_m \setminus C \subseteq dom\ h$);
(d) $dom\ r'_m \subseteq C \cup (S \setminus S_p)$;
$rng\ r'_m = dom\ r'_m$;
(e) $dom\ r''_m \subseteq C \cup C^*$;
$rng\ r''_m \subseteq C \cup S_p$;

From (d), (e) and from (b), (c) we get

(f) $dom\ r'_m \cap dom\ r''_m = C$;
$rng\ r'_m \cap rng\ r''_m = C$;
(g) $r'_m\restriction C \times C = diag\ C$;
$r''_m\restriction C \times C = diag\ C$.

From (b), (c) and the definition of $h$ we get that $r'_n$ and $r''_n$ are functional and injective, and so by (a), (f) and (g) we get that $r_n$ is functional and injective, too. Thus property (i) of $n$-similarity is fulfilled for $r$. Properties (iii) and (iv) follow from (a), (b), (c) and the definition of $h$ with $m = n$. We only have to prove property (ii) of $n$-similarity.

Let $c \in C$; $x$, $g(c,x) \in dom\ r_n$. In the following the functionality of $r_n$, the definition of $g$ and $h$, and points (a), (b), (c) will be used.

- If $x \in C$: $r_n(g(c,x)) = r_n(\gamma) = \gamma = g(c,x) = g(c, r_n(x))$.
- If $x \in C^*$ then we have $r_n(g(c,x)) = r_n(x \circ \langle c \rangle) = r''_n(x \circ \langle c \rangle) = h(x \circ \langle c \rangle) = (x \circ \langle c \rangle, J, n, p, \gamma) = g(c, (x, J, n, p, \gamma)) = g(c, h(x)) = g(c, r''_n(x)) = g(c, r_n(x))$. Here we note that $x, g(c,x) = x \circ \langle c \rangle \in dom\ h$ since they are from $C^* \cap dom\ r_n \subseteq dom\ r''_n \subseteq dom\ h$ (cf. (c)).
- If $x \in S$: $x$ is of the form $(w, I, m, q, d)$. If $w \circ \langle c \rangle \notin Tree(I,m)$, then $r_n(g(c,x)) = r_n(\gamma) = \gamma = g(c,x) = g(c, r'_n(x)) = g(c, r_n(x))$. If $w \circ \langle c \rangle \in Tree(I,m)$ then $g(c,x) \in S$ thus $r_n(g(c,x)) = r'_n(g(c,x)) = g(c,x) = g(c, r'_n(x)) = g(c, r_n(x))$.

□

**Step 5.** Now we define a function *norm* for $\sigma$-type terms and $\sigma$-type temporal-logic formulas

$$norm : Term_\sigma \cup MForm_\sigma \to \mathbb{N}.$$

The definition goes by induction, and instead of $norm(a)$ we simply write $\|a\|$. Let us suppose that $x \in V_g \cup V_l \cup \{\hat{\gamma}\}$; $\tau, \tau' \in Term_\sigma$ and $\phi$, $\psi \in MForm_\sigma$. Then

$$\begin{aligned}
\|x\| &= 1;\\
\|\hat{f}(\tau)\| &= \|\tau\| + 1;\\
\|\hat{g}(\tau,\tau')\| &= max\{\|\tau\|, \|\tau'\|\} + 1;\\
\|\tau = \tau'\| &= max\{\|\tau\|, \|\tau'\|\};\\
\|\neg\phi\| &= \|\phi\| + 1;\\
\|\phi \wedge \psi\| &= max\{\|\phi\|, \|\psi\|\} + 1;\\
\|\exists x\phi\| &= 3 \cdot \|\phi\| + 1;\\
\|1\phi\| &= \|\phi\| + 1;\\
\|\circ\phi\| &= \|\phi\| + 1;\\
\|\Box\phi\| &= \|\phi\| + 1;
\end{aligned}$$

**Step 6.**

**(20.7) Lemma.** *Let $r \rightleftharpoons r(k,k')$ where $k$ and $k'$ are $n$-similar valuations. Let $\tau \in Term_\sigma$ be any term such that $\|\tau\| \leq n$. Then for all $t \in \mathbb{N}$*

*(a) $\tau_{(\mathcal{A},\mathcal{N})}[k,t] \in dom\ r_n$;*
*(b) $r_n(\tau_{(\mathcal{A},\mathcal{N})}[k,t]) = \tau_{(\mathcal{A}',\mathcal{N})}[k',t]$.*

*Proof.* The proof goes by induction. If $n = 0$, then no term $\tau$ satisfies the condition, thus the proposition is true. Now let us suppose that $n \geq 1$, and we know the proposition for $n-1$. We have to verify it for $n$ too. In the proof, we shall use Lemma (20.2) (a), Lemma (20.3) (a), Lemma (20.4), property (ii) of $n$-similarity, and the definition of $f$ and $g$. Since it does not cause any ambiguity we omit the indices representing the corresponding models.

- If $x \in V_g$ then $x[k,t] = k(x) \in dom\ r \subseteq dom\ r_n$. $r_n(x[k,t]) = r_n(k(x)) = r(k(x)) = k'(x) = x[k',t]$.
- If $y \in V_l$ then $y[k,t] = k(y)(t) \in dom\ r \subseteq dom\ r_n$. $r_n(y[k,t]) = r_n(k(y)(t)) = r(k(y)(t)) = k'(y)(t) = y[k',t]$.
- In the case $\hat{\gamma}$, $\hat{\gamma}[k,t] = \gamma \in dom\ r_0 \subseteq dom\ r_n$. $r_n(\hat{\gamma}[k,t]) = r_n(\gamma) = \gamma = \hat{\gamma}[k',t]$.
- In the case $\hat{f}(\tau)$, $\|\tau\| < \|\hat{f}(\tau)\| \leq n$, so by induction $\tau[k,t] \in dom\ r_{n-1} \subseteq dom\ r_n$ and $r_{n-1}(\tau[k,t]) = \tau[k',t]$. Now $\hat{f}(\tau)[k,t] = f(\tau[k,t]) \in C \subseteq dom\ r_0 \subseteq dom\ r_n$, and $r_n(\hat{f}(\tau)[k,t]) = r_n(f(\tau[k,t])) = f(r_n(\tau[k,t]) = f(r_{n-1}(\tau[k,t])) = f(\tau[k',t])) = \hat{f}(\tau)[k',t]$.

- In the case $\hat{g}(\tau,\tau')$ we know that $\|\tau\|$, $\|\tau'\| < \|\hat{g}(\tau,\tau')\| \leq n$, so by induction $\tau[k,t]$, $\tau'[k,t] \in dom\ r_{n-1} \subseteq dom\ r_n$ and $r_{n-1}(\tau[k,t]) = \tau[k',t]$, $r_{n-1}(\tau'[k,t]) = \tau'[k',t]$. Especially, $(\tau'[k,t], \tau'[k',t]) \in r_{n-1}$ from which, by definition, $(g(c,\tau'[k,t]), g(c,\tau'[k',t]) \in r_n$ $(c \in C)$; or equivalently

(*) for any $c \in C$ :

$$g(c,\tau'[k,t]) \in dom\ r_n \text{ and } r_n(g(c,\tau'[k,t])) = g(c,\tau'[k',t]).$$

If $\tau[k,t] \notin C$ then $\hat{g}(\tau,\tau')[k,t] = g(\tau[k,t],\tau'[k,t]) = \gamma \in C \subseteq dom\ r_0 \subseteq dom\ r_n$. Since, by Lemma (20.3a) and Lemma (20.4a), $r_{n-1}(\tau[k,t]) \notin C$, we get $r_n(\hat{g}(\tau,\tau')[k,t]) = r_n(g(\tau[k,t],\tau'[k,t])) = r_n(\gamma) = \gamma = g(r_{n-1}(\tau[k,t]), r_{n-1}\tau'[k,t])) = g(\tau[k',t],\tau'[k',t]) = \hat{g}(\tau,\tau')[k',t]$. If $\tau[k,t] \in C$, from (*) with $c = \tau[k,t]$ we get that $\hat{g}(\tau,\tau')[k,t] = g(\tau[k,t],\tau'[k,t)) = g(c,\tau'[k,t]) \in dom\ r_n$, and $r_n(\hat{g}(\tau,\tau')[k,t]) = r_n(g(\tau[k,t],\tau'[k,t])) = r_n(g(c,\tau'[k,t]) = g(c,\tau'[k',t]) = g(r_{n-1}(c),\tau'[k',t]) =$
$g(r_{n-1}(\tau[k,t]),\tau'[k',t])) = g(\tau[k',t],\tau'[k',t]) = \hat{g}(\tau,\tau')[k',t']$.

□

**(20.8) Lemma.** *Let $r \rightleftharpoons r(k,k')$, where $k$ and $k'$ are $n$-similar valuations. Let $\phi \in MForm_\sigma$ be any formula such that $\|\phi\| \leq n$. Then for all $t \in \mathbb{N}$*

$$(\mathcal{A},\mathcal{N}) \models \phi[k,t] \text{ iff } (\mathcal{A}',\mathcal{N}) \models \phi[k',t].$$

*Proof.* The proof goes by induction, If $n = 0$ then no formula $\phi$ satisfies the condition, thus the proposition is true. Now let us suppose that we know the proposition for all $m < n$, and we have to verify it for $n \geq 1$. For the validity relation "$\models$" recall Definition (17.5).

- The case of $\tau = \tau'$. $(\mathcal{A},\mathcal{N}) \models \tau = \tau'[k,t]$ iff $\tau[k,t] = \tau'[k,t]$. Now $\|\tau\|$, $\|\tau\| \leq \|\tau = \tau'\| \leq n$, thus by Lemma (20.7) $\tau[k,t]$, $\tau'[k,t] \in dom\ r_n$. Since $k$ and $k'$ are $n$-similar, $r_n$ is functional and injective, and so $\tau[k,t] = \tau'[k,t]$ iff $r_n(\tau[k,t]) = r_n(\tau'[k,t])$. Using Lemma (20.7) again, the latter is equivalent to $\tau[k',t] = \tau'[k',t]$, which is true iff $(\mathcal{A}',\mathcal{N}) \models \phi[k',t]$.
- The case of $\neg\phi$. $(\mathcal{A},\mathcal{N}) \models \neg\phi[k,t]$ iff $(\mathcal{A},\mathcal{N}) \not\models \phi[k,t]$. Now $\|\phi\| < \|\neg\phi\| \leq n$, thus, by Lemma (20.3) (b), $k$ and $k'$ are $\|\phi\|$-similar too. Using induction for $m = \|\phi\| < n$, we get that $(\mathcal{A},\mathcal{N}) \not\models \phi[k,t]$ iff $(\mathcal{A}',\mathcal{N}) \not\models \phi[k',t]$ iff $(\mathcal{A}',\mathcal{N}) \models \neg\phi[k',t]$.
- The case $\phi \wedge \psi$. $(\mathcal{A},\mathcal{N}) \models (\phi \wedge \psi)[k,t]$ iff $(\mathcal{A},\mathcal{N}) \models \phi[k,t]$ and $(\mathcal{A},\mathcal{N}) \models \psi[k,t]$. Now $\|\phi\|$, $\|\psi\| < \|\phi \wedge \psi\|$, thus, by Lemma (20.3) (b), for $\mu = max\{\|\phi\|, \|\psi\|\}$ $k$ and $k'$ are $\mu$-similar too. Using induction for $m = \mu < n$, we get that $(\mathcal{A},\mathcal{N}) \models \phi[k,t]$ and $(\mathcal{A},\mathcal{N}) \models \psi[k,t]$ iff $(\mathcal{A}',\mathcal{N}) \models \phi[k',t]$ and $(\mathcal{A}',\mathcal{N}) \models \psi[k',t]$ iff $(\mathcal{A}',\mathcal{N}) \models \phi \wedge \psi[k',t]$.
- The case of modalities. We prove only the case for $\Box\phi$, the other proofs are similar. $(\mathcal{A},\mathcal{N}) \models \Box\phi[k,t]$ iff for each $t' \geq t$: $(\mathcal{A},\mathcal{N}) \models \phi[k,t']$. Now $\|\phi\| < \|\Box\phi\| \leq n$, thus by Lemma (20.3b) $k$ and $k'$ are $\|\phi\|$-similar too.

Using induction for $m = \|\phi\| < n$, we get that for each $t' \geq t$: $(\mathcal{A}, \mathcal{N}) \models \phi[k, t']$ iff for each $t' \geq t$: $(\mathcal{A}', \mathcal{N}) \models \phi[k', t']$ iff $(\mathcal{A}', \mathcal{N}) \models \Box\phi[k', t]$.

- The case of $\exists x \phi$ is the most difficult one. In order to prove it, we need the following lemma.

**(20.9) Lemma.** *If $k$ and $k'$ are $3n+1$-similar valuations, then for all $x \in V_g$*

*(a) for all $a \in A$ there is an $a' \in A'$ such that $k[a/x]$ and $k'[a'/x]$ are $n$-similar and*

*(b) for all $a' \in A'$ there is an $a \in A$ such that $k[a/x]$ and $k'[a'/x]$ are $n$-similar.*

The proof of this lemma is rather complicated, so we postpone it. Now we continue the proof for the case $\exists x \phi$, based on this lemma (observe that, because of quantification, $x \in V_g$).

$(\mathcal{A}, \mathcal{N}) \models \exists x \phi[k, t]$ implies that for some $a \in A$ $(\mathcal{A}, \mathcal{N}) \models \phi[k[a/x], t]$. Let us fix such an $a$. Now $3\|\phi\| + 1 = \|\exists x \phi\| \leq n$, thus by Lemma (20.3) (b), $k$ and $k'$ are $(3\|\phi\| + 1)$-similar too. By Lemma (20.9) (a), we can choose an $a' \in A'$ such that $k[a/x]$ and $k'[a'/x]$ are $\|\phi\|$-similar. Since $\|\phi\| < 3\|\phi\| + 1 \leq n$, we can use induction for $m = \|\phi\|$ and obtain that $(\mathcal{A}, \mathcal{N}) \models \phi[k[a/x], t]$ implies $(\mathcal{A}', \mathcal{N}) \models \phi[k'[a'/x], t]$ which implies $(\mathcal{A}', \mathcal{N}) \models \exists x \phi[k', t]$. Thus we have seen that $(\mathcal{A}, \mathcal{N}) \models \exists \phi[k, t]$ implies that $(\mathcal{A}', \mathcal{N}) \models \exists \phi[k', t]$. The other direction can be proved similarly; we only have to use Lemma (20.9) (b). □

Now we turn to prove Lemma (20.9). However, first we need some further propositions and definitions. The following propositions shows an important consequence with respect to property (iv) of $n$-similarity.

**(20.10) Lemma.**

*(a) Let $n \in \mathbb{N}$, $J \subset C$ and $n \leq m \in \mathbb{N}$. Furthermore let $a = a' \circ a'' \in Tree(J, m)$, and let us suppose that there exists a $w \in C^*$ for which $|w| \geq n$ and $a \circ w \in Tree(J, m)$. Then for any $w' \in C^*$ for which $|w'| \leq n$, it is true that $a' \circ w' \in Tree(J, m)$.*

*(b) Let $J \subset C$ and $m \in \mathbb{N}$. If $a' \circ a'' \in Tree(J, m)$ then $a' \in Tree(J, m)$.*

*Proof.* First we prove the statement (a). If $a' \in J^*$, then from $|w'| \leq n \leq m$ and from the definition of $Tree(J, m)$, we immediately get that $a' \circ w' \in Tree(J, m)$. Otherwise, $a' = a_1 \circ \langle c \rangle \circ a_2$ with some $a_1 \in J^*$, $c \in C \setminus J$. Now from $a_1 \circ \langle c \rangle \circ (a_2 \circ a'' \circ w) = a' \circ a'' \circ w = a \circ w \in Tree(J, m)$ we get that $|a_2 \circ a'' \circ w| \leq m$. Therefore

$$m \geq |a_2 \circ a'' \circ w| = |a_2| + |a''| + |w| \geq |a_2| + |w| \geq |a_2| + n \geq |a_2| + |w'| = |a_2 \circ w'|,$$

i.e. $|a_2 \circ w'| \leq m$ which means that $a_1 \circ \langle c \rangle \circ (a_2 \circ w') \in Tree(J, m)$. Since $a_1 \circ \langle c \rangle \circ (a_2 \circ w') = a' \circ w'$, we have got $a' \circ w' \in Tree(J, m)$ again.

Statement (b) follows from (a) by taking $n = 0$ and $w = w' = \lambda$. □

Now we define a distance *dist* over $A$. First let us define a function $\rho : A \times A \to \mathbb{N} \cup \{\infty\}$ (where $\infty$ behaves as usual with respect to addition and ordering).

$$\rho(x,y) \rightleftharpoons \begin{cases} 0 & \text{if } x,\ y \in C \text{ and } x = y; \\ |z| & \text{if } x,\ y \in C^* \text{ and } y = x \circ z; \\ |z| & \text{if } x,\ y \in S \text{ and they are} \\ & \quad\quad \text{of the form } x = (w, I, n, p, c),\ y = (w \circ z, I, n, p, c); \\ \infty & \text{otherwise.} \end{cases}$$

Note that in the definition, at most one $z$ can satisfy the corresponding conditions, and any such $z \in C^*$. Now let $dist : A \times A \to \mathbb{N} \cup \{\infty\}$ be defined as follows:

$$dist(x,y) = min\{\rho(s,x) + \rho(s,y) \mid s \in A\}.$$

The following statement directly follows from the definition of $\rho$:

**(20.11) Lemma.** *$\rho$ has the following properties (for all $x$, $y$, $z$, $s$, $s' \in A$):*

*(a) if $\rho(x,y) < \infty$ then $x$, $y \in C$ or $x$, $y \in C^*$ or $x$, $y \in S$;*
*(b) $\rho(x,y) = 0$ iff $x = y$;*
*(c) if $\rho(x,y)$, $\rho(y,z) < \infty$ then $\rho(x,z) = \rho(x,y) + \rho(y,z)$;*
*(d) if $\rho(s,y) \leq \rho(s',y) < \infty$ then $\rho(s',s) = \rho(s',y) - \rho(s,y) < \infty$.*

**(20.12) Lemma.** *dist has the following properties (for all $x$, $y$, $z \in A$):*

*(a) if $dist(x,y) < \infty$ then $x$, $y \in C$ or $x$, $y \in C^*$ or $x$, $y \in S$;*
*(b) $dist(x,y) = 0$ iff $x = y$;*
*(c) $dist(x,y) = dist(y,x)$ (symmetry);*
*(d) $dist(x,z) \leq dist(x,y) + dist(y,z)$ (triangle inequality).*

*Proof.* Statement (a) follows from Lemma (20.11) (a) and from the definition of *dist*, since $C$, $C^*$ and $S$ are pairwise disjoint sets. Statement (b) follows from Lemma (20.11) (b) and from the definition of *dist*, while statement (c) follows directly from the definition of *dist*. To prove the triangle inequality we may suppose that both $dist(x,y)$ and $dist(y,z)$ are finite, otherwise the statement is obvious. This means that for some $s$, $s' \in A$ $dist(x,y) = \rho(s,x) + \rho(s,y) < \infty$ and $dist(y,z) = \rho(s',y) + \rho(s',z) < \infty$. Now either $\rho(s,y) \leq \rho(s',y) < \infty$ or $\rho(s',y) \leq \rho(s,y) < \infty$. In the first case, from Lemma (20.11) (d) we get that $\rho(s',s) < \infty$ and $\rho(s',y) = \rho(s',s) + \rho(s,y)$. From this, and from Lemma (20.11) (c) we get:

$$\begin{aligned} dist(x,y) + dist(y,z) &= (\rho(s,x) + \rho(s,y)) + (\rho(s',y) + \rho(s',z)) \\ &\geq \rho(s,x) + \rho(s',y) + \rho(s',z) \\ &= \rho(s,x) + (\rho(s',s) + \rho(s,y)) + \rho(s',z) \\ &\geq (\rho(s',s) + \rho(s,x)) + \rho(s',z) \\ &= \rho(s',x) + \rho(s',z) \\ &\geq dist(x,z) \end{aligned}$$

The case $\rho(s', y) \leq \rho(s, y)$ can be proved similarly. □

The following proposition shows that, in some sense, the distance *dist* describes the connection between the domain/range of an $n$-similarity relation $r \subseteq A \times A'$, and the domain/range of its $n$-th extension $r_n$.

**(20.13) Lemma.** *Let* $r \subseteq A \times A'$, $n \in \mathbb{N}$. *Then*

(a) *if* $v \in dom\ r_n$ *then for some* $u \in dom\ r_0$: $dist(u, v) \leq n$;
(a') *if* $v \in rng\ r_n$ *then for some* $u \in rng\ r_0$: $dist(u, v) \leq n$;
(b) *if* $r \in Sim_n$, $u \in dom\ r$ *and* $dist(u, v) \leq n$ *then* $v \in dom\ r_n$;
(b') *if* $r \in Sim_n$, $v \in rng\ r$ *and* $dist(u, v) \leq n$ *then* $v \in rng\ r_n$.

*Proof.* Statement (a) can be easily proved by induction, using the triangle inequality Lemma (20.12) (d). If $n = 0$ then, by Lemma (20.12) (b), $v \rightleftharpoons u$ will do. If $n > 0$ and we know (a) for $n - 1$, then, from the definition of $r_n$, the following cases are to be considered:

- $v \in r_{n-1}$: Trivial, by the induction hypothesis.
- $v = g(c, a)$ for some $a \in dom\ r_{n-1}$, $c \in C$. If $g(c, a) = \gamma$, then $u = v = g(c, a) = \gamma \in C \subseteq dom\ r_0$ will do. If $g(c, a) \neq \gamma$, then $dist(a, g(c, a)) = 1$. Applying the induction hypothesis for $a \in dom\ r_{n-1}$ we get that for some $u \in dom\ r_0$, $dist(u, a) \leq n - 1$. Now by the triangle inequality (Lemma (20.12d)), $dist(u, v) \leq dist(u, a) + dist(a, v) \leq (n - 1) + dist(a, v) = (n - 1) + dist(a, g(c, a)) = (n - 1) + 1 = n$.
- For some $c \in C$, $g(c, v) \in dom\ r_{n-1}$ and $\gamma \neq g(c, v)$. Thus $dist(g(c, v), v) = 1$, and, by the induction hypothesis, for some $u \in dom\ r_0$ $dist(u, g(c, v)) \leq n - 1$. Now from the triangle inequality, $dist(u, v) \leq dist(u, g(c, v)) + dist(g(c, v), v)) \leq (n - 1) + 1 = n$. (a') can be proved similarly.

To prove (b) we consider the following cases:

- If $u \in C$ then by Lemma (20.12) (a) $v \in C \subseteq dom\ r_0 \subseteq dom\ r_n$.
- If $u \in C^*$ then by Lemma (20.12) (a) $v \in C^*$ and so by Lemma (20.11) (a) there is an $s \in C^*$ such that $\rho(s, u) + \rho(s, v) \leq n$. By the definition of $\rho$ this means that $u = s \circ u'$ and $v = s \circ v'$ with $|u'| + |v'| \leq n$. Since $r \in Sim_n$, $u \in C^* \cap dom\ r$ we get that $(u, (u, I, m, p, \gamma)) \in r$ for some $I \subset C$, $m \geq n$, $p \in C$ and we also know that for some $w \in C^*$, $|w| \geq n$ and $u \circ w \in Tree(I, m)$. Since $u = s \circ u'$, from Lemma (20.10) (a) we know that for any $w' \in C^*$ for which $|w'| \leq n$: $u \circ w' \in Tree(I, m)$. Especially, if $w'$ is an initial segment of $u'$ or $v'$, $s \circ w' \in Tree(I, m)$, since $|u'|, |v'| \leq |u'| + |v'| \leq n$. Therefore, from the definition of extension, from $u = s \circ u'$ and $(u, (u, I, m, p, \gamma)) \in r$, we get that $(s, (s, I, m, p, \gamma)) \in r_{|u'|}$ and then $(s \circ v', (s \circ v', I, m, p, \gamma)) \in r_{|u'|+|v'|}$. Since $s \circ v' = v$ and $|u'| + |v'| \leq n$, we get from this and Lemma (20.2) (a) that $(v, (v, I, m, p, \gamma)) \in r_n$, i.e. $v \in dom\ r_n$.

- If $u \in S$ then by Lemma (20.12) (a) $v \in S$ and so by Lemma (20.11) (a) there is an $s \in S$ such that $\rho(s,u) + \rho(s,v) \leq n$. By the definition of $\rho$ this means that $u$, $s$ and $v$ are of the form $u = (s' \circ u', I, m, p, c)$, $s = (s', I, m, p, c)$ and $v = (s' \circ v', I, m, p, c)$ where $|u'| + |v'| \leq n$; $s' \circ u'$, $s' \circ v' \in Tree(I,m)$. From this, by Lemma (20.10b), we get that if $w'$ is an initial segment of $u'$ or $v'$ then $s' \circ w' \in Tree(I,m)$. Furthermore, since $r \in Sim_n$ and $u \in S \cap dom\ r$, we know that for some $q \in C$ $((s' \circ u', I, m, p, c), (s' \circ u', I, m, q, c)) \in r$. Thus, similarly to the above, we can show that $(v, (s' \circ v', I, m, q, c)) \in r_{|u'|+|v'|}$ and, from this, that $v \in dom\ r_n$.

To prove (b') we note that from $v \in rng\ r$ and $r \in Sim_n$ we get that $v \in C \cup S$. The case $v \in C$ is simple, as in (b). The case $v \in S$ has to be separated into two subcases: one if the corresponding domain element is from $C^*$, and the other if it is from $S$. Both subcases can be proved analogously to (b). □

Now we can turn to prove Lemma (20.9) needed for proving Lemma (20.8) for the case $\exists x \phi$.

*Proof of Lemma (20.9)* By definition, $r \rightleftharpoons r(k,k') \in Sim_{3n+1}$. First we prove statement (a). For every $a \in A$ we need an $a' \in A'$ such that $\hat{r} \rightleftharpoons r(k[a/x], k'[a'/x]) \in Sim_n$. We distinguish two cases with respect to the distance of $a$ from the domain of $r_0$.

**Case 1.** For some $u \in dom\ r_0$, $dist(u,a) \leq 2n+1$. From Lemma (20.3) (b) and Lemma (20.13) (b), we know that $a \in dom\ r_{2n+1}$. By Lemma (20.3) (a), we can define $a' \rightleftharpoons r_{2n+1}(a)$. Now let us define $\hat{r} \rightleftharpoons r(k[a/x], k'[a'/x])$. From the definition of $a'$, and from Lemma (20.2) (a) and Lemma (20.4) (a) we get that $\hat{r}_0 \subseteq r_{2n+1}$, which clearly implies that $\hat{r}_n \subseteq r_{3n+1}$. Thus conditions (i) and (ii) of $n$-similarity are trivially satisfied for $\hat{r}$ since $r \in Sim_{3n+1}$. Obviously $\hat{r} \setminus r \subseteq \{(a,a')\}$, so it is enough to check whether the pair $(a,a')$ satisfies properties (iii) and (iv).

- If $a \in C$ then properties (iii) and (iv) do not concern $(a,a')$.
- If $a \in C^*$ then only property (iv) concerns $(a,a')$. From $dist(u,a) \leq 2n+1$, by Lemma (20.12) (a), Lemma (20.11) (a) and by the definition of $dist$ and $\rho$, we know that $u \in C^*$ and for some $s \in C^*$: $u = s \circ u_1$, $a = s \circ a_1$ where $|u_1| + |a_1| \leq 2n+1$. Since $u \in C^* \cap dom\ r_0 \subseteq dom\ r$ and $r \in Sim_{3n+1}$, we know that $(u, (u, I, m, p, \gamma)) \in r$ for some $I \subset C$, $p \in C$, $m \geq 3n+1$, and there is a $w \in C^*$ such that $|w| \geq 3n+1$ and $u \circ w \in Tree(I,m)$. Now, similarly to the proof of Lemma (20.13) (b), one can control with the help of Lemma (20.10) (a) that $(a, (a, I, m, p, \gamma)) \in r_{|u_1|+|a_1|} \subseteq r_{2n+1}$, thus $a' = r_{2n+1}(a) = (a, I, m, p, \gamma)$. Since $m \geq 3n+1 > n$, it is left to prove that for some $\hat{w}$: $|\hat{w}| \geq n$ and $a \circ \hat{w} \in Tree(I,m)$. Let $\hat{w}$ be any sequence of $C^*$ with $|\hat{w}| = n$. Now $|a_1 \circ \hat{w}| = |a_1| + |\hat{w}| \leq (2n+1) + n = 3n+1$. Since $u = s \circ u_1$ and for some $w$ with $|w| \geq 3n+1$ $u \circ w \in Tree(I,m)$ (as we have seen above), from Lemma (20.10) (a) we get that $s \circ (a_1 \circ \hat{w}) \in Tree(I,m)$, i.e. $a \circ \hat{w} \in Tree(I,m)$.

- If $a \in S$ then only property (iii) concerns $(a, a')$. From $dist(u, a) \leq 2n+1$, we get that $u \in S$ and for some $s \in S$: $u$, $s$ and $a$ are of the form $u = (s' \circ u_1, I, m, p, c)$, $s = (s', I, m, p, c)$, $a = (s' \circ a_1, I, m, p, c)$ where $|u_1| + |a_1| \leq 2n+1$ and $s' \circ u_1$, $s' \circ a_1 \in Tree(I, m)$. Since $u \in S \cap dom\ r_0 \subseteq dom\ r$ and $r \in Sim_{3n+1}$, we know that $((s' \circ u_1, I, m, p, c), (s' \circ u_1, I, m, q, c)) \in r$ for some $q \in C$. Again, similarly to the proof of Lemma (20.13) (b), one can control with the help of Lemma (20.10) (a) that $((s' \circ a_1, I, m, p, c), (s' \circ a_1, I, m, q, c)) \in r_{|u_1|+|a_1|} \subseteq r_{2n+1}$ which means that $a' = r_{2n+1}(a)$ is of the demanded form. Thus we have proved that $\hat{r} \in Sim_n$.

**Case 2.** For all $u \in dom\ r_0$: $dist(u, a) > 2n + 1$. First observe that $a \notin C$, since $C \subseteq r_0$, and if $a \in C$ then with $u \rightleftharpoons a$, by Lemma (20.12) (b), we get $dist(u, a) = 0 < 2n + 1$, a contradiction. Now let $q \in C$ be a parameter such that $S_q \cap rng\ r_{3n+1} = \emptyset$. Such a $q$ can be chosen, since by Lemma (20.2) (d) $Par(r_{3n+1}) = Par(r)$, thus $|Par(rng\ r_{3n+1})| \leq |Par(r_{3n+1})| = |Par(r)| = |Par(dom\ r) \cup Par(rng\ r)| \leq |dom\ r \cup rng\ r| \leq \omega_0 < \omega_1 = |C|$, and so $Q \rightleftharpoons C \setminus Par(rng\ r_{3n+1}) \neq \emptyset$. Therefore any $q \in Q$ will do.

If $a \in C^*$ then let $I \subset C$ be any set such that $a \in I^*$. Let us define $a' \rightleftharpoons (a, I, n, q, \gamma)$. If $a \in S$ then $a$ is of the form $(w, I, m, p, c)$. Let us define $a' \rightleftharpoons (w, I, m, q, c)$. Take

$$\hat{r} \rightleftharpoons r(k[a/x], k'[a'/x])$$
$$r' \rightleftharpoons \{(a, a')\}$$
$$r'' \rightleftharpoons \{(k(x), k'(x)) \mid x \in V_g \setminus \{x\}\} \cup \{(k(y)(t), k'(y)(t) \mid y \in V_l, t \in \mathbb{N}\}.$$

The following statements are true:

(A) $\hat{r} = r' \cup r''$;
(B) $\hat{r}_n = r'_n \cup r''_n$;
(C) $r' \in Sim_n$;
(D) $r'' \in Sim_n$;
(E) $dom\ r'_n \cap dom\ r''_n \subseteq C$;
(F) $rng\ r'_n \cap rng\ r''_n \subseteq C$.

Here (A) is trivial. (B) follows from (A) and Lemma (20.2) (c).

(C) follows from the explicit form of $r'_n$. It is easy to show, by induction, that if $a \in C^*$ then because of the definition of $I$ and because of Lemma (20.10) (b):

$$r'_n = diag\ C \cup \{(a \circ s, (a \circ s, I, n, q, \gamma)) \mid s \in C^*, |s| \leq n\} \cup \{(a_1, (a_1, I, n, q, \gamma)) \mid \exists s \in C^* : |s| \leq n \text{ and } a = a_1 \circ s\}.$$

Similarly, if $a = (w, I, m, p, c) \in S$, using also Lemma (20.10) (b) again,

$$r'_n = diag\ C \cup \{((w \circ s, I, m, p, c), (w \circ s, I, m, q, c)) \mid s \in C^*, |s| \leq n, w \circ s \in Tree(I, m)\} \cup \{(w', I, m, p, c), (w', I, m, q, c)) \mid \exists s \in C^*, |s| \leq n, w = w' \circ s\}.$$

From these forms it is easy to check properties (i) and (iii) of $n$-similarity. To prove property (iv) we have to use the definition of $I$ too ($n \geq n$ and any $w$ with $|w| = n \geq n$ will do). Now we prove property (ii).

- If $a \in C^*$ then $S \cap dom\ r'_n = \emptyset$. Let $x$, $g(c,x) \in dom\ r'_n$. If $x \in C$ then $g(c,x) = \gamma \in C$, and $r'_n(x) = x$; $r'_n(g(c,x)) = r'_n(\gamma) = \gamma = g(c,x) = g(c, r'_n(x))$. If $x \in C^*$ then $g(c,x) = x \circ \langle c \rangle \in dom\ r'_n$, and so $x$, $x \circ \langle c \rangle \in Tree(I,n)$. $r'_n(g(c,x)) = r'_n(x \circ \langle c \rangle) = (x \circ \langle c \rangle, I, n, q, \gamma) = g(c, (x, I, n, q, \gamma)) = g(c, r'_n(x))$.
- If $a \in S$ then $C^* \cap dom\ r'_n = \emptyset$. Let $x$, $g(c,x) \in dom\ r_n$. If $x \in C$ then $g(c,x) = \gamma \in C$ and $r'_n(x) = x$; $r'_n(g(c,x)) = r'_n(\gamma) = \gamma = g(c,x) = g(c, r'_n(x))$. If $x = (w', I, m, p, c) \in S$ and $g(c,x) = \gamma$ then $w' \circ \langle c \rangle \notin Tree(I,m)$. $r'_n(g(c,x)) = r'_n(\gamma) = \gamma = g(c, (w', I, m, q, c)) = g(c, r'_n(x))$. If $g(c,x) \neq \gamma$ then $w' \circ \langle c \rangle \in Tree(I,m)$ and $g(c,x) = (w' \circ \langle c \rangle, I, m, p, c)$. $r'_n(g(c,x)) = r'_n(w' \circ \langle c \rangle, I, m, p, c) = (w' \circ \langle c \rangle, I, m, q, c) = g(c, (w', I, m, q, c)) = g(c, r'_n(x))$.

Thus the proof of (C) is complete.

(D) follows from Lemma (20.2) (b) and Lemma (20.3) (b) since $r'' \subseteq r \in Sim_{3n+1}$.

To prove (E) we note that if for some $v \notin C$: $v \in dom\ r'_n \cap dom r''_n$ then, by Lemma (20.13) (a), for some $u' \in dom\ r'_0$, $u'' \in dom\ r''_0$: $dist(u', v) \leq n$ and $dist(u'', v) \leq n$. Since $v \notin C$, from Lemma (20.12) (a) we get that $u'$, $u'' \notin C$ and so $u' \in dom\ r'$ and $u'' \in dom\ r''$. Necesssarily $u' = a$. Thus from Lemma (20.12) (c), (d): $dist(u'', a) = dist(u'', u') \leq dist(u'', v) + dist(v, u') = dist(u'', v) + dist(u', v) \leq n + n = 2n < 2n + 1$. Since $u'' \in dom\ r'' \subseteq dom\ r \subseteq dom\ r_0$ this contradicts the condition of Case 2.

We turn to prove (F). It is easy to see (e.g. from the explicit form of $r'_n$), that $rng\ r'_n \subseteq C \cup S_q$. On the other hand, since $r'' \subseteq r$, we get from Lemma (20.2) (a), (b) that $r''_n \subseteq r_{3n+1}$, especially $rng\ r''_n \subseteq rng\ r_{3n+1}$. Now (F) follows from the definition of $q$.

Now we are ready to prove that $\hat{r} \in Sim_n$. Property (i) of $n$-similarity follows from (B)-(F) using also Lemma (20.4) (a). Properties (iii) and (iv) follow from (B)-(D) and (i). Property (ii) can be proved as (iii) or (iv) if $x$, $g(c,x) \in dom\ r'_n$ or $x$, $g(c,x) \in dom\ r''_n$. Therefore it is enough to show that if $x$, $g(c,x) \in dom\ \hat{r}_n$ then it is impossible that either $x$, $g(c,x) \in dom\ r'_n$ or $x$, $g(c,x) \in dom\ r''_n$. For this, let us suppose that either $x \in dom\ r'_n$, $g(c,x) \in dom\ r''_n$, $g(c,x) \notin dom\ r'_n$ and $x \notin dom\ r''_n$ or $x \in dom\ r''_n$, $g(c,x) \in dom\ r'_n$, $g(c,x) \notin dom\ r''_n$ and $x \notin dom\ r'_n$. Consider e.g. the first case. From $x \notin dom\ r''_n$ we get that $x \notin C$; from $g(c,x) \notin dom\ r'_n$ we get that $g(c,x) \notin C$, and thus by the definition of $g$ and $dist$ we get that $dist(x, g(c,x)) = 1$. Using Lemma (20.13) (a) we get from $x \in dom\ r'_n$ that for some $u' \in dom\ r'_0$: $dist(u', x) \leq n$, and similarly we get that for some $u'' \in dom\ r''_0$: $dist(u'', g(c,x)) \leq n$.. Since $x$, $g(c,x) \notin C$, from Lemma (20.12) (a) we get that $u'$, $u'' \notin C$ and so $u' \in dom\ r'$, $u'' \in dom\ r''$. Necessarily, $u' = a$. Thus from Lemma (20.12) (c), (d): $dist(u'', a) = dist(u'', u') \leq dist(u'', g(c,x)) + dist(g(c,x), u') \leq n +$

$dist(u', g(c,x)) \leq n + dist(u', x) + dist(x, g(c,x)) \leq n + n + 1 = 2n + 1$. Since $u'' \in dom\ r'' \subseteq dom\ r \subseteq dom\ r_0$ this contradicts the condition of Case 2. The second case is contradictory as well, thus either $x$, $g(c,x) \in dom\ r'_n$ or $x$, $g(c,x) \in dom\ r''_n$, and so $\hat{r} \in Sim_n$.

Now we turn to prove the statement (b) of Lemma (20.9). For every $a' \in A'$ we need an $a \in A$ such that $\hat{r} \rightleftharpoons r(k[a/x], k'[a'/x]) \in Sim_n$. We distinguish two cases with respect to the distance of $a'$ from the range of $r_0$.

**Case 1.** For some $u' \in rng\ r_0$: $dist(u', a') \leq 2n + 1$. From Lemma (20.3) (b) and Lemma (20.13) (b') we know that $a' \in rng\ r_{2n+1}$. Because of the injectivity of $r_{2n+1}$ (see Lemma (20.3) (a)) we can define $a$ by $a' = r_{2n+1}(a)$. Now $\hat{r} \rightleftharpoons r(k[a/x], k'[a'/x])$ is an $n$-similarity. This simply follows from Case 1 of statement (a) since now $a \in dom\ r_{2n+1}$ and so, by Lemma (20.13) (a), for some $u \in dom\ r_0$, $dist(u, a) \leq 2n + 1$, which is just the condition of Case 1 of statement (a), and the $\hat{r}$ given here is the same as the $\hat{r}$ given in Case 1 of statement (a).

**Case 2.** For all $u' \in rng\ r_0$, $dist(u', a') > 2n+1$. Similarly to Case 2 of statement (a) of Lemma (20.9) we can see that $a' \notin C$ and that there is a $q \in C$ such that $S_q \cap dom\ r_{3n+1} = \emptyset$. Since $a' \notin C$, we get that $a' \in S$, thus $a'$ is of the form $(w, I, m, p, c)$ $(I \subset C,\ m \in \mathbb{N},\ p,\ c \in C,\ w \in Tree(I, m))$. Now let us define $a \rightleftharpoons (w, I, m, q, c)$ and let $\hat{r}$, $r'$, $r''$ be defined as in Case 2 of statement (a) of Lemma (20.9). Now statements of the form (A)-(F) of Case 2 of (a) of Lemma (20.9) are true here again, and they can be proved similarly. The only difference is that (E) here can be proved like (F) there, and (F) here can be proved like (E) there.

The proof of $\hat{r} \in Sim_n$ is analogous to the corresponding proof in Case 2 of (a) of Lemma (20.9). We only note that because of the definition of $q$ for all $u \in dom\ r_0$, $dist(u, a) = \infty > 2n + 1$. Therefore the case when neither $x$, $g(c,x) \in dom\ r'_n$ nor $x$, $g(c,x) \in dom\ r''_n$ can be excluded with the same technique as in Case 2 of (a) of Lemma (20.9). □

*Lemmas (20.2)-(20.13) complete the realization of steps (1)-(6), and hence Theorem (20.1) is proved.* □

Note that Theorem (20.1) holds not only for standard Kripke models. Any time structure $\mathcal{T}$ with $|T| \geq \omega_0$ can be used.

The above theorem remains true if we strengthen our temporal logic (as e.g. Pnueli does for his temporal logic, see in Pnueli [1984] or in Lichtenstein, Pnueli, Zuck [1985]) by adding new modalities like "until", "since", "sometime in the past". Namely, we may permit "new modalities" based on addition, multiplication, etc. on time structure $\mathcal{T}$ without affecting the truth of our theorem. Moreover, we can go beyond recursive functions, too. We can add new relations to $\mathcal{T}$, creating e.g. $(T, 0, 1, +, \leq, ..., R_1, ..., R_h)$ and we can base new modalities on this new time structure and the theorem still remains true. Moreover, we can also change the definition of program semantics (e.g. by introducing branching time) leaving the truth of the theorem unchanged. This follows from a careful inspection of the case of the modalities in the proof of Lemma (20.8).

Now let us investigate the interrelation of dynamic and temporal logics in the case of countable models.

Chapter 21

# The Case of Enumerable Models

Countable models play a significant role in programming theory from a pragmatic point of view, since programs are executed in countable models (e.g. on integers). Therefore it is interesting to study the relationship between the two logics in question with respect to the enumerable models. One may expect either that the results of the above chapters are inherited or that dynamic logic is more powerful. However, as we shall see, neither of these expectations is borne out. In fact, temporal logic is of greater expressive power. Before we attempt to investigate their comparative expressiveness we consider an important semantic construction.

Let $(\mathcal{A}, \mathcal{N})$ be a standard Kripke model. Let $k \in Val_{(\mathcal{A},\mathcal{N})}$ be a given valuation, $t \in \mathbb{N}$ a given time moment. Let $p \in rP_\sigma$ be a fixed program. $k_p$ is a shorthand for the valuation $k\restriction_{X \cup X_l}$, where $X$ is $var(p)$ and $X_l$ is the set of variables used to label the node of $gr(p)$.

**(21.1) Lemma.** *For any program $p \in rP_\sigma$ there exists a temporal-logic formula $repeatwork(p) \in Mform_\sigma$ such that for any standard Kripke model $(\mathcal{A}, \mathcal{N})$ and for any valuation $k \in Val_{(\mathcal{A},\mathcal{N})}$ and for any time moment $t \in \mathbb{N}$*

$$(\mathcal{A}, \mathcal{N}) \models repeatwork(p)[k, t]$$

*iff the following two statements hold:*

*(i) for all $t \in \mathbb{N}$ there is a sequence $0 \le t', t'+1, ..., t'+s = t$ $(s \ge 0)$ of time moments such that $k_p(t') = k_p(0)$ and $\lambda(i \le s).k_p(t'+i) \in Trace_{\mathcal{A}}[\![p, var(p)]\!]$.*

*(ii) If $k_0 = k_p(0)$ and $(k_0, ...k_{n+1}) \in Trace_{\mathcal{A}}[\![p, var(p)]\!]$ $(n \ge 0)$ and for some $t_0 < t_1 < ... < t_n$ we have that $k_p(t_i) = k_i$ for all $0 \le i \le n$ then there is a $t_{n+1} > t_n$ such that $k_p(t_{n+1}) = k_{n+1}$.*

*Proof.* Let us take the following formula (with $g = gr(p)$):

$$repeatwork(p) \quad \rightleftharpoons \quad 1\exists X_0 \Bigg($$

$$(r1) \qquad (\check{X} = X_0 \wedge \check{X}_l = start_g) \wedge$$

$$(r2) \qquad \Box \forall U \forall U_l \Big(U = \check{X} \wedge U_l = \check{X}_l \to \exists V \exists V_l \Big(((localstep_g(U, U_l, V, V_l) \vee$$

$$\vee(V = X_0 \wedge V_l = start_g)) \wedge \circ(V = \check{X} \wedge V_l = \check{X}_l))\Big)\Big)\wedge$$

$$(r3) \qquad \Box\forall U \forall U_l \Big( U = \check{X} \wedge U_l = \check{X}_l \rightarrow$$

$$\forall V \forall V_l \big( localstep_g(U, U_l, V, V_l) \rightarrow \Diamond(V = \check{X} \wedge V_l = \check{X}_l)\big)\Big).$$

Here $X \rightleftharpoons var(p)$, $\check{X}$ is the local copy of $X$ and $X_l$ is a set of variables coding the set $node(g)$. $X_0$ is a new global copy of $X$.

The subformula (r1) ensures that the initial value of the corresponding local variables will be equal to the value of the global variable $X_0$. The subformula (r2) is almost the same as subformula $A_{step}$ of $work(g)$. The only difference is that at any time the program can restart its execution at the next time moment. The subformula (r3) guarantees that if at the given moment of time the program is at a certain node then in the future all the possible continuations appear. Therefore, the formula *repeatwork* realizes a particular form of diagonalization. □

**(21.2) Lemma.** *If* $(\mathcal{A}, \mathcal{N}) \models repeatwork(p)[k, t]$ *for some* $k \in Val_{(\mathcal{A},\mathcal{N})}$, $t \in \mathbb{N}$, *then for any* $(k_0, k_1, ..., k_n(, k_{n+1}, ...)) \in Trace_{\mathcal{A}}[\![p, var(p)]\!]$ *with* $k_0 = k_p(0)$, *there are time moments* $t_0 < t_1 < ... < t_n(< t_{n+1} < ...)$ *such that*

$$k_p(t_i) = k_i \text{ for } i = 1, ..., n(, n+1, ...).$$

*Proof.* This can be proved by induction from the statement (ii) of Lemma (21.1). □

The conditions (i) and (ii) of Lemma (21.1) in general are not satisfied. Therefore it is important to investigate whether they can be satisfied.

**(21.3) Lemma.** *If* $\mathcal{A}$ *is a countable model or* $p \in P_\sigma$ *then for any valuation* $\hat{k} \in Val_{\mathcal{A}}$ *there is a valuation* $k \in Val_{(\mathcal{A},\mathcal{N})}$ *such that*

*(a)* $k_p(0){\restriction}_X = \hat{k}{\restriction}_X$ *and*
*(b)* $(\mathcal{A}, \mathcal{N}) \models repeatwork(p)[k, 0]$.

*Proof.* In both cases $Trace_{\mathcal{A}}[\![p, var(p)]\!]$ contains countably many finite paths, starting with the valuation $\hat{k}{\restriction}_X$. By Lemma (21.1), if we form a valuation $k \in Val_{(\mathcal{A},\mathcal{N})}$ such that all these paths occur in $k$ as a slice $k_p(t'), k_p(t'+1), ..., k_p(t'+n), ...$ and $k$ consists of only such slices, then (b) is satisfied ((a) is trivial). The formation of such a $k$ is simple by a Cantor-type diagonalization. □

**(21.4) Theorem.** *Let* $\mathcal{A}$ *be a countable model or* $p \in P_\sigma$ *be arbitrary. Then there exists a temporal-logic formula defining the quasi-total correctness of* $p$ *in* $\mathcal{A}$ *with respect to a given precondition* $\phi$ *and a postcondition* $\psi$.

*Proof.* Let us take the formula

$$\chi \rightleftharpoons (repeatwork(p) \wedge 1(X = \check{X}) \wedge \phi) \rightarrow \\ 1\Diamond(\check{X}_l = stop_p) \wedge 1\Box(\check{X}_l = stop_p \rightarrow \psi[\check{X}/X]).$$

Now, using Definition (10.6), one can show that $(\mathcal{A}, \mathcal{N}) \models \chi$ iff $p$ is quasi-totally correct in $\mathcal{A}$ with respect to $\phi$ and $\psi$. The validity of $\chi$ follows from Lemma (21.2), while the quasi-totally correctness of $p$ follows from the statement (i) of Lemma (21.1) and from Lemmas (21.2) and (21.3). □

**(21.5) Theorem.** *There exists a recursive function mod which assigns a temporal-logic formula $mod(\phi) \in Mform_\sigma$ to any dynamic-logic formula $\phi \in rD_\sigma$ such that for any countable model $\mathcal{A} \in Mod_\sigma$:*

$$\mathcal{A} \models \phi \quad \text{iff} \quad (\mathcal{A}, \mathcal{N}) \models mod(\phi).$$

*Proof.* Fix a formula $\phi \in rD_\sigma$. First we remark that $\phi$ can be built up from open formulas by using only connectives $\neg$, $\wedge$ and $\langle\cdot\rangle$. Indeed, $\exists x\phi$ is equivalent to the formula $\langle x :=?\rangle\phi$.

Let $Z$ be the set of all free or bound variables occurring in the formula $\phi$. Obviously, $var(\phi) \subseteq Z$. For each program $p$ occurring in the formula $\phi$ let $Z_p$ be a new copy of $Z$. Let

$$Z' \rightleftharpoons Z \cup \{Z_p \mid p \text{ occurs in } \phi\}$$

and let $\check{Z}'$ be a new local copy of $Z'$. Moreover, let $\check{Z}_p$ denote the corresponding local copy of $Z_p$ ($\subseteq Z'$).

Let us suppose that $p_1,\ldots,p_n$ are all the programs occurring in the logic operator $\langle\cdot\rangle$ in the formula $\phi$. Take the following program

$$prog(\phi) \rightleftharpoons Z :=?;\ \textbf{choice}\ \big(Z_{p_1} := Z; p_1, \ldots, Z_{p_n} := Z; p_n\big).$$

Let $sl_{p_i}$ be denote the label in $gr(prog(\phi))$ after the program $p_i$.

Let $mod^1$ be the function which assigns a temporal-logic formula to each subformula $\psi$ of the dynamic-logic formula $\phi$. This function is defined by induction as follows.

(i) If $\psi \in Open_\sigma$ then take $mod^1(\psi) \rightleftharpoons \psi$.
(ii) If $\psi \rightleftharpoons \psi_1 \wedge \psi_2$ then take $mod^1(\psi_1 \wedge \psi_2) \rightleftharpoons mod^1(\psi_1) \wedge mod^1(\psi_2)$.
(iii) If $\psi \rightleftharpoons \neg\psi_1$ then take $mod^1(\neg\psi_1) \rightleftharpoons \neg mod^1(\psi_1)$.
(iv) If $\psi \rightleftharpoons \langle p\rangle\psi_1$ then take

$$mod^1(\langle p\rangle\psi_1) \rightleftharpoons 1\Diamond\exists Z_p\big(\check{X}_l = sl_p \wedge Z = \check{Z}_p \wedge Z_p = \check{Z} \wedge mod^1(\psi_1)[Z_p/Z]\big).$$

Now take

$$mod(\phi) \rightleftharpoons repeatwork(prog(\phi)) \rightarrow mod^1(\phi).$$

We are going to prove that $mod(\phi)$ satisfies the theorem. We shall prove that

(i) if $\mathcal{A} \models \phi[k]$ then for all $k \cup k_l \in Val_{(\mathcal{A},\mathcal{N})}$ satisfying $repeatwork(prog(\phi))$,

$$(\mathcal{A},\mathcal{N}) \models mod^1(\phi)[k \cup k_l];$$

(ii) if $(\mathcal{A},\mathcal{N}) \models mod^1(\phi)[k_g + k_l]$ then $\mathcal{A} \models \phi[k_g]$.

Both statements can be proved by induction on the subformulas of $\phi$. The only interesting case is when the subformula is of the form $\langle p\rangle\psi$. We detail the proof of (ii). Let us suppose that

$$(\mathcal{A},\mathcal{N}) \models 1\Diamond\exists Z_p(at(sl_p) \wedge Z = \check{Z}_p \wedge Z_p = \check{Z} \wedge mod^1(\psi)[Z_p/Z])[k_g + k_l].$$

This means that there is a time moment $t$ such that $f_l{\restriction}_{V_l}(t) = sl_p$; and because of Lemma (21.1) (i) there is a time moment $t$ such that $f = \lambda i \leq (t-t').k_l(t+i)$ is a trace of $p$. Because of the construction of $prog(\phi)$: $k_l{\restriction}_{\check{Z}}(t') = k_l{\restriction}_{\check{Z}_p}(t)$, and because of the subformula $Z = \check{Z}_p$ in $mod^1(\phi)$: $k{\restriction}_{\check{Z}_p}(t') = k_g{\restriction}_Z$. So we can conclude that $k_g{\restriction}_Z$ contains the input of trace $f$. However, the output is $k_l{\restriction}_{\check{Z}}(t)$, which satisfies $mod^1(\psi)[\check{Z}/Z]$. Because of the inductive hypothesis it also satisfies $\psi[\check{Z}/Z]$, so $\mathcal{A} \models \langle p\rangle\psi[k_g]$.

Statement (i) can be proved similarly, only Lemma (21.2) has to be used. □

Now let us return to Theorem (17.7):

**(17.7) Theorem.** *The tautologies of $ML_\sigma$ with respect to standard Kripke models constitute a $\Pi^1_1$-complete set.*

*Proof.* According to Theorem (11.12) the set of all tautologies $\chi$ of the form $\chi \rightleftharpoons \langle p_x; p_w\rangle[p_x]\psi$ constitutes a $\Pi^1_1$ complete set. It is enough to prove that this set can be embedded into $Mform_\sigma$ by using a recursive and truth-preserving function. However, $mod(\chi)$ is such a function. It follows from the fact that $p_x \in det\text{-}P_\sigma$ and thus Lemma (21.3) can be applied. Therefore $repeatwork(p_x)$ and $repeatwork(prog(\chi))$ work well in uncountable models too. □

Chapter 22

# Temporal Axiomatization of Program Verification Methods

Temporal logic as a descriptive language allows us to formalize our expectations about the time during which a program runs. Since different program verification methods differ in their view of how they consider program execution we can characterize them axiomatically by using temporal logic. In this chapter we give the required characterization for the Floyd-Hoare method, for the method of intermittent assertions introduced by Burstall [1974] and subsequently propagated by Manna, Waldinger [1978], and for the method introduced by Pnueli [1977]. Sain [1986, 1991] study in detail the axiomatic characterization and interrelation of these program verification methods by means of different induction axiom schemas in the scope of her non-standard dynamic logic.

In Chapter 14 we have already provided a characterization of the Floyd-Hoare method, where we have seen that the induction principle plays a significant role in this axiomatization since only thus can we describe a computational path as a whole process. We introduce different induction axiom schemas in order to axiomatize all the three verification methods as well. By using the axiomatic characterization we also show that the Floyd-Hoare calculus is complete. At the end of this chapter we investigate the interrelation of the Floyd-Hoare, Burstall and Pnueli methods.

**(22.1) Definition.** *Let us fix a similarity type $\sigma$. Let $\phi$, $\psi \in Form_\sigma$ be given formulas and let $p \in rP_\sigma$ be a given program.*

*(i) The temporal representation of the partial correctness formula $\phi\{p\}\psi$ is the formula*

$$\phi\{p\}^m\psi \rightleftharpoons (work(p) \wedge \phi) \to 1\Box(\check{X}_l = stop_p \to \psi[\check{X}/X]),$$

*where $X$, $X_l$, $\check{X}$ and $\check{X}_l$ are as, e.g., in Theorem (18.4).*

*(ii) The total correctness of the program $p$ with respect to precondition $\phi$ and postcondition $\psi$ is represented by the formula*

$$\phi\langle p\rangle^m\psi \rightleftharpoons (work(p) \wedge \phi) \to \Diamond\check{X}_l = stop_p \wedge 1\Box(\check{X}_l = stop_p \to \psi[\check{X}/X]).$$

The first question that could be asked concerning the above defined formulas is whether the formula $work(p)$ is adequate for the required characterization of Floyd-Hoare logic. The formula $work(p)$ sufficiently describes the program executions in standard models, i.e. in the models $(\mathcal{A}, \mathcal{N})$ for any $\mathcal{A} \in Mod_\sigma$. Yet what about the other Kripke models of $MMod_\sigma$? Does $work(p)$ represent the execution of programs in these models too? The answer is no, since this formula describes the possible transitions of the programs. If we wish to derive the entire execution from this description then we need a certain type of induction which allows us to string the step-by-step transitions into computational paths.

Note that we have already seen in Chapter 14 the important role of induction in the description of program properties. Let $\phi \in MForm_\sigma$ be such that $var(\phi) \subseteq V_g$. Let $\check{X}$ be a local copy of a fixed set of variables $X$. Let us suppose that $X \subseteq var(\phi)$. Let us consider the following induction axiom:

$$cont(\phi, X) \rightleftharpoons (1\phi[\check{X}/X] \wedge 1\Box(\phi[\check{X}/X] \to \circ\phi[\check{X}/X])) \to 1\Box\phi[\check{X}/X].$$

This formula says that induction works well along time moments, i.e. if the property described by the formula $\phi$ is inherited from any time moment to the next one, then the property described by $\phi$ must be true always. In other words, the computational paths are continuous with respect to the properties defined by $\phi$. The notation $cont(\phi)$ refers to this *cont*inuity. Let

$$MInd_\sigma \rightleftharpoons \{cont(\phi, X) \mid \phi \in Form_\sigma, X \subseteq var(\phi)\}.$$

In order to give an exact characterization of the program verification methods mentioned above let us define the following sets of formulas:

$$MInd_\sigma^P \rightleftharpoons \{(\phi \wedge \Box(\phi \to \circ\phi)) \to \Box\phi \mid \phi \in MForm_\sigma\};$$

$$MInd_\sigma^B \rightleftharpoons \{(1\phi \wedge 1\Box(\phi \to \circ\phi)) \to 1\Box\phi \mid \phi \in MForm_\sigma \text{ and only modalities of the form } 1 \text{ and } \circ \text{ and } 1\Box \text{ can occur in } \phi\};$$

Let $\Psi \subseteq MForm_\sigma$, $Ax \subseteq Form_\sigma$. We say that a formula $\chi \in MForm_\sigma$ is provable from $Ax$ by using method $\Psi$ iff $Ax \cup \Psi \vdash \chi$. Methods $MInd$, $MInd^B$, $MInd^P$ are called *Floyd-Hoare's method*, *Burstall's method* and *Pnueli's method*, respectively. In cases of Burstall's and Pnueli's methods these induction schemas just coincide with the original definitions (cf. Burstall [1974], Pnueli [1977]).

In the next theorem $\models^m$ denotes the validity relation of the temporal logic $ML_\sigma$ in order to distinguish between the two different notions of validity. The following result is analogous to Theorem (14.30).

**(22.2) Theorem.** *Let $\sigma$ be a fixed similarity type and let $Ax \subseteq Form_\sigma$ be a fixed set of axioms, such that $Ax \models \top \neq \bot$. Let $\phi\{p\}\psi \in rH_\sigma$ be a given partial correctness formula. Then statements (i) and (ii) below are equivalent:*
*(i) $Ax \vdash_H \phi\{p\}\psi$, i.e. $\phi\{p\}\psi$ is Floyd-Hoare provable from $Ax$;*
*(ii) $Ax \cup MInd_\sigma \models^m \phi\{p\}^m\psi$.*

*Proof.* First we prove that statement (i) implies statement (ii). By Theorem (14.30) (i) implies that $Ax \vdash_H \phi\{gr(p)\}\psi$. Thus there is an invariant $\mu : node(gr(p)) \to Form_\sigma$ such that $Ax \vdash \phi \to \mu(start_{gr(p)})$ and $Ax \vdash \mu(stop_{gr(p)}) \to \psi$. Let $g \rightleftharpoons gr(p)$ and let $X \rightleftharpoons var(g)$. Let $X_L$ be a set of variables large enough to code the elements of $node(g)$ and let $\check{X}$ and $\check{X}_L$ be the local copies of $X$ and $X_L$, respectively. Take $\gamma$ as the following formula

$$\bigvee_{c \in node(g)} (X_L = L_c \wedge \mu(c)).$$

It is clear that $\gamma \in Form_\sigma$. Fix a Kripke model $(\mathcal{A}, \mathcal{T}, K) \in MMod_\sigma(Ax \cup MInd_\sigma)$ and let $\hat{k} \in Val_{(\mathcal{A},\mathcal{T},K)}$ be a valuation such that $(\mathcal{A}, \mathcal{T}, K) \models^m (work(g) \wedge \phi)[\hat{k}]$. If $(\mathcal{A}, \mathcal{T}, K) \models^m 1\Box\gamma[\check{X}'/X'][\hat{k}]$ hold (where $X' \rightleftharpoons X \cup X_L$ and $\check{X}' \rightleftharpoons \check{X} \cup \check{X}_L$) then $(\mathcal{A}, \mathcal{T}, K) \models^m 1\Box(\check{X}_L = stop_g \to \psi[\check{X}/X])[\hat{k}]$ would be true. Indeed, if for some $s \in T$, $(\mathcal{A}, \mathcal{T}, K) \models^m \check{X}_L = stop_g[\hat{k}, s]$ then using the validity of $1\Box\gamma[\check{X}'/X']$ with respect to $\hat{k}$ we get that $(\mathcal{A}, \mathcal{T}, K) \models^m \mu(stop_g)[\check{X}'/X'][\hat{k}, s]$. Using $\mathcal{A} \models \mu(stop_g) \to \psi$ we get that $(\mathcal{A}, \mathcal{T}, K) \models^m \psi[\check{X}/X][\hat{k}, s]$. Since $s$ is arbitrary, $(\mathcal{A}, \mathcal{T}, K) \models^m 1\Box(\check{X}_L = stop_g \to \psi[\check{X}/X][\hat{k}]$ holds. This means that $(\mathcal{A}, \mathcal{T}, K) \models^m \phi\{p\}^m\psi[\hat{k}]$. So we have only to check that $(\mathcal{A}, \mathcal{T}, K) \models^m 1\Box\gamma[\check{X}/X][\hat{k}]$. Since $\gamma \in Form_\sigma$ the axiom

$$cont(\gamma, X') \rightleftharpoons (1\gamma[\check{X}'/X'] \wedge 1\Box(\gamma[\check{X}'/X'] \to \circ\gamma[\check{X}'/X'])) \to 1\Box\gamma[\check{X}'/X']$$

belongs to $MInd_\sigma$. We prove that the antecedent of this axiom is true in $(\mathcal{A}, \mathcal{T}, K)$ with respect to the valuation $\hat{k}$. Indeed, by the definition of the validity relation $\models^m$, $(\mathcal{A}, \mathcal{T}, K) \models^m 1\gamma[\check{X}'/X'][\hat{k}]$ is equivalent to $(\mathcal{A}, \mathcal{T}, K) \models^m \gamma[\check{X}'/X'][\hat{k}, 0]$. The latter is equivalent to $\mathcal{A} \models \gamma[\hat{k}(0)]$. Using $(\mathcal{A}, \mathcal{T}, K) \models^m work(g) \wedge \phi[\hat{k}]$ we get that $\hat{k}(0)\restriction_{X_L} = start_g$ and $\mathcal{A} \models \phi[\hat{k}(0)\restriction_X]$. Using $Ax \vdash \phi \to \mu(start_g)$ and the completeness of the first-order calculus we get that $\mathcal{A} \models \gamma[\hat{k}(0)]$, which we wanted to prove.

Now we have to prove that $(\mathcal{A}, \mathcal{T}, K) \models^m 1\Box(\gamma[\check{X}'/X'] \to \circ\gamma[\check{X}'/X'])[\hat{k}]$ or equivalently, that for any $t \in T$, $(\mathcal{A}, \mathcal{T}, K) \models^m (\gamma[\check{X}'/X'] \to \circ\gamma[\check{X}'/X'])[\hat{k}, t]$. Remember, that $(\mathcal{A}, \mathcal{T}, K) \models^m work(g)[\hat{k}]$. This means that $\hat{k}(t) = \hat{k}(t+1)$ or $\mathcal{A} \models onestep_g[\hat{k}(t) + \hat{k}(t+1)[X'/Y']]$. The first case is trivial. In the second case we can use the fact that $\mu$ is an invariant of $g$. This means that if $\mathcal{A} \models \gamma[\hat{k}(t)]$ and $\mathcal{A} \models onestep_g[\hat{k}(t), \hat{k}(t+1)[X'/Y']]$ then $\mathcal{A} \models \gamma[\hat{k}(t+1)]$. However, this implies the validity of the formula $(\gamma[\check{X}'/X'] \to \circ\gamma[\check{X}'/X'])$ in the Kripke model $(\mathcal{A}, \mathcal{T}, K)$ with respect to $(\hat{k}, t)$.

Now we turn to prove the other direction, i.e. we prove that statement (ii) implies statement (i). Let us suppose that for a given $\phi\{p\}\psi \in rH_\sigma$, $Ax \not\vdash_H \phi\{p\}\psi$. We can suppose that $p$ has the form

$$\textbf{repeat } Y' := Y; p^{os} \textbf{ until } Y' = Y.$$

By Theorem (14.50) there is a model $\mathcal{B}$, and there are two valuations $k_1$, $k_2$ and a deterministic weakly transitive closure $Q$ of $D[\![p, Y]\!]$ in $\mathcal{B}$ starting from $k_1$ such that $k_2 \in Q$ and

(1) $\mathcal{B} \models \phi[k_1]$;
(2) $\mathcal{B} \models D[\![p, Y]\!][k_1 + k_2[Y/Y']]$;
(3) $\mathcal{B} \not\models \psi[k_2]$.

We are going to construct a Kripke model $(\mathcal{A}, \mathcal{T}, K) \in MMod(Ax \cup MInd_\sigma)$ such that $(\mathcal{A}, \mathcal{T}, K) \not\models^m \phi\{p\}^m\psi$. Recall Definition (14.11) that

$$D[\![p, Y]\!](Y, Y') \rightleftharpoons \exists W \exists W' \Xi^*(Y, Y') \wedge \Xi(Y', Y'),$$
$$\Xi(Y, Y') \rightleftharpoons D[\![p^{os}, Y]\!](Y, Y').$$

Take $g = gr(p)$. Let $stop_\Xi$ be the node of $g$ just before the start of the assignment $Y' := Y$. Let $Y_L$ be a set of variables large enough to code the elements of $node(g)$.

Let $\mathbb{Z}$ denote the set of all integer numbers. A function $\pi : \mathbb{Z} \to Val_\mathcal{A}[Y \cup Y_L]$ is called a $\mathbb{Z}$-path iff

(a) for all $n \in \mathbb{Z}$, $\mathcal{A} \models localstep_g[\pi(n), \pi(n+1)]$;
(b) for all $n \in \mathbb{Z}$ there is an $n' \in \mathbb{Z}$ such that $n' \leq n$ and $\pi(n')\restriction_Y \in Q$ and $\pi(n')\restriction_{Y_L}$ is equal $stop_\Xi$ or $stop_g$.

Let $\mathbb{Z}path$ denote the set of all $\mathbb{Z}$-paths.

**Claim 1.** Let us suppose that $k, \ell \in Q$ are such valuations that $(k_1, k) \notin TC(\Xi(Y, Y')_\mathcal{B})$ and $\mathcal{B} \models \Xi[k, \ell[Y/Y']]$. There is a $\mathbb{Z}$-path $\pi_{k,\ell}$ such that $\pi(0)\restriction_Y = k$ and for an appropriately chosen $n \in \mathbb{N}$: $\pi(n)\restriction_Y = \ell$.

**Claim 2.** There is a trace $s \in Trace[\![g, Y]\!]$ such that $s(start_g)\restriction_Y = k_1$ and for all $n \in \mathbb{N}$ there is an $n' > n$ such that $s(n')\restriction_Y \in Q$ and $s(n')\restriction_{Y_L}$ is $stop_g$ or $stop_\Xi$.

Let $\prec$ be an arbitrary, but fixed total ordering on $\mathbb{Z}path$. Take $T \rightleftharpoons \mathbb{N} \cup (\mathbb{Z}path \times \mathbb{Z})$. We define an ordering on $T$ in the following way:

$$t_1 \leq t_2 \rightleftharpoons \begin{cases} true & \text{if } t_1,\ t_2 \in \mathbb{N} \text{ and } t_1 \leq t_2; \\ true & \text{if } t_1 \in \mathbb{N} \text{ and } t_2 \in \mathbb{Z}path \times \mathbb{Z}; \\ true & \text{if } t_i = (\pi_i, n_i) \text{ and } \pi_1 \prec \pi_2; \\ true & \text{if } t_i = (\pi, n_i) \text{ and } n_1 \leq n_2; \\ false & \text{otherwise}; \end{cases}$$

Take $0_\mathcal{T} \rightleftharpoons 0 \in \mathbb{N}$. The operation $+1$ can be defined as follows:

$$t + 1 \rightleftharpoons \begin{cases} t + 1 & \text{if } t \in \mathbb{N}; \\ (\pi, n+1) & \text{if } t = (\pi, n) \in \mathbb{Z}path \times \mathbb{Z}; \end{cases}$$

All the other relations and operations can be defined arbitrarily. It is clear that the time structure $\mathcal{T}$ so defined satisfies the axiom system $Nord$. Let $s$ be the trace of $g$ given in Claim 2. Now we define a function $f$ on $T$ as follows:

$$f(t) \rightleftharpoons \begin{cases} s(n)\restriction Y \cup Y_L & \text{if } t \in \mathbb{N}; \\ \pi(n) & \text{if } t = (\pi, n) \in \mathbb{Z}path \times \mathbb{Z}; \end{cases}$$

It is clear that $f : T \to Val_{\mathcal{A}}[Y \cup Y_L]$. Now we are ready to define the set $K$ by taking:

$$K \rightleftharpoons \{\lambda t.f(t)(z) \mid z \in Y \cup Y_L\} \cup \{\lambda t.a \mid a \in \cup_{s \in sort\ \sigma} A_s\}.$$

Let us define a valuation $\hat{k} \in Val_{(\mathcal{A},\mathcal{T},K)}[\check{Y} \cup \check{Y}_L \cup Y]$ by taking $\hat{k}\restriction V_g \rightleftharpoons k_1$ and $\hat{k}(\check{z}) \rightleftharpoons \lambda t.f(t)(z)$ $(z \in \check{Y} \cup Y_L)$. For all other variables $\hat{k}$ is an arbitrary element from $K$. Our aim is to prove the following:

(i) $(\mathcal{A},\mathcal{T},K) \models^m Ax \cup MInd_\sigma$;
(ii) $(\mathcal{A},\mathcal{T},K) \models^m (work(p) \wedge \phi)[\hat{k}]$;
(iii) $(\mathcal{A},\mathcal{T},K) \not\models^m 1\Box(\check{Y}_L = stop_g \to \psi[\check{Y}/Y][\hat{k}]$.

Statement (ii) follows from (1) above and from (a) of the definition of $\mathbb{Z}$-paths. Statement (iii) follows from the facts that $\pi' \rightleftharpoons \lambda n \in \mathbb{Z}.k_2 + (Y_L, stop_g)$ is a $\mathbb{Z}$-path by (2) above, and that for any $n \in \mathbb{Z}$ $(\mathcal{A},\mathcal{T},K) \models^m (\check{Y}_L = stop_g \wedge \neg\psi[\check{Y}/Y])[\hat{k},(\pi',n)]$, by (3) above.

Now we turn to prove statement (i). Since $\mathcal{A} \in Mod(Ax)$, $(\mathcal{A},\mathcal{T},K) \models^m Ax$ obviously holds. Let $\gamma \in Form_\sigma$, $U' \subseteq var(\gamma)$ and $\bar{k} \in Val_{(\mathcal{A},\mathcal{T},K)}$ be given. We prove that $(\mathcal{A},\mathcal{T},K) \models^m cont(\gamma,U')[\bar{k}]$. First we remark that we can suppose that for no $u \in U'$ is $k(\check{u})$ a constant function. Indeed, if $\bar{k}(\check{u})$ were a constant function we could take $U'' \rightleftharpoons U' \setminus \{u\}$ and $\bar{k}' \rightleftharpoons k + (u, \bar{k}(\check{u})(0))$. It is clear that $cont(\gamma,U')[k]$ and $cont(\gamma,U'')[k']$ would be equivalent in the model $(\mathcal{A},\mathcal{T},K)$. We also remark that we can suppose that for all $u \in U'$, $k(\check{u}) = \lambda t.f(t)(u)$. Indeed, by using an appropriate renaming $\iota : U' \to Y$ we can construct a new formula $\gamma' \rightleftharpoons \gamma[\iota(u)/u]_{u \in U'}$ which satisfies this property.

Summarizing, we have to prove that $(\mathcal{A},\mathcal{T},K) \models^m cont(\gamma,U')[\bar{k}]$, where $var(\gamma) \subseteq U' \subseteq Y'$ and for all $u \in U'$: $k(\check{u}) = \lambda t.f(t)(u)$. Now let us suppose that the antecedent of the axiom $cont(\gamma,U')[\bar{k}]$ holds:

$$(\mathcal{A},\mathcal{T},K) \models^m 1\gamma[\check{Y}/Y] \wedge 1\Box(\gamma[\check{Y}/Y] \to \circ\gamma[\check{Y}/Y])[\bar{k}].$$

Take the following $\sigma$-type formula:

$$(*) \qquad \gamma^s \rightleftharpoons \exists Y_L\big(\gamma \wedge (Y_L = start_g \vee Y_L = stop_\Xi \vee Y_L = stop_g)\big).$$

We prove by induction on $Q$ that $\ell \in Q$ implies $\mathcal{B} \models \gamma^s[\ell]$. $\bar{k}(0)\restriction Y = k_1$ and the validity of $1\gamma[\check{Y}/Y]$ in $(\mathcal{A},\mathcal{T},K)$ implies that $\mathcal{B} \models \gamma^s[k_1]$. Now let us suppose that $\ell, \ell' \in Q$ are such valuations from $Q$ that $\mathcal{B} \models \gamma^s[\ell]$ and $\mathcal{B} \models \Xi[\ell, \ell[Y/Y']]$. We must prove that $\mathcal{B} \models \gamma^s[\ell']$.

Let us suppose that $(k_1, \ell) \in TC(\Xi_{\mathcal{B}})$. Let $s \in Trace_{\mathcal{A}}[\![g, Y]\!]$ be the trace defined in Claim 2. Using the fact that $Q$ is a *deterministic* weak transitive closure of $\Xi$ we get that there are natural numbers $n$, $n'$ such that $s(n)\restriction Y = \ell$ and $s(n')\restriction Y = \ell'$ and both $s(n)\restriction Y_L$ and $s(n')\restriction Y_L$ is either $stop_\Xi$ or $stop_g$. Using (*) we have that

$$(\mathcal{A}, \mathcal{T}, K) \models^m \gamma[\bar{k}, t],$$

where $t = n$ or $t = n'$. Using the definition of the validity in Kripke models we get that $\mathcal{B} \models \gamma^s[\ell']$.

Now let us suppose that $(k_1, \ell) \notin TC(\Xi_{\mathcal{B}})$. According to Claim 1 there is a $\mathbb{Z}$-path $\pi$ and a natural number $n\mathbb{N}$ such that $\pi(0)\restriction_Y = \ell$, $\pi(n)\restriction_Y = \ell'$ and both $\pi(0)\restriction_{Y_L}$ and $\pi(n)\restriction_{Y_L}$ is either $stop_\Xi$ or $stop_g$. By inductive hypothesis $\mathcal{B} \models \gamma^s[\ell]$. Thus $(\mathcal{A}, \mathcal{T}, K) \models^m \gamma[\bar{k}, (\pi, 0)]$. By using (*) we get that for all $i \in \mathbb{N}$ $(\mathcal{A}, \mathcal{T}, K) \models^m \gamma[\bar{k}, (\pi, i)]$. By taking $i = n$ we get that $\mathcal{B} \models \gamma^s[\ell']$.

So we have proved that

$$(**) \qquad \gamma^s_{\mathcal{B}} \supset Q.$$

Now we prove that $(\mathcal{A}, \mathcal{T}, K) \models^m 1\Box\gamma[\check{U}'/U'][\bar{k}]$. Let $t \in T$ be arbitrary. If $t \in \mathbb{N}$ then this statement is trival, so we can suppose that $t$ is of the form $(\pi, n)$. By property (b) of $\mathbb{Z}$-paths there is an $n' \in \mathbb{N}$ such that $n' < n$ and $\pi(n')\restriction_Y \in Q$ and $\pi(n')\restriction_{Y_L}$ is either $stop_\Xi$ or $stop_g$. Using (**) $\mathcal{B} \models \gamma^s[\pi(n')\restriction_Y]$ hence $(\mathcal{A}, \mathcal{T}, K) \models^m 1\Box\gamma[\check{U}'/U'][\bar{k}, (\pi, n')]$. Using (*) we get that the same holds for $(\pi, n')$ as well. □

We emphasize that the time structure of the Kripke model constucted in the above proof is also satisfies the axiom system $Npre$ (not only $Nord$).

Now we make a comparative investigation of the other methods. This investigation will be made with respect to their power of expressing partial and total correctness. Therefore, we formulate the partial and total correctness theories for the language $ML_\sigma$. Note that the partial correctness theory is a reformulation of Definition (11.17).

**(22.3) Definition.** *Let $Ax \subseteq MForm_\sigma$ be arbitrary. Define the partial and total correctness theories of $Ax$, respectively:*

$$PC_\sigma(Ax) \rightleftharpoons \{\phi\{p\}^m\psi \mid \phi, \psi \in Form_\sigma, p \in rP_\sigma, Ax \models^m \phi\{p\}^m\psi\},$$

$$TC_\sigma(Ax) \rightleftharpoons \{\phi\langle p\rangle^m\psi \mid \phi, \psi \in Form_\sigma, p \in rP_\sigma, Ax \models^m \phi\langle p\rangle^m\psi\}.$$

**(22.4) Lemma.** *For an arbitrary similarity type $\sigma$ we have*

$$PC_\sigma(MInd) \subseteq PC_\sigma(MInd^B) \subseteq PC_\sigma(MInd^P),$$

$$TC_\sigma(MInd) \subseteq TC_\sigma(MInd^B) \subseteq TC_\sigma(MInd^P).$$

*Proof.* The statement directly follows from

$$MMod_\sigma(MInd) \supseteq MMod_\sigma(MInd^B) \supseteq MMod_\sigma(MInd^P).$$

□

However, the above comparison does not satisfy us. We require sharper results, which also show if two methods prove different sets of partial and total correctness formulas. The required comparative study has been done by Sain [1985c, 1986, 1991], (see also Andréka, Németi, Sain [1991]). Here we give Sain's main results but provide different proofs. For the sake of simplicity we introduce the following abbreviation. Let $Q_1$ and $Q_2$ be two sequences of modal operators, and let $\tau_1$, $\tau_2$ be two terms. $Q_1\tau_1 = Q_2\tau_2$ is a shorthand for the following formula ($y$ is a new global variable):

$$\forall y\, Q_1\big(\tau_1 = y \rightarrow Q_2(\tau_2 = y)\big).$$

E.g. $x = \mathrm{o}y$ means that the actual value of variable $x$ is equal to the value of $y$ at the next time moment. Similarly, $y = 1\Diamond z$ means that the value of $y$ at any time is sometimes equal to the value of the variable $z$.

**(22.5) Theorem.** *For an appropriate similarity type $\sigma$ we have*

$$PC_\sigma(MInd) \subset PC_\sigma(MInd^B).$$

*Proof.* Recall the similarity type $\hat{\eta}$ and axiom system $Next$ from Section 1.6. Let $\sigma \rightleftharpoons \hat{\eta}$. Consider the following program:

$p \rightleftharpoons$ **while** $y \neq 2$ **do while** $x \neq z$ **do** $x := x + 1$ **od** ;
$x := x + 1; y := y + 1$ **od** .

Take $\chi \rightleftharpoons (z \neq 0) \wedge (x = 0) \wedge (y = 0)\{p\}^m false$. We want to prove that

$$MInd^B + Next \models^m \chi^m \quad \text{but} \quad MInd + Next \not\models^m \chi^m,$$

i.e. (by Theorem (21.2)) $Next \not\vdash_H \chi$. The fact that $MInd + Next \not\vdash_H \chi$ can be proved by using the same technique as in the proofs of Theorem (12.9) and Theorem (12.12). The reader can check how one can construct a formula which defines the relation $\leq$ on the data from a Floyd-Hoare derivation of $\chi$. However, such a definition is impossible in $Next$.

Now we prove that $MInd^B + Next \models^m \chi^m$. Let $\breve{x}$, $\breve{y}$ and $\breve{z}$ be the local variables describing the changes of $x$, $y$ and $z$, respectively. Let $l$ be the name of the node just between $x := x + 1$ and $y := y + 1$ in $gr(p)$. Let $(at\ *) \rightleftharpoons \bigvee\{at(c) \mid c \in node\ gr(p), c \neq l\}$. Consider the following formulas

$$\Psi(\breve{x},\breve{y}) \rightleftharpoons \forall u \forall v(u = \breve{x} \wedge v = \breve{y} \rightarrow 1\Box((at\ *) \wedge u = \breve{x} \rightarrow v = \breve{y})) \tag{1}$$

$$\Phi(\breve{x},\breve{y}) \rightleftharpoons \forall u \forall v(u = \breve{x} \wedge v = \breve{y} \wedge u = 0 \rightarrow v = 0) \tag{2}$$

Our aim is to prove that $1\Box\Psi$ is true in the following axiom system:

$$Ax \rightleftharpoons MInd^B + Next + work(p)(x,y,z,\breve{x},\breve{y},\breve{z}) + \big(x = 0 \wedge y = 0 \wedge (z \neq 0)\big).$$

First we check that $1\Box\Phi$ is true in $Ax$. Indeed, $1\Phi$ is true since $1(\breve{x} = 0)$ and $1(\breve{y} = 0)$. The implication $\Phi \rightarrow \mathrm{o}\Phi$ follows from the axiom system $Next$ and the formula $work(p)(\breve{x},\breve{y},\breve{z})$. So by using $cont(\Phi,\{x,y\})$ we have proved $1\Box\Phi$.

Now we prove $1\Box\Psi$ by using the induction axiom $cont(\Psi, \{x, y\})$. $1\Psi$ follows from $1\Box\Phi$, so we have only to check that $\Psi(\check{x}, \check{y}) \rightarrow \circ\Psi(\check{x}, \check{y})$. If $\check{x} = \circ\check{x}$ then this implication trivially holds (because of using $(at\ *)$!). Otherwise $\check{x} + 1 = \circ\check{x}$ obviously.

If $\circ\neg(at\ *)$ then $\circ\Psi(\check{x}, \check{y})$ automatically holds. Hence consider the case when $\circ(at\ *)$ is true and $\check{x} + 1 = \circ\check{x}$. This means that $p$ has carried out $x := x + 1$ in the inner loop. By using the fact that $\Psi(\check{x}, \check{y})$ holds one can check that $\circ\Psi(\check{x}, \check{y})$ also holds. □

Theorem (22.5) means that Burstall's method is more powerful than Floyd-Hoare's method not only with respect to the entire $MForm_\sigma$ but also with respect to the formulas expressing partial and total correctness.

The classical temporal logic systems (see e.g. Prior [1967], van Benthem [1983]) are usually symmetric in that they consider both future and past, to which appropriate modal operators correspond. In order to define the main concept of programming theory and to describe program execution the future fragment of temporal logic is enough. Moreover, this fragment also permits the axiomatic characterization of different program verification methods and also comparison of Floyd-Hoare's and Burstall's methods.

The time structure of the model constructed in the completeness proof may not be a model of successor arithmetic: there may be a $t \in T$ such that there is a no predecessor of $t$ (there is no $t'$ with the property $t' + 1 = t$) and $t$ is different from $0_T$. But in the proof of the completeness theorem for Floyd-Hoare derivation rules we use this possibility of defining $\mathbb{N}$-path as well as $\mathbb{Z}$-paths. However, it is possible to extend our results to those Kripke models for which $-1$ exists. In this section we sketch how this task can be carried out.

**(22.6) Definition.**

*(A) Let $Mform_\sigma^\bullet$ be the least set of formulas satisfying (i)-(iv) of Definition (17.1) and*

*(v) for any formula $\phi \in Mform_\sigma^\bullet$, $(\bullet\phi)$ belongs to $Mform_\sigma^\bullet$.*

*(B) A Kripke model $(\mathcal{A}, \mathcal{T}, K)$ is called strict iff $\mathcal{T} \models Npre$. Let $MMod_\sigma^\bullet$ denote the class of all strict $\sigma$-type Kripke models.*

*(C) Let us extend the validity relation $\models$ to a validity relation $\models^\bullet$ by adding the following assertion to (i) of Definition (17.4):*

$$(\mathcal{A}, \mathcal{T}, K) \models^\bullet (\bullet\phi)[k, t] \text{ iff } (\mathcal{A}, \mathcal{T}, K) \models^\bullet \phi[k, t-1].$$

*(D) The $\sigma$-type strict temporal logic is the language $(MForm_\sigma^\bullet, \models^\bullet, MMod_\sigma^\bullet)$.*

**(22.7) Definition.** *Let us extend the calculus $\vdash_M$ (defined in Definition (17.9)) to a calculus $\vdash_M^\bullet$ by adding the following axioms and rules:*

*5.8'* $\Diamond \circ \phi \leftrightarrow \circ\Diamond\phi$;

*5.9* $\circ \bullet \phi \leftrightarrow \phi$;

*5.10* $\circ\Box(\bullet \circ \phi \leftrightarrow \phi)$;

*6.4* $\phi \vdash_M^\bullet (\bullet\phi)$.

**(22.8) Theorem.** *The calculus* $\vdash^{\bullet}_{M}$ *is complete for* $ML^{\bullet}_{\sigma}$ *which means that for any* $Ax \subseteq Mform^{\bullet}_{\sigma}$ *and* $\phi \in Mform^{\bullet}_{\sigma}$, $Ax \models^{\bullet} \phi$ *iff* $Ax \vdash^{\bullet}_{M} \phi$.

**(22.9) Corollary.** *For any arbitrary set of axioms* $Ax \subseteq Form_{\sigma}$ *and partial correctness formula* $\chi \in rP_{\sigma}$,

$$Ax \vdash_H \chi \quad \text{iff} \quad Ax \cup MInd_{\sigma} \models^{\bullet} \phi\{p\}^m\psi.$$

*Proof.* The proof of Theorem (22.2) is appropriate, because the Kripke model constructed in that proof was strict. □

We note that an analogous form to statements Theorem (22.2) and Corollary (22.9) first has been formulated and proved by Sain for the case when time logical semantics is used for the temporal logic syntax (see e.g. Andréka, Németi, Sain [1991]).

Investigating the interrelation between the extended and unextended temporal logics Sain [1985c] established the following

**(22.10) Theorem.** *Let* $\phi\{p\}\psi \in det\text{-}H_{\sigma}$ *be given. Let us suppose that* $Ax \subseteq Form_{\sigma}$ *is a given set of axioms. The following two statements are true:*

*(i)* $MInd^P_{\sigma} + Ax \models \phi\{p\}^t\psi$ *iff* $MInd^P_{\sigma} + Ax \models^{\bullet} \phi\{p\}^t\psi$;
*(ii)* $MInd^B_{\sigma} + Ax \models \phi\{p\}^t\psi$ *iff* $MInd^B_{\sigma} + Ax \models^{\bullet} \phi\{p\}^t\psi$.

Both statements (i) and (ii) of this theorem generally fail for $rP_{\sigma}$ as it can be seen in Sain [1990], where it was also shown that under certain additional conditions Theorem (22.10) becomes true for the whole $rP_{\sigma}$. We also remark that Theorem (22.10) cannot be generalized to invariance properties from partial correctness formulas.

Let us investigate the interrelation between Burstall and Pnueli program verification methods.

The following result first was proved by Sain [1985c], but here we give it with a new and simpler proof.

**(22.11) Theorem.** *For an appropriate similarity type* $\sigma$ *we have*

$$PC_{\sigma}(MInd^B) \subset PC_{\sigma}(MInd^P).$$

*Proof.* Now we prove that the Pnueli method is stronger than Burstall one. In this proof we use only deterministic programs, so we can use the previous theorem and can always assume that we are working only with strict Kripke models and hence the function $-1$ exists.

Let $p$ be the following program:

$$p \rightleftharpoons \textbf{while } y \neq 0 \textbf{ do } y := y - 1;\ z := z + 1 \textbf{ od}.$$

Take $\chi \rightleftharpoons (y = x \wedge z = 0)\{p\}^m x = z$. First we prove that $MInd^P + Next \models^m \chi^m$. Let us suppose that

$$Next + MInd^P + work(p)(x, y, z, \breve{x}, \breve{y}, \breve{z}) + (y = x \wedge z = 0) + 1\Diamond at(stop_p)$$

holds. We are going to prove that $1\Box(\breve{z} = 1\Diamond\breve{y})$ by induction. Obviously $1(\breve{z} = 1\Diamond\breve{y})$ since $1\breve{z} = 0$, $1\Box(at(stop_p) \to \breve{y} = 0)$ and by assumption $1\Diamond at(stop_g)$. The induction step is trivial by using the formula $work(p)(x, y, z, \breve{x}, \breve{y}, \breve{z})$. Now we turn to"the inverse" , namely: $1\Box(\breve{y} = 1\Diamond\breve{z})$. For a contradiction, let us suppose that $1\Box(\breve{x} \neq \breve{z})$. If this were true then we would use the previous argument to prove $1\Box(\breve{y} \neq 1\Diamond\breve{z})$. Indeed, for the modal operator 1 we get back the indirect assumption, and the inductive step is trivial. However $1\Box(\breve{y} \neq 1\Diamond\breve{z})$ contradicts $1\Box(\breve{z} = 1\Diamond\breve{y})$. Thus we have proved that $1\Diamond(\breve{x} = \breve{z})$. Now by induction we can prove that $1\Box(\breve{y} = 1\Diamond\breve{z})$.

Thus there is a time moment $t$ when $\breve{z} = x$. If at the moment $t$ we have $\breve{y} = 0$ then everything is true. If $\breve{y} \neq 0$ then at the moment $(t+1)$, $\breve{z} = x+1$ and thus there is a time moment $s$ when $\breve{y} = x + 1$, which means that $1\Diamond\breve{y} = x + 1$.

Program $p$ being in the cycle at each third time moment decreases the value of $y$ (which does not change inbetween these moments). For the sake of simplicity let us suppose that a decrease of $y$ with 1 takes place at each moment. The forthcoming Claims 1 and 2 show that in the axiom system $MInd^P$ the continuous decrease never leads to a value which is equivalent to the sum of 1 and of the initial value, while in the case of the axiom system $Mind^B$ there exists a model such that this is not true.

It is very strange that while the value of $y$ continuously decreases a value appears which is "greater" than the initial one. This shows the weakness of the induction schema of $MInd^B$.

**Claim 1.** Let us suppose that $\breve{u}$ is a local variable for which the following formulas hold:

- $1\Box(\circ\breve{u} = \breve{u} - 1)$;
- $1\Diamond(\breve{u} = 0)$.

Then $MInd^P Next \models 1\Box(\breve{u} \neq 1\breve{u} + 1)$.

*Proof of Claim 1.* We prove by induction that

$$(*) \qquad 1\Box(\breve{u} \neq 0 \to \breve{u} \neq \Box \circ \breve{u}).$$

The statement (*) obviously implies Claim 1, since if there is a time moment $t \geq 0$, $\breve{u} = 1\breve{u} + 1$ then at moment $(t + 1)$: $\breve{u} = 1\breve{u}$, which contradicts (*).

First we remark that $1\Box(\breve{u} = 0 \to \Box\breve{u} = 0)$. This can be proved by induction using the fact that $0 - 1 = 0$.

The induction step, i.e.

$$(\breve{u} \neq 0 \to \breve{u} \neq \Box \circ \breve{u}) \to \circ(\breve{u} \neq 0 \to \breve{u} \neq \Box \circ \breve{u})$$

is trivial. The base step, i.e. $1(\breve{u} \neq 0 \to \breve{u} \neq \Box \circ \breve{u}$, is much harder. Let $x = 1\breve{u}$. If $x = 0$ then using $1\Box(\breve{u} = 0 \to \Box\breve{u} = 0)$ we get the desired result. So we can assume that $x \neq 0$. For a contradiction, let us suppose that $\Diamond \circ \breve{u} = x$. By induction we can prove that $1\Box(\breve{u} = \Diamond \circ \breve{u})$. The base step is just $\Diamond \circ \breve{u} = x$. The induction step is trivial using $\circ\breve{u} = \breve{u} - 1$. However, $1\Box(\breve{u} = \Diamond \circ \breve{u})$ contradicts $1\Diamond(\breve{u} = 0)$ and $1\Box(\breve{u} = 0 \rightarrow \Box\breve{u} = 0)$. Indeed, let us suppose that at time moment $t$, $\breve{u} = 0$. (By the second condition such $t$ exists!) Since $x \neq 0$ hence there is a time moment $s$ such that $s + 1 = t$. Obviously, at moment $s$ we have $\breve{u} = 1$. By assumption, at moment $s$ we have $\breve{u} = \Diamond \circ u$. Also, for all $s' \geq t$, at moment $s'$, $\breve{u} = 0$, which gives a contradiction. So we have proved that $1(\breve{u} \neq \Box \circ \breve{u})$. This completes the proof of (*).

Claim 1 gives a contradiction to $1\Diamond\breve{y} = x + 1$ since $x = 1\breve{y}$. Therefore in the case $\breve{z} = x$ we know $\breve{y} = 0$. Indeed, from $1\Box(\breve{z} = 1\Diamond\breve{y})$, since else $work(p)$ in the next time moment $\breve{z} = x + 1$ and this creates a contradiction. According to (*) the value $\breve{y}$ is never repeated, so if $\breve{y} = 0$ then $\breve{z} = x$. This proves $\chi$. So we have proved that $MInd^P + Next \models \chi$.

Now we only have to prove that $MInd^B + Next \not\models \chi$. To do this we need the following

**Claim 2.** Let $M$ be a local variable. There is a model $\mathcal{A}' = (\mathcal{A}, \mathcal{T}, \{f\})$ for which the following hold:

- $\mathcal{A}' \models MInd^B + Next$;
- $\mathcal{A}' \models 1\Box(\circ M = M - 1)$;
- $\mathcal{A}' \models 1\Diamond(M = 0)$;
- $\mathcal{A}' \not\models 1\Box(M \neq 1M + 1)$.

*Proof of Claim 2.* Let $\mathcal{B}$ be a non-standard model of $PA$. Let $\mathcal{T} \rightleftharpoons \mathcal{B}\restriction_{Nord}$ and $\mathcal{A} \rightleftharpoons \mathcal{B}\restriction_{\sigma}$, which means that data and time are isomorphic to each other. Let $M$ be a non-standard natural number. Take

$$f'(t) \quad \rightleftharpoons \quad \begin{cases} M - t & \text{if } M \geq t, \\ 0 & \text{otherwise.} \end{cases}$$

Clearly $T = \mathbb{N} \cup \mathbb{Z} \times \alpha$ where $\alpha$ is some infinite ordered set. Let $h : \alpha \cup \{\uparrow\} \rightarrow \alpha$ be a bijection, where $\uparrow \notin \alpha$. Define $f$ in the following way:

$$f(t) \quad \rightleftharpoons \quad \begin{cases} f'(t) & \text{if } t \in \mathbb{N} \text{ or } t \in \mathbb{Z} \times \{h(\alpha)\}; \\ M + z & \text{if } t = (z, f(\uparrow)) \text{ for some } z \in \mathbb{Z}. \end{cases}$$

So we have defined the generalized Kripke model $\mathcal{A}' \rightleftharpoons (\mathcal{A}, \mathcal{T}, \{f\})$. The last three assumption of Claim 2 and $\mathcal{A}' \models Next$ clearly hold in $\mathcal{A}'$.

To prove $MInd^B$ in $\mathcal{A}'$ let $\phi \in MForm_{\sigma}$. Since $Next$ has the quantifier elimination property and $\phi$ contains only modalitites of the form $1$, $\circ$ and $1\Box$, the formula $\phi$ in $\mathcal{A}'$ is equivalent to the Boolean combination of the following types of atomic formulas:

$$U = V + n, U = x + n, x = y + n, U = m, x = m,$$

where $U, V \in V_L$, $x, y \in V_g$, $n \in \mathbb{N}$ and $m \in \mathbb{Z}$. We remark that this statement is not true for the entire $MForm_{\sigma}$. Indeed, in the case of $MForm_{\sigma}$ the modal operator $\Box$ corresponds to $\leq$, and this fact destroys the quantifier elimination property.

Now let us suppose that $\phi \in \Phi_B$ also holds. We are going to check that $cont(\phi, X)$ holds in $\mathcal{A}'$. Let $u \in \alpha \cup \{\uparrow\}$ and consider the truth of $\phi$ along $\check{z} \times \{u\}$ or $\mathbb{N}$. By construction, the values of $M$ along this time set always differ from each other. Using this fact, the atomic formulas of the above forms have constant value - far enough from parameters. Let us suppose that $1\phi$ and $\phi \to \circ\phi$ are true. If so then $\phi$ is true along $\mathbb{N}$ and therefore $\phi$ is true along $\check{z} \times \{u\}$ - far enough from parameters. However, then using $\phi \to \circ\phi$ we get that $\phi$ is true for the whole $\check{z} \times \{u\}$. Hence $1\Box\phi$ is also true.

Using the model $(\mathcal{A}, \mathcal{T}, \{f\})$ in the claim one can construct a model within which $\chi$ does not hold. $\Box$

Now let us consider how total correctness can be handled in the framework of temporal logic. In order to prove the termination of a program there are two main methods, one of which uses well-founded sets (see e.g. Manna [1974]) whereas the other uses induction over the data structure. This type of induction is also called structural induction (see Burstall [1969]). Both these methods follow the same philosophy by establishing that there is no infinitely long sequence of data while showing that a program has no indefinitely long path. In both constructions the well-founded sets and structural induction are used outside the scope of first-order logic in the program verification methods. The well-founded sets are used as extralogical tools while structural induction is used as a second-order axiom schema.

The first-order time-logical variant of structural induction was introduced in Andréka, Németi, Sain [1981] and was generalized in Sain [1987] while the well-ordered sets were defined in accordance with our approach in Gergely [1987]. Here we give the appropriate definitions in accordance with our philosophy in the temporal logical framework.

Let us consider the well-founded sets. The main question to be answered is how a set can be handled by using only first-order tools. The use of parametrically definable relations offers a good answer.

We shall use the following notations. Let $Z$, $Z'$ and $Q$ be disjoint sets of global variables and let us suppose that $Z'$ is a copy of $Z$. Let $\preceq \in MForm_\sigma$ be a formula with the property $var(\preceq) \subset Z \cup Z' \cup Q$. In this case we write $Z' \preceq Z$ instead of the formula $\preceq$ to express that the intended meaning of the formula $\preceq$ is an ordering. $Z' \prec Z$ is a shorthand for $(Z' \preceq Z) \wedge (Z' \neq Z)$.

**(22.12) Definition.** *Let us fix a Kripke model $\mathcal{B} = (\mathcal{A}, \mathcal{T}, K) \in MMod_\sigma$. A formula $\preceq$ (with variables Z,Z',Q) is called well-founded in $\mathcal{B}$ with respect to a parameter valuation $k_Q \in Val_{\mathcal{A}}[Q]$ iff formulas (i)-(iii) hold in $\mathcal{B}$ with respect to the valuation $k_Q$:*

*(i)* $Z \preceq Z' \to (Z \preceq Z) \wedge (Z' \preceq Z')$;
*(ii)* $Z \preceq Z' \wedge Z' \preceq Z'' \to Z \preceq Z''$;

*(iii)* $Z \preceq Z' \wedge Z' \preceq Z \rightarrow Z = Z'$;

*(iv)* *and for any formula* $\alpha \in MForm_\sigma$ *with* $var(\alpha) \rightleftharpoons Z \cup^* Q \cup^* Q'$ *(where* $Q'$ *is a new set of global and local variables) and for any valuation* $k_{Q'} \in Val_{\mathcal{B}}[Q']$ *the following formula holds in* $\mathcal{B}$ *with respect to the valuation* $k_Q + k_{Q'}$*:*

$$\exists Z\alpha \rightarrow \exists Z'(\alpha[Z'/Z] \wedge \forall Z(\alpha \rightarrow Z' \preceq Z)).$$

*This means that any parametrically definable non-empty subset of the underlying set of the ordering generated by* $\preceq$ *and* $k_Q$ *in* $\mathcal{B}$ *has a* $\preceq$*-least element in* $\mathcal{B}$.

**(22.13) Lemma.** *There is a recursive set of formulas* $WF_\sigma(\preceq) \subseteq MForm_\sigma$ *which expresses the fact that the formula* $\preceq$ *defines a well-founded relation for every parameter.*

If one prefers induction to well-founded relations then instead of $WF_\sigma(\preceq)$ the structural induction on data can be used. This can be formulated as follows.

**(22.14) Definition.**

*(i)* *Let* $\sigma$ *be a given one-sorted similarity type and let* $G \subseteq func\ \sigma$ *be a given finite set. For a temporal-logic formula* $\phi$ *let us consider the following induction axiom:*

$$ind_G(\phi, x) \rightleftharpoons \Big( \bigwedge_{\substack{c \in G \\ ar(c)=0}} \phi[c/x] \wedge \bigwedge_{\substack{f \in G \\ ar(f)=n}} \forall x_1 \ldots \forall x_n \Big( \wedge_{i=1}^{n} \phi[x_i/x] \rightarrow$$

$$\phi\big[f(x_1, \ldots, x_n)/x\big]\Big)\Big) \rightarrow \forall x \phi.$$

*(ii)* *Let* $Dind^P_{G\sigma} \rightleftharpoons \{ind_G(\phi, x) | \phi \in Mform_\sigma, x \in V_g\}$,
$Dind^B_{G\sigma} \rightleftharpoons \{\alpha \in DInd^P_{G\sigma} | \alpha$ contains only modalities $1\Box, 1, \circ\}$,
$Dind_{G\sigma} \rightleftharpoons \{\alpha \in DInd^P_{G\sigma} | \alpha$ contains only modalities $1, \circ\}$.

We note that e.g. the induction principle $Dind^P_{G\sigma}$ approximates the property that constants and functions, names of which belong to $G$, generate the whole data structure. The approximation takes place by using all temporal formulas in $MForm_\sigma$. The main purpose of this induction principle is to ensure that the time of "data generation" and the time represented by the time structure given in Kripke models are the same.

**(22.15) Example.** In the special case when $\sigma$ itself contains a binary relation symbol, say $\leq$, then we can use the formula $z \leq z'$ instead of $\preceq$. In this case $Q = \emptyset$. Similarly, if we have $PA_d$, we can chose $G \rightleftharpoons \{0_d, S_d\}$ and then $Dind_{G\sigma}$ will contain the induction part of $PA_d$.

Using the notations of Definition (22.12) let $(\preceq, Z, Z', Q)$ be a well-founded ordering in $\mathcal{A}$. Let $Y$ be a new local copy of Z. Let $\phi$, $\psi \in MForm_\sigma$ be such formulas that $var(\phi) \cap var(\psi) = \emptyset$. It may happen that $Y \cap var(\psi) \neq \emptyset$. Now we formulate a new proof principle which expresses that the validity of $\Diamond\psi$ can be proved by descending along the ordering $\preceq$. Take the following formula:

$$wfProof(\phi, \preceq, \psi) \rightleftharpoons 1\Box\forall Z\Big((\phi \wedge Z = Y \wedge Z \preceq Z) \rightarrow \\ \Diamond(\psi \vee \exists Z'(\phi \wedge Z' = Y \wedge Z' \prec Z))\Big).$$

**(22.16) Theorem.** *Let $(\preceq, Z, Z', Q)$ be a well-founded ordering and let $\phi$, $\psi \in MForm_\sigma$ be such that $var(\phi) \cap (Z \cup Z') = \emptyset$. Then the following holds:*

$$WF_\sigma(\preceq) \models (wfProof(\phi, \preceq, \psi) \wedge \Diamond\exists Z(\phi \wedge Z = Y \wedge Z \preceq Z)) \rightarrow \Diamond\psi.$$

*Proof.* Let $(\mathcal{B} = (\mathcal{A}, \mathcal{T}, K)$ be a Kripke model and let $k_\phi \in Val_\mathcal{B}[var(\phi)]$ be a given valuation. Moreover let $k_Q \in Val_\mathcal{A}[Q]$ be a valuation such that for all $\alpha \in WF_\sigma(\preceq)$, $\mathcal{B} \models \alpha[k_Q]$. Take

$$H \rightleftharpoons \{k \in Val_\mathcal{A}[Z] \mid \mathcal{A} \models (\phi \wedge Y = Z \wedge Z \preceq Z)[k_\phi, k_Q, k, t] \text{ for some } t \in T\}.$$

Since $\mathcal{A} \models WF_\sigma(\preceq)[k_Q]$ the set $H$ has a $\preceq$-least element, say $\hat{k}$. Let $s \in T$ be the time moment for which $\hat{k} \in H$. Using the minimality of $\hat{k}$ we have

$$\mathcal{B} \not\models \Diamond\exists Z'(\phi \wedge Z' = Y \wedge Z' \preceq Z)[k_\phi, k_Q, \hat{k}, s].$$

Hence by applying the formula $wfProof$ we get $\mathcal{B} \models \Diamond\psi[k_\phi, k_Q, \hat{k}]$. □

**(22.17) Lemma.** *$PA_d \cup MInd_\eta^P \not\models WF_\eta(\leq)$ and $PA_d \cup MInd_\eta^P \not\models DInd_{G\eta}^P$.*

*Proof.* Consider the program

$$p \rightleftharpoons \textbf{while } y \neq 0 \textbf{ do } y := y - 1 \textbf{ od}.$$

It is not hard to prove that

- $PA_d \cup MInd_\eta^P \not\models \langle p\rangle true$, but
- $PA_d \cup WF_\eta(\leq) \models \langle p\rangle true$.

To prove the first statement let $\mathcal{A}$ be a non-standard model of $PA_d$. Take $\mathcal{B} \rightleftharpoons \mathcal{A}^{st}$. It is obvious that for any non-standard input $a$ the program $p$ never terminates in the Kripke model $\mathcal{B}$. However, $\mathcal{B} \models PA_d \cup MInd_\eta^P$.

The second statement can be proved by using the induction principle $wfProof(work(p), \leq, X_l = stop_p)$.

A similar argument shows that the statement is true for $Dind_{G\eta}^P$ as well. □

**(22.18) Example.** At first glance $wfProof$ seems to us a powerful proof principle, however, it is not so. Consider the following program:

$$q \rightleftharpoons y := 0 \textbf{ while } y \neq x \textbf{ do } y := y + 1 \textbf{ od}.$$

Let us prove that $Npre_d \cup WF_\sigma(\leq) \models \langle q \rangle true$. Let us suppose that $work(q)$ holds. Our aim is to prove that $\Diamond x = y$ is true. For a contradiction, let us suppose that $1\Box x \neq y$ is true. Using $WF_\sigma(\leq)$ let $a$ be the least datum for which $1\Box y \neq a$ holds. It is clear that $a \neq 0$. Since $Npre_d$ holds for datum there is a data $b$ such that $b + 1 = a$. By definition, sometime the value of $y$ is equal to $b$. Two time moments later $y$ becomes $b+1 = a$, which gives a contradiction.

Our opinion is that the above proof cannot be carried out by using only the proof principles $wfProof$. Of course, if the data structure also satisfies $PA_d$ then $wfProof$ works correctly because $x - y$ is a good measurement for the time of the termination.

The natural counterpart of Lemma (22.4) remains true:

**(22.19) Lemma.** *For any similarity type $\sigma$ and for an arbitrary $G$ and for an arbitrary $\preceq$:*

$$PC_\sigma(MInd_\sigma \cup DInd_{G\sigma}) \subseteq PC_\sigma(MInd_\sigma^B \cup DInd_{G\sigma}^B) \subseteq PC_\sigma(MInd_\sigma^P \cup DInd_{G\sigma}^P)$$
$$TC_\sigma(MInd_\sigma \cup DInd_{G\sigma}) \subseteq TC_\sigma(MInd_\sigma^B \cup DInd_{G\sigma}^B) \subseteq TC_\sigma(MInd_\sigma^P \cup DInd_{G\sigma}^P)$$

Theorems (22.20)–(22.22) below are due to Sain (see e.g. Sain [1987], [1991]).

**(22.20) Theorem.** *For an appropriate similarity type $\sigma$ and for any non-trivial choice of $G$ (i.e. $G$ contains at least one constant and one unary function symbol) we have*

$$TC_\sigma(MInd_\sigma \cup DInd_{G\sigma}) \subset TC_\sigma(MInd_\sigma^B \cup DInd_{G\sigma}^B),$$
$$TC_\sigma(MInd_\sigma^B \cup DInd_{G\sigma}^B) \subset TC_\sigma(MInd_\sigma^P \cup DInd_{G\sigma}^P).$$

It is an interesting fact that $Dind_{G\sigma}$ does not increase the number of provable partial correctness formulas in the presence of $MInd_\sigma^P$:

**(22.21) Theorem.** *For an arbitrary similarity type $\sigma$ and for an arbitrary set $G$ we have*

$$PC_\sigma(MInd_\sigma^P \cup DInd_{G\sigma}^P) = PC_\sigma(MInd^P).$$

However, for the induction principles $MInd_\sigma$ and $MInd_\sigma^B$ this is not true:

**(22.22) Theorem.** *For an appropriate similarity type $\sigma$ and for any non-trivial choice of $G$ (i.e. $G$ contains at least one constant and one unary function symbol) we have*

$$PC_\sigma(MInd_\sigma \cup DInd_{G\sigma}) \supset PC_\sigma(MInd_\sigma)$$
$$PC_\sigma(MInd^B_\sigma \cup DInd^B_{G\sigma}) \supset PC_\sigma(MInd^B_\sigma)$$

**(22.23)** *Remark.* It is interesting how the above statements will be changed if we consider the axiom system $WF_\sigma(\preceq)$ instead of the structural induction $DInd_{G\sigma}$. It is not hard to prove that if the similarity type $\sigma$ contains symbols $0_d$, $S_d$ and $\leq_d$ with their usual meaning then $WF_\sigma(\leq_d)$ and $DInd^P_{G\sigma}$ are logically equivalent.

Let us call the corresponding $\sigma$-type Kripke models *ordered* ones. It can be established that with respect to the ordered Kripke models if the data structure satisfies $PA_d$ we have the following equalities:

$$TC_\sigma(MInd_\sigma \cup DInd_{G\sigma}) = TC_\sigma(MInd^B_\sigma \cup DInd^B_{G\sigma}) = TC_\sigma(MInd^P_\sigma \cup DInd^P_{G\sigma})$$
$$PC_\sigma(MInd_\sigma \cup DInd_{G\sigma}) = PC_\sigma(MInd^B_\sigma \cup DInd^B_{G\sigma}) = PC_\sigma(MInd^P_\sigma \cup DInd^P_{G\sigma})$$

If we suppose less about the data structure, then it is an open question how these partial and total correctness theories are interrelated.

Part IV

# Programming Logic with Explicit Time

Chapter 23

# Introduction to Part IV

Temporal logic investigated in the previous part represents program execution by taking trace semantics into account. The traces are represented by the changes of local variables. The computational paths are realized according to the time structure of the temporal logic. Note that for a given program $p$ the set $Trace_{\mathcal{A}}[\![p]\!]$ of traces in a given model $\mathcal{A}$, when the input is fixed, forms a tree. Depending on the time structure this tree can be represented in different ways. We considered a time structure which allowed us to represent $Trace_{\mathcal{A}}[\![p]\!]$ as the set of all possible paths from the root (given input) to the leaves (outputs) of the tree. It is important to emphasize that temporal logic uses a fixed linear time structure built into the Kripke models.

Since in temporal logic we cannot use quantifiers over local variables and we cannot refer to single time moments or intervals when considering a program we cannot handle single computation paths but only all possible paths together. Almost all interesting program properties can be expressed in temporal logic except for some connected with counting events (see Wolper [1983]). We have also seen that temporal logic has a complete calculus that permits us to prove all the expressible properties. Note that the description of program properties and their proofs requires a temporal way of reasoning, which is less familiar to logicians than classical logic. In order to make temporal logic adequate to the different recently formulated needs of programming theory it can be augmented with various constructions like new modalities and it also can be allowed to use quantification over local variables. See Manna, Pnueli [1988] for some possible variants of temporal logic. Namely, these necessary extensions have an effect on the entire presence of the three components (data structure, time structure and set of functions) not only in the models of the descriptive language but in its syntax as well. That is, the realization of the second possibility mentioned in Chapter 16 in the formal tools for characterizing program execution becomes necessary. Such extensions, necessary as they are, tend to estrange temporal logic from its modal roots and cause the view it offers to approach that of classical logic.

Therefore, it is quite natural to aim at the development of an appropriate language directly in the frame of classical first-order logic which allows us to handle time at least as in the scope of temporal logic. Moreover, we can also expect to provide more refined time handling, by allowing the language to refer to time moments and to intervals. We also allow the use of functions as appropriate formal objects to represent program semantics not only in the models, as in the case of temporal logic, but also in the object language itself. These functions characterize the data change in time and allow us to build up the computational paths.

Since time, data and functions are different entities it is advisable to have different languages or, at least, different elements of a language correspond to them. This can be provided by a three-sorted language, where the first sort corresponds to data, the second sort corresponds to time and the third one to the set of functions. In the next chapter we introduce a many-sorted first-order language with explicit consideration of data, time and data change in time. This language, called time logic, was introduced in the late 1970s and has been actively investigated under the name of non-standard programming logic by the Hungarian school of programming logic.

By using time logic the characterization of program properties in the abstract computer will be done by appropriate axiom systems. Besides axioms describing the properties of data and time and besides induction principles we use a new kind of axiom, namely the comprehension schemas. Comprehension schemas cannot be formulated in temporal logic because of the lack of quantification over local variables. They give the power of time logic and add new possibilities to use time logic with respect to temporal logic.

Note that an important aim of the axiomatization is to make the set of time moments as close to "standard time" as possible. Also note that explicit time handling always results in the appearance of non-standard models beside the standard models. This means that programs that terminate in a non-standard time moment will become possible. Looking at the program execution from inside the model it will be finite, while looking at it from the outside it will be infinite. Therefore, explicit time handling requires awareness.

From the point of view of programming theory it is an important requirement to have only computable functions, since in this case Church's thesis remains true in the theory with the refined model of the computer. The most powerful comprehension schema, i.e. the most general comprehension schema, is not appropriate for this aim since it proves the existence of non-computable functions as well. Therefore, it is important to provide comprehension schemas appropriate from the point of view of computation theory. We investigate different comprehension schemas even from this point of view. We give all the necessary notions and all the mentioned axiom systems in Chapter 24, where we introduce the time logic and also three different regular time theories.

Programming theory based on time logic will be very flexible since it will process a formalism which permits us to define any theoretically important objects and notions connected with the characterization of programs. This formalism is developed in Chapter 25 as an effective fixed-point theory. Effectivity means that the solution of a fixed-point equation can be obtained in finitely many steps. Moreover, according to the requirement that the objects and notions should be explicitly definable in programming theory, the solutions will be defined in regular time theories. We consider two different fixed-point theories, a finitary and a non-finitary one, to satisfy different needs of the programming theory.

Chapter 26 is devoted to the investigation of the expressive power of time logic. First of all we show that temporal logic can be embedded into time logic. Then we investigate how the extended dynamic logics can be embedded into time logic, which we do by embedding the transitive and inductive extensions. By using the embedding thus established we define the time-logic characterization of different program verification methods. We also compare partial and total correctness theories differing in the underlying theory.

Chapter 24

# Time Logic

In the previous part, temporal logic was introduced to describe program properties. For this logic, traditional modal logic with a temporal interpretation of the modalities was augmented with two kinds of variables, global and local. The use of local variables allows us to describe and characterize the program execution. However, as observed in Wolper [1983] there are some properties, usually referring to counting events, which are not expressible in the considered version of temporal logic where quantification over local variables is not allowed. Moreover, temporal logic does not allow us to refer explicitly to time moments or intervals. The result is that temporal logic handles at once all the computational paths starting from the same input.

To overcome these deficiencies it is possible to extend the expressive power of temporal logic by augmenting it, for example, with new temporal modalities and allowing quantification over local variables or changing linearity of time to branching time or much more sophisticated time notions. For a good survey of these possibilities see Manna, Pnueli [1988]. However, many of these extensions make temporal logic very eclectic. At the same time quantification over local variables changes the modal logical view of temporal logic to the view of classical logic. Therefore, instead of making the different needed extensions of temporal logic we develop a logic appropriate for our programming theory in the framework of classical logic. We introduce the so-called time logic which provides tools to describe and handle data, time and data change in time explicitly.

In Section 24.1 we define the $\sigma$-type time logic which is an extension of $\sigma$-type data structure with new sorts that correspond to time and to data change in time and with the appropriate function and relation symbols to handle time and time functions explicitly. In order to make appropriate the time logic for programming theory we introduce three axiom systems in Section 24.2. In the models of these theories we will built up the first-order programming theory.

## 24.1 Time Extension

Let us fix a similarity type $\sigma$ with equality by the use of which the data environment can be given. Let $t \notin \mathit{sort}\ \sigma$ be a new sort corresponding to time and for each sort $d \in \mathit{sort}\ \sigma$ let us fix a new sort $d^t$, the elements of which allow us to characterize the possible changes of data in time. Informally, the entities of each new sort $d^t$ are functions from the possible time moments to all possible data of sort $d$. Moreover, for each sort $d \in sort\ \sigma$ let $app_d : d^t, t \to d$ be a new function symbol. Let $\sigma^t$ be the minimal similarity type which contains $\sigma$, the above defined new sorts, function symbols and the similarity type $\eta$ of arithmetic whose symbols are considered as $t$-sorted ones.

The elements of a $d^t$-sorted universe are called paths by Kröger [1987] or intensions in Gergely, Úry [1981] and in Sain [1985c] while a few authors use the notion of function. We prefer the latter as the most flexible one since in certain cases functions may behave as paths or, in other cases, as intensions, etc., but function is the appropriate mathematical entity.

**(24.1) Definition.** *Let us fix a similarity type $\sigma$. The time extension of the similarity type $\sigma$ is the pair $(\sigma^t, time)$ where time is defined in such a way that for each model $\mathcal{D} \in Mod_\sigma$:*

$$time(\mathcal{D}) \rightleftharpoons \{\mathcal{A} \mid \mathcal{A} \in Mod_{\sigma^t}, \mathcal{A}{\restriction}_\sigma = \mathcal{D}, \mathcal{A} \models Nord_t \cup Equ_\sigma\},$$

*where $Equ_\sigma$ is the following set of formulas:*

$$Equ_\sigma \rightleftharpoons \{\forall t\ app_d(f,t) = app_d(g,t) \to f = g \mid d \in sort\ \sigma\}.$$

*The elements of $Mod_{\sigma^t}$ are called models with inner time or, for short, time models.*

Note that the function $app_d$ serves to concretize the function name by giving the graph of this function, i.e. for a name $f$, $\lambda t.app_d(f,t)$ is a function that renders to each time moment a $d$-type entity. In the following we often do not distinguish between the name $f$ and the function $app_d(f,\cdot)$ representing it. So we simply write $f(t)$ instead of $app_d(f,t)$.

For the sake of convenience we introduce some notations which carry our intuition beyond the components of the time extension introduced above. Let us denote the set of all $\sigma^t$-type formulas as $TForm_\sigma$ instead of $Form_{\sigma^t}$. Similarly, let $TMod_\sigma$ denote the class of all time models, i.e. $TMod_\sigma \rightleftharpoons \bigcup\{time(\mathcal{D}) \mid \mathcal{D} \in Mod_\sigma\}$. Thus we define the *time logic*

$$TL_\sigma \rightleftharpoons (TForm_\sigma, TMod_\sigma, \models).$$

**(24.2) Definition.** *Let us fix a similarity type $\sigma$.*

*(A) Let the time model $\mathcal{A} \in TMod_\sigma$ be given. The models $\mathcal{A}{\restriction}_\sigma$ and $\mathcal{A}{\restriction}_\eta$ are called the data structure and the time structure (or inner time) of the time model $\mathcal{A}$, respectively and these models are denoted by $\mathcal{D}_\mathcal{A}$ and $\mathcal{T}_\mathcal{A}$, respectively. $\mathcal{A}(t)$, the universe of the time structure, is called the set of time moments and is denoted by $T_\mathcal{A}$.*

*(B) Let $\mathcal{D} \in Mod_\sigma$, $\mathcal{T} \models Nord$ be two given models. Let us suppose that for any $d \in sort\ \sigma$ a non-empty set $B_d$ and a function $K_d : B_d \times \mathcal{T}(t) \to \mathcal{D}(d)$*

*are given such that if* $b, b' \in B_d$ *and* $b \neq b'$ *then at least for one* $t \in \mathcal{T}(t)$, $K_d(b,t) \neq K_d(b,t)$. *Using these entities we can define a unique time model* $\mathcal{A}$ *such that* $\mathcal{T}_\mathcal{A} = \mathcal{T}$, $\mathcal{D}_\mathcal{A} = \mathcal{D}$ *and for any* $d \in sort\ \sigma$, $\mathcal{A}(app_d) = K_d$ *(and hence* $\mathcal{A}(d^t) \rightleftharpoons B_d$*). This time model is denoted by* $(\mathcal{D}, \mathcal{T}, \{K_d \mid d \in sort\ \sigma\})$.

Now we illustrate the notion of model with inner time by giving some examples.

**(24.3) Example.** Let $A$ be an arbitrary but non-empty set. Let the function $\alpha_A : [\mathbb{N} \to A] \times \mathbb{N} \to A$ be defined by taking $\alpha_A(f,n) \rightleftharpoons f(n)$ for each $(f,n) \in [\mathbb{N} \to A] \times \mathbb{N}$.

Let $\sigma$ be a fixed similarity type and let $\mathcal{D} \in Mod_\sigma$ be given. The *standard time extension* of $\mathcal{D}$ is the time model

$$\mathcal{D}^{st} \quad \rightleftharpoons \quad (\mathcal{D}, \mathcal{N}, \{\alpha_{A_d} \mid d \in sort\ \sigma\}).$$

A time model $\mathcal{A}$ is called *standard* iff it is isomorphic to $\left(\mathcal{A}\restriction_\sigma\right)^{st}$. Because $\mathcal{D}^{st}$ always exists, the class $time(\mathcal{D})$ is not empty. Hence the extension $(\sigma^t, time)$ of $\sigma$ is strict for each similarity type $\sigma$.

The following lemma is obvious because only the set $Equ_\sigma$ of axioms contains statements about functions.

**(24.4) Lemma.** *Let* $\mathcal{A} \in Mod_{\sigma^t}$ *such that* $\mathcal{A} \models Nord_t$. *For any sort* $d \in sort\ \sigma$ *let* $\sim_d$ *be the equivalence relation on* $\mathcal{A}(d^t)$ *defined by*

$$f \sim_d g \text{ iff for all } t \in \mathcal{A}(t)\ app_d(f,t) = app_d(g,t).$$

*Let* $B_d \rightleftharpoons \mathcal{A}(d^t)/\sim_d$ *and let* $K_d$ *be the factorization of* $app_d$ *with respect to the equivalence relation* $\sim_d$. *The time model* $(\mathcal{D}_\mathcal{A}, \mathcal{T}_\mathcal{A}, \{K_d \mid d \in sort\ \sigma\})$ *belongs to* $TMod_\sigma$. *This time model is denoted by* $\mathcal{A}/app$.

**(24.5) Example.** Let $\sigma$ be a one-sorted similarity type which contains the similarity type of arithmetics and let $\mathcal{D}$ be an arithmetical model (see Definition (6.6)). We construct a time model $\mathcal{A}$ whose data part is equivalent to $\mathcal{D}$. Let $T \rightleftharpoons nat_\mathcal{D}$ and for any $s \in rel\ \eta \cup func\ \eta$ let $\mathcal{T}(s) \rightleftharpoons \mathcal{D}(s)\restriction_T$. It is clear that $\mathcal{T}$ is an isomorphic copy of $\mathcal{N}$. Take $I \rightleftharpoons D \times nat_\mathcal{D}$. We take $K((b,n),t) \rightleftharpoons \beta_\mathcal{D}(b,t,n)$. Let the time model $\mathcal{A} \rightleftharpoons (\mathcal{D}, \mathcal{T}, \{K\})$. By Lemma (24.4) the time model $\mathcal{A}/app$ belongs to $TMod_\sigma$.

**(24.6) Example.** Now let $\sigma$ be an arbitrary one-sorted similarity type and fix a $\sigma$-type model $\mathcal{D}$. Let us fix a limit ordinal $\alpha$ and consider the set of the first $\alpha$ infinite cardinals, i.e. take

$$T \rightleftharpoons \{\aleph_\nu \mid \nu < \alpha\}.$$

Defining the functions and relations of $\eta$ on $T$ as usual we get a $\eta$-type structure $\mathcal{T}$ on $T$. In the end we define the function $K \rightleftharpoons [T \to D] \times T \to D$ by taking $K(f,t) \rightleftharpoons f(t)$. It is clear that $(\mathcal{D}, \mathcal{T}, \{K\})$ is a time model belonging to $TMod_\sigma$.

## 24.2 On Regular Time Theories

Having the time logic it is important to characterize those models that represent the abstract computers. The characterization may concern all types of entities: data, time and functions. First we have to define the time structure. The axiom system $Nord$ would be appropriate. Moreover, it is important to specify how the formulas describing program properties by concerning data depend on time. This dependency will be formulated with induction axiom schemas. Moreover, we introduce different induction schemas to represent the view of different program verification methods.

Let $\phi \in TForm_\sigma$ be an arbitrary formula. The induction over time with respect to $\phi$ can be formulated with the following axiom:

$$tind(\phi, x) \rightleftharpoons (\phi[0/x] \wedge \forall x(\phi \to \phi[x+1/x])) \to \forall x \phi,$$

where $x \in V_t$.

For an arbitrary set of formulas $\Phi \subseteq TForm_\sigma$ let us define the induction axiom schema generated by $\Phi$ as the set

$$TInd_\sigma^\Phi \rightleftharpoons \{tind(\phi, x) \mid \phi \in \Phi, x \in V_t\} \cup Nord_t.$$

Let us consider the following comprehension axiom schemas:

$$fComp_\phi \rightleftharpoons \forall t \exists! y \phi \to \exists f \forall t\ \phi[app_d(f,t)/y],$$

$$wComp_\phi \rightleftharpoons \forall t \exists! y \phi \to \forall s \exists f \forall t \leq s\ \phi[app_d(f,t)/y],$$

where $t, s \in V_t$, $y \in V_d$ and $f \in V_{d^t}$ for some $d \in sort\ \sigma$. $fComp_\phi$ is called the *full comprehension schema* and $wComp_\phi$ the *weak comprehension schema*. These comprehension axiom schemas state that if a certain formula $\phi$ defines a function $f$ then there is a name for it, or for every finite initial segment of it.

Moreover, let us suppose that $sort\ \sigma$ contains two constant symbols $\top$ and $\bot$ of an arbitrary sort $d$ of $sort\ \sigma$. Let us fix a set of axioms by taking

$$Struct \rightleftharpoons \{\top \neq \bot\} \cup PA_t \cup TInd_\sigma^{TForm_\sigma} \cup Equ_\sigma.$$

Let $\Sigma^+(\sigma^t; \sigma^t)$ be the minimal subset $F$ of $TForm_\sigma$ which satisfies the following conditions:

(i) if $\pi \in Atom_{\sigma \cup \eta}$ then $\pi$, $\neg\pi \in F$;
(ii) if $\phi$, $\psi \in F$ and $x$ is a $sort\ \sigma \cup \{t\}$-sorted variable symbol then $\phi \wedge \psi$, $\phi \vee \psi$, $\exists x \phi$ also belong to $F$;

(iii) if $s_1, s_2 \in V_t$ and $\phi \in F$ then $\forall s_1(s_1 \leq s_2 \rightarrow \phi)$ belongs to $F$.

Now we are ready to define all the three main theories necessary to handle times and functions appropriately. So take

$$\begin{aligned} Reg_\sigma &\rightleftharpoons Struct \cup \{fComp_\phi \mid \phi \in Tform_\sigma\}, \\ wReg_\sigma &\rightleftharpoons Struct \cup \{wComp_\phi \mid \phi \in Tform_\sigma\}, \\ pReg_\sigma &\rightleftharpoons Struct \cup \{fComp_\phi \mid \phi \in \Sigma^+(\sigma^t, \sigma^t)\}. \end{aligned}$$

**(24.7) Definition.** *The theories $Reg_\sigma$, $wReg_\sigma$ and $pReg_\sigma$ are called regular time, weakly regular time and pseudo-regular time theory, respectively. A time model $\mathcal{A}$ which is a model of these theories is also called regular, weakly regular and pseudo-regular time model.*

Regular time theory has been introduced in Gergely, Úry [1981]. Comprehension axiom schemas have also been considered in time logic in Andréka, Németi, Sain [1982]. The expressive power of the descriptive languages with different comprehension axioms has been investigated in Sain [1986, 1987]. It is an interesting question how the theories, defined in time logic so far, are related to each other.

**(24.8) Lemma.** *Let us suppose that the similarity type $\sigma$ contains two constant symbols $\uparrow$ and $\downarrow$ with the same sort. For the time theories defined so far, the following are true:*

(a) $\qquad Mod(Reg_\sigma) \subseteq Mod(pReg_\sigma) \subseteq Mod(wReg_\sigma) \subseteq Mod(Struct)$.

*Moreover, there is a similarity type $\sigma$ such that*

(b) $\qquad Mod(Reg_\sigma) \subset Mod(pReg_\sigma) \subset Mod(wReg_\sigma) \subset Mod(Struct)$.

*Proof.* The statement (a) is almost self-evident. The only interesting part of this statement is the inclusion $Mod(pReg_\sigma) \subseteq Mod(wReg_\sigma)$. To prove it let $\mathcal{A}$ be a pseudo-regular time model. First consider the following formula

$$v_d \rightleftharpoons (t = n \wedge x = b) \vee (t \neq n \wedge x = f(t)),$$

where $d \in sort\ \sigma$, $x, b \in V_d$, $t, n \in V_t$, $f \in V_{d^t}$. It is obvious that $v_d \in \Sigma^+(\sigma^t, \sigma^t)$. Moreover, for any time model $\mathcal{A} \models \forall t \exists! x v_d(f, n)$. This means that in pseudo-regular time models if the value of a function (an element of the $d^t$-sorted universe) is changed at a given time moment then a new function is obtained. Using this fact and the axiom $tind(\exists f \forall t \leq s\, \phi[app_d(f,t)/y], s)$ one can prove by induction on $s$ that the weak comprehension schema holds for an arbitrary time formula $\phi$.

Now we turn to prove that the inclusions of statement (a) are strict.

(i) Let $\mathcal{A}$ be a time model which contains only constant functions, i.e. $\mathcal{A} \models \forall f \forall t f(t) = f(0)$. It is obvious that $\mathcal{A} \in Mod(Struct)$ but $\mathcal{A} \notin Mod(wReg_\sigma)$.

(ii) Let $\mathcal{D}$ be an arbitrary $\sigma$-type model such that $|\mathcal{D}(d)| \geq \omega_0$ for some $d \in sort\ \sigma$. Take $\mathcal{T} \rightleftharpoons \mathcal{N}$ and let

$$A_{d^t} = \{f : \mathbb{N} \to \mathcal{D}(d) \mid \exists t \forall s \geq t f(s) = f(t)\}$$

and take $K_d : [A_{d^t} \times \mathbb{N}] \to \mathcal{D}(d)$ such that $K_d(f,n) \rightleftharpoons f(n)$. Let $\mathcal{A} \rightleftharpoons (\mathcal{D}, \mathcal{T}, \{K_d \mid d \in sort\ \sigma\})$ be the time model obtained in this way. It is clear that $\mathcal{A} \models wReg_\sigma$ but $\mathcal{A} \not\models pReg_\sigma$.

(iii) Let us suppose that $\sigma = \eta$ and let $\mathcal{D} \rightleftharpoons \mathcal{N}$ and $\mathcal{T} \rightleftharpoons \mathcal{N}$ as well and let

$$A_{d^t} \rightleftharpoons \{f : \mathbb{N} \to \mathcal{D}(d) \mid f \text{ recursive in } \mathbb{N}\}$$

and take $K_d : [A_{d^t} \times \mathbb{N}] \to \mathcal{D}(d)$ such that $K_d(f,n) \rightleftharpoons f(n)$. Let $\mathcal{A}$ be the time model obtained in this way. It is obvious that $\mathcal{A} \models pReg_\sigma$. Using the universal recursive function one can check that the following function exists in $Reg_\sigma$:

$$f(e) = \begin{cases} 0 & \text{if the } e\text{-th partial recursive function is total on } \mathbb{N}; \\ 1 & \text{otherwise.} \end{cases}$$

However, it is well known that this $f$ is not recursive in $\mathcal{N}$. Hence $\mathcal{A} \models pReg_\sigma$ but $\mathcal{A} \not\models Reg_\sigma$.

□

Now we show an example of handling time explicitly without using a many-sorted signature.

**(24.9) Example.** Let $\sigma$ be an arbitrary similarity type containing the similarity type $\eta$ of arithmetic which is used to represent data. Let $Ax \subseteq Form_\sigma$ be the set of axioms describing the expectations concerning data, such that $PA \subseteq Ax$.

We introduce a new unary relation symbol ($\zeta \notin \sigma$) to describe time. By $\zeta$ we supply our models with inner time supposing that time can be modeled by data. Let $\sigma'$ be the extension of $\sigma$ by adding the unary relation symbol $\zeta$. To formulate the minimal properties expected for time we introduce the following notations $\zeta'(x) \rightleftharpoons \exists t(x \leq t \land \zeta(t))$. Take

$$\begin{aligned} B_0 &\rightleftharpoons \zeta'(0), \\ B_1 &\rightleftharpoons \zeta'(x) \to \zeta'(x+1). \end{aligned}$$

The satisfaction of the formula $B_0$ provides that the set of time moments is not empty. The induction along $\zeta'$ with respect to an arbitrary formula $\phi \in Form_\sigma$ can be formulated as follows:

$$B_2^{\phi,x} \rightleftharpoons [\phi(0) \land \forall x(\zeta'(x) \land \phi(x) \to \phi(x+1))] \to \forall x(\zeta'(x) \to \phi(x)).$$

The formula $B_1$ and the schema $B_2^{\phi,x}$ provide that the set of time moments is closed under addition and multiplication. According to the above we always suppose that the time satisfies

$$PA' \rightleftharpoons \{B_0, B_1\} \cup \{B_2^{\phi,x} \mid \phi \in Form_\sigma,\ x \in var(\phi)\}.$$

Let $Ax' \rightleftharpoons Ax \cup PA'$ be the set of axioms describing the expectations concerning both data and time. The models of $Ax'$ can be considered as models with inner time. More precisely, let $\mathcal{A} \in Mod(Ax')$ be arbitrary. It is supposed that each element of the universe $A$ can serve as data and a well defined part of data describes or codes time. This part consists of those elements of $A$ which satisfy the relation $\zeta'_{\mathcal{A}}$. Thus the subset $\zeta'_{\mathcal{A}}$ of $A$ is just the inner time of model $\mathcal{A}$.

Now we show how a pseudo-regular time model can be constructed from any model of $Mod(Ax')$. Let $\mathcal{D} \in Mod(Ax')$ be an arbitrary model. Take $T \rightleftharpoons \{a \in D \mid \mathcal{D} \models \zeta'[a]\}$. For any $s \in func\ \eta \cup rel\ \eta$ let $\mathcal{T}(s) \rightleftharpoons \mathcal{D}(s){\restriction}_T$. It is clear that $\mathcal{T} \models PA$. Take

$$I \rightleftharpoons \{f \mid f : T \to D \text{ and } f \text{ is positive existentially definable in } \mathcal{D}\}.$$

Let $K : I \times T \to D$ be defined by $K(f,t) \rightleftharpoons f(t)$. Take $\mathcal{B} \rightleftharpoons (\mathcal{D}, \mathcal{T}, \{K\})$. Clearly $\mathcal{B}/app$ is a time model.

**(24.10) Lemma.** *$\mathcal{B}/app$ is a pseudo-regular time model.*

Details of the programming theory that uses the above model construction can be found in Gergely, Úry [1978,1980a,1981].

**(24.11) Lemma.** *Let us suppose that the similarity type $\sigma$ contains two distinct ground terms $\top$, $\bot$ and $\mathcal{D} \in Mod_\sigma$ is such a model that $\mathcal{D} \models \top \neq \bot$. $\mathcal{D}^{st}$ is a regular time model.*

*Proof.* The statement follows directly from the definitions. □

Chapter 25

# Definability in Regular Time Theories

In order to develop a flexible and powerful programming theory an appropriate formal theory is required which permits us to define all the objects and notions necessary for the theoretical characterization of programs and programming languages in a uniform way. The required formal theory can be ensured by an appropriate definition theory which allows the effective usage of fixed-point equations. Effectivity means that the equations can be solved in finitely many steps. Moreover, in programming theory it is important to work with explicitly defined notions and objects. Therefore we expect that the implicit definitions given in the form of fixed-point equations can be turned into explicit ones. Thus arises the requirement that the solutions of fixed-point equations should be definable.

In this chapter we develop a fixed-point theory in the framework of regular time theories. In this framework the comprehension axiom schema and the possibility of coding finite sequences together ensure the required constructivity and the existence of definable solutions.

In Section 25.1 we show that the weakest comprehension axiom schema is already enough to develop the required fixed-point theory.

Regular time theories allow us to define time-interpreted dynamic logics as a special inductive logic as shown in Section 25.2. Here we also show that regular time theory refutes Church's thesis and the latter is independent of the pseudo-regular time theory. In this section we also show that using time-functions it is easy to define a semantic function and a dynamic logic generated by this semantic function. This so-called dynamic logic with inner time turns out to be equivalent to the time-interpeted dynamic logic. However, the semantic function of this dynamic logic is much more intuitive than the semantic function of time-interpreted dynamic logic.

In Section 25.3 we show that the regular time theory is far too strong, since the truth of the $\eta$-type formulas of arithmetic is definable in it, which forces the consistency of the axiom system $PA$. For defining the required truth function a special non-finitary fixed-point theory will be built up.

## 25.1 Finitary Fixed-Point Theory

The use of a comprehension schema makes the corresponding theory in time logic powerful enough by augmenting it with an appropriate first-order definition tool. Namely, it provides a fixed-point theory which allows us to define all the objects and notions necessary for handling program-theoretic constructions. For example, it makes it possible to define the reflexive and transitive closure of any definable relation, which allows us to define program semantics directly.

**(25.1) Theorem.** *Let us fix a weakly regular time model $\mathcal{A}$ and a data sort $d \in sort\ \sigma$. Let $R$ be a first-order parametrically definable binary relation on $A_d$; i.e. $R \subseteq Val_{\mathcal{A}}[x_1, x_2]$, where $x_1, x_2 \in V_d$. Then there exists a relation $R^*$ that is the minimal first-order parametrically definable binary relation with the properties $R^* = R^* \circ R^* \cup \Delta_{(x_1,x_2)}$ and $R \subseteq R^*$.*

*Proof.* Let $\phi(x_1, x_2, Y) \in Tform_\sigma$ and $k \in Val_{\mathcal{A}}[Y]$ be such that

$$(b_1, b_2) \in R \text{ iff } \mathcal{A} \models \phi[b_1, b_2, k],$$

i.e. $\phi$ defines the relation $R$ with parameter $k$ in $\mathcal{A}$. Let us consider the following formulas

$$Proof(x_1, x_2, Y, f, t) \rightleftharpoons f(0) = x_1 \wedge f(t) = x_2 \wedge \forall s < t\, \phi(f(s), f(s+1), Y)$$
$$\phi^*(x_1, x_2, Y) \rightleftharpoons \exists f \exists t\, Proof(x_1, x_2, Y, f, t)$$

Take $R^* \rightleftharpoons \{(b_1, b_2) \mid \mathcal{A} \models \phi^*[b_1, b_2, k]\}$. It is clear that by substituting the constant 1 for $t$ in the definition of $\phi^*$ we obtain

$$\exists f \exists t (Proof(x_1, x_2, Y, f, t) \wedge t = 1) \leftrightarrow \phi(x_1, x_2, Y),$$

hence $R \subseteq R^*$. To prove that $R^* = (R^* \circ R^*) \cup \Delta_{(x_1,x_2)}$ first we remark that $R^* \subseteq (R^* \circ R^*) \cup \Delta_{(x_1,x_2)}$ is trivial. In order to prove the other inclusion let us fix three elements $b_1$, $b_2$ and $b_3$ of $A_d$ such that $\mathcal{A} \models \phi^*[b_1, b_2, k]$ and $\mathcal{A} \models \phi^*[b_2, b_3, k]$ hold. Let $g_1$, $s_1$, $g_2$, $s_2$ be elements of $A$ such that

$$\mathcal{A} \models Proof[b_1, b_2, k, g_1, s_1], \mathcal{A} \models Proof[b_2, b_3, k, g_2, s_2].$$

Now we define the function g by taking

$$g(t) \rightleftharpoons \begin{cases} g_1(t) & \text{if } t \leq s_1; \\ g_2(t - s_1) & \text{if } t > s_1. \end{cases}$$

By using $wReg_\sigma$ one can prove that there is a $g' \in \mathcal{A}(d^t)$ such that $g{\restriction}_{s_1 + s_2} = g'{\restriction}_{s_1 + s_2}$. We leave it to the reader to prove that $\mathcal{A} \models Proof[b_1, b_3, k, g, s_1 + s_2]$. Therefore $(b_1, b_3) \in R^*$.

Now let $R_1 \subseteq Val_{\mathcal{A}}[x_1, x_2]$ be a parametrically definable relation such that $R \subseteq R_1$ and $R_1 = (R_1 \circ R_1) \cup \Delta_{(x_1,x_2)}$. We have to prove that $R^* \subseteq R_1$. It is enough to prove that for an arbitrary $t \in T$:

$$(*) \qquad \text{if } \mathcal{A} \models \exists f\, Proof(x_1, x_2, Y, f, t)[b_1, b_2, k, t] \text{ then } \mathcal{A} \models \phi_1[b_1, b_2, \hat{k}],$$

where $\phi_1$ is the defining formula for $R_1$ with parameter $\hat{k}$. We prove (*) by induction on $t$.

Basic step: The case $t = 0$ follows from the reflexivity of $R_1$.

Inductive step: Let us suppose that (*) holds. Let us suppose also that

$$\mathcal{A} \models Proof[b_1, b_2, k, g, t+1].$$

It is obvious from the definition that $\mathcal{A} \models Proof[b_1, g(t), k, g, t]$ and $\mathcal{A} \models \phi[g(t), b_2, k]$. From the induction hypothesis we have $\mathcal{A} \models \phi_1[b_1, g(t), \hat{k}]$ and since $R \subseteq R_1$ $\mathcal{A} \models \phi_1[g(t), b_2, \hat{k}]$. Furthermore, from $R_1 \subseteq (R_1 \circ R_1) \cup \Delta_{(x_1,x_2)}$ we get $\mathcal{A} \models \phi_1[b_1, b_2, \hat{k}]$. □

We remark that Theorem (25.1) is true not only for the data sort but for the time sort as well. The main point here is that time moments can be coded by using the axiom system $PA$. However, to extend this theorem to functions as well we have to use pseudo-regular time theory.

**(25.2) Theorem.** *Let us fix a pseudo-regular time model $\mathcal{A}$ and let $R$ be an arbitrary definable many-sorted relation on it: $R \subseteq Val_{\mathcal{A}}[X]$ for some finite set $X \subseteq V$ of variables. The equation $S = S \circ S \cup \Delta_X$ under the condition $R \subseteq S$ has a least, definable solution $R^*$ in $\mathcal{A}$.*

*Proof.* The proof is just the same as the proof of Theorem (25.1). However one must take care over the coding of finite sequences of functions and time moments. The latter can be coded by using the axiom system $PA_t$. The former can be coded in following way: $\langle f_0, ..., f_{k-1}\rangle$ is coded by $f$ iff for all $0 \leq j < k$ and $t \in \mathbb{N}$; $f_j(t) = f(j + t \cdot k)$. To prove that for any $k \in \mathbb{N}$ and for any $f_0, ..., f_{k-1}$ the corresponding function $f$ exists we have to use an appropriately chosen full-comprehension axiom. □

**(25.3) Theorem.** *Let $\Psi$ be a positive existential operator in a pseudo-regular time model $\mathcal{A}$. Then the operator $\Psi$ has a least definable fixed-point in $\mathcal{A}$.*

*Proof.* For the sake of convenience let us suppose that $\Psi$ has the form $\Psi : Sb(A_d \times A_{d^t}) \to Sb(A_d \times A_{d^t})$. By using $\Psi$ we define an operator $R(\Psi)$ on $A_t \times A_{d^t}$ ($k$, $n \in A_t$, $f$, $g \in A_{d^t}$):

$$R(\Psi)(k, f, n, g) \text{ iff } \forall i < n\ (g(i), \lambda t.g(h_i^n(t)) \in \Psi(set(k, f)),$$

where $h_i^n(t) = i + n \cdot (t+1)$ and $set(k, f) \rightleftharpoons \{(f(j), \lambda t.f(h_j^k(t))) \mid j < k\}$. It is not hard to prove that the definition of $R(\Psi)$ can be expressed in $TForm_\sigma$. From Theorem (25.2) we know that $R(\Psi)^*$ exists. Define the following relation:

$$Y\Psi(x, h) \rightleftharpoons \exists i \exists n \exists g\ \big(R(\Psi)^*(0, \lambda t.\top, n, g) \wedge x = g(i) \wedge h = \lambda t.g(h_i^n(t))\big).$$

It is an easy exercise to prove that $Y\Psi$ is the least definable fixed point of $\Psi$ in $\mathcal{A}$. □

It is important to emphasize that the solution of the fixed-point equation in Theorem (25.3) is definable in the pseudo-regular time theory. This means that if we have an object or notion implicitly defined by a fixed-point equation then after solving the latter we obtain an explicit definition for the object or notion in question. However, if this operator is defined on the data structure then this is true in weakly regular time theory as well.

## 25.2 Inductive Extensions Generated by Regular Theories

The power of regular time theory allows us to define an extension of the dynamic logic introduced in Chapter 14 such that it will treat time explicitly as well. For this let us fix a similarity type $\sigma$ which contains two distinct ground terms of the same sort. For any $\mathcal{D} \in Mod_\sigma$ take

$$\begin{aligned} wrg(\mathcal{D}) &\rightleftharpoons \{\mathcal{A} \mid \mathcal{A} \in Mod(wReg_\sigma), \mathcal{A}\restriction_\sigma = \mathcal{D}\}, \\ rg(\mathcal{D}) &\rightleftharpoons \{\mathcal{A} \mid \mathcal{A} \in Mod(Reg_\sigma), \mathcal{A}\restriction_\sigma = \mathcal{D}\}, \\ prg(\mathcal{D}) &\rightleftharpoons \{\mathcal{A} \mid \mathcal{A} \in Mod(pReg_\sigma), \mathcal{A}\restriction_\sigma = \mathcal{D}\}. \end{aligned}$$

It is clear that $(\sigma^t, wrg)$, $(\sigma^t, rg)$, $(\sigma^t, prg)$ are extensions in the sense of Chapter 5. The extensions so obtained are called *the weakly regular time extension, the regular time extension* and *the pseudo-regular time extension* of $\sigma$.

Let $\phi \in \Sigma^+(\sigma; R)$. By Theorem (25.3) the operator ${}_{\mathcal{A}}\Gamma_\phi$ has a least definable fixed point in any model $\mathcal{A} \in Mod(prg)$. Moreover, there is a formula $Y\phi \in TForm_\sigma$ which defines this fixed point independently of $\mathcal{A}$. Take $\nabla\phi \rightleftharpoons Y\phi$. So we have defined two inductive extensions $(\sigma^t, rg, \nabla)$ and $(\sigma^t, prg, \nabla)$ of the similarity type $\sigma^t$. However, $(\sigma^t, wrg, \nabla)$ is an inductive extension of the similarity type $\sigma \cup \eta$.

**(25.4) Theorem.** *$wrg \models \nabla Ind^*_{\sigma\cup\eta}$ and $prg \models \nabla Ind^*_{\sigma^t}$.*

We remark that $rg \models prg$ implies that $rg \models \nabla Ind^*_{\sigma^t}$ also holds.

**(25.5) Definition.** *The inductive logics*

$$\begin{aligned} {}_1DL^{wrg}_\sigma &\rightleftharpoons (rD^1_\sigma, Mod(wrg), \models_{wrg}), \\ {}_1DL^{prg}_\sigma &\rightleftharpoons (rD^1_\sigma, Mod(prg), \models_{prg}), \\ {}_1DL^{rg}_\sigma &\rightleftharpoons (rD^1_\sigma, Mod(rg), \models_{rg}) \end{aligned}$$

*are called dynamic logic with weak inner time, dynamic logic with inner time and dynamic logic with strict inner time, respectively.*

**(25.6) Corollary.** *The dynamic logic with weak inner time, the dynamic logic with inner time and the dynamic logic with strict inner time are compact and complete with respect to consequence.*

*Proof.* This statement is an obvious consequence of Theorem (13.6) since $wReg_\sigma$, $pReg_\sigma$ and $Reg_\sigma$ are recursive sets. □

Let us fix a weakly regular time model $\mathcal{A} \in wrg(\mathcal{D})$ where $\mathcal{D} \in Mod_\sigma$ is an arbitrary data structure. If $p \in rP_\sigma$ then there is a $\sigma^t$-type formula $D[\![p, X]\!]$ which describes the semantics of this program in this inductive extension (see in Chapter 14). However, this semantic function can be defined directly, without using the notion of an inductive extension. Indeed, since $\sigma$ contains two constant symbols of the same sort we can suppose that $onestep_g(X, X_L, Y, Y_L)$ is a $\sigma$-type first-order formula for a given transition graph $g$ belonging to $rG_\sigma$. For any $v \in X \cup X_L$ let $v^t$ be a new $(sort\ v)^t$-sorted variable. The corresponding sets are denoted by $X^t, X^t_L$, respectively. Let $n$ be a $t$-sorted variable. Take the following formula:

$$T[\![g, X]\!](X^t, X^t_L, n) \rightleftharpoons (n > 0) \wedge X^t_L(0) = start_g \wedge$$
$$\forall s < n - 1\ onestep_g(X^t(s), X^t_L(s), X^t(s+1), X^t_L(s+1)).$$

One can define a new semantic function by taking

$$D^t[\![g, X]\!](X, Y) \rightleftharpoons \exists X^t \exists X^t_L \exists n\ T[\![g, X]\!](X^t, X^t_L, n)$$
$$\wedge X^t(0) = X \wedge X^t(n) = Y \wedge X^t_L(n) = stop_g.$$

The following lemma shows that all the "natural" traces are traces in this new sense. For a valuation $k \in Val_{\mathcal{A}}[X^t, X^t_L, n]$ and $s \in T$ let $k \| s \rightleftharpoons \lambda x \in X \cup X_L . k(x^t)(s)$.

**(25.7) Lemma.** *Let $\mathcal{A}$ be a weakly regular time model and let $g \in rG_\sigma$ be given. Let $k \in Val_{\mathcal{A}}[X^t, X^t_L, n]$, $k_Y \in Val_{\mathcal{A}}[Y, Y_L]$ be given. Let us suppose that $\mathcal{A} \models T[\![g, X]\!][k]$ and $\mathcal{A} \models onestep_g[k\|(n-1), k_Y]$. Then there is a valuation $k' \in Val_{\mathcal{A}}[X^t, X^t_L, n]$ such that $\mathcal{A} \models T[\![g, X]\!][k']$, $k'(n) = k(n) + 1$, for each $s < k'(n)$, $k'\|s = k\|s$ and if $s \rightleftharpoons k'(n)$ then $k'\|s = k_Y$.*

*Proof.* The statement is trivial using the fact that in weakly regular time theories the value of a function can be changed at a given time moment. □

**(25.8) Theorem.** *Let $g \in rG_\sigma$ be given. For any finite set of variables $X \supseteq var(g)$ we have*

$$wrg \models D^t[\![g, X]\!] \leftrightarrow D[\![g, X]\!].$$

*Proof.* We only sketch how this theorem can be proved. The most important fact is that $D[\![g, X]\!]$ is defined by using a formula of the form $\Xi^*$. In inductive extensions generated by time models $\Xi^*$ is defined as a least fixed point of an equation formed by using $\Xi^*$. According to Theorems (25.1) the solution of this type of fixed-point equation is defined by using the formula $Proof$ within which $\Xi$ occurs. However, it turns out that $\Xi$ is equivalent to $onestep_g$ and $Proof$ is the same formula as $D^t[\![g, X]\!]$. □

Now we turn to show how a "natural" semantics can be defined for programs and transition graphs with stacks. The formula which describes the trace of these programs is not so evident as in the stack-free case since we must code the stacks into the functions. We mainly follow the coding given in the proof of Theorem (6.7) (B). Let $d \in sort\ \sigma$ be a fixed sort and let $k \in Val_{\mathcal{A}}[\{x^t, n\}]$ be given where $sort\ x^t = d^t$. The value $k$ can be used as a code for an $k(n)$-long stack which has the elements $app_{d\mathcal{A}}(k(x^t), j)$ $(j < k(n))$. By using this coding we can describe the operations and relations on stacks by using the following $TForm_\sigma$-type formulas:

$$tEmpty_d(x, \ell, \hat{x}, \hat{\ell}) \rightleftharpoons (\hat{x} = x \wedge \hat{\ell} = 0),$$

$$tTail_d(x, \ell, \hat{x}, \hat{\ell}) \rightleftharpoons \hat{x} = x \wedge \hat{\ell} = l - 1,$$

$$tHead_d(x, \ell, a, \hat{a}) \rightleftharpoons (l = 0 \wedge \hat{a} = a) \vee (\hat{a} = app_d(x, \ell - 1) \wedge l > 0),$$

$$tPush_d(x, \ell, a, \hat{x}, \hat{\ell}) \rightleftharpoons (\hat{\ell} = \ell + 1) \wedge (\forall t < \ell\ app_d(x, t) = app_d(\hat{x}, t)) \wedge app_d(\hat{x}, \ell) = a.$$

Using these coding principles we can define a $\sigma^t$-type formula

$$onestep^s_g(X, X_S, X_L, Y, Y_S, Y_L)$$

which describes how the transition grpah steps. Here $X_S$ and $Y_S$ are the sets of variables coding the stack variables occuring in the transition graph. This means that to each stack variable $S$ (with sort $d^s$) we associate two new variables $x_S$ and $\ell_S$ to the set $X_S$. The sets of variables $Y$, $Y_S$ and $Y_L$ are new copies of $X$, $X_S$ and $X_L$, respectively.

Let us consider how finite initial segments of finite sequences can be coded. Let $h^n_i(t) \rightleftharpoons i + n \cdot t$. A triplet $(x, \ell, n)$ codes an $n$-tuple the $i$-th member of which is $\lambda t.x(h^{\beta(\ell,i,n)}_i(t))$. This means that the $i$-th finite sequence is $\beta(\ell, i, n)$-long and its $t$-th member is $x$ at $h^{\beta(\ell,i,n)}_i(t)$. We remark that this coding works in weakly regular models as well. Indeed, let $m$ be the maximum of the lengths $\beta(\ell, i, n)$ $(i \leq n)$. It is clear that only the first $n \cdot m$ members of function $x$ play a role, so we can use weak comprehension axioms to define a code for an arbitrary finite sequence of functions and time moments coding stacks. Using the same principles as in defining $D^t[\![g, X]\!]$ we can write down a similar formula denoted by $D^s[\![g, X]\!]$, for transition graphs with stacks, and we can prove a theorem similar to Theorem (25.8).

**(25.9) Definition.** *Let us fix a similarity type $\sigma$ and a program $p \in rP_\sigma$. Let $X$ be a finite set of variables such that $X \supseteq var(p)$. Let $Y$ be a new copy of $X$ and let $n$ be a $t$-sorted variable. We define a formula $TD[\![p, X]\!]$ with free variables $(X, Y, n)$ by taking*

$$TD[\![p,X]\!](X,Y,n) \rightleftharpoons \exists X^t \exists X_L^t\ T[\![gr(p),X]\!](X^t,X_L^t,n)\wedge$$
$$X^t(0)=X\wedge X^t(n-1)=Y\wedge X_L^t(n-1)=stop_{gr(p)}.$$

*If $TD[\![p,X]\!](X,Y,n)$ is true then we say that the program $p$ has an output $Y$ starting from $X$ and running until $n-1$ time moment.*

We remark that because of Theorem (25.8) the above definition is correct in that sense that if we collect the outputs in different time moments then we get the set of "original" outputs.

For the sake of convenience we suppose that $\sigma$ is a one-sorted similarity type and its only sort is $d$. Let us fix an ordering of $d$-sorted variables $V_d$. Let $\lceil\cdot\rceil : rP_\sigma \to \mathbb{N}$ be the Gödel coding of the $\sigma$-type programs with random assignments. Let $vrp$ be a recursive function on $\mathbb{N}$ with the following property:

$$vrp(\lceil p\rceil) \rightleftharpoons \max\ \{i \mid x_i \in var(p)\}.$$

We recall that for any program $p$ there is a set of variables $X_L(p)$ which is large enough to code the labels of $gr(p)$. Let $vro$ be a recursive function on $\mathbb{N}$ such that

$$vro(\lceil p\rceil) \rightleftharpoons \max\ \{i \mid x_i \in var(p)\cup X_L(p)\}.$$

Let $n$, $f$, $\ell$ be three new variable symbols with sort $t$, $d^t$ and $t$, respectively. We use $n$ to code programs and $f$ to code an $\ell$-length trace of the program $p$ coded by $n$. Let $k\in Val_{\mathcal{A}}[n,f,\ell]$ be a fixed valuation. The trace of the program $p$ with code $n$ can be described by using $vro(n)$-many variables. So we can define $vro(n)$-many functions from $k(f)$ by taking

$$Tr(k) \rightleftharpoons \lambda x_i \in var(p)\cup X_L(p).\lambda t\in T_{\mathcal{A}}.f(h_i^{vro(n)}(t)).$$

It is not hard to prove that if $\mathcal{A}$ is a weakly regular time model then $Tr(k)\in Val_{\mathcal{A}}[var(p)^t, X_L(p)^t]$. Now we are ready to form a theorem which states that the program semantics universally definable in weakly regular time theory.

The following theorem is a simple consequence of the fixed-point theory built up in Section 25.1. We left it to the reader to write down a fixed-point equation solution of which gives the formula $\Omega$.

**(25.10) Theorem.** *There is a formula $\Omega\in TForm_\sigma$ with $var(\Omega)=\{n,f,\ell\}$ such that for any program $p\in rP_\sigma$, for any weakly regular time model $\mathcal{A}$ and for any valuation $k\in Val_{\mathcal{A}}[n,f,\ell]$, if $k(n)=\lceil p\rceil$ then*

$$\mathcal{A}\models\Omega[k]\quad \textit{iff}\quad \mathcal{A}\models T[\![gr(p),var(p)]\!][Tr(k),k(\ell)].$$

**(25.11) Corollary.** *There is a formula $\Upsilon(n,f,g)$ (where $sort(n)=t$, $sort(f)$, $sort(g)=d^t$) in such a way that for any program $p\in rP_\sigma$, and for any weakly regular time model $\mathcal{A}$ the relation $\Upsilon_{\mathcal{A}}(\lceil p\rceil,\cdot,\cdot)$ is equal to $D_{\mathcal{A}}[\![p,var(p)]\!]$ in the following sense. Let $X\rightleftharpoons\{x_1,\dots,x_m\}$ list all the variables of the program $p$. Let*

*$Y \rightleftharpoons \{y_1, ..., y_m\}$ be a new copy of the program variables. Let $k \in Val_{\mathcal{A}}[n, f, g]$ be such that $k(n) = \lceil p \rceil$. Let $k_X \rightleftharpoons \lambda x_i \in X.app_{d\mathcal{A}}(k(f), i)$ and let $k_Y \rightleftharpoons \lambda y_i \in Y.app_{d\mathcal{A}}(k(g), i)$. Then*

$$(k_X, k_Y) \in D_{\mathcal{A}}[\![p, var(p)]\!] \quad \textit{iff} \quad \mathcal{A} \models \Upsilon[k].$$

*Proof.* Using $\Omega$ defined in Theorem (25.10) take

$$\Upsilon(n, f, g) \rightleftharpoons \exists F \exists \ell (\Omega(n, F, \ell) \wedge \bigwedge_{i=1}^{n} \Big( x_i \in var(p) \rightarrow F(h_i^{vro(n)}(0)) = f(i) \wedge F(h_i^{vro(n)}(\ell)) = g(i) \Big).$$

The statement immediately follows from Theorem (25.8). (We remark that the coding can be chosen such that the relation $x_i \in var(p)$ as a two-ary relation between $i$ and the code of $p$ is recursive, i.e. it is definable by a formula of the arithmetic.) □

We remark that in this corollary $n$ is a code (or the Gödel number) of a program $p$ and $f$, $g$ are used to code the input and output of the program. The values of $f(i)$ and $g(i)$ give the input and output values of the program variable $x_i$.

Now we show how Church's thesis can be formulated in weakly regular time models. Recall that constructing the time extension $time(\mathcal{D})$ the intended meaning of $d^t$-sorted entities, i.e. functions, was that these functions form the set of all computable functions. In this case Church's thesis means that any function is a computable one. There are many possible formulation of computable functions. We prefer the following: *computable functions are the recursive cutouts of the traces of $P_\sigma$-programs.* (This notion is compatible with the computability in Part I., however, the formulation of this one is much more simple in the present case.)

Let $\{r\}(t)$ be denote the value of $r$th recursive function at time moment $t$. Take

$$CT_\sigma \rightleftharpoons \forall h \exists r \exists n \exists i < vrp(n) \forall \ell \exists f \Big( \Omega(n, f, \ell) \wedge \forall s (\{r\}(s) < \ell \rightarrow h(s) = f(h_i^{vro(n)}(\{r\}(s)))) \Big).$$

This formula expresses the following. For each function $h$ there is a recursive function (coded by $r$), a program $p$ (coded by $n$), there is a program variable $x_i$ (coded by $i$ itself) such that for all $\ell \in \mathbb{N}$, if for some $s$, $\{r\}(s) < \ell$ then the value of $h$ at $s$ is the value of the program variable $x_i$ at time moment $\{r\}(s)$. $\Omega(n, f, \ell)$ states that $f$ codes an $\ell$-long trace of $p$ and the value of the program variable $x_i$ at time moment $\{r\}(s)$ is $f(h_i^{vro(n)}(\{r\}(s)))$. Loosely speaking, this means that $h$ can be formed from an appropriate program in a recursive way.

**(25.12) Corollary.** *The regular time theory refutes Church's thesis, i.e. there is a similarity type* $\sigma$ *such that* $Reg_\sigma \models \neg CT_\sigma$.

*Proof.* The function $f$ constructed in (iii) of the proof of Theorem (24.8) is not computable, but exists in any model of $Reg_\sigma$. □

**(25.13) Theorem.** *Church's thesis is independent of the pseudo-regular time theory.*

*Proof.* Using $rg \models prg$ and Corollary (25.11) we get that $prg \not\models CT_\sigma$. However, using the time model constructed in (iii) of the proof of Lemma (24.8) we get that there is a pseudo-regular time model $\mathcal{A}$ such that $\mathcal{A} \models CT_\sigma$. □

## 25.3 A Non-Finitary Fixed-Point Theory

Now we introduce a non-finitary fixed-point theory for the regular time theory. This fixed-point theory works only for a special type of operators defined below in Definition (25.16). For the sake of better understanding we first introduce a pure set-theoretic version of this fixed-point theory.

**(25.14) Definition.** *An operator* $\Gamma : Sb(B) \to Sb(B)$ *defined on* $B$ *is called quasi-finitary iff* $\Gamma$ *is monotone and there is a function* $norm : B \to \mathbb{N}$ *such that for each* $A \subseteq B$, $a \in \Gamma(A)$ *there is an* $A' \subseteq A$ *such that* $a \in \Gamma(A')$ *and for each* $x \in A'$: $norm(x) < norm(a)$.

**(25.15) Theorem.** *The closure ordinal of a quasi-finitary operator* $\Gamma$ *is* $\omega_0$.

*Proof.* Let $a \in I(\Gamma, v)$ for some $v \in \mathbb{N}$. We prove by induction on $v = norm(a)$ that $a \in I(\Gamma, norm(a))$. If $v = 0$ then $norm(a) = 0$ thus $a \in \Gamma(\emptyset)$, and the statement holds. Now let us suppose that the statement holds for $v$ and let $a \in I(\Gamma, v+1)$ be such that $v + 1 \geq norm(a)$. Since $\Gamma$ is quasi-finitary there is a subset $A \subseteq I(\Gamma, v)$ such that $\max norm(A) < norm(a)$ and $a \in \Gamma(A)$. By the induction hypothesis $A \subseteq I(\Gamma, norm(a) - 1)$. Hence

$$a \in \Gamma(A) \subseteq \Gamma\big(I(\Gamma, norm(a) - 1)\big) = I\big(\Gamma, norm(a)\big).$$

We note that from this also follows that $\Gamma\big(\bigcup_{v \in \mathbb{N}} I(\Gamma, v)\big) = \bigcup_{v \in \mathbb{N}} I(\Gamma, v)$. Now let us suppose that $a \in \Gamma\big(I(\Gamma, \omega_0)\big)$. By definition there is an $A \subseteq I(\Gamma, \omega_0) = \bigcup_{v \in \mathbb{N}} I(\Gamma, v)$ such that $a \in \Gamma(A)$ and $\max(norm(A)) < norm(a)$. By using the first statement of the proof we get that $A \subseteq I(\Gamma, norm(a) - 1)$ and $a \in I(\Gamma, norm(a))$. Thus $\Gamma(I(\Gamma, \omega_0)) = I(\Gamma, \omega_0)$, i.e. $\omega_0$ is the closure ordinal of $\Gamma$. □

Now we give a formalization of this theorem within regular time theory. First we define the first-order version of quasi-finitary operators. Here both the operator $\Gamma$ and the function *norm* are first-order definable. Moreover, the set $A'$ from Definition (25.14) depends on $A$ and $a \in \Gamma(A)$ in a first-order definable way.

Let $\sigma$ be a given similarity type containing two constant terms of the same sort.

**(25.16) Definition.** *Let $\mathcal{A} \in TMod_\sigma$ be a time model. Let $X$ be a finite set of variables such that $sort(X) \subseteq sort\ \sigma$. Let $B \subseteq Val_{\mathcal{A}}[X]$ be a parametrically definable set in $\mathcal{A}$. An operator $\Psi : Sb(B) \to Sb(B)$ is called definable quasi-finitary in $\mathcal{A}$ iff $\Psi$ is parametrically definable in $\mathcal{A}$ and there is a formula $Prev(X, X^t, \hat{X}^t)$ in $TForm_\sigma$ and a definable function $norm : B \to T_{\mathcal{A}}$ such that*

*(i)* $\mathcal{A} \models \forall X \forall X^t \exists \hat{X}^t Prev;$
*(ii)* *If $k \in Val_{\mathcal{A}}[X, X^t, \hat{X}^t]$, $\mathcal{A} \models Prev[k]$ and $k(X) \in \Psi(rng\ k(X^t))$ then $k(X) \in \Psi(rng\ k(\hat{X}^t))$ and for each $k' \in rng\ k(\hat{X}^t)$ we have $norm(k') < norm(k(X))$.*

**(25.17) Definition.** *A time model $\mathcal{A} \in TMod_\sigma$ is called countable iff for any data sort $d \in sort\ \sigma$ there is a function $F \in \mathcal{A}_{d^t}$ such that $rng\ F = \mathcal{A}_d$.*

**(25.18) Theorem.** *Let $\Psi$ be a definable quasi-finitary operator in a countable regular time model $\mathcal{A}$. Then the operator $\Psi$ has a least definable fixed-point in $\mathcal{A}$.*

*Proof.* The proof is similar to the proof of Theorem (25.1). However, we have to show how $\ell$-depth infinite trees and operations on these kind of trees can be defined by using $\sigma^t$-type formulas. Let *Pair* be a definable pairing function on the sort $t$ with definable inverses $D_1$ and $D_2$. Time moments can be used for coding finite sequences. A time moment $n$ codes an $D_2(n)$-long sequence $\beta$ *i*th element of which is $\beta(D_1(n), i, D_2(n))$, i.e. $D_1(n)$ is the code of the sequence. By using this coding two other notions become codable. Let $n + \langle a \rangle$ be a code for a new sequence $n'$ which is the extension of the sequence $n$ by exactly one element $a$. Let $n' \succ n$ be the shorthand for the formula $\exists a(n' = n + \langle a \rangle)$.

To code $\ell$-depth infinite trees we use a new $d^t$-sorted variable $r$. If $\{r\}(s) = \top$ for some $s$ then the sequence coded by $s$ belongs to the tree, otherwise it does not. So define $Tree(r, \ell)$ as the formula

$$\forall s(\{r\}(s) = \top \to D_2(s) \le \ell) \wedge \forall s \forall s'(\{r\}(s) = \top \wedge s \succ s' \to \{r\}(s') = \top).$$

Now let $X$ be a finite set of *sort* $\sigma$ sorted variables and let us suppose that $\Psi$ defined on a subset $Z$ of $Val_{\mathcal{A}}[X]$. Let $R$ be a new relation symbol with arity $X$. Since $\Psi$ is parametrically definable in $\mathcal{A}$ there is a formula $\phi \in TForm_\sigma$ with $var(\phi) \subseteq X \cup^* P$ and a parameter valuation $k_P \in Val_{\mathcal{A}}[P]$ such that for any $Q \subseteq Z$:

$$\Psi(Q) = \{k \in Val_{\mathcal{A}}[X] \mid (\mathcal{A}, Q) \models \phi(X, P)[k, k_P]\}.$$

Now consider the following formula:

$$Proof(X, X^t, r, \ell, P) \rightleftharpoons Tree(r, \ell) \wedge \exists s(\{r\}(s) = \top \wedge X^t(s) = X) \wedge$$
$$\forall s\Big(\{r\}(s) = \top \to \phi[\{X^t(s') \mid \{r\}(s') = \top \wedge s \succ s'\}/R][X'(s)/X]\Big).$$

The sorts of the used variables are as follows: $r$, $s$, $s' \in V_t$, $X \in V_d$ and $X^t \in V_{d^t}$.

As in the proof of Theorem (25.1) we define

$$Y\Psi \rightleftharpoons \{k \in Val_{\mathcal{A}}[X] \mid \mathcal{A} \models \exists X^t \exists r \exists \ell\, Proof(X, X^t, r, \ell, P)[k, k_P]\}.$$

A similar argument as in the proof of Theorem (25.15) proves the following

**Claim.** If $k \in Y\Psi$ then the following formula holds in $\mathcal{A}$:

$$\exists X^t \exists r \exists \ell (Proof(X, X^t, r, \ell, P) \wedge \ell \leq norm(X))[k, k_P].$$

It is clear that $Y\Psi$ is definable by a $\sigma^t$-type formula $\Upsilon$ such that $var(\Upsilon) \subseteq X \cup P$. It is not hard to prove that if S is a definable many-sorted relation on X and $\Psi(S) = S$ then $Y\Psi \subseteq S$. So we have only to prove that if $k \in \Psi(Y\Psi)$ then $k \in Y\Psi$ also holds. Now we use the definable function *norm*. Let $\ell \rightleftharpoons norm(k)$. Since $\Psi$ is quasi-finitary, with the help of *Prev* we can parametrically define a set $Q \subseteq Y\Psi$ such that $k \in \Psi(Q)$ and for any $k' \in Q$: $norm(k') < norm(k)$. By the claim we can suppose that for any $k' \in Q$ there is a $\pi(k') \in Val_{\mathcal{A}}[X^t, r, \ell]$ such that $\mathcal{A} \models Proof[k', \pi(k'), k_P]$ and $\ell < norm(k)$. Using the valuations $\pi(k')$ we can construct a new tree $k_Q \in Val_{\mathcal{A}}[X^t, r, \ell]$ such that $\mathcal{A} \models Proof[k, k_Q, k_P]$. For this construction we have to combine together the trees with the same parameter $k_P$ and then define a new valuation for $X^t$. For this purpose we like to use the full comprehension axiom schema. We can use it only if the formula *Prev* is given and we know that the regular time model is countable. Indeed, in this case for any data sort $d$ let us fix a function $F_d$ which enumerates in $\mathcal{A}$ all the $d$-sorted data. This function can be used to define an ordering on the data structure and then functions as well. The existence of *Prev* guarantees that $Q$ is definable. The above orderings also guarantee that we can choose a unique (namely the least) $\pi(k') \in Val_{\mathcal{A}}[X^t, r, \ell]$. Since everything is unique we can use the appropriate full comprehension schema to define $k_Q$. The existence of such a valuation proves that $\Psi(Y\Psi) \subseteq Y\Psi$. □

Note that the assumption about the time model being countable in the former theorem is necessary because of the form of the comprehension schema which requires in the antecedent the uniqueness of $\phi$, i.e. it has the prefix $\forall\exists!$. If we weaken the antecedent by using only the prefix $\forall\exists$ then we can drop this assumption.

**(25.19) Theorem.** *Let $\mathcal{A}$ be a countable regular time model such that $\mathcal{A} \models PA_d$. Then the truth of d-sorted formulas is definable in $\mathcal{A}$. Hence there is a parametrically definable relation Truth $\subseteq Val_{\mathcal{A}}[n, f, v]$ with the following properties:*

(i) *If $n$ is a Gödel number of a formula $\phi \in Form_\sigma$ with $m$ variables $x_1,...,x_m$, $f$ is a code of a valuation $k : \{x_1, ..., x_m\} \to A_d$ and $(n, f, v) \in Truth$ then $v = \top$ or $v = \bot$ iff $\mathcal{A}_d \models \phi[k]$ or $\mathcal{A}_d \not\models \phi[k]$, respectively.*

(ii) *If $n$ is a Gödel number of a formula with $m$ variables and $k$ is a code of a valuation of this $m$ variables, then there is a unique $v$ such that $(n, k, v) \in Truth$.*

*Proof.* The validity of a formula $\phi$ with respect to a valuation is defined by induction on the complexity of the formula. This induction can be formulised in $Reg_\sigma$ as an operator

$$\Psi : Sb((A_d \times A_d) \times A_d) \to Sb((A_d \times A_d) \times A_d).$$

It is an easy exercise to check that $\Psi$ satisfies the assumptions of Theorem (25.16). So take $Truth \rightleftharpoons Y\Psi$. Obviously, $Truth$ defines the validity of the formulas in the theory $Reg_\sigma$. □

From this theorem we immediately conclude that the consistency of the Peano axiom system for the data sort is provable in regular time theory. This was also obtained by different methods in Sain [1986, 1991].

**(25.20) Corollary.** $Reg_\sigma \cup PA_d \models Con(PA_d)$.

Therefore regular time theory $Reg_\sigma$ is very powerful, but unfortunately it is stronger than would be satisfactory for our programming theory. Namely, the computation theory within this theory does not meet our expectation.

Chapter 26

# Expressive Power of Time Logic

With the time logic introduced in the previous chapter we have three languages for supporting programming theory. How are these languages related to each other? We show in the present chapter that time logic is the most powerful in expressive power. This will be shown by embedding the other two languages, i.e. temporal and dynamic logics, into time logic.

Moreover we provide the characterization of these program verification methods by using the inductive axiom schemas introduced in the previous chapter and we investigate how the corresponding partial and total correctness theories are interrelated. Note that this interrelation in the time logic framework has been investigated in Andréka, Németi, Sain [1982,1991], Sain [1986,1991].

In Section 26.1 we give the embedding of temporal logic into time-logic and we use it to compare different axiomatizations given in the temporal and time-logic framework with respect to their expressive power. In Section 26.2 we present the embedding of transitive and inductive extensions into the time-logic. These embeddings show that time logic is the language which includes all descriptive languages defined so far, and in which the different characterizations defined by them can be represented.

## 26.1 Embedding Temporal Logic

Recall that the temporal-logic formulas may contain both local and global variables. It is clear that local variables in the time-logic framework correspond to $d^t$-sorted functions. Let us suppose that there is a fixed bijection wich assigns to each $d$-sorted local variable $y$ a $d^t$-sorted variable $f_y$.

**(26.1) Definition.** *Let $\sigma$ be a fixed similarity type. Let $Term_t$ denote the set of all time-sorted terms. Let us define a function*

$$\hat{}: (Mform_\sigma \cup Term_\sigma) \times Term_t \to Tform_\sigma$$

*which expresses for any formula $\phi \in Mform_\sigma$ and for any term $\tau \in Term_t$ that $\phi$ is true at the time moment $\tau$. This will be denoted as $\phi\hat{}\tau$.*

$$\tau^{*\frown}\tau \rightleftharpoons \begin{cases} x & \textit{if } \tau^* = x \textit{ is a global variable;} \\ app_d(f_y, \tau) & \textit{if } \tau^* = y \textit{ is a d-sorted local variable;} \\ f(\tau_1{}^\frown\tau, ..., \tau_n{}^\frown\tau) & \textit{if } \tau^* = f(\tau_1, ..., \tau_n); \end{cases}$$

$$\phi^\frown\tau \rightleftharpoons \begin{cases} \rho(\tau_1{}^\frown\tau, ..., \tau_n{}^\frown\tau) & \textit{if } \phi = \rho(\tau_1, ..., \tau_n); \\ (\phi_1{}^\frown\tau) \wedge (\phi_2{}^\frown\tau) & \textit{if } \phi = \phi_1 \wedge \phi_2; \\ \neg(\phi_1{}^\frown\tau) & \textit{if } \phi = \neg\phi_1; \\ \exists x(\phi_1{}^\frown\tau) & \textit{if } \phi = \exists x\phi_1; \\ \forall t^* \geq \tau(\phi_1{}^\frown t^*) & \textit{if } \phi = \Box\phi_1; \\ \forall t^*(t^* = \tau + 1 \rightarrow \phi_1{}^\frown t^*) & \textit{if } \phi = \circ\phi_1; \\ \forall t^*(t^* = 0 \rightarrow \phi_1{}^\frown t^*) & \textit{if } \phi = 1\phi_1. \end{cases}$$

**(26.2) Definition.** *For any formula* $\phi \in Mform_\sigma$ *let us define the formula* $\widetilde{\phi} \rightleftharpoons \forall t_0 \phi^\frown t_0$ *as the time-logic variant of* $\phi$. *Further* $\widetilde{Ax} \rightleftharpoons \{\widetilde{\phi} | \phi \in Ax\}$.

The following statement is an immediate consequence of the above two definitions.

**(26.3) Lemma.** *Let* $Ax \subseteq Mform_\sigma$ *and* $\phi \in Mform_\sigma$ *be arbitrary.* $Ax \models \phi$ *iff* $\widetilde{Ax} \models \widetilde{\phi}$. □

*For the sake of convenience we sometimes simply write* $\phi$ *instead of* $\tilde{\phi}$.
Now we introduce a sublanguage of time formulas.

**(26.4) Definition.** *Let* $TMform_\sigma$ *be the set of all those formulas of* $Tform_\sigma$ *which contain no quantifiers for the variables of* $V_{d^t}$ *for any* $d \in sort\ \sigma$.

An important question with respect to the interrelation between the temporal and time languages is asked in the following

**(26.5)** *Remark.* Is it true that the languages $Mform_\sigma$ and $TMform_\sigma$ have the same descriptive power? More precisely, the question is whether there are two functions (denoted by the same symbol) $int : Mform_\sigma \rightarrow TMform_\sigma$ and $int : TMform_\sigma \rightarrow Mform_\sigma$ such that

(a) for any sets of formulas $Ax_M \subseteq Mform_\sigma$, $Ax_T \subseteq TMform_\sigma$ we have $int(int(Ax_M)) \equiv Ax_M$, $int(int(Ax_T)) \equiv Ax_T$,
(b) if $\phi_M \in Mform_\sigma, \phi_T \in TMform_\sigma$ then $Ax_M \models \phi_M$ iff $int(Ax_M) \models int(\phi_M)$, $Ax_T \models \phi_T$ iff $int(Ax_T) \models int(\phi_T)$.

The answer is yes for the propositional case, which was first proved by Kamp [1968]. One can also find the proof in Gabbay [1986].

Note that $Mform_\sigma$ can be extended by allowing quantification over local variables. Let $MTform_\sigma$ denote this set of formulas. Similarly to the above question one can ask whether $MTform_\sigma$ and $Tform_\sigma$ have the same descriptive power.

In order to characterize the three main program verification methods let us consider the time-logic translation of the induction axioms formulated in temporal logic.

**(26.6) Definition.** *For an arbitrary similarity type $\sigma$:*

$$\begin{array}{lcl} TInd_\sigma & \rightleftharpoons & (MInd_\sigma)^{\sim}; \\ TInd_\sigma^B & \rightleftharpoons & (MInd_\sigma^B)^{\sim}; \\ TInd_\sigma^P & \rightleftharpoons & (MInd_\sigma^P)^{\sim}. \end{array}$$

We remark that there are definitions for the sets $TInd_\sigma$, $TInd_\sigma^B$ and $TInd_\sigma^P$ which do not use the embedding $\tilde{\ }$. For the details see Sain [1985b].

**(26.7) Lemma.** *For an arbitrary similarity type $\sigma$ we have*

$$PC_\sigma(TInd_\sigma) \subseteq PC_\sigma(TInd_\sigma^B) \subseteq PC_\sigma(TInd_\sigma^P);$$
$$TC_\sigma(TInd_\sigma) \subseteq TC_\sigma(TInd_\sigma^B) \subseteq TC_\sigma(TInd_\sigma^P)$$

*Proof.* The statement follows directly from Definition (26.6) and from the fact that any Kripke model can be considered as a time model. □

We can refine the above lemma by establishing inequalities between the partial and total correctness theories.

**(26.8) Corollary.** *For an appropriate similarity type $\sigma$ and for any non-trivial choice of $G$ we have*

$$PC_\sigma(TInd_\sigma) \subset PC_\sigma(TInd_\sigma^B);$$
$$PC_\sigma(TInd_\sigma^B) \subset PC_\sigma(TInd_\sigma^P);$$
$$TC_\sigma(TInd_\sigma^B \cup DInd_{G\sigma}^B) \subset TC_\sigma(TInd_\sigma^P \cup DInd_{G\sigma}^P).$$

*Proof.* The statement follows from Theorems (22.5), (22.11) and (22.20). □

Now let us consider the partial and total correctness theories based on the regular time theory and compare them with partial and total correctness theories corresponding Pnueli's method. Sain [1986,1987] established that regular time theory provides more powerful partial and total correctness theories. Our proof of Sain's theorem uses the main idea of her proof.

**(26.9) Theorem.** *For an appropriate similarity type $\sigma$ and an axiom system $Th$ we have*

$$PC_\sigma(Th \cup TInd_\sigma^P) \subset PC_\sigma(Th \cup Reg_\sigma),$$
$$TC_\sigma(Th \cup TInd_\sigma^P) \subset TC_\sigma(Th \cup Reg_\sigma).$$

*Proof.* Let us suppose that the one-sorted similarity type $\sigma$ contains a copy of the similarity type $\eta$ of arithmetic. It is clear that there exists a function $u$ such that $u(0) = 0_d$ and $\forall t\big(u(t) +_d 1 = u(t+1)\big)$. Take

$$Th \rightleftharpoons PA_d \cup \big\{\forall x \exists t\big(u(t) = x\big)\big\}.$$

Let $p$ be a program which enumerates all the formulas provable from $PA_d$. Thus $p$ starts with a natural number $n$, and terminates with the code of the $n$th true formula derivable from $PA_d$ in its variable $z$. It is clear (using the axiom $\forall x \exists t\big(u(t) = x\big)$) that the program $p$ terminates for all inputs in any model of $Th$. Consider the following formulas:

$$\chi_p \rightleftharpoons true\{p\}(z \neq \lceil x \neq x \rceil) \text{ and } \chi_t \rightleftharpoons true\langle p\rangle(z \neq \lceil x \neq x \rceil).$$

Our aim is to prove that

$$Reg_\sigma \cup Th \models \chi_p \wedge \chi_t \quad \text{but} \quad TInd^P \cup Th \not\models \chi_p \wedge \chi_t.$$

It is trivial that any of the formulas $\chi_p$ and $\chi_t$ implies the consistency of $PA_d$. We prove that $TInd^p \cup Th \not\models Con(PA_d)$. For a contradiction, let us suppose that $TInd^p \cup Th \models Con(PA_d)$. However, $Con(PA_d) \models Con(TInd^p \cup Th)$, i.e. $TInd^p \cup Th \models Con(TInd^p \cup Th)$ which is impossible according to Gödel's second incompleteness theorem.

However, according to Corollary (25.20) we have proved that $Reg_\sigma \cup Th \models Con(PA_d)$. Hence $Reg_\sigma \cup Th \models \chi_p \wedge \chi_t$ as well. □

It is not surprising that the non-standard extension of the similarity type $\sigma$ provides less powerful correctness theories than the ones based on regular inductive time extension $rg$, as we see in the next statement. This result was obtained in Sain [1986].

**(26.10) Lemma.** *For an appropriate similarity type $\sigma$, $PC_\sigma(ns) \subset PC_\sigma(rg)$ and $TC_\sigma(ns) \subset TC_\sigma(rg)$.*

*Proof.* By using Theorems (22.2) and (22.5) we get

$$PC_\sigma(ns) = PC_\sigma(TInd) \quad \text{and} \quad TC_\sigma(ns) = TC_\sigma(TInd);$$
$$PC_\sigma(rg) = PC_\sigma(Reg) \quad \text{and} \quad TC_\sigma(rg) = TC_\sigma(TReg).$$

Therefore the statement just follows from Corollary (26.8) and Theorem (26.9). □

**(26.11) Theorem.** *For an appropriate similarity type $\sigma$:*

$$PC_\sigma(ns) \subset PC_\sigma(wrg) \subset PC_\sigma(prg) \subset PC_\sigma(rg);$$
$$TC_\sigma(ns) \subset TC_\sigma(wrg) \subset TC_\sigma(prg) \subset TC_\sigma(rg).$$

*Proof.* We omit the proof because it needs many new results which, however, are superflous from the viewpoint of the main course of the book. See in Sain [1991]. □

Our knowledge about the relations between different partial and total correctness theories is summarized in the following diagram:

$$\begin{array}{ccccc} & & PC(rg_\sigma) & & \\ & \nearrow & & \nwarrow & \\ PC(TInd_\sigma^P) & & & & PC(prg_\sigma) \\ \uparrow & & & & \uparrow \\ PC(TInd_\sigma^B) & & & & PC(wrg_\sigma) \\ & \nwarrow & & \nearrow & \\ & & PC(TInd_\sigma) & & \end{array}$$

$$\begin{array}{ccccc} & & TC(rg_\sigma) & & \\ & \nearrow & & \nwarrow & \\ TC(TInd_\sigma^P \cup Dind_{G\sigma}^P) & & & & TC(prg_\sigma) \\ \uparrow & & & & \uparrow \\ TC(TInd_\sigma^B \cup Dind_{G\sigma}^B) & & & & TC(wrg_\sigma) \\ & \nwarrow & & \nearrow & \\ & & TC(TInd_\sigma \cup Dind_{G\sigma}) & & \end{array}$$

## 26.2 Embedding Transitive and Inductive Extensions

Having established the embedding of temporal logic into time logic we turn to the investigation of embedding of the extended dynamics logics introduced in Part II. Note that while models of temporal logic are very similar to the models of time logic, in the case of transitive and inductive models this is not so. Therefore, the crucial point if the required embedding is the definition of the time logic models that correspond to the transitive and inductive models.

First we consider how non-standard dynamic logic can be translated into time logic.

**(26.12) Definition.** *Let $\sigma$ be a given similarity type and let $(\phi, X, X', Q) \in \Delta_\sigma$ be a $\sigma$-type $\Delta$-formula. Let $X^f$ be a new function copy of $X$. We often use the following formula:*

$$Chain_\phi(X^f) \rightleftharpoons \forall u \phi(X^f(u), X^f(u+1), Q) \vee X^f(u) = X^f(u+1).$$

*Let $s$ be a t-sorted (time) variable. Take the following formula*

$$Proof_\phi \rightleftharpoons X^f(0) = X \wedge \exists s X^f(s) = X' \wedge Chain_\phi(X^f).$$

*It is clear that $var(Proof_\phi) \subseteq X \cup X' \cup X^f \cup Q$.*

Recall $\hat{\phi}$ from Definition (14.9).

**(26.13) Definition.** *Let $\sigma$ be a given similarity type. We define a translation function $\tilde{}$ : $Form_{\sigma^*} \to TForm_\sigma$ by replacing any occurrences of the atomic formulas of the form $\hat{\phi}(\tau, \tau', \tau_Q)$ by the formula*

$$\exists X^f Proof_\phi[\tau/X, \tau'/X', \tau_Q/Q].$$

**(26.14) Definition.** *Let a time model $\mathcal{A} \in TMod_\sigma$ be given. We define a transitive model $\mathcal{B}$ by taking $\mathcal{B}{\restriction}_\sigma = \mathcal{A}{\restriction}_\sigma$ and for any $\Delta$-formula $(\phi, X, X', Q) \in \Delta_\sigma$ by defining*

$$\mathcal{B}(\hat{\phi}) \rightleftharpoons \{k \in Val_{\mathcal{A}}[X, X', Q] \mid \mathcal{A} \models \widetilde{\phi^*}[k]\}.$$

*This model $\mathcal{B}$ is denoted by $\mathcal{A}^*$.*

**(26.15) Lemma.** *For any time model $\mathcal{A} \in TMod_\sigma$ and $\Delta$-formula $(\phi, X, X', Q) \in \Delta_\sigma$ we have*

$$\{k \mid \mathcal{A} \models \widetilde{\phi^*}[k]\} = \{k \mid \mathcal{A}^* \models \phi^*[k]\}.$$

*Proof.* The statement follows from the definition of $\mathcal{A}^*(\phi^*)$. □

**(26.16) Corollary.** *For any given time model $\mathcal{A} \in TMod_\sigma$ and axiom system $Ax \subseteq Form_{\sigma^*}$:*

$$\mathcal{A} \models \widetilde{Ax} \text{ implies } \mathcal{A}^* \models Ax.$$

**(26.17) Definition.** *Let $\mathcal{B} \in Mod_{\sigma^*}$ be a transitive model. An indexed set of functions*

$$\mathcal{G} \rightleftharpoons \{G_{\phi,k,k_Q} \mid (\phi, X, X', Q) \in \Delta_\sigma, k \in Val_{\mathcal{B}}[X], k_Q \in Val_{\mathcal{B}}[Q]\}$$

*is called fully transitive iff there is an ordinal $\upsilon$ such that for any $(\phi, X, X', Q) \in \Delta_\sigma$, $k \in Val_{\mathcal{B}}[X]$, $k_Q \in Val_{\mathcal{B}}[Q]$ the following hold:*

*(i) the function $G_{\phi,k,k_Q}$ is of the form $\upsilon \to Val_{\mathcal{B}}[X]$;*
*(ii) $G_{\phi,k,k_Q}(0) = k$;*
*(iii) for any $\beta \in \upsilon$, $\mathcal{B} \models \phi[G_{\phi,k,k_Q}(\beta), G_{\phi,k,k_Q}(\beta+1), k_Q]$ or $G_{\phi,k,k_Q}(\beta) = G_{\phi,k,k_Q}(\beta+1)$;*

*(iv) let $k'$, $k'' \in Val_{\mathcal{B}}[X]$ be two valuations such that $\mathcal{B} \models \phi[k', k'', k_Q]$ holds. $\mathcal{B} \models \phi^*[k, k', k_Q]$ iff there is a $\beta \in \upsilon$ such that $k' = G_{\phi,k,k_Q}(\beta)$ and $k'' = G_{\phi,k,k_Q}(\beta+1)$.*

*Moreover, for any $(\phi^i, X^i, X'^i, Q^i) \in \Delta_\sigma$, $k^i \in Val_{\mathcal{B}}[X]$, $k_Q^i \in Val_{\mathcal{B}}[Q]$ and $\beta^i \in \upsilon$ $(i = 1, 2)$ there is a $\beta \in \upsilon$ such that*
*(v) $G_{\phi^i,k^i,k_Q^i}(\beta^i) = G_{\phi^i,k^i,k_Q^i}(\beta)$ and $G_{\phi^i,k^i,k_Q^i}(\beta^i+1) = G_{\phi^i,k^i,k_Q^i}(\beta+1)$.*

**(26.18) Lemma.** *For any $\mathcal{B} \in Mod_{\sigma^*}$ there is a fully transitive indexed set of functions $\mathcal{G}$.*

*Proof.* First we construct an indexed set $\mathcal{G}'$ that satisfies only the properties (i)-(iv). Then we collect all the possible pairs in (v) and choose a large enough ordinal $\upsilon$ and extend any function $G'_{\phi,k,k_Q}$. □

**(26.19) Definition.** *Let $\mathcal{B} \in Mod_{\sigma^*}$ be a given transitive extension and let $\mathcal{G}$ be a fully transitive indexed set. We define a time model $\mathcal{B}^t$ by taking $\mathcal{B}^t\restriction_\sigma \rightleftharpoons \mathcal{B}$ and $\mathcal{T}$ as the natural time structure on $\upsilon$ and by defining*

$$\mathcal{B}^t(d^t) \rightleftharpoons \{f : \upsilon \to \mathcal{B}(d) \mid \exists(\phi, X, X', Q) \in \Delta_\sigma, \exists k_Q \in Val_{\mathcal{B}}[Q], \\ \exists k \in Val_{\mathcal{B}}[X], \exists x \in X, sort(x) = d, \lambda t.G_{\phi,k,k_Q}(x) = f\}$$

*with the obvious applications.*

**(26.20) Theorem.** *For any model $\mathcal{B} \in Mod(Ind^*_\sigma)$ the model $\mathcal{B}^{t*}$ is ismorphic to $\mathcal{B}$. Moreover, for any $\phi \in Form_{\sigma^*}$ if $\mathcal{B} \models \phi$ then $\mathcal{B}^t \models \widetilde{\phi}$.*

*Proof.* It is clear that $\mathcal{B}\restriction_\sigma = \mathcal{B}^{t*}\restriction_\sigma$. We turn to prove that for a given $\Delta$-formula $(\phi, X, X', Q) \in \Delta_\sigma$, $\mathcal{B}^{t*}(\phi^*) = \mathcal{B}(\phi^*)$. Fix three valuations $k$, $\hat{k} \in Val_{\mathcal{B}}[X]$ and $k_Q \in Val_{\mathcal{B}}[Q]$.

First let us suppose that $\mathcal{B} \models \phi^*[k, \hat{k}[X'/X], k_Q]$. Let us consider the following $k^{\mathcal{G}} \in Val_{\mathcal{B}}[X^f]$:

$$k^{\mathcal{G}} \rightleftharpoons \lambda x^f \in X^f.\lambda t.G_{\phi,k,k_Q}(t)(x).$$

By the definition of the fully transitive set $\mathcal{G}$, $\mathcal{B} \models Chain_\phi[k^{\mathcal{G}}]$ and $k^{\mathcal{G}}(0) = k$ and for some $s \in \upsilon$, $k^{\mathcal{G}}(s) = \hat{k}$. Using the definition of $Proof_\phi$ we get $\mathcal{B}^t \models Proof_\phi[k, \hat{k}[X'/X], k^{\mathcal{G}}, k_Q]$, i.e. by definition $\mathcal{B}^{t*} \models \phi^*[k, \hat{k}[X'/X], k_Q]$ also holds.

Now we have only to prove that if $\mathcal{B}^{t*} \models \phi^*[k, \hat{k}[X'/X], k_Q]$, or equivalently

$$(*) \qquad \mathcal{B}^t \models Proof_\phi[k, \hat{k}[X'/X], k^f, k_Q]$$

for an appropriately chosen $k^f \in Val_{\mathcal{B}^t}[X^f]$ then $\mathcal{B} \models \phi^*[k, \hat{k}[X'/X], k_Q]$.

For the sake of simplicity let us suppose that $X$ consists of exactly two elements $x_1$ and $x_2$. By the definition of the time-functions in model $\mathcal{B}^t$ for any

$i = 1, 2$ there is a $\Delta$-formula $(\psi_i, Y_i, Y_i', Q_i) \in \Delta_\sigma$, two valuations $k_i \in Val_{\mathcal{B}}[Y_i]$ and $\ell_i \in Val_{\mathcal{B}}[Q_i]$ such that $x_i \in Y_i$ and $k^f(x_i^t) = \lambda t.G_{\psi^i,k^i,\ell_i}(t)(x_i)$. Let $Y_i''$ be a new copy of $Y_i$ $(i = 1, 2)$. Let $X'$, $X''$ denote the copy of $X$ in $Y_1' \cup Y_2'$ and $Y_1'' \cup Y_2''$, respectively. It is obvious that we can suppose that the sets of variables $Y_1$, $Y_2$, $Y_1'$, $Y_2'$, $Q_1$, $Q_2$ and $Q$ are pairwise disjoint. Our main aim is to prove the following:

$$(**) \qquad \mathcal{B} \models \forall Y_1' \forall Y_2' \forall Y_1'' \forall Y_2'' \left( \bigwedge_{i=1}^{2} (\psi_i^*(Y_i, Y_i', Q_i) \wedge \psi_i(Y_i', Y_i'', Q_i)) \wedge \phi^*(X, X', Q) \to \phi^*(X, X'', Q) \right) [k, k_1, k_2, \ell_1, \ell_2, k_Q].$$

To prove this let us suppose that $k_i$, $k_i'' \in Val_{\mathcal{B}}[Y_i]$ are such valuations for $i = 1, 2$ that

$$\mathcal{B} \models \bigwedge_{i=1}^{2} (\psi_i^*(Y_i, Y_i', Q_i) \wedge \psi_i(Y_i', Y_i'', Q_i)) \wedge \phi^*(X, X', Q) \to$$
$$[k, k_1, k_2, \ell_1; \ell_2, k_Q, k_1'[Y_1'/Y_1], k_2'[Y_2'/Y_2], k''_1[Y_1''/Y_1], k''_2[Y_2''/Y_2]].$$

Now we use the property (iv) of Definition (26.17): there is a $\beta_i \in v$ such that $k_i' = G_{\psi_i,k_i,\ell_i}(\beta_i)$ and $k_i'' = G_{\psi_i,k_i,\ell_i}(\beta_i + 1)$ (for $i = 1, 2$). Using the property (v) of Definition (26.17) there is a $\beta$ such that $k_i' = G_{\psi_i,k_i,\ell_i}(\beta)$ and $k_i'' = G_{\psi_i,k_i,\ell_i}(\beta + 1)$ (for $i = 1, 2$). Let $k' \rightleftharpoons (k_1' + k_2')\restriction_X$ and $k'' \rightleftharpoons (k_1'' + k_2'')\restriction_X$. Using $\mathcal{B} \models \phi^*[k, k'[X'/X], k_Q]$ and the axiom $Cl_\phi \in Ind_\sigma^*$ we get that $\mathcal{B} \models \phi^*[k, k''[X'/X], k_Q]$ holds. So we have proved (**). Let us consider the $\Delta$-formula $(\psi_1 \wedge \psi_2, Y_1 \cup Y_2, Y_1' \cup Y_2', Q_1 \cup Q_2)$. The truth of (**) means that the antecedent of the axiom $Tr_{\psi_1 \wedge \psi_2}(\phi^*)$ holds in model $\mathcal{B}$. Using this axiom we get that if

$$(***) \qquad \mathcal{B} \models \psi_i^*[k_i, k_i'[Y_i'/Y_i], \ell_i]$$

holds for $i = 1, 2$ for a given $k_i \in Val_{\mathcal{B}}[Y_i]$ then $\mathcal{B} \models \phi^*[k, k'[X'/X], k_Q]$ also holds when $k' \rightleftharpoons (k_1' + k_2')\restriction_X$. From (*) we get a $\beta' \in v$ such that $k^f(\beta') = \hat{k}$. Applying (iv) of Definition (26.17) the two valuations $k_i' \rightleftharpoons G_{\psi_i,k_i,\ell_i}(\beta')$ $(i = 1, 2)$ satisfy (***). Therefore $\mathcal{B} \models \phi^*[k, \hat{k}[X'/X], k_Q]$.

Finally we note that by using Corollary (26.16) and the isomorphism just established we obtain that for any formula $\phi \in Form_{\sigma^*}$ if $\mathcal{B} \models \phi$ then $\mathcal{B}^t \models \tilde{\phi}$. □

**(26.21) Definition.** *For any similarity type $\sigma$ let $Reg_\sigma^* \rightleftharpoons (Ind_\sigma^*)^\sim \cup Nord \cup Equ_\sigma$.*

We remark that the axioms of $(Ind_\sigma^*)^\sim$ can be written down without using the translation directly. The respective translations of $Cl_\phi$ and $Tr_\phi(\psi)$ are equivalent to the following formulas:

$$Chain_\phi(X^t) \wedge \exists s(X^t(s) = X) \wedge \phi(X, X') \rightarrow \\ \exists G^t(Chain_\phi[G^t/X^t] \wedge X^t(0) = G^t(0) \wedge \exists s G^t(s) = X'),$$

$$\forall X^t\Big(Chain_\phi(X^t) \wedge X^t(0) = X \rightarrow \psi[X/X'] \wedge \forall s(\psi[X^t(s)/X'] \rightarrow \\ \psi[X^t(s+1)/X'])\Big) \rightarrow \forall X^t(Chain_\phi(X^t) \wedge (X^t(0) = X) \rightarrow \forall s \psi[X^t(s)/X']).$$

From these forms of the axioms we immediately get the following

**(26.22) Corollary.** *For an arbitrary similarity type $\sigma$, $Reg_\sigma \models Reg^*_\sigma$.*

**(26.23) Theorem.** *Let $\sigma$ be an arbitrary similarity type. Let a set $Ax \subseteq Form_{\sigma^*}$ of closed formulas and a closed formula $\phi \in Form_{\sigma^*}$ be given.*

$$Ax \cup Ind^*_\sigma \models \phi \quad \textit{iff} \quad \widetilde{Ax} \cup Reg^*_\sigma \models \tilde{\phi}.$$

*Proof.* Let us suppose that $Ax \cup Ind^*_\sigma \models \phi$. To contradict this let us suppose that there is a time model $\mathcal{A} \in Mod(\widetilde{Ax} \cup Reg^*_\sigma)$ such that $\mathcal{A} \not\models \tilde{\phi}$. Using Corollary (26.16) and Definition (26.21) we get that $\mathcal{A}^* \models Ax \cup Ind^*_\sigma \cup \{\neg\phi\}$ which results in a contradiction.

Now we turn to prove the other direction and we suppose that $\widetilde{Ax} \cup Reg^*_\sigma \models \tilde{\phi}$ but there is a model $\mathcal{B} \in Mod(Ax \cup Ind^*_\sigma)$ such that $\mathcal{B} \not\models \phi$. Using Theorem (26.20) we get a contradiction again. □

**(26.24) Corollary.** *For an arbitrary similarity type $\sigma$ we have $PC(Reg^*_\sigma) = PC(Ind^*_\sigma)$ and $TC(Reg^*_\sigma) = TC(Ind^*_\sigma)$.*

Now we turn to define the translation of the inductive extension. Let $\sigma$ be a given similarity type and let $\phi \in \Sigma^+(\sigma; R_X)$ be a $\sigma$-type positive existential formula with $Q \rightleftharpoons var(\phi) \setminus X$. Let $X^f$ be a new function copy of $X$. Let $j \rightleftharpoons rank(\phi)$. We often use the following formula:

$$\nabla Chain_\phi(X^f) \rightleftharpoons \forall u\Bigg(\phi[false/R][X^f(u)/X] \vee \\ \exists u_1 \ldots \exists u_j \bigwedge_{i=1}^{j} u_i \leq u \wedge \phi\Big[\bigvee_{i=1}^{j} X^f(u_i) = X/R\Big][X^f(u)/X]\Bigg).$$

Let $s$ be a $t$-sorted (time) variable. Take the following formula

$$\nabla Proof_\phi \rightleftharpoons \exists s X^f(s) = X \wedge \nabla Chain_\phi(X^f).$$

It is clear that $var(\nabla Proof_\phi) \subseteq X \cup X^f \cup Q$.

Recall the relation symbol $\hat{\phi}$ from Definition (15.6).

**(26.25) Definition.** *Let $\sigma$ be a given similarity type. We define a translation function$\tilde{}$: $Form_{\sigma^\nabla} \to TForm_\sigma$ by replacing any occurrences of the atomic formulas of the form $\hat{\phi}(\tau, \tau_Q)$ by the formula*

$$\exists X^f \nabla Proof_\phi[\tau/X, \tau_Q/Q].$$

**(26.26) Definition.** *Let a time model $\mathcal{A} \in TMod_\sigma$ be given. We define an inductive model $\mathcal{B}$ by taking $\mathcal{B}\restriction_\sigma \rightleftharpoons \mathcal{A}\restriction_\sigma$ and for any $R_X$, $\phi \in \Sigma^+(\sigma, R_X)$ by defining*

$$\mathcal{B}(\hat{\phi}) \rightleftharpoons \{k \in Val_\mathcal{A}[X,Q] \mid \mathcal{A} \models \widetilde{\nabla\phi}[k]\},$$

*where $Q \rightleftharpoons var(\phi) \setminus X$. This model is denoted by $\mathcal{A}^\nabla$.*

**(26.27) Lemma.** *For any time model $\mathcal{A} \in TMod_\sigma$ and positive existential formula $\phi \in I^+_\sigma$ we have*

$$\{k \mid \mathcal{A} \models \widetilde{\nabla\phi}[k]\} = \{k \mid \mathcal{A}^\nabla \models \nabla\phi[k]\}.$$

*Proof.* The statement follows form the definition of $\mathcal{A}^\nabla(\hat{\phi})$. □

**(26.28) Corollary.** *For any given time model $\mathcal{A} \in TMod_\sigma$ and axiom system $Ax \subseteq Form_{\sigma^\nabla}$:*

$$\mathcal{A} \models \widetilde{Ax} \text{ implies } \mathcal{A}^\nabla \models Ax.$$

**(26.29) Definition.** *Let $\mathcal{B} \in Mod_{\sigma^\nabla}$ be an inductive model. An indexed set of functions*

$$\mathcal{G} \rightleftharpoons \{G_{\phi,k_Q} \mid R_X \in \Omega, \phi \in \Sigma^+(\sigma; R_X), k_Q \in Val_\mathcal{B}[var(\phi) \setminus X]\}$$

*is called fully inductive iff there is an ordinal $\upsilon$ such that for any $R_X$, $\phi \in \Sigma^+(\sigma, R_X)$ with $k_Q \in Val_\mathcal{B}[var(\phi) \setminus X]$ and with $rank(\phi) = j$ the following hold:*

*(i) the function $G_{\phi,k_Q}$ is of the form $\upsilon \to Val_\mathcal{B}[X]$;*
*(ii) for any $\beta \in \upsilon$ there are ordinals $\gamma_i$ $(1 \le i \le j)$ such that if $S \rightleftharpoons \{G_{\phi,k_Q} \mid i \le j\}$ then $(\mathcal{B}, S) \models \nabla\phi[G_{\phi,k_Q}(\beta+1), k_Q]$ or $(\mathcal{B}, \emptyset) \models \nabla\phi[G_{\phi,k_Q}(\beta+1), k_Q]$;*
*(iii) for each $i = 1, ..., j$ let $k \in Val_\mathcal{B}[X]$ be a given valuation. Moreover, let $k \in Val_\mathcal{B}[X]$ be another valuation such that if $S \rightleftharpoons \{k_i \mid i \le j\}$ then $(\mathcal{B}, S) \models \nabla\phi[k]$. $\mathcal{B} \models \phi[k]$ iff there is a $\beta \in \upsilon$ and there are ordinal numbers $\gamma_i \le \beta$ $(1 \le i \le j)$ such that $k = G_{\phi,k_Q}(\beta+1)$ and for $i = 1, ..., j$, $k_i = G_{\phi,k_Q}(\gamma_i + 1)$.*

*Moreover, for any $R_X \in \Omega$, $\phi^n \in \Sigma^+(\sigma, R_X)$, $\ell^n \in Val_\mathcal{B}[var(\phi_n) \setminus X]$, $\beta^n \in \upsilon$ and $\gamma_i \le \beta^n$ $(n = 1, 2,\ 1 \le i \le j)$ if for the set $S^n \rightleftharpoons \{G_{\phi^n,\ell^n}(\gamma^n_i) \mid i \le j\}$*

*we know that* $(\mathcal{B}, S^n) \models \phi^n[G_{\phi^n,\ell^n}(\beta^n+1)$ *then there is a* $\beta \in \upsilon$ *and there are ordinals* $\gamma_i$ $(1 \le i \le j)$ *such that*

*(iv) for* $i = 1, ..., j$, $n = 1, 2$: $G_{\phi^n,\ell^n}(\gamma_i^n) = G_{\phi^n,\ell^n}(\gamma_i)$ *and* $G_{\phi^n,\ell^n}(\beta^n+1) = G_{\phi^n,\ell^n}(\beta+1)$.

**(26.30) Lemma.** *For any model* $\mathcal{B} \in Mod_{\sigma^\nabla}$, *there is a fully inductive indexed set of functions* $\mathcal{G}$.

**(26.31) Definition.** *Let* $\mathcal{B} \in Mod_{\sigma^\nabla}$ *be a given inductive extension and let* $\mathcal{G}$ *be a fully inductive indexed set. We define a time model* $\mathcal{B}^t$ *by taking*

$$\mathcal{B}^t(d^t) \rightleftharpoons \{f : \upsilon \to \mathcal{B}(d) \mid \exists R_X, \exists \phi \in \Sigma^+(\sigma, R_X), \exists k_Q \in Val_{\mathcal{B}}[var(\phi) \setminus X] \\ \exists x \in X, sort(x) = d, \lambda t.G_{\phi,k_Q}(t)(x) = f\}.$$

Similarly to the transitive case one can prove the following

**(26.32) Theorem.** *For any model* $\mathcal{B} \in Mod(Ind_\sigma^\nabla)$ *the model* $\mathcal{B}^{t\nabla}$ *is isomorphic to* $\mathcal{B}$. *Moreover, for any closed* $\phi \in Form_{\sigma^\nabla}$ *if* $\mathcal{B} \models \phi$ *then* $\mathcal{B}^t \models \widetilde{\alpha}$.

**(26.33) Definition.** *For any similarity type* $\sigma$ *let* $Reg_\sigma^\nabla \rightleftharpoons (\nabla Ind_\sigma^*)^\sim \cup Nord \cup Equ_\sigma$.

**(26.34) Corollary.** *For an arbitrary similarity type* $\sigma$, $wReg_\sigma \models Reg_\sigma^\nabla$ *and* $Reg_\sigma^\nabla \models Reg_\sigma^*$.

**(26.35) Theorem.** *Let* $\sigma$ *be an arbitrary similarity type. Let a set* $Ax \subseteq Form_{\sigma^*}$ *of formulas and a closed formula* $\phi \in Form_{\sigma^*}$ *be given.*

$$Ax \cup \nabla Ind_\sigma^* \models \phi \quad \textit{iff} \quad \widetilde{Ax} \cup Reg_\sigma^\nabla \models \tilde{\phi}.$$

**(26.36) Corollary.** *For an arbitrary similarity type* $\sigma$ *we have* $PC(Reg_\sigma^\nabla) = PC(\nabla Ind_\sigma^*)$ *and* $TC(Reg_\sigma^\nabla) = TC(\nabla Ind_\sigma^*)$.

**(26.37) Theorem.** *The following diagram summarizes the connections between the partial correctness theories of different dynamic logics. An arrow "$\longrightarrow$" means that the first partial correctness theory is strictly less then the second. The question mark denotes an open problem. The two partial correctness theories* $PC(TInd_\sigma^P)$, $PC(TInd_\sigma^B)$ *are incompatible with the partial correctness theories* $PC(Reg_\sigma^\nabla)$ *and* $PC(Reg_\sigma^*)$.

$$
\begin{array}{ccccc}
 & & PC(Reg\sigma) & & \\
 & \nearrow & & \nwarrow & \\
PC(TInd^P_\sigma) & & & & PC(Reg^\nabla_\sigma) \\
\uparrow & & & & \uparrow ? \\
PC(TInd^B_\sigma) & & & & PC(Reg^*_\sigma) \\
 & \nwarrow & & \nearrow & \\
 & & PC(TInd_\sigma) & &
\end{array}
$$

*Proof.* The statements of the theorem follow from Theorems (14.37), (22.5), (22.11) and Corollary (26.36). □

A similar result holds for the total correctness theories corresponding to the axiom systems considered in the theorem.

**(26.38) Theorem.** *The following diagram summarizes the connections between the total correctness theories of different dynamic logics. An arrow "→" means that the first total correctness theory is strictly less then the second. The question mark denotes an open problem. The two total correctness theories* $TC(TInd^P_\sigma \cup DInd^P_{G\sigma})$, $TC(TInd^B_\sigma \cup DInd^B_{G\sigma})$ *are incompatible with the total correctness theories* $TC(Reg^\nabla_\sigma)$ *and* $TC(Reg^*_\sigma)$.

$$
\begin{array}{ccccc}
 & & TC(Reg\sigma) & & \\
 & \nearrow & & \nwarrow & \\
TC(TInd^P_\sigma \cup Dind^P_{G\sigma}) & & & & TC(Reg^\nabla_\sigma) \\
\uparrow & & & & \uparrow ? \\
TC(TInd^B_\sigma \cup Dind^B_{G\sigma}) & & & & TC(Reg^*_\sigma) \\
 & \nwarrow & & \nearrow & \\
 & & TC(TInd_\sigma \cup Dind_{G\sigma}) & &
\end{array}
$$

*Proof.* The statements of the theorem follow from Theorem (22.20) and Corollary (26.36). □

**(26.39)** *Remark.* Whether there exists a translation function from the set $Form_{\sigma^*}$ of formulas to $TForm_\sigma$ such that it reflects validity with respect to $Mod(Ind_\sigma)$ and whether there exists a similar translation function for $Form_{\sigma^\nabla}$ reflecting validity with respect to $Mod(\nabla Ind_\sigma)$.

## 26.3 Description of Program Extensions

So far in dealing with program properties we have concentrated on the programming language $rP_\sigma$. However, as we have seen in Chapter 7 the computational power of $rP_\sigma$ is not strong enough; the language is not universal. To make $rP_\sigma$ universal, auxiliary program constructs, for example stacks, should be added.

The new program constructs are added to the language $rP_\sigma$ as extensions introduced in Chapter 5. It is a natural requirement to characterize the extended programming language, i.e. to describe the properties of new program constructs. Note that static control structures, particularly stack extensions, are out of the scope of first-order classical logic (see Corollary (6.2)). However, the extended dynamic logic, temporal logic and time logic can be used to characterize the programs of the augmented programming languages. In this section we show how this characterization works in the case of stacks. Namely, by using the logics mentioned above we define a first-order notion of stacks.

Now let us redefine the stack extension of a given similarity type $\sigma$. Recall the definition of $\sigma_s$ from Example (5.9). Let $Stack_\sigma \subset Form_{\sigma^s}$ consist of the following axioms (for all $d \in sort\ \sigma$):

- $tail^d(empty^d) = empty^d$;
- $pop^d(empty^d, x) = x$;
- $push^d(s, x) \neq empty^d$;
- $tail^d(push^d(s, x)) = s$;
- $pop^d(push^d(s, x), y) = x$;
- $s \neq empty^d \rightarrow push^d(tail^d(s), pop^d(s, x)) = s$;

Of course $Stack_\sigma$ does not describe the main property: applying $tail^d$ sufficiently but finitely many times, in the end we always get an empty stack. To describe this property in extended dynamic logic, temporal logic and time logic, respectively, we have to use the following formulas:

$$EEnd \rightleftharpoons \forall s_1 (s_2 = tail^d(s_1))^* [empty^d / s_2],$$
$$MEnd \rightleftharpoons 1\Box(\hat{s} = s \rightarrow \circ(\hat{s} = tail^d(s))) \rightarrow 1\Diamond\Box\hat{s} = empty^d.$$
$$TEnd \rightleftharpoons \forall i s^t(i+1) = tail^d(s^t(i)) \rightarrow \exists i \forall j \geq i s^t(j) = empty^d,$$

Another property of stacks to be axiomatized is that the elements of a stack (ordering taken into account) define the stack itself. To formulate this property in extended dynamic logic let us consider the following formulas:

$$Edesc(s_1, s_2, u_1, u_2) \rightleftharpoons (s_1 = tail^d(u_1) \wedge s_2 = tail^d(u_2))^*$$
$$ESimilar(s_1, s_2) \rightleftharpoons \forall u_1 \forall u_2 (Edesc(s_1, s_2, u_1, u_2) \rightarrow (u_1 = empty^d \leftrightarrow u_2 = empty^d) \wedge \forall x pop^d(u_1, x) = pop^d(u_2, x)),$$
$$ESame(s_1, s_2) \rightleftharpoons ESimilar(s_1, s_2) \leftrightarrow s_1 = s_2.$$

In a similar way one can describe this property in the frame of temporal logic:

$$Mdesc(\hat{s}) \rightleftharpoons 1\Box\forall s(s = \hat{s} \to \circ(\hat{s} = tail^d(s)))$$

$$\begin{aligned} MSimilar(s_1, s_2) \rightleftharpoons \forall \hat{s}_1 \forall \hat{s}_2 \Big( & MDesc(\hat{s}_1) \land Mdesc(\hat{s}_2) \land \\ & (1\hat{s}_1 = s_1 \land 1\hat{s}_2 = s_2) \land \\ & 1\Box(\hat{s}_1 = empty^d \leftrightarrow \hat{s}_2 = empty^d) \land \\ & 1\Box\forall x(pop^d(\hat{s}_1, x) = pop^d(\hat{s}_2, x)), \end{aligned}$$

$$MSame(s_1, s_2) \rightleftharpoons MSimilar(s_1, s_2) \to s_1 = s_2.$$

It is obvious how these formulas can be written down in time logic. The resulting axiom systems are denoted by $Stack_\sigma$, $MStack_\sigma$ and $TStack_\sigma$ respectively. These sets of formulas are subsets of $SForm_{\sigma^s}$ $MForm_{\sigma^s}$ and $TForm_{\sigma^s}$, respectively.

**(26.40) Lemma.** *Let $\mathcal{A}$ be a $\sigma^s$-type standard transitive extension such that $\mathcal{A} \models Stack_\sigma$. Then the $\sigma^s$-type model $\mathcal{A}\restriction_{\sigma^s}$ and the model $(\mathcal{A}\restriction_\sigma)^s$ are isomorphic.* □

It is clear that a similar theorem is true for temporal and time models as well.

We emphasize that we have defined two different kinds of semantics for programs with stacks. The first kind of semantics was given in an extended dynamic logic frame in Chapter 15 using inductive extensions and a pairing function for the general case. A similar kind of semantics was given in a time-logic frame in Chapter 25. The common aspect of these definition is that we use the same entities to describe stacks which were originally introduced only to describe the semantics of the stack-free programs. The other kind of semantics was given in this paragraph. In this case we use a "double" extension: first we extend the similarity type by new relation and function symbols to describe stacks and then we add further symbols to describe semantics as well. In this frame the programs of $rP_{\sigma^s}$ seem to be stack-free programs because stack operations are treated as normal assignments. The two steps of this extension are "coordinated" by the axioms which describe the iteration of different stack operations, e.g. $pop^d$. It is a natural question about the connection between the two kinds of semantics mentioned above for programs with stacks.

**(26.41) Theorem.** *For any similarity type $\sigma$ and for any $\chi \rightleftharpoons \phi\{p\}\psi \in {}_2rH_\sigma$*

$$wReg_{\sigma^s} \cup Stack_\sigma \models' \chi \quad \text{iff} \quad wReg_\sigma \models \forall X \forall Y(\phi \land D^s[\![p, X]\!] \to \psi[Y/X]),$$

*where $X \rightleftharpoons var(p)$ and $Y$ is a new copy of $X$.*

*Proof.* Let $\mathcal{B} \in Mod(wReg_{\sigma^s} \cup Stack_\sigma)$. It is clear that $\mathcal{B}\restriction_{\sigma^t}$ is a model of $wReg_\sigma$. It is not hard to check that if we add the functions defined by the formulas $tEmpty_d$,...,$tPush_d$ (introduced after Theorem (25.8)) to the model $\mathcal{B}\restriction_{\sigma^t}$ then we get a $\sigma^s$-type structure which is isomorphic to $\mathcal{B}\restriction_{\sigma^s}$. So the two classes of first-order models which influence the validity of the two formulas in the theorem are isomorphic. It is also obvious that the first-order translations of these two formulas are logically equivalent in the classes of models considered. □

We remark that the usage of weakly regular extensions is sufficient because of the axiom $TEnd$.

**(26.42) Definition.** *Let $\phi$, $\psi \in Form_\sigma$ and $p \in rP^s_\sigma$. A partial correctness assertion $\phi\{p\}\psi$ is said to be Hoare-provable iff*

$$\nabla Ind^*_\sigma + Stack_\sigma \vdash \phi\{p\}\psi.$$

**(26.43)** *Remark.* It is an open question whether the Hoare-provable and the $I/O$-provable formulas are the same for the Hoare-formulas with programs containing only one stack for a one-sorted similarity type $\sigma$.

**(26.44)** *Remark.* In Chapter 15 we also define a semantics and therefore a calculus for programs with two (or more) stacks. It is also an open question whether this semantics and that defined above are the same or not. The main problem here is that the semantics defined in Chapter 15 presupposes the existence of a pairing function. This existence is not definable by first-order tools. If we add to the language some new relation and function symbols and axiomatically describe a pairing function then, of course, the two semantics may become identical. In general, however, the question whether an inductive model has a pairing function is not definable by a first-order formula. (We also remark that we can describe by an axiom schema that a model *has no pairing function* at all but this fact is not a useful one...)

# Epilogue

Now that the formal presentation of the subject is completed, let us have a look at it from a distance that enables us to see it from a wider aspect. First of all let us outline the way we have developed our programming theory by using pure classical first-order logic. We recall the main stages in this development.

**Development of first-order programming theory.** *Our main aim was to put first-order classical logic into its rightful place in programming theory* in spite of the widely accepted opinion in programming theory until the 1980s that first-order classical logic is too limited as a formalism to express and prove the important properties of programs. (See papers where first-order logic has been rejected in favor of more complex higher-order formal systems, e.g. Scott [1976].)

Note that the importance of classical first-order logic has not been emphasized only by the members of the Hungarian school, but also by others, see e.g. McCarthy [1978] and Cartwright [1984]. First of all let us see why we give preference to classical first-order logic. From a mathematical viewpoint it is very well developed in both model and proof theoretic aspects. Its automatic theorem proving aspect is also thoroughly investigated, which provides an appropriate background to think about the possibility of making practical use of a programming theory developed in the framework of classical logic. From a pragmatic viewpoint it is important that programmers are also familiar with classical logic. However, *the main argument is that first-order logic is sufficiently powerful to serve as a basis for developing a flexible and powerful programming theory.* It is also clear that variables play a decisive role in programming, and the formal language that we intend to develop to describe programs must handle variables, therefore it should be at least first-order. Of course we could consider second-order logic but it has a very serious disadvantage, namely its incompleteness (non-recursiveness). Therefore, we restrict ourselves to the first-order classical logic. While developing a programming theory in this framework the program variables strictly connected with the data environment are just some of the entities the theory should handle. Another entity is time, which is connected with the representation of program execution.

*It is an important question how and at what level of abstraction time is considered in the programming theory.* It may appear at the metalevel, providing a way to think about time as represented by natural numbers. This view, which we call the $\omega$-view, influences the semantic aspect too. Therefore at this level of abstraction the standard model of arithmetic is associated with time. The programmer's intuition is strictly connected with standard models. Namely, the way of looking at the world of programs allows one to accept only programs which work with standard data and standard time. Therefore, programmers would expect from a programming theory just such a formal first-order language that represents program execution with runs in standard time. The latter means that the program semantics is to be defined by so-called $\omega$-runs or $\omega$-paths. Let us call an imagined language that strictly corresponds to the programmer's intuition a *standard programming* logic. For example, the infinitary language $L_{\omega_1\omega}$ may be such. However, its infinitely long formulas do not allow an appropriate use in programming theory.

It is well known from the theory of arithmetic that neither the model theory nor the proof theory of standard programming logic can be handled in a classical first-order way because of the presence of non-standard models as well. This is the central problem while developing programming theory. The way one deals with this central problem is analogous with the way one tries to axiomatically characterize the standard model $\mathcal{N}$ of arithmetic, or more precisely, its theory $Th(\mathcal{N})$. The Peano axiom system $PA$ is an appropriate axiomatization, however, it does not characterize the standard model.

By using this analogy we developed a programming logic in the classical first-order frame wich was as close to the ideal standard one as possible. First we had to define a "standard computational model" which provides the necessary notions for programs' semantics. Secondly, a descriptive language had to be defined which could be used to describe the properties of programs running in the "standard computational model". These two steps were taken in Parts I and II where we built an abstract computation theory and a descriptive language for it following the standard or $\omega$-view. The main purpose of this development, however, was not just to get the computation theory itself, *but rather to point out the characteristics of this theory which are interesting in the first-order handling of computation.* So we had to *rethink* and *reformulate* all the most well known properties of such theories, and had to recollect the results as well. We chose *a guarded command language without abort and with random assignment* and developed two kinds of semantics for these programs: a *trace* and a *denotational (input/output relational)* semantics. The next step was to select an appropriate descriptive language that allows the characterization of this standard situation. We expected from this language the ability to define different program properties which mostly are related to program execution, i.e. to its semantic characterization. For these purposes we selected the well-known *regular dynamic logic* in Chapter 11. Having investigated this logic first of all on its completeness in Chapter 12 we saw that it is as incomplete as its Floyd-Hoare sublanguage. The efforts that made it complete did not bring us pragmatically satisfactory results.

Having developed an $\omega$-view oriented descriptive language we turned to the development of the classical first-order "alterego" of this language in Chapter 13. Preserving the syntax of regular dynamic logic by using the specially developed method of extension, we introduced the *extended dynamic logic, which is a descriptive language based on classical first-order logic.* This language gives a general frame for the axiomatization of the main properties of program execution although at a far too general level. The extended dynamic logics also allowed us to use a Hoare-type calculus, and in the case of extended dynamic logics, mainly due to their classical first-order nature, this calculus turned out to be complete. *The next step was the concretization of the semantic function used in extended dynamic logic taking into account the computation theory developed in Part I.*

Further effort was made to extend the possibilities of the descriptive language by axiomatizing the program semantics, i.e. either the denotations or the traces. To internalise denotation semantics we considered the notion of *the reflexive and transitive closure* in Chapter 14, which we tried to axiomatise appropriately in different extended languages. We introduced different types of extensions by which we axiomatically defined different types of denotation semantics, which allowed us to define different types of dynamic logics. One of them was the so-called non-standard dynamic logic introduced and investigated by the Hungarian school.

However, the transitive and reflexive closure is not sufficient to describe the semantics of programs satisfying Church's thesis. So in Chapter 15 we defined another extended dynamic logic whose semantic function was based on an appropriate axiomatization of the inductive definitions. The underlying first-order theory of this theory was called *inductive extension.* The dynamic logic with definable trace semantics is already strong enough to describe the properties of programs with one or more stacks. We remark that the usage of the noun "trace" in the names of these extended dynamic logics is based only on historical reasons. Within these logics the trace semantics is not definable at all.

We wished to describe program properties related to program execution processes, therefore we turned to descriptive languages which refer to time at the object level and which are powerful enough to define traces as well. *Temporal logic* was the first one of these languages. Temporal logic allows us to use time as a reference in the characterization of program execution. However, it does not refer explicitly to time moments at the object level but only in the models.

In our version of temporal logic we used a type of Kripke models which contains functions from which the traces can be built up. We have also shown how our version of temporal logic can be used to axiomatize the "standard computational model" and also how different program verification methods can be axiomatically characterized and how they can be compared in respect of their proof power.

According to our aim to have programming theory based on classical first-order logic, we developed the so called *time logic* which allows us to handle not only data but time moments explicitly and also to define, i.e. to internalize, the trace semantics. This logic includes both dynamic and temporal logics and unites the advantages of these logics. *The explicit first-order time consideration allows a refined time handling.* Our expectations and requirements concerning time can be defined by the formulas of the time logic. Of course, beside the standard models the non-standard ones also appear. Despite the non-standard models, this logic is very close to the programmer's intuition, since here program execution plays an important role and is explicitly represented by a special sort of entity called intensions or functions. Time logic allows us to use axiom schemas to postulate the existence of these functions. These axioms are the comprehension schemas.

Given different descriptive languages that allow us to describe and characterize programs, it is important to have appropriate formal tools to prove whether a program has certain properties. Now we turn to consider the proof theoretic aspects of the programming theories introduced in the book.

**Proof Theory.** Speaking about programs we require *finitary proofs.* This also means that the consequences of a recursive or recursively enumerable set should also form a recursively enumerable set. Therefore, *in this book completeness means the recursive enumerability of the set of valid formulas.* Of course, if a language is complete then theoretically there exists a calculus which can enumerate the "true" formulas, among which we are looking in the proof for the one we aim to prove.

Our proof theoretic investigation was concentrated on completeness. First, we investigated whether the introduced descriptive languages are complete, i.e. their true formulas or their certain sets of formulas are recursively enumerable. Second, we provided a concrete calculus and investigated whether it is complete. Our investigation in this direction started with the study of the completeness of dynamic logic and it showed that it is not complete and nor is its Floyd-Hoare sublanguage.

We considered different approaches to make dynamic logic complete. One of them restricted the set of dynamic logical formulas one is allowed to use in program description. But this approach failed because all pragmatically interesting restricted sets of dynamic logical formulas were incomplete. Some other approaches modified the classical notion of completeness, like relative completeness or arithmetic completeness, which presupposed an oracle that handles all tautologies of arithmetic. Dynamic logic is also $\omega$-complete, which means that there is a calculus with an $\omega$-rule which allows us to prove all the true dynamic logical statements.

But we do not accept these modified notions of completeness because we require a finitary notion of proof. Therefore, if we use an inference rule with infinitely many formulas in the antecedent, as we have in an $\omega$-rule, or if it should handle infinitely many formulas as in the case of the oracle, then the criterion of finitariness is not satisfied.

The dynamic logic is not complete if we restrict ourselves to the finitary proof concept. But the extended dynamic logics developed in the framework of classical first-order logic by using extension are complete, and in this case, any calculus of classical first-order logic can be used. To prove program properties a special calculus has been introduced which, in character, is in between the Floyd-Hoare calculus and a standard calculus for classical first-order logic. From the proof theoretic point of view it is important to recall that the extended dynamic logic permitted the axiomatic characterization of the Floyd-Hoare calculus and also of the calculus for the regular dynamic logic introduced by Harel. We also gave a characterization of the new specially developed calculus.

We note that the *comparative investigation* of the expressive and proof power of the logics obtained by different axiom systems is one of the main activities of the Hungarian school. An exhaustive lattice with respect to partial and total correctness has been established among the logics that differ among each other in the axioms that refer to time. We emphasize that in this book the comparative investigation was made using of the axiom systems characterizing the verification methods in three different descriptive languages, in extended dynamic logic, temporal logic and time logic.

Note that the proof theory for the descriptive languages developed in the framework of classical first-order logic is straightforward. We can take any first-order calculus, though of course for the sake of effectiveness special calculi can be introduced. Moreover, the automatic theorem-proving aspect is also well developed and so the chance for practical usability of these languages is better.

Having recalled the way we developed our programming theory in the framework of classical first-order logic and the main proof theoretic considerations, let us see the methods which were specially introduced to support these constructions and investigations.

**Logical methods.** As a basic construction we mention that in order to represent computation processes over the models of classical first-order logic we have introduced an appropriate "shadow universe" to any given model built up from valuations. The computation processes were interpreted by appropriate so-called *many-sorted relations over this universe* which in a natural way corresponds to the model from which it is built up.

*The basic logical methods used in the book are (logical) extension and inductive definition.* The basic form of extension has been introduced in Chapter 5, where it was used to augment the initial programming language $rP_\sigma$ by new program constructs. In Chapter 13 we used extensions to define the notion of extended dynamic logic. The proposed method is very efficient in generating a classical first-order descriptive language such that it is adequate to characterize given notions and to satisfy given requirements regarding its expressive power. Throughout the book we have used several special extensions to describe different kinds of extended dynamic logic. In Chapters 14 and 15 we define the transitive and inductive extension, in Chapter 23 the time extension.

The method of inductive definition is the other basic method used in our investigation. For example in the pure logical characterization of the programming languages with one and two stacks, appropriate modifications of inductive definitions have been used. Inductive extensions provide a very efficient mixture of inductive definition and extension. They allow us to give a first-order axiomatization of the main properties of inductive definitions. This implies the possibility of using fixed-point equations as well. *It is important to emphasize that the initial algebraic approach can be considered as a particular case of this inductive extension approach.*

The *fixed-point theory* of time extension provides the basic method in time logic to define program theoretic notions in an easy and comfortable way. This method can be used to define necessary program theoretic notions as internal entities in the time logic. Note that this method opens up another perspective for investigations in programming theory and also, more widely, in computer science.

Now let us survey some of the main results obtained by the use of these methods.

**Major results.** We developed a computation theory in the framework of classical first-order logic following the $\omega$-view. The basic programming language $rP_\sigma$ of this theory is nondeterministic with random assignment. It can be augmented with different programming constructs by using extensions. It was shown in Theorem (4.30) that for any program from $rP_\sigma$ there exists a canonical form wich consists only of a single **do...od** command. We defined what a computation process over the models of first-order logic means by providing denotational (input-output) and operational (trace) semantics. By using denotational semantics we defined and investigated computability and we formulated Church's thesis (see Thesis (7.15)). The latter says that in an arbitrary $\sigma$-type model the effectively computable relations are just the relations computable by the $\sigma^s$-type programs, i.e. by the programs which can use any number of stacks.

In Chapter 8 it was shown that programming languages can be characterized in a purely logical way by using appropriate versions of the inductive definition method. In particular, Lemma (8.7) says that the relations effectively inductively defined in a fixed model $\mathcal{A}$ are computable in $\mathcal{A}$ with the programs that may use one stack.

The inductively defined relations are $rP\sigma^1$ computable in a fixed model. These statements are combined into statements of comparative schematology; see Theorems (8.9), (8.13), (8.14). The programming language with two stacks is characterized in Theorem (8.25).

The logic characterization of programming languages can be represented as follows:

(i) $rP^0 \approx Rec$;
(ii) $P^1_\sigma \approx EI$;
(iii) $rP^1_\sigma \approx I_\sigma$ (for one-sorted similarity type $\sigma$);
(iv) $P^2 \approx EI^c$.

Turning to the development of an appropriate descriptive language we summed up the most interesting program properties in Chapter 10. Following Kröger [1987] we gave a classification of these properties, and in Chapter 11. we introduced the well known (regular) dynamic logic to describe these properties. While considering dynamic logic we provided a detailed analysis of the problem of completeness. First of all we repeated the well known results by showing that dynamic logic is not complete; see Theorems (12.8) and (12.12). It was also shown that the important restricted partial correctness theories are also incomplete, see Theorem (12.17).

We introduced a new notion of completeness, called *Den*-completeness, with respect to which different versions of Floyd-Hoare logic were investigated; see Theorems (12.20), (12.22) and Corollary (12.21).

In Chapter 13 we gave an axiomatic calculus $\vdash_{dyn}$ about which in Theorem (13.13) it was proved that it is complete under a very general assumption. This theorem guarantees that if the definition of program semantics satisfies some obvious assumptions then we have a Hoare-like (or Harel-like) calculus to prove the formulas of (regular) dynamic logic. Moreover, this calculus is complete with respect to the first-order semantics defined in Chapter 13. The assumption mentioned above is that if the calculus proved that the program semantics is first-order definable then this calculus is complete (see Theorem (13.11)).

We introduced the internalization of the denotation *Den* by providing an appropriate axiomatization of the transitive and reflexive closure. The latter was done by the transitive extension in which we introduced two different sets *Ind* and *Ind** of axioms. By using these axiom systems we introduced the dynamic logic with continuous denotational semantics and that with strongly continuous denotation semantics. The dynamic logic with continuous denotation semantics is the so-called non-standard dynamic logic which was the object of detailed investigation by the Hungarian school. Theorem (14.32) shows that the Hoare calculus and the generalized Hoare calculus are complete with respect to the new extended dynamic logics. Theorem (14.37) and Corollary (14.38) express the interrelation of different dynamic logics. Namely, it is shown that there exists a similarity type $\sigma$ such that

$$rDL_\sigma > rDL_\sigma^{ns} > rDL_\sigma^{ns*}.$$

By using the method of axiomatization which resulted in the calculus $\vdash_{dyn}$ we defined a more detailed calculus $\vdash_{ns'}$ for the extended dynamic logic $rDL_\sigma^{ns*}$. Theorem (14.39) shows the completeness of the new calculus, which can be considered as the classical first-order version of Harel's calculus defined for the (regular) dynamic logic.

We have also shown that the set of pairs of equivalent programs is recursively enumerable in an arbitrary extended dynamic logic, in contrast with the well known theorem saying that in $\mathcal{N}$ the same set is not recursively enumerable (moreover it is $\Pi_1^1$-complete).

In order to characterize program properties of programs with one stack from $rP_\sigma^1$ we introduced the so-called inductive extension. By the use of this extension we introduced two axiom systems $\nabla Ind_\sigma$ and $\nabla Ind_\sigma^*$, and the corresponding extended dynamic logics called dynamic logic with definable and dynamic logic with strongly definable traces, respectively. Corollary (15.14) shows that these logics are compact and complete. We introduced a new kind of calculus, called I/O-calculus, and Theorems (15.20) and (15.21) showed that this kind of calculus is complete with respect to the definable and the strongly definable dynamic logics.

It was also shown that the power of proof of the new calculus is the same for stack-free programs as that of Hoare's calculus (see Theorem (15.23)).

In order to handle program semantics from the viewpoint of trace semantics we consider a version of temporal logic, whose models refer not only to data and time but also to the functions from which the objects to represent traces can be built up. These models are the Kripke ones defined in Definition (17.2). Note that in temporal logic time moments are used only in the models as references with respect to which temporal characterizations like "first" or "sometimes-in-the-future" can be defined. It was proved that the temporal logic is not complete with respect to the standard Kripke models. A temporal calculus was also given.

We have shown how temporal logic can be used to describe program properties; see Theorem (18.4). The main results with respect to temporal logic concern the comparison of standard temporal logic with the dynamic logic. It was shown that, in general, standard temporal and dynamic logic are incomparable with respect to their descriptive power; see Theorems (19.1) and (20.1). However, if we restrict the investigation only to the countable standard models then temporal logic is more powerful than dynamic logic; see Theorem (21.5). The expressive power of the (full) temporal logic is enough to characterize different program verification methods, well known from the literature. This characterization is performed with certain types of induction axiom schemas in Chapter 22.

In Part IV we introduced the time logic which has different sorts to refer to data, time and function. The latter is used to build up traces to represent program execution. We introduced different axiomatizations, which describe different aspects and views of time and changes in time. One of these axiom systems is the regular time theory (and its different variants), which is powerful enough to build a fixed-point theory. The non-finitary fixed-point theory proved in Theorem (25.21) shows that regular time theory has an extraordinary power. Moreover, the formalization of Church's thesis is false in regular time theory. This is why we have introduced pseudo- and weakly regular time theories, which do not fail Church's thesis and have a fixed-point theory as well. Finally, we show how time logical equivalents of different temporal logics can be given. These embeddings are based on some model theoretic constructions which allow us to consider a time model as a transitive or an inductive extension of the data part of a given time model. Different types of regular time theory contain different comprehension axiom schemas and different types of temporal logics contain different induction axiom schemas. So it is not a big surprise that these systems are generally incomparable. (See Theorems (14.37), (22.11)-(22.13), (26.37) and (26.38).)

**Further research.** The development of a powerful programming theory in the framework of classical first-order logic has been successfully carried out. Talking about the future, we have to distinguish at least two main directions of possible research. The first direction is a purely logical one and the second is a programming theoretic one.

First, about the pure logical considerations, the programming theory was developed to be very flexible with the methods of logical extension and inductive definition and also with the combination of these two methods in the method of inductive extension. The latter allows us to use inductive definitions in a pure first-order frame, and thus allows us to solve special fixed-point equations in a first-order manner. These definitions can contain data-valued parameters but cannot contain uninterpreted new relations as parameters. One of the most interesting researches is *to develop a certain kind of inductive extension which also allows us to use relation symbols as parameters.* This development may have some connection with the modularization of logic programming languages.

A fixed-point theory which was independent of inductive definability was used in the time theories. The fixed-point theory was based on the use of comprehension schemas and on the codability of finite sequences. From a pragmatic point of view it would be nice to use less coding. This could be done by *using the set-extension instead of time-extension.* This change can be done because in programming theory we use only the finite slices of time functions. Introducing an appropriate axiomatization for $set_\sigma$, i.e. for the hereditarily finite sets with urelements, we could obtain a set-theoretic background or time-extension. The development of such a programming theory is out of the scope of the present book but is under development. The first results can be found in Úry, Gergely [1981,1986,1987,1990a,1990b].

A *detailed comparison of the different computational families and the defined extended dynamic logics* belongs to the first direction of research. We recall Remarks (15.25), (15.26) and (26.39) which contain several open problems about this question.

Following the second direction of further research the following problems should be solved. The programming theory should be extended to handle *concurrent and parallel computations* as well. To solve this problem (and to describe, for example, operational systems) we have to handle *infinite computations* as well. It seems to us that for this case the finitary coding we used above will not be appropriate. New tools have to be considered. For example, a possible solution may be obtained by *developing λ-calculus and Scott's abstract data types in the classical first-order frame,* as done in Úry, Gergely [1986]. The question mentioned above about the module version of inductive extension is also a program-theoretic one.

The main result we expect from the continuation of the research presented in this book is a flexible foundation not only for a programming theory but also for several problem domains connected with programs and programming, like *logic programming, data base theory, specification theory, software engineering* etc.

# References


Abadi, M. [1989] The power of temporal proofs. Theoretical Computer Science, **64**, 35-84

Aczel, P. [1977] An introduction to inductive definitions. In: Barwise, J. (ed.) Handbook of Mathematical Logic. North Holland, Amsterdam, 739-782

Aho, A.V., Ullman, J.D. [1972] The theory of parsing, translation and compiling, Prentice-Hall, Inc. Englewood Cliffs, N.J.

Alagič, S., Arbib, M.A. [1978] The design of well-structured and correct programs. Springer-Verlag, Berlin

Andréka, H. [1983] Sharpening the characterization of the power of Floyd's method. In: Salwicki, A.(ed.) Logics of Programs and their Applications. Lecture Notes in Computer Science Vol. **148**, Springer-Verlag, Berlin, 1-26

Andréka, H., Gergely, T., Németi, I. [1975a] Easily comprehensive mathematical logic and its model theory. KFKI, Budapest

Andréka, H., Gergely, T., Németi, I. [1975b] On a direction of non-numeric application of computers. Információ- Elektronika 1, (in Hungarian) 52-57

Andréka, H., Gergely, T., Németi, I. [1977] On the completeness of program verification methods. Budapest (Manuscript, in Hungarian)

Andréka, H., Németi,I. [1978] Completeness of Floyd logic. Bull. Section of Logic, Vol. **7**, Wroclaw, 115-120

Andréka, H., Németi, I., Sain, I. [1979a] Henkin-type semantics for program schemas to turn negative results to positive. In: Budach, L. (ed.) Fundamentals of Computation Theory'79, Vol. **2**, Akademie-Verlag Berlin, 18-24

Andréka, H., Németi, I., Sain, I. [1979b] Completeness problems in verification of programs and program schemas. In: Becvár, J. (ed.) Mathematical Foundations of Computer Science. Lecture Notes in Computer Science Vol. **74**, Springer-Verlag, Berlin, 208-218

Andréka, H., Németi, I., Sain, I. [1981] A characterization of Floyd provable programs. In: Gruska, J., Chytil, M. (eds) Mathematical Foundations of Computer Science. Lecture Notes in Computer Science Vol. **118**, Springer-Verlag, Berlin, 162-171

Andréka, H., Németi, I., Sain, I. [1982] A complete logic for reasoning about programs via nonstandard model theory. Theoretical Computer Science, **17:2**, 193-212. 17:3 259-278

Andréka, H., Németi, I., Sain, I. [1991] On the strength of temporal proofs. Theoretical Computer Science, Vol. **87** (to appear)

Apt, K.R. [1981] Ten years of Hoare's logic, a survey, Part I. TOPLAS, **3:4**, 431-483.

Apt, K.R., Delporte C., [1983] An axiomatization of the intermittent assertion method using temporal logic. In: Diaz, J. (ed.) Automata, Languages and Programming. Lecture Notes in Computer Science Vol. **154**, Springer-Verlag, Berlin, 15-27

Banachowski, L., Kreczmar, A., Mirkowska, G., Rasiova, H., Salwicki, A. [1978] An introduction to algorithmic logic. In: Mazurkiewicz, A., Pawlak, Z. (eds.) Mathematical Foundations of Computer Science, Vol **2**, Banach Center Publications, Warsaw, 7-100

Barwise, J. [1975] Admissible Sets and Structures. Springer-Verlag, Berlin

Benthem, J.F.A.K. Van [1983] The Logic of Time. Reidel, Dordrecht

Bergstra, J., Chmielinska, A., Tiuryn, J. [1982] Hoare's logic is incomplete when it does not have to be. In: Kozen, D. (ed.) Logics of Programs. Lecture Notes in Computer Science Vol. **131**, Springer-Verlag, Berlin, 9-23

Brown, S., Gries, D., Szymanski, T. [1972] Program schemas with pushdown stores, SIAM J. Computing **1:3**, 242-268

Burstall, R.M. [1969] Proving properties of programs by structural induction, Comput. J. 12:1, 41-48

Burstall, R.M. [1970] Formal description of program structure and semantics of first-order logic, In: Meltzer, B., Michie, D. (eds.), Machine Intelligence **5**, Edinburgh University Press, Edinburgh, 79-98

Burstall, R.M. [1974] Program proving as hand simulation with a little induction. In: Information Processing'74. North-Holland, Amsterdam, 308-312

Cartwright, R. [1984] Recursive programs as definitions in first-order logic. SIAM J. Computing **13:2**, 374-407

Chandra, A.K. [1974] The power of parallelism and nondeterminism in programming. In: Information Processing '74, North-Holland, Amsterdam, 461-465

Chang, C.C., Keisler, H.J. [1973] Model Theory, North-Holland, Amsterdam, 1973

Constable, R.L. [1977] On the theory of programming logics, Proc. 9th ACM (SIGACT) Symposium on Theory of Computing, Boulder, CO

Constable, R.L., Gries, D. [1972] On classes of program schemata. SIAM J. Computing **1:1**, 66-118

Constable, R.L., O'Donnell, M.J. [1978] A programming logic, Winthrop Publishers, Cambridge, MA

Cook, S.A. [1978] Soundness and completeness of an axiom system for program verification. SIAM J. Computing **7:1**, 70-90

Csirmaz, L. [1980] Completeness theorems of models with nonstandard time. PhD. Thesis, Hungarian Academy of Sciences, Budapest (in Hungarian)

Csirmaz, L. [1981] On the completeness of proving partial correctness. Acta Cybernetica, **5:2**, 181-190

Csirmaz, L. [1985] A completeness theorem for dynamic logic, Notre Dame J. Formal Logic **26:1**, 51-60

Cutland, N. [1980] Computability. An introduction to recursive function theory. Cambridge University Press

Davis, M. [1973] Hilbert's tenth problem is unsolvable. American Mathematical Monthly **80**, 233-269

Davis, M. [1974] Computability. Courant Institute of Mathematical Sciences, New York University

Dickmann,M. A. [1985] Large infinitary languages. In: Barwise, J., Feferman, S. (eds.) Model-Theoretic Logics. Springer-Verlag, Berlin, 317-363

Dijkstra, E.W.A. [1976] Discipline of Programming. Prentice-Hall, NY

Eklof, P.C. [1977] Ultraproducts for algebraists. In: Barwise J. (ed.) Handbook of Mathematical Logic, North-Holland, Amsterdam, 105-138

Engeler, E. [1967] Algorithmic properties of structures, Math. System Theory **1**, 183-195

Engeler, E. [1975] Algorithmic Logic. In: de Bakker, J.W. (ed.) Foundations of Computer Science, Mathematical Centre Tracts, Amsterdam, 57-85

Fischer, M.J., Ladner, R.E. [1979] Propositional dynamic logic of regular programs. J. Computer and System Science

Floyd, R. [1967] Assigning meaning to programs. In: Schwartz, J.T. (ed.) Proc. Symposium in Applied Mathematics, AMS, Providence, RI, 19-32

Friedman, H. [1971] Algorithmic procedures, generalized Turing algorithms and elementary recursion theory. In: Gandy, R.O., Yates C.M.E. (eds.), Logic Colloquium '69, North-Holland, Amsterdam, 361-389

Gabbay, D. [1976] Investigations in modal and tense logics. Reidel, Dordrecht

Gabbay, D. [1986] Executable temporal logic for interactive systems. Dept. of Computing, Imperial College, London (Manuscript)

Gabbay, D., Pnueli, A., Shelah, S., Stavi, J. [1980] On the temporal analysis of fairness. In: Proc. 7th Annual ACM Symposium on Principles of Programming Languages, 163-173

Gergely, T. [1978] May the theory of programming be first order? In: Collection of Abstracts of the Conference on Mathematical Logic in Computer Science, Salgótarján, 1978

Gergely, T. [1987] Non-standard Programming Logic. Hungarian Academy of Science, Budapest, Thesis

Gergely, T., Szőts, M. [1978] On the incompleteness of proving partial correctness. Acta Cybernetica, **4:1**, 45-57

Gergely, T., Úry, L. [1978] Mathematical Theories of Programming, SZÁMKI Technical Report, Budapest

Gergely, T., Úry, L. [1980a] Program behaviour specification through explicit time consideration. In: Lavington, S.H. (ed.) Information Processing '80. North-Holland, Amsterdam, 107-111

Gergely, T., Úry, L. [1980b] Nondeterministic programming within the frame of first order classical logic, Parts I-II. Acta Cybernetica, **4:4**, 333-375

Gergely,T., Úry, L. [1981] Time models for programming logics. In: Dömölki, B., Gergely, T., (eds.) Mathematical Logic in Computer Science. North-Holland, Amsterdam, 359-427

Gergely, T., Úry, L. [1982] Theory of interactive programming, Acta Informatica. **17**, 1-20

Gergely, T., Úry, L. [1983a] A first order theory of dynamic logic. SZÁMALK Technical Working Report, Budapest

Gergely, T., Úry, L. [1983b] Adequate characterization of Hoare logic. Semiotics and Informatics, **22**, 81-101 (in Russian)

Gergely, T., Úry, L. [1983c] First order denotational semantics. SZÁMALK Technical Report, Budapest

Gergely, T., Úry, L. [1985] A uniform approach to programming logics. SZÁMALK Technical Report, Budapest

Goldblatt, R. [1982] Axiomatising the Logic of Computer Programming. Lecture Notes in Computer Science, Vol. **130**, Springer-Verlag, Berlin

Goldblatt, R. [1987] Logics of time and computation. CSLI, Stanford

Gonzalez, M.T.H., Artalejo, M.R. [1985] Hoare's logic for nondeterministic regular programs: A nonstandard completeness theorem. In: Brauer, W. (ed.) Automata, Languages and Programming. Proceedings, Lecture Notes in Computer Science, Vol. **194**, Springer-Verlag, Berlin, 270-280

Grabowski, M. [1984] On relative completeness of programming logics. Proc. 11th ACM Symposium POPL, 1984, 258-261

Hajek, P. [1981] Making dynamic logic first order. In: Gruska, J., Chytil, M. (eds.) Mathematical Foundations of Computer Science 1981. Lecture Notes in Computer Science, Vol. **118**, Springer-Verlag, Berlin, 287-295

Hajek, P. [1986a] Some conservativeness results for nonstandard dynamic logic. In: Demetrovics, J., Katona, G., Salomaa, A. (eds.) Algebra, Combinatorics and Logic. North-Holland, Amsterdam, 443-449

Hajek, P. [1986b] A simple dynamic predicate logic. Theoretical Computer Science **46**, 239-259

Harel, D. [1978] Arithmetical completeness in logics of programs. In: Ausiello, G., Böhm, C. (eds.) Automata, Languages and Programming. Lecture Notes in Computer Science, Vol. **62**, Springer-Verlag, Berlin

Harel, D. [1979] First Order Dynamic Logic. Lecture Notes in Computer Science, Vol. **68**, Springer-Verlag, Berlin

Harel, D. [1980] Proving the correctness of regular deterministic programs: a unifying survey using dynamic logic. Theoretical Computer Science, **12**, 61-81

Harel, D. [1984] Dynamic Logic. In: Gabbay, D., Guenthner, F. (eds.) Handbook of Philosophical Logic, Vol. II. Reidel, Dordrecht, 497-604

Harel, D., Meyer, A.R., Pratt, V.R. [1977] Computability and completeness in logics of programs. In: Proc. 9th Annual ACM Symposium on Theory of Computing, Boulder, CO

Harnik, V. [1975] Effective proper procedures and universal classes of program schemata, J. Computer and System Sciences, **10**, 44-61

Hoare, C.A.R., [1969] An axiomatic basis for computer programming. Comm. ACM, Vol **12**, 576-580, 583

Jech, T.J. [1971] Lectures in set theory with particular emphasis on the method of forcing, Springer-Verlag, Berlin

Kamp, H.W. [1968] Tense logic and the theory of linear order, PhD Thesis, UCLA, Los Angeles, CA

Kripke, S.A. [1963] Semantical considerations on modal logic, Acta Philosophica Fennica, **16**, 83-94

Kröger, F. [1976] Logical rules of natural reasoning about programs. In: (eds.) Automata, Languages and Programming. Edinburgh University Press, 87-98

Kröger, F. [1977] Formalization of algorithmic reasoning. In: Becvar, J. (ed.) Mathematical Foundations of Computer Science 1975. Lecture Notes in Computer Science, Vol. **32**, Springer-Verlag, Berlin, 287-293

Kröger, F. [1978] A uniform logical basis for the description, specification and verification of programs. In: Proc. IFIP Working Conference on Formal Description of Programming Concepts. North-Holland, Amsterdam, 441-457

Kröger, F. [1987] Temporal Logic of Programs. Springer-Verlag, Berlin

Lamport, L. [1977] Proving the correctness of multipocess programs. IEEE Transactions on Software Engineering **3:2**, 125-143

Lamport, L. [1983] What good is temporal logic? In: Mason, R.E.A. (ed.) Information Processing '83, North-Holland, Amsterdam, 657-668

Leivant, D. [1985] Logical and mathematical reasoning about imperative programs. In: Proc. 12th Annual ACM Symposium on Principles of Programming Languages, New Orleans, LA, 132-140

Lichtenstein, O., Pnueli, A., Zuck, L. [1985] The glory of the Past. In: Parikh, R. (ed.), Logics of Programs. Lecture Notes in Computer Science, Vol. **193**, Springer-Verlag, Berlin, 196-218

Makowski, J.A., Sain, I. [1989] Weak second order characterization of various program verification systems. Theoretical Computer Science, **66**, 239-321

Manna, Z. [1969] The correctness of programs, J.Computer and System Sciences **3**, 119-127

Manna, Z. [1974] Mathematical Theory of Computation, McGraw Hill Kogakuska, Tokyo

Manna, Z., Pnueli, A. [1983] Proving precedence properties: the temporal way. In: Díaz, J. (ed.) Automata, Languages and Programming. Lecture Notes in Computer Science Vol. **154**, Springer-Verlag, Berlin, 491-512

Manna, Z., Pnueli, A. [1988] The anchored version of the temporal framework. Technical Report CS 88-21, Weizmann Institute of Science

Manna, Z., Waldinger, R. [1978] Is "sometime" sometimes better than always? Comm. ACM 21, 159-172

McCarthy, J. [1978] Representation of recursive program in first order logic. In: Blum, K. K., Takasu, S. (eds.) Proceedings of the International Conference on Mathematical Studies of Informational Processing, Kyoto

Mendelson, E. [1964] Introduction to Mathematical Logic. D. van Nostrand, Princeton, NJ

Meyer, A.R. [1980] Ten thousand and one logics of programming. Bull. EATCS, January 1980, 11-29

Meyer,A.R. [1982] Contribution to "Transcript of Panel Discussion". In: Kozen, D. (ed.) Logics of Programs, Lecture Notes in Computer Science, Vol. **131**, Springer-Verlag, Berlin, 406-429

Meyer, A.R., Halpern, J.Z. [1982] Axiomatic definitions of programming languages: a theoretical assessment, J. ACM **29:2**, 555-576

Meyer, A.R., Parikh, R. [1981] Definability in dynamic logic, J. Computer and System Sciences, 23, 279-298

Meyer, A., Streett, R.S., Mirkowska, G. [1982] The deducibility problem in propositional dynamic logic. In: Engeler, E. (ed.) Logic of Programs, Lecture Notes in Computer Science, Vol. **125**, Springer-Verlag, Berlin, 12-22

Meyer, A.R., Winklmann, K. [1982] Expressing program looping in regular dynamic logic, Theoretical Computer Science, Vol. **18**, 301-328

Mirkowska, G. [1981] PAL-propositional algorithmic logic. In: Engeler, E. (ed.), Logic of Programs. Lecture Notes in Computer Science, Vol. **125**, Springer-Verlag, Berlin, 29-101

Moldestad, J., Stoltenberg-Hansen, V., Tucker, J.V. [1978] Finite algorithmic procedures and inductive definability, Preprint Series, Institute of Mathematics, University of Oslo

Moschovakis, Y.N. [1974] Elementary Induction on Abstract Structures, North-Holland, Amsterdam

Naur, P. [1966] Proof of algorithms by general snapshots, BIT, **6**, 310-316

Németi, I. [1982] Nonstandard dynamic logic. In: Kozen, D. (ed.) Logics of Programs Lecture Notes in Computer Science, Vol. **131**, Springer-Verlag, Berlin, 311-348

Paterson, M.S., Hewitt, C.E. [1970] Comparative Schematology, AI Laboratory Technical Memo 201, MIT

Pásztor, A. [1986] Nonstandard dynamic logic to prove standard properties of programs. J. Symbolic Computation **2:1**, 59-81

Pásztor, A., Sain, I. [1989] A streamlined temporal completeness theorem. In: Kleine-Büning, H., Richter, M.M. (eds.) Computer Science Logics, Proceedings, Lecture Notes in Computer Science Vol. **440**, Springer-Verlag, Berlin

Pnueli, A. [1977] The temporal logic of programs. In: Proc. 18th IEEE Annual Symposium on Foundations of Computer Science, Providence, RI 1977, 46-57

Pnueli, A. [1981] The temporal semantics of concurrent programs. Theoretical Computer Science Vol. **13**, 45-60

Pratt, V.R. [1976] Semantical considerations on Floyd-Hoare logic. In: Proc. 17th IEEE Annual Symposium on Foundations of Computer Science, Providence, 109-121

Pratt, V.R. [1980] Application of modal logic to programming. Studia Logica **39**, 257-274

Prior, A.N. [1957] Time and Modality. Clarendon Press, Oxford

Prior, A.N. [1967] Past, Present and Future. Clarendon Press, Oxford

Richter, M.M., Szabó, M.E. [1986] Nonstandard computation theory. In: Demetrovits, J., Katona, G., Solomaa, A. (eds.) Algebra, Combinatories and Logic in Computer Science, North-Holland, Amsterdam, 667-693

Rogers, H. [1967] Theory of recursive functions and effective comutability. McGraw-Hill, New York

Sain, I. [1983] Total correctness in nonstandard dynamic logic. Bull. Section of Logic 12:2, Warsaw-Lodz, 64-70

Sain, I. [1984] Structured nonstandard dynamic logic, Zeitschrift für Math. Logic u. Grundlagen der MAth. Heft 3, Band **30** (1984), pp 481-497

Sain, I. [1985a] A simple proof for the completeness of Floyd's method. Theoretical Computer Science Vol. **35**, 345-348

Sain, I. [1985b] Elementary proof for some semantic characterizations of nondeterministic Floyd-Hoare logic. Preprint 59, Institute of Mathematics, Budapest

Sain, I. [1985c] The reasoning power of Burstall's (modal logic) and Pnueli's (temporal logic) program verification methods. In: Parikh, R. (ed.) Logics of Programs, Lecture Notes in Computer Science, Vol. **193**, Springer-Verlag, Berlin, 302-319

Sain, I. [1986] Dynamic Logics with Nonstandard Model Theory. PhD Thesis, Budapest, (in Hungarian)

Sain, I. [1987] Total correctness in nonstandard logics of programs. Theoretical Computer Science **50**, 285-321

Sain, I. [1990] Results on the glory of the past. In Rovan, B. (ed) Mathematical Fundation of Computer Science, Lecture Notes in Computer Science Vol. **452**, 478-484

Sain, I. [1991] Comparing and characterizing the powers of established program verification methods, In: Tucker, J.V., Meinke, K. (eds) Many-sorted Logic and its Applications in Computer Science, John Wiley (to appear)

Salwicki, A. [1970] Formalized algorithmic languages. Bull. Acad. Polon. Sci., Ser. Math. **18**, 227-232

Scott, D. [1976] Data types as lattices, SIAM J. Comput., **5**, 522-586

Shepherdson, J.C. [1973] Computation over abstract structures: serial and parallel procedures and Friedman's effective definitional schemes. In: Rose, J., Sheperson, J.C. (eds.), Logic Colloquium '73, North-Holland, Amsterdam, 445-513

Shoenberg, E., Schwarz, J.T., Sharir, M. [1981] An automatic technique for selection data representations in SETL programs, ACM Trans. Program Lang. and Systems, **3:2**, 126-143

Szalas, A. [1986] Concerning the semantic consequence relation in first order temporal logic. Theoretical Computer Science Vol **47**, 329-334

Tiuryn, J. [1981] Logic of effective definitions. Fundamenta Informaticae, **4**, 629-659

Úry, L., Gergely, T. [1981] On $S$-sorted logical categories. SzÁMALK Technical Report, Budapest

Úry, L., Gergely, T. [1986] A constructive basis for programming and specification theory, Applied Logic Laboratory, Technical Report, Budapest

Úry, L., Gergely, T. [1987] Specification theory based on logical categories, Applied Logic Laboratory, Technical Report, Budapest

Úry, L., Gergely, T. [1990a] Specification theory based on logic categories, Applied Logic Laboratory, Technical Report, Budapest

Úry, L., Gergely, T. [1990b] A constructive specification theory, In: David, G., Boute, R.T. and Shriver, B.D. (eds.) Declarative Systems, Elsevier (North-Holland) 33-82

Wand, M. [1978] A new incompleteness result for Hoare's system. J. ACM **25:1**, 168-175

Wolper, P. [1983] Temporal logic can be more expressive, Information and Control, **56**, 72-99

Wright, G.H. von [1965] And next. Acta Philosophica Fennica **18**, 293-304

# Notations

## Chapter 1

## Chapter 2



## Chapter 4



## Chapter 5

**Chapter 6**



**Chapter 7**



**Chapter 8**



**Chapter 10**



**Chapter 11**



**Chapter 12**

**Chapter 13**



**Chapter 14**



**Chapter 15**



**Chapter 17**



**Chapter 18**



**Chapter 20**



**Chapter 21**

**Chapter 22**



**Chapter 24**



**Chapter 25**



**Chapter 26**

# Subject Index

## EATCS Monographs on Theoretical Computer Science

Vol. 1: K. Mehlhorn
**Data Structures and Algorithms 1:**
**Sorting and Searching**

Vol.2: K. Mehlhorn
**Data Structures and Algorithms 2:**
**Graph Algorithms and NP-Completeness**

Vol. 3: K. Mehlhorn
**Data Structures and Algorithms 3:**
**Multidimensional Searching and Computational Geometry**

Vol. 4: W. Reisig
**Petri Nets**
**An Introduction**

Vol. 5: W. Kuich, A. Salomaa
**Semirings, Automata, Languages**

Vol. 6: H. Ehrig, B. Mahr
**Fundamentals of Algebraic Specification 1**
**Equations and Initial Semantics**

Vol. 7: F. Gécseg
**Products of Automata**

Vol. 8: F. Kröger
**Temporal Logic of Programs**

Vol. 9: K. Weihrauch
**Computability**

Vol. 10: H. Edelsbrunner
**Algorithms in Combinatorial Geometry**

Vol. 11: J. L. Balcázar, J. Díaz, J. Gabarró
**Structural Complexity I**

Vol. 12: J. Berstel, C. Reutenauer
**Rational Series and Their Languages**

Vol. 13: E. Best, C. Fernàndez C.
**Nonsequential Processes**
**A Petri Net View**

Vol. 14: M. Jantzen
**Confluent String Rewriting**

Vol.15: S. Sippu, E. Soisalon-Soininen
**Parsing Theory**
**Volume I: Languages and Parsing**

Vol. 16: P. Padawitz
**Computing in Horn Clause Theories**

Vol. 17: J. Paredaens, P. De Bra, M. Gyssens, D. Van Gucht
**The Structure of the Relational Database Model**

Vol. 18: J. Dassow, G. Păun
**Regulated Rewriting in Formal Language Theory**

Vol. 19: M. Tofte
**Compiler Generators**
**What they can do, what they might do, and what they will probably never do**

Vol. 20: S. Sippu, E. Soisalon-Soininen
**Parsing Theory**
**Volume II: LR(k) and LL(k) Parsing**

Vol. 21: H. Ehrig, B. Mahr
**Fundamentals of Algebraic Specification 2**
**Module Specifications and Constraints**

Vol. 22: J. L. Balcázar, J. Díaz, J. Gabarró
**Structural Complexity II**

Vol. 23: A. Salomaa
**Public-Key Cryptography**

Vol. 24: T. Gergely, L. Úry
**First-Order Programming Theories**